Theories of Personality

Jess Feist
McNeese State University

Theories of Personality

SECOND EDITION

Holt, Rinehart and Winston, Inc.

Forth Worth   Chicago   San Francisco   Philadelphia
Montreal   Toronto   London   Sydney   Tokyo

Publisher	Ted Buchholz
Acquisitions Editor	Eve Howard
Developmental Editor	Tod Gross
Senior Project Editor	Christine Caperton
Production Manager	Tad Gaither
Art & Design Supervisor	John Ritland
Text Designer	Ritter & Ritter, Inc.
Cover Design and Illustration	Kevin Short

Library of Congress Cataloging-in-Publication Data
Feist, Jess.
Theories of personality / Jess Feist,—2nd ed.
Includes bibliographical references.
1. Personality.   I. Title.
BF698.F365   1990   89-36879
155.2—dc20

ISBN: 0-03-027857-0
Copyright © 1990, 1985 by Holt, Rinehart and Winston, Inc.

Address Editorial Correspondence To: 301 Commerce Street, Suite 3700, Fort Worth, TX 76102

Address Orders To: 6277 Sea Harbor Drive, Orlando, FL 32887
1-800-782-4479, or 1-800-433-0001 (in Florida)

Printed in the United States of America

0 1 2 3   039   9 8 7 6 5 4 3 2 1

Holt, Rinehart and Winston, Inc.
The Dryden Press
Saunders College Publishing

Photo Credits
p. 6, Elizabeth Crewes; **p. 22,** Princeton University Press; **p. 53,** Erika Stone/Peter Arnold, Inc.; **p. 67,** Edmund Englman; **p. 74,** UPI/Bettmann Newsphotos; **p. 94,** Jim Anderson/Woodfin

(continued on page 718)

Preface

The nature of humanity has been an issue of interest, concern, and controversy for thousands of years. Historically, the motives and makeup of human beings have been debated by philosophers, scholars, and religious thinkers—often from a viewpoint colored by political, social, or religious considerations. Until near the end of the nineteenth century, however, little systematic progress had been made in humanity's ability to organize, explain, or predict its own actions. The emergence of psychology as an area of inquiry separate from philosophy marked the beginning of a scientific approach to the study of human personality.

Scientifically trained investigators within the realm of psychology called personality have continued to ponder age-old questions. Some of these have been: What factors shape personality? Are people motivated by past events or by their expectations of the future? Do they freely choose their own actions, or is behavior shaped by outside forces? Are human motives mostly conscious, or do they spring from some hidden unconscious source? Do biological or social factors play the more important role in personality development? Is the study of personality best served by an emphasis on the uniqueness of individuals or by a consideration of similarities among people? With the emergence of psychology as a science, the method of answering and investigating these questions began to change.

Psychologists presently ask these and other questions with the purpose of testing hypotheses and reformulating models. In other words, they apply the tools of scientific inquiry and scientific theory to the area of human personality. Science, of course, is not divorced from speculation, imagination, and creativity. All of these qualities are needed in the formulation of theories, and all can be seen in the work of the personality theorists discussed in this book.

Less than 100 years ago Sigmund Freud, a Viennese physician, began formulating a theoretical framework that would give him and others a greater understanding of the human species. His theory was based on clinical observation, but it also was a reflection of the personality of its creator. Since that time others within the scope of psychology have combined clinical or laboratory experience with imaginative speculation to arrive at some theory of human nature. Each of these theories is unique because each theorist has had a unique personality and set of experiences. Though personality theories are based on observations of human behavior, the observations and the accompanying theory are colored by each theorist's individual background, frame of reference, and personal dynamics. It follows, therefore, that within the science of psychology there would be many different and even contrasting theories. Divergent theories, however, may still be useful. The usefulness of a theory depends not on its agreement with some established theory, but on the number of testable hypotheses it generates, the degree to which it integrates existing empirical knowledge, and its ability to suggest practical answers to everyday problems.

COVERAGE

The second edition of *Theories of Personality* provides comprehensive coverage of 18 of the most influential theorists of personality. Emphasis has been placed on normal personality, though also included are brief discussions on the attendant systems of abnormality and the appropriate theory and method of psychotherapy associated with them. As with the first edition, this edition is based on original sources and is concerned with the most up-to-date formulations of each theory. Earlier concepts are included only if they are retained in the later theory, or if they provide vital background for the comprehension of the final theory. Because each theory is an expression of its builder's unique view of the world and of humanity, more biographical information is included than is ordinarily found in survey books on personality theory. Readers, therefore, will have an opportunity to develop an acquaintance not only with the theory but with the theorists' lives as well. Each theorist's concept of humanity is discussed using the framework of the basic questions posed on the previous page. Since these questions might also be answered by philosophers, some scientific criterion must be employed for a systematic evaluation of each theory. Consequently, five criteria of a useful theory are presented in Chapter 1, and each theory is subsequently critiqued using those criteria as a guide.

SCOPE

I have divided *Theories of Personality* into six broad areas, beginning with the *introductory remarks* found in Chapter 1. The so-called *psychodynamic theorists* are discussed in Chapters 2–8. These theorists—Freud, Erikson, Adler, Jung, Sullivan, Horney, and Fromm—based their formulations mostly on clinical observations and tended to emphasize unconscious determinants of personality. Freud, of course, was the first of these to evolve a theory of personality, and the other six were, in one way or another, strongly influenced by him.

Behavioral and cognitive theories comprise Part Three. This unit begins with the classical learning theory of Dollard and Miller, who, with their Freudian inclinations, bridge the span between psychodynamic theories and modern cognitive learning theories. Also included in this group are Skinner's radical behavioral approach, Rotter's social learning theory, and Bandura's social cognitive theory.

Next, I discuss the *dispositional theories,* including the trait and factor theories of Cattell and Eysenck. Also included here is Allport's psychology of the individual, although Allport's emphasis on *personal dispositions* gives his theory a strong humanistic complexion.

The fifth section presents the *humanistic/existential theories,* including those of Kelly, Maslow, Rogers, and May, although Kelly's unique theory almost defies classification.

Finally, in the concluding remarks I present an overview of the various theories and speculate about future directions in personality theory.

WRITING STYLE

Although *Theories of Personality* explores difficult and complex theories, it does so in clear, concise, and comprehensible language. The book is designed for undergraduate students and should be understood by those with a minimum background in psychology. However, I have tried not to oversimplify or violate a theorist's original meaning. I have made ample comparisons between and among theorists where appropriate and have included many examples to illustrate how the different theories can be applied to ordinary day-to-day situations. A glossary at the end of the book contains definitions of technical terms used throughout—many from the view of a particular theorist. Furthermore, the same terms appear in **boldface** and are defined within the text.

INSTRUCTIONAL AIDS

Besides an end-of-book glossary, I have supplied several other features to aid both the student and the instructor. These include:

Case Studies

Every chapter begins with a case study, a brief story of some one person, chosen to help the student relate the subsequent theory to the real world. After introducing the case study at the first of the chapter, additional information on the person is presented throughout the chapter in order to help students better comprehend certain theoretical concepts.

Outlines, Overviews, and Summaries

Chapter outlines orient students to each chapter by previewing major topics to be discussed. Chapter overviews follow the case study and introduce readers to the general tone of the theory. At the end of each chapter is a brief summary, written to give just enough detail for a quick review of important topics.

Box Material

Where appropriate, one or two boxes have been supplied for some chapters. Some of these contain pertinent research, while others are concerned with relevant but not integral information concerning the theory.

Annotated Suggested Readings

At the end of each chapter I have included four or five suggested readings along with a short description of each. These selections have been carefully chosen for their readability, content, and interest level. They direct readers in further study.

Instructor's Manual

An instructor's manual containing learning objectives, key terms, and suggestions for lecture topics accompanies this text. In addition, the instructor's manual contains nearly 1,500 multiple-choice test items. These items are designed to reduce the instructor's work in preparing tests. Of course, each item is marked with the correct answer and the page number in the text on which the answer can be found.

Study Guide

Also available is a student study guide, which includes learning objectives, chapter summaries, and key terms and concepts. In addition, a variety of test items—including matching, fill-in-the-blank, true or false, multiple choice, and short answer questions—are presented. Students will find the study guide helpful in preparing for quizzes and examinations.

ACKNOWLEDGMENTS

Many people have contributed to the completion of this book, and I wish to acknowledge my gratitude to them. First I wish to thank Joanne Durand of the McNeese Library, whose skill and constant good humor made my work much more tolerable. Also, I acknowledge my debt to Greg Feist for his insights on future directions for personality theory. Next, I thank Patrick Moreno for supplying materials, reading parts of the manuscript, and coauthoring the instructor's manual. I also wish to thank Eve Howard, acquisitions editor; Tod Gross, developmental editor; John Haley, editorial assistant; and Christine Caperton, senior project editor at Holt, Rinehart and Winston, for their helpful suggestions during the developmental phase of the manuscript and guidance during the production of the book.

Lynette Babineaux is, without doubt, the world's best secretary. I am deeply indebted to her for the efficient manner in which she helped in the preparation of the manuscript.

To the following reviewers, I am grateful for valuable comments and suggestions: William Arndt, University of Missouri, Kansas City; James Bargar, Missouri Western State College; John Brockway, Davidson College; Clinton Browne, Liberty University; Ana Mari Cauce, University of Washington; Calvin Claus, National College of Education; W. Grant Dahlstrom, University of North Carolina; Boyce Daughtery, East Carolina University; Cooper Holmes, Emporia State University; Ralph W. Hood, Jr., University of Tennessee, Chattanooga; Debra Huntley, Wichita State University; Gary King, Rose State College; Alfred Kornfeld, Eastern Connecticut State College; Phil Lau, DeAnza

College; Paul Lewan, Green River Community College; Mariam London-Hinman, Northern Arizona University; John McBrearty, Temple University; Joseph MacCormack, Washburn University; Kathleen McCormick, Ocean County College; Eugene McCown, Northwest Missouri State College; Sam McFarland, Western Kentucky University; Leslie Morey, Vanderbilt University; Sylvia T. O'Neil, Trenton State College; Richard Pasewark, University of Wyoming; Joseph Philbrick, California State Polytechnic, Pomona; James Pullen, Central Missouri State University; Kathryn Ryan, Lycoming College; Gary Sterner, East Washington State University; Keith Thrasher, Rose State College; Brian Yates, American University; and Edward Yelinek, Wilson College.

I am especially, indebted to the following personality theorists for their kindness in taking time to discuss appropriate sections of the manuscript: Albert Bandura, Raymond B. Cattell, Hans J. Eysenck, Carl R. Rogers (deceased), Julian B. Rotter, and B. F. Skinner.

Most of all, I wish to thank my wife, Mary Jo, for her patience, encouragement, and understanding, and for her work in the preparation of the study guide.

J. F.

Brief Contents

Contents

6 Sullivan: Interpersonal Theory   198

7 Horney: Psychoanalytic Social Theory

8 Fromm: Humanistic Psychoanalysis   266

Part Four
DISPOSITIONAL THEORIES

13 Cattell and Eysenck: Trait and Factor Theories

14 Allport: The Psychology of the Individual   496

Part Five
HUMANISTIC/EXISTENTIAL THEORY   532

18 May: Existential Psychology   648

Part Six
CONCLUDING REMARKS   678

19 A Final Word   679

Glossary   686

References   703

Name Index   719

Subject Index   723

Boxed Features

Theories
of
Personality

Part One

1

Introduction

One hundred years ago a young gifted Viennese neurologist named Sigmund Freud was curious about the nature of humanity. His questions differed little from those asked for centuries by philosophers and theologians. What motivates people? Is there some goal or end toward which people strive? What accounts for similarities among people? For differences? What makes people act in predictable ways? Why are they unpredictable? Do dreams have some meaning? Are there hidden or unconscious forces that control people's behavior? What causes mental disturbances? Are people shaped more by heredity or by environment? By society or biology? What is the nature of human nature?

Unlike many who preceded him, Freud was not content to merely speculate about such questions. He transformed his thoughts into tentative concepts and then searched for evidence that would either confirm his notions or offer insight into how they could be changed. Where could such evidence be found?

As a neurologist, Freud was treating neurotic patients, many of whom suffered from a then common disorder called **hysteria.** He listened to these people, trying to find out what hidden conflicts lay behind their odd assortment of symptoms. "Listening became, for Freud, more than an art; it became a method, a privileged road to knowledge that his patients mapped out for him" (Gay, 1988, p. 70).

Freud's method gradually became more scientific as he formulated hypotheses and checked their plausibility against his clinical experiences. Whether or not Freud was truly scientific is not an issue at this point. What is important is the fact that his early formulations eventually led to a highly structured concept or **theory of personality.**

OVERVIEW

Since Freud's original formulations many others have developed a theory of personality. Some are based largely on philosophical speculation, others mainly on empirical evidence. In this chapter we will see that a useful theory should be founded on *both*.

Many of the advances that have been made in the understanding of human

4

behavior have come from personality theorists who have done two things: (1) They have made observations of behavior, and (2) they have imaginatively speculated on the meaning of those observations. There have been many such men and women, but the ones who are widely recognized as having made significant contributions to our present understanding of personality are Sigmund Freud, Erik Erikson, Alfred Adler, Carl Jung, Harry Stack Sullivan, Karen Horney, Erich Fromm, John Dollard and Neal Miller, B. F. Skinner, Julian Rotter, Albert Bandura, Hans J. Eysenck, Raymond B. Cattell, George Kelly, Gordon Allport, Abraham H. Maslow, Carl Rogers, and Rollo May. The theories of personality formulated by these people are the topic of this book.

But before looking at these theories, we will present a general introduction to the field of personality theory, beginning with a discussion and definition of personality. Nearly everyone seems to be interested in personality, but some students are turned off by the term "theory." After discussing the concept of personality we will examine why theories are essential to science and how they can add to our understanding of personality.

Personality theories differ, not merely in terminology, but on basic issues concerning the nature of humanity. Each personality theory reflects its author's concept of humanity, and we next discuss a structure for organizing the various issues dealing with the nature of human nature. Finally, a brief introduction to research methods in personality theory is presented.

PERSONALITY

Personality is a topic of universal interest, yet it remains a subject clouded with mystery and misunderstanding. All of us have heard such comments as "Jim has a wonderful personality"; "Kathy has an outgoing personality"; or "Jan has no personality at all." Most psychologists, however, believe that personality cannot be adequately described by such simple statements. Before looking at the psychological definition, it might help to define personality according to popular usage.

Popular Definition

For many, the term personality refers to one's social value. People have personality to the extent that they behave in likable ways, are charming, generous, and popular, get along well with others, and generally manifest socially desirable qualities. Personality means being a good conversationalist, witty, socially outgoing, sincere, well-groomed, and inoffensive to others. According to this definition people have "personality" if they have fresh breath, a deodorized aroma, a smiling face, and a soft, pleasant voice.

This layman's conception of personality seems to imply that not everyone has a personality, that some people are either so nasty or so inconspicuous that they are completely devoid of personality.

Politicians are frequently described in terms of this popular definition, pos-

No two people, not even identical twins, have exactly the same personality.

sessing "personality" if they have charisma and charm, are able to project a folksy, relaxed appearance on television, or have an exciting, scandalous, or tragic private life. Again, the implication is that some politicians possess personality while others do not.

Psychological Definition

The popular definition of personality resembles the original meaning of the term, namely, a façade or mask one shows to the world. However, psychologists use the term to refer to what one really is, not to mere surface appearance. Psychologists differ among themselves as to what personality really is and no single definition is acceptable to all of them. Nor would such unanimity be desirable at the present stage of psychological science. The study of personality, including the development of differing theories, is best served by an incomplete tentative definition. Personality theorists evolve unique and vital theories because they lack agreement on the nature of humanity and because each sees personality from an individual reference point.

The person who probably did more than anyone to shed light on the many meanings of personality was Gordon Allport (1937, 1961). In his now classic 1937 book on personality, he traced the history of the term and then listed 50 definitions of it, the final being his own.

Allport pointed out that philologists are in some disagreement as to the exact origin of the word, but that they generally concur that the Latin **persona** (from which personality is derived) referred to a theatrical mask worn in Greek drama by Roman actors before the birth of Christ. The persona was used to project a false appearance to others; that is, the role one plays in life. It is similar to the layman's definition of the term personality. Both indicate a surface appearance, not what one really is.

After an exhaustive discourse in which personality is seen from many angles, Allport (1961, p. 38) offered his definition: "Personality is the dynamic organization within the individual of those psychophysical systems that determine his characteristic behavior and thought."

Allport's definition is acceptable for Allport's theory of personality, but for no other. No single definition can be acceptable to all personality theorists. Of necessity, each must have a unique definition, just as each has a unique concept of humanity and an individual manner of looking at human personality. In general, however, we can say that **personality** refers to all those relatively permanent traits, dispositions, or characteristics within the individual that give some measure of consistency to that person's behavior. These traits may be unique, common to some group, or shared by the entire species, but their pattern is different for each individual. Thus everyone, though like others in some ways, has a unique personality.

THEORY

The word **theory** is a frequently used term, but in everyday language it is seldom employed with the kind of precision necessary to science. Before defining the term it may be helpful to enumerate what a theory is not.

What a Theory Is Not

People sometimes confuse theory with philosophy or idle speculation or hypothesis or taxonomy. Although theory is related to each of these concepts, it is not the same as any of them.

Not a Philosophy

First of all, a theory is a not a philosophy. Philosophy, a much broader term, encompasses the nature of reality **(metaphysics),** the nature of knowledge **(epistemology),** the nature of values **(axiology),** the nature of being **(ontology),** and the nature of causation **(cosmology).** Theory is none of these, although it is a tool used in the scientific pursuit of knowledge (epistemology).

There is no theory about how one should live one's life. This involves values and is the proper concern of axiology. Theories do not deal with "oughts" and "shoulds." They are not sets of principles and how to administer a large corporation, how to plant strawberries, or how to reach heaven.

Philosophy deals with what ought to be or what should be; theory does not. Theory can be seen as a set of *if-then* statements. The goodness or badness of the outcomes of these statements is beyond the realm of theory. For example, theory might tell us that *if* children are brought up in isolation, completely separated from human contact, *then* they will not develop human language, exhibit parenting behavior, and so on. But this statement says nothing concerning the morality of such a method of child rearing.

Not Armchair Speculation

Second, a theory is not mere armchair speculation. Although theories involve speculation, they must never be totally separated from empirical observation. They are closely tied to science and are based on scientifically gathered data.

What is the relationship between theory and science? Science is the branch of study concerned with observation and classification of data and with the verification of general laws through the testing of hypotheses. Theories are useful tools employed by scientists to give meaning and organization to observations. In addition, theories provide fertile ground for the production of testable hypotheses. Without some kind of theory to tie observations together and to point to directions of possible research, science would be greatly handicapped.

Theories are not useless fantasies fabricated by impractical scholars fearful of soiling their hands in the machinery of scientific investigation. In fact, theories themselves are quite practical and are essential to the advancement of any science. Speculation and empirical observation are the two essential cornerstones of theory building, but speculation must not run rampantly in advance of controlled observation. The reader will notice that the later theorists in this book, especially Skinner, Cattell, Bandura, and Rogers, have speculated cautiously and have kept theoretical statements only a small step ahead of laboratory or clinical observation.

Not a Hypothesis

Just as philosophy is a broader concept than theory, the latter is a more generalized term than hypothesis. A good theory is capable of generating many hypotheses. A **hypothesis** is an educated guess or prediction specific enough for its validity to be tested through the use of the scientific method. A theory is too general to lend itself to direct verification. One comprehensive theory, such as Freud's theory of psychoanalysis, may generate thousands of hypotheses. Hypotheses, then, are narrower than theories and flow logically from them. The offspring, however, should not be confused with the parent.

There is, of course, a close relationship between a theory and a hypothesis.

A useful theory will allow the investigator to derive through deductive reasoning a workable hypothesis that can be experimentally tested. The results of such a test, whether they support or contradict the hypothesis, feed back into the theory and, through inductive reasoning, alter it in some way. As the theory grows and changes, other hypotheses can be drawn from it and, when tested, they in turn reshape the theory.

Not a Taxonomy

A **taxonomy** is a classification of things according to their natural relationships. Taxonomies are essential to the development of a science because without classification of data science could not grow. But one must not confuse a taxonomy with a theory. Mere classification of people into, say, introverts and extraverts, or endomorphs, mesomorphs, and ectomorphs does not constitute a theory. Even when several taxonomies are combined, each having several complex subsystems, they do not produce a theory. Unlike theories, taxonomies are not generative. They are dynamic only in the sense that new systems can be added to them, but they ordinarily lead nowhere as far as the production of testable hypotheses are concerned.

Theory Defined

If a theory is not a philosophy, not armchair speculation, not a hypothesis nor a taxonomy, what, then, is it? A scientific theory can be defined as *a set of related assumptions from which, by logical deductive reasoning, testable hypotheses can be drawn.*

This definition needs further explanation. First, a theory is *a set* of assumptions. A single assumption can never fill all the requirements of an adequate theory. A single assumption, for example, could not serve to integrate known facts, something a useful theory should do.

Second, a theory is a set of *related* assumptions. Isolated assumptions could not generate meaningful hypotheses. Neither would they be internally consistent—a criterion for a useful theory.

A third key word in the definition is *assumptions*. The components of a theory are not proven facts in the sense that their validity has been absolutely established. They are, however, accepted *as if* they were true. This is a practical step, taken so that useful research can be conducted and further theory building can proceed.

Fourth, *logical deductive reasoning* is used by the researcher to formulate hypotheses. The concepts of a theory must be stated with sufficient precision and logical consistency to permit the deduction of clearly stated hypotheses. The hypotheses are not components of the theory, but flow from it. It is the job of the imaginative scientist to begin with the general theory and, through deductive reasoning, arrive at a particular hypothesis that can be put to the test. If the general theoretical propositions are illogical, they remain sterile and incapable of generating hypotheses. Moreover, if the researcher uses faulty logic in deducting hypotheses, the resulting research will be meaning-less and will make no contribution to the ongoing process of theory construction.

The final part of the definition includes the qualifier "testable." Unless a hypothesis can be tested in some way, it is worthless. It is not necessary for the hypothesis to lend itself to immediate testing, but there must be some reasonable expectation that at some future time the necessary wherewithal will be acquired so that the hypothesis can be tested.

Theory and Observations

What is the relationship between theory and observations? If a theory is a useful one, the interaction between it and observations is both mutual and dynamic. The relationship generally proceeds as follows.

Theories generate a number of *hypotheses* that can be experimentally inves-tigated. The results from this *experimental research* are called *observations*. These observations then flow back into the theory and restructure it so that, in the future, additional hypotheses can be generated. This cyclic relation-

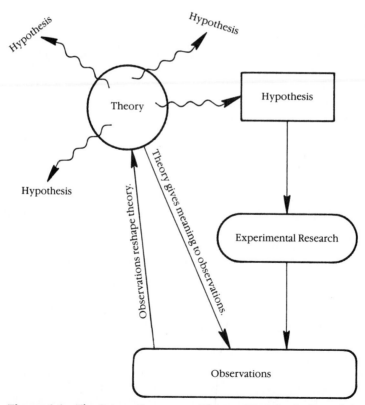

Figure 1.1 The Interaction among Theory, Hypothesis, Experimental Research, and Observations

ship is shown in Figure 1.1. As the theory changes and grows, it extends its utility to a wider range of possible perceptions. More hypotheses can be tested and additional observations made which, in turn, reshape and enlarge the theory even more. This cyclic effect continues for as long as the theory proves useful. When a theory is no longer able to explain related observations, it is set aside in favor of a better one, not because it has been disproven, but because it has ceased to be useful.

What Makes a Theory Useful?

The value of any theory rests on its usefulness, not on its truthfulness. What makes one theory useful and another not? Several standards are used to establish the value of a theory, and each of the theories presented in this book will be evaluated on the basis of the following five criteria.

Organizes Known Data

A useful theory gives organization to observations. This is perhaps a theory's most important function, for without some organization or classification, observations made from research would remain isolated and meaningless. Unless observations are organized into some intelligible framework, a scientist is left with no clear direction to follow in the pursuit of further knowledge. Intelligent questions cannot be asked unless observations have some order. Without intelligent questions, further research is severely curtailed.

A useful theory of personality must be capable of integrating what is currently known about human behavior and personality development. It must be able to shape as many bits of information as possible into a meaningful arrangement. If a personality theory does not offer a reasonable explanation of at least some kinds of behavior, its usefulness is extremely questionable. On the other hand, personality theorists should not force every observation of behavior into their theory, nor should they rationalize every negative research finding. When theorists become compelled to offer their theory as an explanation for *all* personality, they risk mistaking theory for truth. The theory then ceases to be viable and rigor mortis sets in.

Generates Research

Besides giving meaning and synthesis to known data, a useful theory serves as a guide for further research. Without an adequate theory to point the way, many of our present empirical findings would have remained undiscovered. In astronomy, for example, the planet Neptune was discovered because the theory of motion generated the hypothesis that the irregularity in the path of Uranus must be caused by the presence of another planet. Useful theory provided astronomers with a roadmap that guided their search for and discovery of the new planet.

A useful theory will generate two different kinds of research: *descriptive* and *hypothesis testing*. Descriptive research is that which is carried out in order to expand an existing theory. It is concerned with the measurement, labeling, and categorization of the units employed in theory building. Descriptive research has a symbiotic relationship with theory. On one hand, it provides the building blocks for the theory and, on the other, it receives its impetus from the ever-expanding theory. The more useful the theory, the more research generated by it; the greater the amount of descriptive research, the more complete the theory.

The second kind of research generated by a useful theory, hypothesis testing, leads to an indirect verification of the usefulness of the theory. A useful theory will generate many hypotheses which, when tested, add significantly to our understanding of human personality.

Guide to Action

A third criterion of a useful theory is that it must offer the practitioner some guidance over the rough course of day-to-day problems. Psychotherapists, for example, are confronted continually with an avalanche of questions for which workable answers must be found. Good theory provides a structure for finding many of those answers.

For a therapist concerned with such questions as "What are the causes of the patient's neurosis?" or "How can I best treat my client?" a theoretical framework provides a needed shortcut to decision making. Without theory, a practitioner would stumble in the darkness of trial and error. With sound theoretical orientation, a suitable course of action becomes apparent.

For the Freudian analyst and Rogerian counselor, answers to the same question would be very different. To the question "How can I best treat this patient?" the psychoanalytic therapist might answer along these lines:

> If psychoneuroses are caused by childhood sexual conflicts which have become unconscious, then I can help this patient best by delving into these repressions and allowing the patient to relive the experiences in the absence of conflict.

To the same question, the Rogerian therapist might answer:

> If people need empathy, unconditional positive regard, and congruence to grow psychologically, then I can best help this client by providing an accepting non-threatening atmosphere.

Notice that both therapists constructed their answers in an *if-then* framework, even though the two answers call for very different courses of action.

Internally Consistent

A theory can be useful only if its components are logically compatible. For example, the language of a theory must be consistent; that is, the same term must not have two separate meanings nor be applied in more than one way. Also, one tenet of the theory cannot be opposed to another tenet.

A good theory will include a taxonomy that is logical and that has been systematically constructed. It will use concepts and terms that have been clearly and operationally defined and used only in consonance with those definitions. An **operational definition** is one that defines units in terms of specific operations to be carried out by the observer.

An internally consistent theory cannot offer opposing answers to the same question. Also, it does not force incompatible observations into a framework where they do not fit. Its limitations of scope are carefully defined and it does not offer explanations that lie beyond that scope.

Parsimonious

When two theories are equal in their ability to give meaning to observations and to generate testable hypotheses, the simpler one is preferred. This is the law of parsimony. In fact, of course, two theories are never exactly equal in these abilities. In general, however, simple straightforward theories are more useful than ones that bog down under the weight of complicated concepts and esoteric language.

In building a theory of personality, it is usually more desirable to begin on a limited scale and avoid sweeping generalizations that attempt to explain all of human behavior. That was the course of action followed by most of the theorists discussed in this book. For example, Freud began with a theory based largely on hysterical neuroses and, over a period of years, gradually expanded it to include more and more of the personality.

Why Different Theories?

Some might ask, "If theories of personality are truly scientific, why so many different ones?" The answer is that there are many personality theories because the very nature of a theory allows the theory builder to make speculations from a particular point of view. One must be as objective as possible when gathering data, but the decision as to what data are collected and how they are interpreted is based on the theorist's unique perception of human behavior. Theories are not immutable laws; they are built, not on proven facts, but on assumptions that are subject to individual interpretation.

All theories are a reflection of their authors' personal backgrounds. One's childhood experiences, unconscious motivation, philosophy of life, and interpersonal relationships all influence one's view of humanity. Since observations are colored by the individual observer's frame of reference, it follows that there may be many diverse theories. Nevertheless, divergent theories may be useful. The usefulness of a theory depends on its ability to integrate known observations and to generate research, not on its agreement with some other established theory.

There is room for several theories of personality because there are several ways of looking at human personality; several philosophical orientations which allow for different approaches to the scientific study of personality. Scientific investigation cannot exist apart from one's basic assumptions concerning the nature of humanity. A scientist does not operate within a vacuum, but gathers data and makes speculations with some preexisting frame of reference, some preestablished **concept of humanity.**

DIMENSIONS FOR A CONCEPT OF HUMANITY

The basic assumptions concerning human nature rest on several broad dimensions that separate the various personality theorists. Six of these dimensions will serve as a framework for viewing each theory's concept of humanity.

The first dimension is *determinism vs. free choice.* Is one's behavior and personality determined by forces over which one has no control? Can one choose to be what one wills? Can behavior be partially free and partially determined? Although the dimension of determinism vs. free will is more philosophical than scientific, the position theorists take on this issue shapes their way of looking at people and colors their concept of humanity.

A second, perhaps related issue, is one of *pessimism vs. optimism.* Are people doomed to live miserable, conflicted, and troubled lives or can they change and grow into psychologically healthy, happy, fully functioning human beings? In general, those who believe in determinism tend to be pessimistic (Skinner is a notable exception), while those who believe in free choice are usually optimistic.

A third dimension for viewing a theorist's concept of humanity is *causality vs. teleology.* Briefly, **causality** holds that behavior is a function of past experiences, while **teleology** is an explanation of behavior in terms of future goals or purposes. In other words, do people act as they do because of what has happened to them in the past or because they have certain expectations of what will happen in the future?

A fourth consideration that divides personality theorists is their attitude toward *conscious vs. unconscious* determinants of behavior. Are people ordinarily aware of what they are doing and why they are doing it or do unconscious forces impinge upon them and drive them to act without awareness of these underlying forces?

The fifth dimension is one of *biological vs. social* factors. Are people mostly creatures of biology or do social influences play the major role in shaping personality? A more specific element of this issue is heredity vs. environment, that is, are personal characteristics more the result of heredity or are they environmentally determined?

A sixth issue is *uniqueness vs. similarities.* Is the salient feature of people their individuality or their common characteristics? Should the study of personality concentrate on those traits which make people alike or those which make them different?

These are some of the basic issues that separate personality theorists. It should be apparent that differences in personality theories are more than just differences in terminology. They reflect basic differences among the theorists in their concept of humanity. One could not erase the differences among personality theories by adopting a common language. The differences are philosophical and deep-seated. Each personality theory reflects the individual personality of its creator. Each creator has a unique philosophical orientation, shaped in part by early childhood experiences, birth order, sex, training, education, and pattern of interpersonal relationships. These differences help determine whether a theorist will be deterministic or a believer in free choice, pessimistic or optimistic, causal or teleological. They also help determine whether one emphasizes consciousness or unconsciousness, biological or social factors, and the uniqueness or similarities of people. These differences do not, however, negate the possibility that two theorists with opposing views of humanity can be equally scientific in their data gathering and theory building.

RESEARCH IN PERSONALITY THEORY

Earlier we saw that theories and observations have a cyclic relationship: Theory gives meaning to observations, and observations result from experimental research designed to test hypotheses generated by the theory. Not all observations, however, flow from experimental research. Each of us makes many observations everyday. To observe simply means to notice something, to pay attention.

You have been observing human personalities for nearly as long as you have been alive. You notice that some people are talkative and "outgoing"; others are quiet and reserved. You may have even labeled people as extraverts and introverts. Are such labels accurate? Is one extraverted person like another? Does an extravert always act in a talkative, outgoing manner? Are all people either introverts or extraverts?

In making observations and asking questions, you are doing some of the same things psychologists do. They observe human behaviors and try to make sense out of their observations. However, psychologists, like other scientists, try to be *systematic* so that their *predictions* will be consistent and accurate.

Reliability and Validity

To improve their ability to predict, personality psychologists have developed a number of *assessment* techniques, including personality inventories. For these instruments to be useful they must be both **reliable** and **valid.** The reliability of a measuring instrument is the extent to which it yields consistent results. Validity refers to the accuracy of the instrument. Reliability can be determined by several methods: (1) comparing scores on two or more administrations of the same instrument; (2) comparing scores yielded by parallel (equivalent) forms of the same instrument; (3) comparing half the test items with the other half (split-half reliability); or (4) comparing ratings made by two or more judges observing the same phenomenon (interrater reliability).

Reliability is most frequently expressed in terms of **correlation coefficients,** that is, a mathematical procedure for expressing the degree of correspondence between two sets of scores. High positive reliability coefficients (for example, .80 to .90) indicate that subjects obtained nearly the same scores on two administrations of the test. Low scores (near .00) indicate a lack of correspondence, and high negative scores indicate a strong tendency for high scores on one administration of the test to be associated with low scores on a second administration.

Personality inventories may be reliable and yet lack validity or accuracy. Validity is the extent to which an instrument measures what it is supposed to measure. In determining validity, test scores are compared to an independent or outside criterion. For example, a personality inventory designed to measure extraversion and introversion must first be able to differentiate people into an extraverted category and an introverted category. Next, people scoring high in the extraverted direction must be the ones judged by some other criterion to be extraverted, and those scoring in an introverted direction must be independently identified as introverts.

Most of the early personality theorists did not use standardized assessment inventories. Freud, Adler, and Jung all developed some form of projective technique, but none used it with sufficient precision to qualify as a reliable and valid personality inventory. However, the theories of Freud, Adler, and Jung have spawned a number of standardized personality inventories as researchers and clinicians have sought to measure units of personality proposed by those theorists. Later personality theorists, especially Rotter, Cattell, and Eysenck, have developed and used a number of personality measures and have relied heavily on them in constructing their theoretical models.

Bimodal and Unimodal Distributions

Test scores may be distributed in a number of ways, but most personality traits are thought to be either bimodally or unimodally distributed. A **bimodal distribution** is one that has two distinct **modes** (the mode is the most frequent score in a distribution). For example, handedness is bimodally distributed, with most people showing a strong preference for either the right hand or the left. The relatively few ambidextrous people would score in the middle. Similarly, an inventory that categorized people into either introverts or extraverts would yield a bimodal distribution (see Figure 1.2).

A **unimodal** distribution has one distinct mode. Scores from intelligence tests, for example, yield unimodal distributions with the greatest number of people scoring near the **mean** (the arithmetic average score). Figure 1.3 shows a unimodal distribution of scores.

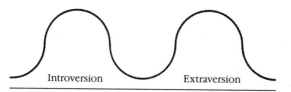

Introversion   Extraversion

Figure 1.2   Example of a Bimodal Distribution

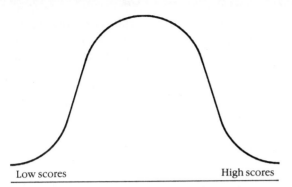

Low scores   High scores

Figure 1.3   Example of a Unimodal Distribution

Research Methods

We said earlier that a useful theory must generate two kinds of research: descriptive and hypothesis testing. An example of descriptive research is the single-subject or case study. Hypotheses are usually tested through means of experimental studies.

Many personality theorists, especially the earlier ones, relied almost exclusively on the *case study.* Freud, Jung, Adler, Horney, and Sullivan based their theories on clinical experiences with one patient at a time. Case studies can have a legitimate role in science provided the investigator is objective, systematic, and thorough. Case studies ordinarily provide more complete analysis of an individual than can be obtained by investigations of many subjects. The main disadvantage of the single-subject study is that it magnifies sampling errors. The error becomes even greater when the person deviates dramatically from the typical person. For example, patients seen in psychotherapy, by virtue of the fact that they are patients, do not constitute a representative sample of personalities, and generalization from clinical experience to people-in-general is problematical.

Experimental studies, on the other hand, use many subjects and are designed to test specific hypotheses. In an experimental study an investigator ordinarily begins with a randomly selected sample of subjects, divides them into two or more equated groups, administers a particular condition to one group, and withholds that condition from the other group. The only difference between the two groups is in their exposure to the **independent variable,** that is, the variable being investigated. Any subsequent differences between the two groups in behavior (the **dependent variable**) can be attributed to the independent variable. For example, in a study to assess the effectiveness of psychotherapy, a number of people seeking therapy are divided into an experimental group that receives therapy and a control group that must wait. The independent variable is the presence or absence of therapy and the dependent variable is the observed changes in behavior, if any, as a consequence of therapy.

In an experiment such as this, people in the control group (those not immediately receiving therapy) sometimes change their behavior in the same direction as do those in the experimental (therapy) group. This is accounted for by the **placebo effect,** that is, changes brought about by people's beliefs or expectations. If people in the control group receive some attention (but not therapy) from the experimenter, they may show positive gains as a consequence of the attention. The placebo effect clouds any conclusions from studies on the effectiveness of psychotherapy.

CHAPTER SUMMARY

Personality is one of the most fascinating topics in psychology. Nearly everyone is interested in personality, although fewer might be attracted to the concept of theory.

The term personality comes from the Latin *persona,* or the mask that people present to the outside world. This original meaning is similar to the *popular definition* of personality, which is associated with charm and charisma.

The *psychological definition,* however, is more likely to include everything that one is. It views personality as comprising all those relatively permanent traits or characteristics that render some consistency to a person's behavior.

A *theory* is defined as a set of related assumptions from which testable hypotheses can be drawn. Theory should not be confused with philosophy, armchair speculation, hypothesis, or taxonomy, although it is related to each of these terms.

Five criteria determine the usefulness of a scientific theory: (1) Does it organize knowledge? (2) Does it generate research?

(3) Does it suggest practical solutions to everyday problems? (4) Is it internally consistent? and (5) Is it simple or parsimonious?

Each personality theorist had either an implicit or explicit *concept of humanity,* and each theorist's view of human nature can be discussed from six dimensions: (1) determinism vs. free choice, (2) pessimism vs. optimism, (3) causality vs. teleology, (4) conscious vs. unconscious determinants, (5) biological vs. social factors, and (6) uniqueness vs. similarities in people.

Because useful personality theories should generate research, several instruments for assessing personality have been developed. These measuring devices must be both reliable (consistent) and valid (accurate). They typically yield either bimodal (two modes) data or a unimodal (one mode) distribution. The two most frequently employed research methods in personality are the case study (single subject) and the experimental design.

Suggested Readings

McCain, G., & Segal, E. M. (1988). *The game of science* (5th ed.). Pacific Grove, CA: Brooks/Cole.
This consistently popular book presents a very readable and interesting account of some of the new developments in science, including a look at the role of scientific theory.
Stanovich, K. E. (1986). *How to think straight about psychology.* Glenview, IL: Scott, Foresman.
Misconceptions about psychology in general and theory in particular are cleared up in this small volume. Basic methods used in psychological research are also included.

Part Two
PSYCHODYNAMIC THEORIES

FREUD

2

Psychoanalysis

Upon approaching George's home, one is immediately impressed by the neatness and orderliness of his yard and house. The lawn has been carefully manicured, with every blade of grass seemingly the same height, the sidewalks and curbs precisely edged, and the flower garden perfectly groomed. The 15-year-old car parked in the driveway is in showcase condition—not a nick has ever marred the waxed exterior, the white walls are snow-white, and the interior is immaculate. The house, though 20 years old, shows no signs of age or deterioration. Because most houses in this suburban neighborhood are attractive and well kept, the exterior of George's house is not altogether remarkable. A look at the interior, however, reveals an unusually clean and orderly appearance. The 20-year-old carpets seem brand-new. Plastic runners lead from one room to the next and it appears that few footsteps have ever ventured off these protective devices. The formal living room looks little used, with plastic covering all the chairs and sofas. The family room appears more informal—rather than plastic covers, bed sheets are used to protect the furniture.

Although he neither cooks nor washes dishes (leaving these chores to his wife), George spends much of his time in the kitchen. Here, while entertaining guests, he habitually and somewhat automatically dusts the furniture, woodwork, and counter top with his white handkerchief. A visitor would be hard pressed to find any dust above the door frame.

George's bedroom and closet are also extremely tidy. Suits and slacks are hung with equal spacings and according to color, shade, and season. Shoes are all neatly placed in a rack, again by color. His bathroom gleams and sparkles. George showers three times a day—once before work, again after work, and finally before retiring. He patiently towels off all the tile after each shower and cleans the faucets until they shine.

George works as a supervisor in an exclusive clothing store. In spite of his modest income, his frugality allows him to afford his luxurious house which is located in a neighborhood where the incomes of most of the residents is two or three times that of George's. At work, of course, George dresses very neatly, though many of his suits are ten years old or more. On weekends, George relaxes around the house, seldom going out to eat or to a movie.

While doing chores around the house and yard he wears blue jeans and a plain white T-shirt. Both, however, are starched and neatly pressed.

George's neatness and orderliness extends to all aspects of his life—his car, house, yard, workshop, and personal appearance. His family must also conform to his standards. George chooses all of his wife's clothes and his two children are well groomed and mannerly. They have learned to never incur their father's wrath by carelessly leaving a newspaper on the coffee table or an empty glass in the family room.

Most readers know someone like George, someone who is uncomfortable amid clutter and who apparently must keep his or her personal possessions in meticulous order. What accounts for such rigid behavior? What theories would Sigmund Freud offer to explain the compulsively neat personality? Later we will address these questions, but first, we will present a brief overview of Freud's personality theory, and then look at the life of the man who created a complex and fascinating approach for reviewing human personality.

OVERVIEW

Sigmund Freud's contributions to personality theory have been both substantial and controversial. Freud's theory, **psychoanalysis,** is not only the most comprehensive of all personality theories; it also has generated the greatest amount of critical interest—both positive and negative.

What makes Freud's theory so interesting? First, the twin cornerstones of psychoanalysis, sex and aggression, are two subjects of continuing popularity. Second, the theory was spread beyond its Viennese origin by an ardent and dedicated group of followers, many of whom romanticized Freud as a nearly mythological and lonely hero. Third, Freud's heavy emphasis on unconscious motivation allows several opposing explanations for the same observed behaviors.

Freud's contributions to our understanding of humanity provide a logical starting point in any discussion of personality theories. Besides originating the most comprehensive of all theories of personality, Freud founded a theory of mental disorders as well as a theory and technique of psychotherapy. Each of these three contributions has served as a foundation stone for the modern edifices of psychiatry and psychology.

The three concerns—normal personality, abnormal development, and psychotherapy—cannot be separated. Each complements and supplements the other two. The present discussion focuses on the first. Abnormal personality and psychotherapy are partially explored, but only to elucidate Freud's theory of personality.

Freud's experiences with patients in psychotherapy provided the basic data for the evolution of his theories. To him, theory followed observation and his concept of personality underwent constant revisions based on his experiences as a practicing psychotherapist. Psychoanalysis, then, always remained an unfinished discipline. Evolutionary though it was, Freud continued to insist that it could not be subjected to eclecticism. Disciples were not permitted to select or reject those ideas which suited their personal preference.

Though Freud regarded himself primarily as a scientist, he made basic observations subjectively and only on a relatively small sample of patients, most of whom were from the upper middle and upper classes. He did not quantify his data, nor did he make observations under rigorously controlled conditions. He utilized the case study approach almost exclusively, typically formulating hypotheses after the facts of the case were known.

Biography of Sigmund Freud

Freud was born either on March 6 or May 6, 1856 in Freiberg, Moravia, which is now a part of Czechoslovakia. (Scholars disagree on his birth date—the first date was but eight months after the marriage of his parents.) Sigmund was the firstborn child of Jacob and Amalie Nathanson Freud, though his father had two grown sons, Emanuel and Philipp, from a previous marriage. Jacob and Amalie Freud had seven other children within 10 years but Sigmund remained the favorite of his young indulgent mother, a fact that may have partially contributed to his lifelong optimism and self-confidence (Jones, 1953, Vol. 1). A scholarly, serious-minded youth, Freud does not seem to have enjoyed a friendship with any of his younger siblings, but was more inclined toward his parents, especially his mother. His earliest playmates were his half-nephew, John, and his half-niece, Pauline. John was about a year older than Sigmund and Pauline was just a little younger than Freud. One of Freud's earliest memories was of him and John taking away a bouquet of flowers from Pauline and causing the young girl to run away in tears (Vitz, 1988).

When Sigmund was three, the two Freud families left Freiberg. Emanuel's family and Philipp moved to London, while at about the same time, the Jacob Freud family moved to Leipzig. The following year, Sigmund moved with his family to Vienna and that city remained his home for nearly 80 years, until 1938 when the Nazi invasion forced him to emigrate to London. He made his home in England until his death on September 23, 1939.

When Freud was about a year old his mother gave birth to a second son, an event that was to have a significant impact on Freud's psychic development. Sigmund was filled with hostility toward his brother and harbored an unconscious wish for his death. When the boy died at eight months of age, Sigmund was left with feelings of guilt at having caused his brother's death. Only in later years was Freud able to understand that the death wish for a sibling was not only common in young children, but also that, in fact, his wish did not produce his brother's death.

This discovery purged Freud of the guilt he had carried into adulthood and, by his own analysis, contributed to his later psychic development (Freud, 1900/1953).

Freud was drawn into medicine, not so much out of love for medical practice but out of an intense curiosity concerning human nature (Ellenberger, 1970). At that time, as throughout his life, he valued the scientific approach to nature over philosophical speculation. He entered the University of Vienna Medical School in 1873, and when he graduated in 1881 he had no intention of practicing medicine. He preferred instead to do research in physiology. To pursue his career, however, he was dependent upon his father and friends for financial support. After his graduation, he remained at the university's Physiological Institute, having primary duties in research as well as some teaching responsibilities.

Freud might have continued his work indefinitely had it not been for two factors. First, he believed (probably without justification) that being a Jew his opportunities for academic advancement would be limited. Second, his father became less able to provide financial aid. Reluctantly, Freud turned from his laboratory to the practice of medicine. He worked for three years in the General Hospital of Vienna, becoming familiar with the practice of various branches of medicine, including psychiatry and nervous diseases (Freud, 1925/1959).

In 1885 he received a traveling grant from the University of Vienna and decided to study in Paris with the famous French neurologist Jean-Martin Charcot. He spent four months with Charcot from whom he learned the hypnotic technique for treating hysteria, a disorder typically characterized by paralysis or the improper functioning of certain parts of the body. It was through hypnosis that Freud became convinced of the psychogenic origin of hysterical symptoms.

From his days as a medical student, Freud developed a close professional association and a personal friendship with Joseph Breuer, a well-known Viennese physician, 14 years older than Freud, and a man of considerable scientific reputation. From Breuer, Freud learned about catharsis, a method of removing hysterical symptoms through "talking them out." He gradually and laboriously discovered the free association technique, which evolved from Breuer's cathartic method. Free association soon replaced hypnosis as Freud's principal therapeutic technique.

From his early years as a physician, Freud was strongly driven by the idea of making some monumental discovery and also of achieving fame (Ellenberger, 1970). His first opportunity to gain recognition came in 1884–1885 and involved the many uses of cocaine. He believed he had achieved an important breakthrough with his experiments with cocaine and was led to proclaim the wonderful virtues of that drug. After taking cocaine himself without any harmful effects, Freud praised it as a near panacea as well as an effective anesthetic (Byck, 1974). However, he was doomed to disappointment when someone else received credit for the discovery of the drug's anesthetic properties. Further trouble followed when he used cocaine in treating a friend for morphine addiction and succeeded in causing him to become a cocaine addict (Ellenberger, 1970).

Two years later, in 1886 and after he had returned from Paris, Freud again believed that he was on the brink of making a major discovery when he presented a paper on male hysteria to the Imperial Society of Physicians of Vienna. Hysteria was originally thought to be a female disorder since it was believed to be the result of a "wandering womb." Freud had learned about male hysteria from Charcot and believed that his paper to the Society would be a major contribution. However, most of the physicians present were already familiar with the illness and, since originality was expected, Freud's paper was not well received. Also, Freud's constant praise of the Frenchman Charcot cooled the Viennese physicians to his talk. Unfortunately, in his autobiographical study (Freud, 1925/1959) he relates a very different story. Freud claims that his lecture was not well received because members of the learned society could not fathom the concept of male hysteria. Freud's account of this incident, now known to be in error, was nevertheless perpetuated for years and, as Sulloway (1979) demonstrates, is but one of many denials created by Freud and his followers to mythologize psychoanalysis and to make a lonely hero of its founder.

Disappointed in his attempts to gain fame, and inflicted with feelings (both justified and otherwise) of professional opposition due to his defense of cocaine and his belief in the sexual factors in neuroses, Freud felt the need to join with a more respected colleague. He turned to Breuer with whom he had worked while still a medical student, and with whom he enjoyed a continuing personal and professional relationship. Breuer had discussed in detail with Freud the case of Anna O, a young woman he had spent many hours treating for hysteria several years earlier. After his rebuff by the Imperial Society of Physicians, and desirous of establishing a reputation for himself, Freud urged Breuer to collaborate with him in publishing an account of Anna O and several other cases of hysteria, along with theoretical and therapeutic considerations of the illness. Breuer, however, was not as eager as the younger and more revolutionary Freud to publish a full treatise on hysteria built on only a few case studies. Finally, and with some reluctance, he agreed to publish with Freud *Studies on Hysteria* (Breuer & Freud, 1895/1955). The beginnings of psychoanalysis are sometimes traced to the original date of this publication, but the embryonic period of Freudian theory lay just ahead.

At about the time *Studies on Hysteria* was published, Freud and Breuer had a professional disagreement and became estranged personally. Freud then turned to his friend Wilhelm Fliess, who, during the late 1890s, served as a sounding board for Freud's newly developing ideas. Fliess was a Berlin physician and Freud's letters to him constitute, perhaps, the most accurate account of the beginnings of psychoanalysis (Freud, 1985).

Freud and Fliess had become friends in 1887, but their relationship became more intimate following Freud's break with Breuer. During the latter part of 1895 and the first few months of 1896, Freud was laboring feverishly on what was called the *Project for a Scientific Psychology* (Freud, 1950/1966). The manuscript was sent to Fliess for criticism, but Freud soon abandoned the "Project" and its existence was not discovered until after World War II. Though the significance of the "Project" is still controversial among Freud scholars, the work does contain many concepts and terms later associated with Freud and psychoanalysis.

The late 1890s were for Freud a time of personal crises and professional isolation. His friendship with Fliess was beginning to cool, eventually to rupture in 1903. He had begun to analyze his own dreams and, after the death of his father in 1896, he initiated the practice of analyzing himself daily. Though his self-analysis continued for a lifetime, it was most difficult for him during the late 1890s. During this period, Freud regarded himself as his own best patient (Ellenberger, 1970). A final contributing factor to his personal crisis was his realization that he was now middle-aged and had yet to achieve the fame he so passionately desired.

During this time he had suffered yet another disappointment in his attempt to make a major scientific contribution. He once again believed himself to be on the verge of an important breakthrough with his "discovery" that neuroses have their etiology in a child's seduction by a parent. Freud likened this finding to the discovery of the source of the Nile. However, by 1897 he came to believe that his seduction theory was not tenable since so many fathers, including his own, would be guilty of seducing their children. Disappointed, he abandoned the seduction theory (see Box—"Parental Practice or Childhood Fantasy? Why Freud Abandoned the Seduction Theory").

Freud's biographer, Ernest Jones (1953, 1955, 1957), believed that Freud suffered from a severe psychoneurosis during the late 1890s, although Max Schur (1972), Freud's personal physician during the final decade of his life, contended that his illness was due to a cardiac lesion, aggravated by addiction to nicotine. Henri Ellenberger (1970), on the other hand, describes this period in Freud's life as a time of "creative illness," a condition characterized by depression, neurosis, psychosomatic ailments, and an intense preoccupation with some form of creative activity. In any event, it is safe to assert that at midlife Freud suffered from self-doubts, depression, and an obsession with his own death.

Despite these difficulties, Freud completed his greatest work, *The Interpretation of Dreams* (1900/1953), during this period. This book, finished in 1899, was an outgrowth of Freud's self-analysis, and contained many of his own dreams, some disguised behind fictitious names. Though it took a few years for the work to create an international stir, it eventually gained for Freud the fame and recognition he had sought.

In the five-year period following the publication of *The Interpretation of Dreams,* Freud, now filled with self-confidence, published several important works that helped solidify the foundation of psychoanalysis (Freud, 1901/ 1953, 1901/1960, 1905/1953a, 1905/ 1953b, 1905/1960). He now was beginning to gain some local prominence in scientific and medical circles, and a group of followers was soon attracted to him. In 1902 the Psychological Wednesday Society was formed with Freud, Alfred Adler, Wilhelm Stekel, Max Kahane, and Rudolf Reitler as participants. In 1908 the name of the organization was changed to the Vienna Psychoanalytic Society. Two years later the International Psychoanalytic Association was founded with Carl Jung of Zurich as president. Jung, a favorite of Freud, had been designated as the "Crown Prince" and "the man of the future," but, like Adler and Stekel before him, Jung quarreled bitterly with Freud and their relationship was terminated in 1913 (McGuire, 1974).

The years of World War I were difficult for Freud. He was cut off from communication with his faithful followers, his psychoanalytic practice dwindled, his home was sometimes without heat, and he and his family had little food. After the

war, despite advancing years and pain suffered from 33 operations for cancer of the mouth, important revisions were made in his theory. The most significant of these were the elevation of the death instinct to a level with the life instinct; the inclusion of repression as one of the defenses of the ego; and the clarification of the female Oedipus complex.

Freud's personal life had many highlights: his marriage to Martha Bernays in 1886 after a long engagement; the birth of their six children between 1887 and 1895; the beginning of his self-analysis in 1897 as a reaction to the death of his father; his trip with Jung to the United States in 1909 to speak at Clark University; his gaining worldwide recognition; and finally, at age 82, his emigration to England after the Nazis had marched into Austria.

What personal qualities did Freud possess? For a more complete insight into his personality the reader is directed to Clark (1980), Ellenberger (1970), Isbister (1985), Jones (1953, 1955, 1957), Sulloway (1979), and Vitz (1988). Briefly, it can be said that Sigmund Freud was, above all else, a sensitive, passionate person. He had the capacity for intimate, almost secretive relationships. While still a young student, he and a close friend, Edward Silberstein, formed a Spanish society with the purpose of learning that language, but also with the effect of solidifying a close union, one which distrusted others and viewed the world with suspicion. Similar relationships were repeated throughout Freud's life. He had the capacity for revealing intimate aspects of his personality to those who were close to him while, at the same time, feeling persecuted by others. He seemed to have needed these intense relationships, which were both exclusive and somewhat distrustful in attitude toward the outside world. His passionate nature is revealed in his correspondence with his intimates (E. Freud, 1960; S. Freud, 1985).

Freud was also an exceptionally gifted writer. He knew several foreign languages, but he was a master of the German tongue. He was an excellent translator, having translated the Englishman, John Stuart Mill, and the Frenchman, Jean-Martin Charcot, among many others. Evidence of his ability as a writer is seen in his winning the Goethe prize for literature in 1930.

Among other qualities, Freud possessed an intense intellectual curiosity; unusual moral courage, demonstrated by his daily self-analysis; extremely ambivalent feelings toward his father and other father figures; the tendency to hold grudges disproportionate to the alleged offense; a burning ambition, especially during his earlier years; strong feelings of isolation even while surrounded by many followers; and an intense and somewhat irrational dislike of Americans, a feeling that became more intense after his trip to the United States in 1909.

Freud's greatest contribution to personality theory is his exploration of the unconscious and his insistence that people are motivated primarily by instinctual forces of which they have little or no awareness. It is fitting, therefore, to begin the discussion of his theory of personality by looking at the different levels of mental life.

LEVELS OF MENTAL LIFE

The fundamental assumption of psychoanalysis is that mental life is divided into two levels, the **unconscious** and the **conscious.** The unconscious, in turn, has two different levels, the unconscious proper and the **preconscious.** (In Freudian psychology the three levels of mental life are used to designate both a process and a location. The existence as a specific location, of course, is merely hypothetical and has no real existence within the body. Yet, Freud spoke of *the* unconscious as well as unconscious processes.)

The unconscious contains all those mental elements which cannot become conscious or which can do so only with great difficulty. The second level, the preconscious, includes those ideas which can more readily become conscious, but which remain in awareness only temporarily. In general, therefore, mental life can be divided into three levels, the unconscious, the preconscious, and the conscious.

Unconscious

Unconscious processes play an important role in determining behavior. Even though unconscious ideas, by definition, are beyond our awareness, Freud believed that they exert an extensive influence on our words, feelings, thoughts, and actions. We may be conscious of overt actions, but ordinarily we are not aware of the mental processes that lie behind our behavior. For example, George (in the case study introduced at the beginning of this chapter) is aware of his desire to maintain a neat and orderly environment, but he has no insight into the origins or causes of his compulsive behavior.

Since the unconscious is not available to the conscious mind, how can one know if it really exists? Freud felt that its existence could be proved only indirectly. To him the unconscious is the only explanation for the meaning behind dreams, slips of the tongue, neurotic symptoms, and certain kinds of forgetting, called repressions. Dreams serve as a particularly rich source of unconscious material. For example, Freud believed that childhood experiences sometimes reappear in adult dreams even though the dreamer has no conscious recollection of them. (For a possible physiological explanation for the unconscious see Box—"Biological Bases for the Unconscious.")

Unconscious processes often enter into consciousness, but, to do so, they must elude censorship through disguise and distortion. Freud used the analogy of a guardian or censor blocking the passage between the unconscious and preconscious and preventing undesirable anxiety-producing memories from entering awareness. To enter the conscious level of the mind, these unconscious processes not only must slip past the primary censor but also must elude a final censor that watches the passageway between the preconscious and the conscious. By that time they are no longer recognized for what they are, but are seen as relatively pleasant, nonthreatening experiences. Sexual and aggressive tendencies, due to their suppression by parents during childhood, often become unconscious through the process of **repression** (Freud, 1917/1963). Repression is the forcing of unwanted, anxiety-ridden experiences into the unconscious in order to defend the person against the pain of that anxiety.

Not all unconscious processes, however, spring from the repression of childhood events. Some, in fact, result not from any personal experience of an individual but from our early ancestors's experiences that have created a vast reservoir of the unconscious, called by Freud our **phylogenetic endowment.** Our phylogenetic endowment refers to our "collective mind," one that has been passed on to us through hundreds of generations of ancestors (Freud, 1917/1923, 1933/1964). Many affective states, such as guilt and anxiety, especially castration anxiety, are explained by Freud's concept of inherited experiences. Inherited phylogenetic endowment is somewhat similar to Carl Jung's idea of a collective unconscious (see Chapter 5). However, while Jung placed primary emphasis on the collective unconscious, Freud relied on the notion of inherited dispositions only as a last resort. That is, when explanations built on individual experiences have been exhausted, Freud

Biological Bases for the Unconscious

Freud's view of the unconscious is sometimes seen as a hypothetical construct—a metaphysical concept with no real biological existence. It is a mythical dumping ground, an explanation for many behaviors, memories, perceptions, and emotions that cannot be explained by any other means. As such, the notion of an unconscious is criticized as being beyond the reach of science. Indeed, few neuroscientists have ever searched for the biological bases for the unconscious. During the past century they have made giant strides in discovering the complex workings of the brain and the nervous system, but these discoveries have never revealed an unconscious mind.

In the meantime, the psychoanalysts have gone their own way—interpreting dreams, slips of the tongue, neurotic symptoms, and other behaviors as springing from an unconscious mind. Although Freud was a neurologist himself, his psychoanalytic followers have been little concerned with locating the neurological base for the unconscious.

Then, in 1985, Jonathan Winson, a neuroscientist with considerable knowledge of psychoanalytic theory, published a book called *Brain and Psyche: The Biology of the Unconscious,* in which he attempts to build a bridge between neurobiology and psychoanalysis, that is, between brain and psyche. Winson believes that the link between brain and psyche began some 140 million years ago when the brains of mammals were undergoing an evolutionary change. As mammals evolved from reptiles they became less dependent on reflexive action and more dependent on organizing and integrating sensory perceptions. This organization and integration is not instantaneous, but takes place over a period of time. In order to survive, mammals, including humans, must be able to integrate new experiences with past memories without necessarily being conscious of such a process. This is done largely during sleep and takes the form of dreams.

Dreams, then, are the bridge between brain and psyche. Winson cites evidence that dreams, defined as rapid eye movement (REM) sleep, are not found in reptiles but are present in nearly all mammals. One exception is the echidna, a small egg-laying mammal found in the forests of Australia. The echidna possesses a large prefrontal cortex, greater in size relative to the rest of its brain than any other mammal, including humans. Winson hypothesizes that the huge prefrontal cortex enables the echidna to correlate new impressions with past experiences, a necessity for mammalian survival. Other mammals, however, with their relatively smaller prefrontal cortex need not accomplish this task while awake, but use REM sleep (dreams) as a means of associating recent experience with the old.

Winson believes that REM sleep is fundamental to mammals and that "in man, dreams are a window on the neural process whereby, from early childhood on, strategies for behavior are being set down, modified, or consulted" (Winson, 1985, p. 209). He further states that "when Freud dissected and analyzed dreams and from them constructed his concept of the unconscious, he was looking at this process" (p. 209).

Winson's basic hypothesis is that *"the phylogenetically ancient mechanisms involving REM sleep, in which memories, associations, and strategies are formed and handled by the brain as a distinct category of information in the prefrontal cortex and associated structures, are in fact the Freudian unconscious"* (Winson, 1985, p. 209).

Winson finds that his neurobiological work supports some of Freud's ideas of the unconscious, but not all. He cannot accept Freud's view of the death instinct, but he does support Freud's notion that most unconscious impulses have a childhood origin. Early experiences in humans, Winson believes, shape the neural connections of a flexible and plastic prefrontal cortex. As the neocortex matures and sets, these experiences are no longer amenable to change. During REM sleep, however, they become associated with more recent experiences and result in dream content with a heavy infantile flavor.

In summary, Winson believes that experiences during the critical first three years of childhood result in the human unconscious and that this unconscious "remains throughout life at the core of the human psyche" (Winson, 1985, p. 241).

used the idea of collectively inherited experiences to fill in the gaps left by individual experiences. These "collective unconscious" experiences are not ones that we as individuals have repressed because they have never been part of our personal experiences.

Unconscious drives may appear in consciousness, but only after undergoing certain transformations. A person may express either erotic or hostile urges, for example, by teasing or joking with another. The original instinct (sex or aggression) is thus disguised and hidden from the conscious minds of both persons. The unconscious of the first person, however, has directly influenced the unconscious of the second. Both gain some satisfaction of either sexual or aggressive urges but neither is conscious of the underlying motive behind the teasing or joking. It is possible, therefore, for the unconscious mind of one person to communicate with the unconscious of another without either person being aware of the process.

It should be clear now that unconscious does not mean inactive or dormant. Instincts in the unconscious constantly strive to become conscious and many of them succeed, although they may no longer appear in their original form. Unconscious ideas can and do motivate the individual. For example, a son's hostility toward his father may masquerade itself in the form of ostentatious affection. In an undisguised form, the hostility would create too much anxiety for the son. His unconscious mind, therefore, motivates him to express hostility indirectly through an exaggerated show of love and flattery. Since the disguise must successfully deceive the person, it often takes an opposite form from the original feelings, but is almost always overblown and ostentatious. (This mechanism, called a reaction formation, will be discussed below under "Defense Mechanisms.")

Dreams, too, are motivated by the unconscious. In Freudian theory, they provide an avenue for repressed material to find expression, but the true nature of the dream lies hidden from the conscious mind of the dreamer.

One may recall the surface level of a dream, but yet remain unaware of the underlying meaning that motivates the dream (Freud, 1900/1953).

Besides being active, unconscious ideas are also intense. The intensity of unconscious urges is vividly seen in neurotic and psychotic symptoms. For example, Freud (1922/1955) believed that the persecution complex of the paranoid patient is a defense against unconscious homosexual urges. Paranoia is thus seen as an expression of unconscious sexual impulses toward the persecutor, who is always a former friend of the same sex. The unconscious impulse becomes quite intense and, at times, dominates the life of the paranoid person even though the person remains completely unaware of any true feelings toward the persecutor (Freud, 1917/1963).

Preconscious

The preconscious level of the mind contains all those elements which are not conscious but can become so quite readily (Freud, 1933/1964). The contents of the preconscious come from two sources, the first of which is conscious perception. What a person perceives is conscious for only a transitory period; it quickly passes into the preconscious when the focus of attention shifts to another idea. For example, you may not now be conscious of what you ate for breakfast this morning, but you can probably recall it without any difficulty. One moment an idea is conscious, then preconscious, and then it can become conscious again. In reality, then, the preconscious is much more similar to the conscious than to the unconscious.

The second source of preconscious content is the unconscious. According to Freud, ideas can slip past the vigilant censor and find their way into the preconscious, albeit in a disguised form. Some of these ideas never become conscious because they are recognized as derivatives of the unconscious. Therefore, they are repressed by the final censor and fall back into the unconscious. Other ideas gain admission to consciousness by their clever disguise, through the dream process, or because they are no longer threatening to the person. Since these ideas slip in and out of awareness quite easily, they are said to be preconscious.

Conscious

Consciousness, which plays a relatively minor role in psychoanalytic theory, can be defined as those mental elements in awareness at any given point in time. It is the only level of mental life directly available to us. Ideas can reach consciousness from two different directions. The first is from the **perceptual conscious** system, which is turned toward the outer world and acts as a medium for the perception of external stimuli. In other words, what we perceive through our sense organs, if not too threatening, enters into consciousness (Freud, 1933/1964).

The second source of conscious elements is from the opposite direction, that is, from within the mental structure. These are the unwelcome guests from the unconscious who have eluded censorship. As we have seen, unconscious ideas can become preconscious by evading the primary censor in the passageway between those two systems by disguising themselves as non-threatening experiences. Once in the preconscious they can come under the eye of consciousness by avoiding a final censor. By the time they reach the conscious system, these ideas are greatly distorted and camouflaged, often taking the form of neurotic symptoms.

The psychologically mature individual is generally more conscious of his or her feelings and the motivation behind behavior than is the psychotic or severely neurotic person, but even the behavior of the mature person is to a large degree guided and controlled by unconscious instincts.

In summary, Freud's concept of the unconscious can be compared to a large anteroom in which many heterogeneous, energetic people are milling

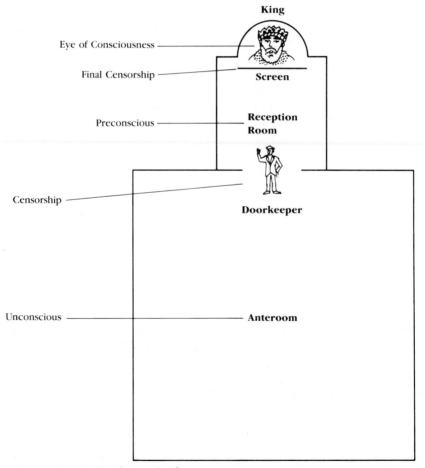

Figure 2.1   Levels of Mental Life

about, crowding one another, and striving incessantly to escape to a smaller adjoining room. Protecting the threshold between the large anteroom and the small reception room is a watchful guardian who serves a dual function. This doorkeeper can either turn back undesirable people at the door, or he can throw out people who originally slipped by. The effect in either case is the same; that is, the people are prevented from coming into view of a king who is seated at the far end of the reception room behind a screen. The meaning of the analogy is obvious. The people in the anteroom represent unconscious mental excitations. The small reception room is the preconscious and the people in the reception room are preconscious ideas. These people may or may not come into view of the king who, of course, represents the eye of consciousness. The doorkeeper who guards the threshold between the two rooms is the primary censor that prevents unconscious ideas from becoming preconscious and renders preconscious ideas unconscious by throwing them back. The screen that guards the king is the final censor, and it prevents many, but not all, preconscious elements from reaching consciousness. The analogy is presented graphically in Figure 2.1.

PROVINCES OF THE MIND

Freud (1933/1964) also divided the mind into three provinces: the "it," almost always translated into English as **id;** the "I," translated as **ego;** and the "above-I," which is rendered into English as **superego.** These provinces or regions have no territorial existence, of course, but are merely hypothetical constructs designed by Freud to better explain his theories. This division of the mind into id, ego, and superego is not identical to the levels of mental life. The ego, for example, cuts across the various levels having conscious, preconscious, and unconscious components. (See Figure 2.2 for the relationship between the provinces of the mind and the levels of consciousness.) The divisions of the mind into the id, ego, and superego are not clear and definite, but allow for certain overlappings and commonalities. Nevertheless, it is convenient, and to a large degree accurate, to consider these provinces separately.

Id

At the core of personality and completely unconscious to the individual is the psychical region called the id, a term derived from the impersonal pronoun meaning "the it," or the not-yet-owned component of personality.

In psychoanalytic theory, the id is home base for the instincts. It constantly strives to satisfy the wish impulses of the instincts by reducing tensions. The id serves the **pleasure principle,** since its sole function is to seek satisfaction of pleasurable drives. The newborn baby may be seen as a personification of an id unencumbered by restrictions of ego and superego. The baby seeks gratification of needs without regard for what is possible or what is proper, sucking when the nipple is either present or absent. Gaining plea-

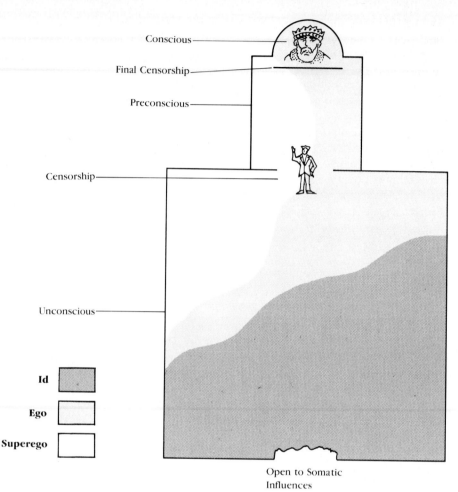

Conscious

Final Censorship

Preconscious

Censorship

Unconscious

Id

Ego

Superego

Open to Somatic
Influences

Figure 2.2   Levels of Mental Life and Provinces of the Mind

sure in either case, the infant receives nutrition only in the former. The extranutritional sucking continues because the id-dominated infant is not in contact with reality. She or he fails to realize that thumb-sucking behavior cannot sustain life.

Since the id has no direct contact with reality, it is not altered by the passage of time or by the experiences of the person (Freud, 1933/1964). Childhood wish impulses remain unchanged in the id for decades. The id is unable to distinguish between objective reality of a juicy steak from a mental image of one. This explains how it is possible for a person to salivate when he or she merely thinks about food.

The id is also illogical. Incompatible ideas can exist side by side within the unsuspecting id. For example, one may possess an unconscious wish for the destruction of another person, while, at the same time, desiring sexual union with that person.

Another characteristic of the id is a lack of morality. It is not immoral, merely amoral, since it cannot make value judgments or distinguish between good and evil. All of the id's energy is spent for one purpose—to seek pleasure (Freud, 1923/1961a, 1933/1964).

In review, the id is primitive, chaotic, inaccessible to consciousness, unchangeable, amoral, illogical, unorganized, and filled with energy received from the instincts and discharged for the satisfaction of the pleasure principle.

Since the id is the region that houses the instincts (primary motivators), it is said to operate through the **primary process.** Because it blindly seeks to satisfy the pleasure principle, its survival is dependent upon the development of a **secondary process** to bring it into contact with the external world. This secondary process functions through the ego.

Ego

The ego, or I, is the region of the mind in contact with reality. It grows out of the id during infancy and, throughout a person's lifetime, it remains the extension of the id which has communication with the external world. The ego is governed by the **reality principle,** which it tries to substitute for the pleasure principle of the id. It is the only one of the three provinces of the mind that has direct contact with reality. In that sense, both the id and the superego are equally unrealistic.

As the sole region of the mind in contact with the external world, the ego becomes the decision-making or executive branch of personality. Not all its choices, however, are made on the conscious level (Freud, 1933/1964). For instance, George's need to be excessively neat and orderly is satisfied not by the id but by the unconscious portion of the ego. Only the ego can decide to daily sweep one's front porch.

Because the ego is partly conscious, partly preconscious, and partly unconscious, decisions are made on each of these three levels. Moreover, when performing its cognitive and intellectual functions, the ego must take into consideration the incompatible, but equally unrealistic, demands of the id and the superego. In addition to these two tyrants, the ego must serve a third master—the external world. It constantly tries to reconcile the blind claims of the id and superego with the realistic demands of the outside world. Finding itself surrounded on three sides by divergent and hostile forces, the ego reacts in a predictable manner—it becomes anxious. Is it any wonder that conflict and anxiety play such an important role in the life of most people (Freud, 1933/1964, 1940/1964)!

As the executive of personality, the ego fights against the pain of anxiety through the mechanisms of repression and its concomitant censorship function. It attempts to reduce anxiety by preventing undesirable or threatening elements from reaching consciousness. This is done by means of the ego-protecting **defense mechanisms.** (The defense mechanisms will be enumerated and discussed more fully later.)

Another function of the ego is to maintain communication between the id and the outside world. The person could not survive without this communication. To accomplish this task the ego must make accurate observations, store these observations, and make use of them at the appropriate occasions.

According to Freud (1933/1964), the ego becomes differentiated from the id when the baby learns to distinguish itself from the outer world. The ego continues to develop and grow while the id remains unchanged. This evolving differentiation between the ego and the id explains many ambiguous feelings in a person. The ego of the adult, for example, may realize that smoking is harmful to health, while the pleasure-seeking id demands oral gratification. The person continues smoking, feels somewhat guilty, but denies both the guilt and the oral gratification by rationalizing that smoking is necessary to keep off excess weight. As the ego develops, the pressures from the outside world may become great enough to force the person to give up smoking, but the id impulse remains unaffected. The need to satisfy oral pleasure may find release in increased eating, gum chewing, fingernail biting, or tongue wagging.

In comparing the ego to the id, Freud (1933/1964) used the analogy of a person on horseback. The rider checks and inhibits the greater strength of the horse, but is at times ultimately at the mercy of the animal. Sometimes the rider permits the horse free rein in order to avoid falling off. Similarly, the ego checks and inhibits impulses, but it is more or less constantly at the mercy of the stronger but more poorly organized id. The ego has no strength of its own but borrows energy from the id. In spite of this dependence on the id, the ego sometimes comes close to gaining complete control. This control is never total, but probably comes closest to being complete during the prime of life of a psychologically mature person.

As the child begins to experience parental rewards and punishments, it learns what to do in order to gain pleasure and avoid pain. This is an ego function, since the child is still exclusively concerned with self. As the child grows older, it identifies with the parents and begins to learn what it should and should not do. This is the origin of the superego.

Superego

In Freudian psychology, the superego, or above-I, is the moral or ethical province of personality. It is guided by the **idealistic principle** as opposed to the pleasure principle of the id and the realistic principle of the ego. The superego grows out of the ego and, like the ego, has no energy of its own. However, the superego differs from the ego in one important respect; it has no contact with the outside world and is therefore unrealistic in its demands for perfection (Freud, 1923/1961a).

The superego has two subsystems, the **conscience** and the **ego-ideal.**

Freud did not clearly distinguish between these two functions, but, in general, the conscience results from experiences with punishments for improper behavior, while the ego-ideal develops when a child is rewarded for proper behavior. A primitive conscience comes into existence when the child conforms to parental standards out of fear of loss of love or approval. Later these ideals are internalized through identification with the mother and father. This identification takes place before and during the Oedipal period. A mature, well-developed superego can result only after the resolution of the Oedipus complex. (The Oedipus complex will be discussed in a later section.)

The well-developed superego acts to control sexual and aggressive impulses through the process of repression. It cannot produce repressions by itself, but can order the ego to do so. The superego watches closely over the ego, judging its actions and intentions. Guilt is the result when the ego acts, or even intends to act, contrary to the moral standards of the superego. Feelings of inferiority will arise if the ego is unable to meet the superego's standards of perfection. Guilt, then, is a function of the conscience; inferiority feelings stem from the ego-ideal (Freud, 1933/1964).

The superego is not concerned with the happiness of the ego. It strives blindly and unrealistically toward perfection. It is unrealistic in the sense that it does not take into consideration the difficulties or impossibilities faced by the ego in carrying out its orders. Not all its demands, of course, are impossible to fulfill, just as not all demands of parents and other authority figures are impossible to fulfill. The superego, however, is like the id in that it is completely ignorant of, and unconcerned with, the practicability of its requirement. One might guess, for example, that George's ego ideal has higher standards for order than even George is able to obtain. This demand for perfection keeps George's ego working hard, but never completely successfully.

Freud (1933/1964) pointed out that the divisions between the different regions of the mind are not sharp and well defined. The development of the three divisions varies widely in different individuals. For some, the superego does not grow after childhood; for others, the superego may dominate the personality at the cost of guilt and inferiority feelings. For yet others, the ego and superego may take turns controlling personality, which results in extreme fluctuations of mood and alternating cycles of self-confidence and self-depreciation. In the healthy individual, the id, ego, and superego are well integrated and operate in harmony with a minimum of conflict. Figure 2.3 shows the relationships among id, ego, and superego in three hypothetical persons. The person dominated by the id has an ego nearly swallowed by the id, and possesses a weak superego, one not capable of counterbalancing the incessant demands of the id. The second person is filled with either guilt or feelings of inferiority and experiences many conflicts due to the dominant superego and the opposing force of the id. The third person is a psychologically healthy individual whose ego has incorporated many of the demands of the id and nearly all those of the superego.

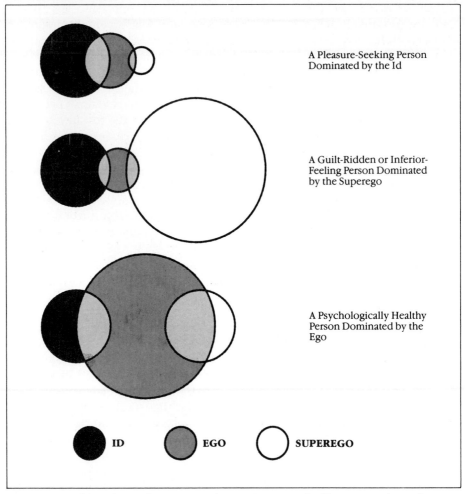

Figure 2.3   The Relationship among Id, Ego, Superego in Three Hypothetical Persons

DYNAMICS OF PERSONALITY

Freud believed that the personality consists of much more than the mental provinces and the levels of mental life. It is energetic or dynamic. Motivation is derived from mental and physical energy within the organism. This energy springs from the instincts.

Instincts

Freud used the German word "Trieb" to refer to a drive or a stimulus within the person. This term is usually translated as **instinct,** but it might more properly be called "drive" or "impulse." An instinct, then, is an internal drive or impulse that operates as a constant motivational force. As an internal stimulus it differs from external stimuli in that it cannot be avoided through flight.

According to Freud (1933/1964), there are many individual instincts, but all of them can be grouped under two major drives: the **life instinct,** generally called Eros or sex, and the **death instinct,** sometimes known as destruction or aggression. Instincts originate from the id, but they come under the control of the ego. Each instinct has its own form of psychic energy. The force by which the sexual instinct works is called **libido;** the psychic energy of the death instinct was never named.

Every instinct is characterized by an impetus, a source, an aim, and an object. Impetus, or pressure, is the amount of force exerted by the instinct. The source of an instinct is the region or zone within the body from which a state of excitation or tension is derived. The aim of an instinct is the removal of that excitation or the reduction of tension. The object is the person or thing that serves as the means through which the aim is satisfied (Freud, 1915/1957a).

The Sexual Instinct

The aim of the sexual instinct is to bring about pleasure within the organism by removing the state of sexual excitation. This pleasure, however, is not limited to genital pleasure. The entire body is invested with libido. Besides the genitals, the mouth and anus are especially capable of producing sexual pleasure and are called **erogenous** or erotogenic zones. The ultimate aim of the sexual instinct (reduction of sexual tension) cannot be changed, but the path by which the aim is reached can be varied. It can take either an active or a passive form or it can be temporarily or permanently inhibited (Freud, 1915/1957). Because the path is flexible and because sexual pleasure stems from organs other than the genitals, much behavior originally motivated by Eros is difficult to recognize as sexual behavior. To Freud, however, all pleasurable activity is traceable to the sexual instinct.

The flexibility of the sexual *object* can bring about a further disguise of Eros. The erotic object can easily be transformed or displaced. Libido can be withdrawn from the original object and placed in a state of free-floating tension, or it can be reinvested in another object, including the self. For example, an infant prematurely forced to give up the nipple may substitute the thumb as an object of oral pleasure.

Freud called the sexual instinct conservative, since the perpetuation of the species is dependent upon the power of its drive. Eros can also be called conservative because it protects individual life. For example, the infant, dominated by the pleasure principle, sucks from the nipple in order to gain sexual pleasure, but, at the same time, it acquires the nourishment essential to life.

Eros manifests itself in many ways. Some of the manifestations of the sexual instinct identified by Freud are narcissism, love, sadism, and masochism. The last two also possess generous components of the death instinct.

Narcissism.   During early infancy the child is primarily self-centered. Its libido, in other words, is invested upon its ego. This condition, which is universal, is known as **primary narcissism.** As the ego develops, there is normally a departure from primary narcissism and a trend toward greater interest in others; that is, narcissistic libido is transformed into object libido. During puberty, however, there is sometimes a redirection of the libido back to the ego and the person takes himself or herself as a sexual object. Such an adolescent is characterized by autoerotic behavior, extreme interest in personal appearance, and preoccupation with self. This pronounced **secondary narcissism** is not universal, but a moderate degree of self-love is common to nearly everyone (Freud, 1914/1957).

Love.   A second manifestation of Eros is love, which develops when the libido is invested in an object other than self. The child's first sexual object is the person who cares for it, generally the mother. During infancy the child of either sex experiences sensual love for the mother, but overt sexual love for members of one's family is ordinarily repressed, and a second type of love comes into existence. This is called aim-inhibited love because the original aim of reducing sexual tension is inhibited or repressed. Aim-inhibited love continues throughout a lifetime with the person loving parents, brothers, and sisters in a nonsexual way.

Obviously, love and narcissism are closely interrelated. Narcissism, of course, involves the love of self, while love is often accompanied by narcissistic tendencies, as when a person loves another who serves as an ideal or model of what one would like to be.

Sadism and Masochism.   Two other instincts that are also intertwined are sadism and masochism. Not only are they inseparable, one from another, but they are interwoven with the life instincts—narcissism and love—as well as being strongly endowed with psychic energy from the death instinct (Freud, 1933/1964).

Sadism is the instinct manifested when sexual pleasure is attained from inflicting pain or humiliation on another. Carried to an extreme, it is considered a sexual perversion, but in moderation sadism is a common need and exists to some extent in all sexual relationships. It is perverted when the sexual aim of erotic pleasure becomes secondary to the destructive aim (Freud, 1933/1964). **Masochism,** like sadism, is a common need, but it becomes a perversion when Eros becomes subservient to the destructive instinct. The masochist experiences sexual pleasure from suffering pain and humiliation inflicted either by self or by another (Freud, 1933/1964). Because the masochist can provide self-inflicted pain, there is no dependency on another person for the satisfaction of such masochistic needs. The sadist, on the other hand, must seek and find another person on whom to inflict pain or humiliation. In this respect, the sadist is more dependent than the masochist.

Sadism and masochism serve as cornerstones to the two-instinct theory. They demonstrate the workings of the sexual instinct and the destructive instinct in combination.

The Destructive Instinct

When Freud first elevated the death instinct to the level of Eros in *Beyond the Pleasure Principle* (Freud, 1920/1955), he did so tentatively and with some caution. With time, however, the destructive instinct became more and more a dogma despite the fact that it was not generally accepted by Freud's close followers.

The aim of the destructive instinct, according to Freud, is to return the organism to an inorganic state. Since the ultimate inorganic condition is death, the final aim of this instinct is self-destruction. As with the life instinct, the death instinct is flexible and the object of destruction is generally transformed from self to others. It then goes under a pseudonym—**aggression.**

The aggressive tendency is present in everyone and is the explanation for wars, atrocities, religious persecution, and murder, as well as malicious gossip, sarcasm, and humiliation. The death instinct also explains the need for the barriers people have erected to check aggression. For example, commandments like "Love your enemies" or "Love thy neighbor as thyself" are necessary, Freud believed, to inhibit the strong, though usually unconscious, drive to inflict injury upon others. These precepts are actually reaction formations. They involve the repression of strong hostile impulses and the overt and obvious expression of the opposite tendency.

Throughout one's lifetime, life and death instincts constantly struggle against one another for ascendancy within the person. At the same time, both must bow to the reality principle, which represents the claims of the outer world. These demands of the real world prevent a direct, unopposed fulfillment of either sex or aggression, create conflict and anxiety, and relegate many sexual and aggressive desires to the realm of the unconscious.

Anxiety

As important as they are, instincts must share the center of Freudian dynamic theory with the concept of **anxiety.** In defining anxiety, Freud emphasized that it is a felt, affective, unpleasant state, accompanied by a physical sensation that warns the person against impending danger. The unpleasantness is often vague and hard to pinpoint, but the anxiety itself is always felt (Freud, 1933/1964).

Only the ego can produce or feel anxiety. There are, however, three kinds of anxiety: *realistic anxiety,* which results from the ego's dependence on the external world; *neurotic anxiety,* which stems from the ego's dependence on the id; and *moral anxiety,* which results from the ego's dependence on the superego (Freud, 1933/1964).

Realistic anxiety is also known as objective anxiety and bears a close resemblance to fear. It is an unpleasant feeling about a known danger. A person may experience realistic anxiety while driving in heavy, fast-moving traffic. The dangerous situation is real and originates in the external world.

The process responsible for neurotic anxiety, on the other hand, originates in the id. Since the id is completely unconscious, neurotic anxiety is defined as apprehension about an unknown danger. The feeling itself exists in the ego, but it originates from id impulses. A person may feel anxious in the presence of a teacher, employer, or some other authority figure. This neurotic anxiety, Freud believed, often stems from early, unconscious feelings of destructiveness directed against the parent of the same sex. These feelings of hostility against the parent were accompanied by fear of punishment and this fear has now become generalized into anxiety.

The third type, moral anxiety, has its origin in the conflict between the ego and the superego. After the establishment of the superego, usually by the age of four or five, a person may experience anxiety as an outgrowth of the conflict between realistic needs and the dictates of the superego. Moral anxiety, for example, would result from sexual temptations if the person believes that yielding to the temptation would be morally wrong. It may also result from the failure to behave consistently with what is regarded as morally right, for example, failing to pay just taxes.

These three types of anxiety are seldom clear-cut or easily separated. They often exist in combination as when fear of water, a real danger, becomes disproportionate to the danger, and hence precipitates neurotic anxiety as well as realistic anxiety. This situation indicates that an unknown instinctual danger is connected with the external one.

Anxiety serves as an ego-preserving mechanism since it acts as a signal to the person that some danger is at hand (Freud, 1933/1964). For example, an anxiety dream signals the censor of an impending danger from the instincts, which allows the person either to awaken and stop dreaming or to better disguise the manifest level of the dream. The ego, constantly vigilant for signs of threat and unpleasure, is alerted to potential danger by the experience of anxiety. This signal then stimulates the person to mobilize for either flight or defense.

Anxiety is also self-regulating. It can precipitate repressions which, in turn, reduce the pain of anxiety (Freud, 1933/1964). If the ego had no recourse to defensive behavior, the anxiety would become intolerable. For example, when people suffering from claustrophobia are prevented from enjoying the defensive behavior of avoiding enclosed spaces, they frequently become overwhelmed with anxiety and paralyzed with fear. Individual differences among people are, in part, explained by the unique ways in which each builds defenses against anxiety.

DEFENSE MECHANISMS

Defensive behaviors, therefore, serve a useful function by protecting the ego against the pain of anxiety. Freud first elaborated on the idea of **defense mechanisms** in 1926 (Freud, 1926/1959), but it remained for his daughter, Anna (A. Freud, 1946), to gather together the various mechanisms in the form of a complete listing. Although defense mechanisms are normal and universally used, when carried to an extreme they lead to compulsive, repetitive, and even neurotic behavior. Because the establishment and maintenance of defense mechanisms require a constant expenditure of energy, any person who makes elaborate use of them has little psychic energy left to satisfy id impulses. This, of course, is precisely the ego's purpose in establishing a defense mechanism—to avoid dealing directly with instinctual demands and to defend itself against the anxiety which accompanies them (Freud, 1926/1959).

The following have been identified by Freud as defense mechanisms: repression, reaction formation, fixation, regression, undoing and isolation, projection, and sublimation.

Repression

The most basic defense mechanism, because it is involved in each of the others, is **repression.** Whenever impulses from the id become too threatening, anxiety is intensified to the point where the ego can no longer tolerate it. To protect itself, the ego represses the instinct, that is, forces the unwanted feeling into the unconscious (Freud, 1926/1959). In many cases the repression is then perpetuated for a lifetime. For example, a young boy may repress his sexual feelings for his mother because this impulse causes too much anxiety. The boy may later marry someone who reminds him of his mother, or, if this would cause too much anxiety, he may marry a woman who is quite opposite from his mother. In either case, a repression of the incestuous impulse is maintained in the unconscious.

No society permits the open direct expression of sexual and aggressive instincts. Their suppression always results in anxiety and eventually leads to their partial or total repression. What happens to these impulses after they have become unconscious? Freud believed that there are several possibilities. First, they may remain unchanged in the unconscious. Second, they force their way into consciousness in an unaltered form, in which case they would create more anxiety than the person could handle; the result would be an extremely painful anxiety attack (Freud, 1933/1964). Fortunately, this seldom happens. A third and much more common fate of repressed instincts is that they find expression in a displaced or disguised form. The disguise, of course, must be good enough to deceive the ego. Repressed drives may disguise themselves as physical symptoms. For example, a man troubled by sexual guilt may develop sexual impotency. The impotency prevents him from having to deal with the guilt and anxiety that would result from normal enjoyable sexual activity. Repressed drives may also find an outlet in dreams, slips of the tongue, or one of the other defense mechanisms.

Reaction Formation

One of the ways in which a repressed impulse may show itself is through adopting a disguise that is directly opposite from its original form. This defense mechanism is called a **reaction formation.** Reactive behavior can be identified by its exaggerated character and by its obsessive and compulsive form (Freud, 1926/1959). An example of a reaction formation can be seen in a girl who deeply resents and hates her mother but, because society demands affection toward parents, such conscious hatred for her mother would produce too much anxiety. Thus to avoid anxiety the girl concentrates on the opposite impulse—love. The girl's "love" for her mother, however, is not genuine. It is showy, exaggerated, and overdone. Close observation will usually reveal to others the true nature of this love, but the girl must deceive herself and cling to the reaction formation, which helps conceal the anxiety-arousing truth that she hates her mother.

Fixation

Psychical growth normally proceeds in a somewhat continuous fashion through the various stages of development. The process of psychologically growing up, however, is not without stressful and anxious moments. When the prospect of taking the next step becomes too anxiety-provoking, the ego may resort to the strategy of remaining at the present, more comfortable psychological stage. Such a defense is called **fixation.** Technically, fixation is the permanent attachment of the libido onto an earlier more primitive stage of development (Freud, 1917/1963). Like other defense mechanisms, fixations are universal. Everyone who continues to derive pleasure from the oral function can be said to have a degree of oral fixation. Anal fixations, too, are not uncommon. George, the middle-aged man we introduced at the beginning of the chapter, may be seen as a person with an anal fixation. His entire life has been characterized by excessive compulsiveness and reluctance to change. His fixation serves to avoid the anxiety that would accompany the novelty and flexibility of situations encountered in normal development. Fixations result in rigid, conforming, and compulsive behavior and make psychological growth or change difficult.

Regression

Once the libido has passed a developmental stage, it may, during times of stress and anxiety, revert back to that earlier stage. Such a reversion is known in psychoanalytic theory as **regression** (Freud, 1917/1963). Regressions are also very common and can be seen readily in children. A completely weaned three-year-old child, for example, may regress to demanding a bottle when a baby brother or sister is born. The attention received by the new baby poses a threat to the older child. Regressions are also frequent in older children and in adults. A common way for adults to react to anxiety-producing situations is to revert to earlier, safer, more secure patterns of behavior. Libido is invested on more primitive and more familiar objects. Under extreme stress one adult may adopt the fetal position, another may return home to her mother, and still another may react by remaining all day in bed, well covered from the cold and threatening world. Regressive behavior is similar to fixated behavior in that it is rigid and infantile. Regressions, however, are usually temporary, while fixations demand a more or less permanent expenditure of psychic energy.

Undoing and Isolation

Two defense mechanisms that are closely related to one another and can be discussed under a single heading are **undoing** and **isolation.** Freud felt that undoing and isolation are important variations of repression and deserve to be considered separately from it (1926/1959).

Undoing and isolation each serve in an auxiliary position to the basic defense mechanism of repression, but they are distinguished from repression by their close association with repetitive and ceremonial acts and with persistent and recurrent thoughts. Freud believed that undoing and isolation emerge when true repression would block out too much reality. The symptoms of undoing and isolation (**compulsions** and **obsessions**) do not remove the ego as far from the real world; that is, they do not block out as much of the earlier, painful experience as do hysteria and amnesia, both symptoms of repression.

Undoing is a type of repression in which the ego attempts to do away with unpleasant experiences and their consequences. It is like negative magic in that ideas or events are made to disappear, erased through a compulsive ceremonial performed for that purpose. The ceremonial act cancels out the earlier event, so that the ego is convinced that it did not happen. A classical example of undoing is found in Shakespeare's account of Lady Macbeth as she ceremonially rubs her hands in an effort to wash away the guilt of Duncan's murder. By cleansing her hands she hopes to undo the part she played in the king's death. Her attempts at repressing guilt, however, do not meet with complete success. When undoing is complete there remains no conscious memory of the guilt-producing event.

According to Freud (1926/1959), undoing is the salient feature in **compulsion neuroses.** (A compulsion involves the irresistible repetition of an act.) Undoing can be either severe or mild. Severe undoing is seen in an extremely compulsive person who repeats in a desirable manner an event that happened in an undesirable way. He thus prevents his ego from having to deal with the unwanted event. The person becomes exceedingly rigid and inflexible in his actions, expending psychic energy to maintain the compulsions and to repress the unwanted experience by doing away with it.

Undoing shades into normal behavior where it may consist of repeatedly making the same mistakes, habitually and ritualistically wasting time, or compulsively looking in the same place for a "lost" possession. In normal undoing the person looks away from an unpleasant experience as if it had never happened. Repression is not complete in normal undoing, but operates with enough strength to keep the repressed experience from regularly intruding on the conscious mind. This differs from severe undoing where the attempt is to make the past completely nonexistent.

A closely related defense mechanism is **isolation.** This defense keeps an unpleasant experience isolated in the unconscious by establishing a period of blacked-out affect immediately following the experience. The person simply does nothing and feels nothing following the painful event. This lack of affect severs the associations between the event and all subsequent experiences. The undesirable event is thus isolated and cannot be reproduced through ordinary thought processes. Though Freud (1926/1959) did not clearly differentiate between undoing and isolation, in general, undoing most often produces compulsions, while isolation leads to obsessive symptoms (an obsession is a persistent or recurrent idea, usually involving an urge toward some action). Also, undoing wipes out or at least partially erases an event, whereas isolation leaves the event intact, but emotionally isolates it from other events in one's experience.

Severe isolation is characterized by persistent and debilitating obsessions, which often have their source in the taboo of touching. Because touching is the immediate aim of both sex and aggression, the obsessive person builds up a prohibition against physical contact. The prohibition becomes abnormal when the obsessive person avoids at all costs physical contact with others, and is plagued incessantly by thoughts of touching. The person refuses to shake hands or kiss another and recoils in horror when inadvertently touched.

Freud (1926/1959) believed that a degree of isolation is common in normal behavior where the ego functions to keep certain thoughts separate. This breaks the chain of associations between those ideas and protects the ego from having to recall an anxiety-arousing experience. For example, a woman may concentrate on the differences between her husband and her father to keep thoughts of their similarities from consciousness, thereby avoiding the guilt that would accompany sexual relations with a father figure.

Projection

When an internal, instinctual impulse becomes too anxiety-provoking, the ego may get rid of it by attributing the unwanted impulse to an external object, usually another person. This is the defense mechanism of **projection,** which can be defined as seeing in others unacceptable feelings or tendencies that actually reside in one's own unconscious (Freud, 1915/1957b). For example, a young woman may consistently interpret the actions of older men as attempted seductions. Consciously, the thought of sexual intercourse with older men may be intensely repugnant to her, but buried in her unconscious is a strong erotic attraction to these men. In general, the more strongly she protests, the more likely it is that she is projecting her own sexual feelings onto others. In this example, the young woman deludes herself into believing that she has no sexual feelings for older men. Thus her anxiety and guilt are erased; the projection, however, maintains the sexual interest while relieving her of responsibility.

An extreme type of projection is **paranoia,** a mental disorder characterized by powerful delusions of jealousy and persecution. Paranoia is not an inevitable outcome of projection, but simply a severe variety of it. According to Freud (1922/1955), a crucial distinction between projection and paranoia is that paranoia is always characterized by repressed homosexual feelings toward the persecutor. Freud believed that the persecutor is inevitably a former friend of the same sex, though sometimes the person may transfer his or her delusions onto a person of the opposite sex. When homosexual impulses become too powerful, the persecuted paranoiac defends himself by *reversing* these feelings and then projecting them onto their original object. The transformation proceeds as follows. Instead of saying, "I love him," the paranoid person says, "I hate him." Since this also produces too much anxiety, he says, "He hates me." At this point, he has disclaimed all responsibility and can say, "I like him fine, but he's got it in for me." The central mechanism in all paranoia is projection with accompanying delusions of jealousy and persecution.

Sublimation

Each of the above defense mechanisms serves the individual by protecting the ego from anxiety, but each is of dubious value from society's viewpoint. According to Freud (1917/1963), one mechanism helps both the individual and the social group. This is **sublimation,** defined as the repression of the genital aim of Eros by substituting a cultural or social aim. The sublimated aim can be seen most obviously in creative cultural accomplishments such as art, music, and literature, but more subtly, in all human relationships and all social pursuits. A prominent example of sublimation, Freud (1914/1953) believed, is the art of Michelangelo, who found an indirect outlet for his libido in painting and sculpting. In most persons sublimations combine with direct expression of Eros and result in a kind of balance between social interests and personal pleasure. Most of us are capable of sublimating a part of our libido in the service of higher cultural values, while, at the same time, retaining sufficient amounts of the sexual instinct for use in the pursuit of individual erotic pleasure.

In summary, all defense mechanisms protect the ego against anxiety. They are universal in that everyone engages in defensive behavior to some degree. Each combines with repression and sometimes with one or more additional mechanisms. Any defense mechanism can be carried to the point of **psychopathology,** but normally defense mechanisms are beneficial to the individual and harmless to society and, in the case of sublimations, they can be beneficial to society.

STAGES OF DEVELOPMENT

Psychosexual development was seen by Freud as proceeding from birth to maturity in ordered, but overlapping stages. The first four or five years of life, or the **infantile stage,** is the most crucial for personality formation. It is followed by a six- or seven-year period of **latency** during which time little or no sexual growth takes place. At puberty there is a renaissance of sexual life and the **genital stage** is ushered in. Psychosexual development eventually culminates in **maturity.**

Infantile Period

One of Freud's (1905/1963, 1923b/1961b) most important assumptions is that infants possess a sexual life and go through a period of pregenital sexual development during the first four or five years after birth. At the time Freud originally postulated the existence of infantile sexuality, the concept, though not new, was met with some resistance, but today nearly all close observers accept the idea that children delight in pleasure gained through the erogenous zones, show an interest in the genitals, and even manifest sexual excitement. Childhood sexuality differs from adult sexuality in that it is not capable of reproduction and it is exclusively autoerotic. With both children and adults, however, the sexual instinct can be satisfied through organs other than the genitals. The mouth and anus are particularly sensitive to erogenous stimulation (Freud, 1933/1964).

Freud (1917/1963) divided the infantile stage into three phases according to which of the three primary erogenous zones is undergoing the most salient development. The oral phase begins first and is followed by the sadistic-anal phase and the phallic phase in that order. The three infantile stages overlap, since the development of an earlier phase continues after the onset of a later one.

Oral Phase

The mouth is the first organ of the body to provide the infant with pleasure. Consequently, the first infantile stage of development is the **oral phase.** The infant obtains life-sustaining nourishment through the oral cavity, but beyond that, it also gains pleasure through the act of sucking.

The sexual aim of *early oral* activity is to incorporate or receive into one's own body the instinctual object-choice, the nipple. During this *oral-receptive* phase the infant feels no ambivalence toward the pleasurable object and its needs are usually satisfied with a minimum of frustration and anxiety. As the baby grows older, however, feelings of frustration and anxiety are more likely to be experienced as a result of scheduled feedings, increased time lapses between feedings, and eventual *weaning.* These anxieties are generally accompanied by feelings of ambivalence toward the love object (mother), and by the increased ability of the budding ego to defend itself against the environment and against anxiety (Freud, 1933/1964).

The infant's defense against the environment is greatly aided by the emergence of teeth. At this point the baby passes into a second oral phase, which Freud (1933/1964) called the *oral-sadistic* period. This phase is characterized by responding to others, through such diverse means as biting, cooing, closing the mouth, smiling, and crying. The baby's initial defense against

Infants satisfy oral needs one way or another.

anxiety takes the usual form of thumb sucking, the child's first experience in autoeroticism. Thumb sucking satisfies the sexual, but not the nutritional, needs of the infant.

As the person grows older, the mouth continues to be an erogenous zone. Oral needs are gratified in a variety of ways, including sucking candy, chewing gum, biting pencils, overeating, smoking cigarettes, "chewing out" other people, and making biting, sarcastic remarks.

Sadistic-Anal Phase

The aggressive instinct originally shows itself during the first year of life in the form of oral sadism. It reaches a fuller development, however, during the second year, at a time when the anus is beginning to emerge as a sexually pleasurable zone. Because this period is characterized by satisfaction gained through aggressive behavior and through the excretory function, Freud (1933/1964) called it the **sadistic-anal phase** of development. The sadistic-anal phase is divided into two subphases, early and late.

During the *early sadistic-anal period* the child receives satisfaction by destroying or losing objects. At this time the destructive nature of the sadistic instinct is stronger than the erotic one. The child takes revenge on the parents for initiating the frustration of *toilet training.*

It is not until the child has entered the late *sadistic-anal period* that a friendly interest toward objects develops. This interest stems from the erotic satisfaction experienced during toilet training. The act of defecating is pleasurable and the product of the act provides the child with a prized object that can be presented to the parents (Freud, 1933/1964). If the parents are loving and praise this behavior, the child is likely to grow into a generous and magnanimous adult. On the other hand, if the parents reject the "gift" in a punitive fashion, the infant may adopt another method of obtaining anal pleasure—withholding the feces until the pressure becomes both painful and erotically stimulating. This mode of narcissistic and masochistic pleasure lays the foundation for the *anal character,* people like our case study, George, who continue to receive erotic satisfaction by keeping and possessing objects and by arranging them in an excessively neat and orderly fashion. People who grow into anal characters were, as children, Freud hypothesized, overly resistant to toilet training, often holding back their feces and prolonging the time of training beyond that usually required. This anal eroticism becomes transformed in the *anal triad* of orderliness, stinginess, and obstinacy, which typifies the adult anal character (Freud, 1933/1964).

Although compulsive neatness is George's most outstanding trait, he also is characterized by a high degree of stinginess and obstinacy. His stinginess might better be termed parsimoniousness because George is exceedingly careful in spending his money, rather than petty or ungenerous. He lives in an expensive house, dresses well, and is a gracious host, always offering guests coffee, tea, or a soft drink. Nevertheless, saving money (as well as childhood toys and possessions) is extremely important to George, and he has accumulated a savings account far in excess of what might be expected from his modest salary.

Similarly, George's obstinacy or stubbornness is well hidden from the casual observer. He is not argumentative or aggressive, but he persists in his beliefs and opinions long after others would have discarded them as childish or immature. George, then, is characterized by the anal triad of compulsive neatness, miserliness, and stubbornness, with neatness being his most visible trait.

Not all anal erotic impulses are transformed into these three adult character traits. Some are more completely repressed and emerge in the form of neurotic symptoms, while others find expression during the phallic and genital periods of development. Freud (1933/1964) believed that, for girls, anal eroticism is carried over into penis-envy during the phallic stage and can eventually be expressed by giving birth to a baby. In the unconscious, Freud believed, the concepts feces, penis, and baby, because of their elongated shapes, mean the same thing and are likely to be represented by the same symbols in dreams.

During the sadistic-anal phase, as in the oral stage, there is no basic distinction between male and female psychosexual growth. Children of either gender can develop an active or a passive orientation. The active is often characterized by what Freud (1933/1964) considered the masculine qualities of dominance and sadism, while the passive orientation is usually marked by the feminine qualities of voyeurism and masochism. However, either orientation, or any combination of the two, can develop in both girls and boys.

Phallic Phase

At approximately age three or four the child enters into a third, or **phallic phase** of infantile development in which the genital area becomes the leading erogenous zone. This stage is marked for the first time by a dichotomy between male and female development, a distinction which Freud (1925/1961) believed to be due to the anatomical differences between the sexes. Freud took Napoleon's remark, "History is destiny" and changed it to "Anatomy is destiny" (Freud, 1924/1961, p. 178). This dictum underlies Freud's belief that physical differences between males and females account for many important psychological differences.

Masturbation, which had its origin in the oral stage, enters a second, more crucial phase during the phallic period. At this time, it is a nearly universal practice, often taking the form of washing or cleansing the genital area. These practices are generally suppressed by the parents, and when the phallic period is terminated the conscious desire to masturbate is usually repressed. The child's experiences with the *suppression of masturbation* help form the foundation of psychosexual development as did earlier experiences with weaning and toilet training (Freud, 1933/1964). The child's experiences with the Oedipus complex, the prominent feature of the phallic phase, play an even more important role in personality development.

Male Oedipus Complex. Freud (1925/1961) believed that, preceding the phallic stage, the infant boy forms an *identification* with his father; that is, he wants to *be* his father. Later the boy develops a sexual desire for his mother; that is, he wants to *have* his mother. These two wishes do not appear mutually contradictory to the underdeveloped ego, so they are able to exist side by side for a time. When their inconsistency is finally recognized, the desire for the mother is retained, since it is more intense than the identification with the father. Inevitably, identification takes on a tone of hostility. The boy sees the father as a rival and desires to do away with him and to possess the mother in a sexual relationship. This condition of rivalry toward the father and incestuous feelings toward the mother is known as the simple **male Oedipus complex.** The term is taken from the Greek tragedy by Sophocles in which Oedipus, King of Thebes, is destined by fate to kill his father and marry his mother.

Freud believed that the bisexual nature of the child (of either sex) complicates the picture. Preceding the Oedipus complex the young boy developed, to some degree, a feminine disposition. During the Oedipal period, therefore, his feminine nature may lead him to display *affection toward his father* and express *hostility toward his mother,* while at the same time, his masculine tendency disposes him toward hostility for father and lust for mother. The ambivalent condition is known as the complete Oedipus complex. Affection and hostility can co-exist because one or both feelings may be unconscious. Freud believed that these feelings of ambivalence in the boy play a role in the evolution of the castration complex, a universal concomitant to the phallic phase of development.

To Freud (1917/1963, 1923/1961b), the castration complex begins after the young boy (who has assumed that all other people, including girls, have genitals like his own) becomes aware of the absence of a penis on girls. This awareness becomes the greatest emotional shock of his life. After a period of mental struggle and attempts at denial, he is forced into the conclusion that the girl has had her penis cut off. He may have been threatened with castration himself or have been punished for his attempts at sexual activity. It is now clear to the boy that the little girl has been punished for masturbation or for seduction of her mother by having her penis removed. The threat of castration now becomes a dreaded possibility. This **castration complex** (in the boy, called **castration anxiety**) cannot long be tolerated. The boy represses his impulses toward sexual activity, including his fantasies of carrying out a seduction of his mother.

Prior to the sudden experience of castration anxiety, little boys may have "seen" the genital area of little girls or their mother, but this sight does not automatically instigate the castration complex. Castration anxiety bursts forth only when the boy's ego is mature enough to comprehend the connection between sexual desires and the removal of the penis. Freud believed that castration anxiety was present in all boys, even those not personally threatened by their fathers or others with removing or stunting the growth of the penis. According to Freud (1933/1964), it is not necessary for each boy to receive a clear threat of castration. Any mention of injury or shrinkage in connection with the penis is sufficient to activate the child's phylogenetic endowment. As we have seen, the phylogenetic endowment is capable of filling the gaps of our individual experiences with the inherited experiences of our ancestors. Ancient man's fear of castration supports the individual child's experiences and results in universal castration anxiety. Freud (1933/1964, p. 86) stated: "It is not a question of whether castration is really carried out; what is decisive is that the danger threatens from the outside and that the child believes in it." He went on to say that "hints at . . . punishment must regularly find a phylogenetic reinforcement in him" (Freud, 1933/1964, p. 86).

Ideally the Oedipus complex should be dissolved and replaced by a mature superego. If, however, the Oedipus complex is merely repressed, it later expresses itself in some neurotic form (Freud, 1924/1961).

Once the Oedipus complex is dissolved or repressed, the boy's incestuous desires become feelings of tender love. He may identify with either the father or the mother, depending on the strength of his feminine disposition. Normally identification is with the father, but it is not the same as pre-Oedipal identification. The boy no longer wants to *be* his father; instead, he uses the father as a model for determining right and wrong behavior. He introjects or incorporates the father's authority into his own ego, thereby sowing the seeds of a mature superego. The budding superego takes over the father's prohibitions against incest and insures the continued repression of the Oedipus complex (Freud, 1933/1964).

Female Oedipus Complex.   The female phallic phase follows a parallel, though more complicated path. To understand it one must go back to the pre-Oedipal period. Freud believed that, for girls, the castration complex *precedes* the Oedipus complex. The opposite is true for the boy, for whom castration anxiety follows and breaks up the Oedipus complex.

The castration complex obviously takes a different form for girls than the one it follows for boys. Again, this is due to the physiological differences between the sexes (Freud, 1925/1961). Like the boy, the pre-Oedipal girl assumes that all other children have genitals similar to her own. Soon she discovers that boys not only possess different genital equipment, but apparently something extra. She becomes envious of this appendage, feels cheated, and desires to have a penis. This experience of **penis envy** is a powerful force in the formation of the girl's personality. Unlike castration anxiety in boys, which is quickly repressed, penis envy may last for years in one form or another. Freud (1933/1964) believed that penis envy is often expressed as a wish to be a boy or a desire to have a man. Almost universally, it is carried over into a wish to have a baby, and eventually it may find expression in the act of giving birth to a baby, especially a boy.

Preceding the castration complex, the girl has established an identification with her mother similar to that developed by the boy, in that she fantasizes being seduced by her mother. These incestuous feelings, according to Freud (1933/1964), are later turned into hostility when the girl holds her mother responsible for bringing her into the world without a penis. Her libido is then turned toward her father, who can satisfy her wish for a penis by giving her a baby, an object which to her has become a substitute for the phallus. The desire for sexual intercourse with the father and accompanying feelings of hostility for the mother are known as the **female Oedipus complex.** (Freud objected to the term Electra complex sometimes used by others when referring to Freud's idea of the female Oedipus complex.) Again, the situation is complicated by the inherent bisexuality of the girl and the degree of masculinity developed by her during the pre-Oedipal period.

The girl must surrender her sexual desires for the father when it becomes apparent that he is not going to satisfy her incestuous fantasies. The Oedipus complex is then broken up, but usually more slowly and less completely than it is with boys. In normal feminine development the girl reestablishes an identification with the mother as a model and develops tender feelings of affection for the father. Not all feminine development, however, proceeds in this manner. If the pre-Oedipal masculine attitude is quite strong, it is possible that the girl will refuse to recognize her femininity, hold permanently to the masculine complex, and resist attempts to suppress masturbation. Another possibility is that a reaction formation will set it. The girl will completely inhibit her masculine disposition, renounce masturbatory activity, turn away from the mother, and repress the greater part of all her sexual instinct (Freud, 1933/1964).

For the girl, too, the superego replaces the Oedipus complex. Her identification with her mother leads to the incorporation of parental authority. Freud (1933/1964) believed, however, that the superego of girls usually is not as severe or well differentiated as is the superego of boys. The reason the girl's superego does not develop as fully as the boy's is traceable to the dif-

Male Phallic Phase	Female Phallic Phase
1. **Oedipus complex** (Sexual desires for the mother; hostility for the father)	1. **Castration complex** in the form of **penis envy**
2. **Castration complex** in the form of **castration anxiety** shatters the Oedipus complex	2. **Oedipus complex** develops as an attempt to obtain a penis (sexual desires for the father; hostility for the mother)
3. **Identification** with the father	3. Gradual realization that the Oedipal desires are self-defeating
4. Strong **superego** replaces the nearly completely dissolved Oedipus complex	4. **Identification** with the mother
	5. Weak **superego** replaces the partially dissolved Oedipus complex

Figure 2.4   Parallel Paths of the Simple Male and Female Phallic Phases

ference between the sexes during their Oedipal histories. For boys, castration anxiety follows the Oedipus complex, breaks it up nearly completely, and renders unnecessary the continued expenditure of psychic energy on its remnants. Energy used to maintain the Oedipus complex now is freed to establish a superego. For the girl, however, the Oedipus complex *follows* the castration complex (penis envy) and, therefore, there is no corresponding sudden shock. The female Oedipus complex is only incompletely resolved by a gradual realization that the girl may lose the love of her mother and that sexual intercourse with her father is not forthcoming. Her libido thus remains partially expended to maintain the castration complex and its relics, thereby blocking some psychic energy which might otherwise be used to build a strong superego (Freud, 1931/1961). The simple male and female Oedipus complexes are summarized in Figure 2.4. As might be expected, Freud's notion of the male and female Oedipus complex is frequently attacked as being less than complimentary to women.

Early in his career, and before he conceived of an Oedipus complex, Freud believed in a seduction theory as providing an explanation for adult personality development. However, he rejected his seduction theory in favor of the now famous Oedipal theory (see Box—"Parental Practice or Childhood Fantasy? Why Freud Abandoned the Seduction Theory").

Latency Period

Freud believed that from the fifth or sixth year until puberty there is a standstill in sexual development. This period in the child's life, the **latency stage,** is brought about partly by the suppression of the sexual instinct and partly by organic factors that owe their existence to prehistoric people. Freud (1913/1953) suggested that the Oedipus complex and the subsequent period of sexual latency could possibly be explained by the following hypothesis. Early in human development a group of brothers, denied the rights to have sexual relations with their mother or sisters, joined together

Parental Practice or Childhood Fantasy? Why Freud Abandoned the Seduction Theory

Growing reports of child sexual abuse cut to the core of Freud's idea of the Oedipus complex. As we have seen, Freud believed that most accounts of childhood seductions were merely wish-fulfillment originating from the fantasy life of the child. This belief perpetuated through the years by psychoanalytically oriented therapists has cast doubt on many reports of sexual abuse. Should these accounts be accepted as fact, or should they be attributed to childhood fantasy?

Before answering this question, let us look at the background of Freud's idea of the Oedipus complex. Prior to his belief that young children possess incestuous wishes toward their parents, Freud had held the opposite view, that is, neurotic symptoms stem from the seduction of children by adults. This "seduction theory" was summarized by Freud (1896/1962, p. 203) in these words.

> I therefore put forward the thesis that at the bottom of every case of hysteria there are *one or more occurrences of premature sexual experience,* occurrences which belong to the earliest years of childhood but which can be reproduced through the work of psychoanalysis in spite of intervening decades. I believe that this is an important finding, the discovery of a *caput Nili* [source of the Nile] in neuropathology.

However, in 1897 Freud repudiated his seduction theory and soon afterward replaced it with the concept of the Oedipus complex. The Oedipus complex was in direct contradiction to the seduction theory because it placed the origin of most parental seductions within the mind of the child.

The history of psychoanalysis would have been quite different if Freud had not reversed himself and shifted emphasis away from his belief that neuroses sprang from actual childhood seductions. In fact, Anna Freud, in a 1981 letter to Jeffrey Masson, stated that if her father had retained the seduction theory "there would have been no psychoanalysis afterwards" (Masson, 1984, p. 113). Actually, Freud never completely abandoned his seduction theory, but always retained some belief in real sexual trauma as a source of neurosis. In his autobiography, Freud (1925/1959) stated that childhood seductions account for some neuroses, but the seducer usually turns out to be other children rather than the father. Since Freud had considered his seduction theory to be equivalent to the discovery of the source of the Nile, why would he deemphasize his treasured theory?

Freud himself offered four reasons in his famous letter of September 21, 1897 to Wilhelm Fliess. First, Freud said, the seduction theory had not enabled him to successfully treat even a single patient. Second, his own father would have to be accused of perversion since Freud, his brother, and several younger sisters all displayed hysterical symptoms at one time or another. Third, there was the possibility (not yet fully conceptualized as the Oedipus complex) that the unconscious mind could not distinguish reality from fiction. And fourth, Freud found that the unconscious memories of advanced psychotic patients did not break through to disclose early childhood experiences (Freud, 1985).

In time, Freud became more and more strongly convinced that neurotic symptoms were related to childhood fantasies rather than to material reality. In his autobiography, he expresses relief that he had corrected the "error" that would have had fatal consequences for psychoanalysis and wonders how anyone could have believed that childhood seductions were so common (Freud, 1925/1959).

In recent years, many observers have come to believe that the seduction theory was not an error, and that Freud went astray when he attributed the fault of seduction to the child rather than to the parent. Balmary (1979/1982) believes that psychoanalysis got off the right track when Freud repudiated the seduction theory and thus set psychological reality above physical reality. Interestingly, she accepts the Oedipal model, but with a different emphasis from the one Freud held. She believes that the key to understanding the Oedipal myth is the transmission of the faults of the father (Laius) to the son (Oedipus). Balmary contends that Freud had an unconscious knowledge of this transmission, but due to his own blind spot, he chose to emphasize Oedipus's sexual desires for his mother (Jocasta) and his hostility for his father.

Lerman (1986) looks more at the standard Freudian view of the Oedipus complex and rejects it as inferior to the original theory as an explanation for neurotic symptoms. She cites evidence from Kinsey that 25 percent of women have had some sexual encounter with an adult by the time they are 13 years old and that 80 percent of the time the adult was a relative or family friend. Masson (1984) believes that psychoanalysis took a wrong turn when Freud abandoned the seduction theory. He says that by shifting emphasis from the reality of child sexual abuse to the inner world of childhood fantasies, "Freud began a trend away from the real world that . . . is at the root of the present-day sterility of psychoanalysis and psychiatry throughout the world" (Masson, 1984, p. 144).

In answer to our original question, it would appear that, while Freud's notion of the Oedipus complex may well have partial validity, psychotherapists and others who work with children and with adults who report childhood sexual experiences must take those reports at face value.

So long as therapists think first of Oedipal wishes, there remains the probability that many real seductions will be treated merely as fantasies.

and killed the father. Because they felt affection as well as hostility toward the father, they were left with strong feelings of guilt. This sense of guilt caused them to instigate strong prohibitions against sexual relations with members of the family and brought about repression of hostility toward the father. Thereafter, they suppressed sexual activity in their own children whenever it became noticeable, probably around age three or four. This suppression became complete and a period of sexual latency resulted. After this experience was repeated in different families, clans, or totems it became an active, though unconscious force in the individual's psychosexual development. This prohibition of sexual activity, then, is part of our phylogenetic endowment and is one possible explanation for the period of latency.

Continued latency is reinforced through constant suppression by parents and teachers and by internal feelings of shame, guilt, and morality. The sexual instinct, of course, still exists, but its aim has been inhibited. The libido is now sublimated and shows itself in social and cultural accomplishments such as school work and the development of friendships. During this period children form groups or cliques, an impossibility during the infantile period when the sexual drive was completely autoerotic.

Genital Period

At puberty there is a reawakening of the sexual aim and the **genital period** is begun. The diphasic sexual life of the person now enters its second stage, which has certain basic differences from the first, or infantile period. The sexual instinct is no longer directed toward self. Autoeroticism is given up and an external object is now desired. The aim of Eros is usually genital union with a person of the opposite sex. Also, reproduction for the first time is a possibility. Freud (1933/1964) believed that, though penis envy may continue to linger, the vagina finally obtains the same status for girls that the male organ had for them during infancy. To boys, the female organ may now be a sought-after object rather than a traumatic threat. The entire sexual instinct takes on a more complete organization. The component instincts, which had operated somewhat independently of one another during the early infantile period, gain a kind of synthesis during adolescence. The mouth, anus, and other pleasure-producing areas take an auxiliary position to the genitals, which now attain supremacy as an erogenous zone.

This synthesis of Eros, the elevated status of the female genital organ, the reproductive capacity of the life instinct, and its direction outward rather than on self represent the major distinctions between infantile and adult sexuality. In several other ways, however, Eros remains more or less unchanged. It may continue to manifest itself in sublimated forms, it may be repressed, or it may be expressed in masturbation or other sexual acts. The subordinated erogenous zones also continue as vehicles of obtaining erotic pleasure. The mouth, for example, retains many of its infantile activities, perhaps dropping thumb sucking but possibly adding smoking or prolonged kissing.

Maturity

The genital period begins at puberty and continues throughout the individual's lifetime. It is a stage attained by everyone who reaches physical maturity. There is an additional stage of *psychological maturity,* which Freud alluded to but never fully conceptualized. Psychological maturity is attained after the person has passed through the earlier stages in an ideal manner. Unfortunately, this seldom happens. There are too many chances for pathological disorders or neurotic predispositions to develop.

Although Freud never fully conceptualized the notion of psychological maturity, it is possible to build a model of the psychoanalytically mature person. Such a person would be characterized by a balance among the structures of the mind. The ego would be in control of the id and superego, but at the same time it would permit them to express themselves (see Figure 2.3). Id impulses would be expressed honestly and without leaving traces of shame or guilt. The superego would complete its task of freeing the person from parental control with no remnants of antagonism or incest. The ego-ideal would be realistic and congruent with the ego. In fact, the boundary between the superego and the ego would become nearly imperceptible.

Consciousness would play a more important role in the behavior of the mature person. Repressed material would be held to a necessary minimum and would emerge in the form of sublimations rather than neurotic symptoms. The Oedipus complex would be completely dissolved, with no traces remaining in the unconscious. Libido formerly directed toward the parent of the opposite sex would be released to search for another person. Tender love and sensual love would be united in the same love-object. In short, the psychologically mature person would come through the experiences of childhood and adolescence in control of psychic energy and with an ego functioning in the center of an ever-expanding world of consciousness.

APPLICATIONS OF PSYCHOANALYTIC THEORY

Freud was an innovative speculator, probably more concerned with theory building than with treating sick people. Much of his time was spent conducting therapy, not only to help patients, but to gain the insight into human personality necessary to expound psychoanalytic theory. A circular relationship existed between his theory and practice. His theoretical framework grew out of his experiences as a practitioner, while his applied psychoanalysis was shaped by his theoretical orientation. The three practical pillars upon which psychoanalytic theory rests are dream analysis, parapraxes, and psychotherapy.

Dream Analysis

The problem of dreams and their meanings was of continuous concern to Freud. Unlike most other aspects of his theory, his ideas on dreams underwent no major revisions from *The Interpretation of Dreams* (1900/1953) until his death in 1939.

In interpreting dreams Freud felt that the **latent** content must be given priority over the **manifest** content. The latent content refers to the unconscious material, while the manifest content is the surface meaning or the conscious description given by the dreamer.

The basic assumption of Freud's dream analysis is that nearly all dreams are *wish-fulfillments*. Some wishes are obvious and are expressed through the manifest content, as when a person goes to sleep hungry and dreams of eating large quantities of delicious food. Most wish-fulfillments, however, are expressed in the latent content and can be known only through interpretation of the dream. The exception to the rule that dreams are wish-fulfillments is found in patients suffering from traumatic neuroses, whose dreams are often composed of repetitions of traumatic experiences. These dreams obey the principle of **repetition compulsion** rather than wish-fulfillment and may be seen in battle-weary soldiers, whose dreams are filled with frightening repetitions of a traumatic experience (Freud, 1920/1955, 1933/1964).

Before discussing Freud's method of dream interpretation, it may be profitable to look at his ideas concerning the construction of dreams. Freud believed that the formation of a dream was not the result of physiological stimuli such as hunger or pain, though at times the manifest content of dreams may come from these sources. Dreams are formed in the unconscious. They originate as attempts of unconscious wishes to find expression in consciousness. To do this, the wishes must slip past both the primary and the final censors (see Figure 2.1). Even during sleep these guardians maintain their vigil, forcing unconscious psychic material to adopt a disguised form. The disguise can operate in two basic ways.

First, the dream content can be distorted through either condensation or displacement. *Condensation* refers to the fact that the manifest dream content is not as extensive as the latent level, indicating that the unconscious material has been abbreviated or condensed before appearing on the manifest level (Freud, 1900/1953). *Displacement* means that the dream image is replaced by some other idea only remotely related to it (Freud, 1900/1953). Condensation and displacement of content both take place through the use of symbols. Certain images are almost universally represented by seemingly innocuous figures. For example, the phallus may be symbolized by any elongated objects such as sticks, snakes, or knives. The female organ often appears as any small box, chest, or oven; parents appear in the form of a king, queen, governor, or president. The dreamer may take the form of a prince or princess. A woman is represented by a room. An open room stands for a sexually promiscuous woman, while a closed room is an unobtainable woman. Sexual intercourse may be disguised as ascending or descending steep inclines like ladders or stairs. Castration anxiety expresses itself in dreams of growing bald, losing teeth, or any act of cutting (Freud, 1900/1953, 1901/1953, 1917/1963).

Second, dreams can deceive the dreamer through the inhibition and reversal of affect. Strong negative emotions, which ordinarily would result in feelings of unpleasantness if allowed to become conscious, might be completely inhibited. The dreamer, though faced with a fearful or anxiety-provoking situation, feels nothing during the dream. The deceptive nature of the manifest content is also illustrated by the reversal of the affect into its opposite. Deeply felt unconscious hostility can be transformed into love by the workings of the dream. The dreamer is fooled into believing that hate is love or that joy is sorrow, as when one mourns the death of a parent whose extinction would be welcomed by the primitive unconscious (Freud, 1900/1953, 1915/1957a, 1917/1963).

After the dream content has been distorted and the affect has been inhibited or reversed, it appears in its manifest form and may be recalled by the

dreamer. The manifest content nearly always relates to conscious or preconscious experience of the previous day (Freud, 1900/1953). Only the latent
content, however, has any psychoanalytic importance.

The unconscious wishes that form the dream usually have their origin in
the infantile years of life (Freud, 1917/1963). The reason for this is that children's wishes are more intense than those of adults. The intensity results
from the suppression or punishment of infantile sexual and destructive
behavior. These desires may remain for years in the unconscious, finding
expression in a disguised form during dreams. Not all dreams originate in
childhood repressions. Some are expressions of adult wishes. The only requisite is that the wish be psychologically intense enough to force its way out
of the unconscious.

In interpreting dreams Freud (1917/1963) ordinarily followed one of two
methods. The first was to ask the person to relate the dream and all associations that occurred to the dreamer, no matter how unrelated or illogical.
These associations reveal the unconscious wish behind the dream. If the
dreamer was unable to relate association material, Freud used a second
method—dream symbols—to discover the unconscious elements underlying
the manifest content. The purpose of both methods (associations and symbols) was to trace the dream formation backward until the latent content was
reached. Freud believed that dream interpretation was the most reliable
approach to the study of unconscious processes, referring to it as the "royal
road" to the unconscious (Freud, 1900/1953, p. 608).

Anxiety dreams offer no contradiction to the rule that dreams are wish-fulfillments. The explanation is that anxiety belongs to the preconscious system,
while the wish belongs to the unconscious. Three typical anxiety dreams
reported by Freud are the embarrassment dream of nakedness, dreams of the
death of a beloved person, and dreams of failing an examination (1900/
1953).

In the embarrassment dream of nakedness the person feels shame or
embarrassment at being naked or improperly dressed in the presence of
strangers. The spectators usually appear quite indifferent, though the
dreamer is very much embarrassed. The origin of this dream is the early
childhood experience of being undressed in the presence of adults. In the
original experience the child feels no embarrassment, but the adults often
register disapproval. The pleasure of nakedness, therefore, is repressed and
replaced by shame and embarrassment. Freud (1900/1953) believed that
wish-fulfillment is served in two ways by this dream. First, the indifference of
the spectators fulfills the infantile wish that the witnessing adults refrain from
scolding. Second, the fact of nakedness fulfills the wish to exhibit oneself, a
desire usually repressed in adults but present in young children.

Dreams of the death of a beloved person also originate in childhood and
are wish-fulfillments. If the person dreams of the death of a younger person,
the unconscious mind is expressing the wish for the destruction of a younger
brother or sister who was a hated rival during the infantile period. When the

dead person is older than the dreamer, for example, a parent, the dreamer is fulfilling the Oedipal wish for the death of a parent. If the dreamer feels anxiety and sorrow during the dream, it is because the affect has been reversed. Dreams of the death of a parent are typical in adults, but they do not mean that the dreamer has a *present* wish for the death of that parent. These dreams were interpreted by Freud (1900/1953) as meaning that, as a child, the dreamer longed for the death of the parent, but the wish was too threatening to find its way into consciousness. Even during adulthood the death wish ordinarily does not appear in dreams unless the affect has been changed to sorrow.

A third typical anxiety dream is of failing an examination in school. According to Freud (1900/1953), the person always dreams of failing an examination that has already been successfully passed, never one that was failed. These dreams usually occur when the dreamer is anticipating a difficult task. By dreaming of failing an examination already passed, the ego can reason, "I passed the earlier test which I worried about, so there is no need to be anxious over tomorrow's task." The wish to be free from worry over a difficult job is thus fulfilled.

In summary, Freud believed that dreams are motivated by wish-fulfillments. Their latent content is formed in the unconscious and usually, but not always, has its origin in childhood experiences. The manifest content often stems from experiences of the previous day. The interpretation of dreams serves as the "royal road" to the unconscious, but dreams should never be interpreted without the dreamer's associations to them. Latent material is transformed into manifest content through the dream work. The dream work achieves its goal by the processes of condensation, displacement, and inhibition of affect. The manifest dream may have little resemblance to the latent material, but accurate interpretation reveals the hidden connection by tracing the dream work backward until the unconscious images are revealed.

Parapraxes

Parapraxis is a term made up by James Strachey, one of Freud's translators. Freud (1901/1960) used the German *Fehlleistung,* or "faulty function" to refer to slips of the tongue or pen, misreadings, incorrect hearing, temporary forgetting of names or intentions, and misplacement of objects. These parapraxes, or faulty acts, are usually referred to as "Freudian slips."

Parapraxes are so common that little attention is paid to them and, ordinarily, no important underlying meaning is attributed to them. Freud, however, insisted that these faulty acts have meaning. They reveal the real, that is, the unconscious intention or purpose of the person: "They are not chance events but serious mental acts; they have a sense; they arise from the concurrent actions—or perhaps rather, the mutually opposing action—of two different intentions" (Freud, 1917/1963, p. 44). One opposing action emanates from the unconscious, the other from the preconscious. Parapraxes, therefore, are similar to dreams in that they are a product of both the unconscious and the preconscious. In parapraxes, the unconscious intention is dominant, interfering with and replacing the preconscious one.

That most people strongly deny any meaning behind their parapraxes is seen by Freud as evidence that the slip, indeed, had relevance to unconscious images that must remain hidden from consciousness. A young man once walked into a convenience store, became immediately attracted to the young woman clerk, and ordered a sex-pack of beer. When the clerk accused him of improper behavior, the young man vehemently protested his innocence. In another instance, a young woman was given a watch by a "boy friend" whom she claimed not to like very much. Her opinion of the watch was also quite low. However, she told her mother that she felt obliged to wear the watch because "he might have spies out to see if I'm wearing the ring." Could it be that she had an unconscious desire to marry this man? Examples such as this can be extended almost indefinitely. Freud provided many in his book, *Psychopathology of Everyday Life* (1901/1960). In all parapraxes the intentions of the unconscious supplant the weaker intentions of the preconscious, thereby revealing the true purpose of the ego.

Psychotherapy

The primary goal of psychoanalytic therapy is to uncover repressed memories. "Our therapy works by transforming what is unconscious into what is conscious, and it works only in so far as it is in a position to effect that transformation" (Freud, 1917/1963, p. 280). More specifically, the purpose of psychoanalysis is "to strengthen the ego, to make it more independent of the superego, to widen its field of perception and enlarge its organization, so that it can appropriate fresh portions of the id. Where id was, there ego shall be" (Freud, 1933/1964, p. 80).

To bring unconscious images to consciousness, Freud (1900/1953, 1905/1953a) utilized two techniques—free association and dream analysis. The technique of free association attempts to arrive at the unconscious by starting with a present conscious idea and following it through a train of associations to wherever it leads. The patient is asked to verbalize every thought that comes to mind, no matter how irrelevant or repugnant it may appear. The process is not easy and some patients never master it.

For this reason, dream analysis remained a favorite therapeutic technique with Freud. In interpreting dreams the analyst asked the patient to reveal the dream and all thoughts associated with it. There is no need to write down the dream or to reproduce it verbatim during treatment. Most important are the associations that come to the patient while revealing the dream.

In addition to the associations of the dreamer, symbolism was used to interpret dreams. With this method the analyst points out meanings of symbols, but the patient has to accept the interpretation and continue to make associations to the dream images. Whether associations and symbols are used

Freud's consulting room, Bergasse 19, Vienna.

singly or in combination, the resulting interpretation usually (but not always) reveals latent content that is sexual in nature.

In order for analytic treatment to be successful, libido previously expended on the neurotic symptom must be freed to work in the service of the ego. This takes place in a two-phase procedure. "In the first, all the libido is forced from the symptoms into the transference and concentrated there; in the second, the struggle is waged around this new object and the libido is liberated from it" (Freud, 1917/1963, p. 455). The transference situation is vital to psychoanalysis. **Transference** refers to the strong sexual or aggressive feelings, positive or negative, that the patient develops toward the analyst during the course of treatment. Transference feelings are unearned by the therapist and are merely transferred to her or him from earlier experiences of the patient, usually with the parents. In other words, the patient feels toward the analyst with the same feeling previously felt toward one or both parents. As long as it manifests itself as interest or love, transference does not interfere with the process of treatment but is an essential tool. When it takes the form of hostility or strong sexual feelings, however, resistance sets in and therapeutic progress is blocked. Resistance is overcome by means of a positive transference, which permits the patient to more or less relive childhood experiences within the nonthreatening climate of the analytic treatment (Freud, 1917/1963).

Several limitations of psychoanalysis were noted by Freud (1933/1964). First, not all old memories can or should be brought into consciousness. Second, treatment is not as effective with **psychoses** or with constitutional ill-nesses as it is with the various transference neuroses such as phobias, hys-terias, and obsessions. A third limitation, by no means peculiar to psychoanalysis, is that a patient, once cured, may later develop another neu-rosis. Recognizing these limitations, Freud felt that psychoanalysis could be used in conjunction with other therapies. However, he repeatedly insisted that it could not be shortened or modified in any essential way.

When analytic treatment is successful, the patient no longer suffers from debilitating symptoms, psychic energy is used to perform ego functions, the ego is expanded to include previously repressed experiences, resistances are overcome, and the transference situation is resolved. The patient does not become a new person, but becomes what he or she might have been under the most favorable conditions.

CONCEPT OF HUMANITY

In Chapter 1 we outlined several dimensions for a concept of humanity. Where does Freud's theory fall on these various dimen-sions? The first of these is *determinism vs. free choice*. On this dimension Freud's views on the nature of human nature would fall easily toward determinism, because he believed that most behavior is determined by past events rather than molded by present goals. We have little or no con-trol over our present behavior, since many of our actions are rooted in uncon-scious strivings that lie beyond present awareness. Though we usually insist that we are in control of our own lives, Freud believed that, in reality, we have little control over the forces that shape our personalities.

Adult personality is largely determined by childhood experiences—espe-cially the Oedipus complex—which have left their residue in the uncon-scious mind. Freud (1917/1955) held that humanity in its history has suffered three great blows to its narcissistic ego. The first was the rediscovery by Copernicus that the earth is not the center of the universe; the second was Darwin's discovery that humans are no different from the other animals; the third, and most damaging blow of all, was Freud's own discovery that we are not in control of our own actions or, as he stated it, "the ego is not master in its own house" (Freud, 1917/1955, p. 143).

A second and related issue is *pessimism vs. optimism*. Again, psychoana-lytic theory must be regarded as essentially pessimistic. According to Freud, we come into the world in a basic state of conflict, with life and death forces operating on us from opposing sides. The innate death wish drives us inces-santly toward self-destruction or aggression, while the life instinct causes us to seek blindly after pleasure. The ego experiences a more or less permanent state of conflict, attempting to balance the contradictory demands of the id and superego while at the same time making concessions to the external world.

Underneath a thin veneer of civilization, we are savage beasts with a natural tendency to exploit others for sexual and destructive satisfaction. Antisocial behavior lies just underneath the surface of even the most peaceful person, Freud believed. Worse yet, we are not ordinarily aware of the reasons for our behavior nor are we conscious of the hatred we feel for our friends, family, and lovers.

A third approach for viewing humanity is the dimension of *causality vs. teleology.* Basically, Freud believed that present behavior is mostly shaped by past causes rather than by our goals for the future. Although present perceptions and fantasies (for example, being seduced in childhood by one's parent) are frequently more important than historical reality, personality is formed more by past events (or belief in those events) than by present expectations of future events. According to Freud, we do not move toward a self-determined goal but instead, are helplessly caught in the struggle between Eros and the death instinct. The two conservative instincts force the person to compulsively repeat primitive patterns of behavior. Adult behavior is one long series of reactions. We constantly attempt to reduce tension; to relieve anxieties; to repress unpleasant experiences; to regress to earlier more secure stages of development; and to compulsively repeat behavior that is familiar and safe.

On the dimension of *conscious vs. unconscious,* Freud's theory obviously leans heavily in the direction of unconscious motivation. Freud believed that everything from slips of the tongue to religious experiences is the result of a deep-rooted desire to satisfy sexual or aggressive instincts. These motives make us slaves to our unconscious. Although we are aware of our actions, Freud believed that the motivations underlying those actions are deeply embedded in our unconscious minds and are frequently quite different from what we believe them to be.

A fifth dimension is *biology vs. culture.* Given his medical training, Freud was disposed to see human personality from a biological viewpoint. True, he (Freud, 1913/1953, 1987) frequently speculated about the consequences of prehistorical social units, but the core of his argument was that customs in these early societies have, through evolution, affected our present biological development. Much of our unconscious and many of our infantile fantasies and anxieties have a biological rather than social origin.

Sixth is the issue of *uniqueness vs. similarities.* On this dimension, psychoanalytic theory takes a middle position. Our evolutionary past gives rise to a great many similarities among people. Nevertheless, our individual experiences, especially those of early childhood, shape each of us in a somewhat unique manner and account for many of the differences among personalities.

CRITIQUE OF FREUD

Although Freud regarded himself primarily as a scientist, his theory-building methods are now considered dated and rather unscientific. They were not based on experimental investigation, but rather on subjective observations

Freud made of himself and his clinical patients. These patients were not representative of people-in-general, but came mostly from the middle and upper classes.

Despite these limitations, Freud developed the most comprehensive and most widely known of all personality theories. This widespread reputation of psychoanalysis is due largely to Freud's gifts as a writer, the comprehensiveness of his psychoanalytic theory, his acceptance of unconscious motivation, and finally his heavy emphasis on sex and aggression. For nearly a century his theory has been honored and condemned, glorified and vilified, praised and disparaged. Apart from this widespread popular and professional interest, the question remains: Was Freud scientific? Present opinions differ on this issue. Paul Kline (1984) argues that Freud used free association as the scientific data base for exploring the unconscious and that his methods were consistent with proper scientific practice. Also, Jonathan Winson (1985), viewing psychoanalysis from the modern field of neuroscience, finds biological evidence to support some of Freud's views (see earlier Box—"Biological Bases for the Unconscious"). On the other hand, another group of writers including Marie Balmary (1979/1983), Hannah Lerman (1986), Jeffrey Masson (1984), and Paul Vitz (1988) have criticized Freud for adopting a male-oriented theory and for allowing many of his personal biases to influence his theories. This latter group generally finds Freud to have been unscientific and to have been greatly influenced by his own unconscious needs, especially those springing from the early periods of his life.

Although Freud has been analyzed by nearly as many people as he himself psychoanalyzed, there remains a need to evaluate his theories against the criteria for a useful theory that were enumerated in Chapter 1. To what extent does Freudian theory reach these standards?

First, how well does psychoanalysis *organize knowledge* into a meaningful framework? Freud's theory of personality is conspicuous by its ability to organize observations. Much of what is known concerning human behavior can be logically shaped into a psychoanalytic framework. The framework, however, is so loose and flexible that seemingly inconsistent data can coexist within its boundaries. Nevertheless, psychoanalysis is a useful theory because it has the power to organize knowledge and also to explain causes of behavior. To the perplexing "Why?" questions, psychoanalysis provides more ultimate answers than any other personality theory. One is not obliged to accept Freud's answers, but they are logical extensions of his basic assumptions. To such difficult questions as "Why does the Oedipus complex develop as it does?" and "Why is there a latency period?" psychoanalysis can provide logical answers. This capacity for dealing with ultimate questions and for tying together loose ends marks Freudian theory as exceedingly useful in its ability to organize observations.

The second criterion of a useful theory is its ability to *generate both descriptive research and testable hypotheses.* By this standard Freudian theory again rates very high. However, it also possesses many inherent problems, especially in the area of generating testable hypotheses. These problems are found in any psychological theory that postulates the existence of an unconscious, a hypothetical concept that lies beyond the scope of direct observation. The unconscious, along with such concepts as the id, ego, and superego, is merely an assumption, and is not capable of being directly verified. The most formidable problem presented by psychoanalysis is the assumption that instincts in the unconscious can be altered, displaced, sublimated, or otherwise transformed. This leads to serious difficulties in the formation and testing of hypotheses.

These problems, however, have not stopped researchers from attempting to explore the validity of nearly every aspect of Freud's theories. A review of hundreds of studies on the efficacy of psychoanalytic theory was reported several years ago by Fisher and Greenberg (1977), and since that time the surge of such research has continued. Not all these studies, of course, have supported Freudian hypotheses, but the value of a theory rests more on its ability to generate research than on its established truthfulness.

Third, a useful theory should serve as *a guide for the solution of practical problems.* Because psychoanalysis is quite comprehensive and because it has the capacity to give organization to a variety of observations, it is generally a useful theory for the practitioner. The psychoanalytically oriented therapist, for example, is aided in finding solutions to practical day-to-day problems by the specific and comprehensive guidelines offered by Freudian theory. Explanations for neurotic symptoms, as well as the behavior of normal individuals, can usually be found within existing psychoanalytic theory and, therefore, psychoanalysis is rated high on this third criterion.

The final two criteria of a useful theory deal with *internal consistency* (including operationally defined terms) and *parsimony.* Psychoanalysis is not parsimonious, but considering its comprehensiveness and the complexity of human personality, it is not needlessly cumbersome. It is an internally consistent theory, if one remembers that Freud wrote over a period of more than 40 years and gradually altered the meaning of some concepts during that time. However, at any single point in time the theory generally possessed internal consistency, though some specific terms were used with less than scientific rigor.

Does psychoanalysis possess a set of operationally defined terms? Here the theory falls short. Such terms as id, ego, superego, conscious, preconscious, unconscious, oral stage, sadistic-anal stage, phallic stage, Oedipus complex, latent level of dreams, and many others are not operationally defined; that is, they are not spelled out in terms of specific operations or behaviors. Investigators must originate their own particular definition of most psychoanalytic terms. This, of course, can lead to chaos, with different researchers defining the same term in different ways.

CHAPTER SUMMMARY

The personal traits and experiences of Sigmund Freud permeate and color nearly all aspects of psychoanalytic theory. Freud's character is clearly stamped on the concepts that comprise his personality theory. First among these concepts are the three *levels of* mental life—*the unconscious, preconscious, and conscious.* Freud's exploration of the unconscious mind, including his own, ranks as one of his greatest contributions to our understanding of human personality. Many years after his original investigation into these three levels of mental life, Freud postulated three *provinces of the mind—the id, ego, and superego.* These three regions of personality overlap with, but are not the same as, the three levels of the mind. The id is a completely unconscious, chaotic "cauldron full of seething excitations" (Freud, 1933/1964, p. 73), serving the pleasure principle and completely out of contact with reality. The ego is the executive branch of personality and is the only province of the mind in contact with the real world. The superego, which serves the moral and idealistic principles, begins to evolve after the resolution of the Oedipus complex, around age four or five.

The two great *instincts* or drives in Freudian psychology are *sex* and *aggression.* These urges are often punished during childhood and, as a result, become repressed. Nevertheless, a sufficient number of these threatening impulses remain to produce anxiety within the ego. In order to protect itself against the pain of anxiety, the ego initiates a number of defense mechanisms, the most basic of which is repression.

Freud suggested three major *stages in the development* of personality—*infancy, latency,* and a *genital period.* The infantile stage lasts from birth to about age four or five and is characterized by the child's first psychosexual experiences. It is the most crucial of the stages in the sense that the foundation for future personality structure is formed then. Infancy is divided into three subphases—the *oral,* the *anal,* and the *phallic,* the last of which is accompanied by the *Oedipus complex.* Following the infantile stage is a period of psychosexual latency that lasts until puberty, at which time the genital stage begins. The genital stage signals the onset of a second, or mature, stage of sexuality. This is the final stage conceptualized by Freud, although a hypothetical period of psychological maturity is suggested by psychoanalytic concepts.

Both *dreams* and *"Freudian slips"* are disguised means of expressing unconscious impulses. Also, both ordinarily express some hidden wish. Freud used dreams along with free association in psychotherapy for the purpose of uncovering portions of the patient's unconscious, thus alleviating neurotic conflicts and symptoms.

The Freudian view of humanity is essentially pessimistic and deterministic. According to Freud, people must perpetually struggle to balance the sexual and aggressive instincts of the id with the realistic demands of the ego and the restrictive prohibitions of the superego. People are seldom aware of the forces underlying their behavior and, for the most part, have little control over their own lives.

Psychoanalytic theory, with its heavy emphasis on such nebulous concepts as the unconscious, presents many difficulties for scientific research. Nevertheless, it has been a very useful theory, with an ability to organize knowledge and to generate research that is unsurpassed by any other personality theory. For many therapists and other practitioners it has been a useful guide for solving practical problems. However, Freudian theory is only moderately parsimonious and is deficient in its use of operationally defined terms.

Suggested Readings

BETTELHEIM, B. (1983). *Freud and man's soul.* New York: Knopf.
In this small book Bettelheim suggests that Americans have been misled by existing translations of Freud from German to English. Born in Vienna in 1903, Bettelheim, as a young man, read Freud's books as they

appeared in his native German. After emigrating to the United States, he began to hear and read English translations that rendered Freud more scientific and less humanistic than he appears to the German reader. Here, Bettelheim attempts to tell us what Freud really said.

FREUD, S. (1952). *An autobiographical study.* (J. Strachey, Trans.) New York: Norton. (Original work published 1925).

Freud's own story of his life and work up to 1925. For a more objective account, the reader may wish to supplement this brief autobiography with the writings of such modern "revisionists" as Ellenberger (1970), Isbister (1985), or Sulloway (1979).

FREUD, S. (1966). *The complete introductory lectures on psychoanalysis.* (J. Strachey, Trans.). New York: Norton. (Original works published 1917, 1933).

The best single-volume introduction to the central ideas of psychoanalysis by Freud himself, this book contains Freud's Introductory Lectures, first delivered at the University of Vienna from 1915 to 1917, and his New Introductory Lectures, which were never delivered, but which contain all the major changes Freud made in his theory after World War I.

GAY, P. (1988). *Freud: A life for our time.* New York: Norton.

By no means an easy book to read, Gay's comprehensive work is up-to-date, scholarly, and complete. This book is "must" reading for the serious Freud student.

MALCOLM, J. (1983). *In the Freud archives.* New York: Knopf.

An intriguing account of the story of Kurt Eissler, guardian of the Freud archives in the Library of Congress and his relationship with two important young Freudian scholars. The first was Jeffrey Masson, who, as provisional Projects Director of the Archives, gained access to early documents that led him to conclude that Freud's abandonment of the seduction theory was a grave mistake that greatly weakened psychoanalysis. The second young scholar was Peter Swales, a self-taught authority on Freud, who finds the father of psychoanalysis to have been much less courageous and virtuous than the image perpetuated by his followers.

ERIKSON

3

Post-Freudian Theory

When she died in 1962, Eleanor Roosevelt was one of the most loved and respected women in the world. Psychologist Abraham H. Maslow (1970) regarded her as a self-actualizing person. If Maslow was right, then Eleanor would have had confidence in her ability to love and be loved and would have had a high degree of self-esteem. In addition, she would have enjoyed a level of psychological health attained by only a very few people, a remarkable achievement for someone whose early life was filled with rejection, misery, and self-doubt.

Anna Eleanor Roosevelt was born in 1884, the oldest of three children and the only daughter of wealthy and socially prominent parents. She idolized her father and enjoyed a warm but brief relationship with him. Unfortunately, Eleanor did not share a close relationship with her mother, who was outspoken in her resentment of her daughter. When Eleanor was eight her mother died of diphtheria at the age of 29. Eleanor's mother had named her own mother as guardian of her three children and specifically excluded Eleanor's father from overseeing their upbringing. Eleanor and her two brothers went to live with Grandmother Hall, but Eleanor's life continued to be one of rejection and sadness. Her father visited occasionally, and these visits were the highlights of Eleanor's life. A few months after her mother died, her four-year-old brother died, also of diphtheria. Her father was a heavy drinker who had been in and out of sanitariums for a number of years. His health quickly deteriorated after a fall from a horse, and he died in 1894 when Eleanor was only 10. His death devastated Eleanor, who felt she had lost the only person who truly cared for her.

When Eleanor was 15 her grandmother, who was having trouble with her own children, decided to send Eleanor to a boarding school in England. There Eleanor developed a warm friendship with Marie Souvestre, the headmistress, and the three years under her tutelage were happy and productive ones for Eleanor. She came to value service to less fortunate people, developed an interest in world affairs, stopped wearing the unattractive dresses that had been her custom, and began to see herself as possessing an inner attractiveness.

When Eleanor returned to New York she wanted to go to college, but her grandmother, who did not believe in formal education for women, refused to allow it. After a year of exhausting and boring debutante parties, Eleanor directed her attention toward more socially useful activities—improving conditions of the underprivileged. At about the same time she met her distant cousin, Franklin Roosevelt, and the two young socialites gradually developed a romantic relationship.

In 1905, at age 21, Eleanor married Franklin. She was given in marriage by her uncle Theodore, who was then President of the United States. Franklin's mother, who had always dominated her son, continued to exercise close control over him and Eleanor long after they were married. In 1908 she built a joint house for herself and her son and his growing family. It took Eleanor years before she was able to stand up to her mother-in-law and lead an independent life. After Franklin developed polio in 1921, his mother felt that his political and social life was over, and she wanted to treat him as an invalid. Eleanor was able to oppose her mother-in-law on this point and refused to allow her husband to be coddled. Finally, in midlife, Eleanor was beginning to exert her independence.

OVERVIEW

According to Erik Erikson, the life of Eleanor Roosevelt, like that of any other person who has lived to old age, proceeded in a series of eight stages. In this chapter we examine in some detail Erikson's psychosocial stages of development and illustrate them with excerpts from the life of Eleanor Roosevelt. But before doing so we compare Erikson's work with that of Freud, a man who had considerable direct and indirect influence on Erikson. In general, Erikson differs from Freud in placing more emphasis on the ego, on social and historical influences, and his extension of developmental stages into adulthood and old age.

Unlike Freud, Erikson is not a physician. In fact he has no college degree of any kind. Yet, he is one of the world's foremost psychoanalysts, having been analyzed by Freud's daughter Anna. In contrast to Adler (Chapter 4) and Jung (Chapter 5), Erikson has never repudiated Freud's ideas. Instead, he has constructed a personality theory on the foundation laid by Freud. Thus, his way of looking at personality can rightly be called post-Freudian theory.

Erikson's theory, like those of others, is a reflection of his background, a background heavily steeped in art.

BIOGRAPHY OF ERIK ERIKSON

The life of Erik Homburger Erikson, like that of Eleanor Roosevelt, has been marked by several "identity crises," a term Erikson began to popularize nearly 50 years ago.

Erikson's early identity crises were in part due to his own clouded origins. He was born June 15, 1902, near Frankfurt, Germany, the son of Karla Abrahamsen and a father of unknown identity. During his first three years he lived alone with his mother, who then married Dr. Theodor Homburger, Erik's pediatrician (Coles, 1970). Erikson grew up in Karlsruhe, a town in southern Germany, believing he was Homburger's son. In his autobiography, Erikson (1975, p. 27) claimed that his parents "kept from me the fact that my mother had been married previously, and that I was the son of a Dane who had abandoned her before my birth." However, Paul Roazen (1976) cited a speech Erikson had given twenty years earlier in which he reported that his father had died around the time of his birth. Roazen further suggested that Erikson may have been born out of wedlock, and that his unknown paternal lineage has contributed to an image of himself as a perpetual stepson. This image is seen in Erikson's persistent loyalty to Sigmund Freud, who, in many ways, became Erikson's mythical stepfather.

Erikson's real stepfather, Theodor Homburger, was from a small Jewish bourgeois family. He was a kindly man who expected his stepson to become a doctor like himself. Erikson's mother, a native of Copenhagen, Denmark, was from a Jewish family, but her own religious affiliation, like that of her son, is not clear. We do know that Erik attended temple where his blond hair and blue eyes made him appear an outsider. At school, on the other hand, his classmates referred to him as a Jew. Erik, therefore, felt out of place in both arenas.

At 18 Erikson completed school at the Gymnasium—the last academic graduation of his life. Feeling "alienated from everything my bourgeois family stood for," he set out in quest of a different style of life (Erikson, 1975, p. 28). Gifted at sketching, he divided his time between art school and wandering throughout southern Germany and northern Italy, hiking and carrying a knapsack with books of his favorite authors. His identity as an artist meant a kind of rebellious way of life rather than a specific occupation, and that way of life was antiestablishment. These were "years of discontent, rebellion, and confusion" (Erikson, 1975).

At 25 he returned to Karlsruhe to teach art. However, a letter from his friend, Peter Blos, was to have a permanent effect on the direction of his life. Erikson had known Blos from their youth in Karlsruhe and the two were friends in Italy. Both were artists and both later became well-known psychoanalysts. Erikson (1975) considers Blos's letter to have rescued him from the life of a wandering artist. The letter asked Erikson to join with Blos in teaching in a newly established school for children in Vienna. The school was run by a friend of Anna Freud, and many of the students were daughters and sons of future psychoanalysts. During the six years he spent in Vienna, Erikson studied psychoanalysis and Montessori education. In addition, he completed a personal analysis with Anna Freud, Sigmund Freud's daughter. Anna, seven years older than Erikson, shared a waiting room with her father, then in his seventies. Erikson rarely addressed the older Freud, not only out of shyness and deference, but also because speech was quite painful for Freud, who wore a prosthetic device in his jaw due to the oral cancer from which he was suffering. Even though Erikson's personal relationship with Freud was minimal, he has remained a life-long ardent admirer of the father of psychoanalysis.

While in Vienna, Erikson met and married Joan Serson, a Canadian-born, American-trained dancer and teacher who had also undergone psychoanalysis. With her psychoanalytic background and her facility with the English language, she has proven to be a capable editor and occasional coauthor of Erikson's books. The Eriksons have three children, a daughter and two sons. The older son, Kai Erikson, is a professor of sociology and has occasionally collaborated with his father.

In 1933 Erikson (still known as Homburger) graduated from the Vienna Psychoanalytic Institute. Then, with fascism on the rise, the Eriksons left Vienna for Denmark, the land of Erik's natural parents. After one summer in Copenhagen they immigrated to the United States, settling first in the Boston area.

With neither medical credentials nor an academic degree of any kind, Erikson was offered a position at the Harvard Medical School. While there, he enrolled in the Ph.D. program in psychology but soon dropped out. While at Harvard, he met Margaret Mead, Ruth Benedict, Henry Murray, Kurt Lewin, and others who had also influenced Harry Stack Sullivan (Chapter 6) and Karen Horney (Chapter 7).

In 1936 Erikson went to Yale where he was associated with the famous Institute of Human Relations and where he also taught at the Medical School. Three years later he moved to the University of California at Berkeley, but not before living among and studying the Sioux Indians in South Dakota. (He later lived with the Yurok Indians in northern California and these experiences in cultural anthropology have added much to the richness and completeness of his theory of personality.)

At about the same time Erikson moved to the West Coast, he became a United States citizen and changed his name. Erikson was not his natural father's name, and his choice of that name is not adequately explained in his autobiography (Erikson, 1975). Perhaps his newly acquired American identity allowed him to identify with Leif Ericsson, the first European explorer to land in North America. Or perhaps Erik's sons wanted to be known as Erikson.

During his California period Erikson gradually evolved a theory of personality, separate from but not incompatible with Freud's. In 1950 he published *Childhood and Society,* a book that has now become a classic, and which made for Erikson an international reputation as an imaginative thinker.

Erikson remained at Berkeley until 1950, when faculty members were being asked to sign a loyalty oath. As a matter of principle, Erikson refused to sign and left California for Stockbridge, Massachusetts where he worked at Austen Riggs, a treatment center for psychoanalytic training and research. He returned to Harvard in 1960 and remained there until his retirement in 1970. After retirement he continued an active career—writing, lecturing, seeing a few patients, and doing research on aging with his wife Joan (Erikson, Erikson, & Kivnick, 1986).

Erikson's best known works include *Childhood and Society* (1950, 1963); *Young Man Luther* (1958); *Identity, Youth and Crisis* (1968); *Gandhi's Truth* (1969), a book that won both the Pulitzer Prize and the National Book Award; *Dimensions of a New Identity* (1974); *Life History and the Historical Moment* (1975); *Identity and the Life Cycle* (1980); and the *Life Cycle Completed* (1982). More recently many of his papers have been compiled in *A Way of Looking at Things* (Schlein, 1987).

Erikson has lived through the eight stages of development and is thus able to see each with a personal perspective. He has traveled extensively and has lived in many geographically and culturally diverse localities. Wherever he lived Erikson has taken his acceptance for granted. Yet, he has not always felt completely at home. In his autobiography (Erikson, 1975, p. 29), he explained his adoption by the Freudian circle with these words.

> I can only surmise . . . that it was a kind of positive stepson identity that made me take for granted that I should be accepted where I did not belong. By the same token, however, I had to cultivate not-belonging and keep contact with the artist in me.

Erikson has kept track, not only of his artist identity, but with his identity as a cultural anthropologist and a clinical psychoanalyst as well.

IMPORTANCE OF THE EGO

Erikson's identity as a clinical psychoanalyst can be traced to his early acceptance into the Freudian circle and his training with Anna Freud. He takes psychoanalysis for granted, and Freudian theory provides the foundation for his life-cycle approach to personality theory. Erikson's theoretical model, however, is more than merely a refinement of psychoanalysis. It is an extension—something Freud might have done in time. For this reason Erikson prefers the term *post-Freudian* rather than *revisionist* or *neo-Freudian*.

Erikson has made three important additions to Freudian theory. First, to Freud's early psychosexual stages (oral, anal, phallic, and latency), he has added four later stages, thus extending the life cycle throughout adulthood and into old age. Second, he has moved beyond the consulting room and has gathered data from historical and cultural sources, thereby elevating social factors above biological explanations. Third, he has emphasized the ego over the id as the key to personality development.

Description of Ego Psychology

In Chapter 2 we saw that Freud used the analogy of a rider on horseback to describe the relationship between the ego and the id. The rider (ego) is ultimately at the mercy of the stronger horse (id). The ego has no strength of its own, but must borrow its energy from the id. Moreover, the ego is constantly attempting to balance blind demands of the superego against the relentless forces of the id and the realistic opportunities of the external world. Freud believed that, in the mature person, it is possible for the ego to rein in the id, but control is always tenuous, and at any time id impulses might erupt and overwhelm the ego.

In contrast, Erikson holds that the ego is more than a mediator between the irrational forces of the id and the unrelenting demands of the superego. The ego is a positive force, one that establishes self-identity and also adapts to the various conflicts and crises of life. The adaptation is not always constructive. At times the ego struggles to defend itself and, on occasion, it may even succumb to the forces of society. In any event it is the ego (the sense of "I" or self-identity) that is the center of personality.

The ego is not synonymous with the individual, but it is indispensable to a person's individuality (Erikson, 1963). The ego is weak, pliable, and fragile during childhood, but by adolescence it should begin to take form and gain strength. Throughout life, it unifies personality and guards indivisibility. Erikson (1963, p. 16) defines the ego as a person's "capacity to unify his experiences and his actions in an adaptive manner."

In formulating his ideas on ego psychology, Erikson (1982) acknowledges his debt to three earlier formulations: Freud's (1923/1961a) conception of the ego as restraint on the biological forces of the id; Anna Freud's (1946) view of a defensive ego; and Heinz Hartmann's (1939/1958) notion of an adaptive ego.

Erikson (1968) sees the ego as a partially unconscious organizing agency that synthesizes present experiences with past selves and also with anticipated selves. There are three interrelated aspects of ego: (1) the *body ego,* which refers to experiences with one's body; (2) the *ego ideal,* which represents the image we have of ourselves in comparison with an established ideal; and (3) *ego identity,* the image we have of ourselves in a variety of social roles. Although adolescence is ordinarily the time when these three components are changing most rapidly, alterations in body ego, ego ideal, and ego identity can and do take place at any stage of life.

In summary, the ego has both a defensive and an adaptive function. Its principal task is to turn the demands of the id and the superego into allies in pursuit of ego identity. The ego operates actively to unify experiences and to guard one's sense of identity.

Society's Influence

Although inborn capacities are important in development, the ego emerges from and is largely shaped by society. Erikson's emphasis on social and historical factors is in contrast with Freud's mostly biological viewpoint. While Freudian theory emphasizes the power of the genetically based id, Erikson sees the ego as developing within a social structure. In an interview with Richard Evans, Erikson said, "The ego can only remain strong in inter-action with cultural institutions and can only remain strong when the child's inborn capacities and potentials are developed" (Evans, 1967, p. 26). In other words, the ego exists as potential at birth, but must emerge from within a cultural environment.

Different societies, with their variations in child-rearing practices, tend to shape personalities that fit the needs and values of their culture. For example, Erikson (1963) found that among the Sioux Indians of South Dakota, pro-longed and permissive nursing of infants (sometimes as long as four or five years) resulted in what Freud would call "oral" personalities. The Sioux place great value on generosity, and Erikson believes that the reassurance resulting from unlimited breast feeding lays the foundation for the virtue of generosity. However, biting is quickly suppressed in infants, and this practice may contribute to the child's fortitude and to the "hunter's ferocity" needed by Sioux society. On the other hand, the Yurok Indians of California have strict regulations concerning elimination of urine and feces, practices that tend to develop "anality." In Western societies orality and anality may be considered undesirable traits or neurotic symptoms. Erikson (1963), how-ever, argues that orality among the Sioux hunters and anality among the Yurok fishermen are adaptive characteristics that help both the individual and the culture within which the individual resides. The fact that Western culture may view orality and anality as deviant traits merely displays its own ethnocentric view of other societies. Erikson (1968, 1974) argues that histor-ically all tribes or nations, including our own, have developed what he calls a **pseudospecies,** by which he means the illusion perpetrated and perpetu-ated by a particular society that it is somehow chosen to be *the* human spe-cies. In past centuries this belief has aided survival of the tribe, but with mod-ern means of world annihilation, such a prejudiced perception (as demonstrated by Nazi Germany) threatens the survival of every nation.

As noted earlier, one of Erikson's principal contributions to personality theory is his extension of the Freudian early stages of development to include youth, adulthood, and old age. Before looking more closely at Erik-son's theory of ego development, it is necessary to understand his view of how personality develops from one stage to the next.

Epigenetic Principle

According to Erikson, the ego develops throughout the various stages of life according to an **epigenetic principle.** This term, borrowed from embry-ology, needs some explanation. In embryology, epigenetic development implies a step by step growth of fetal organs. The embryo does not begin as a completely formed little person, waiting to merely expand its structure and form. Rather, it develops, or should develop, according to a predetermined rate and in a fixed sequence. If the eyes, liver, or other organs do not develop during that critical period when normal development takes place, then they will never attain proper maturity. In similar fashion, the ego follows the path of epigenetic development, with each stage developing at its proper time.

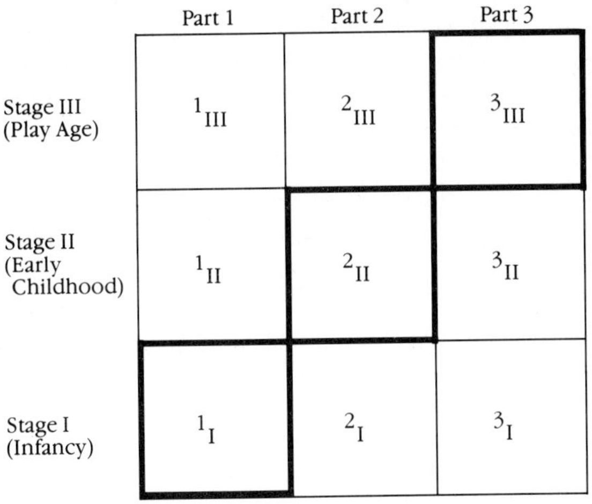

	Part 1	Part 2	Part 3
Stage III (Play Age)	1_{III}	2_{III}	3_{III}
Stage II (Early Childhood)	1_{II}	2_{II}	3_{II}
Stage I (Infancy)	1_{I}	2_{I}	3_{I}

Figure 3.1 The Epigenetic Principle Depicting the First Three Eriksonian Stages (From *The life cycle completed* by E. H. Erikson, 1982, p. 28. Copyright 1982 by W. W. Norton. Adapted by permission.)

One stage emerges from and is built upon its previous stage. In Erikson's words, the epigenetic principle "states that anything that grows has a ground plan, and that out of this ground plan the parts arise, each part having its time of special ascendancy, until all parts have arisen to form a functioning whole" (Erikson, 1968, p. 92). More succinctly, "epigenesis means that one characteristic develops on top of another in space and time" (Evans, 1967, pp. 21–22).

The epigenetic principle is illustrated in Figure 3.1, which depicts the first three Eriksonian stages. The sequence of stages (I, II, III) and the development of their component parts (1, 2, 3) are shown in the heavily lined boxes along the diagonal. Figure 3.1 shows that each part exists before its critical time (at least as biological potential), then emerges at its proper time, and finally continues to develop during subsequent stages. For example, the component parts of Stage II (early childhood) exist during Stage I (infancy) as shown in Box 2_{I}. These component parts reach their full ascendance during Stage II (Box 2_{II}), but continue into Stage III (Box 2_{III}). Similarly, the components of Stage III exist during Stages I and II, reach full development during Stage III, and continue throughout all later stages (Erikson, 1982).

STAGES OF PSYCHOSOCIAL DEVELOPMENT

To appreciate Erikson's eight stages of psychosocial development several points must be understood.

1. As explained above, growth takes place according to the *epigenetic principle*. That is, one component part arises out of another, has its own time of ascendancy, but does not entirely replace earlier components.

2. In every stage of life there is an *interaction of opposites,* that is, a conflict between a **syntonic** (harmonious) element and a **dystonic** (disruptive) element. For example, during infancy *basic trust* (a syntonic tendency) is opposed to *basic mistrust* (a dystonic tendency). Both trust and mistrust, however, are necessary for proper adaptation. An infant who learns only to trust becomes gullible and is ill-prepared for the realities encountered in later development. Of course, an infant who learns only to mistrust becomes overly suspicious and cynical.

3. At each stage the conflict between the dystonic and syntonic elements produces an ego quality or **basic strength.** For instance, from the antithesis between trust and mistrust emerges "hope," an ego quality that allows the infant to move into the next stage.

4. Although Erikson refers to these periods as *psychosocial* stages, he never loses sight of the *somatic* (biological) aspect of human development.

5. Events in earlier stages do not "cause" later personality development. Ego identity is shaped by a *multiplicity of conflicts and events*—past, present, and anticipated.

6. During each stage, but especially from adolescence forward, development is characterized by an **identity crisis,** "a turning point, a crucial period of increased vulnerability and heightened potential" (Erikson, 1968, p. 96). Contrary to popular usage, an identity crisis is not a catastrophic event, but rather an opportunity for either adaptive or maladaptive adjustment.

Erikson's eight stages of psychosocial development are shown in Figure 3.2. The capitalized words are the ego qualities or basic strengths that emerge from the conflicts or psychosocial crises that typify each period. The "vs." separating syntonic and dystonic elements signifies not only an antithetical relationship but also a complementary one. Although only the boxes along the diagonal are filled in, the epigenetic principle suggests that every box would contain some item (see Figure 3.1). Each item in the ensemble is vital to personality development, and each is related to all others. Although it is possible to start at old age and work backward (as Erikson does in *The Life Cycle Completed*), we begin our discussion of psychosocial development with infancy.

Infancy

The first psychosocial stage is **infancy,** a period encompassing approximately the first year of life and paralleling Freud's oral phase of development, although there are important differences between Freud's and Erikson's views. In describing this stage, Freud was concerned almost exclusively with the mouth, while Erikson has adopted a broader focus. To Erikson, infancy is a time of *incorporation,* that is, the infant incorporates or "takes in" not only through the mouth but through the various sense organs as well.

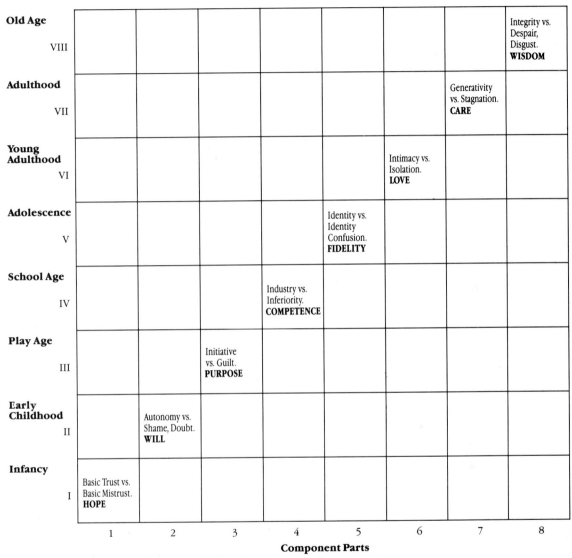

		1	2	3	4	5	6	7	8
Old Age	VIII								Integrity vs. Despair, Disgust. **WISDOM**
Adulthood	VII							Generativity vs. Stagnation. **CARE**	
Young Adulthood	VI						Intimacy vs. Isolation. **LOVE**		
Adolescence	V					Identity vs. Identity Confusion. **FIDELITY**			
School Age	IV				Industry vs. Inferiority. **COMPETENCE**				
Play Age	III			Initiative vs. Guilt. **PURPOSE**					
Early Childhood	II		Autonomy vs. Shame, Doubt. **WILL**						
Infancy	I	Basic Trust vs. Basic Mistrust. **HOPE**							

Component Parts

Figure 3.2   Erikson's Eight Stages of Development with Their Appropriate Psychosocial Crises and Basic Strengths (From *The life cycle completed* by E. H. Erikson, 1982, pp. 56–57. Copyright 1982 by W. W. Norton. Adapted by permission.)

Oral-Sensory Mode

Erikson's expanded view of infancy is expressed in the term **oral-sensory,** a phrase he uses to describe the infant's principal *psychosexual* mode of adapting.

The oral-sensory stage is characterized by two modes of incorporation— receiving and accepting what is given. An infant can receive even in the absence of other people, that is, it can take in air through the lungs and can receive sensory data without having to manipulate others. The second mode of incorporation, however, implies a social context. The infant not only must get but also must get someone else to give. This early training in interpersonal relations helps the infant learn to eventually become a giver. In its experiences with getting others to give, the infant learns to trust or mistrust, which sets up the basic *psychosocial* crisis of infancy.

Basic Trust vs. Basic Mistrust

The infant's most significant interpersonal relations are with the maternal person or primary care giver, ordinarily its mother. If the infant realizes that its mother will provide food regularly, then it begins to learn basic trust; if it consistently hears the pleasant, rhythmic voice of its mother, then more basic trust is developed; if it can rely on an exciting visual environment, then basic trust is solidified even more. In other words, if the infant's pattern of accepting things corresponds with the culture's way of giving them, basic trust will be learned. On the other hand, if the infant finds no correspondence between its oral-sensory needs and its environment, then basic mistrust is developed.

Basic trust is ordinarily syntonic and basic mistrust dystonic. Nevertheless, the infant must develop both attitudes. As noted earlier, too much trust makes one gullible and vulnerable to the vagaries of the world, while too little trust leads to frustration, anger, hostility, cynicism, or depression.

Both trust and mistrust are inevitable experiences of the infant. All babies who have survived have been fed or otherwise cared for, and thus have some reason to trust. In addition, all have been frustrated by pain, hunger, or discomfort and therefore have a reason to mistrust. Erikson believes that some ratio of trust and mistrust is critical to our ability to adapt. He says that "when we enter a situation, we must be able to differentiate how much we can trust and how much we must mistrust, and I use mistrust in the sense of a readiness for danger and an anticipation of discomfort" (Evans, 1967, p. 15).

The inevitable conflict between basic trust and basic mistrust results in the person's first psychosocial crisis which, in turn, leads to the first basic strength—*hope.*

Hope: The Basic Strength of Infancy

Hope emerges from the conflict between basic trust and basic mistrust, and thus becomes the person's first basic strength. In his earlier writings Erikson referred to basic strengths as "virtues," but he abandoned this term because the origin of the word implies manliness or male qualities (Hall, 1983).

Without the antithetical relationship between trust and mistrust there can be no hope. The infant must experience hunger, pain, and discomfort as well as their alleviation, thus giving the baby some reason to expect that future distresses will meet with satisfactory outcomes. This "enduring predisposition to believe in the attainability of primal wishes in spite of anarchic urges and rages of dependency" is called hope (Erikson, 1968, p. 106). To Erikson, "hope is a very basic human strength without which we couldn't stay alive" (Evans, 1967, p. 17). The antipathy of hope is *withdrawal,* which Erikson calls the core pathology of infancy. With little to hope for, the infant retreats from the outside world and begins the journey toward serious psychological disturbance.

According to the epigenetic principle discussed earlier, hope is an element of each of the other basic strengths, that is, it is a component part of will, purpose, competence, fidelity, love, care, and wisdom (see Figure 3.2). For example, in the lower right corner (Box 8), basic trust and basic mistrust meet with wisdom (Erikson, 1979). The seeds of wisdom, then, are planted during infancy as the baby learns to trust and mistrust its mother and the world.

Early Childhood

The second psychosocial stage is **early childhood,** a period paralleling Freud's anal stage and encompassing approximately the second and third years of life. Again, there are differences between the views of Freud and Erikson. As you recall from Chapter 2, Freud regarded the anus as the primary erogenous zone during this period. During the early sadistic-anal phase children receive pleasure in destroying or losing objects while later they take satisfaction in defecating. Once again, Erikson takes a broader view. To him, young children receive pleasure not only from mastering the sphincter muscle, but also from mastering other body functions such as urinating, walking, throwing, holding, and so on. In addition, children develop a sense of control over their interpersonal environment, as well as a measure of self-control. However, this is also a time of experiencing doubt and shame as children learn that many of their attempts at autonomy are unsuccessful. From the conflict between autonomy and shame and doubt there emerges a basic strength called *will.*

Early childhood, then, is characterized by the anal-urethral-muscular psychosexual mode; the psychosocial crisis of autonomy vs. shame and doubt; and the emergence of will as a basic strength.

Anal-Urethral-Muscular Mode

During the second year, the child's primary psychosexual adjustment is the **anal-urethral-muscular** mode. At this time the child learns to control her body, especially in relation to cleanliness and mobility. It is a time of toilet training, but it is also a time of learning to walk, run, hug parents, and hold on to toys and other objects. With each of these activities, the young child is likely to display some stubborn tendencies. She may retain her feces or eliminate them at will; she may snuggle up to her mother or suddenly push her away; she may delight in hoarding objects or ruthlessly discard them.

Early childhood, then, is a time of contradiction, a time of stubborn rebellion and meek compliance, a time of *impulsive* self-expression and *compulsive* deviance, a time of loving cooperation and hateful resistance (Erikson, 1968). This obstinate insistence on conflicting impulses triggers the major psychosocial crisis of childhood: autonomy vs. shame and doubt.

Autonomy vs. Shame and Doubt

If early childhood is a time for self-expression and autonomy, then it is also a time for shame and doubt. As the child stubbornly expresses her anal-ure-thral-muscular mode, she is likely to find a culture that attempts to inhibit some of her self-expression. Her parents may shame her for soiling her pants or for making a mess with her food. They may also instill doubt by questioning her ability to meet their standards. The conflict between autonomy and shame and doubt becomes the major psychosocial crisis of childhood.

Ideally, there should be a proper ratio between autonomy and shame and doubt, and, of course, the ratio should be in favor of autonomy, the syntonic quality. If the child develops too little autonomy, then she will have difficulties in subsequent stages. She will lack the initiative required during the play age and will continue to be handicapped in her later development. According to Erikson's epigenetic diagrams (Figures 3.1 and 3.2), autonomy grows out of basic trust, and if basic trust has been established in infancy, then the child's faith in herself and the world remains intact while she experiences the psychosocial crisis of childhood. Conversely, if basic trust has not been well developed during infancy, then her attempts to gain control of her anal, urethral, and muscular organs during childhood will be met with shame and doubt. Shame is a feeling of self-consciousness, of being looked at and exposed. Doubt, on the other hand, is the feeling of not being certain, the feeling that something remains hidden and cannot be seen. Both shame and doubt are dystonic qualities and both grow out of the basic mistrust that was established in infancy.

Will: The Basic Strength of Childhood

The basic strength of *will* or willfulness evolves from the resolution of the crisis of autonomy vs. shame and doubt. This is the beginning of free will and will power, but only a beginning. Mature will power and a significant measure of free will are reserved for later stages of development, but they have their origins in the rudimentary will that emerges during early childhood. Anyone who has spent much time around two-year-olds knows how willful they can be. Toilet training often epitomizes the conflict of wills between adult and child; but willful expression is not limited to this area. The basic conflict during this stage is between the child's striving for autonomy and the parent's attempts to control the child through the use of shame and doubt.

Rudimentary will can only emerge if the child is permitted some self-expression in the control of her sphincters and other muscles. If her culture instills too much shame and doubt and inhibits autonomy, the child will not adequately develop this second important basic strength. Inadequate will is expressed as *compulsion,* the core pathology of early childhood. Too little will and too much compulsivity carries forward into the play age as lack of purpose and into the school age as lack of confidence.

Play Age

Erikson's third stage of development is the **play age,** a period covering the same time as Freud's phallic phase—roughly ages three to five. Again, we find differences between the views of Freud and Erikson. Freud paid little attention to the child's social development, but instead found great significance in the Oedipus complex, that is, the child's sexual feelings for one parent and hostile feelings for the other. After the Oedipus complex is resolved, the child ordinarily identifies with the parent of the same sex and gives up his sexual feelings for the parent of the opposite sex. While the Oedipus complex is a central theme in Freudian theory, it is but one of several important developments during Erikson's play age. Erikson (1968) says that in addition to identifying with his parents, the preschool child is developing the ability to move around more freely (locomotion), language skills, curiosity, imagination, and the ability to set goals. From these experiences develop the crisis of *initiative vs. guilt* and a realistic sense of *purpose.*

Genital-Locomotor Mode

The primary psychosexual mode during the play age is **genital-locomotor.** Erikson (1982, p. 77) sees the Oedipal situation as a prototype "of the lifelong power of human playfulness." In other words, the Oedipus complex is a drama played out in the child's imagination and includes the budding understanding of such basic concepts as reproduction, growth, future, and death. The Oedipus and castration complexes, therefore, are not always to be taken literally. The child may play at being a mother, a father, a wife, or a husband, but such play is an expression, not only of the genital mode, but also of the child's rapidly developing locomotor abilities. A little girl may envy boys but this is not due to the latter's possession of a penis, but rather to the prerogatives most societies grant to children with a penis. The little boy may have anxiety about losing something, but this refers not only to the penis but to other body parts as well. The Oedipus complex, then, is both more than and less than what Freud believed, and infantile sexuality is "a mere promise of things to come" (Erikson, 1963, p. 86). Unless sexual interest is provoked by cultural sex play or by adult sexual abuse, the Oedipus complex produces no harmful effects on later personality development.

The child's interest in genital activity is accompanied by increasing facility in locomotion. The child is now moving with ease, running, jumping, and climbing with no conscious effort. His play shows initiative and imagination. The rudimentary will developed during the preceding stage is evolving into activity with a *purpose.* His cognitive abilities enable him to manufacture elaborate fantasies including, perhaps, Oedipal fantasies, but also including imagining what it is like to be grown-up, to be omnipotent, or to be a ferocious animal. These fantasies, however, also produce guilt and thus contribute to the psychosocial crisis of the play age, namely, initiative vs. guilt.

Initiative vs. Guilt

As the child begins to move around more easily and vigorously and as his genital interest awakens, he adopts an intrusive head-on mode of approaching the world. He begins to adopt *initiative* in his selection and pursuit of goals. However, many goals, such as marrying one's mother or father or leaving home, must either be repressed or delayed. The consequence of these taboo and inhibited goals is *guilt*. The conflict between initiative and guilt becomes the dominant psychosocial crisis of the play age. Again, the ratio between these two should favor the syntonic quality, initiative. Unbridled initiative, however, may lead to chaos and a lack of moral principles. On the other hand, if guilt is the dominant element, the person may become compulsively moralistic or overly inhibited. *Inhibition* is the core pathology of the play age and the antipathy of purpose.

Purpose: The Basic Strength of the Play Age

The conflict of initiative vs. guilt produces the basic strength of *purpose*. The child now plays with a purpose, competing at games in order to win or to be on top. His genital interests have a direction, with mother or father being the object of his sexual desires. He sets goals and pursues them with purpose. This is also the stage in which the child is developing a conscience, beginning to attach labels such as right and wrong to his behavior. Erikson (1968, p. 119) refers to this youthful conscience as the "cornerstone of morality." However, if the conscience is too strict and uncompromising, the result would be a stifling of initiative, a loss of purpose, and a vindictive attitude toward others. Later in life the person may show unrelenting initiative, overaggressiveness, and strain, all of which may lead to various psychosomatic illnesses.

Erikson (1968, p. 121) sums up the play age this way:

> We may now see what induced Freud to place the Oedipus complex at the core of man's conflicted existence, and this not only according to psychiatric evidence but also to the testimony of great fiction, drama, and history. For the fact that man began as a playing child leaves a residue of play-acting and role playing even in what he considers his highest purposes.

We began this chapter with a brief biography of Eleanor Roosevelt and will use her life story to illustrate her psychological development during each of the five subsequent stages of Erikson's theory. Unfortunately, little is known of her early life with regard to psychosexual development or psychosocial crises. We do know that she remembered her mother telling her during early childhood that she looked like an old woman, without any semblance of spontaneous fun (Steinberg, 1958). Her play age must have been stilted and serious as she strove to acquire the manners and demeanor of adulthood far before her time.

School Age

The **school age** covers the period from about six to 12 or 13 and matches the stage Freud called "latency." As you recall from Chapter 2, Freud called this period latency because he believed that *psychosexual* growth was at a standstill. Only in a general way did he write of the social and academic development taking place during this time. Erikson looks more at the whole child, emphasizing the growth of the ego within a cultural setting. Now for the first time the child's social world has significantly expanded beyond family members to include peers as well as teachers and other adult models. The wish to know becomes strong and is tied to a basic striving for competence. In normal development children industriously strive to read and write, to hunt and fish, or to learn the skills their culture requires.

School age does not necessarily mean formalized schools. In literate cultures schools and professional teachers play a major part in the child's education, while in preliterate societies, less formalized but equally effective methods are used to instruct children in the ways of the society.

In summary, school age is marked by the psychosexual stage of *latency,* the psychosocial crisis of *industry vs. inferiority,* and the emergence of the basic strength of *competence.*

Latency

School age is a time of psychosexual **latency.** Infantile sexuality becomes mostly dormant while full genital maturity has not yet been achieved. Sexual latency is important because it allows the child to divert her energies to learning the technology of her culture and the strategies of meaningful social relations. As the child works and plays hard to acquire these essentials, she begins to form a picture of herself as competent or incompetent. This is the origin of *ego identity*—that feeling of "I" or "me-ness" that evolves more fully during adolescence.

Industry vs. Inferiority

If school age is a period of little psychosexual development, then it is a time of tremendous *psychosocial* growth. The psychosocial crisis of this stage is industry vs. inferiority. Industry, of course, is a syntonic quality and means industriousness, a willingness to remain busy with something and to finish a job. The child learns to work and play at activities directed both toward acquiring job skills and toward learning the rules of cooperation. Erikson (1982) contends that at no other time is the child so eager and ready to learn. As the child learns to make and do things well, she develops a sense of industry. But if her work is insufficient to accomplish her goals, she acquires a sense of inferiority, the dystonic quality of the school age. Earlier inadequacies can also contribute to one's feelings of inferiority. For example, if too much guilt and too little purpose were achieved during the play age, the school age child will likely feel inferior and incompetent. However, failure is not inevitable. Erikson is optimistic in suggesting that a person can successfully handle the crisis of any given stage even though she was not completely successful in previous stages.

The ratio between industry and inferiority should, of course, favor industry, but inferiority, like the other dystonic qualities, should not be avoided. As Alfred Adler (Chapter 4) pointed out, inferiority can serve as an impetus to do one's best. Conversely, an oversupply of inferiority can block productive activity and stunt one's feelings of competence.

Competence: The Basic Strength of School Age

From the conflict of industry vs. inferiority, the person develops *competence*. Erikson (1968, p. 126) defines competence as "the free exercise of dexterity and intelligence in the completion of serious tasks unimpaired by an infantile sense of inferiority." Competence lays the foundation for "cooperative participation in productive adult life" (Erikson, 1968, p. 126).

The antipathy of competence is *inertia*. If the struggle between industry and inferiority favors either inferiority or an overabundance of industry, the child is likely to give up and regress to an earlier stage of development. She may become preoccupied with infantile genital and Oedipal fantasies and spend most of her time in nonproductive play. This regression is called inertia and represents the core pathology of the school-age stage.

For Eleanor Roosevelt school age was a time of doubt, self-pity, deep feelings of inferiority, and sadness. When she was eight, her mother, who had been constantly critical of her, died. This death left no great impression on Eleanor, but when her beloved father died 18 months later, Eleanor was grief-stricken. She regressed into a fantasy life, day-dreaming of many imaginary adventures involving her and her father. Her reaction to her father's death is quite consistent with Erikson's hypothesis that children of school age with overriding feelings of inferiority are likely to regress to Ocdipal fantasies. At this time, Eleanor had little of the basic strength of competence. She was not successful in making intimate friends of her peers and was frequently reminded of her inadequacies as a scholar. Recall that, although Erikson believes that basic strengths build on early ones, he optimistically suggests that people can grow toward maturity in spite of some childhood pathologies. Such was the case with Eleanor Roosevelt.

Adolescence

Adolescence, the period from puberty to young adulthood, is one of the most crucial developmental stages because by the end of this period the person must gain a firm sense of *ego identity*. In the epigenetic configuration, ego identity neither begins nor ends with adolescence, but it is during this time that the crisis between *identity* and *identity confusion* reaches its ascendance. From this crisis emerges *fidelity,* the basic strength of adolescence.

Erikson (1982) sees adolescence as a period of psycho*social* latency, just as school age is a time of psycho*sexual* latency. Although the adolescent is developing sexually and cognitively, he is allowed to postpone lasting commitment to an occupation, a sex partner, or an adaptive philosophy of life. He is permitted to experiment in a variety of ways, trying out new roles and beliefs while seeking to establish a sense of ego identity. Adolescence, then, is an adaptive phase of personality development, a period of trial and error.

Puberty

The principal psychosexual mode of the adolescent stage is *puberty,* defined by Erikson (1968) as genital maturation. Actually, puberty itself plays a relatively minor role in Erikson's concept of adolescence. For most young people, genital maturation presents no major sexual crisis (Erikson, 1967). Nevertheless, puberty is important psychologically because it triggers expectations of adult roles yet ahead—roles that are essentially social and can be filled only through a struggle to attain a clear sense of ego identity.

In Freudian theory puberty ushers in the genital period, but Freud was not specific in describing the psychosocial conflicts of this, the final stage of his developmental theory. Erikson, on the other hand, devotes much attention to youths' quest for identity and their establishment of a stable system of beliefs.

Identity vs. Identity Confusion

The search for ego identity reaches its climax during adolescence as the person strives to find out who he is and who he is not. With the advent of puberty, new roles are presented to the adolescent who now must look to discover his sexual, ideological, and occupational identity.

In his search, the young person draws from a variety of earlier self-images which have been accepted or rejected. Identity, then, begins during infancy and develops through childhood, play age, and school age. During adolescence, for the first time it evolves into an identity crisis as the person copes with the psychosocial conflict of identity vs. identity confusion. The word crisis should not suggest a threat or catastrophe but rather "a turning point, a crucial period of increased vulnerability and heightened potential" (Erikson, 1968, p. 96). An identity crisis may last for many years and can result in either greater or lesser ego strength.

Erikson (1982) holds that identity emerges from two sources: the first is the affirmation or repudiation of childhood identifications; the second is the historical and social context which dictates conformity to certain standards. Young people frequently reject the standards of their elders, preferring instead the values of a peer group or gang. In any event, the society in which one lives plays a substantial role in shaping identity. Identity is defined both positively and negatively. Adolescents decide what they want to become and what they believe, but they also decide what they do *not* wish to be and what they do *not* believe. Often they must either repudiate the values of parents or reject those of the peer group, a dilemma that may intensify their *identity confusion.*

Identity confusion is a syndrome of problems that includes a divided self-

Part of one's identity during late adolescence is the establishment of sexual identity.

image, an inability to establish intimacy, a sense of time urgency, a lack of concentration on required tasks, and a rejection of family or community standards (Erikson, 1968, 1980). As with the other dystonic tendencies, some amount of identity confusion is both normal and necessary. Young people must experience some doubt and confusion about who they are before they can evolve a stable identity. This may involve leaving home (as Erikson did) to wander alone in search of self; experimenting with drugs and sex; identifying with a street gang; joining a religious order; or railing against the existing society, with no alternative answers. Or it may simply involve a quiet consideration of where one fits into the world and what values one holds dear.

Although identity confusion is a necessary part of one's search for identity, too much confusion can lead to pathological adjustment in the form of regression to earlier stages of development. The responsibilities of adulthood are thus postponed for years as the young man or woman drifts aimlessly from one job to another, from one sex partner to another, or from one ideology to another. Conversely, the proper ratio of identity to identity confusion results in (1) the establishment of *faith* in some sort of ideological principle; (2) the ability to freely decide how one should behave; (3) trust in peers and adults who give advice regarding goals and aspirations; and (4) an eventual choice of occupation (see Box—"Identity Crisis during Adolescence").

Fidelity: The Basic Strength of Adolescence

The basic strength emerging from the identity crises of adolescence is *fidelity,* that is, faith in some ideological view or vision of the future (Erikson,

Identity Crisis during Adolescence

Late adolescence, according to Erikson, is a time of *commitment* to personal ideologies and occupational goals. Young people are, or should be, deciding who they are, what they believe, and what kind of work they wish to pursue. Central to Erikson's developmental theory is the notion that late adolescents experience an *identity crisis,* a period of both increased vulnerability and heightened potential.

To assess late adolescent identity, James Marcia (1966) developed an identity status interview that measures both commitment and crisis in the areas of (1) occupation, (2) religion, and (3) politics. On the basis of this interview people are classified into one of four identity status categories. From most mature to least mature they are (1) *identity achievement,* or the completion of a period where questions of identity are asked and successfully resolved; (2) psychosocial *moratorium* in which people are involved in an ongoing crisis of indecision; (3) identity *foreclosure* in which adolescents have not yet begun to question their identity, but instead take on the values and expectations of their parents; and (4) identity *diffusion,* characterized by a lack of commitment and the absence of concern or struggle with problems of identity.

The identity status interview has generated considerable research on ego identity of late adolescents (Marcia, 1980). Under the assumption that identity for each sex has its own path of development, men and women have generally been studied separately.

Because identity *achievement* is the most developmentally mature state, it follows that older, more experienced college students will more likely have reached this stage than younger, less experienced students. Prager (1986) investigated this hypothesis in a study of 86 undergraduates, college-age women from a large American university. An identity status interview was used to assess the "presence or absence of crisis and commitment in the following four areas: occupational goals, religious ideology, political ideology, and sexual values" (Prager, 1986, p. 33). Each subject was classified into one of the four identity statuses for each of these four areas and then assigned an overall rating on identity.

As expected, older subjects (23–24 years old) and those with three or four years of college experience were mostly classified in the identity *achievement* stage, while younger, less experienced college women were predominantly classified in the identity *foreclosure* status. Contrary to prediction, however, Prager found that identity *diffusion* was equally distributed among all subject groups. In general, Prager's study supported Erikson's hypothesis that the most developmentally mature outcome of late adolescent identity crisis is identity achievement.

In an earlier study of college men, Marcia (1976) examined the relationship between identity status and intimacy. He found that subjects classified six years earlier as identity achievement, as well as those currently so classified, were more likely to have established intimate relationships. Subjects who had changed to a foreclosed or diffused status had either stereotyped relationships or were experiencing interpersonal isolation. From these and other studies it appears that the identity status interview has some promise of assessing identity status of late adolescents.

1975). With the establishment of internal standards of conduct, the adolescent is no longer in need of parental guidance. He now has confidence that his religious, political, and social ideologies will provide a consistent standard of conduct.

The trust learned in infancy is basic for fidelity in adolescence. A person must learn to trust others before he can have faith in his own view of the future. He must have developed hope during infancy, but he must follow hope with the other basic strengths of will, purpose, and competence. Each is a prerequisite for fidelity, just as fidelity is required for the acquisition of subsequent strengths.

The pathological counterpart of fidelity is **role repudiation,** or the inability to synthesize various self-images and values into a workable identity. Role repudiation can take the form of either *diffidence* or *defiance* (Erikson, 1982). Diffidence is an extreme lack of trust or confidence in oneself and is expressed as shyness or hesitancy to express oneself. Defiance, on the other hand, is the open act of rebelling against authority. The defiant adolescent stubbornly holds to socially unacceptable beliefs and practices simply because they are unacceptable. Some amount of role repudiation, Erikson believes, is necessary, not only for the formation of personal identity, but also for the injection of new ideas and new vitality into the social structure.

As an adolescent Eleanor had little self-confidence, few friends her age, and no basic ideology. She was still living in a fantasy world, refusing to believe that her late father had been a heavy drinker and had brought shame and disgrace to the family. In searching for her own identity, Eleanor did what many adolescents do—she developed a hero-worship attitude toward a person whom she greatly respected. This person was Marie Souvestre, the headmistress at Eleanor's boarding school. Souvestre became instrumental in forming many of Eleanor's opinions and in shaping her philosophy of life. Eleanor, like all people, was a product of her time and culture. As a woman in early-twentieth century United States, her identity was incomplete until she could find a man and, even after marriage, it was closely tied to that of her husband. For many women, identity is threatened when they change their names with marriage. With Eleanor's marriage to Franklin Roosevelt, no name change was required since Eleanor was born a Roosevelt.

Young Adulthood

Adolescence and the search for identity are indispensable to the subsequent stage—**young adulthood.** The person must have a solid sense of identity in order to fuse her identity with that of another person, a necessary condition of young adulthood. The period of young adulthood is circumscribed not so much by time as by the acquisition of *intimacy* at one end and the development of *generativity* at the other. For some people this is a relatively short time, lasting perhaps only a few years. For others, young adulthood may continue for several decades. During young adulthood mature **genitality** develops, the person experiences the conflict between **intimacy** and **isolation,** and the basic strength of **love** emerges.

Genitality

True *genitality* can develop only during young adulthood. Much of the sexual activity during adolescence is an expression of one's search for identity and is basically self-serving. Genitality during young adulthood is characterized by an absence of compulsivity, overcompensation, and sadistic domination (Erikson, 1963). It involves mutual trust and a more or less permanent sharing of sexual satisfactions with a loved person of the opposite sex. It represents the chief psychosexual accomplishment of young adulthood and can be found only in an intimate relationship.

Intimacy vs. Isolation

Young adulthood is marked by the psychosocial crisis of *intimacy vs. isolation.* Intimacy is the ability to fuse one's identity with that of another without fear of losing it. Intimacy can only be achieved after the formation of a stable ego. Young adolescents may "be in love" and engage in "intimate" relationships, but true intimacy cannot be achieved until identity is established. A person unsure of her identity may either shy away from psychosocial intimacy or desperately seek intimacy through meaningless sexual encounters.

In contrast, mature intimacy means an ability and willingness to share a mutual trust. It involves sacrifice, compromise, and commitment within a relationship of two equals. It should be a requirement for marriage, but many marriages lack intimacy since young people frequently get married as part of their search for the identity they failed to establish during adolescence.

The psychosocial counterpart to intimacy is isolation, which Erikson (1968, p. 137) defines as "the incapacity to take chances with one's identity by sharing true intimacy." Some people become financially or socially successful, yet retain a deep sense of isolation. They are unable to accept the adult responsibilities of productive work, procreation, and mature love.

Again, some degree of isolation is essential to the acquisition of mature love. Too much togetherness can diminish one's sense of ego identity. This leads to psychosocial regression and the inability to face the next developmental stage. The greater danger, of course, is too much isolation, too little intimacy, and a deficiency in the basic strength of love.

Love: The Basic Strength of Young Adulthood

Love, the basic strength of young adulthood, emerges from the crisis of intimacy vs. isolation. Erikson (1968, 1982) defines love as mature devotion that overcomes basic differences between males and females. Although love includes intimacy, it also contains some degree of isolation since each partner is permitted to retain a separate identity. Mature love means commitment, sexual passion, cooperation, competition, and friendship. It is the basic strength of young adulthood, enabling a person to cope productively with the final two stages of development.

The antipathy of love is *exclusivity,* the core pathology of young adulthood. Some exclusivity, however, is necessary for intimacy since a person must be able to exclude certain people, activities, and ideas in order to develop a strong sense of identity. As we have seen, identity is a necessity for true intimacy. Exclusivity becomes pathological when it blocks one's ability to cooperate, compete, or compromise, all prerequisite ingredients for intimacy and love.

As a young woman, Eleanor Roosevelt was much confused in her identity. She had a strong desire to help others, yet little appreciation of human weaknesses. She was shy, awkward, and still lacking in self-confidence (Black, 1940). Despite these traits and before her 21st birthday, she met and married a handsome distant cousin named Franklin Delano Roosevelt. The young couple were much alike in many respects. Both had come from the same aristocratic social class, both had an interest in history, literature, and travel, and both were profoundly immature. Although Eleanor was "in love" with her young debonaire husband, she had not yet achieved true intimacy or love.

Adulthood

The seventh stage of development is **adulthood,** that time when a person begins to take his place in society at large and assume responsibility for whatever that society produces. For most people this is perhaps the longest stage of development, spanning the years from about 31 to 60. Adulthood is characterized by the psychosexual mode of procreativity, the psychosocial crisis of generativity vs. stagnation, and the basic strength of *care.*

Procreativity

Erikson's psychosexual theory assumes an instinctual drive to perpetuate the species. This drive is the counterpart of an adult animal's instinct toward procreation and is an extension of the genitality that marks young adulthood (Erikson, 1982). However, **procreativity** refers to more than genital contact with an intimate partner. It includes assuming responsibility for the care of offspring that result from that sexual contact. Ideally, procreation should follow from the mature intimacy and love established during the preceding stage.

Obviously, people are physically capable of producing offspring before they are psychologically ready to care for the welfare of these children. Intimacy alone is not sufficient for mature adulthood. Two people can be intimate, yet, as a pair, remain isolated from society at large.

Mature adulthood includes more than the procreation of offspring. It means the care of one's children as well as other people's children. In addition, it encompasses productive work and the perpetuation of society. It requires a willingness and readiness to be a part of society and to transmit culture from one generation to the next.

Generativity vs. Stagnation

The syntonic quality of adulthood is *generativity,* defined as "the generation of new beings as well as new products and new ideas" (Erikson, 1982,

p. 67). Generativity is concerned with establishing and guiding the next generation. It includes the procreation of children, the production of work, and the creation of new things and ideas that contribute to the building of a better world.

People have a need not only to learn but also to teach and to instruct. This need extends beyond one's own children to an altruistic concern for other young people. Generativity grows out of earlier syntonic qualities, such as intimacy and identity. As we have seen, intimacy calls for the ability to fuse one's ego to that of another without fear of losing it. This meeting of ego identities leads to a gradual expansion of interests. One-to-one intimacy is no longer enough. Other people, especially children, become part of one's concern. Instructing others in the ways of culture is a drive found in all societies. For the mature adult, this is not merely an obligation or a selfish need, but an evolutionary drive to make a contribution to succeeding generations and to ensure the continuity of human society as well.

The antithesis of generativity is *stagnation and self-absorption.* The generational cycle of productivity and creativity is crippled when people become too absorbed in self, too self-indulgent. A pervading sense of stagnation is said to occur when a person regards himself as his own, or someone else's, one and only child. However, some element of stagnation and self-absorption is necessary. Creative people must, at times, remain dormant and absorbed in themselves (Hall, 1983). The interaction of generativity and stagnation produces care, the basic strength of adulthood.

Care: The Basic Strength of Adulthood

Erikson (1982, p. 67) defines *care* as "a widening commitment to *take care of* the persons, the products, and the ideas one has learned *to care for.*" As the basic strength of adulthood, care arises from each earlier basic strength. One must have hope, will, purpose, competence, fidelity, and love in order to take care of that which one cares for. Care is not a duty or obligation, but a natural desire emerging from the conflict between generativity and stagnation or self-absorption.

The antipathy of care is *rejectivity,* the core pathology of adulthood. Rejectivity is the unwillingness to take care of certain persons or groups (Erikson, 1982). It manifests itself as self-centeredness, provincialism, or *pseudospeciation,* that is, the belief that other groups of people are, by nature, a different species from our own. It is responsible for much of human hatred, destruction, atrocities, and wars. According to Erikson (1982, p. 70), rejectivity "has far-reaching implications for the survival of the species as well as for every individual's psychosocial development."

The long period of adulthood brought many changes in Eleanor's life. She began this stage as a dependent young wife living under the domination of a possessive mother-in-law, and ended it as a respected, admired, and self-confident woman.

This was a period of procreativity as she gave birth to six children from 1906 to 1916. After the birth of her youngest child she suspended sexual relations with her husband when she found evidence that he had been having an affair. Her first impulse was to divorce Franklin, but again, her mother-in-law intervened and threatened to cut off her son's flow of money. Although Eleanor stayed with Franklin she became more emotionally detached from him and began to lead a more independent life style.

Eleanor now entered the generativity stage, nurturing her own children and helping the less fortunate of the world. When Franklin was elected to the presidency in 1932, she knew that all hopes of an intimate life with him were gone and that her mission in life was to care for others.

Old Age

The eighth and final stage of development is **old age,** that period from about 60 to the end of life. Procreation, in the sense of producing children, is now absent, yet old people can remain productive and creative in other ways. They can be good grandparents, not only to their own grandchildren, but also to other younger members of society. Erikson, in an interview with E. Hall, said, "I'm convinced that old people and children need one another and that there's an affinity between old age and childhood that, in fact, rounds out the life cycle" (Hall, 1983, p. 24). Old age can be a time of playfulness, joy, and wonder, but it also can be a time of senility, depression, and despair. The psychosexual mode of old age is generalized sensuality; the psychosocial crisis is integrity vs. despair and the basic strength is wisdom.

Generalized Sensuality

The final psychosexual stage is *generalized sensuality.* Erikson has little to say about this mode of psychosexual life, but one may infer that it means to take pleasure in a variety of different physical sensations—sights, sounds, tastes, odors, embraces, and perhaps genital stimulation. Generalized sensuality may also include a greater appreciation for the traditional life style of the opposite sex. Men become more nurturant and more acceptant of the pleasures of nonsexual relationships including those with their grandchildren and great-grandchildren. Women become more interested and involved in politics, finance, and world affairs (Erikson, Erikson, & Kivnick, 1986). A generalized sensual attitude, however, is dependent on one's ability to hold things together, that is, to maintain integrity in the face of despair.

Integrity vs. Despair

A person's final identity crisis is *integrity vs. despair.* At the end of life the dystonic quality of despair may prevail, but for those with strong ego identity who have found intimacy and have taken care of people and things, the syntonic quality of integrity will predominate. Integrity means a feeling of wholeness and coherence, an ability to hold together one's sense of "I-ness" despite diminishing physical and intellectual powers.

Ego integrity is sometimes difficult to maintain when one finds herself losing familiar aspects of her existence—spouse, friends, body strength, mental alertness, independence, and social usefulness. Under such pressure, despair

Erikson extends the stages of development into old age.

may result. Despair often disguises itself as disgust, depression, or contempt for others. It may also express itself as nonacceptance of the finite boundaries of life.

Despair literally means to be without hope. A reexamination of Figure 3.2 reveals that despair, the last dystonic quality of the life cycle, is in the opposite corner from hope, the person's first basic strength. From infancy to old age, there is always hope. Once hope is lost, despair follows and life ceases to have meaning.

Wisdom: The Basic Strength of Old Age

Some amount of despair is natural and necessary for psychological maturity. The inevitable struggle between integrity and despair produces *wisdom,* the basic strength of old age. Erikson (1982, p. 61) defines wisdom as "informed and detached concern with life itself in the face of death itself." A detached concern does not mean a lack of concern, but rather an active but dispassionate interest. Mature wisdom maintains the integrity of a lifetime of experience in spite of declining physical and mental abilities. It draws from and contributes to the traditional knowledge passed from generation to generation. In old age, it is concerned with ultimate issues, including nonexistence (Erikson, Erikson, & Kivnick, 1986).

The antipathy of wisdom and the core pathology of old age is *disdain,* which Erikson (1982, p. 61) defines as "a reaction to feeling (and seeing others) in an increasing state of being finished, confused, helpless." Disdain

Stages	A Psychosexual Stages and Modes	B Psychosocial Crises	C Radius of Significant Relations	D Basic Strengths
I Infancy	Oral-Respiratory, Sensory-Kinesthetic (Incorporative Modes)	Basic Trust vs. Basic Mistrust	Maternal Person	Hope
II Early Childhood	Anal-Urethral, Muscular (Retentive-Eliminative)	Autonomy vs. Shame, Doubt	Parental Persons	Will
III Play Age	Infantile-Genital, Locomotor (Intrusive, Inclusive)	Initiative vs. Guilt	Basic Family	Purpose
IV School Age	"Latency"	Industry vs. Inferiority	"Neighborhood", School	Competence
V Adolescence	Puberty	Identity vs. Identity Confusion	Peer Groups and Outgroups: Models of Leadership	Fidelity
VI Young Adulthood	Genitality	Intimacy vs. Isolation	Partners in friendship, sex, competition, and cooperation	Love
VII Adulthood	(Procreativity)	Generativity vs. Stagnation	Divided Labor and shared household	Care
VIII Old Age	(Generalization of Sensual Modes)	Integrity vs. Despair	"Mankind" "My Kind"	Wisdom

Figure 3.3 Erikson's Eight Stages of the Life Cycle (From *The life cycle completed* by E. H. Erikson, 1982, pp. 32–33. Copyright 1982 by W. W. Norton. Reprinted with permission.)

is a continuation of rejectivity, the core pathology of adulthood. It means to reject with aloof contempt. It is a natural reaction to human depravity, deceit, and weakness.

When her husband died in 1945, Eleanor was not yet 62 years old and still in the adulthood stage of her life. The 17 years of widowhood were productive ones as she passed easily and gracefully into old age. She emerged from Franklin's shadow and achieved greatness on her own. She traveled throughout the world consulting with world leaders. She lectured, wrote, and worked diligently for her political party. She identified with all humankind in a comfortable and confident manner and displayed the integrity and wisdom that would have been consistent with Erikson's views of old age.

E Core-pathology Basic Antipathies	F Related Principles of Social Order	G Binding Ritualizations	H Ritualism
Withdrawal	Cosmic Order	Numinous	Idolism
Compulsion	"Law and Order"	Judicious	Legalism
Inhibition	Ideal Prototypes	Dramatic	Moralism
Inertia	Technological Order	Formal (Technical)	Formalism
repudiation	Ideological Worldview	Ideological	Totalism
Exclusivity	Patterns of Cooperation and Competition	Affiliative	Elitism
Rejectivity	Currents of Education and Tradition	Generational	Authoritism
Disdain	Wisdom	Philosophical	Dogmatism

Summary

Erikson's cycle of life is summarized in Figure 3.3. Each of the eight stages is characterized by a psychosexual mode as well as a psychosocial crisis. The psychosocial crisis is stimulated by a conflict between the predominating syntonic element and its antithetical dystonic element. From this conflict emerges a basic strength or ego quality. Each basic strength has a basic antipathy that becomes the core pathology of that stage. The person has an ever-increasing radius of significant relations, beginning with the maternal person in infancy and ending with an identification with humanity during old age.

Personality always develops during a particular historical period and within a given society. Nevertheless, the eight developmental stages transcend chronology and geography and are appropriate to nearly all cultures, past or present.

ERIKSON'S METHODS OF INVESTIGATION

Most personality theorists have based their models on experiences with relatively homogeneous populations. For example, Freud, though widely read, limited his investigations largely to upper-middle and upper-class adults who visited his clinic at Berggasse 19 in Vienna. Erikson, on the other hand, has insisted that personality is a product of history, culture, and biology, and this approach is reflected in the breadth of his methods of investigation. No other theorist has studied personality development in such a variety of settings. He has employed anthropological, historical, sociological, and clinical methods to learn about children, adolescents, mature adults, and elderly people. He has studied middle-class Americans, European children, Sioux and Yurok Indian tribes, and even sailors in a submarine. He has written biographical portraits of Adolf Hitler, Maxim Gorky, Martin Luther, and Mohandas Gandhi among others. In this section we look at three approaches Erikson has used to explain and describe human personality—anthropological studies, psychohistory, and play construction.

Anthropological Studies

In 1937 Erikson made a field trip to the Pine Ridge Indian Reservation in South Dakota to investigate the causes of apathy in Sioux children. During this excursion Erikson relied on his clinical training as a psychoanalyst and his experience working with John Dollard and other anthropologists at the Yale Institute of Human Relations. Erikson (1963, Chapter 3) reported on early Sioux training in terms of his newly evolving theories of psychosexual and psychosocial development. He found that apathy was an expression of an extreme dependency the Indians had come to develop on various federal programs. Once courageous buffalo hunters, the Sioux had, by 1937, lost their group identity as hunters and were trying half-heartedly to scrape out a living as farmers. Child-rearing practices, which in the past had trained young boys to be hunters and young girls to be helpers and mothers of future hunters, were no longer appropriate for an agrarian society. As a consequence, the Sioux children of 1937 had great difficulty achieving a sense of ego identity, especially after they reached adolescence.

Two years later Erikson made a similar field trip to northern California to study the Yurok Indians, a tribe that lived mostly on salmon fishing. Although the Sioux and Yurok had vastly divergent cultures, each tribe had a tradition of training its youth in the virtues of its society. The Yuroks, trained to catch fish, had little taste for war, and did not possess a strong national feeling or rigid organizational hierarchy. Obtaining and retaining provisions and possessions were highly valued among the Yuroks. Erikson (1963, Chapter 4) was able to show that early childhood training was consistent with this strong cultural value, and that once again history and society helped shape personality.

Psychohistory

During this century a relatively new discipline called psychohistory has evolved that combines psychoanalytic concepts with historical methods. Freud (1910/1957) originated psychohistory with an investigation of Leonardo Da Vinci and later collaborated with American Ambassador William Bullitt to write a book-length psychological study of President Woodrow Wilson (Freud & Bullitt, 1967). Erikson deplored this latter work and, at one time (Erikson, 1975), suggested that Freud did not knowingly cooperate in writing it. Nevertheless, Erikson took up the methods of psychohistory and refined them, especially in his study of Martin Luther (Erikson, 1958, 1975) and Gandhi (Erikson, 1969, 1975).

Erikson (1974, p. 13) defines psychohistory as "the study of individual and collective life with the combined methods of psychoanalysis and history." He uses psychohistory to demonstrate his fundamental belief that each person is a product of his or her historical time. Psychohistory differs from a case history in that it is more likely to deal with a person who is able to maintain ego identity and integrity in the face of neurotic conflict. Case histories usually depict neurotic individuals who are unable to maintain integrity. Also, in Erikson's psychohistory the effects of the historical period on the protagonist's personal development are documented.

Erikson believes that the author of psychohistory should be emotionally involved in his subject. This involvement is similar to the concept of **countertransference,** first recognized by Freud and extensively elucidated by others. Countertransference is the counterpart of **transference** and refers to the therapist's irrational emotional attachment or attraction to the patient. Erikson, for example, developed a strong emotional attachment to Gandhi which he attributed to his own lifelong search for the father he had never seen (Erikson, 1975).

In *Gandhi's Truth* (Erickson, 1969) Erikson's strong positive feelings for Gandhi are apparent. A central question concerned Erikson: How do healthy individuals such as Gandhi work through conflict and crisis when others are debilitated by strife? In searching for an answer Erikson examined Gandhi's entire life cycle, but concentrated on periods of crisis.

As a child, Gandhi was close to his mother, but experienced conflict with his father. Rather than viewing this situation as an Oedipal conflict, Erikson saw it as Gandhi's opportunity to work out conflict with authority figures— an opportunity Gandhi was to have many times during his life.

Gandhi was born October 2, 1869, in Porbandar, India. As a young man he studied law in London, and was inconspicuous in manner and appearance. Then dressed like a proper British subject, he returned home to practice law. After two years of unsuccessful practice he went to South Africa, another British colony. He intended to remain for a year but his first serious identity crisis kept him there for more than 20 years.

A week after a judge excluded him from a courtroom he was thrown off a train when he refused to give up his seat to a "white" man. These experiences with racial prejudice changed Gandhi's life. By the time he resolved this identity crisis his appearance had changed dramatically. No longer attired in silk hat and black coat, he dressed in the cotton loincloth and shawl that were to become familiar to millions of people throughout the world. During those years in South Africa he evolved the technique of passive resistance known as *Satyagraha* and used it to solve his conflicts with authorities.

After returning to India he experienced another identity crisis when he supported workers against the mill owners in the 1918 strike of Ahmedabad. Erikson (1969) refers to the events surrounding the strike as "The Event." When the workers became discouraged and disillusioned over their lack of success, Gandhi, now 40 years old, began a hunger strike, pledging to eat no more food until the workers' demands were met. Gandhi agonized over his decision, fearing that the mill owners might give in out of sympathy. After four days of fasting, the strike ended and Gandhi had emerged from another identity crisis. Unlike neurotic individuals whose identity crises result in core pathologies, Gandhi developed basic strengths from his critical experiences.

Play Construction

From his clinical experiences with children, Erikson has developed a projective technique that he calls **play construction.** Although he has employed this approach with play age children (see Erikson, 1977), his most famous and controversial use of play construction involved somewhat older children. Three times over a two-year period, Erikson asked 300 preadolescent children to imagine they were movie directors and then to construct an exciting scene from a movie, using a random selection of available toys. The toys included people, animals, furniture, cars, blocks, and other assorted objects. Subjects were 150 girls and 150 boys from a nonclinical population, aged 10, 11, and 12. Interestingly, very few subjects actually created a movie scene or named their dolls after real movie stars. Erikson believes that the stories the children told about the scenes, as well as the scenes themselves, were an unconscious expression of their life history.

Erikson looked for both common and unique elements in play construction. To test for reliability and objectivity, he asked two independent observers to make judgments based on photographs of the completed scenes. The most significant and controversial common element noted was a difference between boys and girls in the way they arranged their scenes. Girls and boys used space differently, with girls tending to construct interior scenes and boys exterior ones. Girls used more furniture, people, and domesticated animals to construct peaceful scenes. If an intruder were included, it was always a male. Boys more often selected blocks, cars, and wild animals to build scenes dominated by height, downfall, and motion. The arrangements of girls were simple, static, and low. Those of boys were complex, action-oriented, and tall or elongated. Girls frequently constructed circular enclosures with low doors and gates that might be either open or closed. In contrast, boys usually built tall towers and included action themes such as rising and falling.

Erikson (1963, 1968) suggested that these differences were at least partially due to anatomical differences between the sexes. He pointed out that play constructions "closely parallel the morphology of the sex organs; in the male, *external* organs, *erectable* and *intrusive* in character, *conducting* highly *mobile* sperm cells; *internal* organs in the female, with a vestibular *access* leading to *statically expectant* ova" (Erikson, 1963, p. 106).

Such an interpretation has not gone uncriticized. Some critics (Janeway, 1971) have accused Erikson of sexism, pointing out that socialization practices might easily explain these differences. Erikson (1975) accepts the argument that social influences might account for some of the differences, but he insists that anatomy is the principle source of gender differences in play constructions. Does this mean that Erikson agrees with Freud that anatomy is destiny? Erikson's answer is yes, anatomy is destiny, but he quickly qualifies that dictim to read: "Anatomy, history, and personality are our combined destiny" (Erikson, 1968, p. 285). In other words, anatomy alone does not determine destiny, but it combines with past events, including socialization practices and various personality dimensions such as temperament and intelligence, to determine who a person will become. "Destiny, for both men and women, depends on what you can make of the fact that you have a specific kind of body in a particular historical setting" (Erikson, 1974, p. 116).

In addition to sex differences (which, incidentally, were not expected at the beginning of the study), Erikson investigated unique elements in play constructions. He found that children consciously or unconsciously arranged scenes and built dramatic plots that were consistent with their life histories. Each of these children was part of a larger study and each had been intensively investigated almost since birth. With this vast information on the child's life history, Erikson was able to see ways in which play constructions were an expression of hidden needs and motives.

Erikson's investigation of play construction is unique among personality theorists. He has used this method as a kind of projective technique in much the same way as Freud used free association and dream interpretation as a means of uncovering unconscious aspects of personality. In the last chapter we saw that Freud believed dreams to be the "royal road" to the unconscious. Similarly, Erikson holds that children's play is the royal road to understanding personal history. He believes that play construction is the "*via regia* to an understanding of growing man's conflicts and triumphs, his repetitive working through of the past, and his creative self-renewal in truly playful moments" (Erikson, 1975, p. 39).

CONCEPT OF HUMANITY

What is Erikson's concept of humanity? How does he see people in terms of the six dimensions for a concept of humanity introduced in Chapter 1?

First, is the life cycle *determined* by external forces or do people have some *choice* in molding their personalities and their lives? Erikson is not as strongly deterministic as Freud, but neither does he believe in complete free choice. His position is somewhere in the middle. Although our destiny lies with anatomy, history, and personality, we retain some limited control over both history and personality, giving us some measure of choice. We can search for our own identities and are not completely constrained by history or society. Individuals, in fact, can change history and alter environment. The two subjects of Erikson's most extensive psychohistories, Luther and Gandhi each had a profound effect on world history and on his own immediate surroundings. Similarly, each of us has the power to determine our own life cycles, even though our global impact may be on a lesser scale.

On the dimension of *pessimism vs. optimism* Erikson tends to be somewhat optimistic. If core pathologies predominate our early stages of development, we are not inevitably doomed to continue a pathological existence in later stages. Although weaknesses in early life make the acquisition of basic strengths more difficult later on, Erikson is sufficiently optimistic to believe that positive change can occur at any stage of life. Each psychosocial conflict consists of a syntonic and a dystonic quality. Each crisis can be resolved in favor of the harmonious element, regardless of past resolutions.

Erikson does not specifically address the issue of *causality vs. teleology,* but his view of humanity suggests that we are influenced more by biological and social forces than by our view of the future. We are a product of a particular historical moment and a specific social setting. Although we can set goals and actively strive to achieve these goals, we cannot completely escape the powerful causal forces of anatomy, history, and sociology. For this reason, Erikson is rated high on causality.

On the fourth dimension, *conscious vs. unconscious* determinants, Erikson's position is mixed. Prior to adolescence, unconscious motivation plays a strong role in shaping personality. Psychosexual and psychosocial conflicts during the first four developmental stages occur before we have firmly established our identity. We are seldom clearly aware of these crises and the ways in which they mold our personalities. From adolescence forward, however, we ordinarily are aware of our actions and most of the reasons underlying them.

Erikson's theory, of course, is more *social* than *biological.* Nevertheless, he does not overlook anatomy and other physiological factors in personality development. Each psychosexual mode, for example, has a clear biological component. However, as we advance through the eight stages, social influences become increasingly more powerful. Also, the radius of social relations expands from the single maternal person to a global identification with all humanity. Erikson's emphasis on social forces is in sharp contrast to Freud's biological theory. Indeed, Erikson's model is sometimes identified as a *social* psychoanalytic theory.

The sixth dimension for a concept of humanity is *uniqueness vs. similarities.* Erikson tends to place somewhat more emphasis on individual differences than on universal characteristics. Although people in different cultures advance through the eight developmental stages in the same order, myriad differences are found in the pace of that journey. Each of us resolves our psychosocial crises in a unique manner, and each uses the basic strengths in a way that is peculiarly ours.

CRITIQUE OF ERIKSON

Erikson's work is widely recognized in both professional and popular circles. The eight stages of human development are frequently cited in the scientific literature as well as in the popular press. A recent survey (Solso, 1987) found that Erikson's first important work, *Childhood and Society* was one of the most frequently recommended books by graduate departments of psychology in the United States and Canada.

Erikson's popularity, in part, is due to his decision to extend Freud's theories rather than to attack them. Many have seen Erikson's work as a continuation of what Freud might have done had he lived another 50 years. Erikson has never repudiated Freud, and thus has avoided much condemnation by orthodox psychoanalysts. More importantly, he has emphasized the ego and normal functioning and thus has gained the favor of many anti-Freudians. Erikson's impact on psychology is demonstrated by a report (Gilgen, 1982) that ranked him in fifth place in importance among psychologists of the last half of the twentieth century. Popularity and influence, however, are not criteria by which scientific theories are evaluated.

Erikson has built his theory largely on ethical principles and not necessarily on scientific data. He came to psychology from art, and acknowledges that he sees the world more through the eyes of an artist than through those of a scientist. In *Childhood and Society* he wrote that he had nothing to offer except "a way of looking at things." His books are admittedly subjective and personal, a fact that undoubtedly adds to their appeal. Nevertheless, Erikson's theory must be judged by the standards of science, not ethics or art.

First, how well does the theory *organize knowledge?* The theory is limited mostly to developmental stages and does not adequately address such issues as personal traits or motivation. This limitation subtracts from the theory's ability to shed meaning on much of what is currently known about human personality. The eight stages of development remain an eloquent statement of what the life cycle should be, and research findings in these areas usually can be fit into an Eriksonian framework. However, the theory lacks sufficient scope to be rated high on this first criterion.

On the second criterion, *generate research,* Erikson's theory is rated somewhat higher. The popularity of his work has sparked numerous studies, both descriptive and experimental. For example, an Ego Identity Status interview (Marcia, 1966) is based on Erikson's theoretical model and has been used to investigate ego identity in a variety of settings. In addition, Hamachek (1988) has recently developed a series of behavioral expressions designed to measure Erikson's first five psychosocial stages. Such an instrument should help future researchers assess levels of development among children and adolescents. A recent developmental psychology textbook by Newman and Newman (1987) has adopted an Eriksonian approach and presents much of the research on Erikson's stages of development. These and other Erikson-based works should add to the continuing heuristic value of this theory.

As a *guide to action,* Erikson's theory provides many general guidelines, but offers little specific advice. Compared to other theories discussed in this book, it ranks near the top in suggesting approaches to dealing with middle-aged and older adults. The growing field of gerontology has made frequent use of Erikson's views of aging, while adolescent psychology has relied extensively on his concept of ego identity. Erikson's ideas about intimacy vs. isolation and generativity vs. stagnation have much to offer to marriage counselors and others concerned with intimate relationships among young adults.

Erikson's theory must be rated high on *internal consistency.* The terms used to label the different psychosocial crises, basic strengths, and core pathologies are very carefully chosen, possibly because English is not Erikson's first language and because of his extensive use of a dictionary while writing. Yet terms like hope, will, purpose, love, care, and so on are not operationally defined. They have little scientific usefulness, although they rank high in both literary and emotional value. On the other hand, Erikson's epigenetic principle and the eloquence of his description of the eight stages of development mark his theory with conspicuous internal consistency.

On the criterion of *parsimony,* the theory has only a moderate rating. The precision of its terms is a strength, but the descriptions of psychosexual stages and psychosocial crises, especially in the later stages, are not always clearly differentiated. In addition, the inclusion of 64 boxes (see Figure 3.2) in his total concept of development renders the theory somewhat cumbersome. In different writings he fills out these boxes with different terms and even different concepts, thus subtracting from the simplicity of the theory.

CHAPTER SUMMARY

The work of Erik Erikson provides a logical extension of Freud's psychoanalysis. An artist by early training, Erikson has offered a "way of looking at things" rather than a theory based on scientifically gathered data. Although he takes for granted most of Freud's work, he has (1) placed more emphasis on the ego and less on the id, (2) extended the stages of development into adulthood and old age, and (3) elevated social influences over the biologically based instincts.

The eight stages of development rest on an *epigenetic principle,* meaning that each component proceeds in a step-by-step fashion with later growth building on earlier development. Also, in every stage there is an interaction of opposites leading to a conflict or *crisis.* Resolution of the crisis produces an appropriate *basic strength* and enables the person to move on to the next stage. In addition, *biological components* lay a ground plan for each individual, but a multiplicity of historical, social, and physiological events shape ego identity.

The first stage of development is *infancy,* characterized by the oral-sensory mode of incorporation, the psychosocial crisis of basic trust vs. mistrust, the basic strength of hope, and the core pathology of withdrawal. Infancy covers the first year of life and is equivalent to Freud's oral stage.

The second stage is called *early childhood* and parallels Freud's anal stage. During early childhood the anal, urethral, and muscular psychosexual modes are in ascendance and the psychosocial conflict of autonomy vs. shame and doubt produces the basic strength called will or its antipathy, called compulsion.

From about ages three to five the child goes through the *play age,* a time corresponding to the phallic or Oedipal period. The play-age child experiences genital-locomotor psychosexual development and undergoes a psychosocial crisis of initiative vs. guilt. Either the basic strength of purpose or the core pathology of inhibition may emerge from the play age.

Erikson's fourth stage, *school age,* covers the period from about six to eleven, and corresponds to Freud's latency stage. The school age child experiences the psychosocial crisis of industry vs. inferiority, from which arises the basic strength of competence or the core pathology of inertia. The school-age child's radius of significant relations has now expanded beyond the family to include peers and teachers who serve as models.

Adolescence is a crucial stage in Erikson's theory because ego identity should emerge from this period. However, identity confusion may dominate the psychosocial crisis, thereby postponing identity. Fidelity is the basic strength of adolescence; role repudiation its core pathology.

The time from about 19 to 30, *young adulthood,* is characterized by genitality, a psychosexual mode that can exist in the absence of intimacy. Ideally, however, intimacy should win out in its conflict with isolation and produce the basic strength of love. If the psychosocial crisis is not completely resolved, the core pathology of exclusivity results.

The seventh and longest stage is *adulthood,* a time not only of procreation but also of productive work and social commitment. The dominant psychosocial crisis is generativity vs. stagnation, while care is the basic strength and rejectivity a possible core pathology.

The final stage, *old age,* is marked by a generalized sensuality and the crisis of integrity vs. despair. Wisdom, the basic strength, is opposed by disdain, the core pathology.

Erikson's concept of humanity is generally optimistic and idealistic. People can overcome early pathologies, but crisis, anxiety, and conflict are a normal and necessary part of living. People cannot be abstracted from society or from the historical period in which they live. Although we are one species, history, culture, and biology lead to individual differences among us.

Erikson's theory has been well received both popularly and professionally. Although not built on an abundance of scientific data, it has sparked a great deal of research and discussion. The theory has an eloquent logic and consistency, but is only moderately successful in organizing knowledge or providing guidelines to practitioners.

Suggested Readings

ERIKSON, E. H. (1950, 1963). *Childhood and society.* New York: Norton.

This is Erikson's first important work, one that laid the foundation to his post-Freudian theory. It is one of the most popular and frequently recommended psychology books in the United States. Erikson added some afterthoughts in the 1985, 35th anniversary edition.

GROSS, F. L. (1987). *Introducing Erik Erikson: An invitation to his thinking.* Lanham, MD: University Press of America.

A brief, concise introduction to Erikson's work, this book supplies a list of novels and films illustrating Eriksonian ideas. Both students and instructors will find much of value in this book.

HALL, E. (1983, June). A conversation with Erik Erikson. *Psychology Today,* pp. 20–30.

In this article, Elizabeth Hall, former managing editor of *Psychology Today,* interviews Erikson at age 81. Erikson talks of the human life cycle, with emphasis on old age. Included is an interesting "box" of Kenneth Keniston's memories of Erikson at Harvard.

NEWMAN, B. M., & NEWMAN, P. R. (1987). *Development through life: A psychosocial approach* (4th ed.). Chicago: Dorsey Press.

Although a text in developmental psychology, this book presents (in Chapters 5–13) a readable account of the life cycle from an Eriksonian perspective. Also included are pertinent research studies into Erikson's theory.

ROAZEN, P. (1976). *Erik H. Erikson: The power and limits of a vision.* New York: Free Press.

Roazen's account of Erikson is more critical than that of Robert Coles (1970), whose biography borders on hero-worship. Throughout, Roazen compares Erikson to Freud and finds him too preachy, utopian, and philosophical. However, he believes that Erikson's hopeful view of humanity may be more helpful in individual therapy than Freud's skeptical attitude toward the human condition.

ADLER

4

Individual Psychology

Christine is a 42-year-old English teacher deeply concerned with her students. She encourages them to talk to her about their personal problems and is always willing to take time to listen and to help. She never seems to object to late night and weekend telephone calls. She apparently is quite willing to sacrifice her own needs to those of others. To many students she seems to be a model of maternal love and concern.

To other students, however, she appears to be weak, petty, insincere, and hypocritical. These students have little to do with her, avoiding personal conversation at almost any cost. To her principal she is mostly a nuisance, constantly asking for favors and adopting the manner of a weak, helpless little girl. Her female colleagues usually find her annoying, overly cheerful, and too self-deprecating. Some of the male faculty members view her as strangely coquettish, a peculiar attitude in light of the fact that Christine is a somewhat large, unattractive woman and not overtly flirtatious.

Christine is completely oblivious to the negative opinions many of her students and colleagues have toward her. How could anyone not like her! She is dedicated, caring, nonaggressive, and willing to do almost anything for anyone.

A gifted student in school, Christine was headed toward a medical career when she met Joe and dropped out of college to get married and start a family. Although her parents and friends encouraged her to remain in school, the decision to leave was an easy one for Christine. People were surprised that she so easily changed her plans, but Christine has had a history of surprising others. Although her behavior toward Joe is usually like that of a passive and compliant daughter, sometimes, for reasons Joe cannot fathom, she will become quite assertive and demanding. For instance, on her fortieth birthday she announced to Joe that she was leaving him for another man—a young teacher with whom she was "in love." However, the young teacher did not share Christine's feelings. Christine never left Joe and, in fact, continued to behave toward him as if nothing had happened.

Christine has two adolescent children, a daughter and a son. Diane and Rusty have always been encouraged to bring their friends home and Christine's house is often filled with young people. Christine takes a personal interest in all of them and is delighted that many see her as a second mother.

OVERVIEW

Christine's concern for others and her self-sacrificing behavior might appear to be a noble expression of maturity and love, but Alfred Adler would see it as a neurotic attempt to strive for personal superiority. Adler, in fact, viewed all motivation as springing from our attempts to gain superiority or success. An original member of the Vienna Psychoanalytic Society, Adler was the first to break from Freud and establish an important and opposing theory. Unlike Erikson, who extended Freud's theory without repudiating it, Adler accepted little of psychoanalysis. In contrast to Freud, Adler was optimistic and idealistic. He emphasized social rather than biological factors; final goals rather than past causes; individual choice and responsibility rather than determinism; and the unity of personality rather than separate and somewhat antagonistic regions of the mind.

Adler's differences from Freud cannot be explained in terms of religion or geography. Both were from middle-class Jewish families and both lived most of their lives in Vienna. Adler himself might explain these differences in terms of birth order, social interest, style of life, and subjective perceptions, all important concepts in Individual Psychology.

BIOGRAPHY OF ALFRED ADLER

Alfred Adler was born on February 7, 1870, in Rudolfsheim, a suburb of Vienna, the second son of a middle class Jewish grain merchant. His older brother, Sigmund, was strong, healthy, intelligent, and successful. Alfred, on the other hand, was weak and sickly, and his earliest memories are concerned with the unhappy comparison between his brother's good health and his own illness. Sigmund was the childhood rival that Adler attempted to surpass. The older brother, however, remained a worthy opponent, having a very successful business in later years (Bottome, 1939).

There are several interesting parallels in the lives of Freud and Adler. Both were born of middle- or lower-middle-class Jewish parents and each lived most of his life in Vienna. Neither was devoutly religious, but Freud was much more conscious of his Jewishness than Adler. While Freud often believed himself to be persecuted because he was a Jew, Adler never claimed to have been mistreated because of his background. Adler later converted to Protestantism, but there is some doubt that he ever held any deep religious convictions. In fact, one of his biographers (Rattner, 1983) regarded Adler as an agnostic.

Like Freud, Adler had a younger brother who died in infancy. In both men this early experience had a profound effect, but in vastly different ways. Freud, by his own accounting, had wished unconsciously for the death of his rival and, in fact, when the boy died, he was filled with guilt and self-reproach, conditions that continued into his adulthood. For Adler, on the other hand, the death of his younger brother, along with his own sickly constitution, brought home to him the reality of death. He saw this experience as a challenge and determined then that his goal in life would be to conquer death; thus he decided at that time to become a physician (Ellenberger, 1970).

While Freud was the oldest and favorite child of his mother, Adler was second-born and enjoyed a warm relationship with his mother for only a short time. He lost that pampered position at age 20 months when his younger sister was born. He then became the favorite of his father and remained so throughout his childhood. Though Freud was surrounded by a large family, including seven younger brothers and sisters, two grown half-brothers, and a nephew and niece about his age, he was more oriented toward his parents than to these other family members. Intellectual analysis and personal courage were more valued by Freud than were intuition and social relationships. For Adler the reverse was true— intuition and social relationships were more important than scientific analysis. Though his family was slightly smaller than Freud's, relationships with siblings and peers played a more pivotal role in Adler's development. He spent much time with friends and schoolmates, and throughout his life was comfortable in group situations. In contrast, Freud developed several intense one-to-one relationships during his lifetime and did not enjoy group activities. Freud's professional organizations, the Vienna Psychoanalytic Society and the International Psychoanalytic

Association, were highly structured in pyramid fashion with an inner circle of Freud's trusted friends forming a kind of oligarchy at the top. Adler, by comparison, was more democratic. He often met with his group, which included patients as well as colleagues and friends, in Vienna coffee houses. The Individual Psychology Society, in fact, suffered from a loose organization, and Adler had a relaxed attitude toward business details that did not enhance his movement (Ellenberger, 1970).

Adler attended elementary and secondary school with neither problem nor distinction (Furtmuller, 1964). He then entered the Vienna Medical School and again completed work with no special distinction. When he received his medical degree near the end of 1895, he realized his childhood goal of becoming a physician. Following a tour of military duty in the Hungarian army (he was a citizen of Hungary until 1911, when he became an Austrian citizen), Adler returned to Vienna for postgraduate study. He began private practice as an eye specialist, but his interest in the whole person led him to give up specialization and to turn to general medicine. During these early years as a general practitioner he demonstrated an intense interest in the complete person, regarding illness as a reflection of the total personality and recognizing the essential unity between the physical and mental aspects of a disease. His concern for the whole person led him to the study of psychiatry, which, of course, did not diminish his interest in general medicine. It did, however, attract the attention of Sigmund Freud.

In 1902 Freud invited Adler to join him in forming the organization that later became the Vienna Psychoanalytic Society. Adler was not a disciple of Freud and did not consider himself a psychoanalyst. He never underwent psychoanalysis and could not accept the heavy sexual emphasis Freud placed on neuroses. Despite the fact that Adler was one of the original members of Freud's inner circle, there was never a warm personal relationship between the two Viennese physicians. Theoretical as well as personal differences grew, especially after publication in 1907 of Adler's *Study of Organ Inferiority and its Psychical Compensation.* (1907/1917).

In 1911 Adler, who was then president of the Vienna Psychoanalytic Society, was asked to present his views before the group. In a series of three papers, he expressed his opposition to the strong sexual proclivities of psychoanalysis and it became obvious to both Freud and Adler that their differences were irreconcilable. Adler resigned his presidency and, along with six other men, left the Freudian circle and formed the Society of Free Psychoanalysis. The following year the name was changed to the Society for Individual Psychology (Ellenberger, 1970). The term individual should not be misunderstood. It does not mean individualism or self-centeredness. Adler stressed social feeling and oneness with humankind. In the Adlerian context "individual" means both unique and indivisible. Each person creates a unique style of life, one which bestows unity or indivisibility on all behavior.

In retrospect, it is not difficult to see that personality differences between Freud and Adler would make a lasting harmonious relationship extremely unlikely. Freud was personally very ambitious and jealously guarded the sacrosanct doctrines of psychoanalysis, while Adler had developed a fierce boyhood rivalry with his older brother, Sigmund, and likely carried over a combative manner in his dealings with the older Freud. Adler was a very vocal member of the Vienna Psychoanalytic Society and often questioned some of the orthodox psychoanalytic views. His quarrelsome attitude was not designed to please Freud, who was quite sensitive to criticism. Adler's competitive nature, it seems, made it necessary for him to become independent of Freud and to establish a psychology that would oppose psychoanalysis.

During his early years of independence, Adler spent much of his time lecturing before audiences of both physicians and lay persons. Then, during World War I, he served as a physician in the Austrian army and, like Freud, his theoretical views were modified by his experiences with war. While Freud erected aggression as the final pillar in his theory, Adler went in a different direction and evolved the concept of social interest.

After the war Adler returned to his lectures in Vienna, established several child guidance clinics, and helped train teachers for the city of Vienna. In his role as an educator of teachers he was ahead of his time, advocating experimental methods and antiauthoritarian attitudes.

From 1926 until his death he frequently visited the United States, holding the position of Visiting Professor for Medical Psychology at Long Island College of Medicine, now Downstate Medical Center, State University of New York. During the last five years of his life he made his home in the United States, but returned to Europe regularly. Unlike Freud, he was impressed by Americans and admired their open-mindedness (Rattner, 1983).

Adler married Raissa Epstein, a Russian, and they had four children. His daughter, Alexandra and his only son, Kurt, became psychiatrists and both continued Adler's work in Individual Psychology.

Adler's favorite relaxation was music, but he also maintained an active interest in art and literature. In his work he often borrowed examples from fairy tales, the Bible, Shakespeare, Goethe, and numerous other literary works. He identified himself closely with the common person and his manner and appearance were consistent with his self-concept. His patients included a high percentage of people from the lower and middle classes, a rarity among psychiatrists of his time.

On May 28, 1937, Adler died of a heart attack in Aberdeen, Scotland, while on one of his many lecture tours.

INTRODUCTION TO ADLERIAN THEORY

After his death, Adler's popularity and prestige waned for a time, but in more recent years his views have come to acquire greater acceptance in both academic and clinical circles. His ideas on the importance of interpersonal relationships have been further developed by Harry Stack Sullivan, Karen Horney, Julian Rotter, Abraham H. Maslow, Carl Rogers, and others. His emphasis on subjective perception is the basis for Albert Ellis's rational-emotive therapy and he has also influenced Rollo May and other existentialists.

Yet Adler remains today less well known than either Freud or Carl Jung. Several reasons account for this. First, he did not establish a tightly-run organization to perpetuate his theories. Second, he was not a particularly gifted writer and most of his books are compiled from scattered lectures. Third, many of his views were incorporated into the works of later theorists and thus became dissociated from his name. Fourth, Adler lacked Freud's drive to gain recognition and fame. He was more content to help individuals and small groups through his clinical work and lectures. .

Although his writings revealed great insight into the depth and complexities of human personality, Adler evolved a basically simple and parsimonious theory of personality. The main tenets of his theory can be stated in outline form. The following is adapted from a list that represents the final statement of Adler's theory (Adler, 1964, pp. 24–25).

1. All psychological phenomena are *unified* within the individual in a self-consistent manner.
2. The *subjective perceptions* of the individual shape behavior and personality.
3. The one dynamic force behind the person's activity is the *striving for success or superiority.*
4. The usefulness of all human activity must be seen from the viewpoint of *social interest.*
5. Social interest develops in accordance with the individual's *style of life.*
6. The style of life is developed by the individual's *creative power.* The creative power, then, is responsible for unity, subjective opinions, the manner of striving, the level of social interest, and, of course, one's unique style of life.

Each of these six tenets is discussed in the following subsections, beginning with unity of personality.

UNITY OF PERSONALITY

All psychological phenomena are unified within the individual in a self-consistent manner.

Individual Psychology insists on the fundamental unity of personality. All of the person's thoughts, feelings, and actions are directed toward a single goal and serve a single purpose. Inconsistent behavior does not exist. When a person such as Christine, in the case study, behaves erratically or unpredictably it is for a single purpose. Such behavior forces other people to be on the defensive, to be watchful so as not to be confused by such capricious actions. When Christine suddenly announced to her husband that she was leaving him for another man, she did so in an emotionless, matter-of-fact way that left Joe bewildered and baffled. Then, just as unexpectedly, she told Joe that she had changed her mind, and their relationship then continued as if nothing had happened. She proceeded to alternate between being warm and cold to Joe. This inconsistent behavior left him puzzled and uncertain about how to react to her. Her behavior, however, merely appears inconsistent. Close examination reveals that her alternating warm and cold attitudes are each consistent with a single goal—the goal of personal superiority over her husband. By consistently baffling and puzzling Joe, Christine subordinates him to her own superiority strivings. Joe became inferior because he was incapable of comprehending her. This situation provided Christine with the upper hand in the marital relationship. The fact that she was successful in her attempts to gain superiority over her husband did not necessitate conscious intent. She probably did not fully understand her goal; that is, she was not aware of her true motive and, undoubtedly, she would never admit that she wanted to gain superiority at the expense of her husband.

All behavior, then, is seen in relation to the final goal of superiority or success and this goal confers unity on one's personality (Adler, 1930).

Adler (1956) recognized several ways in which the entire personality operates with unity and self-consistency. The first of these he called organ dialect.

Organ Dialect

According to Adler, the whole person, mind and body, strives in a self-consistent fashion toward a single goal and all separate actions and functions can be understood only as parts of that goal. The disturbance of one part of the body cannot be viewed in isolation; it affects the entire person. In fact, the diseased organ expresses the direction of the individual's goal, a condition that Adler (1956) called **organ dialect.**

An example of organ dialect is seen in Christine, who suffers from tachycardia, or abnormally rapid heart beat. The symptoms, although quite real and often frightening, nevertheless are not ordinarily life threatening. Once, when her husband was planning to attend an out-of-state conference alone, Christine developed tachycardia just hours before he was to depart. She bravely insisted that he go anyway, that she could survive his absence. Joe, of course, could not leave his sick wife, so he cancelled his travel plans. Christine did not fake her illness, but her physical symptoms speak a dialect of their own. It is as if they say "I am seriously ill and must be attended to." At the same time Christine is saying, "Please go on your trip. I don't need any special attention." Thus, her exaggerated strivings for personal superiority are served in two ways. First, she is able to control Joe's actions and, second, she appears courageous and magnanimous.

Conscious and Unconscious

A second example of a unified personality is the harmony between the conscious and the unconscious. The unconscious is defined by Adler (1956) as that part of the goal which is not clearly formulated nor completely understood by the individual. With this definition Adler avoids a dichotomy between the unconscious and the conscious, which he sees as cooperating parts of the same unified system. Conscious thoughts are those which are understood and regarded by the individual as helpful in striving for success. Whatever the person cannot justify as being helpful is pushed into the unconscious.

> We cannot oppose "consciousness" to "unconsciousness" as if they were antagonistic halves of an individual's existence. The conscious life becomes unconscious as soon as we fail to understand it—and as soon as we understand an unconscious tendency it has already become conscious (Adler, 1929/1964, p. 163).

Consciousness and unconsciousness, rather than being opposing factions, are complementary entities operating under the dominance of a unifying style of life. Whether a thought is conscious or unconscious, it has but one purpose—to realize the goal of superiority or success.

Reason and Emotion

The final goal also gives unity to reason and emotion. The two processes cannot be separated. Thoughts are always accompanied by some measure of affect; feelings are always associated with some degree of cognition.

When a person feels panic upon venturing alone into open spaces, but "knows" there is nothing to fear, emotion and reason may appear to be in conflict. A complete understanding of the person's intentions, Adler said, would reveal that the two processes are simply serving separate aspects of the same goal. The panic serves the goal of superiority in a negative manner. The neurotic has the attitude, "You can't expect too much from me, I'm sick. Just imagine what I could do if only I didn't have this phobia of open spaces." Such an attitude is an expression of self-delusion and an attempt to convince others that this illness is the person's only obstacle to greatness. On the other hand, the "knowledge" that there is nothing to fear in open spaces allows the person to say, "I'm not stupid. I know there is really nothing to fear out there. You must give me credit for thinking straight. I can't help it if this illness possesses me." This apparent conflict can be seen as a unified striving for the goal of personal superiority and for the avoidance of responsibility for facing the problems of life. Neurotics also subordinate others by demanding that they be accompanied outdoors and that they have rendered to them "well-deserved" sympathy. In this way reasoning and emotions work closely together to accomplish the same goal—superiority over other people.

SUBJECTIVE PERCEPTIONS

The subjective perceptions of the individual shape behavior and personality.

Personality is shaped, not by external causes such as organ inferiorities or basic drives, but by the individual's subjective perception of reality. Adler believed that people are motivated more by **fictions,** or expectations of the future, than by experiences of the past. Behavior is consistent with one's perception of the fictional final goal. This goal does not exist in the future but in the person's present perception of the future. It molds contemporary behavior because it is subjectively perceived in the here and now (Adler, 1956).

Fictionalism

Adler's ideas on fictionalism originated with Hans Vaihinger's book, *The Philosophy of "As If"* (1911/1925). Vaihinger believed that fictions are ideas that have no real existence, yet they influence people *as if* they really existed. An example of a fiction might be, "Men are superior to women." Although this notion is a fiction, many people, both men and women, act as if it were a reality. People are motivated not by what is true, but by their subjective perceptions of what is true.

Christine acts as if other people are helpless and in need of her care and concern. When her neighbor's mother died, Christine insisted on driving her to the funeral home and helping make arrangements. After all, a grieving person should not have to drive a car or worry about funeral details. Such "thoughtful consideration" is characteristic of Christine's style of life, but it is also consistent with her final goal of gaining superiority over others by being kinder and gentler than anyone else.

Final Goal

To Adler, the fiction of greatest importance is the final goal of superiority or success. The goal is fictional because it has no objective existence. As a subjective ideal, however, the fictional final goal has great significance. It unifies personality and renders all behavior comprehensible (Adler, 1956).

Each individual has the power to create a personalized fictional goal. It is constructed out of the raw materials provided by heredity and environment, but the goal is neither genetically nor environmentally determined. It is the product of a free creative power (Adler, 1956). By the time children are four or five years of age, their creative minds have reached the state of development that enables them to set their final goals. Infants have an innate drive toward growth, completion, or success. Because they are small, incomplete, and weak, they feel inferior and powerless. To compensate for this deficiency, they eventually set fictional goals—to overcome, to be above, to be big and strong, to be superior or successful. The goal reduces the pain of inferiority feelings and points young children in the direction of superiority wishes and fantasies.

Although the goal is dimly perceived and incompletely understood, Adler (1956) believed that it determines the direction of the child's movement toward power, security, and perfection. The young boy may strive for success by imitating his father or by pretending to be an airplane pilot or an astronaut. His goal to be big, to be powerful, or to be above is unconsciously pursued.

If the child is neglected or pampered the goal remains largely unconscious. Adler hypothesized that one will compensate for feelings of inferiority in devious ways that have no apparent relationship to the fictional goal. The goal of superiority for a pampered girl, for example, may be to make permanent her parasitic relationship with her mother. Her adult behavior often appears self-depreciating and therefore inconsistent with a goal of superiority. It should be remembered, however, that her goal was set at age four or five, a time when Mother appeared large and powerful, and attachment to her became a natural means of attaining superiority.

The fact that the adult behavior of the neglected or pampered person seems inconsistent with a goal of superiority is indicative of an unconscious goal. Conversely, if the child experiences love and security, the goal becomes largely conscious and understood. The secure child strives toward superiority defined in terms of success and social interest. Though the goal never completely becomes conscious, the psychologically mature individual understands and pursues it with a high level of awareness.

In striving for the final goal, many preliminary goals must be created. These subgoals are often conscious, but the connection between them and the final goal usually remains unknown. Furthermore, the relationship among preliminary goals is seldom realized. From the point of view of the final goal, however, they fit together in a self-consistent pattern. Adler (1956) used the analogy of the playwright who builds the characters and the subplots according to the final goal of the drama. When the final scene is known, all dialogue and every subplot acquires new meaning. When an individual's final goal is known, all actions make sense and each subgoal takes on new significance.

Teleology

Adler considered motivation largely from a teleological point of view. **Teleology** is a doctrine that holds that motivation must be considered according to its final purpose or aim, as opposed to **causality,** which considers behavior as springing from a specific cause. Teleology is usually concerned with future goals or ends, while causality ordinarily deals with past experiences that produce some present effect. Freud's view of motivation was basically causal; people are driven by past events that activate present behavior. Adler, on the other hand, adopted a teleological view, in which people are motivated by present perceptions of the future. These fictions need not be true and, in fact, they do not have to be conscious or understood. Nevertheless, they bestow a purpose on all of one's actions and are responsible for a consistent pattern that runs throughout a person's life.

Organ Inferiorities

Adler (1930, 1964) insisted that the whole human race is "blessed" with organ inferiorities, that is, physical handicaps. Feelings of inferiority and their subsequent compensation or overcompensation served as the cornerstone of his early theory. As his thinking matured, they were diminished in importance and became secondary to the striving for success. Nevertheless, the concept of physical inferiorities retains an auxiliary position in Adlerian psychology.

Physical handicaps have no meaning or importance by themselves. Their importance stems from the fact that they stimulate subjective feelings of inferiority (Adler, 1929/1969), and these feelings serve as an impetus toward perfection or completion. History provides many examples of people like Demosthenes or Beethoven overcoming a handicap and making significant contributions to society. Others, however, have overcompensated for feelings of inferiority by becoming criminals or deeply neurotic. The direction of one's compensation depends on one's talent, courage, and social interest.

Birth Order

Another subjective influence on personality development is the child's order of birth in the family. Numerical rank per se is of no importance, but children's perception of the situation into which they are born helps shape personality.

Firstborn children, according to Adler, are likely to have intensified feelings of power and superiority, high anxiety, and overprotective tendencies. They occupy a unique position, being an only child for a time and then experiencing a traumatic dethronement when a younger sibling is born. This event dramatically changes the situation and the child's view of the world. If firstborn children are three or older when a baby brother or sister is born, they incorporate this dethronement into a previously established style of life. They will likely feel hostility and resentment toward the new baby, but, if they have already developed a cooperating style, they will eventually adopt this same attitude toward a new sibling. If the firstborn is less than three, hostility and resentment will be largely unconscious, which make these attitudes more resistant to change in later life. The oldest child may carry hidden hostility toward a younger brother or sister throughout a lifetime (Adler, 1931).

Secondborn children begin life in a better situation for developing cooperation and social interest, Adler claimed. To some extent the personalities of secondborn children are shaped by their perception of the older child's attitude toward them. If this attitude is one of extreme hostility and vengeance, the second child may become highly competitive or overly discouraged. The typical second child, however, does not develop in either of these two directions, but matures toward moderate competitiveness, having a healthy desire to overtake the older rival. If some success is achieved, the child is likely to develop a revolutionary attitude and feel that any authority can be challenged (Adler, 1931).

Again, the child's interpretation of the situation is much more important than her chronological position. If it seems as if the second child is in a favored position, one should recall that Adler himself was a secondborn child. Incidentally, research does not tend to confirm Adler's optimistic view of the second child.

Youngest children are often the most pampered and, consequently, run a high risk of being problem children. They are likely to have strong feelings of inferiority and to lack a sense of independence. Nevertheless, they possess many advantages. They are highly motivated to exceed older siblings and often become the fastest runner, the best musician, the most skilled athlete, or the most ambitious student. The literature and folklore of every nation is filled with examples of the youngest child surpassing older siblings, performing daring deeds, or becoming a conquering hero (Adler, 1931).

The only child is in a unique position of competing, not against brothers and sisters, but against father and mother. This child often develops an exaggerated sense of superiority, an inflated self-concept, and a feeling that the world is a dangerous place, especially if the parents are overly concerned with the child's health. Adler (1931) stated that the only child may lack a well-developed feeling of cooperation and social interest, possess a parasitic attitude, and expect all others to offer pampering and protection.

Christine is a middle child, that is, she is the third of four children, all born about a year apart. The oldest sibling is a sister, followed by a brother, then Christine, then another brother. Interestingly, Adler has little to say about a middle child (other than the secondborn). However, Christine may have some of the characteristics of a second child, competing against a sister only two years older. The sister was strong, active, and very much a "tomboy." Christine adopted quite the opposite style of life, that is, she saw herself as weak, passive, cute, and overly "feminine."

There are many possible family constellations. According to Adler (1931), the situation into which a child is born depends, not solely on rank order, but on the sex of the older and younger siblings, the spread between other members of the family, and, most importantly, on the subjective perception of self and environment.

Summary

In summary, personality is molded, not by reality, but by subjective fictions. The guiding fiction is the goal of superiority or success. The goal is created by the individual during the first four or five years of life, but it remains largely unknown. The subjective, fictional final goal gives unity to personality and, when understood, it confers purpose on all behavior.

STRIVING FOR SUCCESS OR SUPERIORITY

The one dynamic force behind the person's activity is the striving for success or superiority.

The concept of a single governing force behind motivation underwent a metamorphosis in Adler's thinking. As early as 1908 he believed aggression to be the dynamic power behind all motivation. Soon after, he changed the name to "masculine protest," which implied will to power, that is, a striving to dominate others. By 1912, Adler found that masculine protest had become an unsatisfactory term for explaining the motivation of normal people. It retained a subsidiary position in his final theory and is discussed below under his theory of abnormal development. As the central dynamic power, "masculine protest" was replaced by "striving for superiority." This, in turn, was followed in his later writings by "striving for success or perfection," terms more in tune with his final concept of social interest (Adler, 1956).

The Striving Force as Compensation

Every person, whether normal or neurotic, is pulled in the direction of success or superiority. Each person is born with the tendency toward completion or perfection. "The striving for perfection is innate in the sense that it is a part of life, a striving, an urge, a something without which life would be unthinkable" (Adler, 1956, p. 104).

Although the striving for success is innate, it must be developed. At birth it exists as potentiality, not actuality, and it remains for each of us to actualize this potential in our manner. This process is begun during about the fifth year, when we invest direction to the striving force by establishing a goal of superiority. The goal provides guidelines for motivation, shaping our psychological development and giving it an aim.

People strive for superiority or success as a means of compensation for feelings of inferiority or weakness. As noted earlier, all humans are "blessed" at birth with small, weak, and inferior bodies. These physical deficiencies ignite feelings of inferiority only because people, by their nature, possess an innate tendency toward completion or wholeness. People are continually pushed by the need to overcome inferiority feelings and pulled by the desire for completion. The minus and plus situations exist simultaneously and can never be separated, for they are two dimensions of a single force. The force itself is innate, but its nature and direction are due both to feelings of inferiority and to the goal of superiority. Without the innate movement toward perfection, children would never feel inferior; but without feelings of inferiority, they would never set a goal of superiority or success. The goal, then, is set as compensation for the deficit feeling, but the deficit feeling would not exist unless a child first possessed a basic tendency toward completion (Adler, 1956).

The goal is not set as a blind reaction to the deficit feeling nor does it need be set in the exact opposite direction. As a creation of the individual, it may take any form. Even if a person's goals were known, it would not guarantee an accurate prediction of one's specific feelings of inferiority. The goal is not necessarily the mirror image of the deficiency, even though it is a compensation for it. For example, a person with a weak body will not necessarily become a robust athlete, but, instead, may become an artist, an actor, or a writer. Success is an individualized concept and all of us formulate our own definition of it. Our creative power is ultimately responsible for that definition, but it is swayed by the forces of heredity and environment. Heredity establishes the potentiality while environment contributes to the development of social interest and courage. The forces of nature and nurture can never deprive us of the power to set a unique goal or to choose a unique style of reaching for the goal (Adler, 1956).

Methods of Striving

Although each of us strives for completion in a unique manner, there are two general methods of striving. The first is the neurotic attempt to gain personal superiority; the second involves social interest and is aimed at success or perfection for everyone.

Striving for Personal Superiority

Some people strive for superiority with little or no concern for others. Their goals are personal ones and their strivings are motivated largely by exaggerated feelings of personal inferiority. Murderers, thiefs, and con artists are obvious examples of people who strive only for personal gain. However, on a more subtle level, many other people cover their strivings for personal gain behind the cloak of social concern. Christine, for example, appears to the casual observer to be a deeply caring person, taking a much greater interest in her students than any other teacher in her school. She encourages them to talk to her concerning their personal problems and reinforces their revelations of private and painful experiences with conspicuous displays of sympathy and concern. She receives perverted pleasure from her belief that she is the most accessible and dedicated teacher in her school. She never criticizes her colleagues directly because she is far too "professional" to engage in petty bickering. However, Christine has become an expert at nonverbally communicating her displeasure whenever another teacher expresses a lack of concern for a student. She will sigh, gasp, or frown to show her superior standards of professional conduct. To her husband she is overtly and relentlessly critical of her colleagues. If Joe is not yet convinced that his wife is the greatest teacher in the world, it is not because she hasn't told him often enough!

Striving for Success

Psychologically healthy people strive not for personal gain but for the success of all humankind. They are motivated by social interest and are concerned with goals beyond themselves. Unlike Christine, they are capable of helping others without demanding or expecting a personal payoff. They see others not as opponents but as people with whom they can cooperate for social benefit. Their own success is not gained at the expense of others, but as a natural tendency to move toward completion or perfection.

People who strive for success rather than personal superiority maintain a sense of self, of course, but they see daily problems from the view of society's development rather than from a strictly personal vantage point. Their sense of personal worth is tied closely to their contributions to human society. Social progress is more important to them than personal credit (Adler, 1956).

Summary

In summary, each individual begins life with an innate striving force, which is activated by the ever-present physical deficiencies. These weaknesses lead inevitably to feelings of inferiority. All people, both the neurotic and the healthy, possess feelings of inferiority and all set a final goal at around age four or five. However, neurotics develop exaggerated feelings of inferiority and attempt to compensate by setting a goal of personal superi-

Striving for success can take many forms.

ority. They are motivated by personal gain rather than social interest. On the other hand, healthy people, motivated by normal feelings of incompletion and high levels of social interest, strive toward the goal of success, defined in terms of perfection and completion for everyone. Figure 4.1 illustrates the two basic methods of striving.

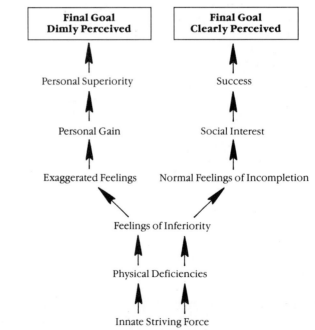

Figure 4.1   Two Basic Methods of Striving toward the Final Goal

By itself, the striving force is without value, being neither good nor bad. It acquires value only in relation to social interest. Striving is useless if it does not benefit other people; it is healthy if it proceeds in the direction of social interest.

SOCIAL INTEREST

The usefulness of all human activity must be seen from the viewpoint of social interest.

In Adlerian psychology, **social interest** occupies a position equal to, but not competitive with, the striving for success. It is a translation from the German word **Gemeinschaftsgefühl,** which could also be translated as "social feeling" or "community feeling." However, *Gemeinschaftsgefühl* has a meaning that is not fully expressed by any English word or phrase. Roughly, it means a feeling with all of humanity; it implies membership in the social community of all people. A person with well-developed *Gemeinschaftsgefühl* strives not for personal superiority but for perfection for all people in an ideal community. Social interest can be defined as an attitude of relatedness with humanity in general, as well as an empathy for each member of the human race. It manifests itself as cooperation with others for social advancement rather than for personal gain (Adler, 1964).

Adler (1964) believed that social interest is part of human nature and that some amount of it exists in everyone—the criminal, the psychotic, and the mentally healthy. Like striving for success, social interest is rooted as potentiality in everyone. However, it must be developed before it can contribute to a useful style of life.

Development in a Social Environment

The development of social interest takes place in a social environment. According to Adler (1956), other people, especially the mother, contribute to this developmental process. Social interest develops early in the mother-child relationship. Before birth a fetus experiences oneness with the mother and after birth the infant strives to reunite with her through the sucking movement of the lips. For several years the child continues to depend heavily on the mother, not merely for physiological needs, but for the satisfaction of psychological needs as well.

Since social interest arises from the mother-child relationship, every living person has some amount of it. The mother's task, according to Adler, is to encourage mature social interest in her child. Her own goal must not be for personal superiority, but should include the social goal of motherhood. She must also possess the ability to cooperate with the child, thus fostering a sense of cooperation. Ideally she has a genuine deep-rooted love for her child—a love that is centered on the child's well-being and not on her own vanity. This healthy love relationship develops from a true caring about people. If she has learned to give and receive love from others, the mother will have little difficulty broadening her child's social interest. On the other hand, if she concentrates affection solely on the child, she will not be able to teach the child to transfer social interest to other people. Her affection for her husband, for her other children, and for society serves as a model for the child. From her demonstration of broad social interest the child learns that there are important people other than one's mother and oneself.

The mother must give equal attention to her three ties: children, husband, and society (Adler, 1956). If she favors the first and shuns the second and third, her children become pampered and spoiled. Conversely, if she directs her attention exclusively to her husband or to society, her children become neglected and unloved. Either mistake brings about a lack of independence and an inability to cooperate within the children. The delicate balance can be achieved only by a woman who feels comfortable with the three major challenges of life—relationships with others (society), sexual love (husband), and occupation (children) (Adler, 1946).

The father is the second important person in the child's social environment. He has a difficult function, one which few fathers are able to successfully fulfill. He must have a good attitude toward his wife, his occupation, and society. In addition, his broad social interest must manifest itself in the relationship with his children. The ideal father treats his children as human beings and cooperates on an equal footing with his wife in caring for them.

According to Adler's standards, a successful father avoids the dual errors of emotional detachment and paternal authoritarianism. These errors may represent two attitudes, but they are often found in the same father. Both prevent the growth and spread of social interest in a child. A father's emotional detachment may influence the child to develop a warped sense of social interest, a feeling of neglect, and possibly a neurotic attachment to the mother. A child who experiences paternal detachment creates a goal of personal superiority rather than one based on social interest. The second error, paternal authoritarianism, also leads to a neurotic style of life. A child who sees the father as tyrannical learns to strive for power and personal superiority (Adler, 1956).

The effects of the early social environment should never be minimized. The relationship children have with their mother and father is so powerful that it smothers the effects of heredity. Adler believed that after age five it is difficult to say with certainty that any characteristic of a child is due solely to genetic factors. By that time learning has modified or shaped nearly every aspect of a child's personality.

Necessity of Social Interest

Adler (1927) believed that social life is the natural condition of the human species and that social interest is the cement that binds society together. It is impossible to conceive of a person in the absence of society. The natural inferiority of individuals necessitates their joining together to form society. Without protection and nourishment from the father and mother a baby would perish. Without protection from the clan the individual would be destroyed by animals that are stronger, more ferocious, or endowed with keener senses. Social interest, therefore, is a necessity and is responsible for every advancement of humanity, even for our existence. Without the willingness of a man and woman to cooperate in the procreation and subsequent protection of a child, the human race could not survive.

Adler believed that the child naturally looks toward others for love and affection. The infant's inadequacy predisposes it toward a mothering person. It is natural, therefore, that individuals develop an early interest in other people. Adler objected to Freud's belief that people are basically narcissistic. If the child later appears self-centered, it is because the mother-child relationship did not foster social interest. Narcissism is a form of neurosis, not an inherent characteristic of people. It grows from neurotic mother-child relationships because an overly indulgent or overly negligent mother teaches her child to be concerned primarily with self-interest (Ansbacher, 1985).

Criterion of Human Values

Social interest was Adler's yardstick for measuring psychological health. It is "the sole criterion of human values" (Adler, 1927, p. 167). To the degree that people possess social interest, they are psychologically mature. A neurotic person lacks *Gemeinschaftsgefühl,* is self-centered, and strives for personal power and superiority over others. The healthy individual is genuinely concerned about people and has a goal of success that encompasses the well-being of all people. Life has no value unless a person contributes to the life of other people and even to the life of future generations. Social interest is the only gauge to be used in judging the worth of a person. Adler (1956) referred to it as the barometer of normality, that is, the standard to be used in determining the usefulness of a life.

Social interest is not synonymous with charity and unselfishness. Acts of philanthropy and kindness may or may not be motivated by *Gemeinschaftsgefühl.* Adler believed that the criterion of all human behavior is social interest and that the value of any deed must be judged on that basis.

Charitable deeds toward others, the establishment of giant foundations for promoting social causes, and do-goodism are sometimes mistaken for true social interest. The motivation behind these acts, however, often arises from personal gain. A wealthy man may regularly give large sums of money to the poor and needy, not because he feels a oneness with them, but, quite to the contrary, because he wishes to maintain a separateness from them. The gift implies, "You are inferior, I am superior, and this charity is proof of my superiority." Most, but not all, charitable behavior is divorced from social interest and married to personal aggrandizement.

Christine consistently gives the appearance of a devoted mother and teacher—a person motivated by an abundance of social interest. However, her need to be the best, most self-sacrificing mother and teacher in the world suggests that she is motivated by personal superiority rather than social interest. She seems intent on convincing her children and her students that she is extra special, a selfless martyr willing to endure personal pain and suffering in order to help others. This self-image supports the grandiose fiction that she is the greatest mother and teacher in the world.

Summary

Social interest cannot be considered apart from striving for success, style of life, and creative power. It stands with striving for success as one of the twin pillars of Adlerian theory. Neither could stand, however, without the support of the other. Striving for success is valueless without social interest, but social interest is nonexistent without the striving. Social interest is also entwined with style of life because no single social act can be evaluated apart from the whole style of life. An act of generosity may be an attempt to gain personal superiority and, therefore, cannot be interpreted as social interest unless it is consistent with a style of life that embodies genuine social interest.

Social interest cannot be separated from the concept of creative power. Ultimately, it owes its development to the creative agent within each individual. At birth social interest exists as potentiality. Then it is partially actualized through the socialization process, but its refinement and final form are created by the individual. Adler believed that the creative power generates not only change but improvement in the human species. This means that in the remote future all persons will possess mature social interest in the same way that they now possess mature lungs and vertebrae. When the evolutionary process reaches that millennium, social interest will be as natural to people as correct breathing or the upright posture. Nevertheless, an individual is not inevitably led toward increased social interest. People can use their creative power to form a useless style of life as well as a useful one.

STYLE OF LIFE

Social interest develops in accordance with the individual's style of life.

Style of life is the term Adler used to refer to the flavor of a person's life. It includes not only the person's goal, but also self-concept, feelings toward others, and attitude toward the world. It is the product of the interaction of heredity, environment, goal of success, social interest, and creative power.

Style of life is similar to Freud's concept of ego in that it is the governing force of personality. Adler's concept, however, includes no id or superego waging war against the self. Style of life is the whole organism plus the person's unique manner of self-expression. Adler (1956) used a musical analogy to elucidate style of life. The separate notes of a composition are meaningless without the entire melody, but the melody takes on added significance when we recognize the composer's style or unique manner of expression.

Formation

Style of life is fairly well established by age four or five. After that time all individual actions revolve around a unified personality. The goal of superiority has been set, and the style of life is formed by the creative power in response to that goal. It would be a mistake to think that, because the goal is singular, style of life should be narrow and rigid. Healthy persons behave in diverse and flexible ways with styles of life that are complex, enriched, and, to some extent, subject to change. They see many ways of striving for success and continually seek to create new options for themselves. Even though the goal remains constant, the way in which it is perceived continually changes for the healthy individual.

Life Style Attitudes

Any attempt to formulate general personality types mutilates the unique life style of the individual. With this severe limitation in mind, and for purposes of illustration only, Adler proposed four general life style attitudes. His proposal was made to classify individuals according to their attitude and behavior toward the outside world. This classification is based on a two-dimensional scheme, with social interest constituting one dimension and **degree of activity** the other (see Figure 4.2). Degree of activity is a person's movement toward the solution of internal and external problems. All individuals have their own degree of activity or energy level, which is usually established during childhood. Activity level itself implies no value and no direction. Only when combined with social interest does it become desirable or undesirable, constructive or destructive, useful or useless (Adler, 1956).

The first of four general life style attitudes identified by Adler (1956) is the *ruling type*. People of this attitude have little social interest, but a high degree of activity. They possess a dominating attitude toward the outside world, approaching the three major problems of life (friendship, sex, and occupation) in an actively aggressive, but socially useless manner. People of the ruling type with an extremely high degree of activity are potentially dangerous. They are the murderers, rapists, tyrants, sadists, and suicides. The high degree of activity of the murderer or the rapist should never be con-

	Degree of Activity	
	Low	High
High Social Interest	(None)	Socially Useful Type
Low Social Interest	Getting Type	Ruling Type
	Avoiding Type	

Figure 4.2   Adler's Two-Dimensional Scheme for Classifying Life Style Attitudes

Understanding Life Style Attitudes Through Early Recollections

The key to understanding individual style of life comes from asking people to relate their earliest recollections. Adler believed that early recollections offer the most productive approach to understanding style of life. The objective validity of the recollection is of no importance. What is important is a person's perception of events. The earliest memory recalled is always consistent with present style of life. The subjective account of this experience yields a clue to understanding a person's goal and also one's style of life (Adler, 1929/1969).

On the surface, many early recollections seem mundane and meaningless, but proper interpretation, Adler believed, will reveal one's underlying style of life. To illustrate this point, Adler used the following example. A seemingly successful man who distrusted everyone, but especially women, reported the following memory: "I was going with my mother and little brother to market. Suddenly it began to rain, and my mother took me in her arms, and then, remembering that I was the older, she put me down and took up my younger brother" (Adler, 1929/1964, p. 123).

What can we make of this early recollection? The older brother, left to fend for himself, was both confused and hurt and felt that another had gained a favorite position with his mother. This memory relates directly to his adult style of life and imbues it with meaning. The pattern or theme running throughout this man's life has been one of distrust and suspicion. Though people may claim to love him and though they give him initial recognition, in the end affection and attention will surely be withdrawn.

If a person's earliest recollection is unpleasant, the life style is likely to be marked by the negative attitude, "Everything bad happens to me." If the first recollection is pleasant, the style of life will be revealed as optimistic and positive (Adler, 1956).

It is important to keep in mind that the early experiences do not *cause* or determine one's style of life. Quite the opposite. One's recollection of early experiences is shaped by present style of life.

If style of life shapes early recollections, then, as style of life changes, we should expect to find that one's early recollections also change. This belief, widely held by Adlerians, has been succinctly stated by one writer with these words: "Early recollections change when therapy has been effective. Either the recollections are new or the old ones are remembered in a different light" (Croake, 1975, p. 517).

This concept is illustrated by the case of a 26-year-old schoolteacher who was in therapy with the author. Near the beginning of therapy, she reported the following earliest recollection: "I remember when I was about two, I was riding in a car with my brothers and sisters. Mother was driving and she got a flat tire on a long bridge. We all got out of the car and Mother tried to change the tire while cars whizzed by us on the narrow bridge. The baby was crying and I thought we were all going to be killed."

After eight months of therapy and presumably some change in her style of life, the client was again asked for her earliest recollection and she now reported the following: "I was riding in a car with my brothers and sisters on the way to visit my favorite grandparents. We crossed a long bridge and I looked out the window and saw several beautiful sailboats on the lake. I remember thinking how pretty they looked." Both recollections, apparently from the same childhood experience, reflect the person's style of life—the first reveals a highly anxious, frightened woman, the second a peaceful, relaxed person.

fused with courage, a quality that demands a combination of social interest and high activity.

The *getting type,* Adler believed, is the most common life style attitude. Individuals with this attitude relate to the outside world in a parasitic manner, depending on others to satisfy most of their needs. Their main concern is getting as much as possible from others. They possess a low degree of activity and little social interest. Their consuming dependency leads to socially useless behavior and, under extreme stress, they are likely to become neurotic or psychotic. They are not especially dangerous, but they contribute little to society (Adler, 1956).

Many of the above statements also apply to the third, or *avoiding type.* Adler (1956) characterized people with this predisposition as having little social interest and low activity. Under traumatic conditions, the avoiding type persons are likely to become neurotic or psychotic. They are characterized by an attitude of avoidance. Fearing defeat more than desiring success, their lives are marked by the socially useless behavior of running away from the tasks of life. They lack the courage to struggle with problems, preferring instead to ignore them or to push them aside. As with people of the getting attitude, they are not directly dangerous to society as long as their degree of activity remains low.

The *socially useful type,* the fourth life style attitude, demands a high level of activity and a high degree of social interest. The person with socially useful attitudes, according to Adler, struggles to solve life's problems in a manner beneficial to society. This person rightly identifies three major social problems—neighborly love, sexual love, and occupation—and knows that the solution to social problems demands cooperation, personal courage, and a willingness to make a contribution to the welfare of another. Adler believed that the socially useful type represents the highest form of humanity in the evolutionary process, the psychologically mature individual who will populate the world of the future (Adler, 1956).

In the two-dimensional scheme, one possible combination is missing: high social interest/low activity. The reason for this is simple. It is not possible to have high social interest without possessing a high degree of activity. People with *Gemeinschaftsgefühl* must *do* something.

No one person can be molded to fit any one of the four life style attitudes. In the end, it is the individual who matters. Our own interpretation of the

Actor James Stewart's unique style comes through, even in the most harrowing circumstances.

world and our unique creative power make each of us different from any other person.

CREATIVE POWER

The style of life is developed by the individual's creative power.

Adler strongly believed that each of us is empowered with the freedom to create our own style of life. Ultimately, we are responsible for who we are and how we behave. We possess a creative power that places us in control of our own lives, and this power is responsible for our final goal, determines the method of striving for the goal, and contributes to the development of social interest. The creative force also produces perception, memory, imagination, fantasy, and dreams, and makes each of us a free individual (Adler, 1964).

Adler acknowledged the importance of heredity and environment in forming personality. Every child is born with a unique genetic makeup and soon comes to have social experiences different from those of any other human. People, however, are much more than a product of heredity and environment. They are creative beings who not only react to their environment but also act on it and cause it to react to them.

Adler (1956) believed that each of us uses heredity and environment as the brick and mortar to build personality, but the architectural design reflects our own style. Of primary importance is not what we have been given, but how we put those materials to use. The building materials of personality are secondary. We are each our own architect. We can build a useful or a useless life, choose to remain healthy or become neurotic, construct a gaudy façade or expose the essence of the structure. There is no inner nature that compels us to be good or forces us to do evil. We do not have to grow in the direction of social interest. Conversely, we have no inherently evil nature from which we must escape. We are who we are because of the use we have made of our brick and mortar.

Creative power is a dynamic concept implying *movement,* and this movement is the most salient characteristic of life. All psychic life involves free movement toward a goal, movement with a direction.

Adler (1929) used an interesting analogy, which he called "the law of the low doorway," to illustrate the free powers of both the neurotic and the healthy individual. If we are trying to walk through a doorway four feet high, essentially two choices are possible. First, we can use our creative power to bend down as we approach the doorway, thereby successfully solving the problem. This is the manner in which the healthy individual solves most of life's problems. On the other hand, if we bump our head and fall back, we must still solve the problem correctly or continue bumping our head. Neurotics often choose to bump their head on the realities of life. When approaching the low doorway, we are neither compelled to stoop nor forced to bump our head. We have a creative power that permits us to follow either course.

ABNORMAL DEVELOPMENT

Adler believed that people are what they make of themselves. Creative power endows humans, within certain limits, with the freedom to be normal or abnormal, healthy or unhealthy, useful or useless.

. Throughout his writings Adler was concerned with abnormal development. Early in his career his experiences and his writings were almost exclusively centered around the inadequate personality. However, after his elevation of social interest, he gave more emphasis to the healthy individual and placed abnormal psychology in a secondary position. A full understanding of Individual Psychology, however, rests on the knowledge of Adler's basic theories of maladjustment.

General Description

What is the essence of maladjustment? According to Adler (1956) the one factor underlying failures of every description is an underdeveloped social interest.

What descriptive phrases characterize those who fail to successfully solve life's problems? In general, failures (1) set their goals too high, (2) have a rigid and dogmatic style of life, and (3) live in their own private world. These three characteristics are inevitable concomitants to lack of social interest. In simple terms, people become failures in life because they are concerned solely with themselves and care nothing about others.

Failures set their goals too high as an overcompensation for exaggerated feelings of inferiority. Extravagant goals lead to dogmatic behavior. The higher the goal, the more rigid the striving. To compensate for deeply rooted feelings of inadequacy and basic insecurity, neurotic individuals narrow their perspective and strive compulsively and rigidly for unrealistic goals.

The exaggerated and unrealistic nature of neurotics' goals set them apart from the community of other people. They live in a private world and endow their goals with private meaning. They approach the problems of friendship, sex, and occupation from a personal angle that precludes successful solutions. Their view of the world is not in focus with that of other individuals and they possess what Adler (1956) called "private intelligence."

External Factors in Maladjustment

Why do some people create maladjustments? Adler (1964) recognized the following three contributing factors, any one of which is sufficient to contribute to abnormality: (1) exaggerated physical deficiencies, (2) a pampered style of life, and (3) a neglected style of life.

Exaggerated Physical Deficiencies

Exaggerated physical deficiencies, whether congenital or the result of injury or disease, are not sufficient to lead to maladjustments. They must be accompanied by accentuated feelings of inferiority. These subjective feelings may be greatly encouraged by a defective body, but they are the progeny of the creative power.

Anyone can develop exaggerated feelings of inferiority, but a child born with physical disabilities has an even greater burden and a higher probability of maladjustment than the physically healthy child. The deficient organ gives the child stronger motivation to compensate and often the striving becomes an overcompensation. A boy small in stature may overcompensate for his inadequate size by becoming extremely aggressive. As a child he may throw rocks at others, bully smaller children, or exhibit destructive behavior. Later, he may find that knives and guns make him a "big man," someone with the power to threaten and frighten other people. This spurious feeling of power helps satisfy his egocentric goal of superiority.

Children with certain deficiencies often try to hide the defect. At times, the concealment is so successful that some people cease to be aware of their abnormality and to deny its existence. Their psychic life, nevertheless, is greatly affected. They are likely to become overly concerned with themselves and to develop exaggerated inferiority feelings, which are manifested as lack of social interest, absence of self-confidence, little courage, and no consideration for others. They feel as if they are living in enemy country, fear defeat more than they desire success, and are convinced that life's major problems can only be solved in a selfish manner (Adler, 1927).

Pampered Style of Life

Adler believed that the pampered style of life lies at the heart of most neuroses. Though discussed separately from exaggerated physical deficiencies and the neglected life style, it is in fact a more basic term. It overlaps and, to a large extent, includes the other two causes of maladjustment.

Children who are pampered have little social interest and low activity level. They possess strong wishes to be pampered, regardless of whether or not they seem to be. Their primary desire is to make permanent the parasitic relationship they originally had with their mother. They expect others to look after them, overprotect them, and satisfy all their selfish needs. They are characterized by extreme discouragement, indecisiveness, oversensitivity, impatience, and exaggerated emotion, especially anxiety.

They believe that other people exist for them and they expect others to pamper them as their mothers once did. They see the world with private vision and believe that they are entitled to be first in everything.

The pampered style of life is not the result of too much love, Adler said. Pampered children are unloved children who have been overprotected, hovered over, smothered, and shielded from responsibilities. Their parents have demonstrated their lack of love by doing too much for them and by treating them as if they were incapable of solving their own problems. At least this is the child's interpretation of the situation and it is the individual's view that matters. If children feel pampered and spoiled, then they *are* pampered and spoiled (Adler, 1964).

Pampered children also feel neglected. Having been protected by a doting mother, they are fearful in her absence. Whenever they must fend for themselves, they feel left out, mistreated, and neglected. These experiences add to the pampered child's stockpile of inferiority feelings (Adler, 1927).

Neglected Style of Life

The third external factor contributing to maladjustments is neglect. Children create neglected styles of life when they feel unloved and unwanted. Orphans and illegitimate children, Adler said, are especially predisposed toward a neglected life style, but any one who feels hated or unwanted is likely to borrow heavily from these feelings in creating a style of life.

Neglect is a relative concept. No one feels totally neglected or completely unwanted. The fact that a child survived infancy is proof that someone cared for that child and that the seed of social interest has been planted.

When children have been abused and mistreated, they are inclined to feel neglected and to create a neglected style of life. Neglected children lack social interest, have little confidence in themselves, and tend to overestimate difficulties connected with life's major problems. They expect society to be cold because people have generally treated them coldly. They are spiteful toward others, distrustful of themselves, and unable to cooperate for the common welfare. They see society as enemy country, feel alienated from all other people, and experience a strong sense of envy toward the success of others. Neglected children have many of the characteristics of pampered ones, but generally they are more suspicious and more likely to be dangerous to others (Adler, 1927).

Safeguarding Tendencies

According to Adler, all neurotic symptoms are created to safeguard the individual's self-esteem. The symptoms themselves serve as **safeguarding tendencies,** protecting an inflated self-image and maintaining a neurotic style of life.

Adler's concept of safeguarding tendencies is similar to Freud's concept of defense mechanisms. Basic to both is the idea that symptoms are formed as a protection of the self or ego. However, there are several differences between the two. First, Freud's defense mechanisms protect the ego against anxiety from instinctual sources, while Adlerian safeguarding tendencies protect the person from outside demands. Also, while Freudian defense mechanisms are common to everyone, Adler discusses safeguarding tendencies only with reference to the construction of neurotic symptoms. It would appear, however, that nearly everyone, the normal as well as the abnormal, relies occasionally on safeguarding tendencies to protect tenuous feelings of self-esteem. Another difference is that, while defense mechanisms operate solely on an unconscious level, safeguarding tendencies may be either conscious or unconscious.

Individual Psychology holds that neurotics fear that their goal of personal superiority will be revealed as erroneous and that they will suffer public disgrace. To compensate for this fiction, they construct safeguarding tendencies that protect them against the embarrassing emergence of exaggerated inferiority feelings.

Excuses, aggression, and withdrawal are three commonly used safeguarding tendencies. They are generally unconscious, but occasionally conscious, devices for protecting the neurotic's life style and for maintaining a fictional, elevated feeling of self-importance (Adler, 1964).

Excuses

The most common safeguarding tendency is **excuses.** The neurotic, as well as the normal individual, typically makes use of the "Yes, but" and the "If only" excuses. In the "Yes, but" excuse people first state what they claim they would like to do—something that sounds good to others—then they follow with an excuse. The housewife protests, "I would like to go to college, *but* my children demand too much of my attention." The executive explains, "I agree with your proposal, *but* company policy will not allow it."

The "If only" statement is the same excuse phrased in a different way. *If only* I had not married Roger I would be very happy now." "*If only* I did not have this physical handicap I could compete successfully for a job." These excuses protect a weak sense of self-worth and deceive people into believing that they are more superior than they really are (Adler, 1956).

Aggression

Another common safeguarding tendency is **aggression.** It is Adler's view that neurotics use aggression to safeguard their exaggerated superiority complex, that is, to protect their delusive self-esteem. Safeguarding through aggression may take the form of depreciation, accusation, or self-accusation.

Depreciation is the tendency to undervalue another's achievement and to overvalue one's own. This safeguarding tendency is evident in such aggressive behaviors as sadism, gossip, envy, and intolerance. The intention behind each act of depreciation is to belittle another so that the neurotic, by comparison, will be placed in a favorable light.

Accusation, the second form of neurotic aggression, is the tendency to blame others for one's failures and to seek revenge, thereby safeguarding one's own tenuous self-esteem. Adler (1956) believed that there is an element of aggressive accusation in all neuroses. Neurotics invariably act to cause people around them to suffer more than they do.

Christine combines the "If only" excuse with aggressive accusation against her husband. She had wanted to attend medical school, but when she married Joe, she gave up those plans in favor of having a family. After her children were in school, she went back to college to finish a degree in education, but she constantly reminds Joe that she would have been a successful doctor, *if only* he had not wanted children. Her accusations against him protect her feelings of self-esteem and keep her from facing the possibility that, even under different circumstance, if she had not married, she might not have become a successful physician.

The third form of neurotic aggression, **self-accusation,** is characterized by self-torture and guilt. Self-torture is evident in masochism, depression, and suicide and it is a means of safeguarding neurotics' power to hurt those people who are close to them. Adler (1956) believed that guilt is often aggressive, self-accusatory behavior.

Self-accusation is the converse of depreciation, though both are aimed toward personal superiority. In depreciation, the other person is devalued to make the neurotic look good by comparison. In self-accusation, neurotics devalue themselves, with the ultimate purpose of inflicting suffering on others, again, to protect their magnified feelings of self-esteem.

Withdrawal

Personality development is sometimes arrested due to a neurotic's tendency to run away from difficulties. Adler referred to this tendency as **withdrawal,** or safeguarding through distance. Neurotics unconsciously escape life's problems by setting up a distance between themselves and the problems.

Adler (1956) recognized four modes of safeguarding through withdrawal:

moving backward, standing still, hesitating, and constructing obstacles. Neurotics are well served by each mode. By making a show of their illness, they gain power over others, are relieved from normal obligations, and generally get their own way.

Adler used the term **moving backward** to refer to any tendency to safeguard the fictional goal of superiority by psychologically reverting to a more secure period of life. Moving backward is similar to Freud's concept of regression in that both involve attempts to return to earlier, less anxiety-ridden phases of life. While regression takes place unconsciously and includes the repression of painful experiences, moving backward may sometimes be conscious and has as its purpose the protection of an inflated goal of superiority. It includes suicide, attempts at suicide, most phobias, hysterical disorders, amnesia, and severe anxiety. The neurotic desires attention from others in order to gain some control over them. For example, attempted suicide usually attracts attention and thus forces other people to worry and fret over the neurotic's well-being. Moving backward is designed to elicit sympathy, the deleterious attitude offered so generously to pampered children.

Psychological distance can also be created by **standing still.** This withdrawal tendency is similar to moving backward but, in general, is not as severe. It is comparable to Freud's concept of fixation, but differs in that it may be partly conscious and, rather than protecting the ego against anxiety, it safeguards the person's inflated feelings of superiority. In standing still neurotics simply do not move in any direction; thus they avoid all responsibility by insuring themselves against any threat of failure. They safeguard their fictional aspirations because they never do anything to prove that they cannot accomplish their goals. Christine never applied to any medical school and therefore was never denied entrance. By doing nothing she was able to safeguard her self-esteem and protect herself against failure.

Closely related to standing still is **hesitating.** Some neurotics hesitate or vacillate when faced with difficult problems. Their procrastinations eventually give them the excuse, "It's too late now." Most compulsions, Adler believed, are attempts to waste time. Compulsive washing, retracing one's steps, excessive orderliness, destroying work already begun, and leaving work unfinished are examples of hesitation. From a social viewpoint, the hesitating tendency is self-defeating because the person wastes time until it becomes too late to accomplish a task. The tendency, however, is useful from the individual's point of view because it protects an inflated sense of self-esteem.

The least severe of the withdrawal safeguarding tendencies is **constructing obstacles.** Some people build a straw house to show that they can knock it down. By overcoming the obstacle, neurotics protect their self-esteem and their prestige. If they fail to hurdle the barrier, they can always resort to an excuse.

Safeguarding tendencies are found in nearly everyone, but when they reach a level of rigidity, they become the essential traits of neuroses. They are created by the oversensitive neurotic as a buffer against the fear of disgrace. They have their origin in accentuated inferiority feelings and are directed toward the elimination of those feelings and the attainment of self-esteem and success. Unfortunately, they are self-defeating, having a built-in goal of self-interest and personal superiority that blocks the attainment of self-esteem. Adler believed that neurotics seldom realize that their self-esteem would be better safeguarded if they gave up their self-interest and developed genuine interest in others.

Masculine Protest

Due to cultural influences, many men, but especially women, overemphasize the importance of being manly. This condition was Adler's definition of **masculine protest.** In most societies, both men and women place an inferior value on being a woman, an unfortunate and unnatural state of affairs that is the cause of much marital discord and many individual problems of superiority and inferiority complexes. In Western societies boys are taught early that being masculine means being courageous, strong, and dominant. The epitome of success for boys is to win, to be powerful, to be on top. Failure is associated with being a "sissy." Girls, on the other hand, often learn to be passive and submissive; they are told of the hardships of menstruation and childbirth; they usually surrender their names and accept those of their husbands. These and many other cultural customs teach young girls that they belong to an inferior gender.

In contrast to Freud, Adler (1930, 1956) believed that the psychic life of women is essentially the same as that of men, and the nearly universal phenomenon of male-dominated cultures is not a natural state of affairs. Rather, it is the product of our historical development. In contemporary Western societies, women are believed to be weak, inferior, and defenseless, an alleged inferiority that causes many women to fight against their feminine roles. Some revolt by developing a masculine orientation and becoming assertive and competitive, while others revolt by adopting a passive "feminine" role, becoming exceedingly helpless, humble, and obedient. Still others become resigned to the belief that they are inferior human beings. They approve of men's privileged position and, in revenge, shift all responsibilities to their husbands or to other men. All these modes of adjustment are the result of cultural influences, not of an inherent psychic difference between the sexes.

Christine possesses many traits associated with the masculine protest. To her husband, she adopts a helpless and defenseless posture. In her eyes she is completely unable to perform any "masculine" task. She has never fixed a faucet, started a lawn mower, or pumped gas into her car. Although she loves to plant flowers, Joe always performs the spade work. Her helplessness in such simple jobs is not due to physical frailty, but is a clever, though unconscious, ploy to seek revenge on men in general and Joe in particular. To her high school students, Christine appears to be an aggressive champion of women's rights. Her support for women's causes, however, is shallow and one-sided. She advocates superiority not equality for women, yet she has given no reflective thought to the views she professes. Her deeply feminine biases are a reflection of a basic belief that women are inferior to men, that is, a masculine protest.

APPLICATIONS OF INDIVIDUAL PSYCHOLOGY

It is convenient to divide the practical applications of Individual Psychology into three areas: early recollections, dreams, and psychotherapy.

Early Recollections

Both early recollections and dreams were part of Adler's practice of psychotherapy, but their individual significance demands that they be discussed separately.

During therapy, Adler invariably asked patients for their earliest memory. The recalled memory yields clues for understanding a patient's personality and goal of superiority, but is never considered to have a causal effect on style of life. It is of no importance whether the recalled experience corresponds with objective reality. People reconstruct events to be consistent with a theme or pattern that runs throughout their lives.

Highly anxious patients often remember fearful and anxiety-producing events, such as auto accidents, temporary or permanent loss of parents, or that they were bullied by other children. For example, two of Christine's early memories reveal frightening experiences. In her earliest recollection, she recalled that when she was about three or four her father had gone away on a business trip and she and her mother were visiting some of his relatives. Several of the older male cousins and uncles began teasing Christine's mother by making reference to her beautiful eyes and pretty long hair. This frightened Christine and she perceived that her mother was also frightened. She and her mother quickly fled from the house, but Christine remained afraid for days afterward.

In the second recollection, Christine was a little older—about five—but the memory is remarkably similar. She was attending a family reunion when she and a girl cousin about her age were confronted by a boy (apparently another cousin) also about her age. Although she could not recall any of the boy's specific actions, she felt threatened by him and became frightened. She avoided danger by maneuvering the other little girl between herself and the boy. Then she ran sobbing to her mother.

In both memories males are seen as menacing and threatening, and females are unsafe in their presence. The threat can be avoided by running away, but the fear lingers.

Pampered people frequently include their mother in early recollections. For example, a 25-year-old man, whose life had been marked by extreme dependence on his mother and neutrality toward his father, recalled: "I was playing with my blocks and Mother was sitting next to me. The blocks fell down and Mother helped me stack them back up." In this recollection, the father is absent, as are the patient's rival siblings. Only he and his watchful, doting mother are recalled. Further exploration of his style of life would show that he has consistently relied on his mother to help him through various difficulties.

Along with Freud's technique of free association (Chapter 2) and Jung's method of the word association test (Chapter 5), Adler's use of early recollections was one of the first projective techniques employed in psychotherapy. Early recollections, however, offer one distinct advantage over free association and word association methods. The technique is not threatening to the patient, arouses little anxiety and resistance, and most patients are usually quite willing to relate their earliest memories (Adler, 1931).

Dreams

The individual's style of life is also expressed in dreams. Adler rejected Freud's notion that dreams are expressions of infantile wishes. On the contrary, he viewed them as forward-looking and as providing clues for solving future problems. Dreams, however, are not prophetic. Though they represent the dreamer's attempt to solve a problem that cannot be solved by common sense alone, dreams are disguised in a manner to deceive the dreamer. The more an individual's goal is inconsistent with reality, the more dreams will be used for self-deception. For example, a man may have the goal of reaching the top, being above, or becoming President. If he also possesses a dependent style of life, his ambitious goal may be expressed in dreams of being lifted onto another's shoulders or being shot from a cannon. A more courageous and independent man with similar ambition may dream of unaided flying. The dream unveils the style of life, but fools the dreamer by presenting him with an unrealistic, exaggerated sense of power and accomplishment.

Since dreams are essentially self-deceptions, they are not easily understood by the dreamer, and thus must be interpreted by a trained person. In interpreting dreams, Adler began with the assumption that every dream creates a mood or emotion that is produced to effectively screen the unconscious style of life from conscious understanding. If dreams were logical and reasonable they would not serve their purpose of deceiving the dreamer. It is the task of the interpreter to help the dreamer make sense out of the illusive feeling tone of the dream (Adler, 1929/1969, 1931).

Psychotherapy

Since maladjustment results from lack of courage, exaggerated feelings of inferiority, and underdeveloped social interest, it follows that Adler would stress these characteristics in his practice of psychotherapy. Courage, self-esteem, and social interest are nurtured by the human relationship between patient and doctor. The warm maternal attitude of the therapist encourages the patient's expanded social interest. In addition, the therapist, in a more paternal role, makes the patient aware of any faulty style of life and helps in finding solutions to the three problems of life: sexual love, social interest, and occupation.

Although Adler was quite active in setting the goal and direction of psychotherapy, he maintained a warm and permissive attitude toward the patient. He established himself as a friendly co-worker, refrained from moralistic preachings, and placed great value on the human relationship. By cooperating with the therapist, the patient establishes contact with another person. The therapeutic relationship awakens the patient's social interest in the same manner that a child gains social interest from the mother. With a neurotic patient, in fact, the therapist must assume the dual functions of motherhood: first, establish a relationship of human fellowship; and second strengthen the patient's independence and courage by increasing and spreading social interest to others. Patients are never allowed to use their neuroses to gain the sympathy of the therapist as they once did with their parents (Adler, 1956).

In understanding the life style of the patient, Adler utilized five possible avenues: early childhood recollections, dreams, birth order, childhood difficulties, and external factors in the illness. All five methods rely on the individual's subjective description of self. Each is used to gain an understanding of the whole person and no method is used to the exclusion of others. They must be consistent with one another in revealing the complete person (Adler, 1946).

Adler innovated a unique method of therapy with problem children by treating them in front of a large group of people in mental health clinics. Receiving therapy in public gives children an understanding that their difficulty is a community problem. Adler was careful not to blame the parents for a child's misbehavior. Instead, he worked to win the parents' confidence and to persuade them to change their attitudes toward the child. With children, as well as adults, he often used the motto, "Everybody can accomplish everything." Except for certain limitations set by heredity, he strongly believed this maxim and repeatedly emphasized that what children do with what they have is more important than what they have (Adler, 1925/1968, 1956).

CONCEPT OF HUMANITY

Adler believed that people are basically self-determined and that they shape their personalities from the meaning they give to experiences. The building material of personality is provided by heredity and environment, but the creative power shapes this material and puts it to use. Adler frequently emphasized that the use one makes of one's abilities and perceptions is the most crucial factor in determining the value of one's style of life. In discussing an individual's relationship to the outside world, Adler wrote:

It is neither heredity nor environment which determines his relationship to the outside. Heredity only endows him with certain abilities. Environment only gives him certain impressions. These abilities and impressions, and the manner in which he "experiences" them—that is to say, the interpretation he makes of these experiences—are the bricks which he uses in his own "creative" way in building up his attitude toward life. It is his individual way of using these bricks, or in other words his attitude toward life, which determines this relationship to the outside world (Adler, 1956, p. 206).

People's interpretations of experiences are more important than the experiences themselves. Adler held that neither the past nor the future determine present behavior. Instead, people are motivated by present perceptions of the past and present expectations of the future. These perceptions do not necessarily correspond with reality but are a reflection of the individual's psychological needs. Adler stated that "meanings are not determined by situations, but we determine ourselves by the meanings we give to situations" (1956, p. 208).

People are forward-moving, motivated by future goals rather than innate instincts or causal forces. These future goals are often fictional or erroneous, but, because we have internal freedom, we can discover the fiction and thereby change our lives. We create our personalities and are capable of reshaping them through the learning of new attitudes. These attitudes encompass an understanding that change can occur, that no other person or circumstance is responsible for what we are, and that personal goals must be subordinated to social interest.

Is the final goal changeable? If not, how can we be free since psychic life revolves around the final goal? Adler's explanation was that the final goal is fixed during early childhood, but, because it is fictional and unconscious, the individual retains an inner freedom to set and pursue temporary goals. The momentary goals are not rigidly circumscribed by the final goal but are created by the person merely as partial solutions. Adler (1927, p. 24) expressed this idea as follows: "We must understand that the reactions of the human soul are not final and absolute: Every response is but a partial response, valid temporarily, but in no way to be considered a final solution of a problem." In other words, even though the final goal is set during childhood, the person is capable of change at any point in life. However, Adler maintained that even though we have a choice, not all our choices are conscious and that style of life is created through both conscious and unconscious choices.

Adler believed that ultimately we are responsible for our own personalities. Our creative power is capable of transforming feelings of inadequacy into either social interest or into the self-centered goal of personal superiority. This means that we remain free to choose between psychological health and neuroticism. Adler regarded self-centeredness as pathological and established social interest as the standard of psychological maturity. Healthy people have a high level of social interest, but throughout their lives they remain free to accept or reject normality and to become what they will.

On the six dimensions of a concept of humanity listed in Chapter 1, Adler could be rated as follows: high on *free-choice,* very high on *optimism,* very low on *causality,* high on *unconscious* influences, high on *social factors* underlying personality, and high on *uniqueness* of individuals. In summary, Adler held that we are self-determining social creatures, forward-moving, and motivated by present fictions to strive toward perfection for ourselves and society.

CRITIQUE OF ADLER

Even though Individual Psychology is philosophically at the opposite pole from psychoanalysis, as a scientific theory of personality it is faced with many of the same problems encountered by Freudian theory.

The first serious limitation of Adlerian psychology is that some of its tenets do not readily lend themselves to *empirical investigation*. Adler's sweeping statement that "everything can also be different" (1956, p. 194) and his claim that present perceptions shape style of life pose important problems to the researcher. For instance, his concept of birth order cannot be definitively studied. Even when the researcher takes into consideration the sex of siblings and the age spread between children, it remains impossible to confidently hypothesize any specific personality traits. Everything can also be different and a second child can see itself in the role similar to that perceived by most firstborns. Because perceptions of birth order are subjective and many variations are possible, studies on family constellations should be taken as neither confirming nor refuting Individual Psychology.

Early recollections are a more appropriate subject of inquiry than birth order because subjects' perceptions are built into early recollections. Studies on early recollections have generally supported Adler's hypothesis that early memories will be consistent with present style of life. For example, Warren (1982) found that, among normal subjects, early recollections predicted present personality patterns, while Rule and Traver (1982) reported that early recollections could be used to predict certain leisure activities.

However, these results do not prove that present style of life shapes one's early recollections. An alternative, causal explanation is also possible; that is, one could counter that early experiences determine present style of life.

Individual Psychology rests on the assumption that present perceptions are of paramount importance. They are responsible for one's unique manner of striving for success as well as one's selective recall of early childhood experiences. Therefore, as one's self-concept is altered, due to therapy or some other experience, one should recall different aspects of one's earliest memories—aspects that are congruent with a changing style of life. This, of course, can be investigated, but it involves longitudinal rather than cross-sectional studies. Unfortunately, this potentially fruitful area of inquiry into the validity of Adlerian psychology has been largely neglected.

A second weakness of Individual Psychology, and one that also applies to Freudian and Jungian theory, is the lack of *precise operational definitions*. Terms like goal of superiority, style of life, social interest, and especially creative power have no scientific definition. Nowhere in Adler's works are they operationally defined and the potential researcher looks in vain for precise definitions that lend themselves to rigorous study.

The term creative power is an especially illusory one. Just what is this magical force that takes the raw materials of heredity and environment and molds a unique personality? How does the creative power translate itself into specific actions or operations needed by the scientist to carry out an investigation? Unfortunately, Individual Psychology does not provide answers to these questions.

The concept of creative power, of course, is a very appealing one. Probably most people prefer to believe that they are composed of something more than the interactions of heredity and environment. Intuitively, most of us feel that we have some agent (soul, ego, self, creative power) within us that allows us to make choices, to be free, and to create our own personality or style of life. As appealing as it is, however, the concept of creative power simply cannot be scientifically studied. Due to lack of operational definitions, therefore, Individual Psychology is rated low on *internal consistency.*

On a more positive note, Adlerian theory has the power and comprehensiveness to *organize knowledge* into a meaningful framework. Though not as global as Freudian theory, it nevertheless is sufficiently broad to encompass possible explanations for much of what is known about human behavior and development. Since all motivation, even seemingly self-defeating and inconsistent behaviors, can be fit into the framework of striving for superiority, Individual Psychology receives a very high rating on this, the first criterion of a useful theory.

Adler's personality theory must be rated high on both its ability to *generate research* and on its *applicability.* Historically, most of the research generated by Adlerian theory has been in the area of family constellation and birth order. More recently, however, there has been an increase in the number of investigations into some of Adler's more difficult concepts, largely due to the construction of several empirically developed scales that measure these various concepts. For example, Thorne (1975) has devised a 200-item questionnaire called The Life Style Analysis, which purports to measure various Adlerian life styles. Also, Rule (1972) and Rule and Traver (1982) have constructed and utilized an Early Recollections Questionnaire, while Altman (1973) has produced a related inventory called the Early Recollections Ratings Scale of Social Interest Characteristics. In addition, considerable research has been reported on the construction, validation, and use of scales for measuring social interest (Crandall, 1975, 1981, 1984; Crandall & Lehman, 1977; Crandall & Putnam, 1980; Greever, Tseng, & Friedland, 1973, 1974; Mozdzierz & Semyck, 1980; Zarski, Sweeney, & Barcikowski, 1977; Zarski, West, & Bubenzer, 1982).

As for *applicability,* Adlerian theory serves the psychotherapist, the teacher, and the child guidance worker with guidelines for the solution to practical problems in a variety of settings. The practitioner gathers information through obtaining the subject's report on birth order, dreams, early memories, childhood difficulties, and organ deficiencies. This information is then used to understand the style of life. By neither pampering nor neglecting the subject and by demonstrating social interest, the practitioner knows which specific techniques to use to bring about increased acceptance of responsibility and greater freedom of choice within the individual.

The final criterion of a useful theory is *parsimony* and on this standard Individual Psychology can be rated about average. The theory itself is quite unified and relatively simple, especially as extracted and edited by Ansbacher and Ansbacher (Adler, 1956, 1964). However, Adler's complete writings are more awkward and unorganized and, therefore, detract from the theory's rating on parsimony.

CHAPTER SUMMARY

The Individual Psychology of Alfred Adler stands in sharp contrast to Freud's pessimistic view of personality. It suggests that people are self-determined, forward-moving, and motivated by present perceptions. They are capable of putting aside personal needs and of striving for the betterment of all humanity.

This chapter looked at six major tenets of Adlerian theory: (1) unity of personality, (2) the subjectivity of perceptions, (3) striving for superiority or success, (4) social interest, (5) style of life, and (6) creative power. In addition, abnormal development and the applications of Individual Psychology were discussed.

Adler held that all aspects of personality are *unified* and that all actions are *consistent* with one's *final goal* or purpose in life.

Behavior is shaped neither by past events nor by objective reality, but rather by our *subjective perceptions.* Objective realities such as organ deficiencies and order of birth have importance only as they relate to our view of ourselves and our environment.

The essential nature of humans dictates that they will *strive for completion* or improvement. Although all people have this innate tendency, not all strive for the welfare of others. Some are motivated more toward personal superiority. However, those with a high level of social interest strive for success, defined as improvement or upward development for everyone.

Social interest, or a deep concern for the welfare of others, is the sole criterion by which human actions should be judged. The three major problems of life—neighborly love, work, and sexual love—can only be solved through social interest.

Social interest develops in accordance with the person's self-consistent *style of life,* which include's one's final goal, self-concept, feelings toward others, and attitudes toward the world.

The style of life is developed by the individual's *creative power.* Personality is forged from the building materials provided by heredity and environment, but our creative power is ultimately responsible for what we make of ourselves.

Adler insisted that neurotics are different from normal individuals to the extent that they lack social interest. People who perceive themselves to have had exaggerated *physical deficiencies,* a *pampered style of life,* or a *neglected style of life* are most likely to become neurotic. All people, but especially neurotics, make use of various *safeguarding tendencies,* among them *excuses, aggression,* and *withdrawal.* Each of these represents conscious or unconscious attempts to protect inflated feelings of superiority against public disgrace.

The *masculine protest,* or the belief that men are superior to women, lies at the root of many neuroses, both for men and for women.

Adler used *early recollections* and *dreams* in his practice of *psychotherapy.* The goal of Adlerian therapy is to foster courage, self-esteem, and social interest through a healthy relationship between the patient and therapist.

Adler's *concept of humanity* is basically optimistic and purposive. People strive toward a final goal of their own creation and have the potential to bring about significant personality change at any time of life. Although social influences are important, ultimately we are all responsible for who we are and what we do with what we have.

As a scientific theory, Individual Psychology is limited by a lack of operationally defined terms and many of its major tenets elude rigorous empirical investigation. Nevertheless, it provides a useful explanation for much of what is known about human personality and is a helpful model for the practitioner.

Suggested Readings

ADLER, A. (1956). *The individual psychology of Alfred Adler: A systematic presentation in selections from his writings.* H. L. Ansbacher & R. R. Ansbacher (Eds.). New York: Basic Books.

A systematic presentation of Adler's theory and practice, edited by two advocates of Individual Psychology.

ADLER, A. (1979). *Superiority and social interest: A collection of later writings* (3rd ed.). H. L. Ansbacher & R. R. Ansbacher (Eds.). New York: Norton.

A compilation of Adler's later writings designed to supplement the 1956 volume.

ELLENBERGER, H. F. (1970). *The discovery of the unconscious* (Chap. 8). New York: Basic Books.

An unbiased, scholarly chapter on Adler's life and work.

ORGLER, H. (1963). *Alfred Adler. The man and his work: Triumph over the inferiority complex.* New York: Capricorn Books.

A readable account of Adler's life and his personality in light of his psychological theories.

RATTNER, J. (1983). *Alfred Adler.* (H. Zohn, Tans.). New York: Frederick Ungar. (Original work published 1983.)

A pro-Adlerian introduction to Individual Psychology intended for both the lay person and the professional.

JUNG

5

Analytical Psychology

The middle-aged doctor sits at his desk in deep contemplation and concern. A six-year relationship with an older friend and mentor has recently ended on bitter terms and the doctor feels isolated and uncertain of his future. He no longer has confidence in his manner of treating patients and has begun to simply allow them to talk, but he does not offer any specific advice or treatment. For some months now he has been having bizarre, inexplicable dreams and seeing strange mysterious visions. None of this seems to make sense to him. He feels lost and disoriented—unsure whether or not the work he has been trained to do is indeed science.

A moderately gifted artist, he has begun to illustrate his dreams and visions with little or no comprehension of what the finished product means. He has also been writing down his fantasies without really trying to understand them. On this particular day he begins to ponder, "What am I really doing?" He doubts if his work is science, but is uncertain as to what it is. Suddenly, to his astonishment, he hears a clear, distinct feminine voice from within him say, "It is art." He recognizes the voice as that of a gifted female patient who has strong positive feelings for him. He protests to the voice that his work is not art, but no answer is immediately forthcoming. Then, returning to his writing he again hears the voice say, "That is art." When he tries to argue with the voice, no answer comes. He reasons that the "woman within" has no speech center so he suggests that she use his. She does so and a lengthy conversation ensues.

The middle-aged doctor talking to the "woman within" was Carl Gustav Jung and the time was the winter of 1913–14. Jung had been an early admirer and friend of Sigmund Freud, but when theoretical differences arose, their personal relationship broke up, leaving Jung with bitter feelings and a deep sense of loss. He then spent more than three years undergoing what Erikson might call a midlife crisis.

The above story is but one of many strange and bizarre occurrences experienced by Jung during his midlife "confrontation with the unconscious." An interesting account of his unusual journey into the deeper recesses of his psyche is found in his biography, *Memories, Dreams, Reflections* (Jung, 1961). I have chosen Jung himself for the case study to open this chapter because his life history seems to closely parallel and vividly illuminate his theory of personality.

OVERVIEW

Jung firmly believed that occult phenomena can and do influence the lives of all of us. At the same time, however, he believed himself to be a tough-minded empirical scientist. His theory is a compendium of opposing polarities. He viewed people as being both introverted and extraverted; rational and irrational; male and female; conscious and unconscious; and pushed by past events while being pulled by future expectations.

This chapter looks with some detail into the long and colorful life of Carl Jung and uses fragments from his life history to illustrate his concepts and theories. Jung believed that each of us is motivated not only by repressed experiences but also by certain emotionally toned experiences we have inherited from our ancestors. These inherited images form what Jung called the "collective unconscious," which includes those elements we have never experienced individually, but rather have come down to us from our ancestors. The "woman within" with whom Jung had a prolonged conversation represents one element of the collective unconscious. Jung's complex theory is one of the most intriguing of all conceptions of personality.

BIOGRAPHY OF CARL JUNG

Carl Gustav Jung was born on June 26, 1875, in Kesswil, a town on Lake Constance in Switzerland. His paternal grandfather, the elder Carl Gustav Jung, was a prominent physician in Basel and one of the best-known men of that city. It was rumored that he was the illegitimate son of the poet, Goethe. Though the elder Jung never acknowledged the rumor, the younger Jung at least sometimes believed himself to be the great-grandson of Goethe and possibly even his reincarnation. In any event, Jung, who had many mystical experiences, believed that he had lived an earlier life during the eighteenth century (Ellenberger, 1970).

Jung's parents were Paul Jung, a minister, and Emilie Preiswerk Jung, the daughter of a theologian. His mother's family had a tradition of spiritualism and mysticism. His maternal grandfather, Samuel Preiswerk, was a believer in the occult and often talked to the dead. He kept an empty chair for the ghost of his first wife and had regular and intimate conversations with her. Quite understandably, these practices greatly annoyed his second wife. His granddaughter, Helene Preiswerk (Carl Jung's first cousin) was also a medium and the subject of Jung's medical dissertation on the occult phenomenon. It seems, therefore, that Jung's interest in spiritualism and the occult was acquired as part of a family tradition (Ellenberger, 1970).

Jung's parents had three children, an older son, who lived only three days, and a daughter nine years younger than Carl. Carl's sister was never an important rival and did not play a prominent role in his life. Thus Carl's early life was that of an only child.

Jung's father was a sentimental idealist, with strong doubts about his religious faith. His mother was earthy, possessed an animal warmth, and seemed to have had a strong attachment to Carl. At age three Carl was separated from his mother, who had to be hospitalized for several months. This separation deeply troubled young Carl and for a long time after he felt distrustful whenever "love" or "mother" were mentioned.

Jung was an emotional and sensitive child. He felt deeply attached to both parents, but seemed to fear a close relationship with either. His parents' frequent disagreements greatly troubled Carl because he disliked having to take sides. His mother compounded this confusion by treating him as an adult when he was still a child. She confided in him by telling him things she could not reveal to her husband. Despite her attempts to drive a wedge between the boy and his father, Carl retained a deep affection for both parents.

Before Carl's fourth birthday his family moved to a suburb of Basel. It is from this period that his earliest dream stems. This dream, which was to have a profound effect on his later life and on his concept of a collective unconscious, will be recounted later (Jung, 1961).

Jung's first career choice was archeology, but he was also interested in philology, history, philosophy, and the natural sciences. Limited financial resources forced him to attend a school near home, so he enrolled in Basel University, which, however, did not have an archeology teacher. Forced to choose another field, he decided to study natural science after twice dreaming of making important discoveries in the natural world (Jung, 1961). His choice eventually narrowed to medicine.

While still in medical school Jung's father died and Carl became the head of the family, which, at the time, included his mother and sister. After completing his medical degree from Basel University in 1900 he became a psychiatric assistant to Eugene Bleuler at Burghöltzli Mental Hospital in Zürich. During 1902–1903 he studied for six months in Paris with Pierre Janet, successor to Charcot. Upon his return to Switzerland in 1903 he married Emma Rauschenbach, a young woman from a wealthy Swiss family. Two years later he began teaching at the University of Zürich while continuing his duties at the hospital.

This was a period of outward growth and activity in Jung's life. Among other activities at this time, he was busily involved with the International Psychoanalytic Association, developed the word association test, established a family, and conducted a private psychiatric practice, all in addition to his work at Burghöltzli. In Jung's own terminology, this was a period of extraverted activity and progression. He had not yet reached the turning point of his life, a time that was characterized by introverted activity and regression.

In 1909 he gave up his position at Burghöltzli, probably because of a difference of opinion with Bleuler. Four years later he surrendered his instructorship at the University of Zürich to give more time to his private practice in psychiatry and especially to devote his energy to his personal rebirth, a critical undertaking that took the form of a long arduous journey into the unconscious. Jung (1961) felt that it would be unfair to continue teaching young students when his own intellectual life was still a mass of doubt and confusion.

Early in his professional career Jung became acquainted with Freud's ideas by reading *The Interpretation of Dreams* (Freud, 1900/1953). Deeply taken with Freud's writings, he became an early defender of psychoanalysis and a correspondence between the two men began. (See McGuire, 1974 for the Freud/Jung correspondence.) In 1907 Freud invited Jung to Vienna and a warm friendship developed. Freud's respect for the younger man led him to groom Jung as his successor and to select him as first president of the International Psychoanalytic Association. In 1909 the two men journeyed to America to deliver a series of lectures at Clark University. En route, they took great interest in interpreting one another's dreams, a pastime likely to strain any relationship.

In *Memories, Dreams, Reflections*

Jung claims that Freud, on the one hand, was unable to interpret Jung's dreams and, on the other hand, he was reluctant to give Jung the details of his personal life, which Jung needed in order to interpret one of Freud's dreams. According to Jung's account, when asked for intimate details, Freud protested, "But I cannot risk my authority!" (Jung, 1961, p. 158). This comment triggered the end of Jung's filial respect for Freud and probably marked the beginning of the end of their relationship. Back in Europe, personal as well as theoretical differences slowly emerged and the friendship between the two men gradually cooled. In 1913 they terminated their personal correspondence, and the following year Jung resigned his presidency and shortly afterward withdrew his membership in the International Psychoanalytic Association (Brome, 1978).

The years immediately following the break with Freud were filled with loneliness and self-analysis for Jung. From December 1913 until 1917 he underwent the most profound and dangerous experience of his life—a trip through the underground of his own unconscious psyche. This experience bears some similarity to Freud's self-analysis. Both men began their search for self while in their late thirties or early forties, Freud as a reaction to the death of his father; Jung following his split with his spiritual father, Freud. Both underwent a period of loneliness and isolation and both were deeply changed by the experience. However, there were also differences. Freud's self-analysis, though not as intense as Jung's, nevertheless lasted longer and became part of his daily routine for the remainder of his life. Freud was filled with outward activity and published his first great book, *The Interpretation of Dreams* during the early phase of his self-analysis. In contrast, Jung published little during the time of his self-analysis and, instead, by his own account, he turned his energies inward and became acquainted with what he termed his collective unconscious mind. During the period of his self-analysis Jung suspended the formulation of new theoretical concepts, and treated his patients by simply listening to and learning from them.

Jung used the techniques of dream interpretation and active imagination to force himself through his underground journey. (These two techniques will be discussed under the heading, "Jung's Methods of Investigation.") By writing down his dreams, drawing pictures of them, telling himself stories, and then following these stories wherever they moved, he came to an acquaintance with his personal unconscious. (See Jung, 1974, for a collection of many of his paintings during this period.) Prolonging the method and going more deeply, he came upon the contents of the collective unconscious—the archetypes. He heard his anima, in a clear feminine voice, speak to him; he uncovered his shadow, the evil side of his personality; he spoke with the old wise man and the great mother archetypes; and finally, near the end of his journey, he achieved a kind of

psychological rebirth called individuation (Jung, 1961).

Even before his association with Freud, Jung had sown the seeds of his own personality theory. His approach to theory and therapy, known as **Analytical Psychology,** was originally influenced by Freud, but his mature theory is uniquely Jungian.

Though he traveled widely in his study of personality, Jung remained a citizen of Switzerland, residing in Küsnacht, near Zürich. He and his wife, who was also an analyst, had five children, four girls and a boy. Jung was born a Christian, but was not a church-goer. He held honorary degrees from several famous universities, including Harvard, Oxford, and the University of Calcutta. Throughout his career he divided his time between conducting research, lecturing, writing, and seeing patients. His hobbies included wood carving, stone cutting, and sailing his boat on Lake Constance. He also maintained an active interest in alchemy, archeology, Gnosticism, Eastern philosophies, history, religion, mythology, and ethnology.

In 1944 he became professor of medical psychology at the University of Basel, but poor health forced him to resign his position the following year. After his wife died in 1955 he was mostly alone, the "old wise man of Küsnacht." He died on June 6, 1961, in Zürich, three weeks short of his 86th birthday. At the time of his death his reputation was worldwide, extending beyond psychology. Jung is popularly regarded as one of the great thinkers of the twentieth century (Brome, 1978).

STRUCTURE OF THE PSYCHE

Jung, like Freud, based his personality theory on the primary assumption that the mind, or psyche, is divided into an unconscious as well as a conscious realm. Unlike Freud, however, he strongly asserted that the ·most important portion of the unconscious springs, not from personal experiences of the individual, but from the distant past of mankind. The psyche, therefore, can be divided into the **conscious** and the **unconscious,** the latter being subdivided into the **personal unconscious** and the **collective unconscious.**

Conscious

Consciousness is a relative concept. There are no psychic images that are completely conscious, but only differing levels of intensity. Since there is no clear line between the conscious and the unconscious, how are they distinguished from one another? Theoretically, they are differentiated by their relationship to the **ego.** Any psychic material sensed by the ego is conscious; material that is not sensed is unconscious. The ego, then, is the center of consciousness and, in Jungian psychology, is always identified with the conscious psyche. It is not the whole personality, but must be completed by the more comprehensive **self.** Therefore, the ego is the subject of the conscious psyche only, whereas the self is the subject of the whole person, conscious and unconscious (Jung, 1951/1959). (The self will be discussed under "Collective Unconscious.")

Unconscious

The unconscious, that part of the psyche which adds depth and completeness to personality, refers to all psychic processes that are not related to the ego. Unconsciousness includes all previously conscious images that have been repressed or have merely fallen below the threshold of consciousness. In addition, it is composed of psychic elements that have never been conscious. Many of these elements form the seeds of future consciousness, but there are probably some that are not capable of becoming conscious.

Personal Unconscious

The top layer of the unconscious, which embraces all repressed, forgotten, or subliminally perceived experiences of the individual, is known as the "personal unconscious." Jung used the term personal because it pertains exclusively to one particular person. One's personal unconscious owes its existence solely to the individual's experiences and, for this reason, the personal unconscious of each human being is unique. It contains repressed infantile memories and impulses, forgotten events, and experiences originally perceived below the threshold of consciousness. Many of these images can be recalled easily, some remembered with difficulty, and still others are beyond the reach of consciousness. This concept of the personal uncon-

scious differs little from Freud's view of the unconscious and the preconscious (Jung, 1931/1960b).

Contents of the personal unconscious are called **complexes.** A complex is
an emotionally toned conglomeration of associated ideas. For example, a
person's experiences with "Mother" become grouped around a core, which
is loaded with affect. The person's mother, or even the word mother, sparks
an emotional response that may block the smooth flow of thought. Complexes are largely personal, but they may also be partly derived from the collective. In the above example, the mother complex comes not only from
one's personal relationship with mother but also from the entire species'
experiences with mother. In addition, there are conscious aspects of the
mother complex. This means that complexes may be partly conscious and
may stem from both the personal and the collective unconscious (Jung,
1928/1960).

Collective Unconscious

The collective unconscious represents Jung's most controversial and, perhaps his most distinctive, concept. In contrast to the personal unconscious,
which results from individual experiences, the collective unconscious has its
roots in the ancestral past of the entire species. Its contents are inherited,
passing from one generation to the next through the germ plasm. Our distant
ancestors' experiences with God, mother, water, earth, and so forth have
been transmitted through the generations so that people in every clime and
time have been influenced by primitive man's primordial images (Jung,
1937/1959).

The contents of the collective unconscious do not lie dormant, but are
active and influence a person's thoughts, emotions, and actions. They are
revealed through their activity. The collective unconscious is responsible for
people's many myths, legends, and religious beliefs. It also produces some
individual dreams, which Jung calls "big dreams," that is, dreams that have
meaning beyond the individual dreamer and are laden with significance for
all people (Jung, 1948/1960b).

Primitive patterns are formed from the collective unconscious and serve as
prototypes for contemporary people. These ancient models are usually called
archetypes, but Jung at various times refers to them as *primordial images,
mythological images, imagos, dominants,* or *collective symbols.* Archetypes
are ancient or archaic images composing the contents of the collective
unconscious. They are similar to complexes in that they are affectively toned
collections of associated images. But whereas complexes are individualized
and make up the contents of the personal unconscious, archetypes are generalized and compose the contents of the collective unconscious. Archetypes
should also be distinguished from **instincts.** Jung defines an instinct as an
unconscious physical impulse toward action, while he sees the archetype as
the psychic counterpart of an instinct. Both archetypes and instincts impel a
person to action and in both cases the person remains unconscious of the
true motives behind the action. Simply, then, instincts are unconsciously

determined physiological drives, while archetypes are unconsciously determined psychological drives (Jung, 1948/1960a).

Jung believed that archetypes originated through the repeated experiences of our early ancestors. The potential for countless numbers of archetypes exists within each person, and when a personal experience corresponds to the latent primordial image, the archetype becomes activated and its effects are felt in personal life.

The archetype itself cannot be directly represented, but, when activated, expresses itself through several modes, primarily dreams, fantasies, and delusions. During his midlife encounter with his unconscious, Jung had many archetypal dreams and fantasies. He frequently initiated fantasies by imagining that he was descending into a deep cosmic abyss. He could make little sense of his visions and dreams at that time, but later, when he began to understand that dream images and fantasy figures were actually archetypes, these experiences took on a completely new meaning (Jung, 1961).

Dreams are the main source of archetypal material and certain dreams offer what Jung considers proof for the existence of the archetype. These dreams produce motifs that could not have been known to the dreamer through personal experience. The motifs often coincide with those known to the ancients or to natives of contemporary aboriginal tribes. A vivid illustration is found in one of Jung's earliest dreams, which took place before his fourth birthday. He dreamed he was in a meadow when suddenly he saw a dark rectangular hole in the ground. Fearfully he descended a flight of stairs and at the bottom encountered a doorway with a round arch covered by a heavy green curtain. Behind the curtain was a dimly lit room with a red carpet running from the entrance to a low platform. On the platform was a throne and on the throne was an elongated object that appeared to Jung to be a large tree trunk.

> It was a huge thing, reaching almost to the ceiling. But it was of a curious composition: it was made of skin and naked flesh, and on top there was something like a rounded head with no face and no hair. On the very top of the head was a single eye, gazing motionlessly upward (Jung, 1961, p. 12).

Filled with terror, the young boy heard his mother say, "Yes, just look at him. That is the man-eater!" This frightened him even more and jolted him awake.

Jung thought often about the dream, but it took 30 years before the obvious phallus became apparent to him and an additional number of years before he could accept the dream as an expression of his collective unconscious rather than the product of a personal memory-trace. In his own interpretation of the dream, the rectangular hole represents death; the green curtain symbolizes the mystery of Earth with her green vegetation; the red carpet signifies blood; and the tree, resting majestically on a throne, is the erect penis anatomically accurate in every detail. After interpreting the dream, Jung was forced to conclude that no three-and-one-half year old boy could produce such universally symbolic material solely from his own experiences. A collective unconscious, common to the species, was the only explanation (Jung, 1961).

Hallucinations of psychotic patients also offer evidence for universal archetypes. In 1906, while working as a psychiatric assistant at Burghöltzli, Jung observed a paranoid schizophrenic patient looking through a window at the sun. The patient begged the young psychiatrist to observe too:

> He said I must look at the sun with eyes half shut, and then I could see the sun's phallus. If I moved my head from side to side the sun-phallus would move too, and that was the origin of the wind (Jung, 1931/1960b, p. 150).

Four years later Jung came across a book by the German philologist Albrecht Dieterich; it had been edited in 1910, but was originally published in 1903, still some years after the patient was committed. The book, written in Greek, dealt with a liturgy derived from the so-called Paris magic papyrus, which described an ancient rite of the worshippers of Mithras, the Persian god of light. In this liturgy, the initiate was asked to look at the sun until he could see a tube hanging from it. The tube, swinging toward the east and west, was the origin of the wind. Dieterich's account of the sun-phallus of the Mithraic cult was nearly identical to the hallucination of the mental patient, who, almost certainly, had no personal knowledge of the ancient initiation rite. Jung offers many similar examples as proof of the existence of archetypes and the collective unconscious (Jung, 1931/1960b).

As noted in Chapter 2, Freud also believed in a collective unconscious, although his concept of "phylogenetic endowment" differs somewhat from Jung's formulation. The first difference is a matter of emphasis. Freud looked first to the personal unconscious; only when individual explanations failed did he resort to the collective. Jung, on the other hand, placed primary emphasis on the collective unconscious and used personal experiences to round out the total personality. The major distinction between the two, though, was Jung's differentation of the collective unconscious into autonomous forces called *archetypes,* each with a life and a personality of its own. Though there is a nearly infinite number of archetypes, a few have evolved to the point where they can be conceptualized. The most notable of these include the persona, shadow, anima, animus, great mother, old wise man, the hero, and the self.

The Persona.   That side of personality one shows to the world is designated as the **persona.** The term is well-chosen, for it refers to the mask worn by actors in the early theater. Society dictates a particular role for each of us. The physician must adopt a characteristic "bedside manner," the truck driver must look and act like a truck driver, and the actress must exhibit the style of life demanded by her public (Jung, 1916/1953).

In Jung's psychology of opposites, the persona is opposed to the individual. To the extent we are conscious of our persona, we remain unconscious of our individuality; to the extent we actualize our individuality, we are unconcerned about our persona. We must acknowledge society, but there is a distinct danger of overidentifying with our persona and losing our individuality completely to unconsciousness. Everyone must strike a balance between the persona and the individual, that is, between the demands of society and what one truly is. To be unaware of one's persona, Jung believed, is to underestimate the importance of society, whereas to be unaware of one's individuality is to be nothing (Jung, 1950/1959).

During Jung's near break with reality from 1913 to 1917, he struggled hard to remain in touch with his persona. He knew that he must retain a normal life, and his work and family provided that contact. He was frequently forced to tell himself, "I have a medical diploma from a Swiss university, I must help my patients, I have a wife and five children, I live at 228 Seestrasse in Künacht" (Jung, 1961, p. 189). Such self-talk kept Jung's feet rooted to the ground and reassured him that he really existed.

The Shadow.   The **shadow,** the archetype of darkness and repression, represents those qualities we do not wish to acknowledge, but attempt to hide from ourselves and others. The inferior or animal side of personality, the shadow consists not only of morally objectionable tendencies but also of a number of constructive creative qualities, such as instincts and other archetypes that we, nevertheless, are reluctant to face (Jung, 1951/1959).

Jung contended that to be whole one must continually strive to know his or her shadow and this quest is a person's *first test of courage.* It is easier to project the dark side of personality onto others, to see in them the ugliness and evil that one refuses to see in oneself. To come to grips with the darkness within oneself is to achieve the "realization of the shadow." Unfortunately, most people never realize their shadow, for to do so would entail a courageous kind of self-analysis, comparable to the one undertaken by Jung during his middle years. Instead, most people choose to identify only with the bright side of their personality. Those who never realize their shadow may, nevertheless, come under its power. These people lead tragic lives, constantly running into "bad luck" and reaping harvests of defeat and discouragement for themselves (Jung, 1954/1959a.).

In *Memories, Dreams, Reflections* Jung (1961) reported a dream in which his shadow, a brown-skinned savage, killed the hero, a man named Siegfried who represented the German people. Siegfried (Sigmund Freud) was no longer needed by Jung, so the task fell to the shadow to eradicate the former hero.

The Anima.   Like Freud, Jung believed that all humans are essentially bisexual and possess both a masculine and a feminine side. The feminine side of man, called the **anima,** originates in the collective unconscious as an archetype and remains extremely resistant to consciousness. Few men become well-acquainted with their anima because this task requires courage of the greatest magnitude. It is far easier to become acquainted with one's shadow, which merely demands that one overcome moral obstacles such as vanity and conceit and admit the inferior side of one's nature. To overcome the projections of the anima, however, a man must, in addition, overcome intellectual barriers, delve into the far recesses of the unconscious, and realize the feminine side of his personality. In Jungian therapy the shadow must be realized before the anima can be recognized (Jung, 1954/1959a, 1954/1959b).

The anima originated from early man's experiences with women—mother, sisters, and lovers—which combined to form a generalized picture of woman. That global concept was embedded in the collective unconscious of all men as the anima archetype. Since the dawn of mankind, every man has come into the world with a predetermined concept of womanhood that shapes and molds all his relationships with individual women. A man is especially inclined to project his anima on his wife and see her not as she really is but as his personal and collective unconscious have determined her. This is the cause of much misunderstanding in marriage, but it is also responsible for the alluring mystique woman has in the minds of men.

The anima is the source of much of man's attitudes and personality. She is responsible for the superhuman qualities men attribute to their mothers, and helps explain why one man might choose to insult another by making disparaging references to his mother. The anima is also responsible for the feeling side in man and is the explanation for certain irrational moods and feelings. During these moods a man almost never admits that his feminine side is casting her spell, but instead, either ignores the irrationality of the feelings or tries to explain them in a very rational masculine manner. In either event he denies that an autonomous archetype, the anima, is responsible for his mood.

At the beginning of this chapter we saw that the cunning, seductive anima was trying to convince Jung that his work was art, not science. Jung (1961, p. 187) interpreted this experience further.

> What the anima said seemed to me full of a deep cunning. If I had taken these fantasies of the unconscious as art, they would have carried no more conviction than visual perceptions, as if I were watching a movie. I would have felt no moral obligation toward them. The anima might then have easily seduced me into believing that I was a misunderstood artist, and that my so-called artistic nature gave me the right to neglect reality. If I had followed her voice, she would in all probability have said to me one day, "Do you imagine the nonsense you're engaged in is really art? Not a bit." Thus the insinuations of the anima, the mouthpiece of the unconscious, can utterly destroy a man.

The Animus. The masculine archetype in women is called the **animus.** While the anima represents irrational moods and feelings, the animus is symbolic of thinking and reasoning. It is capable of influencing the thinking of a woman, yet it does not actually belong to her. It belongs to the collective unconscious and originates from prehistoric woman's encounters with men. In every relationship a woman has with a man she runs the risk of projecting her distant ancestors' experiences with fathers, brothers, lovers, and sons onto the unsuspecting male. In addition, of course, her personal experiences with men, buried in her personal unconscious, enter into her relationships with men. Couple this with projections from the man's anima and with images from his personal unconscious and one has the basic ingredients of any male-female relationship. How much room remains for genuine opinions and feelings based on the individuality of the other person? Is it any wonder that a man and a woman may find one another perplexing and have trouble in relating to one another?

Jung believed that the animus is responsible for thinking and opinion in women just as the anima produces feelings and moods in men. The animus is also the explanation for the irrational thinking and illogical opinions often attributed to women. Many opinions held by women are objectively valid, but according to Jung, on closer analysis it becomes apparent that they were not thought out, but existed ready-made. If a woman is dominated by her animus, no logical or emotional appeal can shake her from her prefabricated beliefs (Jung, 1951/1959a).

Both anima and animus appear in dreams, visions, and fantasies in a personified form. A man may dream about a woman with no definite image and no particular identity. The woman represents no one from his personal experience, but enters his dream from the depths of his collective unconscious. The anima need not appear in dreams as a woman, but can be represented by a feeling or mood (Jung, 1945/1953).

The Great Mother.   Two other archetypes, the great mother and the old wise man, are derivatives of the anima and animus. Everyone, male or female, possesses a **great mother** archetype. This preexisting concept of mother is always associated with both positive and negative feelings. Jung, for example, often spoke of the "loving and terrible mother" (Jung, 1954/1959c). The great mother represents two opposing forces—fertility and nourishment on the one hand and power and destruction on the other. She is capable of producing and sustaining life, but may also devour or destroy her offspring. This all-possessive character of the great mother may sometimes devour the anima in a man and prevent him from separating the concepts of woman and mother. A man dominated by the great mother archetype possesses an incapacitating *mother complex* and never achieves the autonomy necessary to gain psychological maturity since his view of women is stunted.

The fertility and nourishment dimension of the great mother archetype is symbolized by a tree, garden, plowed field, the sea, heaven, home, country, church, the mandala, and hollow objects such as ovens and cooking utensils. Since the great mother also represents power and destruction, she is sometimes symbolized as a *grand*mother, the Mother of God, Mother Nature, Mother Earth, mother-in-law, or a witch. Fertility and power combine to form the concept of *rebirth,* which may be a separate archetype, but its relation to the great mother is obvious. Rebirth is represented by such processes as reincarnation, baptism, resurrection, and individuation. This concept always remains somewhat unconscious due to the fact that it derives from an inherited archetypal image (Jung, 1952/1956, 1954/1959c).

absence of a close personal relationship, was taken by Jung as evidence for the great mother archetype. Legends, myths, religious beliefs, art, and literature of all kinds are filled with symbols of the great mother.

The Old Wise Man.   The archetype of wisdom and meaning, the **old wise man,** symbolizes our preexisting knowledge of the mysteries of life. This archetypal meaning, however, is unconscious and cannot be directly or individually experienced. In fact, it is dangerous to believe that we personally possess this wisdom, and this danger is compounded if the illogical anima is dominant and a man speaks profoundly and prophetically on the major issues of life. His words often sound enlightened and sensible to others who are all too willing to be misled by their own old wise man archetypes. The man dominated by the old wise man archetype may gather a large following of disciples with his impressive verbiage, but his words make little sense, since the collective unconscious cannot directly impart its wisdom to an individual. Political, religious, and social prophets who appeal to reason as well as emotion (archetypes are always emotionally tinged) are guided by this unconscious archetype. The danger to society comes when the man attains power and his pseudoknowledge is mistaken for real wisdom.

The old wise man archetype is personified in dreams as father, grandfather, teacher, philosopher, guru, doctor, or priest. He appears in fairy tales as the king, the sage, or the magician who comes to the aid of the troubled hero and, through superior wisdom, helps him escape from his current misadventures. The old wise man is also symbolized by Life itself. Literature is replete with stories of young men leaving home, venturing out into the world, experiencing the trials and sorrows of Life, and in the end acquiring a measure of wisdom (Jung, 1954/1959a).

The Hero.   The **hero** archetype is represented in mythology and legends as a powerful man, sometimes part god, who fights against great odds to conquer or vanquish evil in the form of dragons, monsters, serpents, or demons. In the end, however, the hero is often undone by some seemingly insignificant person or event (Jung, 1951/1959b). For example, Achilles, the courageous hero of the Trojan War, was killed by an arrow in his only vulnerable spot—his heel. Similarly, Macbeth was a heroic figure with a single tragic flaw—ambition. This was also the source of his greatness, but it contributed to his fate and his downfall.

The image of the hero touches an archetype within us, as demonstrated by our fascination with the heroes of movies, novels, plays, and television programs. When the hero conquers the villain he frees us from feelings of impotence and misery, at the same time, serving as our model for the ideal personality (Jung, 1934/1954).

The origin of the hero motif goes back to earliest human history—to the dawn of consciousness. In conquering the villain, the hero is symbolically overcoming the darkness of prehuman unconsciousness. The achievement of consciousness was one of our ancestors' greatest accomplishments and the image of the archetypal conquering hero represents victory over the forces of darkness (Jung, 1951/1959b).

The Self.   As we have seen, the self represents the whole personality, including the conscious ego, the personal unconscious, and each of the collective unconscious archetypes. Nevertheless, our image of an evolving self (self-realization) is a separate archetype and is symbolized by our ideas of perfection, completion, or wholeness. Like the other archetypes, the self possesses conscious and personal unconscious components, but it is mostly formed by collective unconscious images.

As an archetype, the self is represented by the **mandala** or magic circle. The mandala motif is depicted as a square within a circle, a circle within a square, or any other concentric figure. The mandala represents the strivings of the collective unconscious for unity, balance, and wholeness.

Besides being an archetype the self is the whole personality, including ego-consciousness, the collective and personal unconscious, the persona, shadow, anima, and animus. It must never be confused with the ego, which represents consciousness only. Figure 5.1 shows that the ego is but a part of the total self. Ego-consciousness is represented by the small circle; the personal unconscious is represented by the square; and the collective unconscious is represented by the large circle. Only four archetypes—the persona, shadow, anima, and animus—have been drawn in this mandala. Each is part conscious, part personal unconscious, and part collective unconscious. The figure depicts each as being the same size and shape, but in reality this equality would not be found. In most people the anima and animus are more resistant to consciousness than the shadow, and the shadow in turn is more resistant than the persona. The balance between the ego and the self is also idealistic. Self-realization, however, can only be achieved if a balance does exist. People with inflated egos lack the "soul spark" of personality; that is, they fail to realize the richness and vitality of their personal unconscious and, especially, of their collective unconscious. On the other hand, people whose egos are overpowered by their unconscious are often pathological and possess neither definite egos nor well-balanced personalities (Jung, 1951/1959).

Though the self is almost never perfectly balanced, each person has in the collective unconscious a concept of the perfect, unified self. The mandala represents the perfect self, the archetype of order, unity, and totality. Since self-realization involves completeness and wholeness, it is represented by the same symbol of perfection (the mandala) that sometimes signifies divinity. In the collective unconscious the self appears as an ideal personality, sometimes taking the form of Jesus Christ, Buddha, or other deified figures.

Jung finds evidence for the self archetype in the mandala symbols that appear in dreams and fantasies of contemporary people who have never been conscious of their meaning. Historically, people produced countless mandalas without appearing to have understood their full significance. Further evidence of the mandala as a symbol of order and unity is seen in the increased delusions of psychotic patients at the exact time they are under-

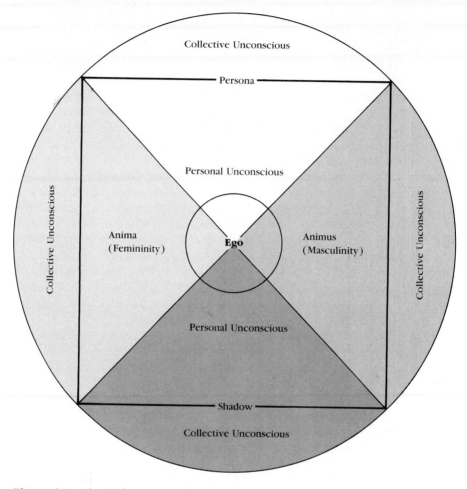

Figure 5.1 The Self

going a period of serious psychic disorder. It is as if the unconscious symbol of order counterbalances the conscious manifestation of disorder (Jung, 1951/1959a).

In summary, the self is the center of personality, including both the conscious and unconscious mind. As the total personality it unites the opposing elements of psyche—male and female, good and evil, light and dark forces. These opposing elements are often represented by the *Yang* and *Yin* (see Figure 5.2), while the self is usually symbolized by the mandala. This latter motif stands for unity, totality, and order; in a word, self-realization. Complete self-realization is seldom if ever achieved, but as an ideal it exists within the collective unconscious of everyone. In order to actualize or fully experience the self, a person must overcome fear of the unconscious; achieve a balance between the persona and the individual; recognize the shadow as

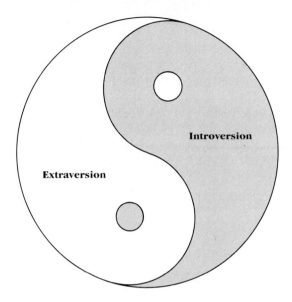

Figure 5.2 The *Yang* and *Yin*

one's own, that is, come to grips with the dark side of the self; and then muster even greater courage to face the anima or animus. Having accomplished all this, the person becomes whole, that is, self-realized.

On one occasion during Jung's midlife crisis he had a vision in which he confronted a bearded old man and a beautiful but blind young girl. The old man explained that he was Elijah and that the young girl was Salome, both biblical figures. A large black snake was living with them. Elijah had a certain, sharp intelligence, although Jung did not clearly understand him. Salome gave Jung a feeling of distinct suspiciousness, while the serpent showed a remarkable fondness for Jung. At the time he experienced this vision, Jung was unable to comprehend its meaning, but many years later he came to see the three figures as archetypes. Elijah represented the old wise man, seemingly intelligent, but not making a good deal of sense; the blind Salome was the anima, beautiful and seductive, but unable to see the meaning of things; and the snake was the counterpart of the hero, showing an affinity for Jung, the hero of the vision (Jung, 1961). Jung believed that he had to identify these unconscious images in order to maintain his own identity and not lose himself to the powerful forces of the collective unconscious. He later wrote:

> The essential thing is to differentiate oneself from these unconscious contents by personifying them, and at the same time to bring them into relationship with consciousness. That is the technique for stripping them of their power. It is not too difficult to personify them, as they always possess a certain degree of autonomy, a separate identity of their own. Their autonomy is a most uncomfortable thing to reconcile oneself to, and yet the very fact that the unconscious presents itself in that way gives us the best means of handling it (Jung, 1961, p. 187).

Attitudes

In addition to the three divisions of the psyche, there are two basic attitudes—introversion and extraversion—and four separate functions—thinking, feeling, sensing, and intuiting—which contribute to the structure of the psyche.

Jung insisted that each person has both an introverted and an extraverted attitude. If introversion is conscious, then extraversion is unconscious; if extraversion is conscious, then introversion is unconscious. Like other opposing forces in Analytical Psychology, introversion and extraversion serve in a compensatory relationship to one another and can be illustrated by the *Yang* and *Yin* motif (see Figure 5.2).

An **attitude** is a predisposition to act or react in a characteristic direction. The term should be distinguished from **type,** which is a more general concept that includes both attitudes and functions. When the two attitudes combine with the four functions, eight possible types or categories are produced.

Introversion

According to Jungian psychology, **introversion** is the turning inward of psychic energy with an orientation toward the subjective. Introverts are tuned in to their inner world with all its biases, fantasies, dreams, and individualized perceptions. These people perceive the external world, of course, but do so selectively and with their own subjective view (Jung, 1921/1971).

The introverted personality is clearly illustrated by Jung himself during his midlife confrontation with the unconscious. His conversations with his anima, his bizarre dreams, and his self-induced visions were the "stuff of psychosis" (Jung, 1961, p. 188). His fantasy life was individualized and subjective. Other people, including even Jung's wife, could not accurately comprehend what he was experiencing. During this time he suspended or discontinued much of his extraverted or objective attitude. He no longer actively treated his patients, he resigned his position as lecturer at the University of Zürich, he stopped his theoretical writing, and for three years, he found himself "utterly incapable of reading a scientific book" (Jung, 1961, p. 193). He was in the process of discovering the introverted pole of his existence.

Jung's voyage of discovery, however, was not totally introverted. He knew that unless he retained some objective hold on the outer world he would risk becoming absolutely possessed by his inner world. Afraid that he might become completely psychotic, he, therefore, forced himself to continue as much of a normal life as possible with his family and his profession. By this technique, Jung eventually emerged from his inner journey and established a balance between introversion and extraversion.

Extraversion

In contrast to introversion, **extraversion** is the attitude characterized by the turning outward of the psychic energy so that the person is oriented toward the objective and away from the subjective. Extraverts are more influenced by their surroundings than by their inner world. They tend to focus on the objective attitude while suppressing the subjective. They are somewhat pragmatic and well-rooted in the realities of everyday life. At the same time, they are overly suspicious of the subjective attitude, whether their own or that of someone else.

No designation of worth should be placed on introversion or extraversion. Each tendency has strengths as well as weaknesses but, unfortunately, there is a common tendency for introverts and extraverts to undervalue one another.

Introversion and extraversion must not be regarded as pure types. They are merely concepts that indicate a person's tendency to be influenced by either the subjective or the objective world.

Functions

Both introversion and extraversion can combine with any one or more of four functions, forming eight possible orientations. The four functions—sensation, thinking, feeling, and intuition—can be briefly defined as follows. **Sensation** tells us what something is; **thinking** enables us to recognize its meaning; **feeling** tells us its value; and **intuition** allows us to "see around corners" and gain knowledge of it without knowing how we know.

Thinking

Logical intellectual activity that produces a chain of ideas is called "thinking." People who habitually use this function in their adaptation to the world are known as thinking types. A thinking type can be either extraverted or introverted, depending on one's basic attitude.

Extraverted thinking flows primarily from objective phenomena and is essentially a conscious process. Extraverted-thinking persons rely heavily on concrete thoughts, but may also use abstract ideas if these ideas have been transmitted to them from without, for example, from parents or teachers. Mathematicians and engineers make frequent use of extraverted thinking in their work. Accountants, too, are extraverted-thinking types since they must be objective and not subjective in their approach to numbers. Not all objective thinking, however, is productive. If too little individual interpretation is brought to objective data, the resulting process is merely the presentation of previously known facts, with no originality or creativity (Jung, 1921/1971).

Thinking involves a subject (the thinker) and an object (the ideas thought about). In this sense, thinking is both subjective and objective, but when the subjective is dominant it is called *introverted thinking*. Introverted-thinking people react to external stimuli, but their interpretation of an event is colored more by the internal meaning they bring with them than by the objective facts themselves. Inventors and philosophers are often introverted-thinking types because they react to the objective world in a highly subjective and creative manner, interpreting old data in new ways. When carried to an extreme, introverted thinking results in unproductive mystical thoughts that are so individualized that they are useless to any other person (Jung, 1921/1971).

Feeling

The process of valuing an idea or event is called "feeling." This definition is more narrow than the one commonly used. In Analytical Psychology, the term feeling is limited to affective *value* responses, such as "I feel sorry for him," or "That is a funny story." It excludes the processes of sensing and intuiting, which are sometimes confused with the feeling function. When a person says, "This surface feels smooth," she is using her sensing function, and when she says, "I have a feeling that this will be my lucky day," she is intuiting, not feeling.

The feeling function is distinguished from emotion. Feeling is the valuation of every conscious activity, even those valued as indifferent. Most of these valuations have no emotional content, but are capable of becoming emotions if their intensity increases to the point of stimulating physiological changes within the person. Feelings, however, are not unique in this ability. Any of the four functions can lead to emotion when their strength is increased.

Like any of the other functions, feeling can be either extraverted or introverted. *Extraverted-feeling types* use objective data to make valuations. They are not guided so much by their subjective opinion, as by external values and widely accepted standards of judgment. They are likely to be at ease in social situations, knowing on the spur of the moment what to say and how to say it. They are usually well liked because of their sociability, but in their quest to conform to social standards they may appear artificial, cold, and unreliable. Their value judgments will have an easily detectable false ring. Extraverted-feeling people often become businessmen or politicians because these professions demand and reward the making of value judgments based on objective information (Jung, 1921/1971).

The *introverted-feeling attitude* is found in people who base their value judgments primarily on subjective perceptions rather than objective facts. Critics of the various art forms make much use of this attitude since their judgments are based heavily on subjective individualized data. When one's entire attitude is colored by subjective valuations, the person is known as an introverted-feeling type. These people have an individualized conscience, a taciturn demeanor, and an unfathomable psyche. They ignore traditional opinions and beliefs, and their nearly complete indifference to the objective (including people) often causes persons around them to feel uncomfortable and to cool their attitude toward them (Jung, 1921/1971).

Sensation

The psychic function that receives physical stimuli and transmits them to perceptual consciousness is called "sensation." Sensation is not identical to the physical stimulus, but is simply the individual's perception of sensory impulses. These perceptions are not dependent on logical thinking or feeling, but exist as absolute, elementary facts within each person.

Sensations may be perceived with either an extraverted or an introverted attitude. People with an *extraverted-sensing attitude* perceive external stimuli objectively, in much the same way that they exist in reality. Their sensations are not greatly influenced by their subjective attitudes. This facility is essential in such occupations as proofreader, house painter, wine taster, or any other job demanding sensory discriminations congruent with those of most people (Jung, 1921/1971).

A person in tune with subjective sensations is said to have an *introverted-sensing attitude.* This attitude can be illustrated by asking several people to describe or reproduce accurately a picture exposed to them for a short length of time. Extraverted-sensing persons will vary little in their reproductions, whereas introverted-sensing persons will differ greatly in their interpretations. Portrait artists, especially those whose paintings are extremely personalized, could be considered to have an introverted-sensing attitude. They give a subjective interpretation to objective phenomena, yet are able to communicate meaning to others. When the subjective-sensing attitude is carried to its extreme, however, it may result in hallucinations or esoteric ramblings that lie beyond the comprehension of other people (Jung, 1921/1971).

Intuition

Intuiting is the most difficult function to understand or describe since it involves perception beyond the workings of consciousness. Intuition, like sensation, is based on the perception of absolute elementary facts, ones which provide the raw material for the thinking and feeling functions. It differs from sensation in that it is more creative, often adding or subtracting elements from conscious sensation.

Intuition, too, can be extraverted or introverted. *Extraverted intuitive people* are oriented toward facts in the external world. Rather than fully sensing them, however, they merely perceive them subliminally. Since strong sensory stimuli interfere with intuition, the intuitive person suppresses many sensations and continues to be guided by hunches and guesses contrary to sensory data. An example of an extraverted intuitive type might be the inventor who must inhibit distracting sensory data and concentrate on unconscious solutions to objective problems. The inventor may create things which fill a need few people realized existed. Often the inventor also remains unaware of the inner workings of the inventive process (Jung, 1921/1971).

Introverted intuition is unconscious perception of facts that are basically subjective. These internal facts usually have little or no resemblance to external reality, but exist in the unconscious as psychological reality. Subjective intuitive perceptions are often remarkably strong and are capable of motivating decisions of monumental magnitude. Introverted intuitive people often appear peculiar to others. One may be a mystic, a prophet, a surrealistic artist, a religious or social fanatic. They may even be martyrs willing to sacrifice their lives, not so much for a logical belief, but for a strongly felt cause. They

ATTITUDES

FUNCTIONS		Introversion	Extraversion
	Thinking	Philosophers, Theoretical Scientists, Certain Inventors	Research Scientists, Accountants, Mathematicians
	Feeling	Subjective Movie Critics, Editorial Writers	Real Estate Appraisers, Objective Movie Critics, Politicians
	Sensation	Artists, Classical Musicians	Wine Tasters, Proofreaders, House Painters, Popular Musicians
	Intuition	Prophets, Mystics, Religious Fanatics	Certain Inventors, Religious Reformers

Figure 5.3 Examples of Different Types

may not clearly comprehend their motivations, but nevertheless are deeply moved by them (Jung, 1921/1971).

The eight Jungian types with some possible examples are seen in Figure 5.3. In addition, Myers (1962) has developed an inventory to assess these and other types (see Box—"The Myers-Briggs as an Indicator of Jungian Typology").

The functions usually appear in a hierarchy, with one occupying a *superior* position, another a *secondary* position, and the other two *inferior* positions. Jung regarded *thinking* and *feeling* as **rational functions** since they require reason and judgment. Both functions rely on raw data gathered through analyzing and synthesizing sensation and intuition, making deductions, and drawing conclusions. In other words, both are involved in the reasoning process; thinking is required in intellectual decisions, feeling in value judgments. The processes of thinking and feeling are always rational but the decisions and judgments are not necessarily valid or "reasonable." *Sensation* and *intuition,* on the other hand, are **irrational functions.** They are not subject to the laws of reason since both involve the immediate perception of data. There is no judgment or reasoning involved. Facts gathered through sensation and intuition have an absolute existence independent of the rational functions.

Since thinking and feeling are both rational, they are competitive with one another, as are the two irrational functions, sensation and intuition. In the hierarchy of functions, if a rational function is superior, an irrational one will be secondary. If an irrational function is superior, the rational function will be inferior. In other words, Jung believed that thinking and feeling normally combine with either sensation or intuition, while sensation and intuition will have either thinking or feeling as a second function.

Most people cultivate only one function so that they characteristically approach a situation relying on the one dominant or superior function. Some people develop two functions, and a few very mature individuals have cultivated three. A person who has theoretically achieved self-realization or individuation would have all four functions highly developed.

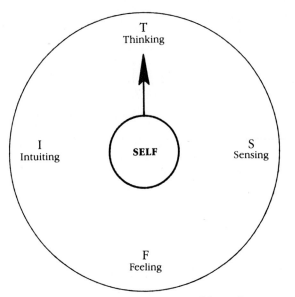

Figure 5.4   The four functions are like points on a compass, with the self facing one direction, but using all four points as guides.

In his later years, long after his journey into the unconscious, Jung came close to developing all four functions. He relied on thinking to construct his theoretical models; on feeling to judge the value of his and other works; on sensation to paint pictures and carve figures; and on intuition to interpret his dreams and fantasies.

The four functions are like the points on a compass, with the self in the center facing a given direction, but using all four points as guides (Jung, 1921/1971) (see Figure 5.4).

DYNAMICS OF THE PSYCHE

We have seen Jung's concept of the structure of personality, that is, the three different layers of consciousness and the basic attitudes and functions. Now we turn to a consideration of the dynamics of the psyche. What is the nature of the energy that moves us?

Jung made no distinction between physical and psychic energy. The same laws or principles apply to both. In this section we look at the principles of *equivalence and entropy,* the concepts of *causality and teleology,* and Jung's ideas on *progression and regression.*

Principles of Equivalence and Entropy

From physics, Jung borrowed the principles of equivalence and entropy to explain human motivation. The first law of thermodynamics is the *principle of equivalence.* It states that when a given quantity of energy is expended in the performance of an activity, an equal amount of energy will appear elsewhere (Jung, 1928/1960). In other words, energy cannot be destroyed, but is merely displaced. Transferred to psychology, this principle holds that for each psychic system a given quantity of energy is available, either actually or potentially. When one psychic function no longer demands a constant expenditure of energy, that same amount of energy is available to perform a second function. The total amount of energy, however, remains the same. For example, the establishment and maintenance of a repression demands the expenditure of a certain amount of psychic energy. If the repressed material continually and forcefully threatens to emerge into consciousness, more energy must be taken from other sources to maintain the repression. As a result, the person is handicapped in intellectual functioning, interpersonal relationships, and other activities demanding free use of psychic energy. Most repressions, however, drain only small amounts of psychic energy, thus freeing the remainder to perform other psychic functions.

An example of the principle of equivalence is found in the adolescent boy deeply in love and infatuated with an older girl. The large amount of energy he expends on his beloved is diverted from that previously used in concentration on academic and athletic activities. After the infatuation wears off, there is a noticeable improvement in both schoolwork and sports.

The second law of thermodynamics is the *principle of entropy,* which states that when objects of different temperatures meet, heat flows from the hotter one into the colder one, bringing about an equalization of temperature. In Jungian psychology the principle of entropy holds that the greater the differences between two poles, the greater the tension generated by them and the longer lasting and more satisfying the resulting attitude.

An example of the principle of entropy is seen in the opposing attitudes of introversion and extraversion. In the beginning, these two opposing forces compete actively against one another, generating great amounts of tension. If the two attitudes are relatively equal in strength, a new attitude somewhere at the midpoint of the poles will emerge and gradually stabilize. If, however, one attitude is relatively unconscious, its influence on its conscious opposing pole will be small and little tension will develop.

The principle of entropy can also be stated this way: the stronger the conflict within a person, the greater the measure of psychic energy flowing from the conflict. Once resolved, strong conflict situations lead to an equalization of tension, a relatively permanent attitude, and the pleasant experience of overcoming a troublesome obstacle. This explains why there is more satisfaction in conquering a formidable opponent than in defeating an easy one.

The principle of entropy is responsible for the stability (sometimes called tranquility or rigidity depending on point of view) of values in older people. After the stormy tensions unleashed in youth by the confrontation of opposites, psychic energy gradually achieves a leveling process and attitudes, opinions, and prejudices become solidified. Older people do not necessarily possess less psychic energy than younger ones; they merely transform the oscillating activity of youth into the balanced stability of old age (Jung, 1928/ 1960).

Causality and Teleology

Does motivation spring from past causes or from teleological goals? Jung insisted that it comes from both. Causality holds that present events have their origin in previous experiences. Freud, for example, relied heavily on a causal viewpoint in his explanations of adult behavior in terms of early childhood experiences. Jung criticized Freud for being onesided in his emphasis on causality, insisting that a causal view could never explain all motivation. Conversely, teleology holds that present events are motivated by future goals and aspirations that direct one's destiny. Adler, for example, held this position, insisting that people are motivated by unconscious perceptions of fictional final goals. Jung was less critical of Adler, but he insisted that human behavior is shaped by *both* causal and teleological forces, and that causal explanations be balanced with teleological ones.

Jung's insistence on balance is seen in his conception of dreams. Many dreams, he contended, have their origins in past events, that is, they are *caused* by earlier experiences, essentially a Freudian view. On the other hand, Jung claimed that some dreams are prophetic, and proper interpretation can reveal *future* events. Dreams can foretell the future because human behavior and dream material are both influenced by the collective unconscious.

Progression and Regression

Not only are people motivated by both causal and teleological events, but psychic energy can also flow in two opposing directions. The forward flow is called **progression,** the backward movement **regression.** Progression is mostly conscious and always involves movement toward adaptation to the external world, while regression is largely unconscious and is directed toward the satisfaction of inner demands. As with extraversion and introversion, neither progression nor regression is valued over the other; both are essential to the achievement of individual growth.

Progression attempts to achieve adaptation to the outer world through an attitude that inclines a person to react consistently to a given set of environmental conditions. Conversely, regression is a necessary backward step in the successful attainment of a goal (Jung, 1928/1960). Regression activates the unconscious psyche, an essential aid in the solution of most problems. Solutions often come only after the conscious mind stops concentrating and allows the unconscious to take over. Most people have had the experience of trying to remember someone's name, but the name does not come until after the conscious psyche has given up and has turned the problem over to the unconscious. The value of regression also shows itself in dreams, which often provide a person with clues to the solution of problems that could not be solved by conscious thought. Unconscious material, distasteful and repugnant though it sometimes is, provides a valuable and necessary resource to the process of individual growth.

Regression is exemplified in the life of Jung, who underwent a prolonged regressive experience from 1913 until about 1917. During that time his psychic life was turned inward toward the unconscious and away from any significant outward accomplishments. He spent most of his energies becoming acquainted with his unconscious psyche and did little in the way of writing or lecturing. Regression dominated his life while progression nearly ceased. Subsequently, he emerged from this period with a greater balance of the psyche, once again becoming interested in the extraverted world, but permanently changed by his profound experiences with the introverted world. Jung believed that the regressive step was necessary for the creation of a balanced personality and for continued growth.

Alone, neither progression nor regression leads to development. Either can bring about too much onesidedness and failure in adaptation; but the two, working together, can activate the process of healthy personality development (Jung, 1928/1960).

DEVELOPMENT OF PERSONALITY

Personality develops through a series of stages that culminate in individuation. In contrast to Freud, Jung emphasized the second half of life, the period after 35 or 40, when a person has the opportunity to bring together the various aspects of personality and to attain self-realization. However, the opportunity for degeneration and neurotic reactions is also present at that time. The direction a person travels depends on one's ability to achieve balance between the poles of the various opposing processes. This ability is proportional to the success achieved in journeying through the previous stages of life.

STAGES OF DEVELOPMENT

The stages of life can be grouped into four general periods—*childhood, youth, middle life,* and *old age.* Jung compares the trip through life with the

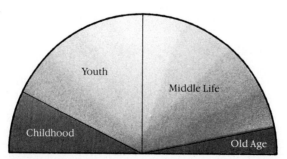

Figure 5.5   Jung compares the four stages of development with the journey of the sun through the sky, with the brightness of the sun representing consciousness.

journey of the sun through the sky, with the brightness of the sun representing consciousness. The early morning sun is childhood, full of potential, but still lacking in brilliance (consciousness); the morning sun is youth, climbing toward the zenith, but unaware of the impending decline; the early afternoon sun is middle life, brilliant like the late morning sun, but obviously headed for the sunset; the evening sun is old age, its once bright consciousness now markedly dimmed (see Figure 5.5). Jung argued that values, ideals, and modes of behavior suitable for the morning of life are inappropriate for the second half. A person must learn to find new meaning in the declining years of life (Jung, 1931/1960a).

Childhood

Jung divided childhood into three substages: (1) the anarchic, (2) the monarchic, and (3) the dualistic. The *anarchic* phase is characterized by chaotic and sporadic consciousness. There may be "islands of consciousness," but there is little or no connection between experiences. Experiences of this phase are either completely undifferentiated from one another or occur on a low level of differentiation, thus making later recall impossible. Experiences of the anarchic phase sometimes enter consciousness as primitive images, incapable of being accurately verbalized.

The *monarchic* phase of childhood is characterized by the development of the ego and by the inception of logical and verbal thinking. During this time the child sees itself objectively, often referring to itself in the third person. The islands of consciousness become larger, more numerous, and inhabited by a primitive ego. Though the ego is perceived as an object, it is not yet aware of itself as perceiver.

Subjectivity, or ego as perceiver, arises during the *dualistic* phase of childhood. The ego is now divided into the objective and subjective. The child now refers to itself in the first person, being aware of his or her existence as a separate individual. During the dualistic periods the islands of consciousness become continuous land, inhabited by an ego-complex that recognizes itself as both object and subject (Jung, 1931/1960a).

Youth

The period from puberty until middle life is called youth. The young man or woman strives to gain psychic and physical independence from his or her parents, find a mate, raise a family, and make a place in the world. According to Jung, it is, or should be, a period of increased activity, maturing sexuality, growing consciousness, and recognition that the problem-free era of childhood is gone forever. The major difficulty facing youth is to overcome the natural tendency (found also in middle and later years) to cling to the narrow consciousness of childhood, thus avoiding problems pertinent to the present time of life. This desire to live in the past is called the *conservative principle*.

People of Western civilization, especially Americans, often place great value on youth, the period of sexual attractiveness, athletic prowess, and general achievement. However, it is also a stage of only moderate consciousness, since the inner workings of the psyche are almost completely ignored during youth. When Jung was young he had the extraverted attitudes of many of his peers. As a student, he joined a fraternity, enjoyed pranks, loved to dance, courted several women, and fell in love. After graduation he was married, pursued a medical career, became a father, and generally was little involved with his inner psyche. His values and behaviors were appropriate for a youthful person.

A person who attempts to hold on to youthful values with advancing age, however, faces a crippled second half of life, handicapped in the capacity to achieve individuation and impaired in the ability to establish new goals and seek new meaning to life (Jung, 1931/1960a).

Middle Life

Jung believed that middle life begins at approximately age 35 for women and 40 for men. The sun has passed its zenith and begins its downward descent, presenting the middle-aged person with increasing anxieties. However, it is also a period of tremendous potentiality.

If the social and moral values of early life are maintained, the middle-aged person becomes rigid and fanatical. The ego is threatened by loss of physical attractiveness and agility, and now, finding one's ideals shifting, the person may fight desperately to hold on to them. Unfortunately, this is the fate of too many middle-aged people. Most of us, Jung said, are unprepared to "take the step into the afternoon of life; worse still, we take this step with the false assumption that our truths and ideals will serve us as hitherto." He goes on to say that "we cannot live in the afternoon of life according to the programme of life's morning; for what was great in the morning will be little at evening, and what in the morning was true will at evening have become a lie" (Jung, 1931/1960a, p. 399).

How can middle life be lived to its fullest? It is much easier for people to find fulfillment during this time if they have lived youth completely. They can then more readily give up the extraverted goals of youth and move in the introverted direction of expanded consciousness. It is not enough for the middle-aged person to be successful in business, prestigious in society, and satisfied with family life. One must look forward to the future with hope and anticipation, surrender the life style of youth, and discover new meaning in middle life. This often, but not always, involves a mature religious orientation, especially a belief in some sort of life after death (Jung, 1931/1960a).

Old Age

As the evening of life approaches, there is a diminution of consciousness just as the light and warmth of the sun diminish at dusk. If a person feared life during the early years, he or she will almost certainly fear death during the later ones. Fear of death is often taken as normal, but in reality, Jung said, death is the goal of life and life can only be fulfilling when death is seen in this light. In 1934, during his 60th year, Jung wrote:

> Ordinarily we cling to our past and remain stuck in the illusion of youthfulness, Being old is highly unpopular. Nobody seems to consider that not being able to grow old is just as absurd as not being able to outgrow child's-size shoes. A still infantile man of thirty is surely to be deplored, but a youthful septuagenarian—isn't that delightful? And yet both are perverse, lacking in style, psychological monstrosities. A young man who does not fight and conquer has missed the best part of his youth, and an old man who does not know how to listen to the secrets of the brooks, as they tumble down from the peaks to the valleys, makes no sense; he is a spiritual mummy who is nothing but a rigid relic of the past (Jung, 1934/1960, p. 407).

Most of Jung's patients were middle-aged or older and many of them suffered from a backward orientation, clinging desperately to goals and life styles of the past and going through the motions of life aimlessly. In treating these people Jung attempted to help them establish new goals and to find meaning in living by first finding meaning in death. This was accomplished through dream interpretation—the dreams of elderly people often being filled with symbols of rebirth, such as baptism, long journeys, or changes in location. These symbols were used to determine the patients' unconscious attitude toward death, thereby helping them discover a meaningful philosophy of life (Jung, 1934/1960).

INDIVIDUATION

Psychological rebirth, or **individuation,** is defined by Jung as the process of becoming an individual or whole person. It is similar to the concept of **self-realization** and the terms are used somewhat synonymously. However, Jung seemed to have conceived of the latter as an idealized product, representing the highest possible level of psychic maturation, while individuation was sometimes seen as a developmental process involving a lower order of attainment. In the present context the two terms are used interchangeably and indicate a high level of psychic development achieved by few people. Another concept with the same general meaning is the *transcendent function,* a term well chosen because it implies an upward movement, a going beyond ordinary development.

Analytical Psychology is essentially a psychology of opposites. Consciousness is opposed to unconsciousness, the personal unconscious to the collective unconscious, persona to individual, ego to self, anima to animus, introversion to extraversion, thinking to feeling, sensing to intuiting, rational functions to irrational functions, causality to teleology, and progression to regression. Individuation is the process of integrating the various poles into a single homogeneous individual. This process of "coming to selfhood" means that the person has all psychological components functioning in unity, with no psychic process atrophying. A person who has gone through

The Myers-Briggs as an Indicator of Jungian Typology

No area of Jungian psychology has been researched as extensively as the concept of types. An important impetus to many of these investigations was the development of the Myers-Briggs Type Indicator (MBTI) (Myers, 1962) and, to a lesser extent, the Jungian Type Survey (JTS) (Wheelwright, Wheelwright, & Buehler, 1964). Of these two type indicators, the JTS is shorter, simpler, and easier to score, but there is some evidence that the JTS has only limited validity due primarily to its brevity (Woehlke & Piper, 1980).

The Myers-Briggs Type Indicator, on the other hand, has had some success in reliably and validly measuring extraversion and introversion. For example, Carlson (1980) found the the MBTI generally supported Jungian type theory and a study by Steele and Kelley (1976) obtained a very high relationship between the extraversion-introversion scale of the MBTI and the extraversion-introversion scale of the factor analytically developed Eysenck Personality Questionnaire (see Chapter 13 for Eysenck's concept of extraversion/introversion). This relationship is especially impressive since the two instruments are based on quite different theoretical approaches. Myers and McCaulley (1985) reported substantial reliability and validity for the MBTI as a measure of Jungian personality types. In addition, a study by Levy and Ridley (1987) found that, over a 10-year period, college women changed their scores very little, thus suggesting that the Myers-Briggs Type Indicator measures relatively stable personality traits.

The MBTI employs terminology slightly different from Jung's. It is based on four bipolar personality dimensions. It opposes extraversion (E) with introversion (I);

sensing (S) with intuition (N); thinking (T) with feelings (F); and judgment (J) with perception (P). This last dimension, (J vs. P), does not reflect basic Jungian typology, but was added by Myers. These combinations yield a potential of 16 personality types, with each type having four dimensions. For example, an ISTJ person is an introverted sensing type who also relies on thinking and judgment. Brief descriptions of the 16 types follows:

ISTJ—Quiet, serious people who are logical and practical. They make up their own minds and take responsibility well.

ISFJ—Quiet, friendly people who are loyal and considerate of other's feelings. They are not interested in technical subjects.

ISTP—These people are quiet, reserved, and detached. They are interested in how mechanical things work and do not exert themselves more than necessary.

ISFP—Quiet and retiring, yet friendly and kind, these people are relaxed and take pleasure in the present moment.

INFJ—These people are conscientious, quietly forceful, and concerned for others. They succeed by perseverance and originality.

INTJ—Independent, original, skeptical, critical, and determined even to the point of stubbornness, these people are often unyielding in their pursuits.

INFP—Interested in ideas and learning, these people are friendly, but often become too involved in what they are doing to be sociable. They don't reveal much about themselves until they know you well.

INTP—These people are quiet, reserved, and ultralogical. Interested in technical and scientific subjects, they are more fascinated by ideas than people.

ESTP—Relaxed, sociable, sometimes blunt and tactless, these people enjoy working with their hands and tend to take things in a matter-of-fact way.

ESFP—Outgoing, friendly, and sociable, these people are more attuned to facts than theories. They rely on common sense and their ability to get along with people.

ESTJ—These people are practical, realistic, and interested in business or mechanics. They like to organize and run activities and are often interested in becoming administrators.

ESFJ—These people are popular, cooperative, talkative, and like to do nice things for people. They are not interested in technical subjects or abstract ideas, but enjoy helping others.

ENFP—Enthusiastic, imaginative, and interested in helping others with their problems, these people are more likely to improvise than to plan ahead.

ENTP—These people are quick, alert, and outspoken. They often argue just for the fun of it and frequently change interests. They are resourceful in solving new and challenging problems.

ENFJ—Responsible, concerned about others' feelings, sociable, and popular, these people are tactful and make good discussion leaders.

ENTJ—These people also make good leaders. They tend to be outspoken, but sometimes are more positive and self-confident than their abilities warrant.

the individuation process has achieved realization of the self; has minimized the persona while actualizing the individual; has become conscious of the anima or animus; has acquired a workable balance between introversion and extraversion; and, perhaps most difficult of all, has elevated all four functions to a superior position.

Individuation is relatively rare, being achieved only by those who are able to assimilate their unconscious into their total personality. To come to terms with the unconscious is a difficult process because it demands courage to face the evil nature of one's shadow and even greater fortitude to accept one's feminine or masculine side. This process is almost never achieved before middle life and then only by men and women who are able to remove the ego as the dominant concern of personality and replace it with the self. One must allow the unconscious self to become the core of personality. To merely expand consciousness is to inflate the ego and to produce a onesided person who lacks the soul spark of personality. The self-realized person is dominated neither by unconscious processes nor by the conscious ego, but achieves a balance between all aspects of personality.

Both progression and regression are necessary for individuation. Progression, the process of adaptation to the demands of the outer world, must be secured before the person can make a satisfactory adjustment to the inner world. One must be in contact with reality before psychological growth can take place; that is, one must make allowances for body functions and for the existence of other people prior to achieving inner development. One should not continue either progression or regression singly for a long period of time; either path would lead to onesided development. If progression is pursued to the neglect of the inner world, the person becomes overly concerned with external values, such as achievement, social status, or material wealth. However, if regression goes unchecked, the person retreats to his or her private world and becomes unable to cope with the problems of the external world.

The self-realized person is able to contend with both the external and the internal. Unlike the psychotic, the healthy person lives in the real world and makes necessary concessions to it. However, unlike the average person, self-realized people are neither ignorant nor distrustful of the regressive process. They regard unconscious images as potential material for new psychic life. They welcome the unconscious and find satisfaction in coming to terms with it in both dreams and introspective reflections (Jung, 1939/1959; 1945/ 1953).

JUNG'S METHODS OF INVESTIGATION

In his methods of investigation, Jung looked beyond psychology in his search for data. He made no apologies for his ventures into the fields of sociology, history, anthropology, physics, philology, religion, mythology, and philosophy. He strongly believed that the study of personality was not the prerogative of any single discipline, and that the whole person could be understood only by pursuing knowledge wherever it exists. This is not to say that Jung considered himself to be a philosopher, theologian, or anything other than a medical psychologist. Far from it. He simply used knowledge obtained through these various approaches to build a scientific psychological theory.

Like Freud, he persistently defended himself as a scientific investigator, eschewing the labels of mystic and philosopher. At the same time, however, he asserted that the psyche could not be understood by the intellect alone, but must be grasped by the total person. Along the same line, he once said, "Not everything I bring forth is written out of my head, but much of it comes from the heart also" (Jung, 1943/1953, p. 116).

Jung gathered data for his theories from extensive reading in many disciplines; but primarily, his basic facts came from a systematic observation of people, including himself. Most of these observations were made on patients through the *word association test, dream analysis, active imagination,* and *psychotherapy.* This information was then combined with readings on medieval alchemy, the other occult sciences, or any other subject in an effort either to confirm or reject the hypotheses of Analytical Psychology.

Word Association Test

Jung was not the first to use the word association technique, but he can be credited with helping to develop and refine the test. He originally used the technique as early as 1903 when he was a young psychiatric assistant at Burghöltzli, but seldom employed it in his later career. In spite of this inattention, the test continues to be closely linked with Jung's name.

His original purpose in using the word association test was to demonstrate the validity of Freud's hypothesis that the unconscious operates as an autonomous process. However, the basic purpose of the test in Jungian psychology today is to uncover feeling-toned complexes. As noted earlier, a complex is an individualized emotionally toned conglomeration of images grouped around a central core. The test is based on the principle that complexes create emotional responses in the subject, and that these responses can then be measured through the use of such devices as a stop watch, a pneumograph, and a galvanometer.

In administering the test, Jung typically used a list of about 100 stimulus words chosen and arranged to elicit an emotional reaction. The subject is instructed to respond to each stimulus word with the first word that comes to mind. Verbal responses are recorded, as are time of response, rate of breathing, and galvanic skin response. Then the experiment is usually repeated, with the subject instructed to duplicate the original verbal responses. Certain types of reactions indicate that the stimulus word has touched a complex.

Critical responses include restricted breathing, as measured by the pneumograph; changes in the electrical conductivity of the skin, detected by the galvanometer; and delayed reactions, or any response time markedly longer than the subject's mean reaction time. Other revealing reactions include multiple responses, that is, those which use many words; disregard of instructions; inability to reproduce a word, for example, errors in pronunciation not usually made; unusual facial expressions, including blushing; nonverbal sounds such as stammering, laughing, coughing, sighing, clearing the throat, or crying; excessive body movement, especially of the hands or feet; repetition of the stimulus word; silence or failure to give a verbal response; and inconsistency on test-retest. Any one, or combination, of these types of responses indicate that a complex has been reached (Jung, 1935/1968; Jung & Riklin, 1904/1973).

Dream Analysis

The subject of dreams is another example of Jung's reconciliation of the opposing views of Freud and Adler. Freud believed that dreams were rooted in past experiences, while Adler held that they were forward-looking. Jung saw validity in both viewpoints, theorizing that dreams reveal the past as well as prophesy the future. As with other psychic events, they have both a *cause* and a *purpose.* Jung insisted that some dreams could be interpreted as infantile wish-fulfillments, others as exaggerated strivings for superiority. However, any attempt to explain dreams solely from either position is too narrow and does an injustice to the full nature of dreams. Jung agreed with much of the Freudian view. To him, dreams spring from the depths of the unconscious and can only be interpreted with the dreamer's associations. Jung also believed that there is a latent meaning to dreams, which is expressed in symbolic form.

He differed from Freud in his insistence that not all dreams are wish-fulfillments and in his reduced emphasis on sexual motifs. His basic difference with Freud, however, was his enlargement of the psychoanalytic causal interpretation to include a finalistic and purposive one. Jung believed that dreams can sometimes foretell the future, not because of any supernatural quality, but because dreams and future actions spring from the same source—the unconscious. This common origin explains how future events can sometimes be foretold through an analytical interpretation of dreams.

The purpose of dreams is often compensatory, that is, feelings and attitudes not expressed during waking life will find an outlet through the dream process. For example, if the anima in a man receives no conscious development, she will express herself through dreams filled with self-realization motifs.

To correctly interpret dreams, one needs to know the dreamer's conscious attitude because the dream is made up of the unconscious opposite. It would be a mistake for the dreamer to interpret his or her dream according to conscious content and apparent meaning; the unconscious meaning must be discovered (Jung, 1916/1960).

It will be recalled that Jung felt certain dreams offered proof for the existence of the collective unconscious. At least three kinds of dreams are considered as archetypal dreams. Under the first heading are *"big dreams,"* those which seem to have special meaning and inexplicable attraction for all mankind. Second are *typical dreams,* those which are common to most people. These include typical themes like flying, entering a cave, losing teeth, or climbing stairs. The third category includes *earliest dreams* remembered. These can be traced back to about age three or four and contain mythological and symbolic images and motifs that could not have reasonably been experienced by the individual child. These early childhood dreams often contain archetypal motifs and symbols such as the hero, the old wise man, the tree, the fish, and the mandala. Jung wrote of these images and motifs: "Their frequent appearance in individual case material, as well as their universal distribution, prove that the human psyche is unique and subjective or personal only in part, and for the rest is collective and objective" (Jung, 1948/1960b, p. 291).

Active Imagination

A technique Jung used during his own self-analysis as well as with many of his patients was active imagination. This method requires the subject to begin with any impression—a dream image, vision, picture or fantasy—and to concentrate until the impression begins to "move." These images are then followed to wherever they lead and the subject must have the courage to face these autonomous images and to freely communicate with them.

The purpose of active imagination is to reveal archetypal images emerging from the unconscious. It can be an aid to an artist or writer in generating creative material, but it can be even more helpful to the thinking person since it enables one to develop the other functions, especially feeling and sensing. Active imagination is a useful technique for anyone who wants to become better acquainted with the collective and personal unconscious and is willing to overcome the resistance which ordinarily blocks open communication with the unconscious.

Jung believed that active imagination has an advantage over dream analysis in that its images are produced during a conscious state of mind. This makes them more clear and reproducible. The feeling tone is also quite specific and the patient ordinarily has little difficulty reproducing the vision or remembering the mood (Jung, 1937/1959).

As a variation to active imagination, Jung sometimes asked patients who were so inclined to draw, paint, or express in some other nonverbal manner the progression of their fantasies. Jung relied on this technique during his own self-analysis and many of these reproductions, rich in universal symbolism and often exhibiting the mandala and the quaternity symbols, are scattered throughout his books. *Man and His Symbols* (1964), *Word and Image* (1979), and *Psychology and Alchemy* (1952/1968) are especially prolific sources for these drawings and photographs.

Jung (1961, p. 192) wrote the following about his experiences with active imagination during his midlife confrontation with the unconscious:

> When I look back upon it all today and consider what happened to me during the period of my work on the fantasies, it seems as though a message had come to me with overwhelming force. There were things in the images which concerned not only myself but many others also. It was then that I ceased to belong to myself alone, ceased to have the right to do so. From then on, my life belonged to the generality. . . . It was then that I dedicated myself to service of the psyche: I loved it and hated it, but it was my greatest wealth. My delivering myself over to it, as it were, was the only way by which I could endure my existence and live it as fully as possible.

Psychotherapy

The hypotheses of Analytical Psychology rest on data gathered from widely scattered sources, but the backbone of Jung's investigations was his observations of patients during psychotherapy.

*Carl G. Jung, the old wise man
Of Küsnacht.*

To Jung, there are at least four basic approaches to therapy. These represent four developmental stages in the modern history of psychotherapy and each has value for some patients. The first is confession of a pathogenic secret. This is the cathartic method practiced by Joseph Breuer and earlier psychiatrists. For patients who merely have a need to share their secrets, catharsis is effective. The second stage involves interpretation, explanation, and elucidation. This approach, used by Freud, gives the patients insight into the causes of their neuroses, but may still leave them incapable of solving social problems. At this point Adlerian therapy may be indicated. This third stage involves the education of the patient as a social being. Unfortunately, Jung said, this development of social interest often leaves the patient merely a normal socially well-adjusted person. To go beyond normality, or adjustment to the outer world, Jung suggested a fourth stage, **transformation,** by which he meant that the doctor must first be transformed into a healthy human being, preferably by undergoing psychotherapy. Only after being free from neuroses (but not necessarily complexes) and having established a philosophy of life is the therapist able to help patients move toward individuaation, wholeness, or self-realization. This fourth stage is especially employed with patients who are in the second half of life and who are concerned with realization of the inner self, with moral and religious problems, and with finding a unifying philosophy of life (Jung, 1931/1954b).

Jung was quite eclectic in his theory and practice of psychotherapy. His treatment varied according to the age, the stage of development, and the particular neurosis of the individual patient. He used both Freudian and Adlerian techniques when appropriate, but these, he felt, were useful primarily for patients with sexual neuroses or power conflicts, problems that are crucial mostly during the first half of life. About two-thirds of Jung's patients, however, were in the second half and a great many of them suffered from a loss of meaning, general aimlessness, and a fear of death. Jung attempted to help these patients find their own philosophical orientation. He was careful not to prescribe a ready-made philosophy, but encouraged each to discover an individual meaning to life and to achieve realization of his or her unique self.

The ultimate purpose of Jungian therapy is to help the neurotic become healthy and to encourage the healthy to work independently toward self-realization. Jung sought to achieve this purpose by using such techniques as dream analysis and active imagination to aid the patient in discovering unconscious material and to bring this in line with the conscious attitude. Jung usually began therapy with four consultations a week, but as soon as possible he would reduce the number of therapeutic hours to one or two a week. This was to encourage patients to try to interpret some of their own dreams and to independently strive toward a unity of ego and self, that is, conscious and unconscious. Ideally, this process should continue after therapy is terminated. "My aim is to bring about a psychic state in which my patient begins to experiment with his own nature—a state of fluidity, change, and growth where nothing is externally fixed and hopelessly petrified" (Jung, 1931/1954a, p. 46). This is essentially what Jung himself accomplished with his journey into his unconscious during the three-year period following his break with Freud.

Though Jung encouraged patients to be independent, he admitted the importance of **transference,** particularly during the first three stages of therapy. He regarded both positive and negative transference as a natural concomitant to the patients's revealing highly personal information to the therapist. He thought it quite all right that a number of male patients referred to him as "Mother Jung" and quite understandable that others saw him as God or savior. Jung also recognized the process of **countertransference,** a term used to describe the therapist's feelings toward the patient. Like transference, countertransference can be either a help or a hindrance to treatment depending on whether or not it leads to a better relationship between doctor and patient, something which Jung felt to be indispensable to successful psychotherapy.

He also emphasized the importance of the unique personality of both therapist and patient and was one of the first to stress the concept that therapy should be a growth-producing experience for the doctor as well as the patient. In 1931 he wrote:

> For two personalities to meet is like mixing two different chemical substances; if there is any combination at all, both are transformed. . . . You can exert no influence if you are not susceptible to influence. It is futile for the doctor to shield himself from the influence of the patient and to surround himself with a smokescreen of fatherly and professional authority (Jung, 1931/1954b, p. 71).

Because there are many goals and an equal number of techniques in Jungian psychotherapy, it is not possible to describe a person who has successfully completed analytical treatment. For the mature person, the goal may be to find meaning in life and strive toward achieving balance and wholeness. The self-realized person is able to assimilate much of the unconscious self into consciousness, but, at the same time, remains fully aware of the potential dangers hidden in the far recess of the unconscious psyche. Jung once warned against digging too deeply in land not properly surveyed, comparing this practice to a person digging for an artesian well and running the risk of activating a volcano.

CONCEPT OF HUMANITY

Jung's opposing forces view of humanity can be described as neither *pessimistic* nor *optimistic,* neither *deterministic* nor *purposive.* Humans are complex organisms composed of many opposing factors. People are motivated partly by *conscious* thoughts, partly by images from their personal *unconscious,* and partly by latent memory traces inherited from their ancestral past. Their motivation comes both from *causal* and *teleological* factors.

The complex make-up of humans invalidates any simple or onesided description. According to Jung, no one is totally good or completely bad; each person is a composition of opposing forces. No one is completely introverted or totally extraverted; all male or all female; solely a thinking, feeling, sensing, or intuitive person; and no one proceeds invariably in the direction of either progression or regression.

The persona is but a fraction of an individual. What one wishes to show others is usually only the socially acceptable side of personality. Every person has a dark side, a shadow, and most try to conceal it from both society and themselves. In addition, each man possesses an anima and every woman an animus, which is even more likely to be hidden. The stronger and more dominant a man appears, the more frantically he is trying to repress his anima. The more helpless a woman seems, the more she is attempting to hide her animus.

The various complexes and archetypes cast their spell over us and are responsible for many of our words and actions and most of our dreams and fantasies. Though we are not master in our own house, neither are we completely dominated by forces beyond our control. We have some limited capacity to determine our lives. Through our will, and with great courage, we can explore the hidden recesses of our psyche. We can recognize our shadow as our own, become partially conscious of our feminine or masculine side, and cultivate more than a single function. This process, which Jung calls individuation or self-realization, is not easy and demands more fortitude than most of us can muster. Ordinarily, it means we have reached middle life and have lived successfully through the stages of childhood and youth. During middle age, we must be willing to set aside the goals and behaviors of youth and adopt a new style appropriate to our stage of psychic development.

Even when a person has achieved individuation, has made an acquaintance with the inner world, and has brought the various opposing forces into balance, that person is still not in complete control of his or her self. Our impersonal collective unconscious remains the source of many of our creations, new ideas, prejudices, interests, fears, and even our dreams.

On the dimension of *biological vs. social* aspects of personality, Jung's theory is decidedly in the direction of biology. The collective unconscious, responsible for so many of our actions, is part of our biological inheritance. Except for the therapeutic potential of the doctor-patient relationship, Jung has little to say about differential effects of specific social practices. In fact, in his studies of various cultures, he found the differences to be superficial, the similarities profound. For this same reason Analytical Psychology can also be rated high on *similarities* among people and low on *individual differences.*

CRITIQUE OF JUNG

Though Jung considered himself to be a medical psychologist and a scientific observer of human behavior, many readers may regard him as a fantasy writer, a philosopher, or an introspective mystic. He is sometimes criticized as being a creator of interesting stories who neglected the rigors of science in his approach to theory building.

Analytical Psychology, like any other theory, can be evaluated in reference to the five criteria of a useful theory established in Chapter 1. It is not necessary that the theory or any major component such as the collective unconscious be absolutely proven. It is only required that the theory meet those criteria of usefulness.

First, does Jungian theory *organize observations* into a meaningful framework? Analytical Psychology is useful because it adds a new dimension to personality theory, namely, the collective unconscious. Those aspects of human personality dealing with the occult, the mysterious, and the parapsychological are not touched upon by most other personality theories. Even though the collective unconscious is not the only possible explanation for these phenomena, and other concepts could be postulated to account for them, Jung is the only modern personality theorist to make a serious attempt to include such a broad scope of human activity within a single theoretical framework.

For a theory to be useful, it must *generate testable hypotheses and descriptive research.* That portion of Jung's theory concerned with classification and typology, that is, the functions and attitudes, can be studied and tested and, in fact, has yielded large amounts of research. However, the crux of his theory, the collective unconscious, does not generate many readily testable hypotheses. Much of Jung's evidence for the archetypes and the collective unconscious came from his own inner experiences which he admittedly found difficult to communicate to others. His attitude is summed up in his statement that "not everything I bring forth is written out of my head, but much of it comes from the heart also" (Jung, 1943/1953, p. 116). In other words, the concepts of archetype and collective unconscious are to be accepted more on faith than on empirical evidence. In a similar vein Jung stated: "Archetypal statements are based upon instinctive preconditions and have nothing to do with reason; they are neither rationally grounded nor can they be banished by rational argument" (Jung, 1961, p. 353). Such a statement may be acceptable to the artist or the theologian, but it is not likely to win adherents from among scientific researchers faced with the problems of designing studies and formulating hypotheses. Perhaps the most serious limitation of Analytical Psychology is its near sterility in generating hypotheses pertinent to the archetypes and the collective unconscious.

A third criterion of a useful theory is its *practicality.* Does the theory aid the therapist, teacher, parent, or others in solving everyday problems? The theory of psychological types or attitudes may be a helpful guide to the practitioner, but, unfortunately, the usefulness of the collective unconscious is largely explanatory. This latter concept does not readily suggest answers to practical questions like "How can I help this patient work through her neurosis?" or "What methods will motivate this student to learn spelling?" A good theory should be practical, but the cornerstone of Analytical Psychology, the collective unconscious, is severely limited in this respect.

Is Jung's theory of personality *internally consistent?* Does it possess a set of operationally defined terms? The first question receives a qualified affirmative answer; the second a definite negative one. Jung generally used the same terms consistently, but he often employed several terms to describe the same concept. The words "regression" and "introverted" are so closely related that they can be said to describe the same process. This is also true of "progression" and "extraverted" and the list could be expanded to include several other terms such as "individuation" and "self-realization," which are not clearly differentiated either. Jung's language is often arcane and many of his terms are not adequately defined. As for operational definitions, they are totally absent from his writings, but, in fairness to Jung, it must be stated that he did not construct his theory with this criterion in mind.

The final criterion of a useful theory is *parsimoniousness.* Jung's psychology is not simple, but neither is human personality. However, his theory is the most complex of all theories and probably more cumbersome than it need be. Jung's proclivity for searching for data from a variety of disciplines and his willingness to explore his own unconscious even beneath the personal level contribute to the great complexities and the broad scope of his theory. The law of parsimony states, "When two theories are equally useful, the simpler one is preferred." In fact, of course, no two are ever equal, and Jung's theory adds a dimension to human personality not greatly dealt with by others.

CHAPTER SUMMARY

The life of Carl Jung provides an appropriate illustration of the basic concepts of Jungian theory. Jung's midlife journey into the deep recesses of his psyche provided the data for his theories concerning a *collective unconscious.* This notion that important segments of our unconscious are inherited from our ancient ancestors is Jung's most distinctive and controversial concept. Repeated experiences of past generations are passed down through inheritance and form the basis of our collective unconscious.

Some of the contents of the collective unconscious become highly developed and are identified as *archetypes.* Jung became acquainted with several of these ancient images during his midlife self-analysis. They included the *anima,* or femine side of men; the *animus,* or masculine disposition in women; the *shadow,* the dark side of our personality; the *old wise man,* the intelligent but deceptive voice of accumulated experience; the *great mother,* the archetype of nourishment and destruction; the *persona,* or mask we show to the outside world; the *hero,* our unconscious image of a person who conquers or vanquishes an evil foe; and the *self,* the archetype of completeness and wholeness.

The layer of the psyche above the collective unconscious is the *personal unconscious,* composed of *complexes* or emotionally toned images revolving around a core concept. Above the personal unconscious is the *conscious,* or those images perceived by the *ego.*

Jung postulated two basic *attitudes— introversion* and *extraversion.* Introversion is a tendency to see the world subjectively, while extraverts tend to take an objective view. When these two attitudes combine with the four *functions—thinking, feeling, sensation,* and *intuition*—eight basic *types* are produced.

In discussing the dynamics of personality Jung relied on the principles of equivalence, entropy, causality, teleology, progression, and regression. The *principle of equivalence* states that energy is never lost or destroyed but merely transformed to another function. The *principle of entropy* provides the foundation for Jung's psychology of opposites. It states that energy flows from the tension produced by opposing poles such as introversion and extraversion.

Jung accepted both *causal* and *teleological* explanations, that is, he believed that some behaviors are caused by past events while others are shaped by our expectations of the future. The concepts of *progression* and *regression* are similar to those of extraversion and introversion and refer to the forward and backward flow of energy necessary to attain eventual balance.

Jung emphasized the last half of life, although he suggested that a healthy *middle life* and *old age* depend on proper solutions to the problems of *childhood* and *youth.*

Early in his career Jung developed the *word association test* which was designed to uncover complexes. Later, during his midlife crisis, he used *dream analysis* and *active imagination* to discover the contents of his own collective unconscious. Subsequently, he made use of these techniques in his practice of *psychotherapy.*

Finally, Jung saw humans as exceedingly complex organisms composed of several opposing forces. He was neither optimistic nor pessimistic, although he believed that people can attain *individuation* or *self-realization* during the second half of life. Analytical Psychology is the most complex of all personality theories, but it falls short of meeting the standards for a scientific theory, especially in its lack of operationally defined terms.

Suggested Readings

JACOBI, J. (1973). *The psychology of C. G. Jung: An introduction with illustrations.* New Haven, CT: Yale University Press.

This brief paperback by one of Jung's former associates is an excellent introduction to Jungian psychology. It includes a lengthy section on the practical application of Analytical Psychology.

JUNG, C. G. (1961). *Memories, dreams, reflections* (A. Jaffe, Ed.). New York: Random House.

Of all of Jung's works, this is possibly the easiest to read and the most interesting. Written by Jung as he entered his ninth decade, this book contains an exciting firsthand account of his midlife confrontation with the unconscious.

JUNG, C. G. (1979). *Word and image* (A. Jaffe, Ed.). Princeton, NJ: Princeton University Press.

This large book is mostly biographical and pictorial. Also included are a chronology and a glossary of technical terms. Anyone interested in Jung will enjoy a leisurely perusal of these pages.

ROBERTSON, R. (1987). *C. G. Jung and the archetypes of the collective unconscious.* New York: Peter Lang.

While the book sometimes strays from Jung's psychology and is not always easy to read, the serious reader will glean much from Robertson's work.

SULLIVAN

6

Interpersonal Theory

Sheila is a popular 20-year-old college student preparing for a secondary school teaching career. Her popularity, however, is limited almost exclusively to men. She has no close women friends even though she lives in a dorm suite with three other women. Her suite mates view Sheila as a pleasant, socially outgoing person who isn't very serious about her schoolwork. Despite Sheila's somewhat effervescent personality, none of her suite mates seem to like her. Indeed, she spends little time with them, but instead prefers the company of men. She has "gone steady" dozens of times since she was 13 and has been engaged twice. Nearly all these relationships became sexual, some almost immediately.

Sheila has a brother who is four years older, but the two have never enjoyed a close relationship. Her father, a drug salesman, spent little time at home and almost none with Sheila. Her mother, a cook in a school cafeteria, tried to fill her husband's absence by pampering Sheila and showering her with gifts and attention. Sheila had few responsibilities as a young girl. Her mother kept her room clean, gave her a generous allowance, inevitably took her side in her frequent disputes and fights with playmates, and often completed her homework after Sheila complained that she didn't understand how to do it.

In early elementary school, Sheila played with both boys and girls, but her insistence on always having things her way made her somewhat unpopular among her peers. She frequently quarreled with playmates, and occasionally these confrontations culminated in angry brawls. By the time Sheila was in the fourth grade she began to feel more isolated from her classmates. The boys showed little interest in any of the girls and the other girls seemed to have their own cliques and small groups. Although Sheila felt left out, neither her mother nor her teachers at this time would have described her as a social isolate. She was frequently seen talking with other children, but these conversations were seldom initiated or welcomed by others. Her classmates tolerated her, and she even seemed to have a few girl friends a year or two younger than herself.

When Sheila reached puberty her life began to change. First, her physical appearance underwent a dramatic metamorphosis. From a rather plain-looking preadolescent she became a physically attractive adolescent. By the time she was 13 she was drawing the attention of older boys. She relished the attention and began to learn how to attain it. She dressed in an attractive though somewhat alluring manner; she kept her hair neat and stylish, and wore makeup in a judicious fashion. In addition, she became quite skillful at inane, meaningless conversation and enjoyed shocking others with graphic sexual and scatological language.

At college, and away from home for the first time, Sheila began to use alcohol and other drugs with some regularity. She relied on them especially to buffer hurt feelings after each of her many love affairs came to an unsatisfactory end. However, she was seldom long without a "boyfriend," but also seldom long with one. She seemed to turn men off almost as quickly as she turned them on.

OVERVIEW

In this chapter we look at the interpersonal theory of Harry Stack Sullivan and attempt to use some of its major concepts to explain the problems Sheila faced in her personal relationships. Like Sheila, Sullivan led a lonely and unsatisfying life as a youngster. Nevertheless, he went on to develop the first comprehensive personality theory by an American.

The outstanding feature of Sullivan's theory of personality is its strong emphasis on interpersonal relationships. Sullivan insisted that personality—healthy or unhealthy—is shaped largely by our relations with other people. He contended that scientific psychiatry deals neither with the mind nor the brain, and that knowledge of human personality can be gained only through the scientific study of interpersonal relations.

BIOGRAPHY OF HARRY STACK SULLIVAN

It may seem ironic that the personality theorist who so emphatically stressed the importance of interpersonal relationships was, himself, the product of isolation and loneliness. Harry Stack Sullivan was born in the small farming town of Norwich, New York, on February 21, 1892, the sole surviving child of poor Irish Catholic parents. His mother, Ella Stack Sullivan, was 32 when she married Timothy Sullivan and 39 when Harry was born. She had given birth to two other sons, neither of whom lived past the first year. As a consequence, she pampered and protected her only surviving child. Harry's father was shy, withdrawn, and taciturn, and never developed a close relationship with his son until after his wife had died and Harry was a prominent physician. He had been a farm laborer and a factory worker who moved to the Stack family farm outside the village of Smyrna, some 10 miles from Norwich, before Harry's third birthday. At about this same time, Ella Stack Sullivan was mysteriously absent from the home and Harry was cared for by his maternal grandmother, whose Gaelic accent the young boy did not easily understand. After more than a year's separation, his mother, who likely had been in a mental hospital, returned. Thereafter Harry had two mothers, and when his grandmother died in 1903, a maiden aunt came to share the duties.

Though both parents were of Irish Catholic descent, his mother regarded the Stack family as socially superior to the Sullivans, and it was not until Harry developed his notions about the similarities among people that he realized the folly of his mother's claims.

As a preschool child Harry had neither friends nor acquaintances of his age, though he did invent several imaginary playmates before age five. After beginning school he still felt like an outsider, being an Irish Catholic in an Anglo-Saxon Protestant community. His Irish brogue and his sharp mind made him unpopular with his classmates throughout his years of schooling in Smyrna.

When Harry was eight and a half he formed a close friendship with a thirteen-year-old boy from a neighboring farm. The chum was Clarence Bellinger who lived a mile beyond Harry in another school district, but was now beginning high school in Smyrna. Arrangements were made for Clarence to pick Harry up and give him a ride to school. Though the two boys were not peers chronologically, they had much in common socially and intellectually. Both were retarded socially but advanced intellectually; both later became psychiatrists and neither ever married.

Chapman (1976) believes that this was probably a homosexual relationship, though Perry (1982) doubts that there was ever any overt sexual activity between the two. In either case, the relationship had a transforming effect on Sullivan's life. It awakened in him the power of intimacy, that is, the ability to love another who is more or less like oneself. In Sullivan's mature theory of personality, he places heavy emphasis on the therapeutic, almost magical power of an intimate relationship during the preadolescent years. This belief, along with many other Sullivanian hypotheses, seems to have grown out of his own childhood experiences.

Sullivan was interested in books and science, not in farming. Though an only child growing up on a farm, he was able to escape many of the chores by absent-mindedly "forgetting" to do them. This ruse was successful because his indulgent mother completed them for him and allowed Harry to receive credit. A bright student, Sullivan graduated from high school as valedictorian at age 16. He then entered Cornell University intending to become a physicist, though he and Clarence also shared an interest in psychiatry. His academic performance at Cornell was less than satisfactory, however, and he was suspended after one year. The suspension may not have been solely for academic deficiencies. He got into trouble with the law at Cornell, probably for mail fraud. It is possible he was a dupe of older, more mature students who were using him to pick up some chemicals illegally ordered through the mail. In any event, for the next two years Sullivan mysteriously disappeared from the scene. Perry (1982) thinks he may have suffered a schizophrenic breakdown at this time and was confined to a mental hospital. His later intense interest in schizophrenia may have its origins in his personal history.

In 1911, with only one year of undergraduate work, he enrolled in the Chicago College of Medicine and Surgery. By Sullivan's claim, this school was little more than a "diploma mill" (Chapman, 1976, p. 27). In reality, however, it was a branch of the respected Valparaiso University. Still a poor to mediocre student, he managed to finish his studies by 1915, but his degree was not granted until 1917.

The period from 1915 until 1921 was again a shadowy and unsettled time in his life. Sullivan claimed to have worked from 1915 until 1917 to pay off the tuition debts that he claimed were the reason his degree was delayed two years. During this time he was also undergoing 75 hours of psychotherapy, probably because he was suffering another schizophrenic episode. During World War I he entered the armed forces as a medical officer and, after the war, continued to serve in that capacity, first for the Federal Board for Vocational Education, and then for the Public Health Service. However, this was still a confusing and unstable period in his life and he showed no promise of the brilliant career that lay just ahead (Perry, 1982).

In 1921, with no formal training in psychiatry, he went to St. Elizabeth's Hospital in Washington, D.C., where he became closely acquainted with William Alanson White, an outstanding neuropsychiatrist. There he had his first opportunity to work with large numbers of schizophrenic patients. The following year he began an association with the Medical School of the University of Maryland and with the Sheppard and Enoch Pratt Hospital in Towson, Maryland. During this "Baltimore period" of his life he conducted intensive studies of schizophrenia, which led to his first hunches about the importance of interpersonal relationships. In trying to make sense out of the speech of schizophrenic patients, Sullivan realized that their illness was a means of coping with anxiety generated from a social or interpersonal environment. His experiences as a practicing clinician gradually translated themselves into the beginnings of an interpersonal theory of psychiatry.

Much of his time and energy at Sheppard was spent selecting and training hospital attendants. Sullivan did little therapy himself, but developed a system where nonprofessional, but sympathetic, attendants treated schizophrenic patients with human respect and care. It was at Sheppard that Sullivan gained a reputation as a clinical wizard. However, he became disenchanted with the political climate at the hospital when he was passed over for the position of head of the new reception center which he had advocated. In March of 1930 he resigned from Sheppard (Perry, 1982).

Later in that year he moved to

New York City and opened a private practice, hoping to enlarge his understanding of interpersonal relations by investigating nonschizophrenic disorders, especially those of an obsessive nature. Times were hard, however, and his expected wealthy clientele did not come in the numbers he needed to maintain his expenses.

On a more positive note, his residence in New York brought him into contact with several psychiatrists and social scientists with a European background. Among these were Karen Horney, Erich Fromm, and Frieda Fromm-Reichmann who, along with Sullivan, Clara Thompson, and others, formed the Zodiac group, an informal organization that met regularly over drinks to discuss old and new ideas in psychiatry and the related social sciences. Sullivan had met Thompson earlier and the two were close friends. Sullivan had persuaded Thompson to travel to Europe to take a training analysis under Sandor Ferenczi, a disciple of Freud. Sullivan learned from all members of the Zodiac group and, through Thompson, his therapeutic technique was indirectly influenced by Freud. Sullivan also credited two other outstanding practitioners, Adolf Meyer and William Alanson White, as having had an impact on his practice of therapy. Despite some Freudian influence on Sullivan's technique, the theory of interpersonal psychiatry is neither psychoanalytic nor neo-Freudian.

During his residence in New York, Sullivan also came under the influence of several noted social scientists from the University of Chicago, which was the center of American sociological study during the 1920s and 1930s. Included among them were social psychologist George Herbert Mead, sociologists Robert Ezra Park and W. I. Thomas, anthropologist Edward Sapir, and political scientist Harold Lasswell. Sullivan formed a close personal friendship with Sapir and Lasswell and the three men were primarily responsible for establishing in 1933 the William Alanson White Psychiatric Foundation in Washington, D.C. This institution, named for the man who had influenced Sullivan's thinking during the previous decade, was founded for the purpose of joining psychiatry to the other social sciences. Sullivan served as president of the foundation from 1933 until 1943 and was coeditor, then editor, of the foundation's journal, *Psychiatry,* from its inception in 1938 until he died in 1949. Under Sullivan's guidance, the foundation also began a training institution known as the Washington School of Psychiatry. Because of these activities in Washington, Sullivan gave up his New York practice, which was not very lucrative anyway, and moved back to the capital city where he remained closely associated with the school and the journal.

In January 1949, Sullivan attended a meeting of the World Federation for Mental Health in Amsterdam. While on his way home, January 14, 1949, he died in a Paris hotel room, a few weeks short of his 57th birthday. Not uncharacteristically, he was alone at the time.

INTRODUCTION TO INTERPERSONAL THEORY

Sullivan believed that people develop their personalities within a social context. The one-to-one relationships people experience are so crucial in the formation of personality, that it can be said that personality does not exist apart from other people. Sullivan (1953a, p. 10) contended that "a personality can never be isolated from the complex of interpersonal relations in which the person lives and has his being." Personality is inextricably tied to interpersonal relations and is defined by Sullivan (1953b, pp. 110-111) as *"the relatively enduring pattern of recurrent interpersonal situations which characterized a human life."* Interpersonal situations, then, provide the subject matter for Sullivan's study of personality.

Sullivan was constantly concerned with the problem of accurate and coherent communication as the crucial ingredient in the interpersonal situation. Though he adopted somewhat technical language, he tried to avoid the use of psychiatric neologisms. In *The Interpersonal Theory of Psychiatry* he wrote, "I think we should try to pick a word in common usage in talking about living and clarifying just what we mean by that word, rather than to set about diligently creating new words by carpentry of Greek and Sanskrit roots" (Sullivan, 1953b, p. 7). Despite this intention, however, much of Sullivan's writings reveal a unique and colorful style of expression, including some esoteric terms not often found in the writings of other personality theorists.

Like Freud and Jung, Sullivan saw personality as an energy system. Energy can exist as *tension* (potentiality for action) or as actions themselves *(energy transformations)*.

TENSIONS

Sullivan defined **tension** as potentiality for action that may or may not be experienced in awareness. In other words, not all tensions are consciously felt by the person. For example, a person may scratch without consciously feeling an itch; yet the fact that energy was transformed into action indicates the presence of this unfelt tension. Many tensions, such as anxiety, premonitions, drowsiness, hunger, and sexual excitement, are felt, but not always on a conscious level.

Tensions are divided into those of *needs* and those of *anxiety*. Tensions of needs represent potentiality for productive actions while tensions of anxiety bring about nonproductive disintegrative behaviors. Needs and anxiety are both opposed to the tension of sleep. In other words, sleep decreases tensions of needs and tensions of anxiety, while strong tensions of either needs or anxiety inhibit sleep and make relaxation difficult. Most people have experienced trouble sleeping because they were anxious, hungry, or in pain.

Needs

Needs are tensions brought on by a biological imbalance between the person and the physiochemical environment, both inside and outside the organism. Needs are episodic—once a person satisfies them they temporarily lose their power, but after a time, they are likely to recur. They differ from tensions of anxiety in that they are integrating or conjunctive whereas anxiety is disjunctive in nature (Sullivan, 1953b).

Though needs originally have a biological component, many of them stem from the interpersonal situation. The most basic interpersonal need is that of **tenderness.** The infant develops a need to receive tenderness from its primary caretaker (called by Sullivan "the mothering one"). During the feeding process the infant not only receives food but also has some of its needs for tenderness satisfied. The tenderness received by the infant at this time demands the cooperation of the mothering one and introduces the infant to the various strategies required by the interpersonal situation. Tenderness, then, is a complex of needs which arises out of the interpersonal situation and which requires the cooperation of a significant other (Sullivan, 1953b).

Tenderness, like the other needs, is associated with and represents potentiality for specific energy transformations. The infant's need to receive tenderness may show itself as a cry, smile, or coo, while the mother's need to give tenderness may be transformed into touching, fondling, or holding. In any of these cases, the infant uses its mouth and the mother her hands to satisfy the need for tenderness.

Many needs, such as oxygen, food, and water, must be satisfied for the general well being of the organism. These are called *general needs* and are opposed to *zonal needs,* which arise from a particula. area of the body, for example, mouth, hands, anus, or genitals. Though these zones of the body are instrumental in satisfying general needs (the mouth, for example, takes in food and oxygen) they possess an additional need for activity or exercise. Manual needs may originate when the infant manipulates the nipple with its hands, but later the needs to handle and feel become satisfying in themselves.

Very early in life these various zones of the body gain importance beyond the satisfaction of general needs and play a significant and lasting role in interpersonal relations. Many of a person's behaviors can be traced back to the various zonal needs. Each zone of interaction expends more energy than necessary for the satisfaction of the general needs for food or water—the excess energy being transformed into consistent and characteristic modes of behavior. One person, for instance, may satisfy oral needs through extranutritional sucking, smoking, or excessive talking. Another may satisfy manual needs by snapping fingers, fondling genitals, or painting pictures.

Anxiety

The second type of tension, *anxiety,* differs from tensions of needs in that it is disjunctive and is not a product of the physiochemical system. In addition, a need is a specific imbalance and requires specific energy transformations to reduce it, whereas anxiety is more diffuse and vague and calls forth no consistent actions for its relief. If an infant lacks food its course of action is clear, but if it is anxious there is little it can do to escape. Sullivan said:

> There is in the infant no capacity for action toward the relief of anxiety.... No action of the infant is consistently and frequently associated with the relief of anxiety; and therefore the need for security, or freedom from anxiety, is highly significantly distinguished from all other needs from its very first hypothetical appearance (Sullivan, 1953b, p. 42).

How does anxiety originate? Sullivan postulates that it is transferred from the parent to the infant through the process of **empathy.** Anxiety in the mothering one inevitably induces anxiety in the infant. Since all mothers have some amount of anxiety while caring for their babies, it follows that all infants become anxious to some degree (Sullivan, 1953b).

Just as the infant does not have the capacity to reduce anxiety, the parent also is ineffective in dealing with the baby's anxiety. Any signs of anxiety or insecurity by the infant are likely to lead to attempts by the parents to satisfy the infants *needs.* For example, a mother may feed an infant whose cries are due to anxiety. If the baby hesitates in accepting the milk, the mother becomes more anxious, thereby generating additional anxiety within the infant. Finally, the baby's anxiety reaches a level where it interferes with sucking and swallowing. Anxiety, then, operates in opposition to tensions of needs and prevents them from being satisfied.

Anxiety has a deleterious effect on adults too. It interferes with foresight, prevents the recall of solutions to past problems, opposes the satisfaction of needs, and is "the chief disruptive force in interpersonal relations." Sullivan likened severe anxiety to a blow on the head. It renders the person incapable of learning, blocks memory, narrows perception, and may result in complete amnesia. It is unique among the tensions in that it maintains the status quo even to the detriment of the individual. While other tensions result in actions directed specifically toward their relief, anxiety produces energy transformations that (1) prevent a person from learning from mistakes; (2) keep him or her pursuing the childish wish for security; and (3) generally insure that the person will remain unchanged (Sullivan, 1953b).

Sullivan held that anxiety and loneliness are unique among all experiences in that they are totally unwanted and undesirable. Since anxiety is painful, it is always shunned and never sought. All people have a natural tendency to avoid it, inherently preferring the state of **euphoria,** or complete lack of tension. Sullivan summarized this concept by stating that *"the presence of anxiety is much worse than its absence"* (Sullivan, 1954, p. 100).

Sullivan distinguished anxiety from fear in several important ways. In their extreme forms fear and uncomplicated anxiety may *feel* alike. However, anxiety is seldom uncomplicated. It usually stems from complex interpersonal situations and is only vaguely represented in awareness; fear is more clearly discerned and its origins more easily pinpointed. Anxiety is always felt, though not necessarily on a conscious level; it produces feelings of uneasiness and uncertainty and is the major ingredient in shame, guilt, embarrassment, and humiliation. Unlike tensions of needs, it has no positive value. Only when transformed into another tension, for example, anger or fear, can it lead to profitable actions. It is opposed to the satisfaction of needs and this opposition is expressed in words that can be considered Sullivan's definition of anxiety: "Anxiety is a tension in opposition to the tensions of needs and to action appropriate to their relief" (Sullivan, 1953b, p. 44).

ENERGY TRANSFORMATIONS

Energy transformations are actions, overt or covert, expended for the satisfaction of tensions of needs and for the reduction of tensions of anxiety. Experience occurs initially as tensions, then this potential energy is transformed into actual or kinetic energy. The resulting actions are labeled energy transformations, a somewhat awkward but technically accurate term. Not all energy transformations are obvious overt actions; many take the form of emotions, thoughts, or covert behaviors that can be hidden from observation.

In summary, there are two kinds of experience—tensions and energy transformations. Tensions, which are potentiality for action, include tensions of needs and tensions of anxiety. Needs arise because of an imbalance between person and environment and are helpful or conjunctive when satisfied. Anxiety, on the other hand, arises from the interpersonal situation and is always disjunctive. Energy transformations literally involve the transformation of potential energy into actual energy or behavior for the purpose of satisfying needs or reducing anxiety.

DYNAMISMS

Energy transformations become organized as characteristic behavior patterns. These patterns, called **dynamisms,** are similar to what others might call traits or habit patterns. Dynamisms can be defined as relatively consistent patterns of action that characterize the person throughout a lifetime (Sullivan, 1953b). Dynamisms are of two major classes: first, those related to specific zones of interaction, including the oral, anal, and genital, and second, those related to tensions. This second class is composed of three categories—the disjunctive, the isolating, and the conjunctive. Disjunctive dynamisms include all those destructive patterns of behavior that are related to the concept of **malevolence;** the isolating dynamisms include those such as **lust,** which are unrelated to interpersonal relations; and the conjunctive dynamisms are those beneficial behavior patterns such as **intimacy** and the **self-system.**

Malevolence

The malevolent transformation is Sullivan's (1953b) concept for that disjunctive dynamism of evil and hatred which is characterized by the feeling that one is living among one's enemies. Malevolence originates during late infancy or early childhood when the responses which earlier had brought about maternal tenderness are instead rebuffed, ignored, or met with anxiety and pain. Many parents attempt to control children's behavior by inflicting punishments, usually in the form of physical pain or reproving remarks. This teaches children to withhold any expression of the need for tenderness and to protect themselves by adopting the malevolent attitude. Parents and peers then find it more and more difficult to react with tenderness, and this, in turn, solidifies the child's negative attitude toward the world. The malevolent attitude manifests itself as timidity, mischievousness, cruelty, or other forms of nonsocial or antisocial behavior.

By the time a child with a malevolent transformation reaches the age of eight or ten, the hostile attitude may have made it nearly impossible to receive tenderness from others. The vicious cycle effect of malevolence makes it the greatest disaster of childhood. Not all children, of course, are afflicted with the malevolent dynamism. Sullivan does not believe that those who develop this condition are inherently evil, but holds that malevolence springs from the interpersonal situation and is therefore learned. The malevolent attitude is expressed by Sullivan with this colorful statement: "Once upon a time everything was lovely, but that was before I had to deal with people" (Sullivan, 1953b, p. 216).

Lust

The dynamism of lust is an isolating tendency requiring no other person for its satisfaction. It is a biological phenomenon evoked by tensions either directly or indirectly related to the genitals. Lust manifests itself as autoerotic behavior even when another person is the object of one's lust. On the other hand, it can combine with intimacy to form consistent homosexual or heterosexual activity. Lust is an especially powerful dynamism during adolescence. At this time it often leads to a reduction in self-esteem since attempts at lustful activity are likely to be rebuffed by authority figures and result in anxiety and surreptitious behavior. For this reason Sullivan considered lust in opposition to self-esteem and personal worth. It may also oppose intimacy. Consider, for example, Sheila, our case study. Her lustful interest in men has made it difficult for her to establish an intimate relationship with either women or men. Her sexual relations with many males may have satisfied her lustful needs but they have not gained for her what she is seeking—intimacy.

Intimacy

During preadolescence the tensions of intimacy normally arise and lead to close interpersonal relationships. The dynamism of intimacy grows out of the earlier need for tenderness, but is a more specific concept. Both tenderness and intimacy are related to the popular term love. Tenderness refers to an increase in euphoria brought on by anyone—mother, father, siblings, friends, or pet animals. Intimacy, however, is restricted to the tender feelings one person has for another individual of more or less equal status. Intimacy confers preadolescents with enough security and courage to try out new behaviors and to reveal hitherto private aspects of their personalities (Sullivan, 1953b). It will be recalled from Sullivan's biography that he experienced the nearly magical power of intimacy during his preadolescence with a boy who, though chronologically older, was a social equal.

Intimacy involves a close relationship between two persons who must react to each other in the give and take of close collaboration. Each is seen by the other as a person of equal value, not merely as an object of gratification. Intimacy must not be confused with sexual interest. In fact, it develops prior to puberty, ideally during preadolescence and, at that time, it usually exists between same-sexed pairs. Ordinarily, it is not until late adolescence that one will have an intimate relationship with a person of the other sex. Because it is a dynamism that requires an equal partnership, it does not usually exist in parent-child relationships. For example, Sheila's relationship with her mother is one of emotional closeness and dependency, but because the two are not equals, the relationship cannot be called intimate.

Intimacy is an integrating and rewarding dynamism, tending to draw out loving reactions from the other person that decrease anxiety and loneliness, two extremely painful experiences (Sullivan, 1953b).

Self-System

Another important conjunctive dynamism is the self-system, the most complex and inclusive of all the dynamisms. Sullivan referred to the self-system as an antianxiety system because it is made up of those dynamisms which protect a person from anxiety. Its primary purpose is to maintain interpersonal security by preventing the progression of anxiety. It is a secondary dynamism "in that it does not have any particular zones of interaction, any particular physiological apparatus, behind it" (Sullivan, 1953b, p. 164). As a complex dynamism it uses all zones of interaction.

The self-system arises out of the interpersonal situation when an infant is about 12 to 18 months of age. At this time the infant begins to learn which behaviors are somehow related to an increase or decrease in anxiety. Prior to this point, fear and pain were the principal forms of unpleasant experience and their arrival seemed independent of the infant's behavior. Now, however, the mothering one begins the process of training by rewarding some behaviors and punishing others. The punishments and disapprovals result in a third unpleasant condition—anxiety. The infant learns that the tenderness of the mothering one is no longer general, but is conditional and depends on specific behaviors. Since good behavior is rewarded and bad behavior is punished, the infant learns to regard itself as "good" or "bad" and the seeds of the self-system are sown (Sullivan, 1953b).

Intelligence and foresight enable people to detect slight increases and decreases in anxiety, and this ability provides the self-system with a built-in warning device. This is a mixed blessing, however. On the one hand, the warning serves as a signal, alerting people to increasing anxiety and giving them an opportunity to protect themselves. On the other hand, this same characteristic makes the self-system resistant to change and prevents people from profiting from anxiety-filled experiences. Since the primary task of the self-system is to protect people against anxiety, it is "the principal stumbling block to favorable changes in personality" (Sullivan, 1953b, p. 169). Personality is not static, however, and is especially subject to change at the beginning of the various stages of development when newly maturing needs begin to emerge (Sullivan, 1964).

As the self-system develops, people begin to form an image of themselves. This self-image is an important and consistent part of the self-system. Interpersonal experiences that are perceived as contrary to self-regard threaten *security.* As a consequence, people attempt to defend themselves against interpersonal tensions by means of **security operations,** the purpose of which is to reduce feelings of insecurity or anxiety that result from endangered self-esteem. People tend to deny or distort interpersonal experiences that conflict with their self-regard. For example, when people who think highly of themselves are called incompetent, they may choose to believe that the other person is stupid or, perhaps, merely joking. Sullivan (1953b, p. 374) called security operations "a powerful brake on personal and human progress."

The pursuit of security is distinguished from the pursuit of *satisfactions.* Satisfactions are end states connected with bodily organization whereas security operations are connected with interpersonal experiences. Sullivan (1953a) listed food, drink, sleep, lust, and loneliness as needs leading to the pursuit of satisfaction. The needs for satisfaction and the needs for security sometimes collide, as when a person on a diet feels hungry, but believes that an attractive physique is essential to maintain self-regard.

Two important security operations are dissociation and selective inattention.

Dissociation

Those impulses, desires, and needs that the self refuses to allow into awareness are said to be dissociated. **Dissociation** includes those infantile experiences not rewarded or punished and which, therefore, do not belong to the self-system. Dissociated tendencies do not cease to exist, but continue to influence personality on an unconscious level. They manifest themselves in dreams, day-dreams, and other unintentional activities outside of awareness and are directed toward the maintenance of interpersonal security (Sullivan, 1953b).

Selective Inattention

The control of focal awareness that involves a refusal to see those things one does not wish to see is called **selective inattention.** This process differs from dissociation in degree and origin. Selectively inattended experiences are more accessible to awareness and more limited in scope. They originate after the self-system has come into being and are a reaction to it. Once the self-system is formed, the person can block out those experiences which are not consistent with it. For example, people who regard themselves as competent drivers may "forget" about the many occasions on which they exceed the speed limit or the times they fail to stop completely at a stop sign. Like dissociated experiences, selectively inattended perceptions remain active though not fully conscious. They are crucial in determining which elements of an experience will be attended and which will be ignored or denied (Sullivan, 1953b).

PERSONIFICATIONS

Personifications are images a person has of self or others. These images may be relatively accurate or grossly distorted, since they are colored both by one's needs and anxieties.

Bad-Mother, Good-Mother

During infancy five elementary personifications are formed: *bad-mother, good-mother, bad-me, good-me,* and *not-me.* The earliest of these is the bad-mother, which grows out of the infant's experiences with the bad-nipple, that is, the nipple that does not satisfy hunger needs. It is of no importance whether the nipple belongs to the mother or to a bottle held by the mother, the father, a nurse, or anyone else. The bad-mother personification is almost completely undifferentiated and includes everyone involved in the nursing situation. For this reason it is a grossly inaccurate image of the "real" mother.

After the bad-mother personification is formed, an infant has a basis for comparing the tender and cooperative behaviors of the mothering one. As a result, the good-mother personification is formed. Ordinarily the good-mother personification ultimately evolves into the concept of "Mother." This is not the "real" mother either, but includes many imaginary positive qualities attributed to the mother. The two personifications, one based on the infant's perception of an anxious malevolent mother and the other on a calm tender mother, combine to form a complex personification composed of contrasting qualities projected onto the same person. Until the infant develops language, however, these two opposing images of mother can exist in the infant with no difficulty (Sullivan, 1953b).

"Me" Personifications

The other three personifications, bad-me, good-me, and not-me, are organized during midinfancy and form the building blocks of the self personification. Each is related to the evolving conception of "me" or "my body."

The bad-me is fashioned from experiences of punishment and disapproval received from the mothering one. The resulting anxiety is strong enough to teach an infant that she or he is "bad," but not so severe that the experience is dissociated or selectively inattended. Like all personifications, the bad-me is shaped out of the interpersonal situation; an infant can learn that it is bad only from someone else, ordinarily from the "bad-mother."

The good-me personification results from an infant's experiences with reward and approval. It is associated with diminishing anxiety and is based on the mother's expression of tenderness to the infant. The not-me personification is formed out of the infant's experiences with sudden severe anxiety. These experiences are either dissociated or selectively inattended. In either case, the infant denies them to the "me" image; that is, they become part of the not-me personification. These shadowy not-me personifications are also encountered by adults and are expressed in dreams, in schizophrenic episodes, and in other dissociated reactions. However, these nightmarish experiences are always preceded by a warning. When sudden severe anxiety strikes adults, they are overcome by *uncanny emotion*. Though this experience incapacitates people in interpersonal relationships, it serves as a valuable signal for approaching schizophrenic reactions. Uncanny emotion may be experienced as dreams, awe, horror, loathing, or a "chilly crawling" sensation. Sullivan (1953b) believed that before the onset of a schizophrenic episode, the perceptive person has a clear signal of approaching dread (Sullivan, 1953b).

Eidetic Personifications

During late infancy or early childhood the three "me" personifications evolve into the self-dynamism. Since this dynamism is an antianxiety system, it has the tools for leveling anxiety inherent in the bad-me and not-me personifications. Its most useful tool is language, which the child uses to raise the self-esteem level. The child conceals the bad-mother and bad-me from perception, but projects remnants of them onto current personifications. These relics from past anxiety-filled situations are called **eidetic personifications** and take the form of imaginary traits attributed to significant others or imaginary people invented to protect self-esteem. Not all interpersonal relations are with real people; children often have eidetic playmates. These imaginary friends may be as significant to a child's development as real playmates (Sullivan, 1964).

Eidetic personifications are not limited to children. Most adults see fictitious characteristics in other people. Eidetic personifications create conflict in interpersonal relations. For example, if a woman marries a man who reminds her of her father, she will project onto him imaginary traits that are remnants from the daughter-father relationship. When the husband reprimands the children, the wife is reminded of her father scolding her. She feels censured and may react with either timidity or boldness, but her reactions are based on an eidetic projection, not only the real personality of the husband.

Eidetic personifications hinder communication and prevent people from functioning on the same level of cognition.

MODES OF COGNITION

Sullivan recognized three levels or modes of cognition: prototaxic, parataxic, and syntaxic. Modes of cognition refer to ways of perceiving, imagining, and conceiving. Experiences on the prototaxic level are impossible to communicate; parataxic experiences are personal, prelogical, and communicated only in distorted form; and syntaxic cognition is meaningful interpersonal communication.

Prototaxic Mode

The earliest and most primitive experiences of an infant are termed **prototaxic.** These experiences are presymbolic, momentary, undifferentiated, incapable of formulation or conceptualization, and therefore noncommunicable. They represent the primary mode of cognition for the neonate and continue into adulthood as an important and common type of experience (Sullivan, 1953b).

Since they cannot be communicated, prototaxic experiences are difficult to describe or define. One can strive to understand the term by attempting to imagine the earliest subjective experiences of a newborn baby. Logically, these experiences must, in some way, relate to different zones of the body. A neonate feels hunger and pain and these prototaxic experiences result in observable action, for example, sucking or crying. The infant does not know the reason for the actions and sees no relationship between its actions and being fed. During early infancy, hunger and pain are prototaxic because they cannot be differentiated from one another nor from any other stimuli. As undifferentiated experiences, prototaxic events are beyond conscious recall.

In adults prototaxic experiences take the form of momentary sensations, images, feelings, moods, and impressions. These primitive images of dream and waking life are dimly perceived, unconscious, and, of course, incapable of being communicated to others.

Parataxic Mode

Parataxic experiences are prelogical and usually result when a person assumes a cause and effect relationship between two events that occur coincidentally. They are more clearly differentiated than prototaxic experiences, but their meaning remains private. Therefore, they can be communicated to others only in a distorted fashion.

The parataxic level of cognition begins very early in infancy and continues to be an important mode of experience throughout a person's lifetime. For example, the infant sucking the nipple at first sees no relationship between sucking and receiving nourishment, but very soon it makes a connection between its behavior and that of its mother. Because sucking and feeding occurred coincidentally, the infant believes that its sucking behavior *caused* the mother's feeding behavior. This process of seeing a cause and effect relationship between two events in close temporal proximity is a *parataxic distortion.*

Parataxic thinking is seen in the conditioning experiences of humans and animals. If children are conditioned to say "please" in order to receive candy, they may eventually reach the illogical conclusion that their supplications caused the appearance of candy. This is a parataxic distortion because uttering the word, "please" does not, by itself, cause the candy to appear. There must be a dispensing person present who hears the word and is able and willing to honor the request. When no other person is present, a child may ask God or imaginary people to grant favors. A good bit of adult behavior comes from similar parataxic thinking. The salient feature of parataxic experiences is that they are personal and private and not capable of being accurately communicated.

Syntaxic Mode

Experiences that are consensually validated and can be symbolically communicated are said to be **syntaxic.** Consensually validated experiences are those upon whose meaning two or more persons agree. Words, for example, are consensually validated because different people more or less agree on their meaning. The most common symbols used by one person to communicate with another are those of language, including words and gestures. Words facilitate communication only if those communicating have had, to some extent, similar experiences. Meaningful communication, therefore, is based on mutually shared experiences.

Sullivan hypothesized that the first instance of syntaxic thinking appears about 12 to 18 months after birth, when a sound or gesture begins to have the same meaning for the mother as it does for the child. For example, the word "ba-ba" after some period of time comes to mean "bottle," or "milk," or "I'm hungry" to both mother and child. Despite this consensually validated experience, the word "ba-ba" may continue to evoke a parataxic distortion if both mother and child attach their own private meanings to the word. To the child it may mean, "I feel lonely and want my bottle, which gives me security," while to the mother it may mean, "I must interrupt what I am doing and feed my baby."

The syntaxic level of cognition becomes more prevalent as the child begins to develop formal language, but it never completely supplants prototaxic and parataxic cognition. *Adult experience takes place on all three levels.*

In summary, Sullivan held that there are two kinds of experience: *tensions,* or potential for action; and *energy transformations,* or actions. There are two categories of tension: needs, which are conjunctive, that is, helpful to development; and anxiety, which is the chief disjunctive force in interpersonal relations, and which interferes with the satisfaction of needs. In addition,

TABLE 6.1   Summary of Sullivan's Concept of Experience and Related Terms

EXPERIENCE (Three levels: prototaxic, parataxic, and syntaxic)
  I. Tensions (potential for action)
      A. Needs (conjunctive)
          1. General needs (concern for overall well-being of the person)
              a. interpersonal (tenderness, intimacy, etc.)
              b. physiological (food, oxygen, water, etc.)
          2. Zonal needs (may also satisfy general needs)
              a. oral
              b. genital
              c. manual, etc.
      B. Anxiety (disjunctive, interferes with satisfaction of needs)
  II. Energy transformations (overt or covert actions designed to satisfy needs or to reduce anxiety)

experience takes place on three levels or modes of cognition: prototaxic, parataxic, and syntaxic. Table 6.1 summarizes Sullivan's concept of experience.

STAGES OF DEVELOPMENT

Sullivan postulated seven epochs or stages of development, each crucial in the formation of human personality. The thread of interpersonal relations runs throughout the stages; other people are indispensable to the person's development from infancy to mature adulthood.

Personality change can take place at any time, but it is most likely to occur during the transition from one stage to the next. In fact, these threshold periods are more crucial than the stages themselves. Experiences previously dissociated or selectively inattended may be permitted entrance into the self-system during one of the transitional periods. Sullivan (1953b, p. 227) hypothesized that, "as one passes over one of these more-or-less determinable thresholds of a developmental era, everything that has gone before becomes reasonably open to influence." His seven stages are infancy, childhood, the juvenile era, preadolescence, early adolescence, late adolescence, and adulthood.

Infancy

The period of infancy begins at birth and continues until the development of articulate speech, usually about 18 to 24 months of age. Sullivan believed that an infant becomes human through tenderness received from the mothering one. The satisfaction of all needs, except breathing, demands the cooperation of another person. The infant cannot survive without a mothering one to provide food, shelter, moderate temperature, cleansing of waste materials, and physical contact.

The mother-infant relationship, however, is like a two-sided coin. The infant develops a dual personification of mother; she is seen as both "good-mother" and "bad-mother," "good" when satisfying the baby's needs and "bad" when stimulating anxiety. The mothering one is always seen in both roles because, while satisfying the infant's needs, she inevitably experiences anxiety herself, thus introducing the infant to the most pernicious force in interpersonal relations.

The emphatic linkage between mother and infant leads inexorably to the development of anxiety for the baby. Being human, the mother enters the relationship with some degree of previously learned anxiety. While her anxiety may spring from any one of a variety of experiences, the infant's first anxiety is always associated with the nursing situation and the oral zone. Unlike its mother, the infant's repertory of energy transformations is not adequate to handle anxiety. So, whenever it feels anxious (a condition originally transmitted to it by the mother), the infant tries whatever means it has to reduce anxiety. These means will most likely take the form of rejection of the nipple, but this neither reduces anxiety nor satisfies the need for food. The infant's rejection of the nipple, of course, is not responsible for the mother's original anxiety, but now adds to it. Eventually the infant discriminates between the good-nipple and the bad-nipple, the former being associated with relative euphoria in the feeding process, the latter with enduring anxiety. This anxiety has all sorts of unwholesome effects, including the obstruction of both memory and foresight (Sullivan, 1953b).

An infant expresses anxiety and hunger in the same way — by crying. This complicates the nursing situation and increases the chances that the infant's anxiety will be mistaken for hunger by the mother and that the nipple will be forced on an anxious but not hungry infant. Conversely, the mother may soon learn that the cry does not always signify hunger and she may neglect to feed the infant even during those times of true hunger. The unsatisfied need leads to rage, which increases the mother's anxiety and interferes with her ability to cooperate with the infant. As tension mounts, the infant loses the capacity to receive satisfaction, but the need for food, of course, continues to increase. Finally, as tension approaches terror, the infant experiences difficulty with breathing. The infant may even stop breathing and turn a bluish color, but the built-in protections of **apathy** and **somnolent detachment** keep it from death. Apathy and somnolent detachment allow the infant to fall asleep despite its hunger; they do not completely abolish the need for food, but they lessen it, thus allowing the infant to return to a relative state of euphoria (Sullivan, 1953b).

At about midinfancy the hands become important zones of interaction. They are used to manipulate the zones, particularly the genital and anal areas. This activity provides an infant with the concepts of "me" and "my body." One particular part of the hand, the thumb, becomes a leading pleasurable zone because it can both feel and be felt. The mothering one, as "carrier of social responsibilities," begins to prohibit thumb sucking and, especially in Western culture, to punish the manipulation of genital and anal areas. These prohibitions, however, always involve anxiety from the mother and eventually cause the infant to deny certain aspects of its world to the self-system and to delegate them to the not-me personification. For example, after repeated punishments for masturbation, an infant may repress feelings of sexual pleasure, thereby removing them from the "me" personification.

Shortly afterward, an infant begins to learn how to communicate through language. In the beginning, language is not consensually validated, but takes place on an individualized or parataxic level. This period of infancy is characterized by **autistic language,** defined as "a primary unsocialized, unacculturated state of symbol activity" (Sullivan, 1953a, p. 17). Early communication takes place in the form of facial expressions and the sounding of various phonemes. Both are learned through imitation and eventually gestures and speech sounds have the same meaning for the infant as they do for other people. This marks the beginning of syntaxic language and the end of infancy.

Sheila, of course, has no memory of her infancy. We do know that her mother did not work outside the home and was never absent for a prolonged period. However, heavy demands were made on her by Sheila's older brother, who was not well-prepared for Sheila's birth and had a difficult time adjusting to it. Sheila's mother felt herself being pulled between the opposing demands of her two children, and, at the same time, found herself resenting her husband who seemed to welcome every opportunity to be away from home.

Childhood

The era of childhood begins with the advent of syntaxic language and continues until the appearance of the need for playmates of an equal status. The age of childhood varies from culture to culture and from individual to individual, but in Western society it covers the period from about 18 to 24 months until age five or six.

During this stage the mother remains the most significant other person, but her role is different from what it was in infancy. The dual personifications of mother are now fused into one and a child has a perception of the mother more congruent with the "real" mother. However, the good-mother and bad-mother personifications are usually retained on a parataxic level. In addition to combining the mother personifications, the child differentiates the various persons forming the mothering one. Mother and father are separated and each has a distinct role in child training. Besides one's parents, the child usually has one other significant relationship—an imaginary playmate. This eidetic friend enables the child to discover more about oneself, and later these experiences aid the child in making friends with real people (see Box—"Imaginary Playmates: A Help or a Hindrance?").

Imaginary Playmates: A Help or a Hindrance?

Preschool children frequently have an imaginary playmate. Many parents have observed their children talking to an imaginary friend, calling the friend by name and possibly even insisting that an extra place be set at the table or space be made available in the car or the bed for this playmate. Also, many adults can recall their own childhood experiences with imaginary playmates. Is the invention of an imaginary playmate a sign of mental instability or simply a harmless phase the child is going through?

Sullivan's answer would be neither. The presence of an imaginary or eidetic playmate can and does have a positive effect on later personality development. These playmates offer children an opportunity to interact with another "person" who is safe and who will not increase their level of anxiety. This comfortable, nonthreatening relationship with another permits children to be more independent of parents and to make friends in later years.

What evidence do we have that imaginary playmates are associated with positive characteristics rather than negative ones? Maya Pines (1978), writing in *Psychology Today,* looked into this question by reviewing the relevant literature and by talking with people conducting research on children's imaginary friends. She reported that one study indicated that 65 percent of three- and four-year-old children had identifiable imaginary playmates. Most of these children were firstborn or only children and most of the playmates were males. This latter finding is due to the fact that little girls may choose either boys or girls as imaginary friends, but boys almost always pick males.

In comparison with children who did not have imaginary playmates, those who did tended to watch far less television and to show a more advanced selection of programs. In addition, these children were more socialized; they showed less aggression and more cooperation. They smiled more, concentrated better, and were less likely to become bored. They also showed more verbal ability and higher levels of intelligence.

These findings, of course, do not indicate that the invention of an imaginary playmate *causes* children to become more intelligent, mature, and sociable. Cause and effect may be in the opposite direction, that is, intelligent, mature, and sociable children may simply have more ability and greater motivation to conjure up an imaginary companion. In any event, it seems that the presence of an imaginary playmate is definitely associated with positive qualities in young children and should not be viewed with concern or alarm.

At about the same time, a child is fusing the me-personifications into a single self-dynamism. Once syntaxic language is established, it is no longer possible to consciously deal with the bad-me and good-me at the same time. The child now labels behaviors as good or bad in imitation of the parents, but these labels differ from the old personifications of infancy. They are on a syntaxic level and originate from the child's behavior rather than from decreases or increases in anxiety. Also, good and bad now imply social or moral value and no longer refer to the absence or presence of that painful tension called anxiety.

During childhood emotions become reciprocal; the child is able to give tenderness as well as receive it. The relationship between the mother and child becomes more personal and is less one-sided. Rather than seeing the mother as good or bad based on how she satisfied hunger needs, the child evaluates the mother syntaxically according to whether she is rejecting, shows reciprocal tender feelings, or develops a relationship based on the mutual satisfaction of needs.

Sullivan (1953b) referred to childhood as a period of rapid acculturation. Besides acquiring language, a child learns cultural patterns of cleanliness, toilet training, eating habits, and sex-role expectancies. Two other important learning processes are *dramatizations* and *preoccupations.* Dramatizations are a child's attempts to act like or sound like significant authority figures, especially mother and father. Preoccupations are strategies for avoiding anxiety and fear-provoking situations by remaining occupied with an activity that has earlier proved useful or rewarding. The malevolent transformation reaches a peak during childhood, giving one the feeling of living in hostile or enemy country. At the same time, the child learns that there are certain restraints on freedom. From these restrictions and from experiences with approval and disapprobation, the child evolves the self-dynamism that provides a useful tool for handling anxiety and for stabilizing personality. In fact, the self-system introduces so much stability that it makes future changes exceedingly difficult.

Although Sheila's childhood was marked by some feelings of living in enemy country, she probably did not experience a fully developed malevolent transformation. Her earliest memory dates back to about age three when she was frightened by a violent argument between her mother and father. She recalled thinking that her father was going to seriously hurt or even kill her mother. This experience left Sheila with the continuing concern that her once secure world might, at any time, come to an abrupt end.

On a more pleasant note, Sheila remembered having an imaginary playmate during her childhood whom she called Boo. Her mother recalled overhearing Sheila talking to Boo and frequently scolding her. She welcomed those peaceful times when Sheila would remain in her room for long periods talking to and frequently scolding Boo. She also indulged Sheila's demands to have an extra place set at the table. Boo was frequently blamed for broken dishes, messy floors, and other minor disasters. Sheila had few playmates prior to attending school and her friendship with Boo provided a safe interpersonal relationship, one in which she could always have her way.

Juvenile Era

The threshold of the juvenile era is marked by the appearance of the need for peers or playmates of equal status. It ends when and if one finds a single chum to satisfy the need for intimacy. In American society the juvenile stage

During the juvenile stage children need to learn competition, compromise, and cooperation.

is roughly parallel to the first three years of school, beginning around age five or six and ending at about age eight and a half. (It is interesting that Sullivan was so specific with the age at which this period ends and the preadolescent stage begins. It will be recalled that Sullivan was eight and a half when he began an intimate relationship with a 13-year-old boy from a nearby farm.)

Three characteristics of the juvenile stage are *competition, compromise,* and *cooperation.* The degree of competition found among juveniles varies with the society, but Sullivan believes that in the United States it has been overemphasized. Parents and teachers conspire to teach the juvenile to be competitive and successful. When success does not come the child is liable to be ridiculed by authorities and peers alike. Compromise, too, can be overdone. A seven-year-old who learns to continually give in to others is handicapped in the socialization process and this yielding trait is likely to remain with the person in adulthood. Cooperation involves more than simply combining competition and compromise; it includes all those processes necessary to get along with others. The juvenile must learn to cooperate with others in the real world of interpersonal relationships. This is essential to becoming socialized, the most important task confronting a person during the juvenile era.

A primary school child associates with other children of equal standing. One-to-one relationships are rare; if they exist, they are more likely to be based on convenience than on genuine intimacy. Boys and girls play with one another with little regard for the sex of the other person. Though permanent dyadic relationships are still in the future, children of this age are beginning to make discriminations among themselves and to distinguish among adults. One teacher appears kinder than another, one parent more indulgent. Authority figures are now seen as people. The real world is coming ever more into focus. This means that the juvenile is beginning to operate increasingly on the syntaxic level, no longer getting by with expressions of fantasy, which were appropriate in childhood. Eidetic playmates are usually surrendered in favor of real ones. Stories and ideas not consensually validated are met with disapprobation, bringing about increased anxiety and consequently diminishing a juvenile's initiative and enthusiasm.

The world begins to appear more complex and complicated during this stage. If the complexity is too anxiety-provoking, a juvenile may simplify matters through the use of selective inattention. This control of focal awareness safeguards a person from having to deal with things that make no sense to the self-system. Selective inattention has both fortunate and unfortunate consequences. On the positive side, details of background noises and sights are tuned out, freeing the person from the burden of meaningless bits of information. On the other hand, some significant experiences inconsistent with the self-system are ignored or distorted, thus blocking syntaxic communication and leading to problems in interpersonal relationships. These interpersonal difficulties are the price one pays for maintaining security.

By the end of the juvenile stage a child should have developed an orientation toward living that makes it easier to consistently handle anxiety, satisfy zonal and tenderness needs, and set goals based on memory and foresight. This *orientation toward living,* readies a person for the deeper interpersonal relationships to follow (Sullivan, 1953b).

The juvenile era was a troubling time for Sheila. Although she had above average intelligence, she did not perform well in school. She dreaded going to school and missed many days because of "illness." She had problems with competition, compromise, and cooperation and often fought (usually verbally) with her classmates. Her mother recognized that Sheila was frequently unhappy and tried to help by blaming the other child for Sheila's many quarrels.

Preadolescence

The period from the appearance of the need for intimacy until puberty is called preadolescence, which begins around age eight or nine and ends with adolescence. It is a time for interest in one particular person of the same sex. All preceding stages have been egocentric, with friendships formed on the basis of self-interest. A preadolescent, for the first time, takes a genuine interest in the other person. Sullivan (1953a, p. 41) called this process of becoming a social being the "quiet miracle of preadolescence," a likely reference to the transformation of personality he experienced during his own preadolescence.

The outstanding characteristic of preadolescence is the genesis of the capacity to love. Previously, all interpersonal relationships were based on personal need satisfaction, but during preadolescence intimacy and love become the essence of friendships. Intimacy involves a dyadic relationship in which there is consensual validation of personal worth. Love exists "when the satisfaction or the security of another person becomes as significant to one as is one's own satisfaction or security" (Sullivan, 1953a, pp.42–43).

The relationships of preadolescence ordinarily involve a person of the same sex and of approximately the same age or status. Preadolescent infatuations with teachers or movie stars are not intimate relationships, since they are not consensually validated. The significant relationships of this age are boy-boy or girl-girl chumships. These pairs are often interlocked so that sociograms with nine- to twelve-year olds will usually show chains of friendships. To be liked by one's peers is more important to the preadolescent than to be liked by teachers or parents. Chums are able to freely express opinions and emotions without fear of humiliation or embarrassment, since the other person means as much as oneself. This free exchange of personal thoughts and feelings initiates the preadolescent into the social world. Each chum becomes more fully human, with an expanded personality and a wider interest in the humanity of all people.

In American society preadolescence is the most untroubled and carefree time of life. Parents are still significant, though they have been reappraised in a more realistic light. There is a lessening of dependence on others for satisfaction of needs. Unselfish love has blossomed, but is not yet complicated by lust. Cooperation acquired during the juvenile era evolves into collaboration, the capacity to work with another, not for self-prestige, but for the well-being of the other.

Preadolescence is critical for the future development of personality. If intimate collaboration is not learned at this time, the person is likely to become a problem and can be seriously stunted in later personality growth. During preadolescence a person may show symptoms of maladjustment that can be traced to unsatisfactory interpersonal relationships in earlier stages. Earlier negative influences, however, can be extenuated by the positive effects of an intimate relationship. Even the malevolent transformation can be reversed and many other juvenile problems, such as loneliness and self-centeredness, are diminished by the achievement of intimacy. The dyadic relationship, however, is not the only therapeutic factor in preadolescence—the peer group itself serves as a microcosm, giving a person experience in various kinds of social situations. This relatively brief and uncomplicated period of life is shattered by the onset of puberty (Sullivan 1953b).

Sullivan might say that many of Sheila's later problems with interpersonal relations were traceable to an unsatisfactory preadolescence. Even though Sheila had some previous interpersonal difficulties, the ones she experienced during the crucial stage of preadolescence were more critical than any others encountered earlier or later. Her self-centered façade and her inability to compete, compromise, or cooperate impeded her ability to establish an intimate interpersonal relationship during this time. While the other girls were

Sullivan believed that chumship during preadolescence is crucial to later psychosocial development.

developing dyadic and chain relationships, Sheila felt left out and lonely. She wanted desperately to be friends with the most popular girl in class, but overtures toward this girl were inevitably rebuffed. Sheila then turned to girls one or two years younger, but in these relationships Sheila always demanded to be the "boss," a situation that eventually led to problems, disagreements, and termination of the relationship. Near the end of preadolescence Sheila became interested in boys, but her male classmates seemed to be more concerned with sports, science fiction, and silliness.

Early Adolescence

Early adolescence begins with puberty and ends with the need for love with one person of the opposite sex. It is characterized by the eruption of genital interest and the advent of lustful relationships. In the United States early adolescence is generally parallel with the junior high school years. As with all stages, however, no great emphasis should be placed on chronological age.

The need for intimacy achieved during the preceding stage continues during early adolescence, but is now accompanied by a parallel, though separate, need—lust. In addition, security, or the need to be free from anxiety, remains active during early adolescence. Intimacy, lust, and security often collide with one another, bringing stress and conflict to the young adolescent. Invariably, lust interferes with security operations since genital activity in American culture is ingrained with guilt, embarrassment, and anxiety. Security is also threatened by a shift in intimacy. During preadolescence intimacy involves a chum of the same sex, but after puberty a person seeks intimate friendships with members of the opposite sex. These attempts are fraught with self-doubt, uncertainty, and ridicule from others, usually leading to loss of self-esteem and an increase in anxiety.

The final collision is that between intimacy and lust. There are at least four reasons why adolescents find it difficult to combine these two dynamisms. First, some adolescents sublimate their genital need, thereby preventing a union of lust and intimacy. Second, intimacy is inclined toward other people; lust is isolating. The powerful genital tensions seek outlet without regard for the intimacy need. Since lust can be satisfied autoerotically or in nonintimate relationships, there is no compelling reason to combine it with intimacy. Third, society divides sexual objects into "good" and "bad," while chums are always seen as "good." Adolescent boys often learn that prostitutes or sexy girls are "bad" while "good" girls are untouchable, though suitable for marriage. This unfortunate state of development is a causal force in many sexual problems, including impotence. A fourth reason for the chasm between lust and intimacy is also culturally induced. Parents, teachers, and other authority figures actively dissuade early adolescent boys and girls from becoming intimate. They sanction same-sex friendships, but for whatever reason (fear of early marriage is one possibility) opposite-sex chumships are discouraged.

Since the lust dynamism is biological, it bursts forth at puberty regardless of the individual's interpersonal readiness for it. A boy with no previous experience with intimacy may become a Don Juan, sexually conquering girls but developing no real interest in them; a girl may become a "teaser," exploiting the lust dynamism but unable to relate to a boy on an interpersonal level. Such was the case with Sheila.

An early adolescent's experiences with masturbation and its suppression also play an important role in forming attitudes toward sex and in the development of self-esteem. A person may have learned that genital pleasure is "bad" and therefore he or she is "bad" when sexual pleasure is experienced. This feeling deprives the early adolescent of self-esteem and leaves the person in a more or less permanent state of anxiety. The boy retains an interest in girls, but his chronic anxiety impairs interpersonal relations with them. The girl, though likely more socially advanced, will have difficulty achieving a chumship of equality with a boy her age.

Sullivan believed that early adolescence is a turning point in personality development. The person either emerges from this stage in command of the intimacy and lust dynamisms, or faces serious interpersonal difficulties in future stages. Though sexual adjustment is important to personality development, Sullivan (1953b) felt that the real issue lies in getting along with other people.

During early adolescence Sheila, perhaps to her ultimate disadvantage, grew into an attractive, sexually sophisticated young lady. The intimacy with other girls that she missed during preadolescence made it very difficult for her to become chums with her boyfriends during early adolescence. Biologically and socially she had less in common with boys than with girls. She shared few common interests, other than sex, with her male companions and was conspicuously incapable of developing an intimate relationship with any of them. Close friendships with girls were also difficult since she still possessed the same personal characteristics that accounted for her previous lack of intimacy. As she became more sexually aggressive and adventuresome, however, her popularity among boys, especially those a couple of years older, began to increase.

Late Adolescence

Late adolescence begins when preferred genital activity becomes stabilized; it terminates in adulthood with the establishment of a lasting love relationship. Late adolescence embraces that period of self-discovery when one is determining one's preferences in genital behavior. In American society late adolescence ideally encompasses the senior high school years, age 15 to 17 or 18. Like all stages of development, however, its attainment is individual—many reach it several years later, others like Sheila never attain it.

The outstanding feature of late adolescence is the fusion of intimacy and lust. The troubled attempts at self-exploration of early adolescence evolve into a stable pattern of sexual activity in which the loved one is also the object of lustful interest. The person of the other sex is no longer desired solely as a sexual object, but as one who is loved as much or nearly as much as self. Unlike the previous stage, which is ushered in by biological changes, late adolescence is completely determined by interpersonal relations.

Successful late adolescence is characterized by growth of the syntaxic mode. At college or work the late adolescent begins "bumping heads" with others, exchanging ideas, and having opinions and beliefs validated or repudiated. The person learns from others how to live in the adult world, but a successful journey through the earlier stages facilitates this adjustment. When previous periods of development have been lacking, one comes to this age with no intimate interpersonal relations, inconsistent patterns of sexual activity, and a great need to maintain security operations. A person relies heavily on the parataxic mode to avoid anxiety, striving to preserve self-esteem through selective inattention, dissociation, and neurotic symptoms. Serious problems are faced in bridging the gulf between society's expectations and one's inability to form intimate relations with persons of the other sex. Believing that love is a universal condition of young people, the late adolescent is often pressured into "falling in love." However, only the mature person has the capacity to love; others merely go through the motions of being "in love" in order to maintain security (Sullivan, 1953b).

Chronologically, Sheila is now a late adolescent. Unfortunately, her interpersonal development has been stunted by her inability to form an intimate relationship during preadolescence. In her search for intimacy she consistently confuses sex with friendship. As a result, each of her sexual relationships has ended in confusion and disappointment. Nevertheless, she continues her quest for that elusive closeness which she has yet to capture.

Adulthood

The successful completion of late adolescence culminates in adulthood, defined as that stage characterized by the establishment of a love relationship with at least one significant other person. Speaking of this love relationship Sullivan (1953b, p. 34) stated that "this really highly developed intimacy with another is not the principal business of life, but is, perhaps, the principal source of satisfaction in life."

Sullivan had little to say about adulthood since he believed that maturity is beyond the scope of interpersonal psychiatry: Those people who have achieved the capacity to love are not in need of psychiatric counsel. His sketch of the mature person is not founded on clinical experience, but is an extrapolation from the preceding stages. Mature adults are perceptive of anxiety or security in others, sensitive to their needs, and genuinely understanding of their problems. They have a low level of anxiety, operate predominantly on the syntaxic level, find life interesting and exciting, and are no problem to themselves or others (Sullivan, 1953b).

MENTAL DISORDERS

According to Sullivan, all mental disorders have an interpersonal origin and can be understood only with reference to the social context. From the simplest lapse of memory to the gravest schizophrenic psychosis, abnormal reactions stem from difficulties in interpersonal relations.

Sullivan believed that the deficiencies found in psychiatric patients are found in every person, but to a lesser degree. There is nothing unique about mental difficulties; they are derived from the same kind of interpersonal troubles faced by all people. Sullivan (1953a, p. 96) insisted "that everyone is much more simply human than unique, and that no matter what ails the patient, he is *mostly* a person like the psychiatrist."

Sullivan believed that most mental disorders emanate from interpersonal relationships and not from organic factors. Most of his early therapeutic work was with schizophrenic patients and many of his subsequent lectures and writings dealt with schizophrenia (Sullivan, 1962). Sullivan distinguished two broad classes of schizophrenia. The first includes all those symptoms originating from organic causes. Illnesses in this category are beyond the study of interpersonal psychiatry and Sullivan was content to classify them under the older term dementia praecox. The second class includes all schizophrenic disorders grounded in situational causes. These were the only ones of concern to Sullivan, since they are the only ones amenable to change through interpersonal psychiatry.

Dissociated reactions often precede schizophrenia. These disorders are characterized by loneliness, low self-esteem, the uncanny emotion, unsatisfactory relations with others, and ever-increasing anxiety (Sullivan, 1953b). A dissociated personality, in common with the normal person, attempts to minimize anxiety by building an elaborate self-system that permits the dissociation of those experiences that threaten security. A normal individual feels relatively secure in interpersonal relations and does not need to constantly rely on dissociation as a means of protecting self-esteem. With mentally disordered individuals, however, dissociation becomes a frequent and persistent strategy, causing them to operate more and more in their own private world with increasing parataxic distortions and decreasing consensually validated experiences (Sullivan, 1956).

PSYCHOTHERAPY

Since mental disorders grow out of interpersonal difficulties, therapeutic procedures must be based on a concentrated effort to improve a patient's relationship with others. To facilitate this process, the Sullivanian therapist serves as a *participant observer,* becoming part of an interpersonal, face-to-face relationship with the patient and providing the patient an opportunity to establish syntaxic communication with another human being. Though a participant in the interview, the psychiatrist avoids getting personally involved. The therapist is not placed on the same level with the patient, but, on the contrary, the first task is to convince the patient of the therapist's expert abilities. In other words, friendship is not a condition of psychotherapy—one must be trained as an expert in the difficult business of making discerning observations of the patient's interpersonal relations (Sullivan, 1954).

Sullivan was primarily concerned with understanding the patient and helping the patient to improve foresight, discover difficulties in interpersonal relations, and restore the ability to participate in consensually validated experiences. To accomplish these goals, he concentrated his efforts on answering three questions constantly facing the therapist. What precisely is the patient saying to me? How can I best put into words what I wish to say to the patient? What is the general pattern of communication between us?

Sullivan divided the interview into four stages: formal inception, reconnaissance, detailed inquiry, and termination.

Formal Inception

The first stage, *formal inception,* involves the therapist's introduction to the patient, including an inquiry into the reason for therapy and the source of referral. The initial contact is extremely important because it is the first instance of communication between therapist and patient. It is crucial to later therapeutic progress that the patient not be humiliated or made more anxious during the formal inception. At this time, the psychiatrist promotes confidence in the patient by demonstrating interpersonal skill, permits the patient to express the reasons for seeking therapy, formulates tentative hypotheses, and decides on a possible course of action (Sullivan, 1954).

Reconnaissance

During the *reconnaissance* stage, the therapist obtains a general personal and social history, makes observations concerning the patient's interpersonal identity, and tries to discover why the patient came to develop a particular personality. At this time the doctor carefully structures the interview, asking questions about the patient's age, birth order, mother, father, education, occupational history, marriage, children, and so forth. The therapist never registers surprise at the information received and continues to impress the patient with an expertise in interpersonal relations. During this period the therapist may use free association, but only indirectly and without the patient's knowledge. The psychiatrist asks open-ended questions, allowing the patient to respond at random until thought patterns circle around to something relevant. The reconnaissance typically lasts from 7 to 15 hours, but may be as brief as 20 minutes when therapy consists of a single interview. At the end of this phase the therapist summarizes the important data, after which the patient amends or adds any details. This ensures that therapy can proceed on a consensually valid basis (Sullivan, 1954).

Detailed Inquiry

The third stage, *detailed inquiry,* varies with the purpose of the interview, but in general it is a time for testing hypotheses formulated during the two preceding stages. The therapist tries to improve understanding by asking a series of detailed questions concerning the patient's personal history and current attitude toward self and significant others. A skillful therapist must listen carefully to all possible meanings behind the patient's utterances. In the search for durable characteristics of the patient, the psychiatrist sifts out communication designed to deceive. The patient unintentionally hides the truth from the psychiatrist believing that the doctor will somehow see the truth as a sign of weakness and failure. This tendency to hide the complete truth and to impress the therapist is a direct result of the patient's anxiety and low self-esteem. High anxiety activates security operations that guard against decreases in euphoria.

During the detailed inquiry the therapist strives to verify impressions formulated during earlier stages. In the quest for the patient's true personal history, the therapist must be careful not to increase the patient's anxiety. Sullivan warned that the psychiatrist must vigilantly guard against the premature introduction of anxiety. Later, after the patient is convinced that help is forthcoming, the therapist can relax the guard somewhat and, if anxiety is accidentally provoked, it will no longer have disastrous results (Sullivan, 1954).

Termination

The fourth and final stage of the interview is *termination* or, in some cases, *interruption*. By termination Sullivan means the therapist does not expect to see the patient again; interruption means the interview is broken, but may be resumed the following day, week, or some other designated time. After each interruption, the psychiatrist gives the patient "homework," something to do or some memory to recall. With either interruption or termination the therapist's main task is to consolidate whatever progress has been made. In doing this a final statement is made of what has been learned of the patient, a course of action is prescribed, the patient is given a final assessment of prognosis, and formal leave is taken. The formal leave-taking must proceed smoothly or else therapeutic benefits so carefully accumulated may be destroyed (Sullivan, 1954).

Parataxic Perceptions in Therapy

Sullivan did not recognize the concept of transference in interpersonal psychiatry, but he did place great emphasis on the importance of the therapist-patient relationship including the parataxic perceptions the patient may have of the doctor. When earlier situations are reviewed during therapy, a patient may develop a distorted view of the therapist so that there are actually three persons present: the imaginary psychiatrist with whom the patient is conversing, the patient who reacts to the imaginary doctor, and the real psychiatrist who is observing and trying to make sense out of the interview. In one example of a parataxic perception, Sullivan (1953a) spoke of a patient who, after about 300 hours of therapy with Sullivan, was surprised to see that he was a thin man with dark, thinning hair. She had previously seen him as a fat old man with white hair.

The therapist attempts to point out the patient's inconsistencies and distortions concerning the doctor and to learn more about the earlier significant authority person who is the source of the patient's delusions. Parataxic attitudes toward the therapist are expressed only after the anxiety has been reduced and the patient begins to feel secure with the doctor. Both therapist and patient can then gain a greater understanding of the patient's past relationships and also facilitate present and future interpersonal relations (Sullivan, 1954).

Sleep and Dreams

Sleep, dreams, and myths are important in interpersonal psychiatry. Sleep relieves a person of the need to maintain security operations. Since sleep and anxiety do not mix well, the self-system is relaxed during sleep. Needs not met during the day are satisfied through dreams. The purpose of the dream is to create a barrier between waking life and sleep by putting into parataxic form problems an individual cannot solve while awake. Since the dream itself is parataxic and, to some extent, prototaxic, it is unreachable. The psychiatrist deals only with a patient's recollection of the dream and these reports are treated in the same way as any other important event—they reveal clues concerning the patient's interpersonal relations. Through dreams the patient acts out interpersonal relations in an illusory, fictional manner.

Myths, like dreams, appear on the parataxic level, but unlike dreams they transcend the individual and pertain to the culture. Sullivan believed that myths originate as general dreams incorporated into the culture because they deal with unsolvable problems common to many people. He also believed that the psychiatrist should not try to translate dreams or myths into syntaxic language. They make sense only on the parataxic level, but this in no way subtracts from their validity (Sullivan, 1953b).

Summary

In summary, the Sullivanian therapist is primarily concerned with uncovering a patient's difficulties in relating to others. The therapist strives to replace disjunctive motivations with conjunctive ones, those which integrate personality and allow needs to be satisfied and security to be enhanced. To accomplish this, the patient must give up some security in dealing with other people and realize that mental health can be achieved only through consensually validated personal relations. The therapeutic ingredient in this process is the face-to-face relationship between psychiatrist and patient, which permits the patient to reduce anxiety and to communicate with others on the syntaxic level.

CONCEPT OF HUMANITY

Sullivan's basic conception of humanity is summed up in his *one-genus hypothesis,* which states that *"everyone is much more simply human than otherwise"* (1953b, p. 32). This was his way of saying that similarities among people are much more important than differences. People are more like people than anything else.

> In other words, the differences between any two instances of human personality—from the lowest grade imbecile to the highest-grade genius—are much less striking than the difference between the least-gifted human being and a member of the nearest other biological genus (Sullivan, 1953b, p. 33).

The one influence separating humans from all other creatures is interpersonal relations. We are born biological organisms, animals with no human qualities except the potential for participation in interpersonal relations. Soon after birth we begin to realize this potential when interpersonal experiences transform us into human beings. Sullivan believed that the mind contains nothing except that which was put there through interpersonal experiences. Unlike Freud and Jung, he contended that there are no human instincts. We are motivated only by environmental influences—interpersonal relationships.

Sullivan insisted that humans have no existence outside the interpersonal situation. As isolated entities we are nothing. Only through our relationships with other humans do we develop personality. Each of us begins life with a somewhat one-sided relationship with a mothering one who both cares for our needs and imparts anxiety to us. Later we are able to reciprocate feelings for the parents and these relationships serve as a foundation upon which subsequent interpersonal relations are built. Next we need to learn to compete, cooperate, and compromise with children who are like us and this provides us with the tools for intimacy and love. It is through our intimate and love relationships that we become healthy personalities and an absence of these relationships leads to stunted mental health and psychological disorders.

Personal individuality is an illusion; we exist only in relation to other people and have as many personalities as we have interpersonal relations. The concepts of *uniqueness* and *individuality* do not concern interpersonal psychiatry. The subject matter of scientific inquiry is the interaction between the observer and the observed, with the observer being a participant in the relationship. This interaction is the essence of personality.

Anxiety and interpersonal relations are tied together in a cyclic manner making significant personality changes difficult. Anxiety interferes with interpersonal relations and unsatisfactory interpersonal relations lead to the use of rigid behaviors that may temporarily buffer anxiety, but, in the long run, they drive us further from positive interpersonal relations. Since they do not solve the basic problem, these behaviors eventually lead to increases in anxiety with the resultant deterioration in interpersonal relations followed by more anxiety, which must be held in check by an ever-rigid self-system. For this reason Sullivan would have to be rated *neither optimistic nor pessimistic* concerning the potential for growth and change within human beings. Interpersonal relations can transform us into healthy personalities, but they can also be restrictive by creating anxiety and its resultant rigid self-structure.

Interpersonal relations are responsible for both positive and negative characteristics in people. If the infant has its needs satisfied by the mothering one, is not disturbed by her anxiety, and receives genuine feelings of tenderness, it can avoid the malevolent transformation in childhood and develop tender feelings toward others. On the other hand, unsatisfactory interpersonal relations may trigger the malevolent transformation and leave us with the feeling that people cannot be trusted and that we are essentially alone among our enemies. Because personality is built solely on interpersonal relations, Sullivan is rated very high on *social influence.*

CRITIQUE OF SULLIVAN

Though Sullivan evolved one of the most comprehensive of all personality theories, over time it has undergone a reduction in popularity, especially among academic psychologists. The value of any theory, however, depends only partially on comprehensiveness and popularity. Ultimately it rests on the five criteria of a useful theory enumerated in Chapter 1.

First, how well does Sullivanian theory provide an organization for all that is known about human personality? Despite its many elaborate postulates, the theory can receive only a moderate rating on its ability to *organize knowledge*. Most of the research findings on interpersonal relationships of children and adolescents are consistent with Sullivan's concepts of the various stages of development. However, the extreme emphasis on interpersonal relations is both a distinguishing feature and a weakness of Sullivan's theory. Much of what is presently known about human behavior has a biological basis and does not easily fit into a theory restricted to interpersonal relations.

The second criterion of a useful theory is its ability to *generate research*. Sullivan's theory regarding the stages of development is not only logical but has the power to generate a multitude of important testable hypotheses as well. Unfortunately, little research has been conducted that specifically tests hypotheses drawn from the theory. One possible explanation for this deficiency is the lack of Sullivan's popularity among those most apt to conduct research—the academicians. Again, this might be accounted for by Sullivan's close association with psychiatry, his isolation from the university setting, and the relative lack of organization in his writings and speeches. A second possible explanation for the paucity of research on Sullivan's stages of development is that such investigations would almost necessitate longitudinal studies and thus would be time consuming. Probably the most important hypotheses that can be drawn from the theory center around Sullivan's notion of the crucial, almost miraculous, stage of preadolescence. He suggests that mistakes made prior to this time can be rectified if the preadolescent is able to establish an intimate relationship with a chum. On the other hand, errors made during this period, that is, the inability to find a chum, cannot easily be remedied during subsequent stages. If longitudinal studies were to lend support to these two hypotheses, then society might better prepare preadolescent children for intimate relationships with another person of equal status.

This leads to the third criterion of a useful theory, namely, its capacity to serve as a *guide for action*. The relative lack of testing of Sullivan's theory diminishes its usefulness as a practical guide for parents, teachers, psychotherapists, and others concerned with the care of children and adolescents. However, if one accepts the theory without supporting evidence, then many practical problems can be managed by resorting to Sullivanian theory. As a guide to action, then, the theory receives a fair to moderate rating.

Is the theory *internally consistent?* Sullivan's ideas suffer from his inability to write well, but the theory itself is logically conceptualized and holds together as a unified entity. His use of terms like prototaxic, parataxic, and syntaxic, though unique, is consistent throughout his writings and speeches. His insistence on the importance of the interpersonal unit is found throughout his work and, to his credit, he does not waver in his belief. Overall, then, his theory is consistent, but lacks the organization that might have been achieved had he committed more of his ideas to the printed page.

Finally, is the theory as *parsimonious* or as simple as it might be? Here Sullivan must receive a low rating. His penchant for creating his own terms and the awkwardness of his writing add needless bulk to a theory which, if streamlined, would be far more useful. A more tightly written theory might have generated more interest in potential researchers which, in turn, would have resulted in a presently more viable theory.

CHAPTER SUMMARY

Harry Stack Sullivan was the first American to develop a comprehensive theory of personality. Like many other theorists, his ideas on personality are a reflection of his own life experiences. Sullivan's early loneliness and isolation led to a theory that emphasized the importance of personal relationships. His isolation also led to a rather esoteric language. However, his insights as a psychotherapist resulted in an eloquent description of six stages of development.

Each developmental stage must be understood by a consideration of the basic concepts of anxiety and interpersonal relations. Anxiety is the chief descriptive force in interpersonal relations and is the cause of much pain and suffering. Interpersonal relations can either create additional anxiety or lead to healthy psychological growth and development.

The first stage is *infancy*—a period lasting from birth to the development of language. During this stage an infant's primary interpersonal relationship is with the mother and its principal source of anxiety is the feeding situation.

When a child begins to develop language, the period of *childhood* begins. This stage continues until about age five or six and is frequently characterized by the creation of an imaginary playmate. Mother still remains the most important "other" in a child's life, but these imaginary playmates can also have lasting effects on later development.

The third Sullivanian stage is the *juvenile era,* a period roughly encompassing the first three years of school in Western culture. At this time a child should learn competition, compromise, and cooperation skills that will enable a person to move successfully through later stages of development.

The most crucial stage of development is *preadolescence* because mistakes made during this phase are exceedingly difficult to overcome later. At this time a child should learn intimacy, ordinarily with a person of the same sex. This close interpersonal relationship is free from the complications of a sexual encounter and is the positive force that allows one to subsequently relate to members of the opposite sex in a personal rather than strictly sexual manner.

As a young person reaches *early adolescence,* sexual interest is stimulated by biological changes. If intimacy was developed during preadolescence, then the person is ready to maintain an intimate relationship with another of the same sex while developing lustful encounters with people of the opposite sex.

When intimacy and lust or both directed toward a single other, *late adolescence* has been reached. This stage, unfortunately, is not achieved by everyone. Many people never combine lust and intimacy in one other person.

Although Sullivan made significant contributions to psychotherapy, especially therapy with schizophrenic patients, his greatest insights revolve around his six interpersonal stages of development and his elucidation of the concept of anxiety.

Suggested Readings

CHAPMAN, A. H. (1976). *Harry Stack Sullivan: His life and his work.* New York: Putnam.
A very readable account of Sullivan's life combined with a discussion of the main principles of interpersonal theory.

PERRY, H. S. (1982). *Psychiatrist of America: The life of Harry Stack Sullivan.* Cambridge, MA: Belknap Press.
Written by the former managing editor of Sullivan's journal, *Psychiatry,* this biography is the result of 20 years of careful research. Sullivan's personality emerges more fully than in any other biography.

SULLIVAN, H. S. (1953b). *The interpersonal theory of psychiatry.* New York: Norton.
As the first book prepared from Sullivan's unpublished lectures, this work contains the most complete account of interpersonal theory, including the six developmental epochs.

YOUNISS, J. (1980) *Parents and peers in social development: A Sullivan-Piaget perspective.* Chicago: University of Chicago Press.
In this attempt to integrate the writings of Sullivan and Jean Piaget, the author argues that children's social development is greatly influenced by their friends and peers.

HORNEY

7

Psychoanalytic Social Theory

When his first wife left him Harold was devastated, confused, and depressed. He had noticed that Nancy was becoming more distant, but he had no notion that she had wanted a divorce. After all, he had been a near perfect husband. He had frequently surprised Nancy with expensive gifts, continually complimented her on her appearance, and routinely praised her cooking. In addition, he tried hard to satisfy her sexually and had remained faithful to her during their five-year marriage. What more could Nancy desire?

For months after the separation Harold struggled in vain to win Nancy back. Then, as he began to accept the permanence of the situation, he started to analyze the reasons for the separation. At first he had blamed himself, but now he was shifting the responsibility to Nancy, criticizing her for her newly formed feminist views. The more he thought of it, the more he began to see that Nancy had been unreasonably influenced by some of her friends, was reacting in an irrational manner, and was showing signs of mental instability. When he became convinced that Nancy's newly acquired ideas and bizarre behaviors were responsible for the separation, he quickly agreed to a divorce.

At about the time he accepted the inevitability of a divorce, Harold's outlook began to improve and his depression lifted. Soon he was seeing another woman and almost as quickly he "fell in love" again.

Harold became completely consumed by his relationship with Denise. Nearly all his time away from work was spent with her. When they weren't physically together, they were talking to one another on the telephone. At first, Denise seemed to be as enamored with Harold as he was with her.

In time, however, she began to feel stifled by the relationship. She wanted to spend more time alone or with other friends. Frequently, she would not be home when Harold called. As Denise became less and less infatuated with Harold, he became more and more demanding of her. He pushed hard for commitment and marriage, but Denise wanted more freedom to see other men. Harold had never dated another woman after he met Denise and he could not understand why she wanted to date other men.

As time went on and Denise became less available to Harold, he became suspicious that she was seeing someone else. He would park his car down the street from her apartment and then follow her when she left. On several of these occasions she, indeed, met another man. Harold never confronted the couple, but when he was alone with Denise he would become enraged and insulting. Repetition of this behavior led Denise to place a restraining order on Harold.

Legally forced to remain away from Denise, Harold was soon dating another woman. Within two months of his breakup with Denise, Harold and Carolyn were married.

After less than a year this second marriage was in trouble. Carolyn was demanding more time for herself and was complaining that Harold was "smothering" her. Harold reluctantly agreed to allow Carolyn more time with her friends, but he was puzzled when she failed to show appreciation for this freedom. In fact, arguments became more frequent, and once again Harold began to blame his wife for his marital problems.

Nevertheless, he desperately desired to hold on to the marriage. He was convinced that if only Carolyn would return to her earlier compliant behavior, their happiness would be assured. However, much to Harold's consternation, Carolyn showed no willingness to recapture the rapture of their early relationship. Harold was unaware that his demands were driving Carolyn farther away. In fact, he was oblivious of any demands whatsoever. He also failed to see any similarities between his previous relationships with Nancy and Denise and the present one with Carolyn.

As he and Carolyn were on the brink of breaking up, Harold once again became devastated, confused, and depressed. Despite his belief that Carolyn was completely responsible for their problems, he tried hard to hold on to the relationship. When he finally realized that a second divorce was inevitable his outlook became less gloomy, and soon, he was once again seeking the companionship of another woman.

As Harold approached his fourth intimate relationship in three years, he had learned little from the previous three.

OVERVIEW

The **psychoanalytic social theory** of Karen Horney offers some insight into Harold's case as well as other normal and neurotic personalities. Horney's theory holds that human relations lie at the core of neuroses and that cultural conditions, especially childhood experiences, are largely responsible for the development of basic anxiety and subsequent unhealthy interpersonal relations.

In order to combat basic anxiety the person adopts one of three basic styles of relating to people: (1) moving toward others, (2) moving against others, or (3) moving away from others. Normal individuals may use any of these, but neurotics are compelled to rigidly employ only one. Their compulsive behavior generates a basic intrapsychic conflict manifested by an idealized self-image on the one hand and self-hatred on the other. The idealized self-image is expressed as (1) neurotic search for glory, (2) neurotic claims, or (3) neurotic pride. Self-hatred can take the form of either self-contempt or alienation from self.

Although Horney's writings are concerned mostly with the neurotic personality, many of her ideas can also be applied to normal individuals. This chapter looks at Horney's basic theory of neurosis, compares her ideas to those of Freud, examines her views on feminine psychology, and briefly discusses her ideas on psychotherapy.

BIOGRAPHY OF KAREN HORNEY

Karen Danielsen Horney was born in Eilbek, a small town near Hamburg, Germany, September 15, 1885 (Quinn, 1987). (A 1978 biography by Rubins erroneously reported the date as September 16 and the town as Blankenese.) Karen was the only daughter of Berndt Danielsen, a sea captain, and Clothilda van Ronzelen Danielsen, a woman nearly 18 years younger than her husband. The only other child of this marriage was a son, about four years older than Karen. However, the old sea captain had been married earlier and had four other children, most of whom were adults by the time Karen was born. Karen was never close to her stern, devoutly religious father who was nearly 50 years older, and who was at sea much of the time. Karen enjoyed a much closer relationship with her mother who both supported and protected her against her father. Nevertheless, Karen's childhood was not a happy one. She resented the favored treatment given to her older brother and, in addition, she worried about the bitterness and discord between her parents.

When she was 14 Karen decided to become a physician, but this was 1899, and there were no universities in Germany that admitted women (Quinn, 1987). Two years later this situation had changed and Karen entered the Gymnasium, a school that would lead to a university and to medical school. She was among the first girls in Germany to attend the Gymnasium. This experience, at age 16, placed her on her own for the first time.

In 1906 she entered the University of Freiburg, becoming one of the first women in Germany to study medicine. There she met Oskar Horney, a political science student. The relationship began as a friendship but eventually became a romantic one. After their marriage in 1909 the couple settled in Berlin where Oskar, now a Ph.D., worked for a coal company and Karen, not yet an M.D., specialized in psychiatry.

By this time, Freudian psychoanalysis was becoming well established and Karen Horney became familiar with Freud's writings. Early in 1910, she began an analysis with Karl Abraham, one of Freud's close associates. After her analysis was terminated, she attended Abraham's evening seminars where she became acquainted with other psychoanalysts. By 1917 she had written her first paper on psychoanalysis, "The Technique of Psychoanalytic Therapy" (Horney, 1917, 1968), which reflected the orthodox Freudian view and gave little indication of Horney's subsequent independent thinking.

The early years of her marriage were filled with many notable personal experiences for Horney. Her father and mother, who were now separated, died within less than a year of each other; she gave birth to three daughters in five years; she received her M.D. degree in 1915 after five years of psychoanalysis; and she had several affairs in her quest for the right man (Quinn, 1987).

After World War I the Horneys lived a prosperous, suburban life style, with several servants and a chauffeur. Oskar was doing well financially and Karen's psychiatric practice was thriving. This idyllic life, however, was not to last. The inflation and economic disorder of 1923 cost Oskar his job and the family was forced to move back to an apartment in Berlin. A year later Karen and Oskar separated and were officially divorced in 1939 after 15 years of separation.

The six years following her separation from Oskar were the most productive of Horney's life. In addition to seeing patients and caring for her three daughters, she became more involved with writing, teaching, traveling, and lecturing. Her papers were now showing important differences with Freudian theory. She believed that culture, not anatomy, was responsible for psychic differences between men and women. When Freud reacted negatively to Horney's position, she became even more outspoken in her opposition.

In 1932 Horney left Germany for a position as associate director of the newly founded Institute for Psychoanalysis in Chicago. Several factors contributed to her decision to immigrate—the anti-Jewish political climate in Germany, (although Horney was not Jewish); increasing opposition to her unorthodox views; and an opportunity to extend her influence beyond Berlin. During the two years she spent in Chicago she met Margaret Mead, Harry Stack Sullivan, and many of the same scholars who had influenced Sullivan (see Chapter 6). In addition, she renewed acquaintances with Erich Fromm and his wife, Frieda Fromm-Reichmann, who she had known in Berlin. For the next 15 years Horney and Fromm (see Chapter 8) became close friends, greatly influencing one another and eventually becoming lovers (Quinn, 1987).

In 1934 Horney moved to New York, where she taught at the New School for Social Research and where she met and was influenced by several other scholars from Europe, including Max Wertheimer. She also became a member of the Zodiac group which included Fromm, Fromm-Reichmann, Sullivan, and others (see Chapter 6).

Although a member of the New York Psychoanalytic Institute, Horney seldom agreed with the established members. Moreover, her book, *New Ways in Psychoanalysis* (1939), made her the leader of an opposition group. The book called for abandoning the instinct theory and placing more emphasis on ego and social influences. In 1941 she resigned from the institute over issues of dogma and orthodoxy and helped form a rival organization, the Association for the Advancement of Psychoanalysis. This new association, however, was also replete with internal strife. In 1943 Fromm (whose intimate relationship with Horney had recently ended) and several others resigned from the AAP, leaving that organization without its strongest members. Despite the rift, the association continued, but under a new name—the Karen Horney Psychoanalytic Institute. In 1952 the Karen Horney Clinic was founded and both organizations have continued to the present time.

Horney published her most important book, *Neurosis and Human Growth,* in 1950. In it she sets forth her own theories which were no longer merely a reaction to Freud, but rather an expression of her own creative and independent thinking.

After a short illness, Horney died of cancer on December 4, 1952.

INTRODUCTION TO PSYCHOANALYTIC SOCIAL THEORY

The early writings of Karen Horney, like those of Adler, Jung, and Erikson have a distinctive Freudian flavor. Like Adler and Jung she eventually became disenchanted with orthodox psychoanalysis and constructed a revisionist theory that reflected her own personal experiences—clinical and otherwise.

Although Horney wrote nearly exclusively about neuroses and neurotic personalities, her works imply much that is appropriate to normal healthy development. Culture, especially early childhood experiences, plays a leading role in shaping human personality, either neurotic or healthy. Horney, then, agreed with Freud that early childhood traumas are important, but she differed from him in her insistence that social rather than biological forces were paramount in personality development.

In this introduction we compare Horney's theories to those of Freud, examine her ideas on the impact of culture, and look at her views on the importance of childhood experiences.

Horney and Freud Compared

Horney criticized Freud's theories on several accounts. First, she cautioned that strict adherence to orthodox psychoanalysis would lead to stagnation in both theoretical thought and therapeutic practice (Horney, 1937). Second, Horney (1937, 1939) objected to Freud's ideas on feminine psychology. (We will return to this subject later.) Third, she stressed that psychoanalysis should move beyond instinct theory and emphasize the importance of cultural influence in shaping personality. "Man is ruled not by the pleasure principle alone but by two guiding principles: safety and satisfaction" (Horney,

1939, p. 73). Similarly, she claimed that neuroses are not the result of instincts, but rather the person's "attempt to find paths through a wilderness full of unknown dangers" (Horney, 1939, p. 10). This wilderness is created by society and not by instincts or anatomy.

Although Horney became increasingly critical of Freud, she continued to recognize his perceptive insights. Her main quarrel with Freud was not so much the accuracy of his observations, but the validity of his interpretations. In general terms, she held that Freud's explanations result in a pessimistic concept of humanity based on innate instincts and the stagnation of personality while hers lead to an optimistic view—one centered on cultural forces that are amenable to change (Horney, 1952).

The Impact of Culture

Although Horney did not overlook the importance of genetic factors, she repeatedly emphasized cultural influences as the primary bases for both neurotic and normal personality development. Modern culture, she contended, is based on *competition* among individuals, even those within the same society. "Everyone is a real or potential competitor of everyone else" (Horney, 1937, p. 284). Competitiveness and the *hostility* it spawns result in feelings of *isolation.* These feelings of being alone in a potentially hostile world lead to intensified *needs for affection.* The needs for affection, on the other hand, cause people to overvalue love in our culture. Many people see love and affection as the solution for all their problems. Genuine love, of course, can be a healthy, growth-producing experience, but the desperate need for love (such as that shown by Harold, our case study) provides a fertile ground for the development of neuroses. Rather than benefiting from the need for love, the neurotic strives in pathological ways to find it. These self-defeating attempts result in low self-esteem, increased hostility, basic anxiety, more competitiveness, and the continual excessive need for love and affection.

According to Horney, our society contributes to this vicious circle in several respects. First, we are imbued with the cultural teachings of brotherly love and humility. These teachings, however, run contrary to another prevailing attitude, namely aggressiveness and the drive to win or be superior. Second, society's demands for success and achievement are nearly endless, so that even when we achieve our material ambitions, further goals are continually being placed before us. Third, our society tells us that we are free, that we can accomplish anything through hard work and perseverance. In reality, however, the freedom of most people is greatly restricted by genetics, social position, and the competitiveness of others.

These contradictions—all stemming from cultural influences rather than biological ones—provide intrapsychic conflicts that threaten the psychological health of normal people and provide nearly insurmountable obstructions for neurotics.

Importance of Childhood Experiences

Neurotic conflict can stem from almost any developmental stage, but, said Horney, childhood is the age from which the vast majority of problems arise. A variety of traumatic events, such as sexual abuse, beatings, open rejection, or pervasive neglect, may leave their impressions on future development, but Horney (1937) insisted that these debilitating experiences can almost invariably be traced to lack of genuine warmth and affection. Horney's own lack of love from her father and her close relationship with her mother must have had a powerful affect on her personal development as well as on her theoretical ideas.

On the other hand, Harold, our case study (who on the surface experienced a childhood similar to Horney's), enjoyed a genuinely close relationship with neither his father nor his mother. His father, like Horney's, was absent much of the time. His job as a truck driver kept him away from home for extended periods. When he was home, he had little time for either Harold or his younger brother. Harold recalls his father as a punitive, grouchy man whose primary paternal task was to discipline his children. Harold, like Horney, turned to his mother for emotional support. Unfortunately, Harold's mother was a deeply troubled woman, herself desperately striving for love and affection. As the firstborn, Harold seems to have been his mother's favorite. She showered him with gifts and attention, possibly in a neurotic attempt to win his love. As a result, Harold developed a deep dependency on his mother and felt isolated and lonely whenever they were separated.

Horney (1939) believed that a difficult childhood, such as Harold's, is primarily responsible for neurotic needs. These needs become powerful because they are the child's only means of gaining feelings of safety. Harold strove to find safety in the relationship with his mother who, unfortunately, was incapable of expressing genuine love for her children. Nevertheless, Harold attached himself emotionally to his mother, and she to him.

It would be an oversimplification, however, to say that Harold's current difficulties in attaching himself to a loving wife are an ongoing expression of his desire to possess his mother in a loving relationship. Horney (1939, p. 152) cautioned that no single early experience is responsible for later personality but that "the sum total of childhood experiences brings about a certain character structure, or rather, starts its development." In other words, she objected to simple explanations, such as Harold's Oedipus complex, as the cause of his present difficulties with women. Instead, she contended that the totality of early relationships molds personality development. "Later attitudes to others, then, are not repetitions of infantile ones but emanate from the character structure, the basis of which is laid in childhood" (Horney, 1939, p. 87).

As noted at the beginning of this section, psychoanalytic social theory holds that childhood experiences are primarily responsible for personality development although later experiences can have an important effect, especially in normal individuals. However, when "the impact of early experiences has been powerful enough to have molded the child to a rigid pattern, no new experience will be able to break through" (Horney, 1945, p. 45). New experiences are interpreted in a manner consistent with the established pattern. For example, Harold's early unsuccessful attempts to win his mother's genuine love have colored his interpretation of his adult experiences with women. His attitude has been "I am determined to use any means, including bribery, to keep from losing this relationship."

BASIC ANXIETY

Horney (1950) believed that each of us begins life with the potential for healthy development, but, like other living organisms, we need favorable conditions for growth. These conditions must include a warm and loving atmosphere, yet one that is not overly permissive. As children, we need to experience both genuine love and healthy discipline. Such conditions provide for feelings of safety and satisfaction and permit us to grow in accordance with our real self.

Unfortunately, a multitude of adverse influences may interfere with these favorable conditions. Primary among these is the parents' inability or unwillingness to love their child. Because of their own neurotic needs, parents often dominate, neglect, overprotect, reject, or overindulge. Horney (1950) pointed out that it is not a single factor but a whole constellation of behaviors that have an adverse affect on a child. As a result, the child fails to achieve feelings of security and belongingness and instead develops profound insecurity and a vague sense of apprehension. This condition is called **basic anxiety,** which Horney (1950, p. 18) defined as "a feeling of being isolated and helpless in a world conceived as potentially hostile." Earlier, she gave a more graphic description, calling basic anxiety "a feeling of being small, insignificant, helpless, deserted, endangered, in a world that is out to abuse, cheat, attack, humiliate, betray, envy" (Horney, 1937, p. 92).

Basic anxiety itself is not a neurosis, but "it is the nutritive soil out of which a definite neurosis may develop at any time" (Horney, 1937, p. 89). Basic anxiety is constant and unrelenting. It needs no particular stimulus such as taking a test in school or giving a speech. It permeates all relationships with others and leads to unhealthy ways of trying to cope with people. Harold, for example, has difficulties with all interpersonal relations. To his wives he was dependent, overly-affectionate, and submissive. To other people he is often hostile, arrogant, sarcastic, and domineering. Both attitudes—the need for affection and the craving for power—have become persistent, yet self-defeating methods of protecting against anxiety and attaining genuine love.

Horney (1937), in fact, identified four basic ways that people in our culture protect themselves against basic anxiety. The first is *affection,* the strategy Harold has used with his mother, wives, and girlfriends. All he wants from these women is to be loved. In his eyes, he demands little and is willing to give much. He has no insights into the real nature of his "love" relationships and is always puzzled when they come to an end.

The second protective device is *submissiveness*. Neurotics may submit themselves either to people or to institutions such as a service organization or a religion. When submissiveness is directed toward other people, it may be another attempt at gaining affection. In his marriages Harold believed that he was completely unselfish, self-sacrificing, and willing to submit his wishes to those of his partner.

Neurotics may also try to protect themselves by striving for *power, prestige,* or *possession*. Power is a defense against the real or imagined hostility of others and takes the form of a tendency to dominate others; prestige is a protection against humiliation and is expressed as a tendency to humiliate others; possession is seen as a buffer against destitution and poverty and manifests itself as a tendency to deprive others.

The fourth protective mechanism is *withdrawal.* Neurotics frequently protect themselves against basic anxiety either by developing an independence of others or by becoming emotionally detached from people. By psychologically withdrawing, neurotics feel that they cannot be hurt by other people.

Horney believed that these protective devices do not necessarily indicate a neurosis. All people use these techniques to some extent. They become unhealthy when the person feels compelled to rely on them and is thus unable to employ a variety of interpersonal strategies. Compulsion, then, is the salient characteristic of all neurotic drives.

COMPULSIVE DRIVES

The same problems that affect normal individuals affect neurotics, except to a greater degree. Both normal people and neurotics use the various protective devices to guard against the rejection, hostility, and competitiveness of others. While normal individuals are able to use a variety of defensive maneuvers in a somewhat useful way, neurotics compulsively repeat the same strategy in an essentially unproductive manner. Normal people usually have some awareness of their protective devices—neurotics do not; normal people find alternate strategies when one particular protective device is frustrated—neurotics cannot.

Horney (1942) insisted that neurotics do not enjoy misery and suffering. They cannot change their behavior by free will, but must continually and compulsively protect themselves against basic anxiety. They are caught in a vicious circle where their compulsive needs to reduce basic anxiety lead to behaviors which perpetuate low self-esteem, generalized hostility, inappropriate strivings for power, inflated feelings of superiority, and persistent apprehension—in short, more basic anxiety.

Neurotic Needs

In 1942 Horney tentatively identified 10 categories of **neurotic needs** that characterize neurotics in their attempts to combat basic anxiety. These categories were overlapping, and a single person, such as Harold, might employ more than one. Readers will note that each of the following neurotic needs relates in some way or another to other people.

1. *The neurotic need for affection and approval.* In their quest for affection and approval neurotics attempt indiscriminately to please others. They try to live up to the expectations of others, tend to dread self-assertion, and are quite uncomfortable with the hostility of others or the hostile feelings within themselves.

2. *The neurotic need for a partner.* Lacking self-confidence, neurotics try to attach themselves to a powerful partner. This need includes an overvaluation of love and a dread of being alone or deserted. Harold clung to his relationships with his wives because he had imbued these women with great power, beauty, and importance. Such a relationship, of course, made him feel important, and the loss of the powerful partner was devastating to his self-esteem.

3. *The neurotic need to restrict one's life within narrow borders.* Neurotics frequently strive to remain inconspicuous, to take second place, and to be contented with very little. They downgrade their own abilities and dread making demands on others. This need characterized Harold's relationships with his wives and girlfriends only. To them he is submissive and deferent. However, on his job as a supervisor for an insurance company he dominates his colleagues and tyrannizes his subordinates.

4. *The neurotic need for power.* Power and affection are perhaps the two greatest neurotic needs. As noted above, the need for power is usually combined with the needs for prestige and possession. It manifests itself as the need to control others and to avoid feelings of weakness or stupidity.

5. *The neurotic need to exploit others.* Neurotics frequently evaluate others on the basis of how they can be used or exploited. At the same time, they fear being exploited by others.

6. *The neurotic need for social recognition or prestige.* Harold was proud that his wives and girlfriends were unusually attractive, and he took pleasure in showing them off. He bought them jewelry and stylish clothes, wore fashionable clothes himself, and always drove an expensive car.

7. *The neurotic need for personal admiration.* This is the need to be admired for what one is rather than for what one possesses. The neurotic's inflated self-esteem must be continually fed by the admiration and approval of others.

8. *The neurotic need for ambition and personal achievement.* Neurotics often have a strong drive to be the best—the best salesperson, the best bowler, the best lover. Other people must be defeated in order to confirm the neurotic's superiority.

9. *The neurotic need for self-sufficiency and independence.* This need reflects a movement away from people so that the neurotic proves that other people are not necessary. The "playboy" who cannot be tied down by any woman exemplifies this neurotic need.

10. *The neurotic need for perfection and unassailability.* By striving

relentlessly for perfection the neurotic receives "proof" of self-esteem and personal superiority. Mistakes and personal flaws are dreaded as the neurotic desperately attempts to hide them from others.

Neurotic Trends

As her theory evolved, Horney began to see that the list of 10 neurotic needs could be grouped into three general categories, each relating to a person's basic attitude toward self and others. In 1945 she identified the three basic attitudes or **neurotic trends** as *moving toward people, moving against people,* and *moving away from people* (Horney, 1945).

Although these neurotic trends constitute Horney's theory of neurosis, they also apply to normal individuals. There are, of course, important differences between normal and neurotic attitudes. While normal people are mostly or completely conscious of their strategy toward people, neurotics are completely unconscious of their basic attitude; while normals are free to choose their actions, neurotics are forced to act; while normals experience mild conflict, neurotics experience severe, insoluble conflict; and while normals can choose from a variety of strategies, neurotics are limited to a single trend.

With each of the neurotic trends, the person attempts to solve **basic conflict** in an essentially nonproductive or neurotic manner. Horney (1950) used the term basic conflict because originally a child is driven in all three directions—toward, against, and away from people. In a healthy child these three drives are not necessarily incompatible. But the feelings of isolation and helplessness Horney described as *basic anxiety* drive some children to act compulsively, thereby limiting their repertoire to a single neurotic trend. Experiencing basically contradictory attitudes toward others, these children attempt to solve this basic conflict by making one of the three neurotic trends consistently predominant. In moving toward people, these children behave in a compliant manner as a protection against feelings of *helplessness;* in moving against people, other children act aggressively to circumvent the *hostility* of others; and in moving away from people, still others adopt a detached manner as a means of alleviating feelings of *isolation* (Horney, 1945).

Moving Toward People

By this time readers should be aware that Horney's concept of **moving toward people** does *not* mean moving toward others in the spirit of genuine love. Rather, it refers to the neurotic need to protect oneself against feelings of helplessness.

In their attempts to protect themselves against feelings of helplessness, compliant people employ either or both of the first two neurotic needs, that is, they desperately strive for affection and approval of others or they seek a powerful partner who will take responsibility for their lives. To a lesser extent, compliant people may adopt the third neurotic need, namely the need to restrict one's life within narrow borders.

Harold's behavior is quite consistent with the first two neurotic needs. His strategy is to find an attractive woman, attribute unusual powers to her, and then subordinate his desires to hers. He is willing to allow his partner to choose his clothes, his house, and his friends. She decides what movies they see, what food they eat, and what hobbies they have. His weakness and helplessness send a message to his partner, "You must constantly love me and protect me because I am weak and helpless." So far, his wives and girlfriends have received that message, but all have found that taking care of helpless Harold does not meet their own needs.

The neurotic trend of moving toward people is similar to Adler's concept of the getting type (see Chapter 4), although no single term such as getting, submissiveness, or dependence can summarize this trend. It is "a whole way of thinking, feeling, acting—a whole way of life" (Horney, 1945, p. 55). Horney also called it a philosophy of life. Neurotics who adopt this philosophy are likely to see themselves as loving, generous, unselfish, humble, and sensitive to other people's feelings. They are willing to subordinate themselves to others, to see others as more intelligent or attractive, and to rate themselves according to what others think of them.

Most of these characteristics describe Harold, but only in relation to the woman with whom he is currently "in love." The fact that Harold is capable of adopting other strategies with other people indicates that his behavior is not sufficiently compulsive to be termed neurotic. Unlike a true neurotic, Harold makes generous use of more than one neurotic trend. He is also capable of moving against people.

Moving Against People

Just as compliant people assume that everyone is nice, aggressive people take for granted that everyone is *hostile* and, as the result, they adopt the strategy of **moving against people.** Neurotically aggressive types are just as compulsive as the compliant types and their behavior is just as much prompted by basic anxiety. Rather than moving toward people in a posture of submissiveness and dependence, these people move against others by appearing tough or ruthless. They are similar to Adler's ruling type and are motivated by a strong need to exploit others and to use them for their own benefit. They seldom admit their mistakes and are compulsively driven to appear perfect, powerful, and superior.

Five of the ten neurotic needs are incorporated in the neurotic trend of moving against people. They include the need to be powerful, to exploit others, to receive recognition and prestige, to be admired, and to achieve.

Harold displays many of these tendencies at work. His subordinates regard him as arrogant, self-centered, and an unreasonable taskmaster. His fellow supervisors and his district manager see him as overly ambitious and somewhat threatening.

Aggressive types play to win rather than for the enjoyment of the contest. They may appear to be hard working and resourceful on the job, but they take little pleasure in the work itself. Their basic motivation is for power, prestige, and personal ambition.

In American society the striving for these goals is usually viewed with admiration. Compulsively aggressive people, in fact, frequently come out on top in many endeavors valued by our society. They may acquire desirable sex partners, high-paying jobs, and the personal admiration of many people. Horney (1945) said that it is not to the credit of our civilization that such characteristics are rewarded while love, affection, and the capacity for true friendship—the very qualities that the aggressive person lacks—are valued less highly.

Moving toward others and moving against others are, in many ways, polar opposites. The compliant person has to like everyone while the aggressive person sees everyone as a potential enemy. For both types, however, "the center of gravity lies outside the person" (Horney, 1945, p. 65). Both need other people. The compliant person needs others to satisfy feelings of helplessness; the aggressive person uses others as a protection against real or imagined hostility. With the third neurotic trend, in contrast, people are of lesser importance.

Moving Away from People

In order to solve the basic conflict of isolation, some people behave in a detached manner and adopt a neurotic trend of **moving away from people.** This strategy, which is similar to Adler's avoiding type, is an expression of needs for privacy, independence, and self-sufficiency. Again, each of these goals has a positive value in our society and, indeed, they are often pursued in a healthy fashion. However, they become neurotic when they are compulsively sought as a means of putting emotional distance between oneself and other people.

Many neurotics find associating with others an intolerable strain. As a consequence, they are compulsively driven to move away from others, to attain autonomy and separateness. They frequently build a world of their own and refuse to allow anyone to get close to them. They value freedom and self-sufficiency and often give the appearance of being aloof and unapproachable. If married, they maintain their detachment even from their spouse. Their wife or husband may complain that they have an impenetrable shell around their feelings and that nothing touches them.

Neurotically detached people fear being tied down, coerced, enslaved, or obligated. Their greatest fear is to need other people. They attempt to restrict their needs so that they will not have to depend on others. They fear illness because then someone might have to take care of them. They dread social functions, especially those with many people. They persist in the illusion of independence by coming late for appointments, ignoring anothers' request, and shunning other's advice.

Moving away from people is a neurotic trend used by many people in an attempt to solve the basic conflict of isolation.

Although all neurotics possess a need to feel superior, detached personalities have an intensified need to be strong and powerful. Their basic feelings of isolation can be tolerated only by the self-deceptive belief that they are perfect and therefore beyond criticism. They dread competition, fearing a blow to their illusory feelings of superiority. Instead, they prefer that their hidden greatness be recognized without any effort on their part (Horney, 1945).

Figure 7.1 summarizes the three neurotic trends and includes their source and their salient characteristic. Although Horney did not explicitly group the 10 neurotic needs within the three neurotic trends, most fit easily into one of these categories. While the neurotic trends best describe neurotic people, each has an analogous set of characteristics that describe normal individuals.

INTRAPSYCHIC CONFLICTS

The neurotic trends flow from basic anxiety which, in turn, stems from a child's relationships with other people. To this point our emphasis has been on culture and interpersonal conflict. However, Horney did not neglect the impact of intrapsychic factors in the development of personality. As her theory evolved she began to place greater and greater emphasis on the inner conflicts experienced by both normal and neurotic individuals. Intrapsychic processes originate from interpersonal experiences, but as they become part

NEUROTIC TRENDS

	Toward People	Against People	Away from People
Basic Conflict or Source of Neurotic Trend	Feelings of Helplessness	Protection Against Hostility of Others	Feelings of Isolation
Outstanding Characteristic	Compliant	Aggressive	Detached
Neurotic Needs	1. Affection and Approval 2. Powerful Partner 3. Narrow Limits to Life	4. Power 5. Exploitation 6. Recognition and Prestige 7. Personal Admiration 8. Personal Achievement	9. Self-sufficiency and Independence 10. Perfection and Unassailability
Normal Analogue	Friendly, Loving	Ability to Survive in a Competitive Society	Autonomous, Serene

Figure 7.1   Summary of Horney's Neurotic Trends

of our belief system they develop a life of their own—an existence separate from the interpersonal conflicts that gave them life.

In this section we look at two important intrapsychic conflicts: the **idealized image** and **self-hatred.** Briefly, the idealized image is an attempt to solve conflicts by painting a godlike picture of self. Self-hatred is an interrelated yet equally irrational and powerful tendency to despise one's real self. As a person builds an idealized image of self, the real self lags farther and farther behind. The key intrapsychic conflict then becomes a growing alienation from self. As the result, the neurotic is bound to hate and despise the actual self which falls so short in matching the glorified self-image (Horney, 1950).

The Idealized Image

Horney believed that human beings, if given an atmosphere of discipline and warmth, will develop feelings of security, self-confidence, and a tendency to move toward *self-realization.* Unfortunately, early negative influences often impede one's natural tendency toward self-realization. This failure leaves the person with feelings of isolation and inferiority. Added to this is a growing sense of alienation from self.

Feeling alienated from self, the person needs desperately to acquire a *sense of identity.* The only way a person can achieve feelings of identity and, at the same time, combat the sense of self-alienation, is to create an *idealized image of self.* This is an extravagantly positive view of self that exists only in the person's mind. The person "endows himself with unlimited powers and exalted faculties; he becomes a hero, a genius, a supreme lover, a saint, a god" (Horney, 1950, p. 22). The idealized image is not a global construction. Neurotics glorify and worship themselves in different ways. Compliant people see themselves as good and saintly; aggressive people build an idealized image of themselves as strong, heroic, and omnipotent; detached neurotics paint their self-portraits as wise, self-sufficient, and independent.

As the idealized self-image becomes solidified, the person begins to believe in the reality of that image. She or he loses touch with the *real* self and uses the *idealized* self as the standard for self-evaluation. Rather than growing toward self-realization, the person moves toward actualizing the idealized self.

In his relations with his wives and girlfriends, Harold truly believed that he was the perfect lover, someone willing to sacrifice his interests and needs to those of the woman in his life. Because he was compulsively driven to live up to his idealized image, he became oblivious to his real problems. His idealized self was now more real to him than his real self.

Horney (1950) recognized three aspects of the idealized image: (1) the neurotic search for glory, (2) neurotic claims, and (3) neurotic pride.

The Neurotic Search for Glory

As neurotics come to believe in the reality of their idealized self, they begin to incorporate it into all aspects of their lives—their goals, their self-concept, and their relations with others. Horney (1950) referred to this comprehensive drive toward actualizing the ideal self as the **neurotic search for glory.**

Besides self-idealization, the neurotic search for glory always includes three other elements: the need for perfection, neurotic ambition, and the drive toward a vindictive triumph.

The *need for perfection* refers to the drive to mold the whole personality into the idealized self. Neurotics are not content to merely make a few alterations. Nothing short of complete perfection is acceptable. They try to achieve perfection by erecting a complex set of "shoulds" and "should nots." Horney (1950) referred to this as the **tyranny of the should.** Neurotics, striving toward an imaginary picture of perfection, "unconsciously tell [themselves]: 'Forget about the disgraceful creature you actually *are;* this is how you *should be*'" (Horney, 1950, p. 64).

Neurotics set outrageous standards for themselves. "I should be honest, generous, dignified, courageous, and unselfish; I should be the perfect lover, father, and husband; I should love everyone; I should anticipate everything; I should not be envious or jealous; I should not become angry or afraid." This list of shoulds and should nots is, of course, unreasonable, endless, and impossible to live up to.

A second key element in the neurotic search for glory is *neurotic ambition,* that is, the compulsive drive toward superiority. Although neurotics have an exaggerated need to excel in everything, they ordinarily channel their energies into those activities that are most likely to bring success. This drive, therefore, may change form several times during a lifetime (Horney, 1950). As a student, the person may direct neurotic ambition toward being the best student in school; later this drive may change to excelling in business or raising the very best show dogs. Neurotic ambition may also take a less materialistic form, such as being the most saintly or most self-actualized person in the community.

The third aspect of the neurotic search for glory is the *drive toward a vindictive triumph,* the most destructive element of all. The need for a vindictive triumph may be disguised as a drive for achievement or success, but "its chief aim is to put others to shame or defeat them through one's very successes; or to attain the power . . . to inflict suffering on them—mostly of a humiliating kind" (Horney, 1950, p. 27). Vindictive triumph can also be gained more subtly by frustrating or outwitting others in personal relations.

The drive for a vindictive triumph grows out of the childhood desire to take revenge for real or imagined humiliations. No matter how successful one is in vindictively triumphing over others, this drive is never diminished; rather, it increases with each triumph. Every success raises the neurotic's fear of defeat and increases feelings of grandeur, thus ensuring the need for further vindictive triumphs.

At work, Harold was not content to get ahead through hard work and equitable competition. He took great pleasure in winning promotions, not so much because he desired the new position, but because it was a way of defeating his rivals for the job. He frequently used his superior verbal skills to berate and humiliate both his fellow supervisors and the employees in his department. Although Harold was unaware of his vindictive tactics, others were quite aware of them and maintained their distance from him whenever possible.

Neurotic Claims

A second aspect of the idealized image is **neurotic claims.** In their search for glory neurotics build a fantasy world—a world which, however, is not synchronized with the real world. They begin to believe that something is wrong with the outside world. They make a claim to the world that they are special and therefore entitled to be treated in accordance with their idealized view of themselves. They fail to see that their claims of special privilege are unreasonable. After all, these claims are quite in accord with the idealized image they have of themselves.

Neurotic claims grow out of normal needs and wishes, but they are quite different. While the nonfulfillment of normal wishes leads to understandable frustration, the nonfulfillment of neurotic claims results in indignation and feelings of bewilderment. Neurotics cannot comprehend why others have not granted their claims. The difference between normal desires and neurotic claims might be illustrated by a situation where many people are waiting in line for tickets for a popular movie. Most people near the end of the line might wish to be up front and some may even try some ploy to get a better position. Nevertheless, these people know that they don't really deserve to cut ahead of others. Neurotic people, on the other hand, truly believe that they are entitled to be near the front of the line, and they feel no guilt or remorse in moving ahead of others.

Neurotic Pride

The third aspect of an idealized image is **neurotic pride,** a false pride based, not on a realistic view of the true self, but on a spurious image of the idealized self.

Neurotic pride is qualitatively different from healthy pride or realistic self-esteem. Genuine self-esteem is based on realistic attributes and accomplishments and is generally expressed with quiet dignity. Neurotic pride, on the other hand, is based on an idealized image of self and is usually loudly proclaimed in order to protect and support the glorified view of oneself (Horney, 1950).

In their imagination neurotics see themselves as glorious, wonderful, and perfect. When others fail to treat them with special consideration, their neurotic pride is hurt. To prevent the hurt, they avoid people who refuse to yield to their neurotic claims, and instead associate themselves with institutions and acquisitions of great social prominence and prestige. Harold, for example, was a member of a prestigious social club, wore a Rolex watch, and usually drove a Mercedes. Like others who strive to realize their inflated image through neurotic pride, claims, and search for glory, Harold was filled with unconscious self-hate.

Self-Hatred

The neurotic search for glory can never be fruitful. When neurotics realize that their real self can never match the insatiable demands of the idealized self, they begin to hate and despise themselves.

> The glorified self becomes not only a *phantom* to be pursued; it also becomes a measuring rod with which to measure his actual being. And this actual being is such an embarrassing sight when viewed from the perspective of a godlike perfection that he cannot but despise it (Horney, 1950, p. 110).

Is self-hate conscious or unconscious? Although the person may, from time to time, utter such statements as "Why am I so stupid?" or even "I hate myself," self-hatred remains an unconscious process. On the other hand, the *expression* of self-hatred may well be conscious. Horney (1950) recognized six major ways in which self-hatred is expressed.

First, self-hatred may result in *relentless demands on the self.* These demands are exemplified by the tyranny of the should discussed above. Harold believed he should be the perfect husband, the greatest lover, the most competent worker, the best golfer in town. The demands he made on himself were unrelenting. Even when he achieved a measure of success at work, for example, he continued to push himself toward perfection.

The second mode of expressing self-hate is *merciless self-accusation.* Neurotics constantly question themselves. "If people only knew me they would realize that I'm pretending to be knowledgeable, competent, and sincere. They don't know that I'm really a fraud." They also analyze their motives and find them ignoble and self-centered. "Perhaps when I gave my friend some advice, I was really trying to demonstrate my superiority." "If I had not allowed my daughter to drive to the store, she would not have had the accident that injured another person." "If only I hadn't introduced Madelyn to Jim, they would have never married and Madelyn would not be living with an abusive husband."

Self-accusation may take a variety of forms, from obviously grandiose expressions, such as taking responsibility for natural disasters, to seemingly realistic self-appraisal. It must not be mistaken for a healthy conscience, however. The latter guards the interests of our real self, while self-accusations are detrimental to the true self and represent unproductive ways of actualizing the ideal self.

Third, self-hate may take the form of *self-contempt.* Belittling, disparaging, doubting, discrediting, and ridiculing oneself are all expressions of self-contempt. Self-contempt prevents us from striving for improvement or achievement. A young man may say to himself, "You conceited idiot! What makes you think you can get a date with the best-looking woman in town!" A father may "modestly" say that his handsome son gets his good looks from his mother. A woman may attribute her successful career to "luck." The person is ordinarily aware of his or her behavior, but not the underlying self-hatred.

A fourth expression of self-hate is *self-frustration.* Horney (1950) distinguished between healthy self-discipline and neurotic self-frustration. The former involves postponing or forgoing pleasurable activities in order to achieve reasonable goals. Self-frustration stems from self-hate and is designed to actualize an inflated self-image.

Neurotics are frequently shackled by taboos against enjoyment. "I don't deserve a new car." "I must not wear nice clothes because many people around the world are in rags." "I must not strive for a better job, because I'm not good enough for it." "I can never hope to lose weight and be more attractive, so I must not try."

Fifth, self-hate may be manifested as *self-torment* or self-torture. Although self-torment may exist in each of the other forms of self-hate, it becomes a separate category when the person's main intent is to inflict harm or suffering on self. A certain masochistic satisfaction is attained through anguishing over a decision, exaggerating the pain of a headache, cutting oneself with a knife, starting a fight that one is sure to lose, or inviting sexual abuse. The list of activities designed to torment or torture one's self is quite extensive.

The sixth and final form of self-hate is *self-destructive actions and impulses.* These may be either physical or psychological; conscious or unconscious; acute or chronic; carried out in action or enacted only in the imagination. Overeating, abusing alcohol and other drugs, working too hard, driving recklessly, and suicide are common expressions of physical self-destruction. Neurotics may also attack themselves psychologically when they quit a job just as it begins to be fulfilling, break off a healthy relationship in favor of a neurotic one, or engage in promiscuous sexual activities.

Self-hatred is sometimes expressed through abuse of alcohol.

Horney (1950, p. 154) summarized the neurotic search for glory and its attendant self-hate with these descriptive words:

> Surveying self-hate and its ravaging force, we cannot help but see in it a great tragedy, perhaps the greatest tragedy of the human mind. Man in reaching out for the Infinite and Absolute also starts destroying himself. When he makes a pact with the devil, who promises him glory, he has to go to hell—to the hell within himself.

FEMININE PSYCHOLOGY

As a woman trained in the promasculine psychology of Freud, Horney gradually realized that the traditional psychoanalytic view of women was skewed. She then set forth her own theory of feminine psychology, one that rejected several of Freud's basic ideas.

For Horney, psychic differences between men and women are not the result of anatomy, but rather cultural and social expectations. If men subdue and rule women or if women degrade or envy men, it is because of the neurotic competitiveness rampant in many societies. Basic anxiety is at the core of men's need to subjugate women and women's wish to humiliate men (Horney, 1937).

Horney (1939) recognized the existence of the Oedipus complex, but insisted that it was due to certain environmental conditions and not to biology. If it were the result of anatomy, as Freud contended, it would be universal (as Freud indeed believed). However, Horney saw no evidence for a universal Oedipus complex. Instead, she held that it is found only in some people and is an expression of the neurotic need for love (Horney, 1967). We have seen that the *neurotic need for affection* and the *neurotic need for aggression* usually begin in childhood and are two of the three basic neurotic trends. A child may passionately cling to one parent and express jealousy toward the other, but these are means of alleviating basic anxiety and not a manifestation of an anatomically based Oedipus complex. Even when there is a sexual aspect to these behaviors, the main goal is *security* and not sexual intercourse.

Horney (1939) found the concept of penis envy even less tenable. Although the concept rests on a biological basis, Horney contended that it is contradictory to biological thinking. There is no more anatomical reason why girls should be envious of the penis than boys should desire a breast or a womb. In fact, boys sometimes do express a desire to have a baby, but this is not the result of a universal male "womb envy."

Horney agreed with Adler (see Chapter 4) that many women possess a masculine protest, that is, a pathological belief that men are superior to women. This perception easily leads to the neurotic desire to be a man. The desire, however, is not an expression of penis envy, but rather "a wish for all those qualities or privileges which in our culture are regarded as masculine" (Horney, 1939, p. 108). (This view is nearly identical to that expressed by Erikson in Chapter 3.)

Neurotic ambition is at the root of a woman's wish to be a man, just as neurotic feelings of helplessness are the bases for her need to submit herself to a man. Since these neurotic needs are cultural rather than biological, they can be eliminated through environmental interventions, including psychotherapy.

PSYCHOTHERAPY

Neuroses, of course, are not limited to women. Society also presents men with a variety of obstacles on the road to psychological health or self-realization.

Neuroses grow out of basic conflict, usually in childhood, and have a way of gradually enveloping more and more of personality. As people attempt to solve the conflict bred by the neurosis, they are likely to adopt one of the three neurotic trends, namely, moving toward, against, or away from others. Each of these tactics may produce temporary relief, but eventually they drive the person farther and farther away from actualizing the real self and deeper and deeper into neurotic spiral (Horney, 1950).

The general goal of Horneyian therapy is to help patients gradually grow in the direction of self-realization. More specifically, the aim is to have patients give up their idealized self-image, relinquish their neurotic search for glory, and change self-hate to acceptance of the real self. Unfortunately, patients are usually convinced that their neurotic solutions are correct and they are reluctant to surrender their neurotic trends. Even though patients have a strong investment in maintaining the status quo, they do not wish to remain ill. They find little pleasure in their handicaps and suffering and would like to be free of them. Unfortunately, they tend to resist change and cling to those behaviors that perpetuate their illness. The three neurotic trends can be cast in favorable terms such as "love," "mastery," and "freedom." Because patients usually see their behaviors in these terms, their actions appear to them to be healthy, right, and desirable (Horney, 1942, 1950).

The therapist's task is to convince patients that their present solutions are perpetuating rather than alleviating the core neurosis, a task that takes time and hard work. Patients may look for quick cures or solutions, but only the long laborious process of self-understanding can effect positive change. Self-understanding must go beyond information and must involve an *emotional* experience. Patients must understand their pride system, their idealized image, their neurotic search for glory, their self-hate, their shoulds, their alienation from self, and their conflicts. Moreover, they must see how all these are interrelated and how they all operate to preserve the basic neurosis.

Although the therapist can help encourage a patient toward self-understanding, ultimately successful therapy is built on self-analysis (Horney, 1942, 1950). A patient must understand the difference between the idealized image of self and the real self. Fortunately, people possess an inherent curative force so that when self-understanding and self-analysis are achieved, they move inevitably in the direction of self-realization.

As to techniques, the Horneyian therapist uses many of the same ones employed by Freud. The two principal approaches are dream interpretation and free association. Dreams are seen as attempts to solve conflicts in either a neurotic or a healthy manner. Proper interpretation helps a patient come closer to an understanding of the real self. "From dreams . . .the patient can catch a glimpse, even in the initial phase of analysis, of a world operating within him which is peculiarly his own and which is more true of his feelings than the world of his illusions (Horney, 1950, p. 349).

In the second major technique, free association (Horney, 1987), patients are asked to say everything that comes to mind, regardless of how trivial or embarrassing it may seem. They are also encouraged to express whatever feelings may arise. As with dream interpretation, free association eventually reveals a patient's idealized image and persistent but unsuccessful attempts at accomplishing it.

When therapy is successful, patients gradually develop confidence in their ability to assume responsibility for their psychological development. They move toward self-realization and all those processes that accompany it. They have a deeper and clearer understanding of their feelings, beliefs, and wishes; they relate to others with feelings, beliefs, and wishes; they relate to others with genuine feelings instead of using them to solve basic conflict; at work, they take a greater interest in the job itself rather than seeing it as a means to perpetuate a neurotic search for glory.

CONCEPT OF HUMANITY

Horney's concept of humanity was based almost entirely on her clinical experiences with neurotic patients; therefore, her view of humanity is strongly colored by her concept of neurosis. Horney presented no estimate of the percentage of people who might be regarded as neurotic, but from her description, it would appear that most of us are guided in part by some neurotic trends.

The prime difference between the healthy individual and the neurotic person is the degree of compulsivity with which each moves toward, against, or away from people. Healthy people move freely and spontaneously and are able to employ all three tactics in their relations with others. In contrast, neurotics are compelled to move. This compulsive drive renders the three movements incompatible, thus setting up basic conflict.

The compulsive nature of neurotic trends suggests that Horney's concept of humanity is deterministic. However, healthy people have a large element of free choice in their lives. Even neurotic individuals, through psychotherapy and hard work, can wrest some control over those intrapsychic conflicts. For this reason Horney's psychoanalytic social theory is rated slightly higher on *free will* than on determinism.

On the same basis the theory is somewhat more *optimistic* than pessimistic. Horney believed that people possess inherent curative powers that lead them toward self-realization. If basic anxiety (the feeling of being alone and helpless in a potentially hostile world) can be avoided, people will feel safe and secure in interpersonal relations and consequently develop healthy personalities. In other words, under conditions of warmth and acceptance people will develop their individual human potentialities. They "will grow, substantially undiverted, *toward self-realization*" (Horney, 1950, p. 17). Earlier, she offered this optimistic observation:

> My own belief is that man has the capacity as well as the desire to develop his potentialities and become a decent human being, and that these deteriorate if his relationship to others and hence to himself is, and continues to be, disturbed. I believe that man can change and go on changing as long as he lives (Horney, 1945, p. 19).

Are we motivated more by *past experiences* or by *present expectations of the future?* Horney's position on this question was a moderate one. Past events, especially those of early childhood, incline us either toward health or neurosis. Horney (1939, p. 153) stated that "the past in some way or other is always contained in the present." However, included in our past experiences is the formation of a philosophy of life and a set of values that give both our present and our future some direction. Our behavior is consistent with our philosophy, our values, and our goals for the future. Despite possible powerful negative influences in early childhood, we can, with great difficulty, surmount the obstacles to change and proceed to grow toward a full realization of our human potentials.

Most people have only *limited awareness* of their motivation. Neurotics especially have little understanding of themselves. They do not see that their behaviors guarantee the continuation of their neuroses. They mislabel their personal characteristics, couching them in socially acceptable terms. Self-effacing people with neurotic needs for love, dependency, and appeasement call their motivations genuine love; hostile people believe they are striving for mastery, strength, or perfection; and detached persons see themselves as desiring freedom. Neurotics are unaware of their compulsive search for glory, their alienation from their real self, or the destructive nature of their shoulds and should nots. They are unconscious of their basic conflict, their self-hate, their neurotic pride and neurotic claims, and their need for a vindictive triumph.

Horney's concept of humanity, of course, emphasized *social influences* more than biological ones. Psychological differences between men and women, for example, are due more to cultural and societal expectations than to anatomy. The Oedipus complex and penis envy are not inevitable consequences of biology, but rather are shaped by social forces. Also, a warm, acceptant social atmosphere in early childhood leads to healthy personality development, while a cold rejecting environment is likely to result in neurosis. Horney did not neglect biological factors completely but her main emphasis was on social influences.

Because Horney's theory looks almost exclusively at neuroses, it tends to highlight *similarities* among people more than uniqueness. Not all neurotics are alike, of course, and Horney described three basic types—the helpless, the hostile, and the detached. Within each category, however, little emphasis was placed on individual differences. Helpless people tend to compensate by attaching themselves to a powerful partner; hostile people move against people, exploiting them for personal gain; and detached people adopt an attitude of indifference and aloofness. On the other hand, one may assume that Horney would see healthy people as quite different from one another since each is realizing his or her own potential.

CRITIQUE OF HORNEY

The strength of Horney's theory is her lucid portrayal of the neurotic personality. No other personality theorist has written so well (or so much) about neuroses. Her comprehensive descriptions of the neurotic, frequently illustrated by interesting case studies, provide an excellent framework for understanding many personalities. However, her nearly exclusive concern with neurotics is a serious limitation to her theory. Her references to the nonneurotic personality are general and not well explicated. She says that people by their very nature will strive toward self-realization, but she paints no clear picture of what self-realization would be.

In fairness to Horney, her theory, like those of Freud, Adler, Jung, and Sullivan, was based largely on clinical experiences. Unlike these other theorists, she was careful not to extrapolate her experiences with neurotics to the broad spectrum of human personality. The reluctance to make assumptions beyond one's basic data is a mark of sound theory building. Nevertheless, the narrowness of Horney's data base is a serious limitation to her theory.

As a result, Horney's theory can be rated very high on its ability to *organize knowledge* of neurotics, but very low on its capacity to explain what is known about people in general.

A second criterion of a useful theory is its power to *generate research.* Here again Horney's theory falls short. Very little research has ever been conducted that would either support or reject hypotheses drawn from this theory. Indeed, Horney's speculations do not easily yield testable hypotheses. The validity of her objections to Freud's assumptions concerning the Oedipus complex and penis envy could be determined, but this would involve tests of Freud's theory rather than Horney's.

As a *guide to action* Horney's theory fares somewhat better. Teachers, therapists, and especially parents can use her assumptions concerning the development of neurotic trends to provide a warm, safe, and acceptant atmosphere for their students, patients, or children. Beyond this, however, the theory is not specific enough to give the practitioner a clear and detailed course of action. On this criterion the theory would receive a moderate rating.

Is Horney's theory *internally consistent,* with clearly defined terms used uniformly? In Horney's book, *Neurosis and Human Growth* (1950), her concepts and formulations are precise, consistent, and unambiguous. However, when all her works are examined, a different picture emerges. Through the years, she used terms such as neurotic needs and neurotic trends sometimes separately and sometimes interchangeably. Also, the terms basic anxiety and basic conflict were not always clearly differentiated. Then too, she used a variety of terms to refer to the three neurotic trends. For example, movement toward people was variously called the neurotic need for affection, helplessness, the self-effacing solution, the appeal of love, and compliance. These inconsistencies render her entire work somewhat inconsistent, but again, her final theory (1950) is a model of lucidity and consistency.

The final criterion of a useful theory is *parsimony.* Horney's final theory is relatively simple and straightforward and is clearly summarized in the last chapter of *Neurosis and Human Growth* (Horney, 1950, Chap. 15). This chapter provides a useful and concise introduction to Horney's theory of neurotic development.

CHAPTER SUMMARY

Karen Horney received her training in Freudian psychology, but objected to the rigidity of its views, especially those regarding women. She insisted that social and cultural influences were more important than biological ones in shaping personality. Our experiences in childhood with warm, accepting parents or with cold, rejecting ones lay the foundation upon which we erect either a healthy or a neurotic personality.

Most of Horney's writings deal with neuroses and neurotic individuals. When children lack warmth and affection their needs for safety and satisfaction are unfulfilled and they develop a feeling of isolation and helplessness in a potentially hostile world. This feeling of *basic anxiety* prevents people from moving spontaneously toward, against, or away from others. The inability to employ different tactics in their relationships with others generates basic conflict in some people. Some neurotics are then compulsively driven to solve their problems by attaching themselves to a partner in a posture of compliance and submissiveness; others strike out against people in an effort to exploit, embarrass, or master them; and still others adopt a detached attitude and try to solve their conflicts through independence and separation from people.

These three *neurotic trends* (moving toward, against, and away from people) are a combination of 10 neurotic needs that Horney had earlier identified and are reactions to *interpersonal conflicts.* In her later writings Horney identifies two major *intrapsychic conflicts*—the idealized image and self-hatred. The *idealized image* represents attempts by neurotics to solve conflicts by constructing a godlike picture of themselves. *Self-hatred* is the tendency for neurotics to hate and despise their real self.

There are three aspects of the idealized image. The first is the *neurotic search for glory,* or the drive toward actualizing the ideal self; second is *neurotic claims,* or unrealistic demands and expectations to be entitled to special consideration and privilege; third is *neurotic pride,* a false pride based on the person's idealized image.

Horney believed that psychological differences between men and women are not due to anatomy, but rather to cultural and social expectations. Many men wish to subjugate women and many women desire to humiliate men, but these needs are neurotic and result from basic anxiety.

Horney's approach to psychotherapy was to bring about growth toward actualization of the real self. To accomplish this, patients must understand that their idealized self-image is a false picture of their true self and they must work toward relinquishing their neurotic search for glory and change self-hate into acceptance of the real self.

Horney's *concept of humanity* is somewhat positive and optimistic. People possess an inherent drive toward self-realization and, in the absence of basic anxiety, will ultimately achieve it. Social influences, especially those of early childhood, sometimes block the road to self-realization, but through therapy and hard work people can overcome those obstacles.

Although Horney's formulation of neurotic development was well-conceived, her general theory of personality rates low on its ability to organize knowledge and to generate research. It is moderately useful as a guide to action and is somewhat parsimonious and internally consistent.

Suggested Readings

HORNEY, K. (1945). *Our inner conflicts: A constructive theory of neurosis.* New York: Norton.
  In this book Horney identifies and discusses the three neurotic trends and sets the stage for her final theory. This book is more readable than *Neurosis and Human Growth* (1950) and provides an excellent introduction to her work.

HORNEY, K. (1950). Theoretical considerations. In K. Horney, *Neurosis and human growth: The struggle toward self-realization* (pp. 366–378). New York: Norton.
  A concise summary of Horney's theoretical position. The writing is more difficult than *Our inner conflicts* (1945), but the two sources together provide a comprehensive view of psychoanalytic social theory.

HORNEY, K. (1967). The flight from womanhood: The masculinity-complex in women as viewed by men and women. In H. Kelman (Ed.), *Feminine psychology* (pp. 54–70). New York: Norton.

Originally published in 1926, this article is important because it represents the first significant opposition to Freud's views on penis envy and the female Oedipus complex written from a woman's perspective.

QUINN, S. (1987). *A mind of her own: The life of Karen Horney.* New York: Summit Books.

An excellent biography of Horney, more readable, accurate, and better balanced than an earlier one by Rubins (1978).

FROMM

8

Humanistic Psychoanalysis

To many of his friends, Richard seems to be wasting his creative talents with a routine job as an assistant cashier in a local bank. Gifted with superior verbal ability, Richard majored in English at the local college, preparing for a career as a creative writer. His intentions were to pursue a master's degree in creative writing and study with a prominent author. While still in college he applied to several graduate schools, but was not accepted because he had not taken the Graduate Record Examination. So Richard took a "temporary" job as a bank teller, waiting for the time when he would further his education. That was 10 years ago and Richard is still no closer to graduate school.

Unmarried and living at home with his parents and younger sister, Richard seems to be settled on a career in banking. Friends and coworkers continually encourage him to make use of his literary talents and return to school. He, too, occasionally speaks of returning to school and, in fact, has applied to several graduate schools during the last decade. Sometimes his applications were late and other times he failed to submit selections of his writing— a prerequisite for acceptance into many creative writing programs. At other times, he was accepted, but he always found several reasons not to go.

Now Richard divides his time between his job as assistant cashier and his hobby of collecting baseball cards. His interest in baseball dates to his early childhood when he and his mother would listen to games on the radio or watch them on television. He began collecting cards of his favorite players, but soon became interested in any baseball card. His collection has mounted to more than 700,000 cards, including rare ones of obscure and famous players from past decades and multiple editions of cards of present players. Richard never trades or sells any of his cards and is constantly vigilant for any new card to add to his collection. As a consequence, his accumulation of cards has spilled over from his bedroom to other rooms vacated by older brothers and sisters who have left home. Richard's father occasionally complains about the huge collection, but his mother is quite tolerant and even encourages his interest. Richard's knowledge of the batting and pitching records of players past and present amazes those who know him. At work, he is frequently called on to settle arguments over baseball facts and figures, which he usually can do from memory alone.

Richard's father, a successful business person, does not understand why his son has no women friends or why he continues to live at home. Preoccupied with his own business, however, he seldom expresses his feeling to Richard and seems content to have two of his seven children still living at home. Richard's mother encourages her son to stay at home by caring for nearly all his needs. She cooks his food, cleans his room, and launders his clothes.

At work, Richard is competent, friendly, and extremely dedicated to his job. He arrives early, stays late, and never complains about organizational policy. Most of his coworkers regard him as congenial and pleasant, but somewhat uncomfortable in social interaction. Despite a knowledge of banking that exceeds that of most of his superiors, Richard displays a glaring lack of self-confidence. To superiors and inferiors alike he is nonaggressive, obsequious, and deferential. No one dislikes Richard, yet he doesn't seem to have any close friends, either male or female.

OVERVIEW

Richard has no signs of psychopathology, yet he lacks the characteristics that Erich Fromm would consider essential to good psychological health. Fromm, trained in Freudian psychoanalysis and influenced by both Harry Stack Sullivan and Karen Horney, developed a theory of personality that is uniquely his own. Compared with Freud, Fromm placed far more emphasis on social influences on personality; compared with Sullivan, he was much more aware of the influence of culture, economics, and class structure; compared with Horney, he was more likely to take an anthropological and historical view of personality.

Fromm was more than a personality theorist. He was a social critic, psychotherapist, philosopher, biblical scholar, cultural anthropologist, and psychobiographer. His humanistic psychoanalysis looks at people from a historical and cultural perspective rather than a strictly psychological one. It is less concerned with the individual and more concerned with those characteristics common to a culture.

Following Karl Marx, Fromm believed that the rise of capitalism has, on the one hand, contributed to the growth of leisure time and personal freedom, and, on the other, it has resulted in feelings of anxiety, isolation, and powerlessness. The cost of freedom, Fromm maintained has exceeded its benefits. The isolation wrought by capitalism has been unbearable, leaving people with two alternatives: to escape from freedom into interpersonal dependencies or to move toward self-realization through productive love and work.

BIOGRAPHY OF ERICH FROMM

Like all personality theorists, Erich Fromm's view of human nature was shaped by childhood experiences. With Fromm, it was Jewish family life, the suicide of a young woman, and the extreme nationalism of the German people that contributed to his concept of humanity.

Fromm was born on March 23, 1900, in Frankfurt, Germany, the only child of middle-class orthodox Jewish parents. His father, Naphtali, was the son of a rabbi and the grandson of two rabbis. His mother, Rosa, was the niece of Ludwig Krause, a well-known Talmudic scholar. As a boy, Erich studied the Old Testament with several prominent scholars, including Rabbi Krause. All of these men were "humanists of extraordinary tolerance and with a complete absence of authoritarianism" (Landis & Tauber, 1971, p. xi). Fromm was especially moved by the compassionate and redemptive tone of the prophets Isaiah, Hosea, and Amos. His humanistic psychology can be traced to the reading of these prophets, "with their vision of universal peace and harmony, and their teachings that there are ethical aspects to history—that nations can do right and wrong, and that history has its moral laws" (Landis & Tauber, 1971, p. x). Though Fromm later abandoned organized religion, these early experiences with the Bible and with the Talmudic scholars contributed to his humanistic views.

Fromm's early childhood was less than ideal. He recalled that he had "very neurotic parents," and that he was "probably a rather unbearably neurotic child" (Evans, 1977, p. 56). He saw his father as being moody and his mother as prone to depression. Moreover, he grew up in two very distinct worlds, one the traditional orthodox Jewish world, the other the modern capitalist world. This split existence created tensions that were nearly unbearable, but it generated a lifelong tendency to see events from more than one perspective (Fromm, 1986; Hausdorff, 1972).

When Fromm was 12 he was both shocked and puzzled by the suicide of an attractive young woman who had been an acquaintance of the Fromm family. The woman was intelligent, artistic, and beautiful. Yet she killed herself so that she could be buried along with her widowed father who had just died. How could such an action be explained? In the eyes of young Erich the father was quite uninteresting and unattractive while the daughter seemingly had much to live for. "How is it possible that a beautiful young woman should be so in love with her father that she prefer to be buried with him to being alive to the pleasures of life and painting?" (Fromm, 1962, p. 4).

How was it possible? This question haunted Fromm for the next 10 years and eventually led to an interest in Sigmund Freud and psychoanalysis. As Fromm read Freud, he began to learn about the Oedipus complex and to understand how such a suicide might be possible. Later, Fromm would interpret the young woman's irrational dependence on her father as a nonproductive symbiotic relationship, but in those early years he was content with the Freudian explanation.

Fromm was 14 when World War I began, too young to fight but not too young to be impressed by the irrationality of German nationalism which he observed first hand. He was sure that the British and French were equally irrational, and once again he was struck by a troubling question. How could normally rational and peaceful people become so driven by national ideologies, so intent on killing, so ready to die? "When the war ended in 1918, I was a deeply troubled young man who was obsessed by the question of how war was possible, by the wish to understand the irrationality of human mass behavior, by a passionate desire for peace and international understanding" (Fromm, 1962, p. 9).

During adolescence Fromm was deeply moved by the writings of Freud and Marx, but was also stimulated by differences between the two. As he studied more he began to question the validity of both systems. "My main interest was clearly mapped out. I wanted to understand the laws that govern the life of the individual man, and the laws of society" (Fromm, 1962, p. 9).

After the war Fromm became a socialist, although, at that time, he did not join the Socialist Party. Instead, he concentrated on his studies in psychology, philosophy, and sociology at the University of Heidelberg, where he received his Ph.D. at the age of 22. Still not confident that his training could answer such troubling questions as the suicide of the young woman or the insanity of war, Fromm turned to the study of psychoanalysis, believing that it promised answers to questions of human motivation not offered in other fields. From 1925 until 1931 he studied psychoanalysis, first in Munich and

then at the Berlin Psychoanalytic Institute, where he was analyzed by Hans Sachs, a student of Freud and the same therapist who later analyzed John Dollard (see Chapter 9).

In 1926 Fromm married Frieda Reichmann, a psychoanalyst who later would obtain an international reputation for her work with schizophrenic patients. In 1930 Fromm, Fromm-Reichmann, and others founded the South German Institute for Psychoanalysis in Frankfurt. With the Nazi threat becoming more intense, Fromm moved to Switzerland, where he joined the International Institute of Social Research in Geneva.

In 1933 Fromm accepted an invitation to deliver a series of lectures at the Chicago Psychoanalytic Institute. The following year he emigrated to the United States and opened a private practice in New York City. There, he and his wife renewed their acquaintance with Karen Horney, whom they had known casually at the Berlin Psychoanalytic Institute. They also met Harry Stack Sullivan, Clara Thompson, and other prominent psychotherapists then living in New York.

In 1941 Fromm joined Horney's newly formed Association for the Advancement of Psychoanalysis (AAP), but after two years of dissension, he resigned from the association. Fromm and Horney had previously been lovers, but by 1943 they were rivals. When students requested that Fromm, who did not hold an M.D. degree, teach a clinical course, the organization split over his qualifications. With Horney siding against him, Fromm, along with Sullivan, Thompson, and several other members, quit the AAP and immediately made plans to begin an alternative organization (Quinn, 1987). In 1946 this group established the William Alanson White Institute of Psychiatry, Psychoanalysis, and Psychology, with Fromm as both Chairman of the Faculty and Chairman of the Training Committee.

Fromm's marriage to Frieda Fromm-Reichmann ended in divorce, and in 1943 he married Henny Gurland. In 1949 the Fromms moved to Mexico and a more favorable climate for Henny Fromm who, by then, was in poor health. Fromm joined the faculty at the National Autonomous University in Mexico City, where he established a psychoanalytic department at the Medical School. Although his wife died in 1952, he continued to live in Mexico and commuted between his home in Cuernavaca and New York, where he continued as adjunct professor at the William Alanson White Institute. In 1974 Fromm and his third wife, Annis Freeman, moved to Muralto, Switzerland, where he died, March 18, 1980, five days short of his 80th birthday.

During his long professional career, Fromm held faculty positions at a number of distinguished schools, including the University of Frankfurt, Columbia, Bennington College, Yale, Michigan State, New York University, National University of Mexico, the William Alanson White Institute, and the New School for Social Research. Throughout his professional career he worked as a practicing psychotherapist. At first he followed an orthodox psychoanalytic technique, but after 10 years he became "bored" with the Freudian approach and developed his own methods which were more active and confrontational (Fromm, 1986; Sobel, 1980).

Fromm's ideas have attained a wide audience. Among his best-known books are *Escape from Freedom* (1941), *Man for Himself* (1947), *Psychoanalysis and Religion* (1950), *The Sane Society* (1955), *The Art of Loving* (1956), *The Heart of Man (1964), The Anatomy of Human Destructiveness* (1973), and *To Have or To Be* (1976).

Humanistic psychoanalysis is a broadly based theory, borrowing ideas from Freud, Marx, sociology, cultural anthropology, and religion. Landis & Tauber (1971) listed five important influences on Fromm's thinking: (1) the teachings of the humanistic rabbis, (2) the revolutionary spirit of Karl Marx, (3) the equally revolutionary ideas of Sigmund Freud, (4) the rationality of Zen Buddhism as espoused by D. T. Suzuki, and (5) the writings of Johann J. Bachofen (1815–1887) on matriarchal societies.

BASIC ASSUMPTIONS

Fromm's most basic assumption is that individual personality can only be understood in the light of human history. "The discussion of the human situation must precede that of personality" and "psychology must be based on an anthropologico-philosophical concept of human existence" (Fromm, 1947, p. 45).

In their evolutionary history, humans, unlike other animals, have been "torn away" from their prehistoric union with nature. They have no powerful instincts that allow them to adapt to a changing world. Instead, they have acquired the facility to reason. Fromm (1947) referred to this condition as the *human dilemma*. People experience this basic dilemma because they have become separate from nature, and yet have the capacity to be aware of themselves as isolated beings. Our ability to reason, however, is both a blessing and a curse. On the one hand, it permits us to survive, but on the other, it forces us to attempt to solve basic insoluble dichotomies. Fromm (1947) referred to these as "existential dichotomies" because they are rooted in our very existence. We cannot do away with these existential dichotomies; we can only react to them relative to our culture and our individual personalities.

The first and most fundamental dichotomy is that between life and death. Self-awareness and reason tell us that each of us will die. We can try to negate this dichotomy by postulating life after death, but this attempted solution does not alter the fact that our lives end with death.

A second existential dichotomy is that we are capable of conceptualizing complete self-realization, but, because life is short, we can never reach it. "Only if the life span of the individual were identical with that of mankind could he participate in the human development which occurs in the historical process" (Fromm, 1947, p. 42). Some people try to solve this dichotomy by assuming that their own historical period is the crowning achievement of humanity, while others postulate a continuation of development after death. Still others deny personal growth and devote their lives to the welfare of the community.

The third existential dichotomy is that we are ultimately alone, yet we cannot tolerate isolation. We are aware of ourselves as separate individuals and, at the same time, we are aware that our happiness depends on uniting with our fellow human beings. Although we cannot completely solve the problem of aloneness vs. union, we must make an attempt or else run the risk of insanity.

HUMAN NEEDS

As humans, we are motivated by a number of physiological needs—hunger, sex, and safety, for example—which we share with other animals, but satisfying these needs can never resolve our human dilemma. Only the distinctive human needs can move us toward a reunification with the natural world. Human needs, or **existential needs,** are those that have emerged during the evolution of human culture and have grown out of our attempts to find an answer to our existence. Human needs also represent attempts to avoid insanity. Indeed, Fromm (1955) contended that one important difference between mentally healthy individuals and neurotic or insane ones is that healthy people find answers to their existence—answers that more completely correspond to their total human needs. In other words, healthy individuals are better able to find ways of reuniting to the world through the human needs of relatedness, transcendance, rootedness, a sense of identity, and a frame of orientation.

Relatedness

The first human or existential need is **relatedness,** the drive for union with another person or persons. There are three basic ways in which a person may relate to the world: (1) submission, (2) power, and (3) love. A person can submit to another, to a group, or to an institution in order to become one with the world. "In this way he transcends the separateness of his individual existence by becoming part of somebody or something bigger than himself and experiences his identity in connection with the power to which he has submitted" (Fromm, 1981, p. 2).

Submissive people often search for domineering persons to submit to while those who seek power over others welcome submissive partners. When a submissive person and a domineering person find each other they frequently establish a *symbiotic relationship,* one that is satisfying to both partners. Although such symbiosis may be gratifying, it blocks growth toward integrity and psychological health. The two partners "live on each other and from each other, satisfying their craving for closeness, yet suffering from the lack of inner strength and self-reliance which would require freedom and independence" (Fromm, 1981, p. 2).

Richard, our case study, seeks relatedness through dependency and submission. He and his mother enjoy a symbiotic relationship, each depending on the other for satisfaction of needs. His mother provides him with nurturance and affection; he provides her with a dutiful and considerate son. The idyllic relationship may appear to be love, but it is founded on mutual dependency and not an authentic love that would permit each to grow toward independence and individuality.

People in symbiotic relationships are drawn to one another, not by love, but by a desperate need for relatedness, a need that can never be completely satisfied by such a partnership. Underlying the relationship are unconscious feelings of hostility. Each partner blames the other for not being able to completely satisfy his or her needs. Each finds himself or herself seeking more and more submission or power. As a result, each person becomes more and more dependent on the other, and less and less of an individual.

The only route by which a person can become united with the world and, at the same time, achieve individuality and integrity is **love,** which Fromm (1981, p. 3) defines as a "*union* with somebody, or something outside oneself *under the condition of retaining the separateness and integrity of one's own self.*" Love involves sharing and communion with another, yet it results in a freeing of the person to be unique and separate. It enables a person to satisfy the need for relatedness without surrendering integrity and independence. In love, two people become one, yet remain two.

In *The Art of Loving* (1956) Fromm identified care, responsibility, respect,

Relatedness can take the form of submission, power, or love.

and knowledge as four basic elements common to all forms of genuine love. To love another we must *care* for that person and be willing to take care of him or her. Love involves an active concern for the other person, an interest in that person's growth and development.

Love also means *responsibility,* that is, a willingness and ability to respond. If we love another, we respond to that person's physical and psychological needs.

Responsibility does not mean taking over another's life. It must be tied to *respect,* which permits the other person to be separate, to be a unique individual. If we respect others, we allow them to grow. We neither exploit nor dominate our loved ones, but respect them as fellow humans. We accept them for who they are without trying to change them.

We can respect others only if we have *knowledge* of them. To know others means to see them from their own point of view. Knowledge of another, however, always remains imperfect "The further we reach into the depth of . . . someone else's being, the more the goal of knowledge eludes us. Yet we cannot help desiring to penetrate into the secret of man's soul" (Fromm, 1956, p. 29).

Care, responsibility, respect, and knowledge are interrelated. One must *know* another person in order to *respect* her or him; *care* and *responsibility* must be guided by *knowledge;* and knowledge would be shallow if it were not motivated by care and concern (Fromm, 1956).

Transcendence

Like other animals, humans are thrown into the world without their consent or will and then removed from it, again without their consent or will.

But unlike other animals, human beings are driven by the need for **transcendence,** that is, the urge to rise above their passive and accidental existence and into "the realm of purposefulness and freedom" (Fromm, 1981, p. 4). Just as there are productive and nonproductive methods of relatedness, there are positive and negative approaches to transcendance. We can transcend our passive nature by either creating life or by destroying it. Though other animals can create life through reproduction, only humans are aware of themselves as creators. Also, humans can be creative in other ways. They can create art, religions, ideas, laws, material production, and love.

To create means to be active, to care about that which one creates. To create new human lives takes more than an act of sex—it takes love and care until children are able to take care of their own needs. To create great art or literature demands care and interest. To create laws requires lawmakers to be involved, to care about their creation.

People can also transcend life by destroying it. Through killing, a society or a person rises above the slain victims in a nonproductive attempt to transcend life. In *The Anatomy of Human Destructiveness* (1973) Fromm argued that humans are the only species to use **malignant aggression,** that is, to kill for reasons other than survival. Although malignant aggression is a dominant and powerful passion in some individuals and cultures, it is not common to all humans. It apparently was unknown to many prehistoric societies, as well as some contemporary "primitive" societies. Malignant aggression stems from *"the interaction of various social conditions with man's existential needs"* (Fromm, 1973, p. 218).

During human evolutionary history, as the human brain, particularly the neocortex, grew in size and complexity, reliance on instincts diminished. Then, using their ability to reason, humans evolved a number of social conditions including the various forms of malignant destruction. Humans are the only species known to kill their fellow members merely for revenge, excitement, or pleasure. This noninstinctual destruction of others represents a misplaced attempt to satisfy the existential need for transcendence.

Rootedness

A third existential need is for **rootedness,** that is, the need to establish roots or to feel at home again in the world. When humans evolved as a separate species they lost their home in the natural world. At the same time, their capacity for thought enabled them to realize that they were without a home, without roots. The consequent feelings of isolation and helplessness became unbearable. As with the other human needs, people would lose their sanity if they could not find ways to satisfy the need for rootedness. Very early in life a child receives roots from the mother, who is experienced as "the fountain of life, as an all-enveloping, protective, nourishing power. Mother is food; she is love; she is warmth; she is earth. To be loved by her means to be alive, to be rooted, to be at home" (Fromm, 1955, p. 39).

Rootedness can be sought in either productive or nonproductive strategies. With the productive strategy, the person is weaned from the "all-enveloping orbit of the mother" and becomes fully born.

> To the extent that man is fully born, he finds a new kind of rootedness; that lies in his creative relatedness to the world, and in the ensuing experience of solidarity with all man and with all nature. From being *passively* rooted in nature and in the womb, man becomes one again—but this time actively and creatively with all life (Fromm, 1981, p. 7).

In other words, when people move beyond the protective orbit of their mother or mother substitute, they actively and creatively relate to the world and become whole or integrated. This new tie to the natural world confers security and reestablishes a sense of belongingness and rootedness.

People may also seek rootedness through the nonproductive strategy of **fixation,** which, in its extreme form, is characterized by a desire to return to the mother's womb. It is seen as a tenacious reluctance to move beyond the protective security provided by one's mother.

A person may become fixated or blocked at a childish stage of development and crave the security of a mother or mother substitute. Our case study, Richard, although seemingly independent and capable in many ways, is still dependent on his mother for security and incapable of severing the bonds that tied him to her and home. In addition, the bank for which (whom) he works is like a second mother to him. He sees himself as a loyal member of a family of coworkers and becomes angry whenever he hears criticism of any aspect of the bank. Although young and in good health, he is more concerned with the health insurance and retirement programs of his parent company than with his salary.

People who strive for rootedness through fixation are "afraid to take the next step of birth, to be weaned from the mother's breast. [They] . . . have a deep craving to be mothered, nursed, protected by a motherly figure; they are the externally dependent ones, who are frightened and insecure when motherly protection is withdrawn" (Fromm, 1955, p. 40).

Rootedness can also be seen phylogenetically in the evolution of the human species. Fromm agreed with Freud that incestuous desires are universal. However, he disagreed with Freud's belief that they are essentially sexual. According to Fromm (1955, pp. 40–41), incestuous feelings are based on "the deep-seated craving to remain in, or to return to the all-enveloping womb, or to the all-nourishing breasts." Fromm was influenced by J. J. Bachofen's (1861, 1967) ideas on early matriarchal societies. According to Bachofen, in the earliest form of social organization, the mother, not the father, was the central figure. It was she who provided roots for her children and motivated them to either develop their individuality and reason or become fixated and incapable of psychological growth.

Sense of Identity

The fourth human need is for a **sense of identity,** our capacity to be aware of ourselves as a separate entity. Because we have been torn away from nature we need to form a concept of ourself, to be able to say, "I am I," or "I am the subject of my actions." Fromm (1981) believed that primitive people identified themselves more closely with their clan and did not see themselves as individuals existing apart from their group. Even during medieval times people were identified largely by their social role in the feudal hierarchy. The rise of capitalism and of democracies has given people more economic and political freedom, but only a minority of people have achieved a true sense of "I" as a result. Many still identify with others or with institutions. One's nation, religion, occupation, or social group provides a substitute sense of identity.

> Instead of the pre-individualistic clan identity, a new herd identity develops in which the sense of identity rests on the sense of an unquestionable belonging to the crowd. That this uniformity and conformity are often not recognized as such, and are covered by the illusion of individuality, does not alter the facts (Fromm, 1981, p. 9).

Without a sense of identity we could not retain our sanity. This threat provides a powerful motivation for us to do almost anything to acquire a sense of identity. This may explain why Richard identifies himself so closely with the bank where he works. Also, his expert knowledge of baseball marks him as a person apart from the crowd. Thus Richard has acquired some sense of identity, although it is an illusory one.

Healthy people have less need to conform to the herd, less need to give up their sense of self. They do not have to surrender their freedom and individuality in order to fit into society. They know who they are and what they want. They experience themselves as the center of their lives and possess an authentic sense of identity.

Frame of Orientation

A final human need is for a **frame of orientation.** Being split off from nature, we need a roadmap, a frame of orientation, to make our way through the world. Without such a map we would be "confused and unable to act purposefully and consistently" (Fromm, 1973, p. 230). A frame of orientation enables us to organize the various stimuli that impinge on us. "Man finds himself surrounded by many puzzling phenomena and, having reason, he has to make sense of them, has to put them in some context which he can understand" (Fromm, 1955, p. 63).

Every person has a philosophy, a consistent way of looking at things. Many take this philosophy or frame of reference for granted. Anything at odds with their view is judged as "crazy" or "unreasonable." Anything consistent with it is seen simply as "common sense." People will do nearly anything to acquire and retain a frame of orientation, even to the extreme of following irrational, bizarre, or fanatical philosophies such as those espoused by Hitler, Charles Manson, or leaders of the Ku Klux Klan.

A roadmap without a *goal* or destination is worthless. As humans, we have

	Negative Components	Positive Components
Relatedness	⟨ Submission Domination	Love
Transcendence	Destructiveness	Creativeness
Rootedness	Fixation	Wholeness
Sense of Identity	Adjustment to a Group	Individuality
Frame of Orientation	Irrational Goals	Rational Goals

Figure 8.1   Summary of Human Needs

the mental capacity to imagine many alternative paths to follow. To keep from going insane, however, we need a final goal or "object of devotion." According to Fromm (1973) this goal or object of devotion focuses our energies in a single direction, enables us to transcend our isolated existence, and confers meaning to our lives.

Richard's goal apparently is to make permanent his symbiotic relationship with his mother or mother substitute. His frame of orientation tolerates few deviations, and the familiarity of home and bank provide him with comfort, security, and a consistent way of viewing his life.

Summary

In addition to physiological or animal needs, people are motivated by five distinctively human needs—relatedness, transcendence, rootedness, a sense of identity, and a frame of orientation. These needs have evolved from our existence as a separate species and are aimed at moving us toward a reunification with the natural world. Fromm believed that lack of satisfaction of any of these needs is unbearable and results in insanity. Thus, we are strongly driven to fulfill them in some way or another, either positively or negatively.

Figure 8.1 shows that relatedness can be satisfied through submission, domination, or love, but only love produces authentic fulfillment; transcendence can be satisfied by either destructiveness or creativeness, but only the latter permits joy; rootedness can be satisfied by either fixation to the mother or by moving forward into full birth and wholeness; the sense of identity can be based on adjustment to the group or it can be satisfied through creative development toward individuality; and a frame of orientation may be either irrational or rational, but only a rational philosophy can serve as a basis for the growth of total personality (Fromm, 1981).

THE BURDEN OF FREEDOM

The central thesis of Fromm's writings is that humans have been torn from nature, yet they remain part of the natural world, subject to the same physical limitations as other animals. As the only animal that possesses self-awareness, imagination, and reason, humans are "the freak of the universe" (Fromm, 1955, p. 23). Reason is both a curse and a blessing. It is responsible for our feelings of isolation and loneliness, but it is also the process that enables us to become reunited with the world.

Historically, as people gained more and more economic and political freedom, they came to feel increasingly more isolated. For example, during the Middle Ages, people had relatively little personal freedom. They were anchored to prescribed roles in society, roles that provided security, dependability, and certainty. Then, as they acquired more *freedom to* move socially and geographically, they found they were *free from* the security of a fixed position in the world. They were no longer tied to one geographic region, one social order, or one occupation. They became separated from their roots and isolated from one another. A parallel experience is seen on a personal level. As children become more independent of their mothers, they gain more *freedom to* express their individuality, to move around unsupervised, to choose their friends and clothes, and so on. At the same time they experience the burden of freedom, that is, they lose the security of being one with the mother. This burden of freedom results in **basic anxiety,** a feeling of being alone in the world.

Mechanisms of Escape

Because basic anxiety produces a frightening sense of isolation and aloneness, people attempt to flee from freedom through a variety of escape mechanisms. In *Escape From Freedom,* Fromm (1941) identified three primary mechanisms of escape—authoritarianism, destructiveness, and conformity. Unlike Horney's *neurotic* trends (see Chapter 7), Fromm's mechanisms of escape are the driving forces in *normal* people, both individually and collectively.

Authoritarianism

Fromm (1941, p. 141) defined **authoritarianism** as "the tendency to give up the independence of one's own individual self and to fuse one's self with somebody or something outside oneself in order to acquire the strength which the individual self is lacking." Authoritarianism takes two forms— **masochism** and **sadism.**

Masochistic strivings result from basic feelings of powerlessness, weakness, and inferiority, and are aimed at joining the self to a more powerful person or institution. Such feelings often are disguised as love or loyalty, but, unlike love and loyalty, they can never contribute positively to independence and authenticity. Richard appears to love his mother and to be loyal to his employer, but his attachment to both is motivated by masochistic striving, and is ultimately self-defeating.

Compared with masochistic strivings, sadistic tendencies are more neurotic and more socially harmful. Like masochism, sadism is aimed at reducing basic anxiety through achieving unity with another person or persons. Fromm (1941) identified three kinds of sadistic tendencies, all more or less clustered together. The first is manifested as the need to make others dependent on oneself and to gain power over those who are weak. The second is the need to exploit others, to take advantage of them and use them for one's benefit or pleasure. A third sadistic tendency is the desire to see others suffer, either physically or psychologically.

Sadistic tendencies are frequently disguised as a reaction formation and appear as exaggerated kindness and an overconcern for the welfare of others. Richard's obsequious manner may well mask a sadistic tendency to dominate and control. By being kind and gentle he influences others to treat him in an amiable and benign manner.

Sadism and masochism, of course, are usually found within the same person, resulting in a "constant oscillation between the active and the passive side of the symbiotic complex" and making it "difficult to determine which side of it is operating at a given moment. In both cases individuality and freedom are lost" (Fromm, 1941, pp. 158–159). Both sadism and masochism are characterized by the belief that our lives are determined by forces outside ourselves. In other words, the authoritarian escape mechanism is a self-defeating attempt to find happiness by submitting to a force outside one's self.

Destructiveness

Destructiveness is similar to authoritarianism in that it is rooted in the feelings of aloneness, isolation, and powerlessness. However, unlike sadism and masochism, which depend on a continual relationship with another, destructiveness would eliminate the other.

Both individuals and nations can employ destructiveness as a mechanism of escape. By destroying people and objects a person or a nation attempts to restore lost feelings of power. Serial killers are typically lonely people, searching for union with another person. Their contact with their victims, however, is usually short and ends with the destruction of a human who might have provided intimacy and unity. Obviously, destructiveness is self-defeating, for in destroying, one can no longer unite. The destructive person, however, is attracted to a kind of perverted isolation that would be achieved if one could eliminate the outside world.

> I can escape the feeling of my own powerlessness in comparison with the world outside myself by destroying it. To be sure, if I succeed in removing it, I remain alone and isolated, but mine is a splendid isolation in which I cannot be crushed by the overwhelming power of the objects outside of myself. The destruction of the world is the last, almost desperate attempt to save myself from being crushed by it (Fromm, 1941, p. 179).

Conformity

The most common means of escape in American society, Fromm believed, is **conformity.** With conformity, a person tries to escape from a sense of aloneness and isolation by giving up individuality and becoming whatever other people desire. The person thus becomes an automaton, a robot reacting predictably and mechanically to the whims of others.

Richard tries very hard to do as other desire of him. He wants to please his mother and father, his coworkers and boss, and even the people he meets casually. Although an intelligent and knowledgeable person, he never expresses an opinion that may anger or disturb someone else. His tastes in cars, clothes, entertainment, and food are quite conventional and pedestrian. In many ways he is like an automaton—predictable, stiff, and mechanical. No one can dislike Richard, but because he lacks authenticity and individuality, no one can really love him either.

Conformists usually give themselves credit for more individuality than they deserve. They say, "I think so and so," or "I believe this or that," but the "I" to whom they refer is often merely an extension of society and represents a general belief or attitude. They tend to value the same music and movies that everyone else values. They feel the way they are supposed to feel in a given situation and thus lose their identity as unique persons.

In summary, people in the modern world are free from many external bonds and free to act according to their own will. But they do not know what they want, think, or feel. They conform like automatons to some anonymous authority and adopt a self that is not authentic. The more they conform, the more powerless they feel; the more powerless they feel, the more they must conform. People can break this cycle of conformity and powerlessness only by achieving self-realization or positive freedom (Fromm, 1941).

Positive Freedom

The emergence of political and economic freedom need not lead inevitably to the bondage of isolation and powerlessness. A person "can be free and not alone, critical and yet not filled with doubts, independent and yet an integral part of mankind" (Fromm, 1941, p. 257). A person can attain this kind of freedom through self-realization and by a full expression of both rational and emotional potentialities. "These potentialities are present in everybody; they become real only to the extent to which they are expressed. In other words, *positive freedom consists in the spontaneous activity of the total, integrated personality*" (Fromm, 1941, p. 258). To achieve **positive freedom** a person must be spontaneously active. Spontaneous activity is frequently seen in small children and artists who have little tendency to conform to whatever others want them to be. They act according to their basic natures and not according to conventional rules. Richard has natural talents as a writer, but his needs to conform, to seek safety and security, prevent him from realizing his creative potentials. His primary mechanisms of escape—authoritarianism and conformity—free him from the unbearable pain of total isolation and aloneness. However, they also prevent him from being an individual and from pursuing positive freedom. Positive freedom represents a successful solution to the human dilemma of being part of the natural world and yet separate from it. Through positive freedom and spontaneous activity we overcome the terror of aloneness and achieve a union of the self with the world, but with no loss of individuality.

Fromm (1941) held that love and work are the twin components of positive freedom. Through active love and work we unite with others and with the world without sacrificing our integrity. We affirm our uniqueness as individuals and achieve full realization of our potentialities. Love and work comprise the lone *productive character orientation.*

CHARACTER ORIENTATIONS

Fromm (1947, p. 50) defined personality as "the totality of inherited and acquired psychic qualities which are characteristic of one individual and which make the individual unique." The most important of the acquired qualities of personality is **character,** defined as *"the relatively permanent system of all noninstinctual strivings through which [people relate themselves] to the human and natural world"* (Fromm, 1973, p. 226).

People relate to the world in two ways: by acquiring and using things *(assimilation)* and by relating to self and others *(socialization).* Both assimilation and socialization come through experience, not instinct. In general, people can relate either *nonproductively* or *productively.* The nonproductive orientation includes *receiving, exploiting, hoarding,* and *marketing;* the single productive orientation has three dimensions—*working, loving,* and *reasoning.* Personality is always a blend or combination of several orientations, though one orientation is usually dominant.

Nonproductive Orientations

Fromm used the term nonproductive to suggest strategies that fail to move a person closer to positive freedom and self-realization. Nonproductive orientations are, however, not entirely negative; each has both a negative and a positive aspect.

Receptive

Receptive people feel that the source of all good lies outside themselves and that the only way they can relate to the world is to receive things, including love, knowledge, and material possessions. They are more concerned with receiving than with giving, and want others to shower them with love, ideas, and gifts. In return they are willing to be loyal, accepting, and trusting. The negative aspects of a receptive character include passivity, submissiveness, servility, and lack of self-confidence. Each of these describes Richard, at least to some extent. However, Richard also possesses most of the positive characteristics of the receptive orientation; he is devoted, modest, polite, and trusting.

Exploitative

Exploitative people, like receptive ones, believe that the source of good is outside themselves. However, unlike receptive people, they aggressively take what they desire, rather than passively receive it. In their social relationships they are likely to use cunning or force to take someone else's friend. An exploitative man may "fall in love" with a married woman, not so much because he is truly fond of her, but because he wishes to exploit her husband. In the realm of ideas, exploitative people prefer to steal or plagiarize rather than create. Unlike receptive characters, they are willing to express an opinion, but it is usually an opinion that has been pilfered.

On the negative side, exploitative characters are egocentric, conceited, arrogant, and seducing. Their positive qualities include pride, impulsiveness, and self-confidence. They are active, captivating, and able to take initiative.

Hoarding

Rather than valuing things outside themselves, **hoarding** characters seek to save that which they have already obtained. They hold everything in and do not let go of anything. They keep their money, their feelings, and their thoughts for themselves. In a love relationship they try to possess the loved one and to preserve the relationship rather than allowing it to change and grow. They tend to live in the past and are repelled by anything new. They are similar to Freud's anal character (see Chapter 2) in that they are excessively orderly, stubborn, and miserly. However, Fromm (1964) believed that the hoarding character's anal traits are not the result of sexual drives, but rather are part of the person's general interest in all that is not alive, including the feces.

Richard obviously has many of the traits, both negative and positive of the hoarding character. He is pedantic, obsessive, possessive, and anxious; more positively, he is orderly, cautious, methodical, and loyal. His enormous collection of baseball cards is not for sale or trade. He carefully arranges his cards in a neat and orderly manner and preserves them so that older ones always appear brand-new.

Marketing

The **marketing** character is an outgrowth of modern commerce. Trade is no longer personal but carried out by large, impersonal corporations. Marketing characters see themselves as commodities, with their personal value being dependent on their exchange value, that is, their ability to sell themselves.

Marketing personalities must see themselves as being in constant demand; they must make others believe that they are skillful and salable. Their personal security rests on shaky grounds since they must adjust their personality to that which is currently in fashion. They play many roles and are guided by the motto "'I am as you desire me'" (Fromm, 1947, p. 73).

Marketing characters are aimless, opportunistic, inconsistent, and wasteful.

They are without a past or a future and have no permanent principles or values. They have fewer positive traits than the other orientations because they are basically empty, waiting to be filled with whatever characteristic is most marketable. Some of the positive qualities Fromm (1947) used to describe the marketing personality include changeability, open-mindedness, undogmatic, adaptable, and generous.

The Productive Orientation

The productive person is the most healthy of all character types. This orientation is directed toward positive freedom and a continuing realization of one's potentials. Only through productive activity can a person solve the basic human dilemma, that is, to become united with the world and with others, while, at the same time, retaining uniqueness and individuality. This can be accomplished only through productive work, love, and thought. The productive orientation, therefore, is a single type with three interrelated dimensions.

Healthy people value *work,* not as an end in itself, but as a means of creative self-expression. They do not work to exploit others, to market themselves, to withdraw from others, or to accumulate needless material possessions. They are neither lazy nor compulsively active, but use work as a means of producing life's necessities.

Productive *love* is characterized by the four qualities of love discussed earlier—care, responsibility, respect, and knowledge. Healthy people have a passionate love of life and all that is alive **(biophilia).** They desire to further all life—the life of people, animals, plants, ideas, and cultures. They are concerned with the growth and development of themselves as well as others. Biophilic individuals want to influence others through love, reason, and example, not by force. Fromm believed that love of others and self-love are inseparable, but that self-love must come first. Everyone has the capacity for productive love, but few achieve it because they cannot first love themselves.

Productive *thinking* cannot be separated from productive work and love. It is motivated by a concerned interest in another person or object. Healthy people see others as they are and not as they would wish them to be. Similarly, they know themselves for who they are and have no need for self-delusion.

Fromm (1970) believed that healthy people rely on some combination of all five character orientations. Their survival as healthy individuals depends on their ability to *accept* things from other people, to *take* things when appropriate, to *preserve* things, to *exchange* things, and to *work, love,* and *think* productively.

PERSONALITY DISORDERS

If healthy people are able to work, love, and think productively, then unhealthy personalities are characterized by a failure to use their full potentials, especially their power to love. In our previous discussion of the non-productive orientations—receptive, exploitative, hoarding, and marketing—the emphasis was mostly on modes of assimilation, that is, one's method of acquiring and using objects or things. However, serious psychopathology has its roots in modes of socialization, that is, one's pattern of relating to other people. Fromm (1981) held that the psychologically disturbed person is one who is incapable of love and has failed to establish union with others.

Fromm recognized three severe personality disorders—necrophilia, malignant narcissism, and incestuous symbiosis.

Necrophilia

The term **necrophilia** means love of death and usually refers to a sexual perversion where a person desires sexual contact with a corpse. However, Fromm (1964, 1973) used necrophilia in a more generalized sense to denote any attraction to death. Necrophilia is an alternative character orientation to *biophilia.* People naturally love life, but when social conditions stunt biophilia, a person may adopt a necrophilous orientation.

Necrophilous personalities hate humanity. They are the racists, warmongers, and bullies of the world; they love bloodshed, destruction, terror, and torture. Their greatest achievement is to destroy life. They are strong advocates of law and order; love to talk about sickness, death, and burials; and are fascinated by dirt, decay, corpses, and feces. They prefer night to day and love to operate in darkness and shadow.

Necrophilous people do not simply *behave* in a destructive manner; rather, their destructive behavior is a reflection of basic *character.* All of us behave aggressively and destructively at times, but the necrophilous person's entire life revolves around death, destruction, disease, and decay.

Malignant Narcissism

If all of us display some necrophilous behavior, so too are all of us **narcissistic.** In its benign form narcissism is manifested as a greater interest in one's own body and concerns than in those of others. In its malignant form narcissism impedes one's perception of reality so that everything belonging to self is highly valued and everything belonging to another is devalued. One's face, physique, car, house, and ideas are far superior to those of others.

Narcissistic people are preoccupied with themselves, but this overconcern is not limited to admiring themselves in a mirror. Preoccupation with one's body often leads to **hypochondriasis** or an obsessive attention to one's health. Fromm (1964) also recognized **moral hypochondriasis,** which is a preoccupation with *guilt* about previous transgressions. In other words, people who are fixated on themselves are likely to internalize experiences and to dwell on both physical and moral aspects of their being. "The narcissism underlying physical or moral hypochondriasis is the same as the narcissism of the vain person" (Fromm, 1964, p. 69). Each stems from an intense interest in one's self.

Narcissistic personalities possess what Horney (Chapter 7) calls "neurotic claims." They achieve security by holding on to a distorted belief that their extraordinary personal qualities give them superiority over everyone else. Since what they *have*—looks, physique, wealth—is so wonderful, it is not necessary that they *do* anything to prove their value. Their sense of worth depends on their narcissistic self-image and not on their achievements. When their efforts are criticized by others they react with anger and rage, frequently striking out against their critics, trying to destroy them. If the criticism is overwhelming, they may be unable to destroy it, and so they turn their rage inward. The result is *depression,* a feeling of worthlessness that marks unconscious narcissism. While depression, intense guilt, and hypochondriasis may appear to be anything but self-glorification, Fromm believed that each of these could be symptomatic of deep underlying narcissism.

Incestuous Symbiosis

A third pathological orientation is **incestuous symbiosis,** or an extreme dependence on the mother or mother surrogate. Incestuous symbiosis is an exaggerated form of the more common and more benign *mother fixation.* Men with a mother fixation need a woman to care for them, comfort them, and admire them; they feel somewhat anxious and depressed when their needs are not fulfilled. This condition is relatively normal and does not greatly interfere with one's daily life.

However, with incestuous symbiosis people are inseparable from the *host* person; their personalities are blended with the other person and individual identities are lost. Incestuous symbiosis originates in infancy as a natural attachment to the mothering one. The attachment is more crucial and fundamental than any sexual interest that may develop during the Oedipal period. Fromm agreed more with Sullivan than with Freud with his suggestion that attachment to the mother rests on the need for security and not for sex. "Sexual strivings are not the cause of the fixation to mother, but the *result*" (Fromm, 1964, p. 99).

People living in incestuous symbiotic relationships feel extremely anxious and frightened if that relationship is threatened. They believe that they cannot live without the other. (The host need not be another human—it can be a family, clan, church, country, and the like.) The incestuous orientation distorts reasoning powers, destroys the capacity for authentic love, and prevents people from achieving independence and integrity.

In summary, Fromm (1964, p. 107) wrote:

> The tendency to remain bound to the mothering person and her equivalents—to blood, family, tribe—is inherent in all men and women. It is constantly in conflict with the opposite tendency—to be born, to progress, to grow. In the case of normal development, the tendency for growth wins. In the other case a severe pathology, the regressive tendency for symbiotic union, wins, and it results in the person's more or less total incapacitation.

In some severely pathological personalities, such as Adolph Hitler, necrophilia, malignant narcissism, and incestuous symbiosis are combined into

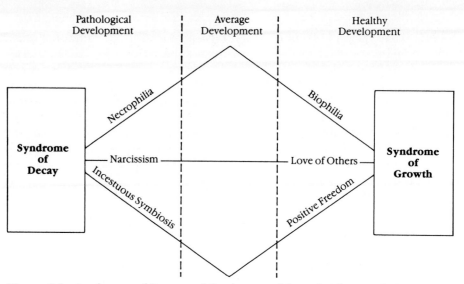

Figure 8.2   Syndromes of Decay and Syndromes of Growth. Three pathological and three healthy orientations converge to form each syndrome, but most people are probably in the middle.

what Fromm (1964) termed the *syndrome of decay.* Such people are attracted to death, take pleasure in destroying those who are regarded as inferiors, and act in the name of the homeland, the clan, or the party. Fromm contrasted the syndrome of decay with the *syndrome of growth.* With pathological individuals necrophilia, malignant narcissism, and incestuous symbiosis converge to form the syndrome of decay; with the syndrome of growth, biophilia, love, and positive freedom converge, as shown in Figure 8.2. Note that both the syndrome of decay and the syndrome of growth are extreme forms of development; most people are probably in the average range.

PSYCHOTHERAPY

Fromm was trained as an orthodox Freudian analyst, but became bored with standard analytic techniques. "With time I came to see that my boredom stemmed from the fact that I was not in touch with the life of my patients" (Fromm, 1986, p. 106). He then evolved his own system of therapy, which he called *humanistic psychoanalysis.* Compared to Freud, Fromm was much more concerned with the interpersonal aspects of a therapeutic encounter. He agreed with Adler, Sullivan, and Horney that therapy is built on a personal relationship between therapist and patient and that accurate communication is essential to therapeutic growth.

Fromm believed that patients come to therapy seeking satisfaction of their basic human needs—relatedness, transcendence, rootedness, a sense of identity, and a frame of orientation. The task for the therapist, then, is to relate "as one human being to another with utter concentration and utter sincerity" (Fromm, 1963, p. 184). In this spirit of relatedness the patient will once again feel at one with another person. Although transference and even countertransference may exist within this relationship, the important point is that two real human beings are involved with one another.

Therapists must be able to put themselves in the place of the patient, to understand every negative, neurotic, or nonproductive need of the patient, even before it is verbalized. There is nothing within the patient that is foreign to the therapist. In an interview with Richard Evans (1966, p. 46) Fromm referred to this concept as the *human premise*.

> There is nothing human which is alien to [me]. Everything is in me: I'm a little child, I'm a grownup, I'm a murderer, and I'm a saint; I'm narcissistic, and I'm destructive. There is nothing in the patient which I do not have in me. And only insofar as I can muster within myself those experiences about which the patient is telling me either explicitly or implicitly, only if they arouse an echo within myself, can I know what the patient is talking about and give back to him what he is really saying. Then something very strange happens: the patient does not have the feeling that I'm talking about something alien to him—he does not feel that I'm talking about him or that I'm talking down to him—instead he feels that I'm talking about something we both share.

As part of his attempt to achieve shared communication, Fromm asked patients to reveal their dreams. He believed that dreams as well as fairy tales and myths are expressed in symbolic language—the only universal language humans have developed (Fromm, 1951). Because dreams have meaning beyond the individual dreamer, it is not necessary to ask for the patient's associations to the dream material. Not all dream symbols, however, are universal; some are accidental and depend on the dreamer's mood before going to sleep; others are regional and national and depend on climate, geography, and dialect. Many symbols have several meanings because of the various experiences connected with them. For example, fire may symbolize warmth and home to some people and death and destruction to others. Similarly, to desert people, the sun may represent a threat, while to people in cold climates, it stands for growth and life.

Fromm adopted a middle position between Freud's view of dreams as wish-fulfillments and Jung's notion of the prophetic nature of dreams. Fromm felt that many dreams express sexual wishes and fantasies, but that others provide insight into the future, insight that is not present during waking life. Dreams are not really prophetic, but they sometimes come true because the insights gained while sleeping are often learned later while the person is awake. For example, cowards may dream that they defeat a formidable opponent in a contest. This is their first insight into their ability to muster courage. Eventually, through therapy and dream interpretation, they may realize their courage and act upon it while awake.

Fromm (1963) believed that the therapist should not try to be too scientific in understanding the patient. Only in the attitude of relatedness can another person be truly understood. The patient should not be viewed as an illness or a thing, but as a person, with all of the same human needs as the therapist.

RESEARCH METHODS

Fromm gathered data on human personality from many sources, including psychotherapy, cultural anthropology, and psychohistory. In this section we look briefly at his anthropological study of life in a Mexican village and his psychobiographical analysis of Adolph Hitler.

Social Character in a Mexican Village

During the late 1950s and extending into the mid-1960s, Fromm and a group of psychologists, psychoanalysts, anthropologists, physicians, and statisticians studied social character in an unidentified Mexican village about 50 miles south of Mexico City. The team interviewed every adult and half the children in this isolated farming village of 162 households and about 800 inhabitants.

The people of the primitive village were mostly farmers, earning a living from small plots of fertile land. As Fromm and Michael Maccoby (1970, p. 37) described them:

> They are selfish, suspicious of each others' motives, pessimistic about the future, and fatalistic. Many appear submissive and self-deprecatory, although they have the potential for rebelliousness and revolution. They feel inferior to city people, more stupid, and less cultured. There is an overwhelming feeling of powerlessness to influence either nature or the industrial machine that bears down on them.

Could one expect to find Fromm's character orientations in such a society? After living among the villagers and gaining their acceptance, the research team employed an assortment of techniques designed to answer this and other questions. Included among the research tools were extensive interviews, dream reports, detailed questionnaires, and two projective techniques—the Rorschach Inkblot Test and the Thematic Apperception Test.

No evidence for Fromm's *marketing* personality was found. Recall that Fromm believed that this character orientation was a product of modern commerce, where trade is no longer personal and where people regard themselves as commodities. Not surprisingly, these peasant villagers were still immune to the marketing orientation.

However, the researchers did find evidence for several other character types, the most common of which was the *nonproductive-receptive* type. These people tended to look up to others and devoted much energy in trying to please those they regarded as superiors. Working men identified as belonging to this type would, on paydays, accept their pay in servile fashion, as if they had somehow not earned it.

The second most frequently found personality type was the *productive-hoarding* character. These people were hard working, productive, and independent. They usually farmed their own plot of land and relied on saving part of each crop for seed and for food in the event of future crop failure. Thus, hoarding rather than consuming was essential to their lives.

The *unproductive-exploitative* personality was identified as a third character orientation. Men of this type were most likely to get into knife or pistol fights while "the women are the most malicious gossip mongers" (Fromm & Maccoby, 1970, p. 123). Only about 10 percent of the population were dominantly exploitative, a surprisingly small percentage considering the extreme poverty of the village.

An even smaller number of inhabitants could be described as *productive-exploitative*—no more than 15 individuals in the whole village. Among them were the richest and most powerful men in the village, who had taken advantage of the unproductive-receptive villagers by keeping them economically dependent.

In general, Fromm and Maccoby (1970) reported a remarkable similarity between character orientations in this Mexican village and the theoretical orientations Fromm had suggested some years earlier. This anthropological study, of course, cannot be considered as confirmation of Fromm's theory. Since Fromm was one of the investigators, it is quite possible that he simply found what he had expected to find.

A Psychohistorical Study of Hitler

Following the lead of Freud (Chapter 2) and Erikson (Chapter 3), Fromm examined historical documents in order to sketch a psychological portrait of a prominent person, a technique known as psychohistory or psychobiography. The subject of Fromm's most complete psychobiographical study was Freud (see Fromm, 1959), but Fromm (1941, 1973, 1986) also wrote at length on the life of Adolph Hitler.

Fromm regarded Hitler as the world's most conspicuous example of a person suffering from the *syndrome of decay,* that is, a combination of necrophilia, malignant narcissism, and incestuous symbiosis. Hitler displayed all three pathological disorders: he was attracted to death and destruction; he was narrowly focused on self-interests and greatly delighted in self-aggrandizement; and he was driven by an incestuous devotion to the Germanic "race," being fanatically dedicated to preventing its blood from being polluted by Jews and other "non-Aryans."

Unlike some psychoanalysts who look only to early childhood for clues to adult personality, Fromm believed that each stage of development is important and that nothing in Hitler's early life bent him inevitably toward the syndrome of decay. As a child, Hitler was perhaps spoiled by his mother, but her indulgence did not cause his later pathology. It did, however, foster narcissistic feelings of self-importance. "Hitler's mother never became to him a person to whom he was lovingly or tenderly attached. She was a symbol of the protecting and admiring goddesses, but also of the goddess of death and chaos" (Fromm, 1973, p. 378).

Adolph Hitler personified the syndrome of decay.

Hitler was an above average student in elementary school, but a failure in high school. During adolescence he experienced some conflict with his father who wanted him to be more responsible and to take a reliable civil service job. Hitler, on the other hand, somewhat unrealistically desired to be an artist. Also during this time he began to lose himself more and more in fantasy. His narcissism ignited a burning passion for greatness as an artist or architect, but reality brought him failure after failure in this area. "Each failure caused a graver wound to his narcissism and a deeper humiliation than the previous one; in the same degree as his failures, grew also his indulgence in fantasy, his resentment, his wish for revenge, and his necrophilia" (Fromm, 1973, p. 395).

The terrible realization of his failure as an artist was blunted by the outbreak of World War I. His fierce ambition could now be channeled into being a great war hero fighting for his homeland. Though he was no great hero, he was a responsible, disciplined, and dutiful soldier. After the war, however, he experienced more failure. Not only had his beloved nation lost, but revolutionaries within Germany had "attacked everything that was sacred to Hitler's reactionary nationalism, and they won. . . . The victory of the revolutionaries gave Hitler's destructiveness its final and ineradicable form" (Fromm, 1973, p. 394).

We saw earlier that necrophilia does not simply refer to *behavior;* it pervades a person's entire *character.* So it was with Hitler. After he came to power he demanded that his enemies not merely surrender but that they be annihilated as well. His necrophilia was expressed in his mania for destroying buildings and cities, his orders to kill defective people, his boredom, and his slaughter of millions of Jews.

Another trait Hitler manifested was narcissism. He was interested only in himself, his plans, and his ideology. His conviction that he could build a "Thousand-Year Reich" shows an inflated sense of self-importance. He had no interest in anyone unless that person was of service to him. His relations to women lacked love and tenderness; he seemed to have used them solely for perverted personal pleasure, especially for voyeuristic satisfaction.

According to Fromm's analysis, Hitler also possessed an incestuous symbiosis, manifested by his passionate devotion, not to his real mother, but to the Germanic "race." In addition, his perception of reality was flawed, he was sadomasochistic and withdrawn, and he completely lacked feelings of love or compassion. All these characteristics, Fromm contended, did not make Hitler psychotic. They did, however, make him a sick and dangerous man.

Insisting that Hitler not be seen as inhuman, Fromm (1973, p. 433) concluded his psychohistory with these words: "Any analysis that would distort Hitler's picture by depriving him of his humanity would only intensify the tendency to be blind to the potential Hitlers unless they wear horns."

CONCEPT OF HUMANITY

Fromm's concept of humanity begins with this definition: *"The human species can be defined as the primate who emerged at that point of evolution where instinctive determinism had reached a minimum and the development of the brain a maximum"* (Fromm, 1976, p. 137). Human beings, then, are freaks of nature, the only species ever to have evolved this combination of minimal instinctive powers and maximal brain development. "Lacking the capacity to act by the command of instincts while possessing the capacity for self-awareness, reason, and imagination . . . the human species needed a *frame of orientation* and an *object of devotion* in order to survive" (Fromm, 1976, p. 137).

Human survival, however, has been paid for by the price of basic anxiety, loneliness, and powerlessness. In every age and culture people have been faced with the same fundamental problem: How to escape from feelings of isolation and find unity with nature and with other people?

How *optimistic* was Fromm that people could reunite with others and achieve positive freedom? On this dimension for a concept of humanity Fromm receives a moderate rating. He was realistic enough to recognize that most people remain isolated and lost, but he was hopeful enough to believe that some people realize their potentials and become reunited with other people and with nature. Fromm had a rather pessimistic attitude toward modern capitalism, insisting that most people in capitalistic societies feel isolated, lack individuality, and cling desperately to the illusion of independence and freedom. They do not act according to their own will because they are unaware of their own feelings and beliefs. They feel powerless, have little sense of identity, and hide behind a façade of happiness (Fromm, 1968).

However, Fromm was also optimistic. He believed that positive freedom, a sense of identity, and growing individuality were possible. In *Man For Himself* (1947, p. x) he wrote: "I have become increasingly impressed by . . . the strength of the strivings for happiness and health, which are part of the natural equipment of man." Most people, Fromm felt, are relatively happy in spite of adverse social conditions.

On the dimension of *free choice vs. determinism* Fromm again took a middle position. He insisted that this issue cannot be applied to the entire species. One person may be free to choose and another not free. Choice itself is relative, seldom being an either/or dichotomy. Instead, Fromm (1964) believed, there are degrees of inclinations toward action and individuals are seldom aware of all the possible alternatives.

Fromm believed that our actions are subject to those forces that have determined human nature, but our ability to reason enables us to understand the motivation behind our behavior. This ability allows people to take an active part in their own fate and to "strengthen those elements which strive for the good" (Fromm, 1947, p. 233).

On the dimension of *causality vs. teleology* Fromm tended to favor teleology. Although the history of our species has created the present human dilemma, we as individuals set goals that guide our actions. We constantly strive for a frame of orientation, a roadmap, by which to plan our lives into the future.

Fromm believed that one of the uniquely human traits is *self-awareness*. Humans are the only animals who can reason, visualize the future, and consciously strive toward self-erected goals. Self-awareness, however, is a mixed blessing, and many people repress their basic character in order to avoid mounting anxiety. Others, though, are mostly conscious of the reasons for their behavior. People in a productive love relationship, for example, must, of necessity, have a high level of awareness since productive love requires the conscious qualities of mutual care, responsibility, respect, and understanding.

Though he did not entirely overlook biological forces, Fromm strongly emphasized *social influences* on personality. The distinctively human needs of relatedness, transcendence, rootedness, sense of identity, and frame of orientation are all products of a social environment. There is no biologically fixed human nature. Human personality is historically and culturally determined. As a species we are exceedingly adaptable, but as individuals we are not always flexible. For most people, once a characteristic is established by social forces, it becomes very difficult to change. Culture, then, makes us human and shapes our character. Fromm (1956, p. 11) wrote: "Life in its biological aspects is a miracle and a secret, and man in his human aspects is an unfathomable secret."

Finally, Fromm placed moderate emphasis on *similarities* among people. Though history and culture impinge heavily on personality, people retain some degree of uniqueness. We are one species sharing many of the same human needs. Nevertheless, interpersonal experiences throughout a person's life bestow a measure of uniqueness on the individual.

CRITIQUE OF FROMM

Fromm, perhaps, was the most brilliant essayist of all personality theorists. He wrote beautiful essays on international politics (Fromm, 1961), on the relevance of the biblical prophets for people today (Fromm, 1986), on the psychological problems of the aging (Fromm, 1981), on Marx, Hitler, Freud, Christ, and myriad other topics. Regardless of the subject matter, at the core of all Fromm's writings was an unfolding of the essence of human nature.

Like all the theorists so far discussed, Fromm's primary source of data was his experiences as a psychotherapist. Also like the other psychodynamic theorists, he tended to take a global approach to theory construction, erecting a grand, highly abstract model that was basically philosophical. His insights into human nature strike a responsive chord, as evidenced by the popularity of his books; but are they scientific?

How do Fromm's ideas rate on the five criteria of a useful theory. First, the breadth of the theory enables it to *organize and explain* much of what is known concerning human personality. However, its lack of precision makes prediction difficult.

Indeed, imprecise and vague terms have rendered the theory nearly sterile as a *generator of empirical research.* Unlike Bandura (Chapter 12), Fromm did not evolve his theory as a consequence of continuing research. The study of the Mexican village (Fromm & Maccoby, 1970), and later studies by Maccoby (1976, 1981) on character types of American business leaders, came well after Fromm's theory had been established, and findings from these studies did not modify the theory.

As a *guide to action,* Fromm's writings have little value, except to stimulate readers to think productively. Unfortunately, neither the researcher nor the therapist receives much practical information.

Fromm's humanistic psychoanalysis is internally consistent in the sense that a single theme runs throughout his writings. However, the theory lacks a structured taxonomy, a set of operationally defined terms, and a clear limitation of scope. Like many of the psychodynamic theories, humanistic psychoanalysis is rated low on *internal consistency.*

Finally, is the theory *parsimonious?* Once again, Fromm does not fare well. He was reluctant to abandon earlier concepts and formulations or to relate them precisely to his later ideas. As a consequence, the theory lacks simplicity and unity. For example, the three major personality disorders—necrophilia, malignant narcissism, and incestuous symbiosis—are not integrated into the different character orientations. Also, the mechanisms of escape would seem to be related to both the character orientations and the personality disorders, but Fromm did not specify the nature of this relationship.

CHAPTER SUMMARY

Fromm's basic thesis is that people, during their history, have been torn away from their prehistoric union with nature and also with one another. Moreover, they have the power of reasoning, foresight, and imagination. This combination of lack of animal instincts and the presence of rational thought makes humans the freaks of the universe. Self-awareness contributes to feelings of loneliness, isolation, and homelessness. To escape from these feelings, people strive to become reunited with others and with nature.

Only the uniquely *human needs* can move people toward reunification. These needs include *relatedness,* or the need to unify with another person through submission, power, or love; *transcendence,* or the need to rise above a passive existence and create or destroy life; *rootedness,* or the need to establish roots; a *sense of identity,* or a feeling of "I;" and a *frame of orientation,* or the need to develop a consistent way of looking at the world.

During our history as a species, we have gained a degree of economic and political freedom, but this achievement has brought about ever greater feelings of isolation and separation from the world. This burden of freedom has produced *basic anxiety,* or a sense of being alone in the world. To relieve basic anxiety we employ various *mechanisms of escape,* especially *authoritarianism, destructiveness,* and *conformity.* These strategies are the driving forces in normal people, not a sign of pathology. Authoritarianism is the tendency to establish a dominant/submissive symbiotic relationship; destructiveness attempts to eliminate other people or objects; and

conformity is the need to give up one's identity and become what others desire.

Some people, Fromm believed, succeed in becoming one with the world. These people acquire *positive freedom,* or the spontaneous activity of a whole, integrated personality.

In his early writings Fromm identified four nonproductive and one productive *character orientations.* The *nonproductive types* have both positive and negative traits. These orientations include *receiving,* or relating to the world by taking in knowledge, love, or material possessions; *exploiting,* or taking things away from others either by cunning or force; *hoarding,* or holding on to possessions, feelings, and ideas; and *marketing,* or seeing one's self as a commodity to be bought and sold. The *productive orientation* has three dimensions: loving, working, and thinking. Healthy people are characterized by all three and also by *biophilia,* or a passionate love of life and all that is living.

The opposite of biophilia is *necrophilia,* or the love of death, destruction, decay. Necrophilia is one of three traits making up the *syndrome of decay,* the other two being *malignant narcissism,* or infatuation with self, and *incestuous symbiosis,* or the tendency to remain bound to the mothering person or her equivalents.

The goal of Fromm's humanistic *psychotherapy* is to establish union with patients so that they can become reunited with the world. Psychotherapy was the chief source of Fromm's data, but he also employed *cultural anthropology* and *psychohistory* as research methods.

In his concept of humanity Fromm takes a middle road position on free will vs.

determinism, optimism vs. pessimism, conscious vs. unconscious forces, and uniqueness vs. similarities. His theory is rated high on teleology and very high on social influences.

As a scientific theory, unfortunately, the theory cannot be rated high. It has above average ability to organize knowledge, but has generated very little empirical research. It is also rated low on being a practical guide to action, on internal consistency, and on parsimony.

Suggested Readings

FROMM, E. (1947). *Man for himself: An inquiry into the psychology of ethics.* New York: Holt, Rinehart and Winston.

In this book Fromm discusses the various character orientations and suggests that the productive type is the highest achievement of humanity. He also insists that psychology cannot be separated from philosophical and ethical issues.

FROMM, E. (1956). *The art of loving.* New York: Harper & Brothers.

This is perhaps Fromm's most popular book, though many readers may have been attracted to it believing that it concerned sexual techniques. Fromm's discussion of the various aspects of love remain fresh today.

FROMM, E. (1981). Values, psychology, and human existence. In E. Fromm. *On disobedience and other essays* (pp. 1–15). New York: Seabury Press.

This short chapter is an excellent introduction to Fromm's most recent thinking. Emphasis is on the five human needs—relatedness, transcendence, rootedness, sense of identity, and a frame of orientation.

FROMM, E. (1986). *For the love of life* (H. J. Schultz, Ed.; R. Kimber & R. Kimber Trans.). New York: Free Press. (Original works published 1972, 1974, 1975, 1983).

Originally delivered in German as radio talks, these eight essays reflect the wide range of Fromm's interests—from a discussion of affluence and ennui in modern society, to a dialogue with the editor on the character of Hitler, to a final question on the nature of humanity.

Part Three
BEHAVIORAL AND COGNITIVE THEORIES

DOLLARD AND MILLER
9   Classical Learning Theory

SKINNER
10   A Behavioral Analysis

ROTTER
11   Social Learning Theory

BANDURA
12   Cognitive Learning Theory

DOLLARD AND MILLER

9

Classical Learning Theory

Amy, a 22-year-old college senior, has a serious problem. Jeff, a successful young business executive, has asked her to marry him after she graduates. She originally accepted his offer, but now she is having second thoughts. Although marriage to Jeff offers a seemingly secure financial future, Amy feels as if she doesn't love him.

Amy is scheduled to graduate with a degree in psychology but has no particular plans to pursue an advanced degree in that area. For as long as she can remember, she has more or less expected to get married after college, and marriage to an established young businessman would have been especially appealing. At the same time, however, she has strongly believed that love is the basis for a successful marriage. Now, she has a conflict. Marriage to Jeff has both negative and positive aspects. On the one hand, it offers financial security, but on the other, it promises a life with a person she doesn't love.

In trying to solve her problem, Amy has confided in and sought advice from several friends as well as her mother. Some of her friends have told her to forget about Jeff, arguing that love is essential for a happy marriage. Others have suggested that money can solve many problems in marriage and that, in time, she would learn to love Jeff. In addition, she has already given her word that she would marry him. Amy's mother has refused to give her opinion, encouraging Amy to make her own decision. To complicate matters, Amy is in love with Jason, a high school dropout who seems to love her, but who does not match her ideal of a suitable husband.

Amy is experiencing a conflict. A desirable goal (marriage to Jeff, a likable wealthy young man) is accompanied by an equally undesirable quality (she doesn't love him). How can Amy solve her conflict? How did she acquire the value that marriage should be based on love? Why is money and financial security important to her? What is behind her need to confide in her mother and friends and to ask for their advice?

OVERVIEW

The classical learning theory of John Dollard and Neal E. Miller provides possible answers to these questions. In general, the theory holds that Amy

302

learned the values that brought about her conflict and that learning principles can also help her solve the problem.

Dollard and Miller insisted that most of personality is learned and that all learning, from the very simple to the extremely complex, is acquired on the basis of four fundamental factors. First, people must have a *drive* or motivation; second, they must attend to some *cue* that determines how they are to act; third, they must make some kind of *response;* and fourth, that response must be *reinforced.*

Both Dollard and Miller were trained in psychoanalysis, and their theory can be seen as a bridge spanning the gap between Freud and modern learning theory. Using their backgrounds in Freudian psychology and the social sciences, they have been able to apply the fundamental principles of learning to the higher mental processes of human beings. Their effort to explain complex thinking, cultural acquisition, and unconscious learning is their most significant contribution to personality theory.

BIOGRAPHIES OF JOHN DOLLARD AND NEAL E. MILLER

John Dollard was born on August 29, 1900, in the small American community of Menasha, Wisconsin; he was the oldest son of a railroad engineer and a former schoolteacher. His family lived in Menasha until his father was killed in a train wreck at about the time John was approaching college age. His mother then moved the family to Madison so the children could more easily attend the University of Wisconsin (Miller, 1982).

After a short time in the U.S. Army, Dollard enrolled at the University of Wisconsin where he studied English and commerce. After he graduated with a bachelor of arts degree in 1922, he remained at the University as a fund-raiser for the Wisconsin Memorial Union. In that capacity he met and became friends with Max Mason, who became like a second father to Dollard. When Mason became president of the University of Chicago, Dollard went with him as

one of his assistants, a position he held from 1926 until 1929. In 1930 Dollard earned a master of arts degree in sociology from Chicago and the following year was awarded a Ph.D. in sociology. At Chicago he was influenced by the same social scientists who had helped shape the thinking of Harry Stack Sullivan, Karen Horney, and Erich Fromm.

During the year 1931–1932 Dollard went to Germany as a research fellow to study psychoanalysis. As part of his training he was analyzed by Hans Sachs, a close associate of Sigmund Freud and the same therapist who analyzed Fromm. On returning from Germany, he took a position as assistant professor of anthropology at Yale University, and the following year he moved to the newly created Institute of Human Relations at Yale as assistant professor of sociology. The institute was established as a multidisciplinary organization, and included a number of well-known scholars from the fields of psychology, psychiatry, anthropology, and sociology, including O. Hobart Mower, Robert Sears, and Clark Hull. It was at the institute that he formed a close working relationship with Neal Miller. A man of broad interests and abilities, Dollard held positions in three academic departments at Yale—anthropology, sociology, and psychology. In 1969 he became professor emeritus, a position in which he remained active until his death on October 8, 1980.

Dollard's versatility is evidenced by a review of his major titles. In 1935 he wrote *Criteria for the Life History,* a book which pulls together the case history methods of two disciplines—sociology and clinical psychology—and which establishes criteria for examining both biological and cultural factors in a person's life. Next came *Caste and Class in a Southern Town* (1937), a now classic field study of the black person's social role in the South during the 1930s. This book, which was an outgrowth of Dollard's master's thesis, created such a stir that it was banned in Georgia and South Africa. A companion volume, *Children of Bondage* (1940), was coauthored with Allison Davis, a social anthropologist. During World War II Dollard served as consultant to the Secretary of War and, partially as a result of this experience, he published two books, *Victory over Fear* (1942) and *Fear in Battle* (1943), which deal with the causes and cures of battle neuroses. His interest in the practice of psychotherapy, the training of therapists, and the desirability of brief psychotherapy led to *Steps in*

Psychotherapy (1953), a book coauthored with Frank Auld and Alice White, which contained verbatim accounts of therapy sessions from audio recordings. He also collaborated with Auld in writing *Scoring Human Motives* (1959), which continued efforts to objectively analyze psychotherapy interviews.

Dollard's early collaboration with Neal E. Miller produced three volumes, which comprise the core of the Dollard and Miller theory of personality. The first was a joint project by several members of the Yale group, *Frustration and Aggression* (1939). In 1941 Miller and Dollard published *Social Learning and Imitation* and, in 1950, their most important work, *Personality and Psychotherapy,* appeared. (In this latter book, Dollard was the senior author, but in the 1941 publication, Miller's name appears first. Therefore, the theory has variously been referred to as the Miller and Dollard theory or the Dollard and Miller theory. Either, of course, is acceptable.)

Neal E. Miller, also a Wisconsin native, was born in Milwaukee on August 3, 1909. He received a B.S. from the University of Washington in 1931, and a M.S. from Stanford the following year. He then went to Yale to continue his education. While working toward his doctoral degree, he held the position of assistant in psychology at the Institute of Human Relations. After completing his Ph.D. in 1935 he journeyed to Austria to study psychoanalysis at the Vienna Institute of Psychoanalysis, thus paralleling Dollard's training four years earlier. As part of his psychoanalytic training he underwent analysis with Hans Hartmann, a pupil of Freud.

In 1936 Miller returned to Yale to accept a position as instructor at the Institute of Human Relations, where he worked to integrate the disciplines of economics, sociology, anthropology, psychiatry, psychology, and law. With the outbreak of World War II, he served in the U.S. Army Air Force as an officer in charge of research. From 1944 until 1946 he served as director of a psychological research project for the Air Force. After the war he returned to Yale. Then in 1966 he became professor of psychology and head of the Laboratory of Physiological Psychology at Rockefeller University, where he conducted research in a variety of areas, especially biofeedback and brain functioning. An outgrowth of this research has led to an involvement in the newly emerging fields of behavioral medicine, behavioral

health, and health psychology (Miller, 1983, 1984a, 1984b). In 1986 Miller moved back to Yale, where he continues his work in health related areas.

Miller is recognized as a meticulous and productive experimentalist as well as an innovative theorist. His work in experimental psychology led to his selection as President of the American Psychological Association, a position he held during the year 1960–1961. Other honors include serving as James Rowland Angell Professor at Yale from 1952 until 1966; being selected for membership in the National Academy of Science; receiving the Warren medal from the Society of Experimental Psychologists in 1957 and being elected president of Division 38 (Health Psychology) of the American Psychological Association. In addition, Miller is one of the few behavioral scientists to receive the President's Medal of Science.

FUNDAMENTALS OF LEARNING

Dollard and Miller believed that, for the most part, human behavior is learned. We learn to be who we are and what we are. We learn our fears, our feelings of guilt, anxiety, shame, and loneliness; we learn to set goals, develop aspirations, and to strive toward our goals and aspirations; we learn to adjust to our social environment, to adopt normal and abnormal patterns of adjustment, and to erect a multitude of neurotic symptoms.

No matter how different two learning situations may appear on the surface, the same four fundamental factors apply. From the simplest to the most complex, all learning is based on **drive, cue, response,** and **reinforcement.**

Dollard and Miller (1950) use a simple experiment to illustrate the four principles of learning. The experiment involves a six-year-old girl learning to find candy hidden under a particular book in a bookcase. The girl is sent out of the room while a small piece of her favorite candy is placed under the middle book on the bottom shelf of the bookcase. The girl is then called back into the room and informed that a piece of candy is hidden under one of the books in the bookcase; she is instructed that she must replace each book after removing it to look for the candy. During the first phase of the experiment, the little girl engages in so-called random behavior. She looks under books on the top shelf—some of them more than once. She searches under magazines in the bookcase and under a book on a nearby table. Finally, after 210 seconds and 36 incorrect books, she finds the candy, and as her reward, she is allowed to eat it. She is then sent out of the room a second time while another piece of candy is hidden under the same book. Upon reentering the room, the little girl is given the same instructions, but this time she goes directly to the lower shelf and after 13 books and only 86 seconds she finds the candy. The experiment is repeated for a total of 10 trials, by which time the girl is making no errors and has reduced her time to two seconds.

With this simple experiment in mind, let us turn to a discussion of each of the four fundamentals of learning.

A drive is any stimulus strong enough to impel action. In the experiment above, the little girl's drive was hunger. (The experimenters' drive would be a little more complicated, but a noble fraction of it must have been curiosity.) Specifically, the girl had to be hungry for that particular kind of candy, and her hunger drive must have remained strong enough to motivate her throughout the experiment. If the experiment had continued beyond the tenth trial to a point where the girl had become satiated with candy, she would no longer have been impelled to act. This assumes, of course, that hunger was the sole drive. In reality, she was probably motivated by several drives, including, perhaps, the desire to please the experimenters or, more likely, the excitement of playing a game and having fun. One might assume also that this latter motivation would have weakened if the experiment had continued much longer.

Cues tell one when, where, and how to respond. In the present example, the little girl responded on the basis of auditory cues she received from the experimenters as well as visual ones of the room, bookcase, and individual books. In order to follow the experimenters' directions and correctly solve the task of finding candy, she must be able to understand language, that is, to distinguish one word from the other and to bring meaning to them. She must also distinguish the bookcase from the coffee table, to differentiate one shelf from another, as well as make fine distinctions among similar appearing books. *Cues, then, are stimuli that are distinctive enough to guide responses.*

A response is the behavior that occurs as a reaction to drives and cues. Before they can be reinforced, responses must first occur. The little girl had to eventually lift the correct book in order to receive her reward. This response had to be within her repertoire of responses—an obvious fact, but one which should never be overlooked. The little girl's reinforcement was eating the candy she had found, or perhaps it was merely finding the candy and thus correctly solving the puzzle. This reward, or more technically, reinforcement, tends to increase the probability that the girl will make the same response on a future trial. *Reinforcement is any event that strengthens the connection between a cue and a response, thereby increasing the tendency for a response to be repeated.*

Before continuing with a more detailed explanation of the fundamental factors of learning, let us look at a quotation from Dollard and Miller summarizing the relationship among the four factors.

> The drive impels responses, which are usually also determined by cues from other stimuli not strong enough to act as drives but more specifically distinctive than the drive. If the first response is not rewarded by an event reducing the drive, this response tends to drop out and others to appear. The extinction of successive nonrewarded responses produces so-called random behavior. If some one response is followed by reward, the connection between the cue and this response is strengthened, so that this response is more likely to occur. *This strengthening of the cue-response connection is the essence of learning* (Dollard & Miller, 1950, pp. 29–30; italics added).

Drive

The term drive can be used interchangeably with motivation. All drives are stimuli, but not every stimulus is a drive. As pointed out earlier, Dollard and Miller believed that any stimulus can become a drive if it is strong enough to impel action. According to Dollard and Miller there are two major classes of drives—*innate drives* and *learned drives.*

Innate Drives

Innate, or primary, drives are those not weakened by lack of reinforcement. They include pain, hunger, sex, thirst, fatigue, cold, and oxygen deprivation. That they are not weakened by nonreinforcement is illustrated by the example of a hungry man driven to seek food. If he is reinforced by food he will learn what steps to take in the future to reduce his drive. On the other hand, if his hunger drive goes unreinforced—that is, if he does not get anything to eat—he remains hungry and continues to be motivated by the hunger drive. In fact, the less the reinforcement, the more powerful the drive; ordinarily, the longer the man goes without eating, the stronger his drive becomes. Innate drives are not dependent upon learning. Eating in a certain restaurant involves both a learned drive and an innate drive. A diner finds the food in a particular establishment especially reinforcing and so learns to frequent that eating place. Hunger itself, however, exists in the absence of any prior learning and is not dependent on reinforcement for its continued strength.

Society prevents primary drives from becoming excessively strong by providing opportunities for people to breathe, drink, eat, and regulate body temperature. As for the sex drive, its unrestrained expression is not permitted by most societies; however, all societies allow their members to satisfy this drive under certain conditions, for instance in marriage or through such disguised forms as sublimations and inhibitions.

Because innate drives are usually gratified within the trappings of society, and because they are often disguised, their importance in most learning situations is generally underestimated. Only under unusual conditions, such as war or natural disaster, does it become evident to what extremes people will go in order to satisfy a primary drive. In a smoothly functioning society, however, innate drives are normally satisfied with little cognizance of their primary nature. They are hidden behind the veneer of secondary or learned drives. In American culture, as an example, food is ordinarily eaten within a social context, in the presence of friends or family. Not only is the food reinforcing but so, too, is the pleasant conversation, soft music, sparkling plates and dishes, candlelight, and proper etiquette, which often accompany satisfaction of the hunger drive. These social drives are learned, of course, but they may be dominant enough to obliterate the basic hunger drive, which is relegated to an accessory position. Dollard and Miller (1950) said that the importance of innate drives is often overlooked because society permits their convenient satisfaction and because they are frequently hidden behind a screen of learned drives.

Learned Drives

Learned, or secondary, drives are those which are governed by the principles of learning and extinction and which can be strengthened through reinforcement. Secondary drives are not easily distinguishable from primary drives. For example, fear can be either a primary or a secondary drive depending on whether or not it is learned. In general, however, learned drives are those which, at one time in a person's life, were neutral, but which take on drive value during the course of learning. Money, for example, has neither positive nor negative value to an infant, but acquires drive properties as a child learns to attach value to it. Functionally, learned drives have the same value as innate drives; that is, they impel action.

Secondary drives are learned on the basis of innate drives and often so completely hide the primary drive that we do not recognize the connection between the learned and the innate drive. For example, let us look at Amy, our case study. Her motivation for love in marriage and her drive to acquire money have both been learned, but behind each is an innate drive. Love (a learned drive) may disguise the primary drive of sex, while striving for money (another learned drive) may mask such innate drives as hunger, safety, and avoidance of extreme temperatures.

Learned drives differ from primary drives in two important ways. First, learned drives are much more varied. The reason for this is obvious. Innate drives, such as hunger and sex, are the same in all cultures, while learned drives differ from culture to culture. In fact, learned drives account for the differences among cultures as well as the differences among individuals within a culture. One person may be driven to achieve various sexual conquests, another to hoard money, a third to acquire social acceptance, and so on. The personality of each individual is characterized by the specific learned drive that motivates much of that person's behavior.

A second distinction is that innate drives cannot be extinguished; learned drives can. This difference might well be the criterion for identifying innate drives. If a motivation cannot be extinguished, it is a primary drive. Hunger, of course, is not dependent on reinforcement for its drive value and cannot be extinguished through nonreinforcement or counterconditioning. All secondary drives, because they have been learned, can be unlearned, that is, extinguished. Some learned drives, however, are extremely resistant to extinction. These are the ones Allport (Chapter 14) would term functionally autonomous. (In Allport's concept of functional autonomy, the original drive may be replaced by a new motive so that behavior becomes self-sustaining.) Dollard and Miller (1950), however, did not allow for functionally autonomous motivation and insisted that any learned drive is subject to the laws of extinction.

Cue

Cues, like drives, are stimuli, but they differ from drives in that they are not strong enough to impel action, but instead are distinctive enough to determine when, where, and how responses will be made. The same stimulus could serve as either a drive or a cue depending on its intensity and its distinctiveness. The five o'clock whistle is a cue for the employees to stop work. They can differentiate its sound from all others and are thus told by it what response they should make. However, for employees working next to the whistle, the intensity of the sound serves as a drive, impelling them to action. Their immediate response might be to move away from the whistle or to hold their hands over their ears. Only after they have made such a response does the cue value of the sound have meaning. Then they, too, pack up their belongings and go home.

Internal stimuli like hunger and pain may also have cue as well as drive value. A very hungry person is driven to eat—almost anything will do. A moderately or slightly hungry person will differentiate among internal stimuli and recognize a specific hunger, for example, salty foods rather than sweets. The person is guided by olfactory and visual cues to select popcorn rather than candy.

Single cues quite often provide inadequate information. A single letter or even a word may mean very little, but sentences and paragraphs form *patterns* of cues and carry much more meaning. Most human learning is complex and results from a pattern of cues. We develop a preference for a song, not by hearing a single note, but by listening to the entire melody. Even the whole song may take on a different character depending on the context in which it is heard. A Christmas carol, which may elicit a positive response in December, may, in July, be met with disdain.

Some cues are so weak that they are perceived on an extremely low level of differentiation. Most of us have had the experience of walking into a familiar room and somehow feeling that something is missing or out of place. We do not quite know what it is, yet we perceive that something is wrong. Likewise, a baseball scout may observe two players and judge one to be a better prospect than the other even though his batting average is not as high. When asked his criteria for such a judgment, the scout is lost for words and simply responds that "something inside tells me this player is better than that one." Dollard and Miller (1950) believed that much of human personality is learned on the basis of weak cues or cues that have never been verbalized. These experiences form a portion of their definition of the unconscious.

Response

"Drive impels the individual to respond to certain cues. Before any response to a specific cue can be rewarded and learned, this response must occur" (Dollard & Miller, 1950, p. 35). This seems rather obvious, but it must not be overlooked in any analysis of learning or in any attempt to teach a person a specific behavior. Learning cannot occur unless the response to be learned is within the repertoire of the learner. No matter how hard one tries, one cannot teach a neonate to recite Lincoln's Gettysburg Address!

Learning from one's mistakes is a time-honored cliché, but without much validity in learning theory. One never learns correctly by making an incorrect response. The only thing learned by trial and error is that a particular trial was an error. One must still find and make the right response. Much time is saved if the learner makes the correct response first. In learning to ride a bicycle, one must respond to the cue of leaning to the left by shifting one's weight to the right. Jumping from the bike, slamming on the brakes, or leaning more to the left will never result in learning the correct response.

Responses need not be overt actions. Those which involve the higher mental processes, such as thinking, are not overt, yet they are learned and subject to the same principles of learning as are more readily observable behaviors. These higher mental processes, especially language, are a major distinction between animal and human learning. Moreover, language greatly facilitates the learning of additional behavior. Teaching a person to drive an automobile is made easier simply by telling the learner what to do (Dollard & Miller, 1950).

Hierarchies of Responses

Dollard and Miller pointed out that the more often a response occurs, the more frequently it can be reinforced and, therefore, the more likely it is to occur in future situations. This cyclic effect results in an increasing probability that a given response will occur in a particular learning pattern. Other responses have less likelihood of appearing, depending on the strength of the drive and the frequency of reinforcement of these responses in past similar situations. The probability of any response occurring can be placed on a **hierarchy of responses.** Dollard and Miller (1950) recognized two hierarchies in any learning situation—the initial hierarchy, and the resultant hierarchy.

The *initial hierarchy* of responses may be due either to previous learning or to hereditary factors and is the one present at the beginning of a learning experiment. If it is the result of heredity it is called an innate hierarchy, but, in any case, the order of responses in the initial hierarchy can be changed through learning. Initially an infant secures physical contact by crying. Later this response may drop from the dominant position to be replaced by stretching forth one's arms or by verbalizing, "Hold me."

After learning has shifted response positions, the new hierarchy is called the *resultant hierarchy*. Resultant hierarchies indicate the establishment of a habit that will persist for as long as the dominant response maintains its position at the top of the hierarchy. A person who has previously been rewarded by self-contradictory behaviors makes a habit of befuddling others through confusing statements and bewildering actions. Self-contradiction is the dominant response in the resultant hierarchy. As long as it is reinforced by self or others it will retain its position.

Anticipatory Responses

Responses with a tendency to occur earlier than they did in the original learning situation are called **anticipatory responses** (Dollard & Miller, 1950). Anticipatory responses have both positive and negative effects. On the one hand, they make learning more efficient; on the other, they may lead to more errors. In typing, for example, when the word "the" is to be written, skilled typists begin reaching for the letter "e" even before the "h" is struck. This enables them to type whole words at one time and to greatly improve speed. However, anticipating can also lead to an incorrect response, as when the word "any" is to be typed, but the more common "and" is written instead. The anticipatory tendency is involuntary and does not depend on the learner's insight. Typists need not understand the mechanics of how they are able to type whole words at one time, they simply do it. On the other hand, knowing that they are likely to write "any" for "and" gives them no particular advantage in correcting this persistent error.

Responses in a sequence can each in turn become anticipatory. A young child playing in the mud for the first time may anticipate punishment upon seeing its mother with a belt in her hand. The next time the child plays in the mud, punishment may be anticipated when the mother comes into view. With additional reinforcement, a spanking is anticipated merely by thinking of the mother while enjoying a mud bath. In this same fashion all of us eventually learn important shortcuts that save time and make learning more efficient.

Reinforcement

In order to be learned a response must be reinforced. Dollard and Miller (1950, p. 39) defined reinforcement as "any specified event . . . that strengthens the tendency for a response to be repeated."

This brief definition needs further elucidation. First, it may appear to be circular. If reinforcement is merely that which increases the tendency for a response to recur, then learning could simply be defined as the acquisition of new responses through reinforcement. This reasoning would tell us little about the nature of reinforcement. Dollard and Miller escaped this dilemma by pointing out that what serves as a reinforcement in one cue-response situation may also act as a reinforcement in others. In other words, if little Jimmy is praised whenever he produces while seated on the potty chair, a cue-response connection is strengthened. Therefore, he learned a response as the result of some type of reinforcement. But how do we know that praise and not something else is the specific reinforcement? The answer, of course, is that praise can be identified as the reinforcing agent if it can also be used to train Jimmy to clean his room, to dress himself, or to learn any other desired response.

A second point needs to be made regarding the nature of reinforcement. From the above definition it may seem that the strengthening of the cue-response connection will continue to increase *ad infinitum* as long as the reinforcement is present. This is only partially true. Many learning situations have a built-in mechanism that prevents a single response from continuing indefinitely. A hungry person is reinforced by eating, but this response is reinforced only as long as the drive remains strong. Food, however, weakens the drive so that after one has become satiated there is no longer a stimulus strong enough to impel eating. As the hunger drive weakens, it is replaced by stronger drives that impel other responses like, perhaps, sleeping or exercising. Reinforcement continues to strengthen the cue-response connection only for as long as the drive remains strong (Dollard & Miller, 1950).

Third, Dollard and Miller say that reinforcement is often automatic; that is, it is independent of any thought or insight. For example, infants severely punished for defecating in their pants may learn to be neat and orderly without having to think about how to avoid future punishment. They need not say to themselves, "I must not be messy or I'll be punished." This belief in automatic and unconscious reinforcement is an important difference between the social learning theories of Dollard and Miller and of Albert Bandura (see Chapter 12). Bandura believes that learning does not take place without cognitive mediation, which means that the person is actively involved in evaluating the desirability of various reinforcements. On the other hand, Dollard and Miller (1950), while recognizing the role of higher mental processes in selecting and evaluating many reinforcement events, insisted that an adequate theory of learning must make room for automatic, unconscious reinforcements.

Finally, the concept of *secondary* reinforcement must be considered. Like secondary drives, secondary reinforcements are learned. Whenever a previously ineffective reward causes learning to take place, we can say that that particular reward is learned. Money is a good example of a secondary reinforcer. An infant attaches no value to a dollar bill, and paper money cannot be used to motivate it. Later in life a person learns the value of money. Indeed, one may continue to work for it even though all primary drives are satisfied. The money per se becomes a reinforcement and may be hoarded with no intention to spend it for food or shelter.

Most secondary reinforcers, including money, are learned in association with primary drives. Money is originally sought in order to secure food. Compliments are reinforcing because they may have initially been associated with a reduction of the hunger or thirst drive. A parent gives a child a cookie or a drink of milk while offering praise for being good. Later, praise alone serves as a reinforcement. Most adult learning is the result of secondary reinforcements, but a major portion of these learned reinforcers can be traced back to primary drives.

Gradient of Reinforcement

Dollard and Miller (1950) further speculated that with most learning there is a sequence of responses leading to the final reinforced one. A hungry person may have to plan a meal, go to the grocery store, purchase food, bring it home, prepare it, cook it, and finally eat it. Is only the eating response rewarded? No, for if the preceding behaviors were not reinforced they would not occur. But if they, too, are rewarding, why should the person continue to the final response of eating? In other words, if shopping for groceries is reinforcing (and we know that it is or else it would not occur), why is it not the final response in the sequence? The answer is that eating is more strongly reinforced than cooking, cooking more than preparing food, and so on back to the beginning of the sequence. This progressive strengthening of responses in sequence is called the **gradient of reinforcement** and results in the final response securing a stronger reinforcement than earlier ones.

The gradient of reinforcement explains why people increase the tendency to approach a goal the closer they are to it. Long-distance runners put forth a greater and greater burst of effort the nearer they come to the finish line. Automobile drivers traveling a thousand miles to visit friends find themselves going faster and faster as they approach their destination. The gradient of reinforcement can also be illustrated by Amy, our case study. As she nears graduation, she has found that her interest in school has increased and her grades have improved. During her freshman and sophomore years she was far from her goal of graduation and her school work floundered as she spent much time socializing and going to parties, but now as she approaches her goal (graduation) she finds herself working harder at her studies.

The gradient of reinforcement also explains why, other things being equal, immediate reinforcements are more effective than delayed ones. Children punished by their parents immediately after scribbling on the wall will learn more effectively than those punished five hours later. Students who receive immediate feedback on term papers have their scholarly responses strengthened more than those who must wait three months to receive reinforcement.

Drives and Reinforcement

We have seen that the same object can be either a drive or a reinforcement. Money can be a secondary drive or it can be a secondary reinforcement. However, the same event cannot be both a drive and a reward *at the same time,* but it may produce two effects that fluctuate in rapid succession so that they become closely associated. Cooking food, for instance, can be a drive provided it is associated with, or sometimes leads to, the reduction of the hunger drive. Cooking can also be a reward so that in the aggregate experience of preparing and eating food the drive and reward become closely interwoven. Cooking is a reward because cooks know they will eventually eat their preparation. If they did not subsequently eat their own food (for example, a chef in a restaurant), the act of cooking would not be a reward, but instead would be motivated by a drive to acquire a later reward (money), which will enable them to purchase food and other reinforcers.

Summary

Reinforcement strengthens the tendency for a response to be repeated. Nonreinforced responses tend to drop out and are not repeated in subsequent learning trials. The fact that nonrewarded responses tend to disappear gives other responses a chance to be reinforced. Eventually, some response will be followed by reinforcement and will then tend to occur earlier in subsequent learning trials. If it continues to be strengthened through reinforcement, this response will become a habit. Only reinforcement can strengthen or maintain a habit. Repetition does nothing by itself.

Reduction of a drive serves as a reinforcement so that after a drive has been satiated it loses its power to impel action. Other drives then replace it. This leads to variety in human behavior and explains why reinforcement of a specific response does not lead to a perpetual repetition of that response.

HIGHER MENTAL PROCESSES

To this point we have been discussing basic learning theory. The concepts of drive, cue, response, and reinforcement can be applied to animal as well as human learning. In fact, much of the experimentation employed to develop these concepts was based on animal studies. Results of these studies generalize easily to simple human learning. But what about more complex human learning—those higher mental processes which help differentiate humans from other animals? Dollard and Miller (1950) hypothesized that the same four factors that apply to simple learning are equally applicable to higher mental processes like thinking and abstract problem solving.

In psychoanalytical terms, higher mental processes are ego functions. They are used to solve problems of an emotional or social nature, as well as simple physical problems. They include complex functions like abstract reasoning, intention and planning, language acquisition, and foresight. They are also responsible for such superego functions as shame, guilt, identification, and the formation of the concept of an ideal self.

In learning-theory terms, higher mental processes differ from automatic habits or responses in that they involve no immediate overt response to cues. "The final overt response follows a series of internal responses, commonly called a train of thought" (Dollard & Miller, 1950, p. 98). For example, a man walking on frozen ground slips and falls. He responds automatically by thrusting his hands forward in order to protect his head and body from striking the ground first. This is a simple response to the immediate cue of falling and is done without thinking and involves no higher mental processes. Another person walking on frozen ground thinks, "I must be careful. I have seen others fall so I, too, might slip. Therefore, I must take shorter steps." A final response of slowing the pace follows a series of internal responses and results from the use of higher mental processes.

We have seen that responses are impelled by drives and elicited by cues. So how can there be a *series* of internal responses? How can one response follow another without an intervening drive or cue? The answer is that one internal response does not follow directly from another response. Instead, Dollard and Miller said, some responses generate cues which, in turn, elicit other responses. These **cue-producing responses** should be distinguished from instrumental responses. The latter simply produce an immediate change in the learning environment. Removing an obstacle in one's path, taking a drink of water, and scratching an itch are examples of instrumental responses. Cue-producing responses form the basis of higher mental processes such as thinking, reminiscing, fantasizing, and improvising. As the term implies, they are responses that produce cues which, in turn, become part of a stimulus pattern leading to a later response.

Cue-producing responses may be either overt or covert. An example of an overt cue-producing response would be making a list of errands one must run. The response of writing the list evokes a cue that shapes a later response. Covert cue-producing responses function the same way but the responses and cues take place internally and are not perceptible to others. A hostess planning a party employs many covert cue-producing responses. Her silent thoughts produce cues that mediate further thoughts. She thinks, "I plan to invite Mr. Jones, but if I do I should invite Mr. Brown, his best friend. That reminds me, Mrs. Brown doesn't get along with Mrs. Smith, whom I'd hoped would bring her card table and chairs." In this sequence, one internal response produces a cue that elicits another internal response which, in turn, produces still another cue and so on.

There are two different ways in which cue-producing responses can be used. First, they can serve as cues to other people as when one person gives a command to another. Next, they can serve as cues to the person producing them. This second form, which usually but not always involves internal behavior, is more central to higher mental processes than the first (Dollard & Miller, 1950).

Foresight

When words and thoughts serve as stimuli for learning they are called **mediated drives.** Higher mental processes, especially verbal responses, enable us to respond to words and thoughts about the future. People do not live solely in the here and now. Having learned the concept of future, our responses are often mediated by cue patterns consisting of words or thoughts about coming events. An employee works diligently for a whole month in order to obtain a reward at the end of that period. This seems to be contrary to the gradient of reinforcement principle, which hypothesized that immediate reinforcements are more effective than delayed ones. However, foresight and mediated drives generate immediate reinforcement by keeping the worker continuously mindful of a paycheck at the end of the month.

Foresight makes it possible for us to be motivated over a long period of time. Without it, we would not invest money in land, plan a trip, seek revenge, and so on. Foresight is largely, but not completely, dependent on language. Verbal ability aids us in thinking about the future. We provide ourselves with nearly continuous reinforcement through thoughts about receiving compliments, reassurances, threats, or disapprovals (Dollard & Miller, 1950).

Reasoning

A second higher mental process, also facilitated by language, is reasoning. Reasoning shortens the time of learning by substituting cue-producing responses for instrumental ones (Dollard & Miller, 1950). The importance of reasoning is shown in the old cliché "Think before you act." Without reasoning, people would be doomed to carry out overt trial and error responses in each new learning situation. The hunger drive would impel us to scratch continually for food. Without reasoning we would never have planted crops or domesticated animals. Each response designed to make life easier would be trial and error, and no complex inventions could be possible.

Reasoning enables us to skip many of the instrumental responses required in problem solving and to replace them with verbal responses. Reasoning, however, is not limited to verbal trial and error behavior. If it were, it would be more efficient than performing overt trial and error responses, but it would still necessitate a long laborious sequence of symbolic behavior beginning with the problem and leading to the solution. Since reasoning utilizes cue-producing responses, many trial and error steps are omitted and certain previously reinforced responses move *forward* in the sequence. A second course of reasoning begins with the goal and proceeds *backward* until the correct response is found. Most of us have solved problems in this manner. We see the solution to the problem and ask ourselves, "Now how can this goal be reached?"

Social Training

One of humanity's great advantages over other animals is its capacity to use higher mental processes to preserve culture. Great trial and error or insightful discoveries of the past are handed down from one generation to the next, obviating their continual rediscovery. Without social training each generation would be forced to begin culture anew.

Probably our most beneficial cultural heritage is language. Through imitation we quickly learn the language of our parents and our society. This useful tool is our most highly developed form of cue-producing responses. We use it to think and to give ourselves private verbal cues that greatly facilitate learning. Language, a cultural inheritance, is itself the primary vehicle of cultural inheritance, is itself the primary vehicle of cultural transmission. It is used to train children to become adult members of a society. Verbal suggestions and advice from parents and other experienced persons, as well as verbal rewards and punishments, help children learn the ways of their society.

A part of social training is learning independence and conformity. Independence is learned whenever the child's internal drives are stronger than the external verbal cues received from parents. If the child is hungry enough, admonitions not to eat the cookies for the bridge party will go unheeded. Similarly, curiosity may win out over the advice to stay away from the abandoned house down the street. Conformity is learned whenever a child is reinforced for socially desirable responses. Again language offers a prime example. A child learns to speak because to be verbally understood is rewarding; not to be understood offers few rewards. The child conforms to society by using the same word for an object that others use.

Not all conforming behavior entails higher mental processes. One form, imitation, may be based on either instrumental acts or on cue-producing responses.

IMITATION

Dollard and Miller originally saw imitation as learned behavior, but Miller (see Evans, 1976) has since stated that people have strong *innate* dispositions to imitate. These innate tendencies, however, can be greatly modified through learning.

Same Behavior

Dollard and Miller identified three levels or types of imitative behavior. The first is **same behavior,** which may be learned either with or without imitation. Each person learns independently to respond in the same way to a given cue. For example, when the five o'clock whistle blows each worker puts away his or her tools, cleans up, walks to the parking lot, gets into a car, and drives away. Each worker's behavior is independent of the other employees, even though some may have learned the routine originally through imitating another worker (Miller & Dollard, 1941).

Copying Behavior

The second type of imitation is **copying,** in which people attempt to minimize perceived differences between their behavior and that of another. The principal difference between same behavior and copying lies in the intention of the imitator. In the first case there is no intention, active or automatic, to

One type of imitation is copying. This picture shows students being reinforced for minimizing the differences between their behavior and that of others.

adopt behavior similar to that of another. In copying, the imitator feels uncomfortable (nonreinforced) whenever perceiving a discrepancy between one's own and another's behavior. Copying is illustrated by the worker who imitates the quitting time routine of coworkers because not doing so would cause anxiety. The worker may observe that the other employees begin putting away their tools and cleaning up at 4:30. By five o'clock they are lined up at the gate, and when the whistle blows they dash to the parking lot, jump into their cars, and speed away. Not learning to copy these responses means the worker would become a social outcast and feel lonely and somewhat stupid working a half-hour after everyone else has stopped (Miller & Dollard, 1941).

Matched-Dependent Behavior

The third level of imitation is **matched-dependent** behavior. As with copying, imitators in matched-dependent behavior use another's responses as cues for their own behavior, but, unlike copying, they do not respond to the differences between their behavior and that of the other person. In copying, imitators observe their own and another's behavior, note the differences between the two, and attempt to close the gap by copying the other person's responses. In matched-dependent imitation one person uses another's behavior as a cue and then follows that person; it is not necessary to respond to differences or similarities between one's behavior and that of the leader. Copying usually involves social equals, while matched-dependent behavior ordinarily involves unequals. In the latter, one imitates another who is seen as older, wiser, more experienced, or more skillful.

Matched-dependent behavior is observed in most families where there are two girls or two boys about two or three years apart. The younger sibling is likely to follow in the footsteps of the older, imitating his or her manner of talking, walking, sitting, and so on. Much social training is learned through matched-dependent imitation. Children follow the lead of parents, teachers, and older siblings. Adults, too, learn a great deal through matched-dependent behavior. An apprentice carpenter imitates the master, a beginning teacher uses an older instructor as a model, a young woman tries to be the same kind of wife and mother as her mother (Miller & Dollard, 1941).

The divisions among the three types of imitation are not clear and absolute; one shades into another. The important point is that imitation, though it may have an innate basis, is learned in accordance with the same four fundamental factors (drive, cue, response, and reinforcement) that apply to other learning situations.

FEAR AND ANXIETY

Two other responses that lend themselves to the four fundamentals of learning are fear and anxiety, both strong motivational forces in the behavior of people. In the classical learning theory of Dollard and Miller, fear and anxiety can serve as drives, cues, and responses. Furthermore, their reduction is a reinforcement. Fear is usually thought of as apprehension of a known or specific danger, either external or internal, real or imagined, while anxiety is seen as a fear whose source is vague and often concealed by repression. The connection between fear and anxiety is so close that they may be discussed as a single concept.

Fear as a Drive

Fear and anxiety are drives because they can motivate new responses. Fear can motivate us to drive safely or to build a bomb shelter. Anxiety motivates us to study more or to bite our fingernails. People vary considerably in their responses to fear depending on previous learning. Typical responses to fear (uncomplicated by the presence of other drives) include immobility, flight, and strong physiological changes such as rapid heart beat, dryness of the mouth and throat, frequent urination, muscular tension, and increased perspiration (Dollard & Miller, 1950).

Fear is a learnable drive. However, its neurological basis is innate, which explains why fear of shock or pain seems to be inherent in humans. Most fears, however, are learned and are subject to the same principle of learning as other responses. Fears are learned whenever previously neutral stimuli assume fearful qualities and thus impel new responses. People differ in their capacity to learn fear responses, but many fears are acquired very easily. For example, most people quickly learn to be afraid of falling trees or wild animals. Other fears, such as fear of the number 13 or fear of women with red hair, are learned much more individually. In either case, fears can become extremely strong drives, quite resistant to extinction. Some fears are carried for a lifetime simply because the person avoids any opportunity to extinguish them. In time the fear may actually become stronger and generalize to similar stimuli. A person with a phobia of the number 13 may eventually show fear of the numbers 12, 14, or 31. This fear impels that person to avoid any contact or reminder of these numbers (Dollard & Miller, 1950).

Fear as a Response

Fear and anxiety are internal responses, but they often cue external responses so that their effects are observable to others. Both fear and anxiety produce a variety of external behaviors, but fear is often followed by flight, while anxiety is followed by defensive mechanisms.

We have seen that fear responses are quite resistant to extinction, but when fear shades into anxiety extinction is even more difficult, especially when repression is involved. If a person has repressed the original traumatic experience that produced the anxiety, it may be almost impossible to extinguish the response. Once extinguished, fears are quite likely to be **spontaneously recovered,** that is, to suddenly reappear without additional reinforcement. Extinction merely inhibits the fear response; it does not completely eliminate it (Dollard & Miller, 1950).

Fear as a Cue

Fear also has cue value since it is a stimulus and can become distinctive from other stimuli. People learn to respond to certain internal cues by labeling them "fear." This labeling facilitates the learning of fear and spreads it to a variety of other internal cues and responses which, without labeling, the person could never learn to fear. Thus, the ability to use language accounts for many human fears.

Not all cues are easily distinguishable and fear can sometimes be confused with anger and other internal cues, while anxiety often arouses internal cues that are confused with hunger. For example, an anxious person feels a definite emptiness inside and attempts to alleviate it by eating. Since the internal cues are changed by a full stomach, the person is reinforced by eating and therefore continues in future similar situations to eat when anxious. This can have a disastrous cyclic effect on overweight people whose anxiety may, in part, be due to their obesity. Eating leads to a gain in weight, which increases anxiety, which results in more eating. Anger, too, is sometimes confused with fear due to mislabeling of internal responses. This explains why frightened people sometimes strike out against the fear-provoking object rather than fleeing from it (Dollard & Miller, 1950).

Fear as a Reinforcement

Fear itself is not a reward, but its reduction or promised reduction can serve as a reinforcement. This concept is included in Miller's (1951, p. 463)

Drive-Reduction: The Usefulness of a Disproven Hypothesis

In Chapter 1 we said that a useful theory is one that generates testable hypotheses and subsequent research. The hypotheses need not be proven true. Useful research can be generated by hypotheses that are eventually disproven. Early in their collaboration Dollard and Miller proposed their well-known drive-reduction hypothesis, which implied that a reduction in the drive stimulus is a necessary and sufficient condition for reinforcement.

Almost immediately a storm of controversy arose, leading to thoughtful criticism and a substantial amount of research. Gordon Allport (Chapter 14) believed the hypothesis to be restrictive. He pointed out that people are not always motivated to reduce a drive—sometimes they strive to maintain or even increase tension. Studies of the drive-reduction hypothesis tended to support Allport in demonstrating that sometimes *increases* in drive are reinforcing. For example, Olds and Milner (1954) presented evidence that showed that reinforcement can be produced by an increase in stimulation and, therefore, is not exclusively the result of stimulus reduction. They implanted electrodes in the brains of 15 male rats and, using no other reinforcement, conditioned the rats to press a lever in order to receive the electrical stimulation.

Sheffield (1966a, 1966b) has suggested an alternative to the drive-reduction hypothesis, which he called *drive-induction* theory of reinforcement. He presented evidence from studies of rats that tends to support his notion that animals, at least, will learn responses that initiate or arouse motivation and that a reduction in drive is not an essential of reinforcement. In one study, for example, male rats learned a response that led to copulation without subsequent reduction of the sex drive through ejaculation. Learned reward was ruled out since the rats had no experience with ejaculation either prior to or during the experiment.

It is through studies of this kind that theoretical formulations prove their usefulness. Even when research fails to demonstrate the validity of a particular hypothesis, science is served because inadequate formulations can be eliminated in favor of more fruitful ones. When competing evidence is found, a synthesis can sometimes be accomplished or modifications can be made in the original theory.

The controversy has led Miller (1959) to modify the dogmatic stance of the original drive-reduction hypothesis and to suggest that a sudden reduction in drive is a *sufficient* condition for reinforcement, but it is not a *necessary* one. In other words, a reduction in drive is rewarding, but other conditions such as drive arousal or stimulation may also be reinforcing.

famous *drive-reduction hypothesis* which states in part that "stimulus situations . . . acquire reward value if responses that reduce stimulation are reinforced." (See Box—"Drive-Reduction: The Usefulness of a Disproven Hypothesis"). Attending a terrifying movie offers a reward because the person understands that the fright will not last forever. A fearful roller-coaster ride is reinforcing as long as the rider eventually experiences a reduction in fear.

Of course, most stimulus situations producing fear are not voluntary: frightening movies and rickety roller coaster rides are exceptions. A frightened person does not ordinarily choose to be frightened. In fact, people are strongly motivated to escape from fearful stimuli or to reduce fear in some way. In an original fearful state people usually attempt trial and error responses to accomplish this reduction. Any trial followed immediately by fear reduction will tend to be learned since it produces reinforcement. Probably the easiest learned response to fear is flight. A child who is afraid of a large dog runs away. A person frightened by a tornado flees to safety. The act of running is not in itself rewarding, but it instigates drive reduction, which serves as the reinforcing agent (Dollard & Miller, 1950).

We have seen that fear can be a stimulus or a response. As a stimulus it can have either drive or cue value depending on its strength and distinctiveness. As a response, fear itself is unobservable, but the typical reactions to it, both internal and external, can be both observed and recorded. Since strong fear is an unpleasant sensation, its sudden reduction becomes a reinforcement. Fear and anxiety are typically the principal ingredients in conflict situations.

CONFLICT

The anatomy of conflict, based on a social learning theory model, has been investigated in the laboratory by Miller (1944) and applied to psychotherapy by Dollard and Miller (1950). Conflict exists whenever two equally valued but incompatible responses are desired or required. The two responses are not only incompatible, but they cannot follow one another in sequence. If both responses could be produced, no conflict would exist. People in conflict typically react with tension, anxiety, vacillation, or blocking. They are often unable to make any response, but once an appropriate response is made, the degree of conflict is progressively lessened.

Basic Assumptions

Before proceeding to a discussion of the different kinds of conflict, it is necessary to understand four fundamental principles about approach (positive) and avoidance (negative) gradients.

1. "The tendency to approach a goal is stronger the nearer the subject is to it" (Dollard & Miller, 1950, p. 352). This is called the **gradient of approach** and is a specific form of the gradient of reinforcement discussed above.
2. "The tendency to avoid a feared stimulus is stronger the nearer the subject is to it" (Dollard & Miller, 1950, p. 352). This is the **gradient of avoidance** and explains why people show more and more apprehension the closer they get to a fearful stimulus.
3. "The strength of avoidance increases more rapidly with nearness than does that of approach" (Dollard & Miller, 1950, p. 352). This explains why, when a goal has both positive and negative value, a person's tendency to avoid becomes stronger than the tendency to approach as one

nears the goal. When the tendency to approach a stimulus is stronger at a distance than the tendency to avoid, a person will move toward the goal, then stop at the point where the avoidance gradient crosses the approach gradient (see Figure 9.1).

4. "The strength of the tendencies to approach or avoid varies with the strength of the drive upon which they are based" (Dollard & Miller, 1950, p. 353). In other words, the stronger the drive, the greater the tendency to approach a positively valued goal and to avoid a negatively valued one. Strong drives, therefore, increase the height of the gradient at any distance from the goal. Figure 9.2 shows that when the drive is strong enough, the gradient to approach may be higher than the gradient to avoid under weak drive. A very hungry person will eat mildly distasteful food.

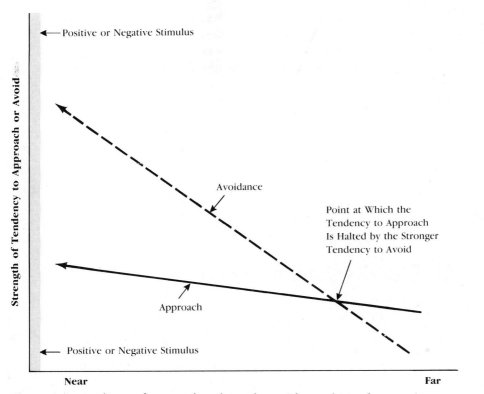

Figure 9.1 Gradients of Approach and Avoidance. The gradient of approach increases as one nears a positive stimulus, but as one nears a negative stimulus, the gradient of avoidance increases at an even faster rate. (From Miller, N. E., Experimental studies of conflict. In J. McV. Hunt (Ed.), *Personality and the behavior disorders.* New York: Ronald Press, 1944, p. 434; adapted in Dollard, J., & Miller, N. E., *Personality and psychotherapy.* New York: McGraw-Hill, 1950, p. 356. Copyright 1944 by The Ronald Press Co. Adapted by permission.)

The tendency to approach a goal becomes stronger as one gets closer to the goal. Long-distance runners put forth more effort as they approach the finish line.

Types of Conflict

Dollard and Miller did not originate the concept of approach-avoidance and avoidance-avoidance conflicts. They did, however, conceptualize conflicts within social learning theory, and Miller (1959) conducted extensive research that both supported and enlarged existing theory.

When people are midway between two equally desirable goals, it is sometimes said that they experience an approach-approach conflict. Dollard and Miller (1950), however, do not consider this situation to be a conflict. The donkey halfway between two haystacks will *not* starve to death. First of all, it is not likely that a person would ever be exactly midway between two goals and second, even minor changes in the perceived value of one or the other goals would pull the person slightly toward one goal or the other. Since the approach gradient increases the nearer the person comes to the stimulus, even minor shifts are sufficient to make one goal more desirable than the other. No vacillation, tension, or blocking will occur in these situations.

Approach-Avoidance

In our case study we saw that Amy was having second thoughts about her decision to marry Jeff. She is attracted to Jeff because of his money and his pleasant disposition. However, she also has a strong belief that one should

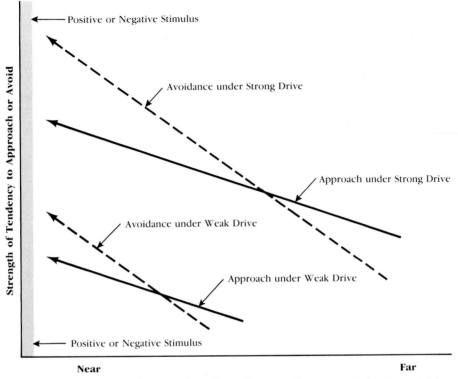

Figure 9.2 Gradients of Approach and Avoidance under Strong Drive. Strong drive increases the height of both the approach and avoidance gradient. Approach under strong drive may be greater than avoidance under weak drive. (From Miller, N. E., Experimental studies of conflict. In J. McV. Hunt (Ed.), *Personality and the behavior disorders.* New York: Ronald Press, 1944, p. 440; adapted in Dollard, J., & Miller, N. E., *Personality and psychotherapy.* New York: McGraw-Hill, 1950, p. 358. Copyright 1944 by The Ronald Press Co. Adapted by permission.)

marry for love, and she does not love Jeff. Amy is experiencing an **approach-avoidance conflict,** which Dollard and Miller (1950, p. 355) define as any "situation in which a person has strong tendencies to approach and avoid the same goal."

Approach-avoidance conflicts exist because the avoidance gradient is steeper than the approach gradient. When Amy first accepted Jeff's proposal, there was no serious conflict. The positive aspects of the marriage out-weighed the negative ones. As she approached the wedding date, however, the thought of a loveless marriage became stronger until the negative aspects of marriage to Jeff equaled the desirable ones. At that point, Amy's conflict became intense and her ability to make a decision became impaired.

In an approach-avoidance conflict a person approaches a negative goal or event until the approach gradient is crossed by the steeper avoidance gradient. At that intersection the tendencies to approach and to avoid are equal

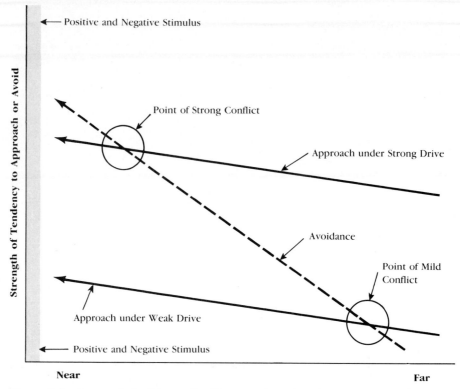

Figure 9.3 Approach-Avoidance Conflict. As a feared goal is approached, the avoidance becomes stronger and the person retreats to a point where the two gradients cross, that is, where the approach tendency is equal to the avoidance tendency. Increasing the motivation to approach without reducing the fear merely intensifies the conflict. (From Miller, N. E., Experimental studies of conflict. In J. McV. Hunt (Ed.), *Personality and the behavior disorders.* New York: Ronald Press, 1944, p. 440; adapted in Dollard, J., & Miller, N. E., *Personality and psychotherapy.* New York: McGraw-Hill, 1950, p. 361. Copyright 1944 by The Ronald Press Co. Adapted by permission.)

and conflict results. The person remains approximately at this point, not able to move nearer the goal because the tendency to avoid is now stronger than the tendency to approach. If the person is far from the goal and the drive to approach is weak when it meets the avoidance gradient, only mild conflict is experienced. However, as the drive becomes stronger it intersects the avoidance gradient at a point nearer the feared goal. The person then experiences intense conflict because the drive to approach and the tendency to avoid are quite strong. Figure 9.3 shows that increasing the motivation of the person without reducing the avoidance gradient (fear and anxiety) may result in more severe conflict and still leave the person short of the goal. This happened to Amy when she heard suggestions from some of her friends that she might eventually learn to love Jeff. Increasing the strength of the drive to marry (that is, the approach gradient) has simply delayed and intensified Amy's conflict.

Everyone experiences approach-avoidance conflicts, but the lives of troubled and neurotic persons seem to be defined by them. These people are perpetually stuck in neutral gear. They would like to accomplish their goals, but that would require that they surmount "impossible" obstacles. Their fear of the goal is always equal to the tendency to approach it. They remain constantly at the point of conflict, neither able to diminish fear, which in many cases is self-erected, nor able to reduce the drive by accepting the idea that the goal cannot be reached. Either a reduction in fear or a reduction in the drive would lessen the conflict. Inability to make a decision becomes a way of life for troubled persons. One complains, "I would like to divorce my husband, but it's too scary." Another worries, "I'd like to quit my job, but my wife would be furious with me."

Approach-avoidance conflicts can be overcome in two ways. First, the motivation can be made stronger than the fear to avoid the goal. Since the avoidance gradient is steeper than the approach gradient, this can be accomplished only if the fear is relatively weak or the original drive is quite strong. Then the approach gradient reaches the goal before being intersected by the avoidance gradient. The person eventually reaches the goal, but only at the expense of experiencing ever-increasing anxiety.

A second and usually more successful method of overcoming approach-avoidance conflicts is to reduce the negative value of the goal. Most therapists give priority to this attack, attempting first, by one technique or another, to lessen the patient's anxiety and to alleviate unreasonable fears. The progressive relaxation of Edmond Jacobson (1938) and the meditative relaxation of Herbert Benson (1975) have both been used extensively by psychotherapists.

Avoidance-Avoidance

A person caught between the devil and the deep blue sea is experiencing an **avoidance-avoidance** conflict. This type of conflict is illustrated in Figure 9.4, where two negative stimuli are opposed to each other. They are placed in contradiction so that as one attempts to escape from the first he or she draws nearer the other. The conflict results either in vacillation near the point of conflict or in escape by some third route. This alternate route is seen where a person resorts to a psychological breakdown in order to escape the conflict resulting from, say, a domineering spouse on the one hand and fear of divorce on the other. Most avoidance-avoidance conflicts, especially those of a physical nature, are resolved by resorting to an alternate route.

When no third pathway can be found, the person must remain near the point of conflict until circumstances change the strength of one of the negative goals, thereby changing the angle of intersection. This will either alter the point of conflict or eliminate it completely. Take, for example, the would-be watermelon thief who is caught between an angry farmer and a threatening dog. The thief may smile and speak in a friendly manner, thereby reducing the farmer's anger and lowering that negative stimulus, or it may come

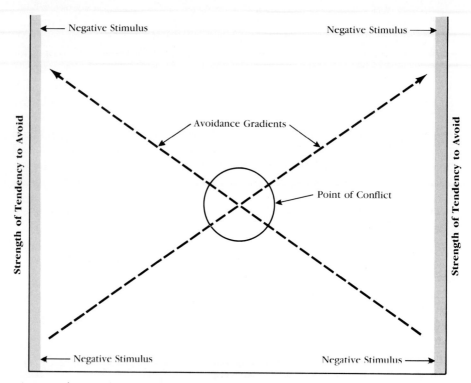

Figure 9.4 Avoidance-Avoidance Conflict. As one retreats from one negative stimulus, one comes nearer to another negatively valued goal. If this tendency to avoid the two negative stimuli is equal, the person reaches a point of conflict midway between the two. If one goal is more dreaded than the other, the point of conflict is pushed nearer the less feared one. When the strength of the drive increases one gradient but not the other, the conflict point is placed closer to the lower gradient. (From Miller, N. E., Experimental studies of conflict. In J. McV. Hunt (Ed.), *Personality and the behavior disorders.* New York: Ronald Press, 1944, p. 442; adapted in Dollard, J., & Miller, N. E., *Personality and psychotherapy.* New York: McGraw-Hill, 1950, p. 364. Copyright 1944 by The Ronald Press Co. Adapted by permission.)

to the thief's attention that the dog is chained to a post, thus restricting its range of movement and allowing for escape in that direction (Dollard & Miller, 1950).

Double Approach-Avoidance

A third type of conflict is that of **double approach-avoidance.** Most situations involving human responses are so complex that simple avoidance-avoidance conflicts are rare. In the majority of instances each of the two goals has both a positive and negative valence. When a person has difficulty escaping a single avoidance-avoidance conflict, it is possible that both goals also possess some positive value.

In a single approach-avoidance conflict, if the approach gradient is higher

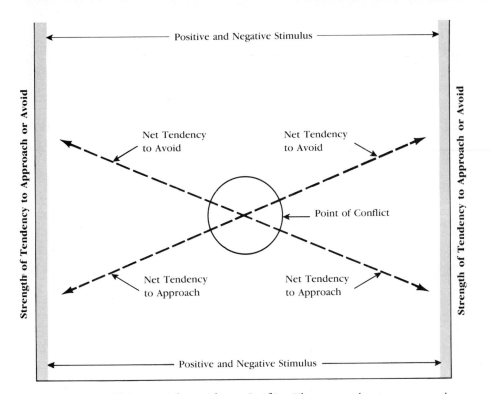

Figure 9.5 Double Approach-Avoidance Conflict. The net tendency to approach an ambivalent goal decreases as the subject nears the goal. In the double approach-avoidance conflict the subject is trapped within the point of conflict midway between two equally valued ambivalent goals. (From Miller, N. E., Experimental studies of conflict. In J. McV. Hunt (Ed.), *Personality and the behavior disorders.* New York: Ronald Press, 1944, p. 447; adapted in Dollard, J., & Miller, N. E., *Personality and psychotherapy.* New York: McGraw-Hill, 1950, p. 367. Copyright 1944 by The Ronald Press Co. Adapted by permission.)

at the goal than the avoidance gradient, a person will achieve the goal, but at the expense of experiencing greater and greater amounts of anxiety. The reason for this progressive anxiety is simple. The avoidance gradient is subtracted from the approach gradient to determine the net tendency to approach. Since the avoidance gradient is steeper than the gradient of approach, the net tendency to approach becomes weaker and weaker the nearer the subject is to the goal.

In a double approach-avoidance conflict a person is caught between two goals each carrying both a positive and a negative value. Each goal is desired and feared at the same time. Since the net tendency to approach an ambivalent stimulus decreases as the subject nears the goal, distant goals are seen as more desirable than close ones. With double approach-avoidance conflict (see Figure 9.5), the point of conflict between two equally valued ambivalent goals is midway between the goals, but, because the net tendency to approach becomes progressively weaker as one nears the goal, there is single approach-avoidance conflict all along each gradient. The double conflict arises whenever the subject nears the intersection of the two gradients. The approach-avoidance conflict felt in nearing one ambivalent goal is now equaled by the approach-avoidance conflict experienced in pursuing a contradictory ambivalent goal. Prior to reaching the point of conflict, a person was progressing toward a feared goal despite ever-increasing anxiety. Eventually that ambivalent goal would be reached, but when a second ambivalent goal is opposed to the first, progression stops and the person is left vacillating near the point of conflict (Dollard and Miller, 1950).

Amy, our case study, is actually experiencing a double approach-avoidance conflict because she knows that Jason, the man she loves, would willingly marry her. However, Jason dropped out of high school, has been heavily involved with cocaine, and is completely unacceptable to Amy's parents. Her dilemma is now more difficult to resolve than the simple approach-avoidance conflict. She can't marry both Jeff and Jason, although there is some attraction to both. Marrying either one also carries a negative value—on the one hand a loveless marriage, on the other a life of insecurity.

Amy used both *foresight* and *reasoning* to solve her double approach-avoidance conflict. Seeing possible misery in marriage to either Jeff or Jason, she decided to escape by marrying neither. Instead she applied to more than a dozen graduate schools and received acceptance from one. She used this as an excuse to break her promise to Jeff. She knew that Jeff's business would prevent him from following her out of state where she would be attending school. She also realized that Jason would be unwilling to spend several years away from his friends while she worked toward a Ph.D. Although her decision was not easy, she saw it as the only way to escape her dilemma.

REPRESSION AND THE UNCONSCIOUS

Those drives, cues, and responses which have never been verbalized or which are inadequately labeled become unconscious. These include most experiences prior to the development of fluent language. Unlabeled experiences, however, are not limited to early childhood. Adults, too, repress thoughts, especially those associated with strong unpleasant drives like pain, fear, anxiety, and guilt. In agreement with Freud, Dollard and Miller (1950) believed that sexual and aggressive responses, in particular, are likely to be unlabeled or mislabeled.

Before proceeding with our discussion of repression and the unconscious, it is well to differentiate among the following terms: repression, suppression, overt inhibition, and overt restraint.

Repression refers to *thoughts not* under verbal control, that is, those for which a person has no adequate label. Since it is automatic and preverbal, repression cannot be stopped or reversed by conscious effort. Trying to remember repressed experiences is an exercise in futility (Dollard & Miller, 1950).

Suppression involves *thoughts* that *are* under verbal control. One can suppress an idea or image by intentionally stopping thinking about it. "That's a horrible idea. I should get it out of my mind." Other people may also be involved, as when someone says, "Let's stop this gruesome topic of conversation and talk about something more pleasant." The consequences of suppression are similar to those of repression, but, because it is not automatic, it operates much more selectively and usually can be stopped or reversed by conscious effort (Dollard & Miller, 1950).

Overt inhibition refers to *actions not* under verbal control. A response is inhibited when a contradictory response prevents its occurrence. Sexual pleasure, for example, can be inhibited by intense anxiety or guilt. It is not possible to be extremely anxious and enjoy relaxed sexual pleasure at the same time. Overt inhibition is related to repression in that neither involves verbalization (Dollard & Miller, 1950).

Overt restraint involves *actions* that *are* under verbal control. A response can be restrained when a conflicting response under verbal control is opposed to it, thereby preventing its occurrence. Overt restraint occurs when one tells oneself, or is told by another, to stop making a particular response. As a golfer, for example, you may make a conscious effort to slow down your swing. Eventually you substitute a slow smooth swing for a hurried, jerky one. Since overt restraint and suppression are both under verbal control, they offer more hope for unlearning maladaptive behavior than do overt inhibition and repression (Dollard & Miller, 1950).

After Amy moved to another state to attend school, she became more involved in her work and with making new friends. Because she cannot easily see either Jeff or Jason, she has used overt restraint to solve her conflict.

Figure 9.6 outlines Dollard and Miller's concepts of repression and the unconscious.

Repression occurs because it is rewarding to stop thinking about a certain experience. Stopping thinking is a response just as is stopping talking. Like any response, it is impelled by a drive, elicited by cues, and learned through reinforcement. Stopping thinking about painful and fearful experiences is reinforcing because it reduces unpleasant stimuli. For example, if a child is punished for playing with his genitals or for hitting his baby sister, he soon learns to dissociate these experiences and many of their attendant feelings from himself. Since sexual and aggressive thoughts are unrewarded, he eventually gives them up and represses his infantile sexual feelings as well as his hostility for his little sister.

For repression to occur it is not necessary that punishment follow the

	Thoughts	Actions
Not Under Verbal Control	**Repression**	**Overt Inhibition**
Under Verbal Control	**Suppression**	**Overt Restraint**

Figure 9.6   Dollard and Miller's Concept of Repression and the Unconscious

socially disapproved behavior immediately. Even when punishment is delayed, the parents usually inform children of the reason they are being punished. Their words elicit the same cues that were present during the performance of the forbidden act and henceforth the same cues produce a repression.

Since repressions involve stopping thinking, they often prevent our seeing connections between cues. This may lead to denial or feelings of inhibition of response. Children, for example, may learn that anger is acceptable under certain circumstances and that it is all right to break a dish, if done so accidentally. But if they deliberately break a dish *because* they are angry, they are likely to be punished. They then refuse to see the connection between anger and destructive behavior. Thereafter, when they are angry they inhibit their aggression to the point that they deny any desire to be destructive. Conversely, when they act aggressively and destructively it may be with a smile and a denial of anger.

Repression prevents people from labeling thoughts and feelings and makes it impossible for them to think rationally about their problems. This leads to what Dollard and Miller call "stupid" behavior, that is, behavior not mediated by verbal and other cue-producing responses that form the basis of the higher mental processes, Stupid behavior is difficult to unlearn because there is no language available to adequately label cues and responses. People may be highly intelligent in some ways, but in the areas of repression they remain stupid (Dollard & Miller, 1950).

ABNORMAL DEVELOPMENT

According to Dollard and Miller (1950), stupidity is one of three chief ingredients in abnormal behavior. The other two are misery and symptoms. Abnormality is learned as the result of conflict, repression, and reinforce-

---

Does Frustration Always Result in Aggression? Is Aggression Always Caused by Frustration?

In 1939 a five-man team from the Yale Institute of Human Relations—John Dollard, Leonard Doob, Neal Miller, O. Hobart Mowrer, and Robert Sears—published a work called *Frustration and Aggression* in which they proposed the controversial idea that frustration always leads to some sort of aggression and, conversely, that aggression inevitably stems from frustration. This *frustration-aggression hypothesis,* as the proposition

came to be known, is not a critical element in Dollard and Miller's subsequent theory of personality. It is, however, a bold, clearly stated, and easily testable hypothesis and, like the later drive-reduction formulation, it engendered both controversy and research.

The negative reaction to this hypothesis was immediate. A. H. Maslow (1941) and Karl Menninger (1942), among others, criticized the notion, claiming that common sense alone tells us that frustration does not always lead to aggression. Subsequently, the Yale group amended the original statement to read, "Frustration produces instigations to a number of different types of response, one of which is an instigation to aggression" (Miller, 1941, p. 338). In other words, frustration can lead to a variety of responses, including aggression. The group, however, did not retract the second half of the hypothesis, namely that aggression is always a consequence of frustration. This truncated frustration-aggression hypothesis continued to generate debate and study.

One of the most persistent critics of the frustration-aggression hypothesis has been Arnold H. Buss. Finding exceptions to both parts of the original hypothesis, Buss (1961) presented evidence that indicated that aggression has antecedents other than frustration; for example, "both attack and annoyers clearly lead to aggression" (Buss, 1961, p. 28). This, of course, does not disconfirm the amended hypothesis proposed by Miller in 1941. However, Buss also believed that the second part of the hypothesis could not be supported. He reported that "aggression does not necessarily have identifiable antecedents," and he was further convinced that "the frustration-aggression hypothesis should be discarded" (Buss, 1961, p. 28).

Another author who has written extensively on the frustration-aggression hypothesis is Leonard Berkowitz. In 1958 he suggested that both attack and insult can lead to aggression, but moderated his criticism by stating that attack and insult were forms of frustration (Berkowitz, 1958). Four years later he again pointed out that aggression can be caused by factors other than frustration, but he still insisted that the Dollard et al. hypothesis was "the best theoretical framework for the analysis of social aggression" (Berkowitz, 1962, p. xi). By 1969 he was saying that frustration increases the probability of aggressive action, but denied that frustration always leads to aggression or that aggression is an inevitable consequence of frustration (Berkowitz, 1969). In what amounts to an epilogue of his history of the frustration-aggression hypothesis, Berkowitz (1978) restated the position that aggression is caused by conditions other than frustration and reviewed several studies which dispelled the idea that all aggression is instigated by frustration. He pointed out that a Mafia "hitman" may act aggressively toward his target for monetary motives and not out of frustration. Also, a businessman may behave aggressively toward a competitor without any feelings of frustration. Finally, Berkowitz suggested that pain, not frustration, is the primary source of aggression.

The frustration-aggression hypothesis can now be laid to rest, but during its 40-year history it served the worthwhile purpose of generating an abundance of research, having the total effect of yielding much useful information about the causes of aggression and the consequences of frustration. In a conversation with Richard Evans (1976), Miller admitted that there are other outcomes of frustration as well as other causes of aggression. What, then, are the answers to the two basic questions? Does frustration always result in aggression? No, but it usually does, particularly if no other outlet is found for it. Is aggression always caused by frustration? Again, the answer is no, but it ordinarily arises either from frustration or from some other unpleasant stimulus.

ment. Conflict produces misery; repression leads to stupidity; and reinforcement is essential for the acquisition of those abnormal symptoms which are learned.

Not all abnormal symptoms, however, are learned. Some are direct physiological effects of strong conflicted drives such as fear, anxiety, guilt, anger, and so on. Abnormal symptoms acquired in this fashion take such forms as muscular tension, agitation, or stomach acidity. They are generally accompanied by other, more numerous, symptoms that are learned.

How are abnormal behaviors learned when society does not idealize abnormality? Most are learned in childhood and are taught unintentionally by parents and other socializing agents. Children can learn abnormal behaviors despite parents' attempts to reinforce healthy responses and to withhold reward for unhealthy ones. This is possible for at least three reasons. First, parents are not always present to reinforce behavior, which allows for self-reinforcement and maladaptive responses. Second, the parents' delayed rewards for proper behavior may not be as strong as the immediate reward a child receives for an improper response. The third, and probably most important, reason is that many rewards are unconscious and more than balance the punitive effect of an experience. For example, for some children a spanking may be more rewarding than it is punishing, but neither parent nor child is aware of this fact.

Strong drives, especially fear, are instrumental in learning abnormality. Fear can have a threefold effect on a person's behavior. First, it can lead to *flight* or *escape,* which results in drive reduction. Since fleeing is rewarding, the person learns to run away from fear-provoking stimuli. This can be a productive response and is in no way associated with the acquisition of a neurosis. However, it may also be maladaptive, especially when one learns that society sometimes demands that one stand and face one's fears, thereby generating conflict between fear and social pressure.

The second pathway fear can take in affecting a person's behavior is through *conflict.* We have already seen that fear is a major component in conflict and that conflict prevents a person from reaching a desired goal. Since conflict does not reduce the drive, the person is left in a more or less permanent state of high drive, which leads to a feeling of tension and irritability called *misery.* A person suffering from misery has a variety of symptoms including sleeplessness, apathy, phobias and irrational fears, restlessness, and a general lack of zest for living. Misery results from overt inhibition, that is, from conflict that prevents the occurrence of responses which would ordinarily reduce the drive (Dollard & Miller, 1950).

Whenever conflict leads to the inhibition of thoughts, *repression* has taken place. This is the third effect fear can have on behavior. When fear results in repression no verbal cues are available for the learning of new responses. Without labels the person is not able to properly discriminate among the various cues appropriate to a specific learning situation. Repression erases the person's ability to think about differences between responses that are followed by punishment and those that are not. Some people are unable to distinguish between intentional and unintentional injury inflicted upon another; they feel guilty when they accidentally harm someone and no amount of logical reasoning can change their feelings. In this one area, at least, their thought processes are characterized by *stupidity*. Like miserable persons, stupid ones behave in a self-defeating manner. Being unable to think intelligently about their maladaptive behaviors, they are not capable of conscious actions that would either reduce their drive or solve their conflict. At the same time, their stupidity contributes to their misery and to the ever-lengthening list of neurotic symptoms. Since they are unable to resolve their conflicts, they may blame themselves and behave in ways that reflect a self-deprecating attitude. Then again, they may blame others and develop tendencies toward rationalization, projection, hallucination, delusion, or displacement. When conflicts are both strong and unconscious, the person does not profit from experiences and continues making the same mistakes. This compulsive behavior can itself be reinforcing, since it leads to a reduction of anxiety (Dollard & Miller, 1950).

In summary, the pattern of abnormality consists of a vicious circle of strong drive, usually fear, which is not reduced but instead results in conflict, misery, repression, and stupidity. The person is then unable to discriminate—that is, to properly label drives and cues—and the lack of ability to learn in the area of the neurosis leads to a perpetuation of neurotic symptoms. The symptoms themselves are usually compromises and often represent attempts to escape from an avoidance-avoidance conflict.

PSYCHOTHERAPY

If neuroses and maladaptive responses are learned, then they may be unlearned. In essence, this is the thrust of Dollard and Miller's psychotherapy. They hypothesized that neurotics have learned to be ill and are unable to use higher mental processes to solve personal problems, and that therapy is a matter of learning new ways to make better adjustments.

Though Dollard and Miller (1950) used many Freudian techniques, for example, transference, dream interpretation, and free association, they explained the therapeutic process in terms of learning theory.

The therapist must be a healthy person, possess prestige in the eyes of the patient, and be willing to listen empathetically and noncritically. By showing faith in an ultimate cure and by being permissive, the therapist encourages the client to express feelings verbally. The therapist is tolerant and noncondemning of the client's sexual and aggressive feelings, which might normally produce fear, anxiety, and guilt when expressed to a less accepting person. The calm, healthy therapist serves as a model to be imitated, thereby reducing the patient's anxiety.

In using free association, the therapist encourages the patients to say everything that comes to mind. This frees the clients from having to use logic or make sense, thus allowing them to express themselves without threat of cross-examination or nonacceptance. This experience is different from the reaction clients usually receive in social situations. The cathartic effect of free expression in the absence of negative reinforcement serves to weaken fear, anxiety, and guilt.

The client or patient is taught to use higher mental processes to solve problems. This is possible because repressions and overt inhibitions have been removed. The patient now uses foresight, reasoning, realistic hope, adaptive planning, and insight to solve personal problems. The patient, of course, and not the therapist, must gain the insight. Awareness of the problem and its unrealistic basis encourages the patient to employ new methods of problem solving (Dollard & Miller, 1950).

Dollard and Miller did not accept verbal changes as a goal of therapy. Patients must *do* something different. They must make new responses, which are now rewarded or, at least, no longer punished. For therapy to be effective the newly learned responses must not be punished by others, as might happen if patients were married to neurotic or punitive spouses. Instead, they must receive positive reinforcement either from others or from themselves (Dollard & Miller, 1950).

CONCEPT OF HUMANITY

Dollard and Miller viewed people as complex organisms capable of acquiring enormously intricate and subtle patterns of behavior through the process of learning. To them, people are neither innately good nor inherently evil, but endowed with the potential to learn (within the limitations set by society and by one's native abilities) to become healthy or neurotic. Because Dollard and Miller said that personality is determined mostly by learning within a social context, they are rated high on *determinism* and low on *free choice.*

Dollard and Miller's concept of humanity can be seen as both *pessimistic and optimistic.* We begin life with the possibility of learning maladaptive behavior during early socialization, especially during the feeding situation, cleanliness and sex training, and anger-anxiety conflicts. In addition, there are numerous other possible pitfalls in our path. Nonproductive behaviors can be learned in a wide variety of ways. Behavioral patterns adopted during early childhood may continue to be reinforced throughout a lifetime, resulting in a more or less permanent nonproductive life style. However, potentially troublesome learnings do not predetermine that we will develop in a negative direction. If conflicts are kept to a minimum and if parents are reasonably permissive, we can emerge from this period with healthy habits of coping with our environment. Even when maladaptive responses are learned, there always remains the possibility of relearning them. This process of relearning is facilitated by the acquisition of language and through the higher mental processes.

The concept of higher mental processes adds to the completeness of Dollard and Miller's personality theory and elevates it above those less integrative learning theories which concern themselves largely with lower order human habits. Dollard and Miller were able to apply their basic principles of learning to the most complex of human responses, namely, thinking. The ability to think makes us essentially different from other animals, but does not exempt us or our behavior from the same laws of learning that apply to all animals. Dollard and Miller were willing to generalize from animal studies in developing a theory of human personality, but they never lost sight of the fact that we have a far greater capacity to learn and that our unique social patterns set us apart from all other species.

Not only are humans different from other animals, but each person is unique, different from all others in intelligence and the ability to learn. Dollard and Miller were also cognizant of the role *society* plays in shaping individual personality. Given these hereditary and environmental factors, no two people will learn exactly the same thing, in precisely the same way, and at the same rate of speed. These differences greatly lessen the possibility that predictions about human behavior will be completely valid. However, there are enough *similarities among people* so that reasonably accurate prognostications can be made and generally valid hypotheses can be stated concerning human behavior.

The Dollard and Miller theory is basically, but not completely, a *causal* one. Behavior, they contended, is shaped by previous experiences with reinforcement, but higher mental processes such as foresight enable us to think about the future and to respond on the basis of these thoughts.

Contributing also to the richness of Dollard and Miller's concept of humanity was their recognition of the role *unconscious learnings* play in molding personality. Their Freudian training helped them to see people as being motivated by unconscious as well as by conscious forces. Much of what we learn is acquired prior to verbalization and is therefore beyond our ability to recall. Many of our later learned thoughts and actions are either repressed or overtly inhibited so that they become unconscious. They may continue to influence behavior and to shape future learnings, but they are not under verbal control and cannot be consciously manipulated.

CRITIQUE OF DOLLARD AND MILLER

How well does the classical learning theory of Dollard and Miller meet the criteria of a useful theory? First, does it *organize knowledge* in a meaningful way? The Dollard and Miller view of learning integrates behavioral principles with psychoanalysis and the social sciences and consequently is able to offer an explanation for a broad base of human personality. It was the first learning theory to emphasize the importance of verbal behavior (covert and overt) as both a cue and a response. The concept of cue-producing responses enables one to explain thinking in terms of reinforcement theory.

The theory has sometimes been criticized because its basic hypotheses have been suggested by animal studies and most have been tested by the use of animals rather than humans. Can animal studies tell us anything about humans other than those characteristics the two species hold in common? Dollard and Miller would say that, first, there are many characteristics that humans have in common with lower-order animals. Fear, hunger, sex, and aggression, for example, are experienced by rats as well as people. To study the physiological bases for these motivations in humans would present many practical and ethical problems. It is simply more feasible to use rats. Second, Dollard and Miller believed that most characteristics possessed by rats are also possessed by humans, but that humans have many characteristics that other animals do not. In extrapolating from animals to humans, therefore, they began with animal studies, but then proceeded to check these results against less well-controlled clinical and naturalistic studies of people and also against cross-cultural comparisons of human behavior.

Overall, Dollard and Miller's learning theory is unusually useful in its ability to organize knowledge and to explain how human behavior is acquired. All acquired behavior can be traced to the drive, cue, response, and reinforcement. However, this heavy emphasis on learning, with only a glancing nod toward biology, is also a limitation of the theory. Hereditary factors and individual constitutional differences are not adequately accounted for by Dollard and Miller.

A useful theory must also *generate research* and testable hypotheses. The theory of Dollard and Miller has been especially prolific in stimulating both research and lively discussion. The drive-reduction theory, though neither original to Dollard and Miller nor crucial to their final theory, is most often associated with Miller, and he and Dollard are usually cited in the numerous studies investigating this hypothesis. Similarly, the frustration-aggression hypothesis, originally suggested by Dollard, has been subjected to heated debate and study. Though results of studies of both hypotheses are not generally supportive of Miller and Dollard's positions, they do not markedly detract from the usefulness of the theory. Appropriately, Dollard and Miller have modified their theoretical formulations when change was warranted by the evidence. But they have also allowed some questionable hypotheses to remain until more research data was forthcoming, knowing that these hypotheses would stimulate additional research and lead to sounder theory. In this manner, the Dollard and Miller theory has been a useful one, allowing subsequent learning theorists to expand and amend the original formulations.

In evaluating a theory, these first two criteria carry the greatest weight, and the Dollard and Miller learning theory would receive high ratings on both standards. The theory offers an explanation for much of what is known concerning human behavior and it has stimulated a wealth of relevant research. The third criterion by which a useful theory is judged is its *practicality*. Does it serve as a useful guide to the practitioner? Does it tell the parent, teacher, or therapist what to do in order to shape or control behavior? Learning theory of various kinds is especially useful in guiding action. The practitioner can employ learning theory technqiues to help others both to acquire desirable behaviors or to extinguish nonproductive ones. Inappropriate behaviors can be viewed as being acquired in accordance with certain specific principles and capable of being eliminated by a learning process that is spelled out by Dollard and Miller's theory of personality.

Internal consistency is another secondary criterion of any theory. Like most learning theorists, Dollard and Miller are precise in defining their terms and are aware of the importance of internal consistency. When they were forced to make modifications in formulations, as with the drive-reduction hypothesis, for example, they were careful to spell out the new definitions.

Finally, a useful theory must be as *parsimonious* or straightforward as possible. Dollard and Miller attempted to formulate a scientific theory based on observations gleaned from experimentation. To their credit, they did not venture into the realm of story-telling and myth-making which pervade other theories, notably those of Jung and Freud. However, unlike Skinner (Chapter 10), they postulated the existence of hypothetical internal states such as drives, cues, conflicts, and cue-producing responses. Skinner argues that these hypothetical fictions are not only unnecessary to the scientific analysis of behavior but also interfere with an accurate understanding of human personality. The Dollard and Miller personality theory, therefore, receives a moderate rating on parsimony.

CHAPTER SUMMARY

The classical learning theory of John Dollard and Neal E. Miller provides a bridge between Freudian psychoanalysis and modern learning theory. Dollard's background in the social sciences, Miller's experience as an experimental psychologist, and the psychoanalytic training of both give their personality theory a unique flavor.

According to Dollard and Miller, personality is largely learned. Whether it is simple or complex, conscious or unconscious, all learning is based on four fundamentals—drive, cue, response, and reinforcement. A *drive* is any stimulus strong enough to instigate action; a *cue* is any stimulus distinctive enough to guide action; a *response* is the behavior that occurs as a result of drives and cues; and *reinforcement* is any event that strengthens the connection between a cue and a response.

Although much of their theory is based on animal studies and simple experiments with humans, Dollard and Miller hypothesized that these same four principles apply to *higher mental processes* such as foresight, reasoning, and language acquisition. The principal difference between higher mental processes and the learning of simple habits is that higher mental processes involve a series of internal or *cue-producing responses.*

Personality is partly formed by our *imitation* of other people. Dollard and Miller recognized three types of imitation. The first is *same behavior,* in which different people respond in the same way to a given cue. In the second, *copying,* a person attempts to duplicate the behavior of another, while in the third, *matched-dependent behavior,* the person initiates the behavior of another who is seen as socially or physically superior.

Much of human misery and many neurotic symptoms are the result of nearly insoluble *conflict.* The three most difficult conflicts are the *approach-avoidance,* in which the same stimulus is both desired and feared, *avoidance-avoidance,* in which the person is stuck half way between two equally undesirable stimuli, and the *double approach-avoidance,* in which the person is in between two stimuli, each of which carries both a positive and a negative value.

Abnormal development, including fears and anxiety, is learned as the result of conflict, repression, and reinforcement. Since neurotic symptoms are learned, they can also be unlearned through the process of *psychotherapy.*

Dollard and Miller see humans as complex animals whose personalities are largely determined by social forces outside the individual's personal control. People can use higher mental processes such as reasoning and foresight to solve problems, but, ultimately, even these solutions lie beyond individual choice.

Although few studies are currently being conducted on it, Dollard and Miller's classical learning theory has a history of generating much research, especially on the drive-reduction and frustration-aggression hypotheses. Moreover, the theory still retains its ability to give meaning and organization to observed data. Also, it continues to be a useful guide to the practitioner.

Suggested Readings

BERKOWITZ, L. (1962). The frustration-aggression hypothesis. In L. Berkowitz, *Aggression: A social psychological analysis* (pp. 26–50). New York: McGraw-Hill.
Berkowitz investigates Dollard and Miller's frustration-aggression hypotheses and finds that not all aggression results from frustration and that frustration does not lead inevitably to aggression.

DAVIS, A., & DOLLARD, J. (1940). *Children of bondage: The personality development of negro youth in the urban south.* Washington: American Council on Education.
A classical investigation of the personality development and the socialization of eight black youths in New Orleans and Natchez during the late 1930s. The book is more valid as a historical study than as a contemporary description of black adolescents in the South.

DOLLARD, J., & MILLER, N. E. (1950). *Personality and psychotherapy: An analysis in terms of learning, thinking, and culture.* New York: McGraw-Hill.
An indispensable resource for Dollard and Miller's classical learning theory. It extends their 1941 volume to include a description of neuroses, conflict, and psychotherapy.

MILLER, N. E. (1984). Learning: Some facts and needed research relevant to maintaining health. In J. D. Metarazzo, S. M. Weiss, J. A. Herd, N. E. Miller, & S. M. Weiss (Eds.). *Behavioral health: A handbook of health enhancement and disease prevention* (pp. 199–208). New York: Wiley.
Miller summarizes his later ideas on reinforcement and motivation. He also points out the wide range of effects that learning has on maintaining health. Thus, Miller combines his three historical interests— learning theory, biofeedback, and behavioral health.

MILLER, N. E., & DOLLARD, J. (1941). *Social learning and imitation.* New Haven, CT: Yale University Press.
In this scholarly and well-written book, Miller and Dollard introduce their four fundamentals of learning and apply them to higher mental processes and imitation. Also included are chapters on crowd behavior and lynching.

SKINNER

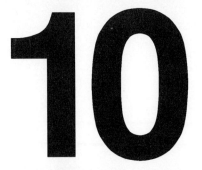

A Behavioral Analysis

Fred, an aspiring young writer, was away from home for the first time, attending a small liberal arts college. Although not really homesick, he missed his old friends and family. As a member of the college glee club, Fred was touring with that group during Easter vacation, and when the tour ended he went home to visit his parents and younger brother, Ed.

Fred and his brother were neither rivals nor close friends. They had little in common except mutual respect and affection. Fred was somewhat shy, scholarly, and avidly interested in literature and music; Ed was sociable, athletic, and more emotionally dependent on his parents. In spite of these differences Fred was pleased to be visiting with his only sibling.

On the Sunday following Easter, Fred and Ed dropped their mother and father at church (Fred had stopped attending several years earlier) and then drove downtown to enjoy an ice cream sundae with one of Ed's friends. After eating their sundaes they went back to their house, where Ed asked his friend and Fred to wait in the car while he ran in to use the bathroom. After an unusually long time, Ed emerged from the house complaining of a severe headache. The three young men went into the house, where Ed then lay down in his bed in great pain. A doctor was called and after he arrived Fred drove back to the church to get his mother and father. When they got home they were greeted by the maid who told them that Ed had died.

Years later when Fred wrote of this incident he failed to reveal how he *felt* when his brother died. He noted that the death had a devastating effect on the family and he described in some detail the *behavior* of the various family members. He recalled that his mother threw her arms around her dead son and that his father walked from the room saying "For heaven's sake, for heaven's sake." Fred also described his grandfather's behavior at the funeral and how he looked at the body of his dead grandson and declared his willingness to trade places with him. At no time in his account of his brother's death, however, did Fred report his own emotions or speculate concerning the inner feelings of others.

For a person who aspired to be a poet, how could Fred have been without emotion at such a time? *He wasn't.* By the time Fred described this event more than fifty years later, he had become a writer of a different kind. He was by then a psychologist, a radical behaviorist, a man who, though he believed

344

in inner states such as emotions, insisted that the science of psychology should deal with observable data and not hypothetical events such as feelings. Fred, of course, is Burrhus Frederic Skinner, probably the most influential and best-known American psychologist of the twentieth century.

OVERVIEW

The learning theory of Dollard and Miller can be seen as a bridge spanning the psychodynamic theory of Freud, which relies heavily on speculation gleaned from clinical observations, and the behavioral theory of B. F. Skinner, which minimizes speculation and focuses almost entirely on observable behavior. Dollard and Miller, though experimentalists, were not reluctant to postulate the existence of internal events such as drives, cues, foresight, reasoning, unconscious processes, and conflict.

Skinner, in contrast, contends that psychology as a natural science must limit itself to the study of observable phenomena. He does not claim, however, that observable behavior is limited to external events. Instead, he includes within the scope of observable behavior such private events as thinking, remembering, and anticipating. Skinner's strict adherence to observable behavior has earned his approach the label "radical behaviorism."

Radical behaviorism insists that the scientific study of human behavior must avoid all hypothetical constructs (such as id, ego, superego, style of life, social interest, archetypes, cues, drives, needs, and so forth) often used by other theorists to explain human personality. To Skinner, behavior, not fictional constructs, is the basic data of psychological science.

In addition to being a radical behaviorist, Skinner can rightfully be regarded as a determinist and an environmentalist. As a determinist he rejects the notion of volition or free will. Human behavior, like any observable phenomenon, is lawfully determined and can be studied scientifically.

As an environmentalist Skinner holds that psychology must not explain behavior on the basis of the physiological or constitutional components of the organism. It is not that genetic factors are unimportant, but that, because they are fixed at conception, they are of no help in the control of behavior. The *history* of the individual, rather than the anatomy, provides the most useful data for predicting and controlling behavior.

BIOGRAPHY OF B. F. SKINNER

Skinner was born on March 20, 1904, in Susquehanna, Pennsylvania, the first child of William and Grace Madge Burrhus Skinner. His father was a lawyer and an aspiring politician who never quite became successful in politics, but who, nevertheless, earned a comfortable living as an attorney. Both parents had lived in Susquehanna as children and both had attended high school there. All four grandparents lived in the same town and young Fred (he was almost never called Burrhus or B. F.) often visited with them after school and on weekends. The family's roots were deeply embedded in Susquehanna and Skinner grew up in a comfortable, happy, upper-middle-class home where his parents practiced the values of temperance, service, honesty, and hard work. The Skinners were Presbyterian, but Fred began to lose his faith during high school and thereafter never practiced any religion.

When Fred was two-and-a-half, a second son, Edward James, was born. Fred and Ebbie (as he was known) got along well considering the fact that they did not share many interests and that Fred felt Ebbie was treated more leniently and loved more by both parents. However, Fred did not feel unloved. He was simply more independent and less emotionally attached to his mother and father. But after Ebbie died during Fred's first year at college, the parents became less and less willing to let the older son go. They wanted him to become "the family boy," and indeed succeeded in keeping him financially obligated even after B. F. Skinner became a well-known name in American psychology.

As a child, Skinner was inclined toward the arts. He learned to play the piano and the saxophone well enough to form a jazz band during his late teenage years. From an early age he was interested in writing, and by the time he was in high school he had experimented with writing novels, poems, movie scenes, song lyrics, and plays. His ambition was to be a professional writer and he made a serious attempt to realize that goal. Besides music and literature, he also enjoyed painting and had a propensity toward inventing and building a variety of gadgets. This latter ability has served him well in his career as a behavior psychologist by enabling him to design and build much of the equipment used in his experiments.

Skinner attended public school in Susquehanna. Not only were all 12 grades in the same building, but one teacher (whom he greatly admired and respected) moved with him through most of his elementary and high school years. After graduating, his family moved to Scranton, Pennsylvania, where his father had taken the position as general counsel for the Hudson Coal Company. Immediately thereafter Skinner entered Hamilton College, an all-male liberal arts school in Clinton, New York. Throughout his four years at Hamilton he longed to become a creative writer. During his junior year he wrote a three-act play in one day, a feat he attributed to "automatic writing."

After taking his bachelor's degree in English he set about to realize his ambition. When he informed his father that he wished to spend a year at home working at nothing except creative writing, his request understandably was met with lukewarm acceptance. His father wrote him, warning of the necessity of making a living, but reluctantly agreed to support him for the one year on condition that Fred would get a job if his writing career was not successful. This unenthusiastic letter was quickly followed by a more encouraging one from Robert Frost who had read some of Skinner's writings. Skinner returned to Scranton, built a study in the attic, and every morning went to work at writing.

But nothing happened. His efforts were unproductive. He had nothing to say and had no firm position on any current issue. In his autobiography, Skinner (1976) refers to this period as his "Dark Year." Elms (1981) regards this time as Skinner's first, but not last, major identity crisis.

At the end of this unsuccessful year, he was faced with the task of looking for a new career. Science beckoned. Wanting to understand people better, he turned to psychology. He was accepted as a graduate student at Harvard for the Fall 1928 term. He had never taken an undergraduate course in psychology, but just prior to entering Harvard he read about John B. Watson in Bertrand Russell's *Philosophy.* He bought a copy of Watson's *Behaviorism,* read some Pavlov, and determined at that early date to be a behaviorist. He never wavered from that determination.

Before leaving for Cambridge, Skinner spent several months living in Greenwich Village in New York City and followed this experience with a summer touring Europe. These experiences, which may have better prepared him to be a writer, ironically came after rather than before his ill-fated attempt to carve for himself a career in creative writing.

At Harvard he quickly became a leader of a small group of graduate students dedicated to behaviorism. Upon finishing his Ph.D. in 1931 he was granted a fellowship by the National Research Council to continue his laboratory research at Harvard. His experiments were exclusively with animals, mostly rats, though he also used squirrels and even lobsters. At this same time he drew up a plan for himself outlining his goals for the years 1930–1960. The plan also reminded him to adhere closely to behavioristic methodology and not to "surrender to the physiology of the central nervous system" (Skinner, 1970, p. 155). By 1960 it could be said that Skinner had reached the most important phases of the plan, though not all specifics were realized.

When his fellowship ended in 1933 he was faced for the first time with the chore of hunting for a permanent job. Positions were scarce during this depression year and prospects looked dim, but soon his worries were alleviated. In the spring of 1933 Harvard created the Society of Fellows, a program designed to promote creative thinking among young intellectually gifted men at the university. Skinner was selected as a Junior Fellow and spent the next three years doing laboratory research. Conditions were ideal! He worked independently, was paid for doing what he loved, and lived sumptuously in a suite in Winthrop House.

At the end of his three-year term as a Junior Fellow he was again in the position of having to look for a job. Curiously, he knew almost nothing of academic psychology and was not interested in learning about it. He had a Ph.D. in psychology, five-and-a-half additional years of laboratory research, but was ill-prepared to teach within the mainstream of psychology, having "never even read a text in psychology as a whole" (Skinner, 1979, p. 179).

In 1936 he began a teaching and research position at the University of Minnesota, where he remained for nine years. While at Minnesota he continued to work in his laboratory, teach, and write. His first book, *The Behavior of Organisms* (1938), was published during this time and two of his most interesting ventures, the baby-tender and the pigeon-guided missile, came out of the Minnesota period.

Almost immediately after moving to Minneapolis, Skinner married Yvonne Blue following a short and erratic courtship. Two daughters were born to them, Julie in 1938 and Deborah in 1944. It was the second daughter who gained both fame and notoriety by living her first two-and-a-half years in a baby-tender that Skinner built.

The baby-tender, variously called the Air-Crib, Heir Conditioner, baby-box, and, erroneously, the "Skinner Box," was essentially an enclosed crib with a large window and a continual supply of fresh warm air. After *Ladies Home Journal* published an article on the baby-tender, Skinner was both condemned and praised for his invention. Interest from other parents persuaded him to market the device. However, difficulties in securing a patent and his association with a business partner who,

according to Skinner (1979), was both incompetent and unscrupulous caused him to eventually abandon the commercial venture; and when Debbie outgrew the baby-tender, it unceremoniously became a home for some of Skinner's pigeons.

During World War II Skinner had trained pigeons to pilot missiles into enemy targets, but that project, too, ended in disappointment. The disappointments and frustrations with the baby-tender and especially the missile project led to what Elms (1981) has referred to as Skinner's midlife crisis. Furthermore, when he left Minnesota in 1945 for a position as chairman of the psychology department at the University of Indiana, the move was not without added frustrations. His wife had ambivalent feelings about leaving friends, his administrative duties proved irksome, and he still felt out of the mainstream of scientific psychology. However, his personal crisis was soon to end and his professional career would take another turn.

In the summer of 1945, while on vacation, Skinner wrote *Walden Two,* a utopian novel that portrayed a society in which problems were solved through behavioral engineering. The book was written with great speed and emotional catharsis. It was 1948 before *Walden Two* was published and another decade before it began to become a popular book, but the writing provided immediate therapy for Skinner. At last he had done what he failed to accomplish during his Dark Year nearly 20 years earlier. Elms (1981) considers his midlife crisis to have come to an end with the writing of *Walden Two.* The book was also a benchmark in Skinner's professional career. No longer would he be confined to the laboratory study of rats and pigeons, but hereafter he would be involved with the application of behavioristic findings to the technology of shaping human behavior. His concern with the human condition was elaborated in *Science and Human Behavior* (1953) and reached philosophical expression in *Beyond Freedom and Dignity* (1971).

Since his retirement in 1974, Skinner has remained active, publishing several books, including three important ones on human behavior: *About Behaviorism* (1974), *Reflections on Behaviorism and Society* (1978), and *Upon Further Reflection* (1987a). In addition, he has written his three-volume autobiography, *Particulars of My Life* (1976), *The Shaping of a Behaviorist* (1979), and *A Matter of Consequences* (1983). He is currently the Edgar Pierce Professor Emeritus at Harvard University and continues an active life as a writer and lecturer.

SCIENTIFIC BEHAVIORISM

To understand Skinner's radical behaviorism, it is first essential to know something about his technology of behavior and his philosophy of science.

A basic assumption made by Skinner is that human behavior is subject to the laws of science and can be studied just as any other natural phenomena. Natural phenomena are best studied when no inner motivations are attributed to them. The wind does not blow because it wants to turn windmills; rocks do not roll downhill because they possess a sense of gravity; birds do not migrate because they like the climate better in other regions; and people do not eat because they feel hungry. Physical and biological scientists can easily accept the idea that the behavior of the wind, rocks, and birds can be studied without reference to an internal motive; but many scientists of human behavior assume that people are motivated by internal drives and that an understanding of the drives is essential.

Skinner disagrees. Why postulate an inner mental function that is outside the scope of scientific analysis? People do not eat because they are hungry. Hunger is an inner condition not directly observable. If one wants to increase the probability that a person will eat, one must first observe the variables related to eating. If deprivation of food increases the likelihood of eating, then one can deprive a person of food in order to better predict and control subsequent eating behavior. Both deprivation and eating are physical events clearly observable and therefore within the province of science. To say that a person eats due to hunger is to assume an unnecessary and unobservable mental condition between the physical fact of deprivation and the physical fact of eating. This clouds the issue and relegates much of psychology to that realm of philosophy known as **cosmology** or the concern with causation. In order to be scientific, Skinner contends psychology must avoid internal mental factors and confine itself to observable physical events (Skinner, 1953, 1987a).

Although Skinner rejects internal states as being outside the domain of science, he does not deny their existence. Such conditions as hunger, paranoia, values, self-confidence, aggressive needs, religious beliefs, and spitefulness exist, but they are not explanations for behavior. To use them as explanations is not only fruitless but also limits the advancement of scientific behaviorism. Other sciences have made greater advances because they have long since abandoned the practice of attributing motion (behavior) of objects and living things to motives, needs, or will power. Skinner's scientific behaviorism follows their lead (Skinner, 1945).

Philosophy of Science

Scientific behaviorism allows for an interpretation of behavior, but never offers an explanation of its causes. Interpretation permits generalization from the simple learning condition to the more complex. For example, Skinner generalized from animal studies to children and then to adults. Any science, including that of human behavior, begins with the simple and eventually evolves generalized principles that permit interpretation of the more complex. Skinner employs principles derived from laboratory studies to interpret the behavior of human beings, but interpretation is not to be confused with explanation. Events in everyday life take on meaning through knowledge of laboratory studies because the same conditions of learning apply in both cases. However, no explanation should be offered as to why people behave. Explanations are mentalistic fictions created by wishful thinking and beyond the scope of physical events that can be observed by science (Skinner, 1978).

The purpose of science, Skinner (1953) says, is not only to predict behavior but to control it as well. Science is also concerned with the description of behavior and the conditions under which it occurs. Prediction, control, and description are possible in scientific behaviorism because behavior is both determined and lawful. Human behavior, like that of physical and biological entities, is neither whimsical nor the outcome of free will. It is determined by certain identifiable variables and follows definite lawful principles which, hypothetically at least, can be known. When behavior appears to be capricious or individually determined, it is simply because some of it is beyond our present capacity to predict or control. Potentially, the conditions under which behavior occurs can be discovered and, therefore, behavior can be predicted, described, and, to some extent, controlled. Skinner has devoted much of his time to trying to discover these conditions using a procedure he calls operant conditioning.

Operant Conditioning

Skinner (1953) recognizes two kinds of conditioning, respondent and operant. In **respondent conditioning,** also called classical or Pavlovian, a response is drawn out of the organism by a specific, identifiable stimulus. The simplest examples include reflexive behavior. Light shined in the eye stimulates the pupil to contract; food placed on the tongue brings about salivation; and pepper in the nostrils results in the sneezing reflex. With reflexive behavior, responses are unlearned, involuntary, and common not only to the species but across species as well. Respondent conditioning, however, is not limited to simple reflexes. It can also be responsible for more complex human learning like phobias, fears, and anxiety. A child bitten by a dog shows a fear response whenever confronted by that dog. A specific stimulus (the dog) now elicits a response (fear) that was not present prior to the time the child was bitten.

A more comprehensive approach to behavior, Skinner believes, is **operant conditioning.** The key to operant conditioning is the immediate reinforcement of a response. The organism first *does* something and then is reinforced by the environment. Reinforcement, in turn, increases the probability that the same behavior will occur again. This is called operant conditioning because the organism operates on the environment to produce a specific effect. Operant conditioning changes the frequency of a response or the probability that a response will occur through the systematic use of reinforcement. The reinforcement does not cause the behavior, but merely makes it more likely that it will be repeated.

One distinction between respondent and operant conditioning is that in respondent conditioning behavior is *elicited* from the organism, while in operant conditioning behavior is *emitted.* Skinner makes a distinction between elicited and emitted behavior. An elicted response is drawn from the organism while an emitted response is one that simply appears. Emitted responses do not previously exist inside the organism and no stimulus or internal cause is responsible for their occurrence. They simply appear because of the organism's individual history of reinforcement or the species' evolutionary history.

An example of operant conditioning can be seen in a parent who wishes to increase the frequency of smiles emitted by a child. He watches the child constantly and gives her candy every time she smiles. In this example, as in all instances of operant conditioning, there are three essential conditions: the *situation,* the *behavior,* and the *consequence.* The situation is the environment or setting in which the behavior takes place. In our example this would include the home, school, playground, the parent, and the child. This is an extremely problematic situation because the parent ordinarily could not follow the child all day dispensing rewards. This is one reason Skinner worked in a laboratory setting employing a rigidly controlled environment in the form of a box or cage usually called the "Skinner box."

The second essential in the operant conditioning paradigm is the response or behavior. In the above example the behavior is smiling, a relatively simple response that will undoubtedly occur without any previous training. More complex behavior must be gradually "shaped" through the use of "successive approximations," terms explained below. The response must be within the organism's repertoire and must not be interfered with by competing or antagonistic behaviors.

The third factor in operant conditioning is the consequence. If no consistent consequence follows an operant behavior during the history of the organism, no learning will occur; that is, there will be no change in the frequency of the behavior. But if there is a consequence (and there always is one of some sort), then there will follow an increase or decrease in the probability of the response being emitted. In the above example, candy is a reward and it acts to reinforce the behavior of smiling and to increase its frequency. However, if a parent gave a child candy every time she smiled, the child would eventually reach her fill. To insure that an organism remained at a certain level of deprivation, Skinner carefully rationed the amount of food given to the animal prior to training and used body weight as a measure of deprivation. He also employed various intermittent schedules of reinforcement so that the organism was not reinforced for every desired response and would thus remain in a state of partial deprivation. This sort of rigorous control is usually not available with the conditioning of humans.

Shaping

In the above experiment, the child was reinforced whenever she emitted the desired behavior, namely smiling. In most cases the desired behavior is more complex and will be emitted only through the process of **shaping.** This procedure entails first the rewarding of gross approximations of the behavior, then closer approximations, and finally the desired behavior itself. Through this process of reinforcing **successive approximations,** the final complex set of behaviors is gradually shaped (Skinner, 1953).

Shaping can be illustrated by the example of training a severely mentally retarded boy to dress himself. The ultimate behavior is to have the child put on all his own clothes. If reinforcement were withheld until this target behavior occurred, the child would never successfully complete the chore. To train the boy, the complex behavior of dressing must be broken down into simple segments. First, the child is reinforced with a reward, say, candy, whenever he approximates the behavior of positioning his left hand near the inside of the left sleeve of his shirt. Once the behavior is sufficiently reinforced, reward is withheld until the child places his hand into the proper sleeve. Then he is rewarded only for putting his left arm entirely through the sleeve. Following this, the same procedures are used with the right sleeve, the buttons, trousers, socks, and shoes. After the child learns to dress himself completely, reinforcement need not follow every successful trial. By this time, in fact, the ability to put on all his clothes will probably become a reward in itself. Quite apparently, the final target behavior could only have been reached by breaking up complex behavior into component parts and by reinforcing successive approximations to each response. Shaping allows conditioning to take place quite quickly. In only two or three minutes Skinner has conditioned pigeons to raise their heads to heights never before reached. Chickens have been trained to play a facsimile of baseball and dogs have been conditioned to jump through hoops in a very short time.

Even complex behavior, such as learning to play Ping-Pong, is acquired through shaping and successive approximations.

If reinforcement increases the probability that a given response will recur, then how can behavior be shaped from the relatively undifferentiated into the highly complex. In other words, why doesn't the organism simply repeat the old reinforced response? Why does it emit new responses that have never been reinforced, but which gradually move it toward the target behavior? The answer is that behavior is not discrete, but continuous, that is, one usually moves slightly beyond the previously reinforced response. If behavior were discrete, shaping could not occur since the organism would become locked into simply emitting previously reinforced responses. Since behavior is continuous, the organism moves slightly beyond the previously reinforced response and this slightly exceptional value can then be used as the new minimum standard for reinforcement. (The organism may also move slightly backward or slightly sideways, but only movements toward the desired target are reinforced.) Skinner (1953) compares shaping behavior to a sculptor molding a statue from a large lump of clay. In both, the final product seems to be different from the original form, but the history of the transformation reveals continuous behavior and not a set of discrete steps.

Operant behavior always takes place in some environment and the environment has a selective role in shaping and maintaining behavior. The organism, throughout its history, will have been reinforced by reacting to some elements in the environment but not to others. This history of differential reinforcement results in **operant discrimination.** Discrimination can be observed when a pigeon is reinforced for pecking at a circular key but not when an octagonal one is presented. Reinforcement is therefore contingent upon a pecking response within one environment but not another.

Discrimination does not exist within the pigeon, Skinner claims, but is a consequence of the organism's reinforcement history. Discrimination, therefore, is not an ability possessed by the organism. It is a function of environmental variables and the organism's previous experiences with reinforcement. We do not come to the dinner table because we discern that the food is ready, but because our previous experiences of reacting in a similar way have been mostly reinforced. This distinction may seem to be splitting hairs, but to Skinner it has important theoretical and practical implications. The first explanation sees discrimination as a cognitive function, existing within the person; the second accounts for it by environmental differences and by individual history. The first is beyond the scope of empirical observation; the second can be scientifically studied.

If a pigeon is reinforced for pecking at a circular key but not when an octagonal one is presented, discrimination takes place. If, on the other hand, the pigeon is rewarded for pecking a round key and has no training with an octagonal one, then something quite different happens. Now the pigeon pecks at the octagonal key even though it has never been reinforced for this behavior. A response to a similar environment in the absence of previous reinforcement is called **stimulus generalization.** Skinner has observed, however, that the pigeon will not peck with the same frequency in the new situation. The frequency diminishes as the size, color, or shape of the key varies from the original one. Technically, the organism does not generalize from one situation to another, but reacts to the second situation in the same manner it reacted to the first because the two situations possess *identical elements.* Skinner (1953, p. 94) puts it this way: "The reinforcement of a response increases the probability of all responses containing the same elements."

Reinforcement

We have seen that reinforcement increases the probability that an operant response will be emitted and we have described the role of reinforcement in shaping behavior. It is time to examine this powerful force more closely.

Reinforcement is anything within the environment that strengthens a behavior. Actually, Skinner (1987a) says that reinforcement has two effects: it *strengthens the behavior* and it *rewards the person.* Reinforcement and reward, therefore, are not synonymous. Not every behavior that is reinforced is rewarding or pleasing to the person. For example, people are reinforced for working, but may find their jobs boring, uninteresting, and unrewarding. Reinforcers exist in the environment and are not something felt by the organism. Food is not reinforcing because it tastes good; rather, it tastes good because it is reinforcing (Skinner, 1971).

Any behavior that increases the probability that the species and the individual will survive tends to be strengthened. Since food, sex, and parental care are necessary for survival of the species, behavior that produces these conditions is reinforced; since injury, disease, and extremes in climate are detrimental to survival, any behavior that tends to reduce or avoid these conditions is likewise reinforced. Reinforcement, therefore, can be divided into that which produces a beneficial environmental condition and that which reduces or avoids a detrimental one. The first is called positive reinforcement and the second, negative reinforcement.

Kamikaze Pigeons

Are pigeons intelligent enough (or stupid enough) to be trained to fly suicide missions during wartime? The answer, interestingly, is "Yes."

Using the principles of positive reinforcement, Skinner trained pigeons during World War II to peck at keys that controlled the bomb they were riding. As the enemy ship moved, the pigeons would peck the controls to maintain the missile on track of its target. The Kamikaze pigeons and their guided missiles never saw battle, but simulated tests proved successful.

The history of Project Pigeon is an interesting one, but to Skinner personally it was both disappointing and frustrating. After Germany invaded Norway and Denmark in April 1940, almost two years before the United States's entry into the war, Skinner purchased a flock of pigeons for the purpose of training them to guide missiles. At that time the U.S. government showed very little interest. After Pearl Harbor, Skinner resumed Project Pigeon, this time with some help from the University of Minnesota. Major financial resources, however, were needed and in 1942 the National Defense Research Committee again backed away from granting support.

Undaunted, Skinner obtained an appropriation from General Mills Inc. to continue the project. He was granted a sabbatical leave from the university and went to work for General Mills. The project was begun anew, but he still lacked governmental support.

In an effort to secure the needed funds he prepared a film of trained pigeons pecking at the control of a missile and guiding it toward a moving target. Interest was rekindled and after officials visited Minneapolis, General Mills was given $25,000 to develop the project. Nevertheless, frustrations lay ahead. Skinner felt the pigeon-driven weapons could be ready for combat by the summer of 1944, but the government was more cautious.

A final presentation in Washington in 1944 was particularly disillusioning. Skinner had demonstrated the feasibility of the project by producing a live pigeon that unerringly tracked a moving target. Despite the spectacular demonstration, there was some laughter and considerable skepticism. Finally, after four years of work, more than two of which were full time, Skinner was notified that the project could no longer be continued. In the final analysis, Project Pigeon was probably scuttled not because of the unconventional proposal to use animals to fly missiles but because it was in competition with a much more devastating weapon—the atomic bomb (Skinner, 1960, 1979).

Any stimulus which, when added to a situation, increases the probability that a given behavior will occur is termed a **positive reinforcer** (Skinner, 1953). Food, water, sex, money, social approval, and physical comfort are examples. When made contingent on behavior, each has the capacity to increase the frequency of a response. For example, if clear water appears whenever a person turns on the kitchen faucet, then that behavior is strengthened because a beneficial environmental stimulus has been added.

The removal of an aversive stimulus from a situation also increases the probability that the preceding behavior will occur. This removal is called a **negative reinforcer** (Skinner, 1953). The reduction or avoidance of loud noises, shocks, and hunger pangs would be negatively reinforcing because they strengthen the behavior immediately preceding them. Negative reinforcement differs from positive reinforcement in that it requires the removal of an aversive condition whereas positive reinforcement involves the presentation of a beneficial stimulus. The effect of negative reinforcement, however, is identical to that of positive reinforcement; both strengthen behavior. Some people eat because they like a particular food; others eat to diminish hunger pangs. For the first group, food is a positive reinforcer; for the second, removal of hunger is a negative reinforcer. In both instances, the behavior of eating is strengthened because the consequences are rewarding.

There is an almost unlimited number of aversive stimuli, the removal of which may be negatively reinforcing. Anxiety, for example, is an aversive stimulus and any behavior that reduces it (repression, making excuses, and the like) is reinforcing. Other examples include guilt, illness, pain from burns, scoldings, threats of imprisonment, and fear of damnation. Behavior that reduces or avoids any of these conditions tend to be strengthened. On the other hand, the presence of any of these aversive stimuli is called punishment.

Punishment

Negative reinforcement must not be confused with punishment. Negative reinforcers remove, reduce, or avoid aversive stimuli while **punishment** is defined as the presentation of an aversive stimulus such as an electric shock or the removal of a positive one such as disconnecting an adolescent's telephone. A negative reinforcer strengthens a response; punishment does not. Though punishment does not strengthen a response, neither does it inevitably weaken it. The effects of punishment are therefore less predictable than those of reward (Skinner, 1953).

The control of human and animal behavior is better served by positive and negative reinforcement than by punishment. The effects of punishment are not opposite those of reinforcement. When the contingencies of reinforcement are strictly controlled, behavior can be precisely shaped and accurately predicted. With punishment, however, no such exactitude is possible. The reason for this is simple. Punishment is ordinarily imposed to prevent people from acting in a particular way. When successful, people stop behaving in that manner, but they still must do something. What they do cannot be accurately predicted since punishment does not make it clear what they should do, but merely suppresses the tendency to behave in the undesirable fashion. One effect of punishment, consequently, is to *suppress* behavior. For example, if a boy teases a younger sister he can be made to stop by a spanking, but, unfortunately, this does not improve his disposition toward the younger child. It merely suppresses teasing temporarily or while in the presence of parents.

Another effect of punishment is the *conditioning of a negative feeling.* This is accomplished through the use of a strong aversive stimulus that is incompatible with the behavior being punished. In the above illustration, if the pain of the spanking is strong enough, it will instigate a response (crying, withdrawal, attack) which is incompatible with the behavior of teasing a younger sibling. In the future, when the boy thinks about mistreating his younger sister, the thought elicits, through classical conditioning, the conditioned response of fear, anxiety, guilt, or shame. This negative emotion then serves to prevent the undesirable behavior from recurring. Lamentably, it offers no positive instruction to the child.

A third outcome of punishment is the *spread of its effects.* Any stimulus associated with the punishment may be suppressed or avoided. In our example, this might include the younger sister, the parent, the paddle, or the place where the spanking occurred. The boy may deny the feelings of hostility toward his parents or he may avoid almost all contact with his sister. As a result, his behavior toward them becomes maladaptive. Yet this inappropriate behavior serves the purpose of preventing future punishment. Skinner recognizes the classical defense mechanisms as effective means of avoiding pain and its attendant anxiety. The punished person may fantasize, project feelings onto others, rationalize aggressive behaviors, or displace them toward other people or animals.

Punishment has several characteristics in common with reinforcement. Just as there are two kinds of reinforcements (positive and negative), there are two types of punishment. The first requires the presentation of an aversive stimulus, the second involves the removal of a positive reinforcer. An example of the former would be pain encountered from falling as the result of walking too fast on an icy sidewalk. An example of the latter is a fine levied against a motorist for driving too fast. This first example (falling) results from a natural condition; the second (levying a fine) follows from human intervention. This is a second characteristic common to punishment and reinforcement: both can derive from either natural consequences or from human imposition. A third common ingredient is that both punishment and reinforcement are means of controlling behavior, whether the control is by design or by accident. Skinner obviously favors planned control and his ideas on the control of human behavior are discussed later.

Schedules of Reinforcement

Operant conditioning is based on the fact that any behavior immediately followed by the presentation of a positive reinforcer or the removal of an aversive stimulus tends thereafter to occur more frequently. The frequency of that behavior, however, is subject to the conditions under which training occurred, more specifically, to the various schedules of reinforcement (Ferster & Skinner, 1957).

Reinforcement can follow behavior either on a continuous schedule or on an intermittent one. **Continuous schedules** call for reinforcing the organism for every trial, a procedure which leads to an increase in frequency of the response, but which is an inefficient use of reinforcers. More effective are the **intermittent schedules** where the organism is not reinforced for every response. Intermittent schedules are based either on the behavior of the organism or on elapsed time; they can be set either at a fixed rate or can vary according to a randomized program. Accordingly, four basic intermittent schedules are recognized: fixed-ratio, variable-ratio, fixed-interval, and variable-interval. In addition, an assorted number of combinations among the various schedules is possible. At least nine of these combinations are identified by Ferster and Skinner (1957), but we need be detained only by the four principal intermittent schedules.

Fixed-Ratio.   With a **fixed-ratio schedule,** the organism is reinforced intermittently according to the number of responses it makes. Ratio refers to the ratio of responses to reinforcers. An experimenter may decide to reward a pigeon with a pellet of grain for every fifth peck it makes at a disc. The pigeon is then conditioned at a fixed-ratio schedule of 5 to 1, that is, FR 5.

Nearly all intermittent schedules begin by reinforcing the organism for every desired response, that is, on a continuous basis. But soon, continuous reward can be ended and reinforcement can proceed intermittently. In the same way, extremely high fixed-ratio schedules, like 200 to 1, must begin at a low rate of responses and gradually build to a higher one. A pigeon can be conditioned to work long and rapidly in exchange for one food pellet provided it has been previously reinforced at lower rates. Fixed-ratio schedules generate rapid responses in pigeons, some emitting more than ten pecks per second.

Technically, almost no pay scale follows a fixed-ratio or any other schedule, since workers ordinarily do not begin with a continuous schedule of immediate reinforcement. Bricklayers, for example, working by piece-rate, approximate a fixed-ratio schedule, but they are not paid immediately after laying one brick or even 100 bricks. In fact, several individual responses are required to lay a single brick and these responses have never been rewarded by pay. They were, of course, reinforced by immediate feedback during early training, but never on a fixed-ratio basis.

Variable-Ratio.   With a fixed-ratio schedule the organism is reinforced after every nth response. With the **variable-ratio schedule** it is reinforced after the *n*th response *on the average.* Again, training must start with continuous reinforcement, proceed to a low response number, and then increase to a higher rate of response. A pigeon rewarded every third response on the aver-

Because slot machines pay off on a variable ratio schedule, some people become compulsive gamblers.

age can build to a VR 6 schedule, then VR 10, and so on. An organism working on a VR 10 schedule might be reinforced after the second response, the eighth, the sixteenth, the fourteenth, and so on, but the average is one reinforcement for every 10 responses. The mean number of responses must be increased gradually to prevent extinction. After a high mean is reached, say, VR 500, responses become extremely resistant to extinction. (More on rate of extinction later.)

For humans, playing slot machines is an example of a variable-ratio schedule. The machine is set to pay off at a certain rate, but the ratio must be flexible, that is, variable, to prevent players from predicting payoffs. Probably no jobs pay on a variable-ratio schedule, but a close approximation would be bonuses handed out unpredictably after a given amount of work.

Fixed-Interval.   With the **fixed-interval schedule** the organism is reinforced for the first response following a designated period of time. For example, FI 5 indicates that the organism is rewarded for its first response after every five-minute interval. Setting reward dependent on elapsed time results in an interesting pattern of responses. As the end of the time period nears, the organism responds at a high rate and will almost certainly emit a response immediately after the end of the designated time. After reinforcement is obtained, however, there is a slowing of response rate until near the end of the next interval. This is not unlike the student working hard immediately before midterm exams, taking it easy after the tests, then putting forth another push as finals approach.

Employees working for salary or wages approximate a fixed-interval schedule. They are paid every week, every two weeks, or every month, but this is not strictly a fixed-interval schedule. Why do workers distribute their efforts fairly evenly over time rather than loafing most of the time and then showing an end of the period spurt characteristic of the fixed-interval schedule? The answer is that there are many other controls affecting their work, such as watchful supervisors, threats of dismissal, or promises of promotion. Another reason salaries are not technically fixed-interval schedules is that reinforcement does not follow the first response after a designated interval. An employee may even be at home when the paycheck arrives in the mail. (Trips to the mailbox are sometimes reinforcing.)

Variable-Interval.   A **variable-interval schedule** is one in which the organism is reinforced after the lapse of random or varied periods of time. For example, VI 5 means that the organism is reinforced following random-length intervals that average five minutes. Such schedules result in more responses per interval than do fixed-interval schedules. With a variable-interval schedule the organism can make no correlation between behavior and reinforcement. With a fixed-interval schedule the organism's behavior includes many pauses, while the variable-interval schedule results in a constant rate of responding.

In daily life reinforcement results more often from one's effort rather than the passage of time. For this reason, ratio schedules are more common than interval ones and the variable-interval schedule is probably the least common of all. For example, workers are seldom paid on a variable-interval basis. A hypothetical example would be bonuses paid throughout the year with varying lengths of time between them, the worker's production being unrelated to the timing of the bonus. Payment does not occur this way. Human behavior, however, is sometimes reinforced on a variable-interval schedule. Television addicts watch their favorite program every week, hoping it will be enjoyable. Sometimes it is, often it is not. Fisherman waiting patiently and passively to get a nibble are rewarded at various intervals by fish striking the line and through little of their own effort.

Conditioned and Generalized Reinforcers

To a pigeon, food is a reinforcer because it removes a condition of deprivation. Food is also a reinforcer for humans and generally for the same reason. But how can money be reinforcing since it cannot directly remove a condition of deprivation? The answer, of course, is that money is a **conditioned reinforcer.** Conditioned reinforcers are those things which are not by nature satisfying, but become so because they are associated with such unlearned reinforcers as food, water, sex, or physical comfort. Money is a conditioned reinforcer because it can be exchanged for a great variety of primary reinforcers. Because it is associated with more than one primary reinforcer, money is also considered a **generalized reinforcer.**

Skinner (1953) recognizes five important generalized reinforcers that sustain much of our behavior. Attention, approval, affection, submission of others, and tokens (money) are all conditioned generalized reinforcers since they are only indirectly related to primary reinforcers and since they can each be used as reinforcers in a variety of situations. Attention, for example, is a conditioned generalized reinforcer because it is associated with such primary reinforcers as food and physical contact. When children are being fed or held, they are also receiving attention. After food and attention are paired a number of times, attention itself becomes reinforcing through the process of respondent conditioning, discussed above. Children, and adults too, will work for attention with no expectation of receiving food or physical contact. In much the same way, approval, affection, submission of others, and money acquire generalized reinforcement value. Behavior can be shaped and responses learned with generalized conditioned reinforcers supplying the sole reinforcement.

Extinction

Once learned, responses can be lost for at least four reasons. First, they can simply be forgotten during the passage of time. Second, and more likely, they can be lost because preceding or subsequent learnings interfere. Third, they can disappear due to punishment, repression being included in this category. A fourth cause of lost learnings is extinction.

There are two kinds of extinction, respondent and operant. **Respondent extinction** follows respondent conditioning and involves the presentation of the conditioned stimulus in the absence of the unconditioned stimulus. The response elicited by the conditioned stimulus eventually disappears.

Operant extinction is the systematic withholding of reinforcement previously contingent upon a response until the probability of the response diminishes to zero (Skinner, 1953). Rate of operant extinction depends largely on the schedule of reinforcement under which learning occurred. However, the curve may be complicated by emotion, since a person might respond more often or more violently while angry. If reinforcement follows a continuous schedule, extinction occurs at a fast rate. A child receives a dollar every time she cleans her room. But after cleaning the room several times with no remuneration, she may soon stop, provided no aversive stimuli such as threats or nagging are present.

Behavior trained on an intermittent schedule is much more resistant to extinction. Skinner (1953) has observed as many as 10,000 nonreinforced responses with intermittent schedules. Such behavior appears to be self-perpetuating and is practically indistinguishable from functionally autonomous behavior, a concept suggested by Allport and discussed in Chapter 14. In general, the higher the rate of responses per reinforcement, the slower the rate of extinction; the fewer responses an organism must make or the shorter the time between reinforcers, the more quickly extinction will occur. This suggests that praise and other reinforcers should be used sparingly in training children.

When reinforcement occurs intermittently, the desired behavior may persist a lifetime in the absence of further reinforcement because it is in the process of becoming extinct. Extinction, however, is seldom systematically applied to human behavior outside therapy or behavior modification. Because we live in relatively uncontrolled environments, we almost never experience the methodical withholding of reinforcement. If a behavior persists for a lifetime, it is probably receiving some periodic reinforcement, though the nature of that reinforcement may be obscure to the individual.

THE HUMAN ORGANISM

Our discussion of Skinnerian theory to this point has dealt primarily with the technology of behavior, a technology based exclusively on the study of animals. But do the principles of behavior gleaned from rats and pigeons apply to the human organism? Skinner's (1974, 1987a) view is that an understanding of the behavior of laboratory animals can generalize to human behavior just as physics can be used to interpret what is observed in outer space and an understanding of basic genetics can help in interpreting complex evolutionary concepts.

Skinner believes that if psychology is to advance as a science, then it must be confined to a scientific study of observable phenomena, namely behavior. Science must begin with the simple and move to the more complex. This sequence might proceed thus: from animal behavior, to psychotics, to retardates, to children, and finally to adult behavior (Skinner, 1974, 1987a). Skinner, therefore, makes no apology for beginning with the study of animals, a practice, incidentally, he abandoned some 40 years ago.

According to Skinner (1987a) human behavior (and human personality) is shaped by three forces. The first is the individual's personal history of reinforcement which we have just discussed; the second is natural selection or the evolutionary history of the species; and the third is the evolution of social environments or cultures.

Natural Selection

The human organism is the product of a long evolutionary history. As individuals, our behavior is determined by genetic composition and especially by our personal histories of reinforcement. As a species, however, we are shaped by the contingencies of survival. Natural selection plays an important part in human behavior (Skinner, 1974, 1987a).

Individual behavior that is reinforcing tends to be repeated; that which is not tends to drop out. Similarly, those behaviors which, throughout history, were beneficial to the species have tended to survive while those which were only idiosyncratically reinforcing have tended to drop out. For example, natural selection has favored those individuals whose pupils dilated and contracted with changes in lighting. Their superior ability to see during both daylight and nighttime enabled them to avoid life-threatening dangers and to survive to the age of reproduction. Similarly, infants whose heads turned in the direction of a gentle stroke on the cheek were able to suckle, thereby increasing their chances of survival and the likelihood that this rooting characteristic would be passed on to their offspring. These are but two examples of several reflexes that characterize the human infant today. Some, such as the pupilary reflex, continue to have survival value while others, like the rooting reflex, are of diminishing benefit (Skinner, 1969, 1978).

The contingencies of reinforcement and the contingencies of survival interact with one another so that in practice it is often difficult to separate the two. For example, sex is reinforcing to the individual and behavior followed by sexual satisfaction tends to be reinforced. Furthermore, sexual behavior has natural selection value, since those individuals who are more strongly aroused by sexual stimulation are also the ones who are most likely to produce offspring capable of similar patterns of behavior.

Not every remnant of natural selection continues to have survival value. In our early history overeating was adaptive because it allowed people to survive during those times when food was less plentiful. Now, in societies where food is continuously available, obesity has become a health problem to many and overeating has lost its survival value.

Although natural selection helped shape some human behavior, it is probably responsible for only a small number of our actions. Skinner (1989) says that the contingencies of reinforcement, especially those that have shaped our culture, account for most of our behavior.

> We can trace a small part of human behavior . . . to natural selection and the evolution of the species, but the greater part of human behavior must be traced to contingencies of reinforcement, especially to the very complex social contingencies we call cultures. Only when we take those histories into account can we explain why people behave as they do (Skinner, 1989, p. 18).

Cultural Evolution

Recently Skinner (1987a, 1989) has elaborated more fully on the importance of culture in shaping human behavior. *Selection* is responsible for those cultural practices that have survived, just as selection plays a key role in our evolutionary history and also with the contingencies of reinforcement. "People do not observe particular practices in order that the group will be more likely to survive; they observe them because groups that induced their members to do so survived and transmitted them" (Skinner, 1987a, p. 57). In other words, there is no group mind or corporate decision to do what is best for the society; but those societies whose members behaved in certain ways tended to survive. For example, verbal behavior obviously has had tremendous survival value because it is found in all contemporary societies. Those societies that evolved verbal behavior have had the added advantage of using language as a means of transmitting other cultural practices.

Cultural practices such as tool making and verbal behavior begin when an individual is reinforced for using a tool or uttering a distinctive sound. Eventually, a cultural practice evolves that is reinforcing to the group, though not necessarily to the individual. Both tool making and verbal behavior have survival value for a group, but few of us now make tools and some (for example, monks who have taken the vow of silence) do not emit verbal behavior.

The remnants of culture, like those of natural selection, are not all adaptive. For example, the division of labor that evolved from the Industrial Revolution has helped society to produce more goods, but it has led to work that is no longer directly reinforcing. Another example is warfare, which in the preindustrialized world benefited certain societies, but then evolved as a threat to human existence before other cultural practices could be invented to countercontrol it.

In summary, Skinner (1987a, p. 55) writes that

> human behavior is the joint product of (1) the contingencies of survival responsible for the natural selection of the species and (2) the contingencies of reinforcement responsible for the repertoires acquired by its members, including (3) the special contingencies maintained by an evolved social environment. (Ultimately, of course, it is all a matter of natural selection, since operant conditioning is an evolved process, of which cultural practices are special applications.)

The Self

Skinner criticizes those who view the self as something possessed by the organism. The self is not a homunculus, or small man, inside the organism, directing all its moves. Neither is the self an autonomous being, ultimately responsible for its own behavior. The self is the organism; the organism is the self, or at least it becomes the self when it acquires a consistent pattern of behavior. More specifically, Skinner has offered these definitions of self. In *Science and Human Behavior* he stated that "a self is simply a device representing a *functionally unified system of responses* (Skinner, 1953, p. 285). Later, he defined a self as "a repertoire of behavior appropriate to a given set of contingencies" (Skinner, 1971, p. 199). A slightly different definition appeared three years later. "A self or personality is at best a repertoire of behavior imparted by an organized set of contingencies" (Skinner, 1974, p. 149).

These definitions imply individual differences among selves; unity or consistency within a single self; and, most important, a self as nothing other than behavior. To say the self is "functionally unified" or "organized" does not suggest that the self is incapable of novel behaviors. Through shaping, drugs, deprivation, emotion, or changes in environment, the organism may emit responses that have never before appeared in its repertoire. There is, however, no autonomous self that is responsible for these new behaviors, but only environmental contingencies of reinforcement.

Inner States

If the environment is accountable for behavior, are there then no inner states which affect personality? Though Skinner (1974) rejects explanations of behavior founded on nonobservable hypothetical constructs, he does not deny the existence of these internal states. Internal or private events can be studied just as any other behavior, but their observation is, of course, limited. Skinner says, "I believe it is possible to talk about private events and, in particular, to establish the limits with which we do so accurately. I think this brings so-called 'nonobservables' within reach" (B. F. Skinner, personal communication, June 13, 1983).

Radical behaviorism, then, does not ignore various states of the mind, but holds that explanations of behavior in terms of them is fruitless and retards the advancement of scientific behaviorism. Just as physics and biology began to make strides after abandoning the practice of attributing motion to the willpower of physical things and living organisms, so too will psychology become scientific after it rejects explanations of observable behavior based on fictitious constructs. What, then, is the role of such inner states as self-awareness, drives, emotions, and purpose or intention?

Self-Awareness

Skinner (1974) believes that humans not only have consciousness but also they are aware of their consciousness; they are not only aware of their environment but also they are aware of themselves as part of their environment; they not only observe external stimuli but also they are aware of themselves observing that stimuli.

Behavior is a function of the environment, and part of that environment is within one's skin. This portion of the universe is peculiarly one's own and is therefore private. Each of us is subjectively aware of our own thoughts, feelings, recollections, and intentions. These private events are real; they have physical properties and thus are potentially subject to the same scientific analysis as any other physical phenomena (Skinner, 1974).

Self-awareness and private events can be illustrated by the following example. A worker reports to a friend, "I was so frustrated today that I almost quit my job." What can we make of such a statement? First, the report itself is verbal behavior and, as such, can be studied in the same way as any other behavior. Second, the statement that she was on the verge of quitting her job refers to a nonbehavior. Responses never emitted are not responses and, of course, have no meaning to science. Third, a private event transpired "within the skin" of the worker. This private event, along with her verbal report to the friend, can be scientifically analyzed. At the time the worker felt like quitting, she might have observed the following covert behavior. "I am observing within myself increasing degrees of frustration, which are raising the probability that I will inform my boss that I am quitting." This is more accurate than saying "I almost quit my job," and it refers to behavior which, though private, is within the boundaries of scientific analysis.

Drives

From the view of radical behaviorism drives are not causes of behavior, but merely explanatory fictions. To Skinner (1953) drive simply refers to the effects of deprivation and satiation and to the corresponding probability that the organism will respond. To deprive a person of food increases the likelihood of eating; to satiate a person decreases that likelihood. However, deprivation and satiation are not the only correlates of eating. Other factors that increase or decrease the probability of eating are internally observed hunger pangs, availability of food, and previous experiences with food reinforcers.

If drives are defined in terms of intervening states between deprivation and response, then they are unnecessary concepts and have no place in a scientific analysis of behavior. Hypothetically, if we knew enough about the three essentials of behavior (situation, behavior, and consequences), then we would know *why* a person behaves, that is, what drives are related to specific behaviors. At that time drives would have a legitimate role in the scientific study of human behavior. Until then, however, explanations based on fictionalized constructs like drives or needs are merely untestable hypotheses.

Emotions

It would be difficult to convince someone that emotions do not exist. All of us have experienced fear, anger, joy, sorrow, and elation and usually these feelings have been associated with behavior. We strike out when angry, smile when joyful, cry when sad, and shout when elated. Like most people, we probably thought that our actions were caused by our emotions. They were not. Throughout history people have attributed behavior to emotions, but to Skinner, this explanation is not only a waste of time; it also impedes the advancement of scientific analysis. Psychology must be concerned with observable behavior and emotions themselves are not directly observable. Physiological concomitants of emotion, obviously, can be measured, but those data are not the subjectively felt emotion. In fact, the physical changes accompanying fear are quite similar to those of anger and cannot reliably be used to identify the emotion (Skinner, 1953).

When Skinner (1976) wrote about the death of his younger brother (as described in the opening of this chapter), he avoided any account of his own behavior in terms of emotions. He didn't tell us if he was sad, frightened, or confused. He simply described his and others' behavior. It wasn't that he had no feelings, but that feelings are inner behaviors beyond the observation of others.

Skinner, then, does not deny the existence of emotions. He accounts for them by the contingencies of survival and the contingencies of reinforcement. Throughout the millennia individuals most strongly disposed toward fear or anger were those who escaped from or triumphed over danger and thus were able to pass on those characteristics to their offspring. On an individual level, those experiences followed by delight, joy, pleasure, and other pleasant emotions tended to be reinforcing, thereby increasing the probability that they would recur in the life of that person.

Though emotions are subjectively real, Skinner (1974) believes that it is a mistake to attribute behavior to them. To say "She slammed the door because she was angry" makes an inference that is unnecessary and misleading. If one wished to know what contingencies accompany door-slamming behavior, then one must observe the environment, not postulate an internal intermediary cause. The probability of door-slamming behavior can be increased by environmental contingencies such as depriving the person of a certain positive reinforcer or by adding certain aversive stimuli. If anger *caused* people to slam doors, there would be many more broken door jambs in the world!

Purpose and Intention

The concepts of purpose and intention are recognized by Skinner, but again, he would caution against attributing behavior to them. Purpose and intention exist within the skin, but are not subject to direct outside scrutiny (Skinner, 1974).

A felt ongoing purpose may itself be reinforcing. If I believe that my purpose for jogging is to feel better and live longer, then this thought per se acts as a reinforcing stimulus, especially while undergoing the drudgery of running or when trying to explain the reasons for jogging to a nonrunner.

A person may "intend" to see a movie Friday evening because viewing similar films has been reinforcing. At the time the person intends to go to the movie she feels a physical condition within the body and labels it an "intention." What are called intentions or purposes, therefore, are physically felt stimuli within the organism, and not mentalistic events responsible for behavior. "The consequences of operant behavior are not what the behavior is now for; they are merely similar to the consequences that have shaped and maintained it" (Skinner, 1987a, p. 57).

Complex Behavior

Radical behaviorism holds that when a response is followed immediately by either reinforcement or by punishment, the probability of that response recurring is correspondingly increased or decreased. Human behavior, however, is exceedingly complex and these complexities need to be understood if behavior is to be predicted or controlled. Skinner does not deny "higher mental processes" such as cognition, reason, and recall; nor does he ignore other complex human endeavors like creativity, unconscious behavior, dreams, and social behavior. He does, however, warn against attributing these behaviors to functions of the mind.

Higher Mental Processes

Dollard and Miller (Chapter 9) theorized that the higher mental processes can be explained by the same four factors that apply to simple learning, namely, drive, cue, response, and reinforcement. They postulated the concept of cue-producing responses which allow for a series of internal responses or the so-called "train of thought." Skinner also recognizes the various higher mental processes, but he does not include the hypothetical concepts of cues and cue-producing responses and he does not reify the concept of drives.

Human thought, Skinner (1974) admits, is the most difficult of all behaviors to analyze, but potentially, at least, it can be understood so long as one does not resort to such hypothetical fictions as mind or cue-producing responses. His approach to studying higher mental processes is to investigate the contingencies under which they occur. Thinking, problem solving, and reminiscing are covert behaviors that take place within the skin, but not inside the mind. As behavior, they are amenable to the same contingencies of reinforcement as overt behavior. For example, when a woman has misplaced her car keys she searches for them because similar searching behavior has been previously reinforced. In like manner, when she is unable to recall the name of an acquaintance she searches for that name covertly because this type of behavior has earlier been reinforced. However, the acquaintance's name did not exist in her mind any more than did the car keys. Skinner (1974, pp. 109–110) sums up this procedure with the statement: "Techniques of recall are not concerned with searching a storehouse of memory but with increasing the probability of responses."

Problem solving also involves covert behavior and often requires the person to covertly manipulate the relevant variables until the correct solution is found. Ultimately these variables are environmental and do not spring magically from the person's mind. A chess player seems to be hopelessly trapped, surveys the board, and suddenly makes a move that allows his marker to escape. What brought about this unexpected burst of "insight"? He did not solve the problem in his mind. He manipulated the various markers (not by touching them but in covert fashion), rejected moves not accompanied by reinforcement, and finally selected the one that was followed by internal reinforcement. The solution may have been facilitated by his previous experiences of reading a book on chess, listening to expert advice, or playing the game; but it was initiated by environmental contingencies and not manufactured by mental machinations.

Creativity

How does the radical behaviorist account for creativity? Logically, if behavior were nothing other than a predictable response to a stimulus, there would never be novel or creative behavior since only previously reinforced behavior would be emitted. Skinner answers this problem by comparing creative behavior with natural selection in evolutionary theory. "As accidental traits, arising from mutations, are selected by their contribution to survival, so accidental variations in behavior are selected by their reinforcing consequences" (Skinner, 1974, p. 114). Just as natural selection explains differentiation among the species without resorting to an omnipotent creative mind, so behaviorism accounts for novel behavior without recourse to a personal creative mind.

In both natural selection and creative behavior the concept of mutation is crucial. In evolutionary theory the mutations are random, while in reinforcement theory the responses are not technically random, but nevertheless they have the same effect. In both cases, new or accidental conditions are produced that have some possibility of survival. Creative writers change their environment, thus producing responses that have some chance of being reinforced. When their "creativity dries up" they may move to a different location, travel, read, talk to others, put words on paper with little expectancy that they will be the finished product, or try out various words, sentences, and ideas covertly. To Skinner, then, creativity is simply the result of "random" or "accidental" behaviors (overt or covert) that happen to be rewarded. If some people are more creative than others, it is due both to differences in genetic endowment and to experiences that have shaped creative behavior.

Unconscious Behavior

As a radical behaviorist, Skinner cannot accept the notion of unconscious motivation where the unconscious is seen as a storehouse of repressed ideas or emotions. He does, however, accept the idea of unconscious *behavior*. In fact, nearly all behavior is unconscious since the relationship between genetic and environmental variables and one's own behavior is rarely observed by the behaving organism. In this sense, most behavior is the product of unconscious contingencies of reinforcement (Skinner, 1987a).

In a more limited sense, behavior is labeled unconscious when the person, in order to avoid emitting that behavior, no longer thinks about it (Skinner, 1953). Specifically, this refers to behavior that has been suppressed through punishment. Behavior that has aversive consequences has a tendency to be ignored or not thought about. A child repeatedly and severely punished for sexual play may both suppress the sexual behavior and repress any thoughts or memories of such activity. Eventually the child may deny that the sexual activity took place. Such *denial* avoids the aversive aspects connected with thoughts of punishment and is thus a negative reinforcer. In other words, the child is rewarded for *not thinking* about certain sexual behavior.

Repression also takes place when a person avoids certain thoughts or actions by engaging in opposite or competing forms of behavior. For example, a man troubled by problems at home may enmesh himself in work, thereby not only physically avoiding home life but also blocking out any thoughts of it.

A more severe example of not thinking about aversive stimuli is seen in a child who behaves in hateful ways toward her mother. In doing so, she will also exhibit some less antagonistic behaviors. If the loathsome behavior is punished, it will become suppressed and replaced by the more positive behaviors. Eventually the child will be rewarded for gestures of love and these, therefore, will begin to increase in frequency. After a time, her behavior becomes more and more positive and might resemble what Freud would call "reactive love." The child no longer has any thoughts of hatred toward her mother and behaves in an exceedingly loving and subservient manner. Skinner (1953) would account for this "reaction formation" as the effect of contingencies of reinforcement. No unconscious feelings of hatred can be observed, only slightly stilted signs of love.

Dreams

Dreams are not left unaccounted for in Skinner's behavioral analysis. As covert and symbolic forms of behavior, they are subject to the same contingencies of reinforcement as any other behavior. Skinner (1953) agrees with Freud that dreams may serve a wish-fulfillment purpose.

Dream behavior is reinforcing when repressed sexual or aggressive stimuli are allowed expression. To act out sexual fantasies and to actually inflict damage on an enemy are two behaviors likely to be associated with punishment. To even covertly think about these behaviors may also have punitive effects. However, in dreams these behaviors may be expressed symbolically without any accompanying punishment. In fact, there is evidence to suggest that dreams themselves are positively reinforcing. When people are denied an opportunity to dream for several consecutive nights, they will show an increasing need to dream. Dement (1960), using rapid eye movements (REMs) as an indicator of dreaming, demonstrated that people ordinarily dream about four or five times a night, but when deprived of REM sleep, and then given a chance to dream, they not only dream more frequently (as measured by REMs) but also for longer periods. This suggests that dreaming behavior itself is reinforcing to humans.

Social Behavior

It is always the individual who behaves, never the group. Individuals establish groups because it is satisfying to do so. People form clans so that they (individually) might be protected against animals, natural disasters, or enemy tribes. People also form governments, establish churches, or become part of lynch mobs because they are reinforced for that behavior.

The social environment, however, is not always reinforcing. People are sometimes ridiculed, insulted, or physically abused within the context of a group, yet, for many reasons, they continue to remain part of that group. First, because the group consists of several people, the abused person may be receiving positive reinforcement from one or more persons while incurring the punishment from some others. For example, a child abused by the father may be reinforced by family life because of a nurturant mother. This suggests a second possibility for remaining in a group though suffering abuse: The person (in this case, a child) may not possess sufficient means of counter-control and, therefore, can neither change the behavior of other members nor physically flee from the group. Third, reinforcement may occur on an intermittent schedule so that the abuse suffered by the individual is intermingled with occasional reward. If the positive reinforcement is strong enough and occurs on a variable-ratio or variable-interval schedule, then its effects will be more powerful than those of punishment.

Control of Human Behavior

Ultimately, an individual's behavior is controlled by environmental contingencies. Those contingencies may have been erected by society, another individual, or oneself, but it is the environment, not free will, which is responsible for behavior.

Social Control

Individuals act to form social groups because such behavior tends to be reinforcing. Groups, in turn, exercise control over their members by formulating written or unwritten laws, rules, and customs that have physical existence beyond the lives of individuals. The laws of a nation, the rules of an organization, and the customs of a culture transcend any one individual's means of countercontrol and serve as powerful controlling variables in the lives of individual members. In addition, social control includes the influence one individual exercises over another in a one-to-one relationship (Skinner, 1974).

Social forces control our behavior in a nearly infinite variety of ways, but all these techniques can be grouped under the following headings: operant conditioning, describing contingencies, deprivation and satiation, and physical restraint (Skinner, 1953).

Operant Conditioning.   Society exercises control over its members through the four principal methods of operant conditioning: positive reinforcement, negative reinforcement, and the two techniques of punishment (adding an aversive stimulus and removing a positive one). Each of these can be illustrated by observing the controlling techniques available to a fourth-grade teacher.

The teacher shapes the behavior of her students through the use of positive reinforcement when she gives high grades for excellent work, compliments socially desirable behaviors, or awards prizes for perfect attendance. She can also reward acceptable behavior through negative reinforcement. She can shorten the time of detention if the punished student remains silent and gives the appearance of hard work, or she can stop scolding a child when he begins to cry. On the other hand, she can rely on two methods of punishment. She can assign extra work for disobedient behavior, give low grades for poor work, or scold the child for fighting on the playground. Finally, there is available to her the removal of positive reinforcers. She can rearrange seating so that a very talkative child can no longer sit next to a friend or she can revoke a child's special privileges when the child abuses them.

In all examples, the teacher makes reward or punishment contingent on the behavior of the child. The effectiveness of each technique depends on the consistency with which it is employed, the individual student's genetic makeup and personal history of reinforcement, and the existence of any other conflicting modes of behavioral control.

Describing Contingencies.   A second technique of social control is to describe to a person the contingencies of reinforcement. This is different from arranging contingencies, a procedure crucial to operant conditioning. Describing contingencies involves language, usually verbal, where the controlled person is made aware of the consequences of not-yet-emitted personal behavior.

There are many examples of describing contingencies. Motorists are warned to watch out for ice on the next bridge. "Look out below," warns a construction worker after dropping a hammer. Threats are also a means of describing contingencies. "If you don't buy me a gift for my birthday, I will divorce you." Advertising is another method of control through describing contingencies. "Invest your money with our bank and receive the highest rate of interest allowed by law." "Use our brand of toothpaste and you will improve your love life." In none of these examples will the attempt at control be perfectly successful, yet with each of them there is an increased likelihood that the desired response will be emitted. Also, none of these attempts is designed to change a person's "mind," but rather to alter the environment.

Deprivation and Satiation.   Behavior can also be controlled either by depriving people or by satiating them with reinforcers. Again, even though deprivation and satiation are internal states, the control originates with the environment. Deprived individuals are more likely to respond in ways designed to alleviate deprivation. When children have no appetite at mealtime, the chances of them eating dinner will be increased if they are deprived of snacks between meals. A sailor deprived for long periods of physical love is more likely to respond with sexual behavior when the opportunity arises.

Satiating a person is also a means of control. A satiated person is less likely to respond with behavior that is undesirable to the controlling person. A parent can diminish, at least temporarily, the likelihood that children will nag by giving them many interesting toys. A government can decrease the chances that its citizens will revolt by establishing generous social welfare programs. In the long run, social control through satiation has the obvious disadvantage of cost to the controller and therefore is likely to be used only by those who can afford those costs.

Physical Restraint.   Another example of social control involves physically restraining individuals so that they cannot behave in a particular manner. We erect fences to keep others from trespassing on our property; society builds prisons to restrain criminals; and we hold back a child who plays near a deep ravine. Physical restraint acts to counter the effects of conditioning and results in behavior contrary to that which would have been emitted had the person not been restrained.

At first glance it appears that physical restraint is a means of denying an individual's freedom. However, Skinner (1971) does not recognize personal freedom, holding that all behavior is shaped by the contingencies of survival, the effects of reinforcement, and the contingencies of the social environment. Therefore, the act of physically restraining a person does no more to negate freedom than any other technique of control, including self-control.

Self-Control

If personal freedom is a fiction, then is not self-control also a myth? Does not self-control depend on one's ability to make a free choice? Skinner would

Physical restraint is one means of social control.

answer in the negative. Just as one person can alter the variables in another's environment, one can also manipulate variables within one's own environment, thus exercising some measure of self-control. The contingencies of self-control, however, do not reside within the individual and cannot be freely chosen by the person. When people control their own behavior, they do so by the same techniques they would use in controlling someone else's behavior and ultimately these variables lie outside the organism.

How does one manipulate outside variables so that these variables in turn will shape one's own behavior? Skinner (1953) and Skinner and Vaughan (1983) point to several techniques, some of which are also used in social control.

Physical restraint is used not only in social control but also for self-control. It is physically impossible to hold oneself back so that one will not behave in an undesirable way. Nevertheless, it is quite possible to arrange environmental contingencies so that these contingencies will restrict behavior. An angry person can clench his teeth to prevent himself from speaking inappropriately. A dieting person can ask a friend to hold the money as they walk through the candy store.

Self-control can also be produced through the use of *physical aids* such as tools, machines, and financial resources. A carpenter speeds work by using powered equipment; a shopper increases the likelihood of spontaneous purchases by bringing enough money.

Another means of self-control is *changing the stimulus,* thereby increasing the probability of the desired behavior. Students wishing to concentrate on studies can turn off a distracting television set. People desiring to stop smoking may no longer carry cigarettes with them. A person who wishes to call a friend more frequently can tape the telephone number some place where it will be frequently seen. All these techniques involve the manipulation of environmental variables, which increases the probability that one's own behavior will be changed.

Earlier, we saw that social control could be exercised through depriving or satiating another person. Similarly, self-control can be produced with the same procedures. Athletes are often advised to abstain from sex prior to an important competition. (Incidentally, there is little evidence to suggest that this form of *self-deprivation* is successful.)

Satiation is probably a more effective means of self-control than it is social control, because in the latter situation the controller must possess nearly unlimited assets. Self-satiation can utilize smaller quantities of resources. A smoker chews gum to satiate an oral craving and thereby reduces the likelihood of lighting a cigarette. An alcoholic constantly sips on soft drinks to keep from drinking liquor. A worker labors hard so that exhaustion will facilitate sleep. Note again that self-control is not dependent on free will, but on altering environmental variables.

Another technique of self-control is to arrange the environment so that one can escape from *aversive stimulation* only by producing the proper response. Skinner (1953) uses the illustration of setting an alarm clock so that the aversive sound can be stopped only by getting up to shut off the alarm. Dieters weigh themselves daily and frequently view their reflection in the mirror to produce an undesirable image that can be avoided only by losing weight. Self-commands are also examples of using aversive stimulation. A golfer hits a bad shot and responds with a personally insulting name. A prowler hears the sound of someone approaching and says, "I'm getting out of here." Verbal commands like these are aversive stimuli and, therefore, a means of self-control.

Skinner (1953) also listed *drugs,* especially alcohol, as a frequent means of self-control. Tranquilizers are ingested to make one's behavior more placid. A disgruntled employee takes several drinks, knowing that this will increase the chances of telling off the boss. A drug addict injects heroin to prevent withdrawal discomfort. Nicotine is smoked to induce relaxation. Examples of self-control through the use of drugs can be expanded almost endlessly.

The technique of *doing something else* is used solely with self-control and cannot be applied to social control. We do something else in order to avoid behaving undesirably. This procedure is effective only if the substitute behavior is prepotent, that is, more powerful than the unwanted behavior. An obsessive neurotic counts repetitious patterns in wallpaper to avoid thinking about earlier guilt-laden experiences. A person tempted to behave sexually goes jogging instead. In these examples counting patterns and jogging attain prepotency over guilt-ridden thoughts and sexual activity because of the aversive stimuli associated with the latter two responses. The substitute behaviors are therefore negatively reinforcing, permitting the person to avoid unpleasant thoughts.

THE UNHEALTHY PERSONALITY

Unfortunately the techniques of social control and self-control sometimes produce detrimental effects, which result in inappropriate behavior and unhealthy personality development. When social control is excessive there are three basic strategies for counteracting it: The individual can escape, revolt, or use passive resistance (Skinner, 1953).

Counteracting Strategies

With the defensive strategy of *escape,* a person withdraws from the controlling agent either physically or psychologically. Since the original controlling agent is ordinarily the parents, and very young children have little means of running away from home, a frequent mode of escape is to psychologically withdraw from parents and later to seclude oneself from society. People whose behavior is characterized by escape find it difficult to become involved in intimate personal relationships, tend to be mistrustful of people, and prefer to live lonely lives of noninvolvement.

People who *revolt* against society's controls behave more actively, counterattacking the controlling agent. Children oppose their parents' control by openly defying their authority, or more indirectly, by writing on the walls and mistreating the furniture. Older people rebel through public vandalism, tormenting teachers, verbally abusing others, pilfering equipment from employers, provoking the police, or overthrowing established organizations such as religions or governments.

Those who counteract control through *passive resistance* are more subtle than the rebels and more irritating to the controllers than those who utilize escape. Skinner believes that passive resistance is most likely to be employed where escape and revolt have failed. The conspicuous feature of this strategy is stubbornness. A child with homework to do finds a dozen excuses why it cannot be finished; then, after completing it, the child still makes a failing grade. The employee slows down progress by undermining the work of others, and the husband allows important chores to pile up by staying busy with trifles.

Inappropriate Behaviors

Inappropriate behaviors follow from self-defeating techniques of counteracting social control or from unsuccessful attempts at self-control, especially when either of these failures is accompanied by strong emotion. Like all behavior, inappropriate or unhealthy responses are learned. They are shaped

Walden Two—Utopia or Tedium?

If it is inevitable that human behavior will be shaped by the environment, then why not design a culture that will mold behavior in the most favorable manner possible? This, of course, was Skinner's prime motivation in writing *Walden Two* (1948). In the summer of 1945, as World War II was coming to a close, Skinner decided to create a society that would give returning soldiers a model for the "good life" after the war. He was at a point in his personal life when he needed self-therapy, and the writing of *Walden Two* filled that need. The book's principal characters, Frazier and Burris, represent Skinner's attempts to reconcile two aspects of his own personality (Skinner, 1967). But the ultimate importance of *Walden Two* is in its blueprint for a utopian society, based on Skinner's experimental analysis of behavior.

Briefly, the book is an account of a fictional rural community, Walden Two, where about 1000 people are living the "good life" in a deliberately controlled society. The community has been established by the book's protagonist, T. E. Frazier, and none of its inhabitants have to be coerced into living there. In Walden Two the people work only four hours a day, the children are well cared for, food is plentiful, medical care is excellent, and music, art, and literature flourish. Indeed, this must be the "good life."

Some people, however, have questioned the desirability of residing in Walden Two. Some of the most frequent criticisms of a behaviorally engineered society are (1) the citizens would have no individual freedom, (2) there would be no one to control the controllers, (3) there would be little motivation to achieve since the environment rather than the person is

credited with accomplishments, and (4) even if such a society were feasible, there would be reluctance to live in such a dull, antiseptic environment. Skinner (1969) has responded to each of these criticisms as follows:

First, he would insist that people are not free anyway, if by freedom one means free from the restraints of environmental contingencies. If, on the other hand, one defines freedom as the opportunity to live in a culture that maximizes positive reinforcers and minimizes punishment, then the people of Walden Two would enjoy more freedom than others. According to Skinner (1969), they would also be free to behave in ways that would change the society so that it could meet emergencies and survive into the future.

At present, people act as if freedom exists and they behave as if they are pursuing freedom. Fictional freedom is a powerful incentive for most contemporary people. However, in a well-designed society people could enjoy the "good life," which is, after all, the goal of those now seeking freedom. "The problem, in short, is not to design a way of life which will be liked by men *as they now are,* but a way of life which will be liked by those who live it" (Skinner, 1969, p. 41).

Second, Skinner would note that in our current culture we daily see misuse of power and therefore understandably distrust those who possess it. Skinner obviously was concerned with this problem when he wrote *Walden Two* because he imbued Frazier, the founder, with "negative charisma" and had him abdicate any position of authority. In Walden Two, as in any society, leaders are themselves controlled through the use of countercontrol. The principal difference is that in Walden Two measures of countercontrol are specifically designed into the community so that there is no reward for flagrant abuse of authority.

Third, Skinner would respond that currently we admire people who apparently behave for the good of society rather than for self-interest. They are especially commended when it seems that they were not forced to act for the good of the whole. What happens to personal credit in a behaviorally engineered society? The fact that personal credit is a positively valued commodity reflects an evolutionary history of haphazard control. It now seems necessary to attribute personal credit to individuals in order to assure the survival of the species. In a well-designed society, however, contrived or artificial reinforcers could be minimized. Personal credit would no longer have any positive value; people would be reinforced by natural contingencies such as food, sex, art, music, literature, and friendship.

Skinner (1969) responds to the fourth criticism by saying that people who complain that Walden Two is too well designed, with too little spontaneity, are themselves the product of their own culture. Such people, Skinner says, blindly fear anything that might be better than what they are accustomed to. They are compared to children who say "I'm glad I don't like broccoli because if I liked it, I'd eat a lot of it, and I hate it" (Skinner, 1969, p. 42).

by the contingencies of positive and negative reinforcement and especially by the effects of punishment.

Obviously, inappropriate behavior takes many forms and Skinner (1953) lists several of the more common patterns along with their reinforcement contingencies. The first of these is taking *drugs*. The effects of alcohol and other drugs are reinforcing because they enable the person to avoid aversive stimuli, but their long-term consequences may be detrimental, leading to dependence or to a chronic mode of escape from the problems of everyday life.

Another inappropriate pattern is *excessively vigorous behavior,* which makes no sense in terms of the contemporary situation, but might be reasonable in terms of past history. Excessively vigorous behavior may stem from repression or reaction formation and is likely to manifest itself as extreme restlessness, perseveration, or a compulsive tendency to repeat a response. An opposite pattern is *excessively restrained behavior,* a pattern which develops out of a history of punishment. The individual learns responses that avoid the aversive stimuli associated with punishment and these responses frequently take passive forms like shyness, stubbornness, inhibition, or hysterical paralysis.

Another type of inappropriate behavior is simply *blocking out reality.* This is similar to Sullivan's concept of selective inattention (see Chapter 6), in which the person pays no attention to aversive stimuli like a nagging spouse or the punitive thoughts associated with an earlier guilt-producing experience.

A fifth form of undesirable behavior listed by Skinner reflects *defective self-knowledge* and is manifested in such self-deluding responses as boasting, rationalizing, or believing oneself to be Jesus Christ or Julius Caesar. This pattern is usually an unsuccessful attempt at self-control and continues to be reinforcing because the person avoids the aversive stimulation associated with thoughts of inadequacy.

A final detrimental effect of control on behavior is *aversive self-stimulation,* exemplified by self-punishment or the arrangement of environmental variables so that one is punished by others. How can this "masochistic" behavior be rewarding? There are several possibilities. First, aversive self-stimulation may permit the person to avoid even more painful stimuli as when a soldier shoots himself in the foot in order to escape battle. Also, masochistic behavior is negatively reinforcing when it avoids the aversive conditions of guilt or sin by inflicting "deserved" punishment on the person. Finally, self-punishment can be learned through respondent conditioning. When an aversive stimulus (pain) is paired with a strong reward (sex), the pleasure may override the pain so that the entire event (sexual pleasure coupled with pain) becomes reinforcing and, in some cases, the aversive stimulus (pain) may become, by itself, reinforcing. As a result, a person gains enjoyment from pain inflicted by self or others.

You have probably recognized that most of these inappropriate patterns are behavioral descriptions of several Freudian defense mechanisms (repression, regression, reaction formation), Adlerian safeguarding tendencies (excuses, aggression, withdrawl), as well as Sullivan's notion of selective inattention. While the psychodynamic theorists view these behaviors as totally or partially motivated by unconscious urges within the person, Skinner sees them simply as overt behaviors shaped by the environmental contingencies of reward and punishment. Whereas the older theorists would see these mechanisms as expressing some hidden purpose of the individual, the radical behaviorist attributes no special purpose to them other than the avoidance of aversive stimulation and the attainment of positive reinforcement.

PSYCHOTHERAPY

Skinner (1987b) believes that psychotherapy is one of the chief obstacles blocking psychology's attempt to become scientific. Nevertheless, his ideas on the shaping of behavior (both "neurotic" and "therapeutic") have had a significant impact on the current behavior therapy movement. However, his notions on treatment are not limited to the approach called behavior therapy, but extend to a description of how *all* therapy works.

The therapist, whether psychoanalytic, client-centered, or behavioral, is a controlling agent. Not all controlling agents, however, are harmful and the patient must learn to discriminate between punitive authority figures (both past and present) and the permissive therapist who dispenses positive reinforcers. Where the parent was cold and rejecting, the therapist is warm and accepting; where the parent was critical and judgmental, the therapist is supportive and empathic. The shaping of any behavior takes time and therapeutic behavior is no exception. The therapist molds desirable behavior by reinforcing slightly improved changes in behavior. The nonbehavioral therapist may do this accidentally or unknowingly, while the behavioral therapist attends specifically to this technique (Skinner, 1953).

Traditional therapists generally explain behaviors by resorting to a variety of fictional constructs such as the Oedipus complex, strivings for superiority, collective unconscious, approach-avoidance conflicts, and self-actualization needs. Skinner, however, believes that the psychotherapist should work on the assumption that fantasies, slips of the tongue, defensive mechanisms, safeguarding tendencies, and so on are behaviors that can be accounted for by learning principles. No explanatory fictions or inner causes are needed to explain "neurotic" or inappropriate behavior and no therapeutic purpose is enhanced by postulating them. Skinner reasons that if behavior is shaped by inner causes, then some force must be responsible for the inner cause. Traditional theories must ultimately account for this cause, but behavior therapy merely skips it and deals directly with the history of the organism; and it is this history which, in the final analysis, is responsible for any hypothetical inner cause.

A variety of techniques have been developed by behavioral therapists over the years, most based on operant conditioning, though some are built around the principles of respondent conditioning. In general, behavior therapists play an active role in the treatment process. They point out to the patient the positive consequences of certain behaviors and the aversive effects of others and they also suggest behaviors which, over the long haul, will result in positive reinforcement. More specifically, behavioral therapists suppress inappropriate behaviors such as phobias by a technique called **systematic desensitization** (Wolpe, 1973); they teach assertiveness training (Rimm & Masters, 1979); and they employ a variety of techniques for preventing problems and enhancing positive behaviors (Krumboltz & Thoresen, 1976). The interested reader may wish to consult these or other sources for a more detailed account of behavior therapy techniques.

CONCEPT OF HUMANITY

There can be no doubt that B. F. Skinner has a *deterministic view* of human nature. Concepts like free will and individual choice have no place in his thinking. People are not free, but are controlled by environmental forces, and, when it appears that they are motivated by inner causes, closer examination reveals that those causes can be traced to sources outside the individual. Self-control depends ultimately on environmental variables and not on some inner strength. When people control their own lives, they do so by manipulating their environment which, in turn, shapes their behavior. Therefore, it is unnecessary to postulate any hypothetical constructs such as will power or responsibility. Human behavior can be perfectly predicted if all genetic and environmental factors are known. At the present stage of the science of human behavior, of course, these factors are not completely known. Human behavior is extremely complex, but people behave under many of the same laws as do machines and animals.

The notion that human behavior is completely determined is an extremely problematic one for many people who believe that they observe daily many examples of free choice in both themselves and others. What accounts for this illusion of freedom? Skinner (1971) holds that freedom and dignity are reinforcing concepts because people tend to find satisfaction in the belief that they are free to choose and also in their faith in the basic dignity of the human being. Since these fictional concepts are reinforcing in many modern societies, people tend to behave in ways that increase the probability that these constructs will be perpetuated. Once freedom and dignity lose their reinforcement value, people will stop behaving *as if* they existed.

There is no spontaneous generation of behavior any more than there was a spontaneous generation of maggots on dead animals in the days preceding Pasteur (Skinner, 1974, p. 54). If behavior appears to be free, haphazard, or random, it is only because the environmental and genetic conditions are not conspicuous, and behavior is therefore not readily predictable. In other words, people are not autonomous, but the illusion of autonomy persists because of our ignorance of the individual's history. We attribute free will to humanity simply because we do not take the time to understand behavior. Every action we fail to understand we assign to some internal concept such as beliefs, intentions, values, or motives. Skinner does not deny that people are capable of reflecting upon their own nature, but he insists that this reflective behavior can be observed and studied just like any other.

Is Skinner's concept of humanity *optimistic or pessimistic?* At first thought, it may appear that a deterministic stance is necessarily pessimistic. However, Skinner's view of human nature tends, if anything, to be somewhat optimistic. Since human behavior is shaped by the principles of reinforcement, the species is quite adaptable. Of all behaviors, the most satisfying ones tend to increase in frequency of occurrence. People, therefore, learn to live quite harmoniously with their environment. The evolution of the species is in the direction of greater control over environmental variables. This results in an increasing repertoire of behaviors beyond those essential for mere survival. However, Skinner (1987a) is also concerned that present cultural practices have not yet evolved to the point where nuclear war, overpopulation, and depletion of natural resources can be stopped. In this sense, he is more of a realist than an optimist.

Nevertheless, he has provided a blueprint for a utopian society (see *Walden Two,* Skinner, 1948). If his recommendations were followed, then people could be taught how to arrange the variables in their environments so that the probability of correct or satisfying solutions would be increased. Skinner has long been interested in improving humanity and his efforts with the baby tender and with teaching machines are but two examples of this interest.

Is humanity basically good or evil? Skinner hopes for an idealistic society where people behave in ways that are loving, sensible, democratic, independent, and good, but people are not by nature this way. But neither are they essentially evil. Within limits set by heredity, people are flexible in their adaptation to the environment, but no evaluation of good or evil should be placed on an individual's behavior. If a person typically behaves altruistically for the good of others, it is because this behavior, either in the species' evolutionary history or in the individual's personal history, has been previously reinforced. If one behaves cowardly, it is because the rewards for cowardice outweigh the aversive variables (Skinner, 1978).

On the dimension of *causality vs. teleology* Skinner's theory of personality is very high on causality. Behavior is caused by the person's history of reinforcement as well as by the species' contingencies for survival and the evolution of cultures. Though people behave covertly (within the skin) to think about the future, all those thoughts are determined by past experiences.

The complex of environmental contingencies responsible for these thoughts, as well as for all other behaviors, are beyond our awareness. We rarely have knowledge of the relationship between all genetic and environmental variables and our own behavior. For this reason Skinner would be placed very high on the *unconscious dimension of personality.*

The history of the person determines behavior, and because all of us have our own histories of reinforcement contingencies, behavior and personality are relatively unique. Genetic differences also account for *uniqueness among people.* Biological and historical differences make us unique individuals, and Skinner emphasizes those differences more than he does our similarities.

Though he believes that genetics play an important role in personality development, Skinner holds that human personality is largely shaped by the environment. Since an important part of that environment is other people, Skinner's concept of humanity inclines more toward social than toward biological determinants of behavior. As a species, *Homo sapiens* has developed to its present form because of particular environmental factors with which it has interacted. Climate, geography, and strength relative to other animals have all helped shape the species. But the *social environment,* including family structures, early experiences with parents, educational systems, governmental organization, and so forth, have played an even more important role in development of personality.

Skinner would wish for people to be trustworthy, understanding, warm, and empathic, characteristics which his friendly adversary Carl Rogers (see Chapter 17) believed to be at the core of the psychologically healthy personality. While Rogers believed that these positive behaviors, to some extent, are the result of our capacity to be self-directed, Skinner holds that they are completely under the control of environmental variables. We are not by nature good, but we can become so if we are exposed to the proper contingencies of reinforcement. Although his view of the ideal person would be similar to those of Rogers and Abraham H. Maslow (see Chapter 16), Skinner believes that the means of becoming autonomous, loving, and self-actualizing must not be left to chance, but should be specifically designed into the society.

CRITIQUE OF SKINNER

Except for Freud's psychoanalysis, the radical behaviorism of B. F. Skinner is the most maligned, criticized, and condemned personality theory of the twentieth century. It has been blamed, by one source or another, for nearly every ill facing society today—the failure of our educational system, the dehumanization of psychology, and even political assassination (Skinner, 1971). Many worry that Skinner's view of utopia would include a citizenry of automatons under strict control of a not-too-benevolent dictator. All such views of radical behaviorism, of course, are grossly in error and miss the fundamental point of Skinner's writings, namely that human behavior is not different in kind from any other observable phenomena and can therefore be scientifically studied and predicted.

As a scientific theory, Skinner's view of personality must be evaluated by the same criteria used to assess all other theories. First, how well does it *organize all that is known about human personality?* On this criterion the theory must receive only a moderate rating. Skinner's approach is to describe behavior and the environmental contingencies under which it takes place. His purpose is to bring together these descriptive facts and to generalize from them. Many personality traits can be accounted for by the principles of operant conditioning and Skinner even offers explanations for such human characteristics as defense mechanisms, neurotic reactions, altruistic behaviors, and dreams. To date, however, many of these explanations have yet to be fully developed. In addition, other concepts such as insight, creativity, motivation, inspiration, and self-concept do not fit easily into an operant-conditioning framework.

A second criterion of a useful theory is that it should *generate research.* Neither Skinner nor his disciples have conducted much research designed specifically to test hypotheses drawn from his theory of personality. Indeed, Skinner is opposed to hypothetico-deductive systems and the testing of fabricated hypotheses. On the other hand, the quantity of descriptive research generated by Skinner's ideas is exceeded in the arena of personality theory only by investigations of Freud's psychoanalytic concepts.

The abundance of descriptive research turned out by Skinner and his followers has made operant conditioning an extremely practical procedure. For example, Skinnerian techniques have been applied to programmed instruction and teaching machines, training mentally retarded children to speak and dress themselves, conditioning phobic patients to overcome their fears, and various self-improvement procedures such as giving up cigarettes, assertiveness training, or going on a diet. In fact, there are few areas of training, teaching, or psychotherapy where Skinnerian theory cannot be applied. As a *guide to action,* therefore, the theory must be evaluated very highly.

The fourth criterion of a useful theory is *internal consistency* and, judged by this standard, Skinnerian theory again would be rated very high. Terms are defined operationally, a process greatly aided by the avoidance of fictionalized mentalistic concepts. Skinner defines his terms precisely and his scientific attitude results in a theory that not only possesses internal consistency but also is consistent with data gathered from laboratory research.

Is the theory *parsimonious?* On this final criterion Skinner's theory is difficult to rate. On the one hand, it is free from cumbersome hypothetical constructs, but, on the other hand, it demands a novel expression of everyday phrases. For example, instead of saying, "I got so mad at my husband, I threw a dish at him, but missed," one would need to say, "The contingencies of reinforcement within my environment were arranged in such a manner that I observed my organism throwing a dish against the kitchen wall."

CHAPTER SUMMARY

As a radical behaviorist, B. F. Skinner avoids all hypothetical concepts such as mind or personality and bases his concept of humanity solely on observable behavior. Although most of his observations were made on rats and pigeons, Skinner believes that these observations can be generalized to human behavior. Rather than testing hypotheses, Skinner has simply observed behavior for the purpose of describing, predicting, and controlling it. His philosophy of science permits the interpretation of behavior, but not an explanation of its causes.

Although Skinner recognizes the existence of inner states such as thinking and feeling, he insists that they are beyond the realm of behavioral analysis. Thoughts and feelings can be observed by the individual, but only overt behavior can be studied by the scientist.

Human behavior, Skinner believes, is shaped by three forces: the individual's personal history of *reinforcement, natural selection,* and the *evolution of cultural practices.* Skinner's views on natural selection and cultural evolution are based largely on speculation, while his ideas on reinforcement are founded on his laboratory work on *operant conditioning.* In operant conditioning, reinforcement (or punishment) is contingent upon the occurrence of a particular behavior.

There are two types of reinforcement— positive and negative. A *positive reinforcer* is any event which, when added to a situation, increases the probability that a given behavior will occur. *Negative reinforcement* also increases the probability of a given behavior, and refers to the removal of an aversive stimulus. Similarly, there are two types of *punishment;* the first is the presentation of an aversive stimulus and the second involves the removal of a positive stimulus. The effects of reinforcement are more predictable than those of punishment.

Reinforcement can be either *continuous* or *intermittent,* but intermittent schedules are more efficient. The four principal intermittent *schedules of reinforcement* are the *fixed-ratio,* where the organism is reinforced after a predetermined number of responses; the *variable-ratio,* where reinforcement occurs after every *n*th response on the average; the *fixed-interval,* where reinforcement occurs according to a designated period of time; and the *variable-interval,* where reinforcement occurs after a lapse of random or variable periods of time.

Skinner offers several means by which human behavior is controlled. The first is *social control,* where another person, a group, a society, or a nation shapes an individual's behavior. This is accomplished through (1) operant conditioning, (2) describing the contingencies of reinforcement, (3) depriving or satiating a person, or (4) physically restraining the individual. People can also control their own behavior through *self-control,* but all control ultimately rests with the environment. Self-control, therefore, is not a function of free will.

Unhealthy behaviors are learned in the same way as any other behaviors, that is, mostly through operant conditioning. In order to change unhealthy behaviors many behavior therapists have employed a multitude of techniques based on the principles of operant conditioning.

In his concept of humanity Skinner can be regarded as a *determinist* and an *environmentalist.* As a determinist he rejects the notion of free choice and insists that all behavior is lawfully determined and potentially, at least, can be perfectly predicted and controlled. As an environmentalist he de-emphasizes anatomy and stresses the environment, including natural selection, as the final shaper of human behavior.

Skinner's behavioral analysis has generated volumes of research, most of it descriptive rather than hypothesis testing. The theory also receives high marks for being internally consistent and for guiding the practitioner. However, it is only moderately successful in organizing all that we currently know about human behavior.

Suggested Readings

MINDESS, H. (1988). The denial of personality. In H. Mindess, *Makers of psychology: The personal factor* (pp. 84–109). New York: Insight Books.

An interesting and readable chapter on the life of Skinner, a man Mindess calls "the personality that denies personality."

SKINNER, B. F. (1953). *Science and human behavior.* New York: Macmillan.

Skinner's first and most complete work on the science of *human* rather than animal behavior, this book provides a comprehensive foundation for the scientific analysis of behavior.

SKINNER, B. F. (1971). *Beyond freedom and dignity.* New York: Knopf.

In this, his most controversial book, Skinner argues that the concepts of freedom and dignity are detrimental to the building of an effective society. *Beyond Freedom and Dignity* was on nearly every bestseller list in 1971.

SKINNER, B. F. (1974). *About behaviorism.* New York: Knopf.

Skinner defines, analyzes, and defends behaviorism. In his introduction he presents twenty commonly held beliefs about behaviorism, all of which, he believes, are wrong.

SKINNER, B. F. (1987). *Upon further reflection.* Englewood Cliffs, NJ: Prentice-Hall.

A collection of Skinner's later works, this brief book challenges the reader in such areas as survival of the world, the importance of cultural evolution, and cognitive science. Also included is a chapter updating *Walden Two.*

ROTTER

Social Learning Theory

As a senior majoring in psychology, Gerry has been trying to decide about her future. Since her freshman year she has wanted to get a Ph.D. in clinical psychology and has worked hard to maintain a high grade point average throughout her college career. She has already been accepted by several graduate schools, but has yet to apply to any of the three prestigious schools she would really like to attend.

Moreover, her uncle in another state has told her that after she graduates she can have a potentially high-paying position as an advertising salesperson for his independent telephone-book publishing company. In addition, Chuck, her boyfriend of several years, wants her to marry him but he is not willing to move out of state with her.

Gerry is not too worried about her ability to do graduate-level work at any of the schools that have already accepted her. However, she is less confident in her ability to complete a Ph.D. program in the more prestigious schools. In fact, her reluctance to even apply to these schools reflects not only a fear of being rejected but also of being accepted—and then failing.

In the past Gerry has been able to reach most of her goals, academic as well as nonacademic. In high school she tried out for the tennis team and made it. In college she joined the staff of the school paper and worked her way up to editor by her junior year.

Although her failures have been few, she has nearly always taken responsibility for them. When she was not chosen for a lucrative and highly prestigious scholarship, she did not blame the selection committee or attribute her loss to luck or fate. She realized that very few students could be accepted and that her scholastic record was not as good as those of the people selected.

Now Gerry is at a crucial point in her life. She is undecided about applying to the most prestigious graduate schools. Would she be accepted? Could she succeed? Should she attend one of the regional universities that has already accepted her? How about her uncle's offer? What about Chuck?

What will Gerry do? Can her behavior be predicted? What factors should be considered in such a prediction?

OVERVIEW

The social learning theory of Julian B. Rotter attempts to answer questions such as those raised by Gerry's situation. Rotter's personality theory represents an attempt to pull together reinforcement theories on the one hand, and cognitive theories on the other. As a learning theory, it is a sharp departure from both the radical behaviorism of Skinner and the classical learning theory of Dollard and Miller. Rotter objects to Skinner's notion that reinforcement takes place automatically, without any intermediary agent reacting to the reinforcement. He believes that *cognitive* factors at least partially determine how environmental contingencies will be perceived. He also departs from Skinner in his emphasis on *social* aspects of learning.

Unlike Dollard and Miller, Rotter has not evolved a theory with a Freudian inclination; rather, his theory shows the imprint of Alfred Adler. Goals and social relations are more important than drive reduction and conflict; unity of personality is stressed more than separate drives; and people are basically motivated not to reduce tensions but to achieve future rewards. Rotter, then, believes that reinforcements are maximized when behavior is seen as moving the person in the direction of a goal. His theory is *future-oriented,* allowing for the person's *expectations* of future events.

Rotter also differs from Dollard and Miller and from Skinner in his insistence that an adequate theory of human personality must be built on a *study of humans* and not extrapolated from animal studies. People are capable of cognitively and purposefully acting upon their environments and do not merely react passively to them.

BIOGRAPHY OF JULIAN ROTTER

Julian B. Rotter was born in Brooklyn, New York, on October 22, 1916, the third son of Jewish immigrant parents. As an elementary school and high school student he was an avid reader and by his junior year had read nearly every book of fiction in the local library. That being the case, he turned one day to the psychology shelves where he found Adler's *Understanding Human Nature,* Freud's *Psychopathology of Everyday Life,* and Karl Menninger's *Human Mind.* He was particularly impressed by Adler and Freud and soon returned for more (Rotter, 1982).

By the time he entered Brooklyn College he was seriously interested in psychology, but curiously, did not major in it. By his own account, he chose chemistry because it seemed to be a more employable degree during the Depression of the 1930s. As a junior at Brooklyn College, he learned that Adler was, at the time, professor of medical psychology at Long Island College of Medicine, and he attended Adler's medical lectures and several of his clinical demonstrations. Eventually, he came to know Adler personally and was invited to attend meetings of the Society for Individual Psychology in Adler's home.

When he graduated from Brooklyn College in 1937, Rotter had accumulated more credits in psychology than in chemistry and gave little consideration to a career in chemistry. Instead, he entered graduate school in psychology at the University of Iowa. Solomon Asch at Brooklyn College had awakened in him an interest in Kurt Lewin's field theory; thus Rotter journeyed to Iowa to study with Lewin.

After receiving the master's degree in psychology from Iowa in 1938, he completed an internship in clinical psychology at Worcester State Hospital in Massachusetts. There he met Clara Barnes who later became his wife. Next, Rotter went to the University of Indiana from which he received the Ph.D. in clinical psychology in 1941. At Indiana he came under the influence of J. R. Kantor, who furthered his understanding of philosophy of science and theory building that had begun under Herbert Feigl at Iowa.

In 1941 Rotter accepted a position as clinical psychologist at Norwich State Hospital in Connecticut. Part of his duties consisted of training interns and assistants from the University of Connecticut and Wesleyan University. This work, which was his first real teaching experience, was interrupted in 1942 when he was drafted into the United States Army, where he spent more than three years as a psychologist. After the war he returned briefly to Norwich and then took his first academic position at Ohio State University.

The years at Ohio State were productive ones for Rotter. He attracted a number of outstanding graduate students, evolved a theory of personality, and published the original formulations of that theory in *Social Learning and Clinical Psychology* (1954). When George A. Kelly (see Chapter 15) gave up the directorship of the Psychological Clinic at Ohio State, Rotter became director, a position that increased his sphere of influence.

Wanting to return to New England and unhappy with the political effects of McCarthyism in Ohio, he took a position at the University of Connecticut in 1963, where he served as professor of psychology and director of the Clinical Psychology Training Program.

Rotter's early contributions to personality theory were unique because they combined the scientific rigor of learning theory with the human-oriented experiences of clinical psychology. He has been influenced not only by Adler, Thorndike, Hull, Kantor, and Lewin but also by his colleagues and students. Following Lewin, the field theorist, he views the person as interacting with the psychological environment or field and believes that mathematical formulas can, at least hypothetically, predict outcomes of that interaction.

Among Rotter's publications are *Social Learning and Clinical Psychology* (1954); *Clinical Psychology* (1964); *Applications of a Social Learning Theory of Personality,* with J. E. Chance and E. J. Phares (1972); *Personality,* with D. J. Hochreich (1975); *The Development and Application of Social Learning Theory: Selected Papers* (1982); the Rotter

Incomplete Sentences Blank (Rotter, 1966); and the Interpersonal Trust Scale (Rotter, 1967). Rotter has been active in professional organizations, having served as president of the Eastern Psychological Association and the divisions of Social and Personality Psychology and Clinical Psychology of the American Psychological Association. He has also served two terms on the APA Education and Training Board. In 1988 he received the prestigious APA Distinguished Scientific Contribution Award. He and his wife have two children and live in Storrs, Connecticut.

BASIC ASSUMPTIONS

Rotter's social learning theory is predicated on several basic postulates or assumptions. First, prediction of human behavior rests on an understanding of the *interaction* of people with their meaningful environments (Rotter, 1982). People do not react equally to every element in their environment; rather their reactions depend on the meaning or importance they attach to an event. Perception and cognition, then, are key concepts in Rotter's theory. How people perceive their environments is shaped both by individual history and by one's expectations of future events.

As an interactionist, Rotter holds that neither the environment itself nor the individual is responsible for behavior. In this respect he differs from Skinner, who believes that reinforcement ultimately stems from within the environment. To Rotter, reinforcements are not solely dependent on external stimuli, but are given meaning by the individual's cognitive capacity. Likewise, personal characteristics such as needs or traits cannot, by themselves, cause behavior. Rather environmental and personal factors in interaction provide the best predictor of human behavior. Take for instance Gerry, our case study. Her past experience of reinforcement for academic work is not, by itself, sufficient motivation to apply to graduate school, but it interacts with her present belief or expectation that she will be successful.

A second assumption of Rotter's theory is that human personality is *learned* (Rotter, 1982). Thus, it follows that personality is not set or determined at any particular age of development, but can be changed or modified as long as people are capable of learning. Although the accumulation of previous experiences gives our personalities some stability, we are always amenable to change through new experiences. We learn from past experiences, but those experiences are not absolutely constant; they are colored by intervening experiences which then affect present perceptions.

Rotter's third assumption is that personality has a *basic unity* (Rotter, 1982), which means that our personalities possess relative stability. As we become more experienced, we learn to evaluate new experiences on the basis of previous reinforcement. This relatively consistent evaluation leads to greater stability and unity of personality.

Rotter's fourth basic assumption is that motivation is *goal directed* (Rotter,

1982). He rejects the drive-reduction hypothesis of Dollard and Miller, Freud, and others as being inadequate as an explanation of human behavior. People are not primarily motivated to seek pleasure or to reduce drives, but by their expectations that their behaviors are advancing them toward goals. For example, Gerry knows that four years of graduate school will be hard work. Rather than reducing tension, the prospect of graduate school promises to increase it.

Other things being equal, people are most strongly reinforced by behaviors that move them in the direction of anticipated goals. This refers to Rotter's **empirical law of effect,** which "defines reinforcement as any action, condition, or event which affects the individual's movement toward a goal" (Rotter & Hochreich, 1975, p. 95). Rotter believes that any adequate theory of personality must take into consideration the assumption that people are capable of anticipating events and that, therefore, their criterion for evaluating reinforcers is movement in the direction of the anticipated event.

FOUR VARIABLES OF PREDICTION

Rotter's primary concern is with the prediction of human behavior. Four variables and their interaction must be analyzed in order to make accurate predictions. These are *behavior potential, expectancy, reinforcement value,* and the *psychological situation.* Behavior potential refers to the likelihood that a given behavior will occur in a particular situation; expectancy is a person's expectation of being reinforced; reinforcement value is preference a person gives to any reinforcement; and the psychological situation refers to a complex pattern of cues perceived by the person for a specific time period.

Behavior Potential

Broadly considered, **behavior potential** (*BP*) refers to the possibility that a particular response will occur at a given time and place. More specifically, Rotter and Hochreich (1975, p. 95) define it as "the potential for any given behavior to occur in a particular situation or set of situations as calculated in relation to any single reinforcement or set of reinforcements."

In any situation there are several behavior potentials, some strong, some weak. For example, in the case of Gerry, the psychology major, we might be interested in predicting her behavioral potential with reference to her immediate future. Several behaviors are possible. She might apply to one or more highly prestigious graduate programs, attend one that has already accepted her, work toward a master's degree, or not go to graduate school. She might stay in town and marry Chuck or move out of state and take her uncle's job offer. How can one predict which behaviors are most or least likely to occur? *The behavior potential in any situation is a function of both expectancy and reinforcement value.*

If we wish to know the likelihood that Gerry will attend School A rather than School C, for example, we could hold expectancy constant and vary reinforcement value. Assume each of these behavior potentials carried a 90 percent expectancy of being reinforced, that is, Gerry believes that she has a 90 percent chance of being successful at either School A or School C. Then her choice would be based solely on the reinforcement value of each. If completing the program in prestigious School A has greater reinforcement value than earning a Ph.D. at mediocre School C, then Gerry is more likely to attend School A.

The second approach to prediction is to hold reinforcement value constant and vary expectancy. If total reinforcements from each possible behavior are of equal value, then the one with the greatest expectation of reinforcement is most likely to occur. More specifically, if graduation from one school has exactly the same reinforcement value as graduation from any other school, then the response with the highest behavior potential is the one that is most likely to produce a reinforcement. In other words, Gerry is most likely to attend the school where she will be successful.

Rotter employs a broad definition of behavior, which refers to any response, implicit or explicit, that can be observed or measured, directly or indirectly. This comprehensive concept allows Rotter to include as behavior such hypothetical constructs as generalizing, problem solving, thinking, analyzing, and so forth.

Expectancy

Rotter and Hochreich (1975, p. 96) define **expectancy** (E) as "the probability held by the individual that a particular reinforcement will occur as a function of a specific behavior on his part in a specific situation or situations." The probability is not determined by the individual's history of reinforcements, as Skinner contends, but is subjectively held by the person. History, of course, is a contributing factor, but so too are unrealistic thinking, expectations based on lack of information, and fantasies, so long as the person sincerely believes that a given reinforcement or group of reinforcements is contingent on a particular response.

Expectancies can be general or specific. Generalized expectancies (GEs) are learned through previous experiences with a particular response or similar responses and are based on the belief that certain behaviors will be followed by positive reinforcement. For example, since Gerry has been previously reinforced by high grades for hard work, she has a generalized expectancy of future reward and will work hard in a variety of academic situations.

Specific expectancies are designated as E' (E prime). In any situation the expectancy for a particular reinforcement is determined by a combination of a specific expectancy (E') and the generalized expectancy (GE). For example, Gerry has a general expectancy that a given level of academic work will be rewarded by good grades and yet she believes that an equal amount of hard work in her French class will go unrewarded. Total expectancy of success is a function of both one's generalized expectancy and one's specific expectancy. This total expectancy partially determines how hard one will work in French class and is, therefore, one of the variables that enables us to predict behavior.

Reinforcement Value

Another variable in the prediction formula is **reinforcement value** (*RV*), which is defined as "the degree of preference for any reinforcement to occur if the possibilities of their occurring were all equal" (Rotter & Hochreich, 1975, p. 97). Reinforcement value can be illustrated by a vending machine with several possible selections, each costing the same. A woman approaches the machine willing and able to pay 50 cents in order to receive a snack. The vending machine is in perfect working condition so that there is a 100 percent probability that her response will be followed by some sort of reinforcement. Her expectancy of reinforcement, therefore, for the candy bar, corn chips, potato chips, popcorn, tortilla chips, and Danish pastry are all equal. Her response, that is, which button she presses, is determined by the reinforcement value of each snack. When expectancies and situational variables are held constant, behavior is shaped by one's preference for the possible reinforcements, that is, reinforcement value. In most situations, of course, expectancies are seldom equal and prediction is made difficult by the fact that both expectancy and reinforcement value vary.

In determining reinforcement value, one must consider both positive and negative aspects of reinforcement. Rotter agrees with Skinner that positive reinforcement is any event or condition that increases the probability that a particular behavior will occur again under the same or similar circumstances. However, his definition of negative reinforcement is different. It will be recalled that Skinner defined negative reinforcement as the removal of an aversive stimulus, which consequently increases the probability that a particular behavior will occur. Rotter, on the other hand, uses the term in much the same way that Skinner talks about punishment; that is, it is the occurrence of a negatively valued event. Negative reinforcement, therefore, decreases the likelihood that a particular behavior will occur again (Rotter, Chance, & Phares, 1972).

Positive and negative reinforcement values can be illustrated by Gerry's situation with regard to graduate school. Gerry has also considered applying to School B, one that is equally prestigious and positively reinforcing as School A. However, School B is located in a particularly cold area of the country and Gerry hates cold weather. This negative value must be subtracted from School B's positive value in predicting which school Gerry is more likely to prefer.

What determines the reinforcement value for any event, condition, or action? First, the individual's perception contributes to the positive or negative value of an event. Rotter calls this **internal reinforcement** and distinguishes it from **external reinforcement,** which refers to events, conditions or actions that one's society or culture values. Internal and external reinforcements may be either in harmony or at a variance with one another. For example, both School A and School B have outstanding reputations, so that acceptance to either would carry strong external reinforcement. However, Gerry does not regard School B as positively as do other people. In this case internal and external reinforcements are discrepant, but with School A, Gerry's internal and external reinforcements are in harmony.

Another contributor to reinforcement value is one's needs. Generally, a specific reinforcement tends to increase in value as the *need* it satisifes becomes stronger. A starving child places a higher value on a bowl of soup than does a moderately hungry one. (Needs are more fully discussed below).

Reinforcements are also valued according to their expected consequences for future reinforcements. People are capable of using cognition to anticipate a sequence of events leading to some future goal. The ultimate goal contributes to the reinforcement value of each event in the sequence. For example, a young law student desires a position with a prestigious law firm headed by Mr. Bigshot. She knows that Bigshot will be attending the same party as one of her friends. Obtaining her friend's invitation has positive reinforcement value only because of its expected relationship with future reinforcements. Ordinarily, she might regard the party as tedious and insipid, but now the invitation is valued because it offers her a chance to talk to Mr. Bigshot. Conversation with him is reinforcing only because it increases her chances of receiving a job offer; otherwise, talking to him may be a terrible bore. Reinforcements seldom occur independent of future related reinforcements, but are likely to appear in **reinforcement-reinforcement sequences,** which Rotter (1982) refers to as clusters of reinforcement.

Humans are goal-oriented, and they anticipate achieving a goal if they behave in a particular way. Other things being equal, goals with the highest reinforcement value are most desirable. Desire alone, however, is not a sufficient variable for predicting behavior. The potential for any behavior is a function of both expectancy and reinforcement value, as well as the psychological situation.

The Psychological Situation

The **psychological situation** (*s*), the fourth variable in the prediction formula, refers to that part of the external and internal world to which the person is responding. It is not synonymous with external stimuli, though physical events are usually important.

Behavior is a function neither of environmental events nor of central traits or characteristics within the person, but rather of the interaction of the person with his or her meaningful environment. If physical stimuli alone determined behavior, then two individuals would respond in exactly the same way to identical stimuli; if personal traits were responsible for behavior, then a person would always respond in a consistent and characteristic fashion, even to different events. Since neither of these conditions is valid, something other than the environment or personal traits must shape behavior. Social learning theory hypothesizes that the interaction between person and environment is a crucial factor in shaping behavior.

The psychological situation is "a complex set of interacting cues acting upon an individual for any specific time period" (Rotter, 1982, p. 318). A person never behaves in a vacuum, but rather responds to cues within his or her perceived environment. These cues serve to determine for the individual certain expectancies for behavior-reinforcement sequences as well as for reinforcement-reinforcement sequences. The time period for the cues may vary from momentary to lengthy; thus, the psychological situation is not limited by time. One's marital situation, for example, may be relatively constant over a long period of time, whereas the psychological situation faced by a driver during a blowout may be extremely short. The psychological situation must be considered along with expectancies and reinforcement value in determining the probability of a given response.

BASIC PREDICTION FORMULA

To predict behavior, Rotter has proposed a basic formula that includes all four variables of prediction. He does not claim that the basic prediction formula can precisely predict behavior; it represents an idealistic rather than practical means of prediction. The formula can be illustrated by Gerry in a situation where she is listening to a dull and lengthy lecture by one of her professors. To the internal cues of boredom and the external cues of seeing slumbering classmates, what is the likelihood that she will respond by resting her head on the desk in an attempt to sleep? The psychological situation alone is not responsible for her behavior, but it interacts with her expectancy for reinforcement plus the reinforcement value of sleep in that particular situation. Her behavior potential can be estimated by Rotter's basic formula for the prediction of goal-directed behavior:

$$BP_{x,s_1,R_a} = f(E_{x,R_a,s_1} \ \& \ RV_{a,s_1})$$

This formula is read: The potential for behavior x to occur in situation 1 in relation to reinforcement a is a function of the expectancy that behavior x will be followed by reinforcement a in situation 1 and the value of reinforcement a in situation 1 (Rotter & Hochreich, 1975, p. 99).

Applied to the above example, the formula is a means of determining the likelihood (behavior potential or *BP*) that Gerry will rest her head on her desk (behavior x) in a dull and boring classroom with other students slumbering (the psychological situation or s_1) with the goal of sleep (reinforcement or R_a), is a function of her expectation that such behavior (E_x) will be followed by sleep *(Ra)* in this particular classroom situation (s_1), plus a measure of how highly she desires to sleep (reinforcement value or RV_a) in this specific situation (s_1).

Consider a second example. David, who has worked for 18 years in Hoffman's Hardware Store, has just been informed that, due to a business decline,

People do not behave in a vacuum, but rather respond to cues within their perceived environment.

there is a strong possibility that a cut in the work force will result in the loss of his job. How can we predict David's subsequent behavior? Will he beg his boss to let him remain with the company? Will he strike out in violence against the store or the owner? Will he displace his anger and behave aggressively toward his wife or children? Will he begin drinking heavily and become apathetic toward searching for a new job? Will he immediately and constructively begin looking for another position?

Since most of these possible behaviors are new to David, how can we predict what he will do? At this point the concepts of **generalization** and **generalized expectancy** enter into Rotter's personality theory. If, in the past, David has generally been rewarded for behaviors that have resulted in his increased social status, for example, then there is only a slight probability that he will beg his boss for a job, since this behavior is contrary to increased social status. On the other hand, if his previous attempts at responsible independent behaviors have generally been reinforced and if he has the *freedom of movement,* that is, the opportunity to apply for another job, then, assuming he needs work, there is a high probability that he will apply for another job or otherwise behave independently. This prediction, while not as specific as the one predicting Gerry's likelihood of sleep, is nevertheless, more useful for situations where rigorous control of pertinent variables is not possible. Predicting David's reaction to the probable loss of a job is a matter of knowledge of how he views the options available to him and of information concerning his present *needs*.

NEEDS

Unlike Skinner, Rotter is willing to hypothesize the existence of inner states such as needs, goals, and expectancies. Social learning theory assumes that people are goal-oriented. Any behavior or set of behaviors that people see as moving them in the direction of the goal can be said to satisfy a need. Needs are not seen as states of deprivation or arousal but as indicators of the direction of behavior. The difference between needs and goals is semantic only. When focus is on the environment, Rotter (1982) speaks of goals; when it is on the person, he talks of needs.

The concept of needs allows for more generalized predictions than that permitted by the four specific variables that comprise the basic prediction formula. Ordinarily, personality theory deals with broad predictions of human behavior. We know, for example, that a person with strong needs for dominance will usually try to gain the power position in a variety of situations. In specific situations, however, there may be times when a dominant person will behave in a nondominant or even submissive fashion. The basic prediction formula cited above permits specific predictions, assuming, of course, that all relevant information is at hand. It is the more appropriate formula for controlled laboratory experiments, but not as relevant to the prediction of day-to-day behaviors. For this reason Rotter introduces the concept of needs and their accompanying *general prediction formula,* which will be cited later.

Categories of Needs

Rotter lists six broad categories of needs (Rotter & Hochreich, 1975), each representing a group of functionally related behaviors, that is, behaviors that lead to the same or similar reinforcements. For example, we can have our recognition needs met in a variety of situations and by many different people. Therefore, we can receive reinforcement for a group of functionally related behaviors, all of which satisfy our need for recognition. The following list is not intended by Rotter to be exhaustive, but it does represent most of the important needs humans have.

Recognition-Status

The need to be recognized by others and to achieve status in their eyes is a powerful need for most people. Recognition-status includes the need to excel in those things one regards as important, for example, school, sports, occupation, hobbies, and physical appearance. It also includes the need for socioeconomic status and personal prestige. Playing a good game of bridge would be an example of a specific behavior listed under this category.

Dominance

Dominance, the need to control the behavior of others, includes any set of behaviors directed at gaining power over the lives of friends, family, colleagues, superiors, and subordinates. Talking fellow workers into accepting one's ideas is a specific example of dominance.

Independence

Independence is the need to be free of the domination of others. It includes those behaviors aimed at gaining the freedom to make one's own decisions, to rely on oneself, and to attain goals without the help of others. Declining aid in repairing a bicycle is a demonstration of the need for independence.

Protection-Dependency

An opposite set of needs involves protection-dependency. This category includes the needs to have others take care of us, keep us from experiencing frustration and harm, and help us satisfy the other needs. A specific example of protection-dependency would be asking our spouse to stay home from work and take care of us when we are ill.

Love and Affection

Most people have a strong need for love and affection. This includes a need for acceptance by others that goes beyond recognition and status to include an indication of liking or affection. The need for love and affection includes those behaviors aimed toward securing warm regard, interest, and devotion from others. An example of this need is seen in a young man who does a favor for his girlfriend, hoping that she will tell him that she loves him.

Physical Comfort

Perhaps the most basic need, in the sense that other needs are learned in relation to it, is the need for physical comfort, including the need for food, good health, and physical security. Other needs are learned as an outgrowth of our needs for pleasure, physical contact, and well-being. Behavior resulting in sexual gratification is an example of the need for physical comfort.

Need Components

A need complex has three essential components: *need potential, freedom of movement,* and *need value,* which are analogous to the more specific concepts of behavior potential, expectancy, and reinforcement value (Rotter, Chance, & Phares, 1972).

Need Potential

Need potential (*NP*) refers to the possible occurrence of a set of functionally related behaviors directed toward the satisfaction of the same or similar goals. Need potential is analogous to the more specific concept of behavior potential. The difference between the two is that need potential refers to a *group* of functionally related behaviors, while behavior potential is the likelihood that a particular behavior will occur in a given situation in relation to a specific reinforcement.

Need potential cannot be measured solely through observation of behavior. Different people behaving in apparently the same manner may be realizing different need potentials. For one person eating in a fancy restaurant, the need being satisfied may be physical comfort; for another it may be love and affection, if that person is with a loved one; for another the need may be recognition-status. In fact, probably any of the six broad needs could be satisfied by this action. Whether or not one's need potential is realized, however, depends not only on the value or preference one has for that reinforcement but also on one's freedom of movement in making responses leading to that reinforcement.

Freedom of Movement

We have seen that behavior is, in part, determined by one's expectancies, that is, one's best guess that a particular reinforcement will follow a specific response. In the general prediction formula (discussed below), **freedom of movement** (*FM*) is analogous to expectancy. It is defined as the "mean expectancy of obtaining positive satisfactions as a result of a set of related behaviors directed toward obtaining a group of functionally related reinforcements" (Rotter, Chance, & Phares, 1972, p. 34). In other words, freedom of movement is one's overall expectation of being reinforced for performing those behaviors which are directed toward the satisfaction of some general need. To illustrate, a person with a strong need for dominance could behave in a variety of ways to satisfy that need. She might select the clothes her husband will wear, decide what college curriculum her son will pursue, direct actors in a play, organize a professional conference involving dozens of colleagues, or perform any one of hundreds of other behaviors aimed at securing reinforcement for her dominance need. The average or mean level of expectancies that these behaviors will lead to the desired satisfaction is a measure of her freedom of movement in the area of dominance needs.

Freedom of movement can be determined by holding need value constant and observing one's need potential. For example, if a person places exactly the same value on dominance, independence, love and affection, and each of the other needs, then that person will perform those behaviors judged to have the greatest expectancy of being reinforced. If the person performs behaviors leading to physical comfort, for example, then there will be more freedom of movement in that need complex than any others. Ordinarily, of course, need value is not constant since most people prefer the satisfaction of one need over others.

Need Value

The degree to which a person prefers one set of reinforcements to another is called **need value** (*NV*). Rotter, Chance, and Phares (1972, p. 33) define need value as the "mean preference value of a set of functionally related reinforcements." In the general prediction formula, need value is the analogue of reinforcement value. When freedom of movement is held constant, people will perform those behavior sequences which lead to satisfaction of the need most preferred. If people have equal expectancies of obtaining positive reinforcement for behaviors aimed at the satisfaction of any need, then the value they place on a particular need complex will be the principal determinant of their behavior. If they prefer independence to any other need complex, and if they have an equal expectation of being reinforced in the pursuit of any of the needs, then their behavior will be directed toward achieving independence.

General Prediction Formula

The basic prediction formula cited above is limited to highly controlled situations where expectancies, reinforcement value, and the psychological situation are all relatively simple and discrete. In most situations, prediction of behavior becomes more complex since behaviors and reinforcements usually occur in functionally related sequences. Consider our case study, Gerry, the psychology major. The basic prediction formula gives us some indication of the likelihood that in the specific situation of a boring lecture, she will rest her head on her desk. However, a more generalized prediction formula is needed to predict her need potential for pursuing a Ph.D. degree. To make these more generalized predictions, Rotter introduces the following general prediction formula:

$$NP = f(FM \ \& \ NV)$$

This equation means that need potential (NP) is a function of freedom of movement (FM) and need value (NV). The formula is analogous to the basic prediction formula and each factor is parallel to the corresponding factors of that basic formula (Rotter & Hochreich, 1975). To illustrate the general prediction formula, we can look at Gerry's situation with regard to her future. To predict her *need potential* for any of the possible alternative behaviors we would have to measure her *freedom of movement,* that is, her mean expectancy of being reinforced for a series of behaviors needed to reach her goal, plus *need value* of all those reinforcements, that is, the value she places on recognition-status, independence, or any other need she associates with receiving a Ph.D. in clinical psychology. Gerry's needs for recognition-status, love and affection, and so on can be satisfied through a *set* of behaviors. For instance, her need for recognition-status might be satisfied by completing all the steps necessary for receiving a Ph.D. Her need for love and affection might be satisfied by marriage to Chuck. The value she places on these various needs (need value), plus her average expectancy of being reinforced for performing the required series of behaviors (freedom of movement), equals her potential for pursuing the set of required behaviors (need potential). A

BASIC PREDICTION FORMULA

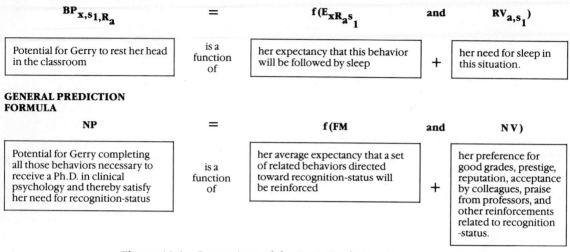

Figure 11.1   Comparison of the Basic Prediction Formula and the General Prediction Formula

comparison of the basic (specific) prediction formula and the generalized prediction formula is shown in Figure 11.1.

Generalized Expectancies

Rotter's general prediction formula allows for the fact that people use similar experiences from the past to anticipate present reinforcement. If Gerry fills out an application to School A, it is not only because that specific behavior has a history of reinforcement but also because she perceives that other similar experiences have been reinforced. In other words, Gerry has a **generalized expectancy** for success in this situation. Her past similar experiences of being accepted upon applying for jobs or to other schools have, to some extent, influenced her expectation of being reinforced by applying to School A. Her perceived chances of success may not be the same as they were for other applications, but they have been altered by those similar experiences.

Rotter's two most famous scales for measuring generalized expectancies are the Internal-External Control Scale and the Interpersonal Trust Scale.

Internal vs. External Control of Reinforcement

In our introductory case study, we saw that Gerry has generally, but not always, been successful in reaching her goals. When she failed to win an important scholarship, she did not blame the selection committee or luck—she recognized that her scholastic record was not quite good enough. Her behavior was a reflection of a generalized expectancy for *internal* control of reinforcement. Gerry believes that reinforcement is generally contingent on

Are You the Master of Your Fate?

The Internal-External Control Scale is an attempt to measure the degree to which people perceive a causal relationship between their own efforts and environmental consequences. People will strive to reach their goals, not so much because of the nature of the goals or even a strong internal desire to reach them, but because of a generalized expectancy that such strivings will be successful. A basic assumption of Rotter's research with the I-E scale is that people who believe that they can control their own fate will behave differently in a variety of situations from those who believe that their destiny is controlled by luck, chance, or powerful others (Rotter & Hochreich, 1975).

Rotter's I-E Scale has been a consistently popular research topic since its inception, with the volume of studies now numbering in the thousands. However, the concept is not always clearly understood. Rotter (1975) has pointed out several common misconceptions concerning internal and external control of reinforcement (he seldom refers to it as "locus of control"), misuse of the instrument continues. First, scores on the scale are not determinants of behavior. They are indicators of generalized expectancies (*GE*s) and must

be considered along with *reinforcement value (RV)* when predicting behavior potential. A second misconception of locus of control is that it is specific and can predict achievement in a specific situation. Again, the concept refers to generalized expectancies of reinforcement and indicates that people ordinarily believe that they are in control of their lives or that they generally expect that luck or outside forces control what happens to them. The third common misconception is that the scale divides people into two distinct types, with high internal scores signifying social desirability and high external scores indicating socially undesirable characteristics. Extreme scores in either direction would be undesirable. That is, very high external scores might be related to apathy and despair, with people believing that they have no control over their environments; extremely high internal scores would mean that people accept responsibility for everything that happens to them—accidents, business failure, delinquent children, and so forth. Scores somewhere in between these extremes, but inclined in the direction of internal control, would probably be most healthy or desirable.

either her actions or her own personal characteristics and not on fate or on other people. Gerry would likely score high on Rotter's (1966) Internal-External (I-E) Control Scale (see Box—"Are You the Master of Your Fate?").

Interpersonal Trust Scale

Another example of a generalized expectancy *(GE)* that has provoked considerable interest and research is the concept of interpersonal trust. Rotter (1980, p. 1) defines interpersonal trust as "a generalized expectancy held by an individual that the word, promise, oral or written statement of another individual or group can be relied on." It does not refer to the belief that people are naturally good or that we live in the best of all possible worlds. Neither should it be equated with gullibility. Rotter (1980) sees trust as a

The Interpersonal Trust Scale

Because we have differential experiences with the words of others, it follows that there should be individual differences among people with regard to interpersonal trust. To measure these differences Rotter (1967) developed an Interpersonal Trust Scale, which asked people to respond to 25 items such as: "In dealing with strangers one is better off to be cautious until they have provided evidence that they are trustworthy"; and "Most elected public officials are really sincere in their campaign promises" (Rotter, 1967, p. 654). Scores for each of the 25 items were added so that high scores indicate the presence of interpersonal trust and low scores mean a generalized expectancy of distrust.

Is it more desirable to score high or low on the scale, to be trustful or distrustful? When trust is defined independently of gullibility, then it can be argued that high trust is not only desirable but essential for the survival of civilization. We trust that the food we buy is not laced with poison; that the gasoline in our cars will not explode on ignition; that airline pilots know how to fly the plane in which we travel; and even that the postal service will deliver our mail without tampering with it. Despite the prevalence of a good deal of cynicism, suspicion, and distrust, society continues to function because people generally have at least a moderate amount of trust in each other.

Rotter (1980) has summarized results of studies that indicate that people who score high in interpersonal trust as opposed to those who score low are (1) less likely to lie; (2) probably less likely to cheat or steal; (3) more likely to give others a second chance; (4) more likely to respect the rights of others; (5) less likely to be unhappy, conflicted, or maladjusted; (6) somewhat more likable and popular; (7) more trustworthy; (8) neither more nor less gullible; and (9) neither more nor less intelligent. In other words, high trusters are not stupid or naive and, rather than being harmed by their trustful attitude, they seem to possess many of the characteristics that other people regard as positive and desirable.

Interpersonal trust, as well as internal/external control, are generalized expectancies and therefore consistent and predictable characteristics of an individual. Rotter believes that when one knows a person's score on the Interpersonal Trust Scale, then one can make reasonably accurate predictions as to the degree of trust that person will show in novel situations (Rotter, 1971).

belief in the communications of others when there is no evidence of disbelieving, whereas gullibility is a belief that most others would regard as foolish or naive.

Social learning theory hypothesizes that since many reinforcements come from other people, individuals will develop generalized expectancies that positive or negative reinforcements will follow from verbal promises or threats made by others. Sometimes these promises and threats are kept; other times they are broken. In this way each of us learns to trust or distrust the words of others (see Box—"The Interpersonal Trust Scale").

Team figure skating demands a high level of interpersonal trust.

MALADAPTIVE BEHAVIOR

Maladaptive behavior in Rotter's social learning theory is any persistent behavior that fails to move a person closer to a desired goal. It frequently, but not inevitably, arises from the combination of high need value and low freedom of movement (Rotter, 1964).

High need value often stems from a condition of setting goals unrealistically high. A person may have realistic needs for love and affection, but unrealistically sets a goal to be loved by everyone. In this example, need value will nearly certainly exceed freedom of movement and the resulting behavior is likely to be defensive or maladaptive. When goals are set too high, the person cannot learn productive behaviors because the goals are beyond reach. Instead, the person learns how to avoid failure or how to defend against the pain that accompanies failure. For example, a woman whose goal is to be loved by everyone inevitably will be ignored or rejected by someone. She may be aggressive toward others with the rationalization that people are stupid or evil because any decent person would shower her with love; or she may withdraw from people in order to avoid being hurt by them.

Setting goals too high is only one of several possible contributors to maladaptive behavior. Another frequent cause is low freedom of movement. People may have low expectancies of success because they lack information or ability to perform the behaviors that will be followed by positive reinforcement. A person who values love, for example, may lack the interpersonal skills necessary to obtain it.

People may also have low freedom of movement because they make a faulty evaluation of the present situation. For example, people sometimes underestimate their intellectual abilities because, in the past, they have been told that they were stupid. Even though their need values are not unrealistically high, they have low expectations of success because they wrongly believe that they are incapable of performing well in school or competing successfully for a higher level job.

People may also have low freedom of movement because they generalize from one situation in which, perhaps, they are realistically inadequate to other situations in which they could have sufficient ability to be successful. For example, a physically weak adolescent who lacks the skills to be an accomplished athlete may erroneously see himself as unable to compete for a role in the school play or to be a leader in a social club. He inappropriately generalizes his inadequacies in sports to lack of ability in unrelated areas.

In summary, maladjusted individuals are characterized by unrealistic goals, inappropriate behaviors, inadequate skills, or unreasonably low expectancies of being able to execute the behaviors necessary for positive reinforcement. Since they have learned inadequate ways of solving problems within a social context, it is possible to unlearn these behaviors or to learn more appropriate ones within the controlled social environment provided by psychotherapy.

PSYCHOTHERAPY

In Rotter's theory, "the problems of psychotherapy are problems of how to effect changes in behavior through the interaction of one person with another. That is, they are problems in human learning in a social situation" (Rotter, 1964, p. 82).

Though Rotter adopts a problem-solving approach to psychotherapy, he does not limit his concern to quick solutions to immediate problems. His interest is more long range, involving a change in the patient's orientation toward life. In general, the goal of therapy is to bring freedom of movement and need value into harmony, thus reducing defensive and avoidance behaviors. The therapist assumes an active role as a teacher and attempts to accomplish the therapeutic goal in two basic ways: changing the importance of goals and eliminating unrealistically low expectancies for success (Rotter, 1964; 1970, 1978; Rotter & Hochreich, 1975).

Changing Goals

Many patients are unable to solve life's problems because they are pursuing skewed or distorted goals. The role of the therapist is to help patients understand the faulty nature of their goals and to teach them constructive means of striving toward realistic goals. There are at least three sources of problems connected to inappropriate goals (Rotter & Hochreich, 1975).

First, there may be two important goals in conflict, as when a person values both independence and protection-dependency. Adolescents frequently have problems in this area. On the one hand, they wish to be free from their parents' domination and control, but, on the other, they still desire to have a nurturing person care for them and protect them from painful experiences.

Their ambivalent behaviors are confusing both to themselves and to their parents. In this situation, the therapist may try to help patients see how specific behaviors are related to each of the needs and proceed to work with them in changing the value of one or both needs. By gradually altering need value, patients begin to behave more and more consistently and to experience greater freedom of movement in obtaining their goals.

A second source of problems is a destructive goal. Some patients persistently pursue self-destructive goals that inevitably result in failure and punishment. The job of the therapist is to point out the detrimental nature of the pursuit and the likelihood that it will be followed by negative reinforcement. One possible technique used by a therapist in these cases is to positively reinforce movements away from destructive goals. Rotter, however, is not bound to a specific set of techniques for each conceivable problem. He is both pragmatic and eclectic. The appropriate procedure is the one that works with a given patient.

Many people find themselves in trouble because they set their goals too high and are continually frustrated because they cannot reach or exceed them. This is the third area of inappropriate goals and, perhaps, the most common one. High goals lead to failure and pain, so instead of learning constructive means of obtaining a goal, the person learns nonproductive ways of avoiding pain. Avoidance through flight or repression is the chief symptom and may evolve into an end in itself. Therapy consists of realistically reevaluating and lowering exaggerated goals by reducing their reinforcement value. Since high reinforcement value is often learned through generalization, the therapist works toward teaching patients to discriminate between past legitimate values and present spurious ones. For example, a patient may have been previously rewarded with food or affection for association with his mother. At the same time, his mother may have praised him for cleanliness behaviors. As a consequence, he learned to place an unrealistically high value on compulsive neatness and, as an adult, is never quite comfortable amid clutter and disarray. The therapist must teach him that nourishment and love are independent from compulsively neat and orderly behavior. Rotter, however, does not stop with insight and the elimination of maladjustive behaviors. He also attempts to teach patients new behaviors that will lead to the reinforcement they seek.

Eliminating Low Expectancies

The second general approach of a social learning therapist is to attack low expectancies of success and its analogue, low freedom of movement. As noted in the section on maladjustment, people may have low freedom of movement for at least three reasons.

First, they may lack the skills or information needed to successfully strive toward their goals (Rotter, 1970). The therapist then becomes a teacher, "warmly" and empathetically instructing patients in more effective techniques for solving problems and satisfying needs. If a patient, for example, has difficulties in interpersonal relationships, there is an arsenal of techniques that might be employed. The therapist could extinguish inappropriate behaviors by simply ignoring them; use the therapist/patient relationship as a model for an effective interpersonal encounter which may then generalize beyond the therapeutic situation; or advise the patient of specific behaviors to try out when in the presence of those other people who are most likely to be receptive.

A second source of low freedom of movement is faulty evaluation of the present situation. For example, an adult may lack assertiveness with her colleagues because, during childhood, she was punished for competing with her siblings. The patient now must learn to differentiate between past and present, between siblings and colleagues. The therapist's task is to help her make these distinctions and, with the present example, teach her assertiveness techniques in a variety of appropriate situations.

Finally, low freedom of movement can spring from inadequate generalization. Patients often use failure in one situation as proof that they cannot be successful in other areas. Earlier we saw the example of the physically feeble adolescent who, because he was unsuccessful in sports, generalized his failure to nonathletic areas. His present problems come from faulty generalization and the therapist must reinforce even small successes in social relationships, academic achievements, and other situations. Eventually the patient will come to discriminate between realistic shortcomings in one area and successful behaviors in other situations.

Though Rotter recognizes that therapists should be flexible in their techniques and utilize different approaches with different patients, he does suggest several interesting techniques that he has found to be effective. The first is to teach patients to look for alternative courses of action (Rotter, 1978). Patients frequently complain that their spouse, parent, child, or employer does not understand them, treats them unjustly, and is the source of their problems. In this situation, Rotter would simply teach the patient to change the other person's behavior. This can be accomplished by an examination of the patient's behaviors, which normally lead to negative reactions by spouse, parent, child, or employer. If the patient can find an alternative method of behaving toward important others, then there is a strong probability that those others will change their behavior toward the patient. The patient thereafter will be rewarded for behaving in a more adaptive and appropriate fashion.

A related approach is to help patients develop a more accurate understanding of other people's motives (Rotter, 1978). Many patients have a suspicious or distrustful attitude toward others. They believe that their spouse, teacher, or boss is intentionally and spitefully trying to harm them. Rotter attempts to teach these patients to look at ways in which they may be contributing to the other person's defensive or negative behavior. Patients can be taught to realize that these other people are frequently frightened or threatened by the patient and not simply nasty or spiteful.

A third technique of social learning therapy is to help patients look at the long-range consequences of their behavior (Rotter, 1978). People sometimes engage in maladaptive behavior because the secondary gains of their immediate symptoms outweigh their present frustration and any possible long-term reinforcement. For example, a woman may adopt the role of a helpless child in order to gain control over her husband. She complains to her therapist that she is dissatisfied with her helplessness and would like to become more independent, both for her sake and for the benefit of her harried husband. What she probably does not realize, however, is that her current helpless behavior is gaining for her the satisfaction of her dominance needs. The more helpless she acts, the more control she exercises over her husband and children. This present positive reinforcement is stronger than the accompanying negative reinforcement. In addition, the long-range positive consequences of self-confidence and independence are weak and not clearly seen. The task of the therapist is to train the patient to postpone minor contemporary satisfactions for more important future ones.

Another novel technique suggested by Rotter (1978) is to have patients enter into a previously painful social situation, but rather than speaking as much as typical, they are asked to remain as quiet as possible and largely to observe. In observing, patients have a better chance of learning the motives of others. They can then use that information in the future to alter their own behavior, thereby changing the reactions of others and reducing the painful effects of future encounters with those other persons.

In summary, the therapist is an active participant in social interaction with the patient. An effective therapist possesses the characteristics of warmth, empathy, acceptance, and understanding, not only because these attitudes encourage the patient to verbalize problems, but also because reinforcement from a warm, accepting therapist is more effective than that from a cold, rejecting one (Rotter, Chance, & Phares, 1972). The therapist attempts to minimize the discrepancy between need value and freedom of movement by helping patients alter their goals or by teaching effective means of obtaining those goals. Even though the therapist is an active problem solver, Rotter (1978) believes that eventually patients must learn to solve their own problems.

CONCEPT OF HUMANITY

Rotter's concept of humanity is more in the tradition of humanistically oriented theorists such as Adler (Chapter 4), Allport (Chapter 14), Maslow (Chapter 16), and Rogers (Chapter 17) than learning theorists such as Dollard and Miller (Chapter 9) or Skinner (Chapter 10).

Rotter sees people as cognitive animals whose perceptions of events are more important than the events themselves. People are capable of perceiving reinforcement in a variety of ways and this cognitive perception is more influential than the environment in determining the value of the reinforcer. While it can be assumed that food represents a reward to a deprived rat, no such comparable assumption can be made with regard to humans. What a parent views as a reward, a child may see as a punishment and vice versa. Human cognition enables different people to see reinforcement differently. This assumption, in fact, is at the basis of Rotter's idea of internal and external locus of control. Internals tend to see reward as contingent upon their behavior, while externals view reward as contingent upon forces outside themselves. Since perceptions and need values differ among people, it is not possible to say that a particular individual will react to a specific event in a predictable fashion. When need value and freedom of movement for an individual are known, then it becomes possible to predict need potential, that is, generalize behaviors for that individual.

Humans are both purposive and goal-directed. They do not merely react to their environments; they *interact* with their *meaningful* environments. Rotter's view of humanity is more *teleological* or future-oriented than it is causal, but it does not overlook past causes. The goals people set for themselves help shape the meaning of their reinforcements. Events people perceive as moving them closer to their goals are positively valued, while those which prevent them from reaching goals are negatively valued. Goals, then, serve as criteria for evaluating events. People are motivated not as much by past experiences with reinforcement as they are by their expectations of future events.

People move in the direction of goals they have established for themselves. These goals, however, can change as need value and freedom of movement change. Because people are continually in the process of setting goals, they have some choice in directing their lives. *Free choice* is not unlimited, however, since past experiences with reinforcement, present need value, as well as present freedom of movement all determine behavior.

Rotter can be described as neither *optimistic nor pessimistic,* but rather as realistic and pragmatic. He believes that people can be taught constructive strategies for problem solving and that they are capable of learning new behaviors at any point in life. However, he does not hold that people have within themselves an inherent force that moves them inevitably in the direction of psychological growth.

On the issue of *conscious vs. unconscious* motives, Rotter generally leans a little in the direction of conscious forces. People can consciously set goals for themselves and consciously strive to solve old and new problems. People, however, are not always aware of their need value nor are they conscious of the underlying motivation for much of their present behavior.

On the issue of personality being shaped by *social or biological influences,* Rotter is clearly an advocate of social factors. He does not deny the effects of genetics, but rather insists that the most significant aspects of personality are learned within a social context.

As for stressing *uniqueness or similarities,* Rotter can probably be placed most accurately in a middle position. People have individual histories and unique experiences that allow them to set personalized goals, but there are also enough similarities among people to allow for the construction of mathematical formulas which, if sufficient information were available, would permit reliable and accurate prediction of behavior. In summary, people are forward-looking, purposive, unified, cognitive, social creatures who are capable of evaluating present experiences and anticipated future events on the basis of goals they have chosen for themselves.

CRITIQUE OF ROTTER

Rotter's personality theory is attractive to those who value the rigors of learning theory and the speculative assumption that people are forward-looking, cognitive beings. Rotter has evolved a learning theory for thinking, valuing, goal-directed humans rather than for laboratory animals. Whether the theory is philosophically satisfying or not, its value must rest on how it rates on the five criteria for a useful theory.

First, how well does his theory *organize knowledge?* Most observable behaviors can be made meaningful by the general prediction formula and its components of need potential, freedom of movement, and need value. When behavior is seen as a function of these variables, it takes on a different hue. Even bizarre or "self-destructive" behaviors can be viewed in terms of freedom of movement and need value. In Rotter's framework, for example, "self-destructive" behaviors indicate that the person generally expects to be reinforced for those actions (freedom of movement). In addition, the type of reinforcements received are, on the average, positively valued (need value). This schema renders comprehensible much seemingly unintelligible and inappropriate behavior.

A second criterion of a useful theory is its ability to *generate significant research.* Rotter's concept of locus of control has been, and continues to be, one of the most widely researched topics in recent psychological literature (Lefcourt, 1982; Rotter, 1982; Strickland, 1989; Wallston, Wallston, & DeVellis, 1978; Weisz & Stipek, 1982). Locus of control, however, is not the core of Rotter's personality theory and the theory itself has not generated a comparable level of research.

Does Rotter's personality theory serve as a useful *guide to action?* On this criterion the theory would be rated only moderately high. Rotter's ideas on psychotherapy are quite explicit and are a helpful guide to the therapist, but his theory of personality is not as practical. The mathematical formulas serve as a useful framework for organizing knowledge, but they do not suggest any specific course of action for the practitioner since the value of each factor within the formula cannot be known with mathematical certainty.

Is the theory *internally consistent?* Rotter is careful in defining terms so that the same term does not have two or more meanings. In addition, separate components of the theory are logically compatible. The basic prediction formula, with its four specific factors, is logically consistent with the three broader variables of the general prediction formula.

Is Rotter's social learning theory *parsimonious?* In general, it is relatively

simple and does not purport to offer explanations for all of human personality. However, its language, though internally consistent, is not always in
agreement with commonly accepted meanings. For example, he uses the
term negative reinforcement in the same way that Skinner and other learning
theorists use punishment.

CHAPTER SUMMARY

Rotter's social learning theory attempts to
synthesize the strengths of reinforcement
theories with those of the cognitive theories.
According to Rotter, how a person behaves in
a specific situation is a function of that
person's expectations of reinforcements and
the strength of needs satisfied by those
reinforcements. The cognitive processes of
thinking and memory allow one to anticipate
possible reinforcements in situations that are
unique and unfamiliar.

In specific situations behavior is estimated
by the *basic prediction formula* that suggests
that the potential for a given behavior to
occur, in a particular situation in relation to a
specific reinforcement, is a function of the
expectancy that the specific reinforcement
will follow the given behavior, plus the value
of the reinforcement in that particular
situation.

Because the basic prediction formula is
limited to specific situations, Rotter proposed
an analogous formula that predicts
functionally related behaviors in specific
situations. This *general prediction formula*
states that need potential is a function of
freedom of movement and need value.

Need potential refers to the possible
occurrence of a set of functionally related
behaviors directed toward the satisfaction of
a goal or a similar set of goals. *Freedom of
movement* is the average expectancy that a
set of related behaviors will be reinforced.
Need value is the degree to which a person
prefers one set of reinforcements to
another.

In many situations people develop
generalized expectancies for success because
a similar set of experiences has been
previously reinforced. One such generalized
expectancy is an internal or external *locus of
control.* People who score high on the
Internal-External Control Scale tend to feel
helpless in a world controlled by others or by
chance; people who score in the direction of
interval control generally believe that success
is due to their own efforts.

A second measure of generalized
expectancies is the *Interpersonal Trust Scale.*
Interpersonal trust is a generalized
expectancy that the word of another can be
relied on. People with high interpersonal
trust are themselves more trustworthy and
less likely to lie, cheat, or steal. In addition,
they are more likable, better adjusted, and
happier than people who lack interpersonal
trust.

Rotter defines *maladaptive behavior* as
those actions that fail to move a person closer
to a desired goal. Because it usually arises
from a combination of distorted goals and
low expectancies for success, Rotter's method
of *psychotherapy* aims toward changing goals
and eliminating low expectancies.

Rotter's concept of humanity breaks from
traditional learning theory and is more in the
spirit of humanistic theories. People are
motivated by goals, and they use their
cognitive abilities to evaluate their movement
toward those goals.

Social learning theory is useful because it
organizes and gives meaning to much of what

is known about human behavior. In addition, Rotter's concept of locus of control has been one of the most widely researched topics in psychology during the past 25 years. However, the core of Rotter's theory has failed to generate comparable research.

Suggested Readings

PHARES, E. J. (1988). Perceived control. In E. J. Phares. *Introduction to personality* (2nd ed.) (pp. 463–493). Glenview, IL: Scott, Foresman.
  In this chapter Phares, a student of Rotter who helped develop the Internal-External Control Scale during the late 1950s, discusses the research on perceived control, learned helplessness, and internal-external control of reinforcement.
ROTTER, J. B. (1980). Interpersonal trust, trustworthiness, and gullibility. *American Psychologist, 35,* 1–7.
  In this article Rotter defines interpersonal trust and discusses research on the relationship between trust and both prosocial behavior and gullibility.
ROTTER, J. B. (1982). Introduction. In J. B. Rotter. *The development and applications of social learning theory: Selected papers* (pp. 1–12). New York: Praeger.
  In this brief introduction to social learning theory, Rotter puts forth seven postulates that underlie his theory of personality.
ROTTER, J. B. (1982). Social learning theory. In N. T. Feather (Ed.), *Expectations and actions: Expectancy-value models in psychology* (pp. 241–260). Hillsdale, NJ: Erlbaum. Reprinted in J. B. Rotter. *The development and applications of social learning theory: Selected papers* (pp. 301–323). New York: Praeger.
  In this chapter Rotter describes the basic principles of social learning theory and applies them to motivation, beliefs, attribution theory, and the psychological situation.

BANDURA

Social Cognitive Theory

One Sunday afternoon Jim received a call from his friend Kevin who invited him to play tennis. Jim usually enjoyed a good fast-paced singles match, but on this day Kevin asked him to join Mark and one of Mark's friends in a game of doubles. Jim knew Mark only casually and had never met Mark's friend. Ordinarily, Jim might have declined because he didn't care for doubles—not enough exercise. However, the football game he was watching on television was one-sided and he wasn't much interested in it. Besides, his wife and daughter had gone to visit his mother-in-law so Jim had little else to do. He accepted the invitation, changed clothes, and drove to the tennis courts.

Although he and Greg—Mark's friend—lost the match, Jim enjoyed the company. When Kevin suggested that the four of them go to his house for a cold drink, Jim went along. At Kevin's, he got to know Greg better. Greg was a young assistant professor of history at the state university and was visiting Mark during the semester break. Since Jim was a high school history teacher, he and Greg quickly began talking about history. Eventually, Greg suggested that Jim might wish to further his studies in history and pursue an advanced degree.

Jim was in his third year of teaching American history at the local high school and had never really considered changing jobs. He enjoyed teaching and was considered a good teacher by his students and colleagues. However, the more Greg talked, the more Jim thought he might be better suited to do research and teach at the college level. Greg encouraged him to apply at his university and Jim replied that he would consider it.

The next day, however, Jim had lost some of his enthusiasm about graduate school. He knew it would be a hardship for his wife, Laura, and their young daughter, Angela. Laura would either have to quit her job as an elementary school teacher and move with him or the two would be separated for three or four years. Neither course of action seemed feasible, and Jim was sure that Laura would object to either.

When Jim told Laura of his encounter with Greg, he was surprised that she encouraged him to go to graduate school. She said that she could probably find another teaching job and that Angela could go to nursery school while he studied history.

With Greg's recommendation and his own superior academic record, Jim not only was accepted into the Ph.D. program but was awarded a teaching fellowship as well. So Jim, Laura, and Angela left friends and relatives in their home town and embarked on a new professional career. From that time on Jim's life would be dramatically changed because of his chance meeting with Greg on the tennis court.

OVERVIEW

The learning theories of Dollard and Miller, Skinner, and Rotter hold that our personality, in part, is shaped by the reinforcements we receive from our environment. However, none of them consider that the particular environment in which we live can shift dramatically with little participation from us. The lives of most of us have been substantially changed by chance encounters, such as Jim's meeting with Greg, or fortuitous events, such as a boring football game. The *social cognitive theory* of Albert Bandura, however, takes fortuity into consideration. Personality is molded by an interaction of behavior, personal factors, and environment, but chance frequently plays a role in determining which environment we live in and even which behaviors we will enact.

Bandura differs from the earlier learning theorists in several fundamental ways. Unlike Dollard and Miller, he believes that responses need not occur in order to be learned. According to Bandura, we can learn by observing another person's performance. For example, we might watch a magician do a particular trick, see how it was done, go home and perform the trick ourselves. Learning obviously occurred prior to our performance.

Bandura's theory also differs from Skinner's in several ways. First, Bandura gives more consideration to the cognitive capacities of the individual and less to environmental factors. Second, he stresses the idea that reinforcement can be vicarious; that is, we can be reinforced by observing another person receive a reward. This indirect reinforcement accounts for a good bit of human learning. A third difference is Bandura's insistence that behavior is not ultimately a function of the environment, but of the interaction among the environment, the behavior of the person, and personal factors, especially cognition. Bandura also differs from Skinner on the relationship between reinforcement and cognition. Whereas Skinner holds that there is no learning without reinforcement, Bandura asserts that there is no reinforcement without prior cognition. In order for an event to be reinforcing, Bandura says, we must be cognizant of the connection between actions and their outcomes. Conditioning is cognitively mediated; it is not an inevitable consequence of the environment alone.

Compared to Rotter, Bandura places more emphasis on the acquisition of learning. More specifically, he stresses the importance of modeling and learning through observation of others. He is less concerned with mathematical formulas for predicting behavior and less involved with the measurement of individual differences.

BIOGRAPHY OF ALBERT BANDURA

Albert Bandura is a native of Canada, but has spent his professional career in the United States. He was born on December 4, 1925, in Mundare, a small town in northern Alberta, where he attended elementary and secondary grades at the only school in town. Though the school was understaffed (there were only two teachers and twenty students in the high school), either the educational climate or the native ability of the students must have been outstanding since most of Bandura's classmates went on to college and successful professional careers. After graduating from high school, Bandura spent a summer in Alaska working on the Alaska highway, an experience that brought him into contact with a wide variety of fellow workers, many of whom manifested various degrees of psychopathology. Thus an interest in clinical psychology was kindled.

Bandura attended the University of British Columbia in Vancouver, and after only three years, he graduated in 1949 with a major in psychology. In looking for a graduate program, he chose the University of Iowa because of its strong emphasis on learning theory. At Iowa he was a student of Kenneth Spence, who had been a colleague of Clark Hull at Yale. Indirectly, then, his early thinking was molded by the same learning-theory tradition that had influenced Dollard and Miller. Indeed, Bandura was directly influenced by Miller and Dollard's *Social Learning and Imitation* (1941), which provided a stimulus for his early work. He completed a master's degree in 1951 and was awarded the Ph.D. in clinical psychology the following year.

After leaving Iowa City, he spent a year in Wichita, Kansas, completing a postdoctoral internship at the Wichita Guidance Center. In 1953 he joined the faculty at Stanford University where, except for one year, he has remained until the present time. In his early years at Stanford, Bandura was influenced by Robert Sears who had moved there after an active career as a member of the Yale Institute of Human Relations, which also included John Dollard and Neal Miller.

Most of Bandura's early publications were in clinical psychology, dealing primarily with psychotherapy and the Rorschach test. Then, in 1958, he collaborated with the late Richard H. Walters, his first doctoral student, to publish a paper on aggressive delinquents. The following year their book *Adolescent Aggression* (1959) appeared. Since then, Bandura has continued to publish on a wide variety of subjects, often in collaboration with his graduate students. His most monumental work is *Social Foundations of Thought and Action* (1986).

Bandura is married to Virginia Varns whom he met at the University of Iowa where she was an instructor in the School of Nursing. They have two daughters, Mary and Carol. His hobbies include attending opera and hiking in the Sierra Mountains and along the coastal ridges of California.

Many honors and awards have come to Bandura. In 1969 he spent a year away from Stanford as a fellow at the Center for Advanced Study of the Behavioral Sciences. He received the Guggenheim Fellowship in 1972 and the Distinguished Scientist Award from Division 12 (Clinical) of the American Psychology Association (APA) in the same year. In 1974 he was elected president of APA and also was awarded an endowed chair at Stanford, the David Starr Jordan Professor of Social Science in Psychology. In 1977 he received the James McKeen Cattell Award. In 1980 he was elected fellow, American Academy of Arts and Sciences; and the same year he won the Distinguished Contribution Award from the International Society for Research on Aggression, as well as the prestigious Award for Distinguished Scientific Contribution from the American Psychological Association.

INTRODUCTION TO SOCIAL COGNITIVE THEORY

More than any other personality theorist, Bandura has evolved a model of human functioning based on careful research and cautious speculation. His theorizing is never far ahead of his base of knowledge. To some extent he has built his model on the work of earlier learning theorists such as Hull, Dollard and Miller, Skinner, and Rotter, but the larger portion of his data base results from studies he and his colleagues conducted.

Rather than using animal studies as a model for human behavior, Bandura has keyed his interest on those aspects of humanity that make us different from other animals, namely, our cognitive abilities. Cognition alone, however, does not account for our behavior. Bandura's social cognitive theory views people as driven neither exclusively by the forces of cognition nor automatically by events within the environment. Instead, human functioning is molded by the reciprocal interaction of behavior; personal factors, including cognition; and environmental events. Bandura calls this triadic model **reciprocal determinism**.

Bandura also holds that people are symbolizing animals. Their ability to use symbols, especially language, enables them to "transform transient experiences into internal models that serve as guides for future action" (Bandura, 1986, p. 18). These transformations give some consistency and structure to the *self system*. Without this capacity people would merely react to sensory experiences and would lack the capacity to anticipate events, create new ideas, or use internal standards to evaluate present experience. People have the capacity for reflective self-consciousness. They can not only think, but they can think about thinking. "They monitor their ideas, act on them or predict occurrences from them, judge the adequacy of their thoughts from the results, and change them accordingly" (Bandura, 1986, p. 21).

Finally, while biology plays some role in personality formation, Bandura contends that humans are largely a product of *learning*. We can and do learn through direct experience, but much of our behavior is shaped through the observation of others. Bandura (1986, p. 19) states that "virtually all learning phenomena, resulting from direct experience, can occur vicariously by observing other people's behavior and its consequences for them."

In Bandura's theory reciprocal determinism, the self system, and learning are interrelated, but for convenience we discuss them separately.

RECIPROCAL DETERMINISM

In Chapter 10 we saw that Skinner believes that behavior is a function of the environment; that is, behavior ultimately can be traced to forces outside the person. As environmental contingencies change, behavior changes. But what impetus changes the environment? Several, including human behavior. Thus, Skinner believes that, though behavior is determined by the environment, the human organism also exercises some measure of countercontrol over the environment. Behavior, in Skinnerian theory then, is a function of the interaction of environment and the organism; but, in the final analysis, it is environmentally determined.

Bandura adopts quite a different stance. In his theory there is a reciprocal interaction among three variables—the environment, the behavior, and the person. In this scheme, behavior is, to some extent, a function of the environment and, conversely, the environment is, at least partially, a function of behavior. However, a crucial third factor has been added—the person. By "person" Bandura means largely, but not exclusively, internal factors such as cognition. Because of cognitive capacities of memory and anticipation, the person is able to influence both environment and behavior. Cognition determines, at least partially, which environmental events will be attended, what value will be placed on these events, and how they will be organized for future use. Cognition, however, is not an autonomous entity, independent of behavior and environment. Bandura (1986) criticizes those theorists who attribute the source of human behavior to internal forces such as instincts (Freud), drives (Dollard and Miller), needs (Maslow), or intentions and conscious judgments (Allport). Cognition is itself determined. It is formed by both behavior and environment, just as it has some determining effect on these other two variables. Personal conduct, then, is seen in terms of *reciprocal determinism,* a term used by Bandura to suggest a triadic interaction of environment, behavior, and person (Bandura, 1977b, 1978b, 1982a, 1986).

Reciprocal determinism is represented schematically in Figure 12.1, where B signifies behavior; E is the external environment; and P represents the person, including physical characteristics such as sex, social position, size, and physical attractiveness, but especially the internal state of cognition, which includes thought, memory, judgment, foresight, and so on.

An example of reciprocal determinism is in order. A child begging her father for a cookie is, from the father's viewpoint, an environmental event. If the father automatically (without thought) were to give the child a cookie, then the two would be conditioning one another's behavior in the Skinnerian

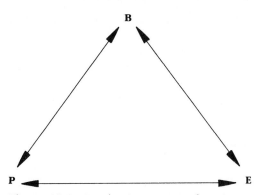

Figure 12.1　Bandura's Concept of Reciprocal Determinism. Human functioning is a product of the interaction of behavior (B), personal variables (P), and environmental events (E). (From *Social foundations of thought and action: A social cognitive theory* © 1986, p. 24, by Albert Bandura. Reprinted by permission of Prentice-Hall, Inc., Englewood Cliffs, NJ.)

sense. The behavior of the father would be controlled by the environment, but his behavior, in turn, would have a countercontrolling effect on the environment, namely the child. In Bandura's theory, however, the father is capable of thinking about the consequences of rewarding or ignoring the child's behavior. He may think, "If I give her a cookie, she will stop crying temporarily, but in future cases she will be more likely to persist until I give it to her. Therefore, I will not allow her to have a cookie." Hence the father has an affect on both his environment (the child) and his own behavior (rejecting his daughter's request). The child's subsequent behavior (father's environment) helps shape the cognition and the behavior of the father. If the child stops begging the father may then have other thoughts. For example, he may evaluate his behavior by thinking, "I'm a good father because I did the right thing." The change in environment also allows the father to pursue different behaviors. Thus, his subsequent behavior is partially determined by the reciprocal interaction of his environment, cognition, and behavior.

In this illustration the reciprocal interaction is completed. The child's pleas affected the father's behavior (E→B); they also partially determined the father's cognition (E→P); the father's behavior helped shape the child's behavior, that is, his own environment (B→E); his behavior also impinged on his own thoughts (B→P); and his cognition partially determined his behavior (P→B). To complete the cycle, P (person) must influence E (environment). How can the father's cognition directly shape the environment, without first being transformed into behavior? It cannot. However, P does not signify cognition alone; it stands for person. Bandura (1978b, p. 346) hypothesizes that, "People activate different environmental reactions, apart from their behavior, by their physical characteristics (e.g., size, physiognomy, race, sex, attractiveness) and socially conferred attributes, roles, and status." The father then by virtue of his role and status as a father, and perhaps in conjunction with his size and strength, has a decided effect on the child. Thus the final determination is completed (P→E).

Differential Contributions

Bandura uses the term reciprocal to indicate a mutual interaction of forces, not a similar or opposite counteraction. The three reciprocal factors need neither to be of equal strength nor to make an equal contribution. The relative potency of the three varies with the individual and with the situation.

At times behavior might be the most powerful, as when a person plays the piano for her own enjoyment. Other times the environment exerts the greatest influence, as when a lifeboat overturns and every survivor begins thinking and behaving in a very similar fashion. At still other times cognition (person) may gain ascendancy, as when a person believes that there are sinister plans being plotted to destroy her.

The relative influence of behavior, environment, and person depends on which of the triadic factors are strongest at a particular moment as the reciprocal interaction changes (Bandura, 1982a).

Meaning of Determinism

"Determinism" must not be understood to mean that behavior is completely determined by forces outside the individual. Bandura (1988a) sees no incompatibility between human agency and determinism. He is not an absolute determinist who believes that all behavior is caused by external events, but neither does he accept the concept of complete free will. Human personality and behavior are influenced by external events, but they are not inevitably determined by them. They are also partly molded by the internal state of cognition, which at least partially determines which environmental events will be perceived, evaluated, and acted upon. In other words, it is not the environment itself, but our perception of the environment which helps determine behavior. Within limits, then, people can choose to behave in a manner that increases the probability that the environment will interact with them in a somewhat predictable way. Behavior, therefore, is not only a dependent variable, but also an independent variable, exerting an influence on both the environment and the person.

Attempts to trace behavior ultimately to environmental causes are futile. The theory of reciprocal determinism holds that for every environmental cause there is a previous action that partially produced it, just as every action is partially shaped by prior environmental influences (Bandura, 1982a).

Chance Encounters and Fortuitous Events

Bandura believes that people are remarkably flexible and resilient. They "must develop their basic capabilities over an extended period, and they must continue to master new competencies to fulfill changing demands throughout their life span" (Bandura, 1986, p. 20). Resilience is possible

Can Chance Change Your Life?

We have seen that people have limited choice to act upon and react to their environments. Many situations in life, however, are beyond one's deliberate control. These are *chance encounters* and *fortuitous events.* A chance encounter is defined as "an unintended meeting of persons unfamiliar to each other" (Bandura, 1986, p. 32). A fortuitous event is an environmental experience that is unexpected and unintended.

The everyday lives of people are affected to a greater or lesser extent by the people they chance to meet. One's marital partner, occupation, place of residence, and the like may largely be the result of a fortuitous meeting that was unplanned and unexpected.

Fortuity adds a separate dimension in any scheme used to predict human behavior and makes accurate predictions practically impossible. However, this does not mean that chance encounters have a separate position in the reciprocal determinism paradigm. Once they occur, they enter the triadic interlocking system at point E (environment) and add to the mutual interaction in the same manner as do planned events. At that point, people behave toward their new acquaintance on the basis of their prior history of reinforcements, their expectations for this new relationship, and the other person's reaction to them (Bandura, 1982a).

There are many examples of chance encounters and fortuitous events permanently altering the path of a person's life or even the course of history. A number of years ago a young graduate student became bored with his reading assignment so he and a friend decided to play golf. By chance, this male twosome happened to be playing behind two women golfers. During the course of the round, two twosomes became one foursome, an acquaintanceship became a romantic interest, which eventually led to a marriage. By this fortuitous meeting Virginia Varns became the wife of Albert Bandura (Bandura, 1982b).

Choice of career is also often a matter of chance, and those careers which have made a lasting impression on civilization are no less likely than others to have been fortuitously chosen. Raymond Dart, the renowned paleoanthropologist, was a physician in need of baboon bones to instruct medical students to distinguish between human and animal skeletons. By chance, one of his students brought in a skull, previously used as a paperweight, which turned out to be the remains of *Australopithecus africanus,* an early human ancestor. This chance event influenced Dart to change careers and his subsequent work in anthropology has had a significant impact on our understanding of the evolution of the species.

because any of the three triadic factors—environment, behavior, or person— may be altered at any time. Two important potential changes are **chance encounters** and **fortuitous events.**

In our introductory case study we saw that Jim's career as a historian was set in motion by a chance meeting with Greg, the young assistant professor of history. Without this fortuitous encounter, Jim might have spent his professional life as a high school teacher in his home town. By changing careers he changed his environment, behavior, and personal factors, including cognition. Each change has had a reciprocal effect on each of the other triadic factors. However, Jim did not become a new person after he switched careers. His previous experiences had provided him with a relatively stable way of interpreting events. For years Jim had seen himself as a person who was academically gifted, intellectually curious, and historically oriented. Even though Jim changed his geographic location, his new environment was self-selected on the basis of a preexisting interest. In other words, Jim did not become a new person as a result of his chance encounter with Greg, but he did change his life path.

SELF SYSTEM

Bandura deviates from Skinner's radical behaviorism in postulating the existence of a **self system,** which acts upon both the environment and behavior. If behavior were completely a function of the environment, Bandura reasons, then there would be more variability within a person. Our behavior would be less consistent because we would constantly be reacting to the great diversity of environmental stimuli. "If actions were determined solely by external rewards and punishments, people would behave like weathervanes, constantly shifting direction to conform to whatever momentary influence happened to impinge upon them" (Bandura, 1986, p. 335). Though personality is largely learned and can be quite complex and variegated within any one person, some consistencies of speech, self-expression, and behavioral traits are difficult to account for on the bases of environmental contingencies alone. Cognitive factors such as memory and foresight bring some unity and consistency to personality (Bandura, 1978b).

However, Bandura does not go to the other extreme and suggest that there is an autonomous agent within the person shaping behavior to conform to a preexisting self-concept. In fact, Bandura believes that the behavior of an individual is generally more varied than it appears and that it is a grave error to attribute different behaviors to single or dual motives like striving for success (Adler) or sex and aggression (Freud). If behavior were regulated by a single motive, people would be more consistent. For example, a person who is usually moral would never behave immorally, but we know that this frequently happens. In Chapter 14 we will see that Gordon Allport argues that people possess personal dispositions or traits that have the power to render divergent stimuli functionally equivalent. Bandura would not countenance such an argument. An aggressive person, for example, is not always aggressive because the environment does not always reinforce aggressive behavior. Differential experiences with reward and punishment, to a large degree, shape one's behavior.

Bandura uses the term self system carefully. Unlike Sullivan's concept of self-system, which evolves mainly as a mechanism to avoid or reduce anxiety, Bandura's term does not refer to an independent agent with such a narrow purpose. It "refers to cognitive structures that provide reference mechanisms and to a set of subfunctions for the perception, evaluation, and regulation of behavior" (Bandura, 1978b, p. 348). This implies that people are capable of observing and symbolizing their own behavior and of evaluating it on the basis of memories of past reinforced or nonreinforced behavior as well as anticipated future consequences. Then, using this cognition as a reference point, they are able to exercise some measure of self-regulation (Bandura, 1982a).

Self-Regulation

Though people have no independent self with the capacity to manipulate the environment at will, they are capable of some degree of self-regulation. By using reflective thought they can manipulate their environments and produce consequences of their actions. These consequences feed back into the reciprocal determinism paradigm and enable people to partially regulate their own behavior. Three component processes are involved in self-regulatory behavior: self-observation, judgmental processes, and self-reaction (Bandura, 1978b, 1986).

Self-Observation

The first requirement for self-regulation is *self-observation* of performance. We must be able to monitor our own performance, even though the attention we give to it need not be complete or even accurate. We attend selectively to some aspects of our behavior and ignore others altogether. What we observe depends on interests and other preexisting self-conceptions. In achievement situations such as painting, playing games, or taking examinations we pay attention to the quality, quantity, speed, or originality of our work; in interpersonal situations such as meeting new acquaintances or reporting on events, we monitor the sociability of morality of our conduct (Bandura, 1986).

Judgmental Process

Self-observation alone does not provide a sufficient basis for regulating our own behavior. We must also evaluate our performance. This second, or *judgmental process* helps people regulate their behavior through the process of cognitive mediation. We are capable not only of reflective self-awareness but also of judging the worth of our action on the basis of goals we have set for ourselves. More specifically, the judgmental process depends on personal standards, referential performances, valuation of activity, and performance attribution.

Personal standards allow us to evaluate our performances without comparing them to the conduct of others. To a mentally retarded 10-year-old child, the act of tying his shoelaces may be highly prized. He need not devalue his accomplishment simply because other children can perform this same act at a younger age.

Personal standards, however, are a limited source of evaluation. For most of our activities, we evaluate our performances by comparing them to a *standard of reference*. Students compare their test scores to those of their classmates, the middle-aged jogger compares times and distances to those compiled by others of the same age, and the bridge player judges personal skill against that of others. In addition, we use our own previous levels of accomplishment as a reference for evaluating present performance. "Are my bowling scores higher than they were last year?" "Has my singing voice improved over the years?" "Is my teaching ability better now than ever?" Also, we may judge our performance by comparing it to that of a single individual, a brother, sister, parent, or even a hated rival; or we can compare it to a standard norm such as par in golf or a perfect score in bowling.

Besides personal and reference standards, the judgmental process is also dependent upon the overall *value* we place on an activity. If the ability to wash dishes or dust furniture receives minor value, the person will spend little time or effort in trying to improve these abilities. On the other hand, if getting ahead in the business world or attaining a professional or graduate degree is highly valued, the person will spend much effort in order to achieve success in these areas.

Finally, self-regulation also depends on how we judge the causes of our behavior, that is, *performance attribution.* If we believe that our success is due to our own efforts, we take pride in our accomplishments and tend to work harder to attain our goals. However, if we attribute our performance to external factors, we do not derive as much self-satisfaction and are not as likely to put forth strenuous effort to attain our goals. Conversely, if we believe that we are responsible for our own failures or inadequate performance, we will work more readily toward self-regulation than if we are convinced that our shortcomings and our fears are due to factors beyond our control (Bandura, 1983, 1986).

Self-Reaction

The third and final component of the self-regulatory function is *self-reaction.* We respond positively or negatively to our behavior depending on how it measures up to our personal standards. That is, we create incentives for our own actions through self-reinforcement or self-punishment. For example, a diligent student may reward herself for completing a reading assignment by watching a favorite television program.

Self-reinforcement does not rest on the fact that it immediately follows a response. The consequences of behavior are mediated by the person. We set standards for performance which, when met, tend to regulate behavior by such self-produced rewards as pride and self-satisfaction. When standards are not met, behavior is followed by self-dissatisfaction or self-criticism.

This concept of self-mediated consequences is a sharp contrast to Skinner's notion that the consequences of behavior are environmentally determined. Bandura hypothesizes that we work to attain rewards and to avoid punishments according to self-erected standards. Even when rewards are tangible, they are often accompanied by self-mediated intangible incentives such as a sense of accomplishment. The Nobel Prize, for example, carries a cash award, but its greater value to most recipients must be the feelings of pride or self-satisfaction in performing the tasks that led to the award.

External Factors in Self-Regulation

We have seen that personal conduct is controlled neither by autonomous internal entities such as ego or conscience nor by environmental determinants. Rather, behavior is regulated by the reciprocal interaction of person, environment, and prior behavior. People, therefore, have some limited capacity to regulate their own behavior. What processes contribute to this self-regulation?

First, people are capable of monitoring their own behavior and evaluating it in terms of both proximate and distant goals. In addition, self-regulation demands that people possess some capacity to manipulate the external factors that feed into the reciprocal interactive paradigm. Finally, they must be able to perceive the consequences of the manipulation of these external factors. Behavior, then, stems from a reciprocal influence of external factors with personal variables (Bandura, 1977b, 1978b).

Standards of Evaluation

External factors affect self-regulation in at least three ways (Bandura, 1978b). First they provide us with a standard for evaluating our own behavior. Standards do not stem magically from internal forces. Environmental factors, interacting with personal influences, shape individual standards for evaluation. By precept we learn from parents and teachers the value of honest or friendly behavior; by direct experience, we learn to place more value on being warm and dry than cold and wet; and through observing others, we evolve a multitude of standards for evaluating self-performance. In each of these examples personal factors affect which standards we will learn, but environmental forces also play a role.

External Reinforcement

Second, external factors aid self-regulation by providing the means for reinforcement (Bandura, 1977b). Intrinsic rewards are not always sufficient; we also need incentives that emanate from external factors. An artist, for example, may require more reinforcement than self-satisfaction to complete a large mural; environmental support in the form of a monetary retainer, praise and encouragement from others, and especially periodic self-reward may also be necessary.

The incentives to complete a lengthy project usually come from the environment and often take the form of small rewards contingent upon the completion of subgoals. The artist may enjoy a cup of coffee after having completed painting the hand of one of the subjects or break for lunch after finishing another small section of the mural. However, self-reward for inadequate performance is likely to result in environmental sanctions. Friends may criticize or mock the artist's work, patrons may withdraw support, or the artist may be self-critical. When performance does not meet self-standards, people tend to withhold rewards from themselves.

Selective Activation

A third external factor affecting self-regulation is **selective activation,** which refers to Bandura's (1986) belief that there is no automatic controlling agent within the person. Self-regulatory influences, he insists, operate only if they are activated. How and when one activates the self-regulatory function is influenced both by self-evaluation and by environmental conditions. When it is obvious that one particular course of action is inconsistent with one's self-concept and will result in injury to another, the self-regulatory process is strongly activated. If it is clear that striking another person will result in injury to that person and a jail term for oneself, then selective activation allows one to choose a different behavior. However, when the propriety of one's action is more ambiguous, the person may disengage evaluative standards from the behavior.

Disengagement of Internal Control

After we have adopted social and moral standards of conduct we can regulate our behavior by disengaging ourselves from the injurious consequences of our actions. Bandura (1986) refers to this as **disengagement of internal control.** Disengagement of behavior from self-evaluative consequences entails the use of either environmental or cognitive factors to justify otherwise reprehensible behavior. This can be accomplished in four ways. First, the nature of the *behavior* itself can be redefined. Second, the *relationship* between one's actions and their effects can be obscured by displacement or diffusion of responsibility. Third, the detrimental *consequences* of one's behavior can be distorted, minimized, or ignored. Fourth, the *victim* can be dehumanized or become the recipient of blame (Bandura, 1986, 1988d). Figure 12.2 illustrates the various points at which the disengagement may occur.

Redefinition of Behavior.   With the first technique (redefinition of behavior), otherwise reprehensible behavior is justified by a cognitive restructuring, thus allowing perpetrators to minimize or escape responsibility for their actions. At least three techniques can be employed which allow people to disengage themselves from responsibility for their behavior (see upper-left box in Figure 12.2).

The first is *moral justification* in which otherwise culpable behavior is made to seem defensible or even noble. Bandura (1988d) cites the example of World War I hero Sergeant Alvin York who, as a conscientious objector, believed that killing was morally wrong. Then after his battalion commander quoted from the Bible the conditions under which it was morally justified to kill, and after a long prayer vigil, York became convinced that killing enemy soldiers was morally defensible. After redefining killing, York became one of

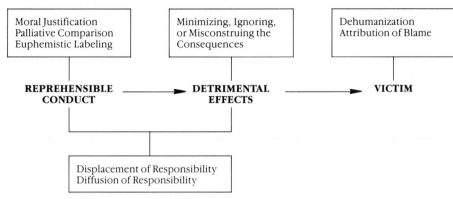

Figure 12.2 Mechanisms through which internal control is selectively activated or disengaged from reprehensible conduct at different points in the regulatory process. (From *Social foundations of thought and action: A social cognitive theory* © 1986, p. 376, by Albert Bandura. Reprinted by permission of Prentice-Hall, Inc., Englewood Cliffs, NJ.)

the greatest war heroes in American history, killing and capturing dozens of German soldiers.

A second method of reducing responsibility through the redefinition of wrongful behavior is to make advantageous or *palliative comparisons* between that behavior and the even greater atrocities committed by others. The incumbent politician claims to be stealing from public funds at a much lower pace than other elected officials. The child who vandalizes a school building uses the excuse that others broke even more windows. Terrorists justify their acts as minor defensive maneuvers against major powers.

A third technique in redefining behavior is the use of *euphemistic labels.* The murder of millions of Jews was called "purification of Europe" or "the final solution" by some Nazis. Bombing raids into neutral countries have been called "preemptive strikes," murder is sometimes called "wasting" or "terminating" people, and theft of private property has been termed "liberation," "confiscation," or "redistribution of wealth."

Displacement of Responsibility.   The second method of disengagement is the displacement or diffusion of responsibility (see lower box in Figure 12.2).

With *displacement,* the consequences of one's actions are minimized by placing responsibility on an outside source. A rapist blames his mother, who, he feels, never showed him physical affection. Normally conscientious and sympathetic civil service workers shift responsibility for their actions to a higher authority. "This is not my idea. I was told to do it." Nazi prison officers were "carrying out orders" from higher officers.

A related procedure is to *diffuse responsibility*—to spread it so thin that no one person is responsible. The civil servant, rather than blaming the boss, may diffuse responsibility throughout the entire bureaucracy. "That's the way things are done around here," or "That's just policy," are two frequently heard comments.

Disregard or Distortion of Consequences.

If behavior cannot somehow be disengaged from self-evaluative consequences through redefinition or displacement of responsibility, then a third method of disengagement might be employed. This involves distorting or obscuring the relationship between the behavior and its detrimental consequences (see center of Figure 12.2).

Bandura recognizes at least three techniques of disengaging the detrimental consequences of one's actions. They can be minimized, ignored, or misconstrued. An example of *minimizing consequences* is seen when a driver runs a red light and strikes a pedestrian. As the injured party lies bleeding and unconscious on the pavement, the driver is heard to say, "She's not really hurt badly. She's going to be okay."

Second, the consequences of one's actions can be disregarded or *ignored,* as when one does not see firsthand the harmful effects of those actions. In wartime, heads of state and army generals seldom view the total destruction and death resulting from their decisions.

Third, consequences can be distorted or *misconstrued.* A parent beats a child badly enough to cause serious bruises, but explains that the child needs discipline in order to mature properly.

Blame the Victims.

The fourth set of disengagement involves either dehumanizing the victims or attributing blame to them (see upper-right box in Figure 12.2).

In time of war the enemy is seen as subhuman. One is no more culpable for killing enemy soldiers (so the belief goes) than for swatting flies or spraying mosquitoes. At various times, Jews, blacks, American Indians, Orientals, beggars, the elderly, and criminals have become *dehumanized* victims. Acts of violence, insult, or other forms of mistreatment have been perpetrated against these groups by otherwise kind, considerate, and gentle people in order to disengage the perpetrator from an ambiguous situation.

When victims are not dehumanized, they are sometimes *blamed* for the perpetrator's culpable conduct. Victims of political assassination have been accused of inviting their own murder. An employee may steal from his employer because "The boss is stupid for making it so easy to take this merchandise. She deserves to lose it."

Disengagement and Defense Mechanisms.

The reader may see some similarity between Bandura's concept of disengagement and Freud's idea of defense mechanisms or Adler's notion of safeguarding tendencies. These similarities, however, are more superficial than substantive. With all three, a person is protected from conditions of discomfort, but aside from this, differences outweigh similarities. The defense mechanisms operate unconsciously and automatically to protect the ego from anxiety. Safeguarding tendencies are erected for the purpose of protecting a person against external threats to fictionalized feelings of personal superiority. They operate automatically, can be conscious as well as unconscious, and are directed toward gaining superiority over other people.

On the other hand, disengagement procedures are neither unconscious nor automatic, but are cognitively mediated. They protect a person from neither instinctual demands nor external threats; instead, they permit one to minimize or avoid responsibility in an ambiguous situation by justifying behavior that ordinarily would be foreign to one's self-evaluation. Unlike safeguarding tendencies, they are not specifically directed toward other people, but are employed to justify to oneself behavior that would otherwise be devalued or condemned by that person.

Self-Efficacy

How people will act in a particular situation depends on the reciprocity of environmental and cognitive conditions, especially those cognitive factors related to their expectations that they can or cannot execute the behavior necessary to effect a successful change in that situation. These expectations refer to Bandura's concept of **self-efficacy.**

In the reciprocal determinism paradigm, which postulates that the environment, behavior, and person have an interactive influence on one another, self-efficacy refers to the P (person) factor. Though it has a powerful influence, it is not the sole determiner of behavior. It combines with environment, prior behavior, and other personal variables to produce behavior.

Self-Efficacy Defined

What does Bandura mean by self-efficacy? Briefly, it is people's expectations that they are capable of performing the behavior that will produce desired outcomes in any particular situation. People with high self-efficacy believe that they can do something to alter environmental events; those with low self-efficacy regard themselves as essentially incapable of executing consequential behavior. Bandura (1986, p. 391) defines perceived self-efficacy as "people's judgments of their capabilities to organize and execute courses of action required to attain designated types of performances."

Self-efficacy is not the expectation of the outcomes of an event and is therefore different from Rotter's concepts of expectancy and freedom of movement. With Rotter's terms, the focus is on the *reinforcement,* that is, the probability that reinforcement will follow a specific behavior. With self-efficacy, on the other hand, the focus is on *behavior,* that is, the expectation that one is capable of executing the behavior necessary to produce an effect.

Bandura (1984, 1986) distinguishes between *efficacy* expectations and *outcome* expectations. Efficacy refers to people's confidence that they have the ability to perform certain behaviors, whereas an outcome expectancy refers to one's prediction of the likely *consequences* of that behavior. Outcome should not be confused with successful accomplishment of an act; it refers to the consequences of behavior, not the completion of the act itself.

For example, a job applicant may have confidence that she will perform well during an interview, have the ability to answer any possible question, remain relaxed and controlled, and exhibit an appropriate level of friendly behavior. Therefore, she has high self-efficacy in regard to the employment interview. However, despite these high efficacy expectations, she may have low outcome expectations. A low outcome expectancy would exist if she believes that she has little chance of being offered a position. This judgment might be due to unpromising environmental conditions, such as high unemployment, depressed economy, or superior competition. In addition, other personal factors such as age, gender, height, weight, or physical health may negatively affect outcome expectancies.

Self-efficacy also differs from Rotter's concept of locus of control. Internal locus of control is not synonymous with high self-efficacy, nor is external locus of control synonymous with low self-efficacy. Rotter holds that people with internal locus of control believe that events are shaped by causes over which they exercise a measure of control, whereas Bandura believes that people with high self-efficacy believe they are capable of behavior that can affect environmental forces, and, therefore, impinge on the ultimate outcome of an event. Conversely, in Rotter's theory, people with an external locus of control see the environment rather than themselves as being primarily responsible for events, whereas in Bandura's view, low self-efficacy is not necessarily a denial of responsibility, but rather a belief that one cannot execute actions that effect desired environmental change. It is possible, of course, for one to have low self-efficacy due to lack of skill and still believe that the control of behavior resides within the individual. Though the concepts of efficacy and locus of control are related, there are important differences between them. Efficacy refers to the judgment that one can or cannot execute certain behaviors, while locus of control centers on the belief that outcomes are determined either by one's actions or by forces beyond one's control.

Besides being different from outcome expectancies and locus of control, there are other concepts that must not be confused with self-efficacy. First, efficacy does not refer to the ability to execute basic motor skills such as walking, reaching, or grasping. Also, personal efficacy does not imply that designated behaviors can be performed without anxiety, stress, or fear; it is merely our judgment, accurate or faulty, as to whether or not we can execute the required actions. Finally, judgments of efficacy are not the same as levels of aspiration. Heroin addicts, for example, often aspire to be drug-free, but may have little confidence in their ability to successfully beat the habit (Bandura, 1982c).

Sources of Self-Efficacy

Personal efficacy is acquired, enhanced, or decreased through any one or combination of four sources: (1) enactive attainments, (2) vicarious experiences, (3) verbal persuasion, and (4) physiological arousal (Bandura, 1986). With each method, information about oneself and the environment is cognitively processed and, together with recollections of previous experiences, alters perceived self-efficacy. Besides these four sources, efficacy is affected by one's internal standards of conduct.

The most influential source of self-efficacy is *enactive attainments,* or performance (Bandura, 1977a, 1986). In general, successful performance raises efficacy expectancies while failure tends to lower them. There are several corollaries to this general statement. First, successful performance raises self-efficacy in proportion to the difficulty of the task. A good tennis player gains little by defeating a clearly inferior opponent, but if one performs well against a superior opponent, self-efficacy is enhanced. Second, tasks successfully accomplished by oneself are more efficacious than those completed with the help of others. In sports, team accomplishments do not increase personal efficacy as much as do individual achievements. Third, failure is most likely to decrease efficacy when we know that we put forth our best effort. To fail when only half-trying is not as inefficacious as to fall short in spite of one's best efforts. Also, failed performance under conditions of high emotional arousal are not as self-debilitating as failure under maximal conditions: "I know I failed that test, but I was worried about my father's health at the time." This, by the way, is not an excuse uttered for public consumption—self-efficacy is contingent on information processed (accurately or not) by the individual, with no aim toward deception of others. Another corollary to the general statement that successful performance enhances efficacy while failure decreases it is that occasional failure has little effect on efficacy, especially for people with a generally high expectancy of success. However, people with low efficacy seldom give themselves credit even for those occasional successful performances.

A second source of efficacy is **vicarious experiences** (Bandura, 1977a). Observing others succeed raises self-efficacy (Bandura et al., 1980); observing another of equal competence fail at a task tends to lower one's efficacy (Brown & Inouye, 1978). When the model is dissimilar to the observer, vicarious experiences have minimum effect on efficacy. An old, sedentary coward watching a young, active, brave circus performer successfully walk a high wire will undoubtedly have little enhancement of efficacy expectations for duplication of the feat.

Vicarious experiences are strongest when people have had little prior experience with the activity. Observing a professional golfer correctly execute the proper swing will be less efficacious to the experienced golfer as opposed to the novice. In general, the effects of modeling are not as strong as those of personal performance in raising levels of efficacy, but they can have powerful effects where inefficacy is concerned. Observing a swimmer of equal ability fail to negotiate a choppy river will likely dissuade the observer from attempting the same task. The effects of this vicarious experience may last a lifetime.

Self-efficacy can also be acquired through *verbal persuasion* (Bandura, 1977a). The effects of this source are limited, but under proper conditions verbal persuasion can raise or lower self-efficacy (Chambliss & Murray, 1979). First, a person must believe the persuader. Exhortations from a credible

The most powerful source of self-efficacy is enactive attainment or performance.

source have more efficacious power than those from an uncredible person. This explains some of the success of groups such as Alcoholics Anonymous and Synanon. It may also have been the reason Jim, our case study, became persuaded that he could successfully work toward a Ph.D. in history. Recall that both an assistant professor of history and his wife verbally encouraged him to pursue the degree.

Second, the activity one is being exhorted to attempt must realistically be within one's repertoire of behavior. No amount of verbal persuasion can alter someone's efficacy judgment on the ability to limbo dance under a stick 12 inches from the floor. Jim's past academic record offered evidence that he might successfully attain a Ph.D. Specific knowledge or skills alone do not increase efficacy sufficiently to pursue a particular career. Social skills, the ability to communicate, and the capacity to organize and manage one's time all combine with knowledge and skill to affect perceived self-efficacy. Bandura (1986) believes that occupational preferences are determined more by self-efficacy than by the rewards a person expects to receive from the job.

Bandura hypothesizes that the efficacious power of suggestion is directly related to the perceived status and authority of the persuader. Status and authority, of course, are not identical. For example, a psychotherapist's suggestion to phobic patients that they can ride in a crowded elevator is more likely to increase self-efficacy than if spouses or children made the same suggestion; but if that same therapist tells patients that they have the ability to

Verbal persuasion can raise or lower self-efficacy.

change a faulty light switch, there may be no enhancement of self-efficacy. Also, verbal persuasion is most effective when combined with successful performance. Persuasion may convince someone to attempt an activity, and, if performance is successful, both the accomplishment and the subsequent verbal rewards emanating from the persuader combine to increase future efficacy.

The final source of efficacy is *physiological arousal* (Bandura, 1977a, 1986). Strong emotion ordinarily lowers performance and most people have learned to judge their ability to execute a given task using their emotional arousal as a cue. People experiencing intense fear or acute anxiety are likely to have lower efficacy expectancies. The actor in a school play knows the lines during rehearsal, but realizes that the fear felt opening night may block recall. Most people, when not afraid, have the ability to successfully handle snakes. The task merely requires that one grasp the snake firmly behind the head. For most of us, however, the fear that accompanies that activity is debilitating and greatly lowers our performance expectancy.

Therapists have long recognized that a reduction in anxiety or an increase in physical relaxation can facilitate performance. Arousal information is related to several variables. First, of course, is the level of arousal; we are ordinarily cognizant of our emotional states. Incidentally, for some situations emotional arousal is associated with increased performance; the anxiety felt by the actor on opening night, if not too intense, may raise efficacy expectancies. The second variable is the perceived realism of the arousal. If one knows that the fear is realistic, as when driving on an icy mountain road, personal efficacy may be raised. However, when one is cognizant of the absurdity of the phobia, for example, fear of the outdoors, then the emotional arousal tends to lower efficacy. Finally, the nature of the task is an added variable. Emotional arousal may facilitate the successful completion of simple tasks, but it is likely to interfere with performance of complex activities.

Self-Efficacy as a Predictor of Behavior

Self-efficacy is not a stimulus that controls response, but it is one of several self-influences that affect our behavior. For Bandura, the source of control does not reside in the stimulus or the environment, but lies in the reciprocation of environmental, behavioral, and personal factors. An important personal variable is self-efficacy, and when it is combined with specific goals and knowledge of performance, it can serve as an important contributor to future behavior (Bandura, 1988b; Bandura & Cervone, 1983). Bandura believes that people produce their future by how they behave and not by simply predicting what will happen in a specific situation.

Bandura (1981) is critical of self-theories, such as the one developed by Carl Rogers (Chapter 17), that center on a composite self-concept rather than many specific self-precepts. Self-efficacy, then, is not a global concept. It varies from situation to situation depending on the competencies required for different activities; the presence or absence of other people; the perceived competence of these others, especially if they are competitors; the person's predisposition to attend to failure of performance rather than to success; and the accompanying physiological states, particularly the presence of anxiety, apathy, or despondency (Bandura, 1982c).

High and low efficacy combine with responsive and unresponsive environments to produce four possible predictive variables (Bandura, 1982c). When efficacy is high and the environment is responsive, outcomes are most likely to be successful. When low efficacy is combined with a responsive environment, people may be become depressed when they observe that others are successful at tasks that seem too difficult for them. When people with high efficacy encounter unresponsive environmental situations, they will intensify their efforts to change the environment. They may use protest, social activism, or even force to instigate change, but if all efforts fail, Bandura hypothesizes, they will either give up that course and take on a new one or they will seek a more responsive environment. Finally, when low self-efficacy combines with an unresponsive environment, there is a prediction of apathy, resignation, and helplessness. For example, when the difficulties of becoming company president become apparent to a junior executive with low self-efficacy, the person will develop feelings of discouragement, give up, and fail to transfer productive efforts toward a similar goal.

LEARNING

In the previous section we saw that one source of self-efficacy was vicarious experience. Bandura believes that much of what we learn is acquired through observing others. "If knowledge could be acquired only through the effects of one's own actions, the process of cognitive and social development would be greatly retarded, not to mention exceedingly tedious" (Bandura, 1986, p. 47).

Not all learning, however, comes through observing others. We also learn by experience. We enact or perform behaviors that have consequences and thereby learn from the effects of our actions. Bandura (1986) discusses two major kinds of learning—*observational* and *enactive.*

Observational Learning

Bandura distinguishes between learning and performance. He believes that people can learn without performing any behavior. Responses need not occur in order for learning to take place; that is, we can learn through observation. We observe natural phenomena, plants, animals, waterfalls, the motion of the moon and stars, and so forth, but especially important to social cognitive theory is the assumption that we learn through observing the behavior of other people. In this respect, Bandura differs from Skinner, who holds that enactive behavior is the basic datum of psychological science. He departs from both Skinner and Dollard and Miller in his belief that reinforcement is not essential to learning. True, reinforcement facilitates learning, but it is not a necessary condition for it. We can learn, for example, by observing models being reinforced.

Bandura (1977b, 1986) believes that observational learning is much more efficient than learning through direct experience. By observing others we are spared countless responses that might be followed by punishment or by no reinforcement. Children observe characters on television, for example, and repeat what they hear or see; they need not enact random behaviors, hoping that some of them will be rewarded.

Modeling

The core of observational learning is *modeling.* Learning through modeling involves adding and subtracting from the observed behavior and generalizing from one observation to another. In other words, modeling involves cognitive processes and is not simply mimicry or imitation. Modeling is a much broader term. It is more than matching the actions of another. It involves symbolically representing information and storing it for use at a future time (Bandura, 1986).

Modeling takes into account the psychological effects of being exposed to a model. What are some of these psychological influences upon modeling? First, the characteristics of the model are important. We are more likely to model high-status people rather than those of low status, competent individuals rather than unskilled or incompetent ones, and powerful people rather than impotent ones. Second, the characteristics of the observer affect the likelihood of modeling. People who lack status, skill, or power are most likely to model. Children model more than old people and novices are more likely to model than experts.

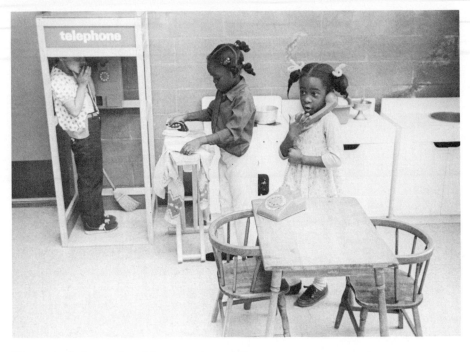

The core of observational learning is modeling.

Third, the consequences of the modeling behavior have an effect on modeling. The greater the value a person places on the observed behavior, the more likely it will be learned. Also, behavior that is rewarding to the observer is learned faster than that which is punishing or not reinforcing. However, the observation of a model receiving severe punishment may facilitate learning. This is one instance of where we can learn without performing the behavior. Seeing another receive a severe shock from touching an electric wire teaches us a valuable lesson.

Processes Governing Observational Learning

Bandura (1977b, 1986, 1988c) recognizes four processes that govern observational learning: attention, representation, behavioral production, and motivation (Bandura, 1977b; 1986).

Attention.   Before we can model another person we must attend to that person. What factors regulate attention? First, we are most likely to attend to the people with whom we associate, since we have more opportunities to observe these individuals. Second, attractive models are more likely to be observed than unattractive ones; popular figures on television, in sports, or in movies are often closely attended. Also, the nature of the behavior being modeled affects our attention; we observe behavior that we think is important to us and from which we believe we can profit.

Representation.   In order for observation to lead to new response patterns, those patterns must be symbolically represented in memory. Symbolic representation need not be verbal. Some observations are retained in imagery and can be summoned in the absence of the physical model. This process is especially important in infancy when verbal skills are not yet developed.

Verbal coding, however, greatly speeds the process of observational learning. With language we can talk to ourselves and verbally evaluate those observed behaviors and decide which ones we wish to discard and which we desire to try. Verbal coding also helps us to rehearse the behavior symbolically, that is, to tell ourselves over and over again how we will perform the behavior once given the chance. Rehearsal can also entail the actual performance of the modeled response and this, too, aids the retention process.

Behavioral Production.   After attending to a model and retaining what we have observed, the next process of modeling involves behavioral production. In converting cognitive representations into appropriate actions, we must ask ourselves several questions about the behavior to be modeled. First we ask, "How can I do this?" After symbolically rehearsing the relevant responses, we try out our new behavior. While performing, we monitor ourselves with the question, "What am I doing?" Finally, we evaluate our performance by asking, "Am I doing this right?" This last question is not always easy to answer, especially if it pertains to a motor skill such as ballet dancing or platform diving in which we cannot actually see ourselves. Carroll and Bandura (1982, 1985), however, found that self-monitoring by use of a video recorder facilitates the learning of some motor skills.

Motivation.   Observational learning is most effective when learners are motivated to perform the modeled behavior. Attention and representation can lead to the acquisition of learning, but performance is facilitated by motivation to enact that particular behavior. Even though observation of others may teach us *how* to do something, we may have no desire to perform the necessary action. One person can watch another use a power saw or run a vacuum cleaner and not be motivated to try either activity. Most sidewalk superintendents have no wish to emulate the observed construction worker.

Observing a model being punished for performance will diminish one's likelihood of enacting the same behavior. For example, if you notice a classmate receiving an embarrassing admonition from a professor after asking a question, you will probably learn not to ask questions in that class. In summary, then, modeling is facilitated by observing appropriate activities, properly coding the events for representation in memory, actually performing the behavior, and being sufficiently motivated.

Enactive Learning

Every response a person makes is followed by some consequence. Some of these consequences are satisfying, some are dissatisfying, but others are simply not cognitively attended and hence have little effect.

Reinforcers can be either positive or negative, but Bandura believes that their effects do not follow automatically from the consequences of a response. Complex human behavior involves the cognitive mediation of the individual in order for the consequences of a response to have an effect. Verbal reinforcement, for example, must be attended and comprehended before it can have meaning. The meaning for the receiver, however, may be different from that intended by the sender. A dance instructor compliments pupils for performing a particularly difficult maneuver, hoping to encourage them and to improve their skill level. However, the words may have an opposite effect or no effect on the dancers, who may reason that if they really possessed the potential to be great performers, their teacher would not need to compliment them for such a simple move.

Bandura (1977b) recognizes at least three functions served by response consequences. They can impart information, motivate future behavior, or reinforce present behavior.

Impart Information

The first function of response consequences is an informative one. We notice the effects of our actions, retain this information, and use it as a guide for future actions. Bakers who have previously been reinforced for faithfully following directions may choose to ignore a recipe item calling for two tablespoons of baking powder. Why? Because in the past they have also been reinforced for noticing the approximate ratio of baking powder to flour and also that printed material sometimes contains typographical errors. Therefore, they conclude, the correct amount of baking powder is two teaspoons, not two tablespoons. Information retained from earlier reinforcing situations, therefore, enables people to deviate from their normal procedure of closely following a recipe. Their previous histories of being reinforced for following directions do not dictate that they will respond automatically. The consequences of using the lesser amount of baking powder on this occasion undoubtedly will be noted and likely retained for future reference.

Motivate Future Behavior

A second function of response consequences is to motivate anticipatory behavior. People are capable of symbolically representing future outcomes and acting accordingly. They not only possess insight but are also capable of foresight. We do not have to suffer the discomfort of cold before deciding to wear a coat when going outside in freezing weather. Instead, we anticipate the effects of cold, wet weather and dress accordingly. The symbolic representation of discomfort serves as a stimulus for our thinking about wearing a coat, and it also increases the likelihood that we will actually wear one and thus be reinforced for that behavior. Receiving reinforcement for wearing warm clothing in cold weather then becomes a motivator in future similar situations.

Reinforce Present Behavior

The consequences of responses also serve to reinforce behavior, a function that has been firmly documented by Skinner (Chapter 10) and other reinforcement theorists. Bandura (1986), however, contends that, though reinforcement may at times be unconscious and automatic, complex behavioral patterns are greatly facilitated by cognitive intervention. A fledgling basketball player practices free throws with little consistent success. Soon the player realizes that the shots that find their mark are the ones in which the knees were bent and backspin was applied to the ball. Without this cognitive intervention, Bandura believes, performance is likely to remain at a low level. If responses did not impart specific information with which the learner interacts, then progress would be slow or nonexistent. The question at this point then becomes: Is immediate feedback by itself sufficient to shape a player's shooting behavior toward greater and greater accuracy? It is quite possible that slow improvement may be made where the learner knows when, but not why, an attempt is successful. However, Bandura maintains that learning will occur much more efficiently when the learner is cognitively involved in the learning situation and understands what behaviors precede successful responses.

DYSFUNCTIONAL BEHAVIOR

Bandura's concept of reciprocal determinism assumes that behavior is learned as a result of the interaction of person, behavior, and environment. Dysfunctional behavior is no exception. It is determined by a mutual interaction of the person, including cognition and neurophysiological processes; the environment, including interpersonal relations and socioeconomic conditions; and behavioral factors, especially previous experiences with reinforcement.

Bandura's concept of dysfunctional behavior lends itself most readily to depressive reactions, phobias, and aggressive behaviors.

Depressive Reactions

High personal standards and goals can lead to achievement and self-satisfaction. However, when people set their goals too high, they are likely to fail. Failure frequently leads to depression and depressed people often undervalue their own accomplishments. The result is chronic misery, feelings of worthlessness, lack of purposefulness, and pervasive depression. Bandura (1986) believes that dysfunctional depression can occur in any of the three self-regulatory subfunctions.

First, during *self-observation* people can misperceive their own performance or distort their memory of past accomplishment. Depressed people are more likely to underestimate their successes and overestimate their failures. More frequently, however, depression relates to distorted recollections. Depressed people tend to exaggerate their past mistakes and minimize their prior accomplishments.

Second, the *judgmental processes* of depressed people are likely to be faulty. They set their standards unrealistically high so that any performance attainments will be judged as a failure. Even when they achieve success in the eyes of others, they continue to berate their own accomplishments. Depression is especially likely when goals and personal standards are much higher than one's perceived efficacy to attain them.

Finally, the *self-reactions* of depressed inividuals are quite different from those of nondepressed persons. Depressed people not only judge themselves harshly, but they also are inclined to treat themselves badly for their short-comings. Bandura (1986, p. 361) suggests that depressed people "generally evaluate themselves less favorably and reward themselves less than the non-depressed, who are more inclined to savor their successes. The depressed are also inclined to punish themselves more severely for poor performances."

Phobias

Phobias are fears that are strong enough and pervasive enough to have severe debilitating effects on one's daily life. For example, snake phobias (a seemingly favorite topic of Bandura) prevent people from holding a variety of jobs and from enjoying many kinds of recreational activities. Phobias and fears are learned by direct contact, inappropriate generalization, and obser-vation of models. They are difficult to extinguish because they produce avoid-ance behavior and, unless the fearsome object is somehow encountered, the phobia will endure.

Once established, phobias are maintained by consequent determinants; that is, a person continues to receive negative reinforcement for avoiding the fear-producing situation. For example, if a person expects to receive aversive experiences (encountering a snake) while walking through a vacant lot, he will reduce the feeling of threat by not entering the field. (If he is a real estate salesperson, he may remove himself farther from the fearsome situation by quitting his job.) In this example, dysfunctional (avoidance) behavior is pro-duced by the mutual interaction of the person's expectancies (belief that snakes inhabit the open field), the external environment (the vacant field), and behavioral factors (his prior experiences of strong fear when approach-ing open fields).

Aggressive Behaviors

Aggressive behaviors, when carried to extremes, can also be dysfunctional. Bandura rejects the frustration-aggression hypothesis of Dollard and Miller (Chapter 9) and the instinct theory of Freud (Chapter 2). Instead, he con-tends that aggressive behavior is acquired through observation of others, direct experiences with positive and negative reinforcements, training or instruction, and bizarre beliefs (see Box—"Is TV Violence Contagious?").

Once established, people continue to aggress for at least five different rea-sons: they enjoy inflicting injury on the victim (positive reinforcement); they avoid or counter the aversive consequences of aggression by others (negative reinforcement); they receive injury or harm for not behaving aggressively (punishment); their aggressive behavior enables them to live up to personal

Is TV Violence Contagious?

That aggression can be learned through observing others was demonstrated by Bandura, Ross, and Ross (1963) in a now classic study that found that children who observe others behaving aggressively displayed more aggression, after being mildly frustrated, than a control group of children who did not view aggressive acts but were equally frustrated. In this study 96 Stanford University Nursery School boys and girls from about three to five-and-one-half years of age were divided into three matched experimental groups and one control group of 24 subjects each.

The first experimental group observed a live model behaving with both verbal and physical aggression toward a number of toys, including a large inflated Bobo doll; the second experimental group observed a film showing the same model behaving in an identical manner; the third experimental group saw a fantasy film in which a model, dressed as a black cat, behaved equally aggressively against the Bobo doll; the control group, matched with the experimental groups on previous ratings of aggression, was not subjected to an aggressive model, but otherwise was treated identically to the three experimental groups.

After subjects in the three experimental groups observed a model scolding, kicking, punching, and hitting the Bobo doll with a mallet, they were brought into another room where they were mildly frustrated. Immediately following this frustration the child was brought into the experimental room, which contained some toys (such as a smaller version of the Bobo doll) that could be played with aggressively. In addition, some essentially nonaggressive toys such as a tea set and coloring materials were present. The subjects' aggressive or nonaggressive response to the toys was observed through a one-way mirror.

As hypothesized, children exposed to an aggressive model displayed more aggressive responses than those who had not been exposed. Also, as hypothesized, boys were more aggressive than girls. Contrary to expectations, there was no difference in the amount of total aggression shown by subjects in the three experimental groups. Those who observed the cartoon character were at least as aggressive as those exposed to a live model or to a filmed model. In general, children in each experimental group exhibited about twice as much aggressive behavior as did those in the control group. In addition, the particular kind of aggressive response was remarkably similar to that displayed by the adult models. Children scolded, kicked, punched, and hit the doll with a mallet in close imitation to the behavior that had been modeled.

standards of conduct (self-reinforcement); and they observe others receiving rewards for aggressive acts or punishment for nonaggressive behavior (Evans, 1976).

THERAPY

According to Bandura, deviant behaviors are not caused by characterological weaknesses, a single master motive, or unhappy childhood experiences. They are initiated on the basis of social cognitive learning principles and they are maintained because, in some ways, they continue to serve some function. Therapeutic change, therefore, is difficult because it involves the elimination of behaviors that have become associated with satisfying conditions of reinforcement. Smoking, overeating, and drinking alcoholic beverages, for example, generally have positive effects initially and their long-range aversive consequences are usually not sufficient to produce avoidance behavior.

The ultimate goal of therapy is self-regulation. To achieve this end, the therapist introduces strategies designed not only to induce behavioral change but to maintain it as well. Performance accomplishments are emphasized, not the treatment of illnesses or the facilitation of vague achievements such as self-actualization or psychological health.

Bandura (1978a) visualizes three levels of treatment accomplishments. The first level is the *induction of change.* Therapy, if it is to have any degree of effectiveness, must at least instigate some change in behavior. For example, if a phobic response to height is extinguished, a previously acrophobic person is able to climb a 20-foot ladder; thus change has been induced.

The second level of treatment accomplishment is *generalization.* The acrophobic person will not only be able to ascend a ladder but also will generalize that behavior to other situations. This is a more effective level than simple induction of change, and it allows the person to ride in airplanes or look out windows of tall buildings.

Some therapies induce change and facilitate generalization, but, in time, the therapeutic effects are lost and the person reacquires the dysfunctional behavior. This is particularly true with extinguishing maladaptive habits such as smoking and overeating. The most effective therapy reaches the third level of accomplishment, which is *maintenance* of newly acquired functional behaviors.

Since dysfunctional behavior is produced by reciprocal determinism, "the likelihood that a given behavior will be performed can vary markedly in different environmental settings toward different people, and at different times" (Bandura, 1978a, p. 96). This broad conceptualization of both maladaptive behavior and treatment permits a variety of therapeutic techniques and strategies. The first criterion of any approach is that it bring about behavioral change. Beyond that, generalization and maintenance become important goals.

Bandura suggests several basic treatment approaches, one of which is overt or vicarious modeling. Observing live or filmed models performing threatening activities can help extinguish anxieties and fears and permit the observer to perform those same activities (Rosenthal & Bandura, 1978).

In a second treatment mode, covert or cognitive modeling, subjects are trained to visualize models performing fearsome behaviors. (Bandura et al., 1980). Overt and covert modeling strategies are most effective, however, when combined with performance-oriented approaches (Bandura, 1977b).

A third procedure, called enactive mastery, requires the subjects to perform those behaviors which have previously produced incapacitating fears.

Enactment, however, is not ordinarily the first step in treatment. The subjects typically begin by observing models or by having their emotional arousal lessened through **systematic desensitization** (Wolpe, 1973), the extinction of anxiety or fear through self-induced or therapist-induced relaxation. Fearsome situations are placed on a hierarchy from least to most threatening. Subjects, while relaxed, enact the least threatening behavior and then gradually move through the hierarchy until they can perform the most threatening activity, all the while remaining at a low state of emotional arousal (Bandura, Blanchard, & Ritter, 1969).

Bandura has demonstrated that each of these strategies can be effective and that they are most powerful when used in combination with one another (Bandura, 1977a; Bandura & Adams, 1977; Bandura et al., 1980). Bandura (1977b) believes that the reason for their effectiveness can be traced to a common mechanism found in each of these approaches, namely, *cognitive mediation.* When people use cognition to increase self-efficacy, that is, when they become convinced that they can perform difficult tasks, then, in fact, they become able to cope with previously intimidating situations.

Motivation to change dysfunctional behaviors is enhanced when people set realistic goals and then receive feedback on how they are doing relative to achieving those goals. The goals themselves do not provide motivation; rather, people use performance feedback to evaluate their progress toward goals. When self-satisfaction is contingent upon narrowing the gap between performance and adopted goals, the "people give direction to their actions and create self-incentives to persist in their efforts until performances match their goals" (Bandura, 1988b, p. 41). Goals should be challenging, yet reasonable. But most of all, people must have knowledge of their performance in relation to their goals.

CONCEPT OF HUMANITY

Bandura sees humans as having the capacity to become many things. "Human nature is characterized by a vast potentiality that can be fashioned by direct and observational experience into a variety of forms within biological limits" (Bandura, 1986, p. 21). Humans have evolved neurophysiological mechanisms for symbolizing their experiences. They have the capacity to store past experiences and to use this information to chart future actions.

Our capacity to use symbols provides us with a powerful tool for understanding and controlling our environment. It enables us to solve problems without resorting to inefficient trial-and-error behavior, to imagine the consequences of our actions, and to set goals for ourselves (Bandura, 1988a).

As humans, we are *goal directed,* purposive animals. The future can be seen in the present and we can bestow it with meaning by our cognitive awareness of possible consequences of future behavior. We anticipate the future and behave accordingly in the present. The future does not determine behavior, but its cognitive representation can have a powerful effect on present actions. "By representing foreseeable outcomes symbolically, people can convert future consequences into current motivators and regulators of foresightful behavior" (Bandura, 1986, p. 19).

Though we are basically *goal-oriented,* Bandura believes that we have specific rather than general intentions and purposes. We are not motivated by a single master goal such as striving for superiority or self-actualization, but rather by a multiplicity of goals, some distant and some proximate. These individual intentions, however, are not ordinarily anarchical; they possess some stability and order. Cognition gives us the capacity to evaluate probable consequences and to eliminate behaviors that do not meet our standards of conduct. Personal standards, therefore, tend to give human behavior a degree of consistency, even though that behavior lacks a master motive to guide it.

Bandura's concept of humanity is more *optimistic* than pessimistic. People are seen as capable of learning new behaviors at any time of their lives. Some dysfunctional behaviors persist due to low self-efficacy or because they are perceived as being reinforced. However, their continuation is not inevitable, and most people have the capacity to change their unproductive modes of behavior through modeling productive behaviors of others and through various cognitive strategies.

Biological factors are not completely overlooked in social learning theory. However, since they are but one aspect of one of three variables that interact to produce behavior, they are not heavily emphasized by Bandura. Instead, cognition gains ascendance within that variable termed *person* (P), while *social factors* are important ingredients in each of the other two variables—*environment* (E) and *behavior* (B).

Are humans free to control their own actions? Bandura's answer is qualified. Reciprocal determinism postulates a mutual interlocking system in which person, behavior, and environment all influence one another. Therefore, neither outside forces nor personal factors are solely responsible for human behavior. People have some capacity to control their behavior. Though they are affected by both the environment and their experiences with reinforcement, they, in turn, have some power to mold these two external conditions. To some extent, people can manage those environmental conditions which will shape their own future behavior and they can choose to ignore or augment their previous experiences. People can "serve as a causal contributor to their own life course by selecting, influencing, and constructing their own circumstances" (Bandura, 1986, p. 38).

This concept of self-regulation goes beyond Skinner's notion of counter-control. Skinner holds that ultimately the environment is the force behind the organism's behavior, while Bandura believes that people are *partially free* to create those environments which later impinge upon them. Personal freedom, then, is limited; it is restricted by physical constraints such as laws, prejudices, regulations, and the rights of other people. In addition, personal factors such as perceived inefficacy and lack of confidence restrict individual freedom. Some people, then, have more freedom than others. "Given the same environmental conditions, persons who have the capabilities for exercising many options and are adept at regulating their own behavior will have greater freedom than will those who have limited means of personal agency" (Bandura, 1986, p. 39). Bandura (1986, p. 42) defines freedom as "the number of options available to people and their right to exercise them."

Bandura believes that neither freedom nor responsibility should be considered antithetical to determinism. To him, outside influences operate deterministically on human behavior, but the person retains some measure of self-influence, which also operates deterministically on behavior. Since a degree of self-regulation is always possible, personal responsibility cannot be abdicated. As people recognize the possibility of alternative actions, they must assume partial responsibility for their actions (Bandura, 1982a, 1986).

It may appear that Bandura straddles the fence on the issue of freedom and determinism since he says that behavior is determined by an interaction of self-regulation and external source of influence. Philosophically, however, the question of freedom is an either/or issue. Partial freedom *is* freedom. No one seriously holds that behavior is completely free. All personality theorists recognize that outside forces have at least some influence on behavior. They may argue over the degree of restriction, but if they grant even one iota of free human agency, then they must be viewed as believers in personal freedom. If one holds, as does Bandura, that people are partially free, then one must eventually be concerned with the ultimate origin of that freedom. To say that it stems from reciprocal determinism begs the question. Granted, people are influenced by their interaction with environment and the contingencies of reinforcement, but the ultimate source of free choice must reside within that part of the reciprocal determinism paradigm labeled "person." Though Bandura is not greatly concerned with the question of ultimate choice, his belief in partial freedom places him within the camp of those who recognize personal freedom.

On the issue of *causality or teleology,* Bandura's position would be described as moderate. Human functioning is a product of environmental factors interacting with behavior and personal variables, especially cognitive activity. We move with a purpose toward goals that we have set, but motivation exists neither in the past nor the future. It is contemporary. Although future events cannot motivate us, our conception of them is "converted into current motivators and regulators of behavior" (Bandura, 1988b, p. 37).

Social cognitive theory emphasizes *conscious thought* over unconscious determinants of behavior. Self-regulation of actions relies on self-monitoring, judgment, and self-reaction, all of which are ordinarily conscious during the learning situation. "People do not become thoughtless during the learning process. They make conscious judgments about how their actions affect the environment" (Bandura, 1986, p. 116). After learnings are well established, especially motor learning, they may become unconscious. We do not have to be aware of all our actions while driving a car or swinging a golf club.

Bandura recognizes the limitations that biological forces place on us. Nevertheless, we have a remarkable plasticity. Our social environments allow us a wide range of behaviors. We observe other people and use them as models. All of us live in a number of social networks and are thus influenced by a variety of people. Modern technology, in the form of computers and the media, facilitates the spread of social influences.

Because people have a remarkable plasticity and capacity for learning, there are vast individual differences among them. Bandura's emphasis on *uniqueness,* however, is moderated by biological and social influences, both of which contribute to some similarities among people. Bandura, then, would be rated high on the uniqueness dimension.

CRITIQUE OF BANDURA

Bandura has evolved his social cognitive theory by a careful balance of the two principal components of theory building—innovative speculation and accurate observation. Unlike many earlier personality theorists (namely Freud, Adler, Jung, and Sullivan), who based their observations on clinical experiences, and contrary to the theories of Dollard and Miller and Skinner, which were built largely on studies of animals, Bandura's personality theory rests on data carefully obtained from dozens of studies conducted by him and his associates using human subjects. In contrast to Maslow, Allport, and some of the self theorists, his speculations seldom outdistance his data, but, rather, are carefully advanced, only one step in front of observations. This scientifically sound procedure increases the likelihood that testing of hypotheses will yield positive results and that the theory will generate additional testable hypotheses.

Bandura is currently the most active of all personality theorists. His work is currently receiving a great deal of attention, some supportive, some critical. Though a review of the criticisms is beyond the scope of the present volume, the interested reader is referred to Borkovec (1978), Eastman and Marzillier (1984), Eysenck (1978), Kazdin (1978), Kirsch (1980, 1982, 1990), Kirsch and Wickless (1983), Lang, (1978), Marzillier and Eastman (1984), Olsen, (1979), Pereboom (1979), Rychlak (1979), Wolpe (1978), and Woolfolk and Lazarus (1979). In fairness to Bandura, it must be added that he is quite capable of answering his critics (see, for example, Bandura, 1979, 1983, 1984).

The usefulness of Bandura's personality theory, however, does not rest on its current popularity, but, as with other theories, its value lies in its ability to organize knowledge and generate important research. In addition, it must serve as a practical guide to action, be internally consistent, and parsimonious. How does Bandura's theory rate on these five criteria?

On its ability to *organize knowledge* it receives a very high rating. In his most recent book, *Social Foundations of Thought and Action* (1986), Bandura has tied together many of the loose ends of his theory. Much of the important psychological research findings of the past decade can be organized by social cognitive theory. Reciprocal determinism is a comprehensive concept that offers a viable explanation for the acquisition of nearly all observable behavior. The inclusion of three variables in this paradigm gives Bandura's theory more flexibility to organize and explain behavior than Skinner's radical behaviorism, which relies nearly exclusively on environmental variables.

Bandura's theory must be given a very high rating on its capacity to *generate research*. This is a theory's heuristic value, that is, its usefulness in stimulating investigation. Bandura and his colleagues have done much of the research, but other researchers, too, have been attracted to the theory. Bandura may be the most meticulous writer of all the personality theorists included in this volume. His carefully constructed formulations lend themselves to the generation of numerous testable hypotheses. Unfortunately, his concepts and phraseology are so precisely stated that they become esoteric. The uninitiated reader, for example, would find *Social Foundations of Thought and Action* (Bandura, 1986) nearly incomprehensible.

How *practical* is Bandura's social cognitive theory? To the therapist or anyone interested in the acquisition and maintenance of new behaviors, it is an extremely useful guide to action. In addition to possessing the practical value of other learning theories, Bandura's theory presents the useful dimension of observational learning. Therapists, teachers, and trainers can use themselves as models or introduce other forms of observational learning, including such a simple procedure as cognitive modeling, which Bandura has shown to be an effective method of instigating change.

Is the theory *internally consistent?* In terms of language, Bandura's theory is remarkable in its consistency. Words are carefully chosen and no single term carries more than one definition. The theory itself, because it is not highly speculative, has outstanding internal consistency. Bandura is not afraid to speculate, but he never ventures far beyond the empirical data available to him. The result is a carefully couched, rigorously written, and internally consistent theory.

The final criterion of a useful theory is *parsimony*. Again, Bandura's social cognitive theory meets high standards. The theory is simple, straightforward, and unencumbered by hypothetical or fanciful explanations.

CHAPTER SUMMARY

Bandura's social cognitive theory holds that human functioning is a product of the mutual interaction of environmental events, behavior, and personal factors, especially cognitive activity. This triadic model is called *reciprocal determinism*. The three reciprocal factors do not necessarily make an equal contribution to thought and action. At different times and under different conditions, any one of the three may be the most powerful. However, none of the factors is ever solely responsible for behavior. All three constantly operate in mutual interaction.

The important environmental factors, often overlooked by other theorists, are *chance encounters* and *fortuitous events*. Bandura believes that many of the crucial influences in our life originate from these unplanned and unexpected events. Once they occur, however, they enter into the triadic model in the same manner as do planned events.

As cognitive animals, we have the capacity to use symbols, especially language, to transform contemporary experiences into relatively consistent patterns of behavior. This gives the *self system* some stability. The self system refers to cognitive structures that enable us to perceive, evaluate, and regulate our behavior.

Within limits, we have the capacity for *self-regulation.* The three component processes of self-regulation are (1) *self-observation,* that is, monitoring our own behavior; (2) *judgmental processes,* that is, self-evaluation based on personal standards, standards of reference, the value we place on our actions, and whether or not we attribute success or failure to our own efforts; and (3) *self-reaction,* that is, self-produced rewards or punishment.

External factors are also involved in self-regulation. These include (1) *standards of evaluation* which stem least partially from the environment; (2) *external reinforcement* in the form of rewards received from others; (3) *selective activation,* which refers to Bandura's notion that self-regulatory influences operate only if they are activated; and (4) *disengagement of internal control,* that is, separating ourselves from the injurious consequences of our actions. We can disengage ourselves from responsibility by redefining our behavior, displacing or diffusing responsibility, distorting the harmful effect of our actions, or by blaming the victim of our negligent behavior.

Performance is generally enhanced when we have high *self-efficacy,* that is, high expectations that we can perform those behaviors that will produce desired outcomes in a particular situation. Self-efficacy is enhanced by (1) enactive attainment or performance, (2) vicarious experiences, (3) verbal persuasion, and (4) low levels of physiological or emotional arousal.

Bandura believes that people can learn without performing any behavior. He refers to this as *observational learning* and distinguishes it from *enactive learning.* In order to learn through observation we must attend to our model, organize and retain our observations, try out our new actions, and be motivated to perform the modeled behavior.

Enactive learning takes place when our responses produce consequences. Response consequences can impart information, motivate future behavior, or reinforce present behavior.

Like all human behavior, *dysfunctional behavior* is acquired through the reciprocal interaction of environment, personal factors, and behavior. Bandura has most intensely investigated depressive reactions, fears and phobias, and aggressive behaviors.

Social cognitive theory has influenced a number of behaviorally oriented therapies, but Bandura's chief emphasis is on cognitive mediation, especially perceived self-efficacy.

Bandura conceives humans as having a unique potential to learn a variety of responses through their ability to symbolize experiences. We can recall the past, set goals for the future, but we live in the present. We have some limited capacity for personal freedom, but our behavior is also constricted by social and biological influences.

Overall, Bandura's social cognitive theory receives the highest marks of any theory discussed in this book. It is rated very high on four of the five criteria for a useful theory—generate research, organize knowledge, internal consistency, and parsimony. In addition, it is rated high as a guide to the practitioner.

Suggested Readings

BANDURA, A. (1982b). The psychology of chance encounters and life paths. *American Psychologist, 37,* 747–755.

Chance encounters and fortuitous events cannot be predicted by the science of psychology, yet they frequently exert a major influence on a person's life. Here Bandura argues that in chance encounters the separate chain of events have their own causal determinants and having once occurred, they enter the reciprocal determinism paradigm and can be analyzed in the same manner as other environmental events.

BANDURA, A. (1986). *Social foundations of thought and action: A social cognitive theory.* Englewood Cliffs, NJ: Prentice-Hall.

As the most complete and updated expression of social cognitive theory, this book is ''must'' reading for any serious student of Bandura. However, the esoteric language and lack of organization make for difficult reading.

BANDURA, A. (1988c). Social cognitive theory. In A. Vasta (Ed.), *Annals of child development* (Vol. 6). Greenwich, CT: JAI Press.

This chapter presents in brief form the major components of Bandura's social cognitive theory. A good introduction to Bandura's most recent ideas.

EVANS, R. I. (1976). *The making of psychology: Discussion with creative contributors* (pp. 242–254). New York: Knopf.

Richard Evans's interview with Bandura offers some glimpses into the personal side of Bandura as well as Bandura's earlier views on learning and aggression.

Part Four
DISPOSITIONAL THEORIES

CATTELL AND EYSENCK
13 Trait and Factor Theories

ALLPORT
14 The Psychology of the Individual

CATTELL AND EYSENCK

Trait and Factor Theories

Holly, a 25-year-old nurse, is dissatisfied with her job. She has few opportunities to make important decisions and resents the preferential treatment demanded by and given to doctors. A first-born child with a sister 10 years younger, Holly has always been independent. Lack of autonomy at work, however, is creating an almost unbearable situation for her.

Holly has lived with her boyfriend, Tom, for two years, and his tolerant and nonpossessive attitudes toward her are a large measure of her attraction to him. Tom is quite accepting of Holly, even those risk-taking behaviors that he personally finds frightening. Holly smokes, drinks heavily at times, drives her sports car at a high rate of speed, and smokes marijuana regularly. In addition, she likes to climb small mountains and skydive, even though both activities arouse fear in her.

While in high school and college, most of Holly's friends were gay men. She enjoyed their company partly because of their artistic interests but mostly because they were "different." She frequently went to gay bars with several of these men and was sometimes propositioned by gay women. Although she occasionally fantasized about having sex with some of these women, she never did. However, she has had a number of sexual affairs with men, both before and after she began living with Tom.

Holly takes personal pride in her acceptance of those people who are not always understood or accepted by others. She continues to have many friends who are homosexual, black, poor, or artistic. Many of her colleagues at work see her as a "radical" with ultraliberal ideas. She antagonizes some of the other hospital staff members with her honest, forthright manner of speaking and many of the male physicians are irritated by her assertiveness, self-sufficiency, and lack of deference. However, Holly is not a troublemaker. She is sensitive and nurturant to her patients, and they generally respond positively to her. Unfortunately, patient care is becoming an increasingly smaller part of her job and Holly is seriously considering quitting.

OVERVIEW

In this brief description of Holly we have used several adjectives to describe her characteristic behavior. These descriptive and distinguishing qualities of Holly can be called **traits.** A trait is a relatively permanent disposition of an individual, which is inferred from that person's behavior.

In Chapter 14 we will see that Gordon Allport developed a personality theory that utilized the concept of traits or dispositions. Allport, however, relied more on intuition and deductive reasoning than on mathematical procedures. Raymond B. Cattell and Hans J. Eysenck, on the other hand, have each applied a more systematic method to the problems of identifying traits. The approach they use is **factor analysis,** a technique that will be briefly described later. Because they employ different factor analytic procedures, Cattell and Eysenck have arrived at different traits. Cattell has identified a comparatively large number of traits, while Eysenck is convinced that only three basic factors underlie human personality.

Cattell has spent his professional life mapping the entire sphere of human personality. He found a number of both normal and abnormal temperament or structural traits and then turned his attention to measuring the dynamics of personality. To that end he discovered a variety of motivational traits. With knowledge of both the structure and the dynamics of personality, it becomes potentially possible to predict human behavior.

On the other hand, Eysenck has used factor analysis to extract only three general factors or types—extraversion/introversion, neuroticism/stability, and psychoticism/superego.

BIOGRAPHY OF RAYMOND B. CATTELL

Raymond Bernard Cattell was born in Staffordshire, England, on March 20, 1905, of proper Victorian middle-class parents. The second of three sons, he was protected by his mother from a domineering father who centered his scrutiny on the oldest child. This relative freedom allowed young Raymond to roam the beach of Devonshire, where his family had moved when he was six, and to explore the coast in boats he had learned to sail at an early age (Cattell, 1974a). Though three years younger, he nearly caught up to his older brother in school, but the rivalry between the two was lessened when the older boy was moved to a different school.

His relatively carefree childhood was dampened by World War I.

Cattell was too young to be a soldier, but he had viewed the devastation of war and had watched the trainloads of bloodstained wounded. Suddenly the tranquility of childhood had vanished: "Silently there came an abiding sense of seriousness into my life, compounded of a feeling that one could not be less dedicated than these [wounded soldiers], and of a new sense, for a boy, of the brevity of life and the need to accomplish while one might" (Cattell, 1974a, p. 63).

At 16 he entered King's College of the University of London and at 19 graduated with highest honors with a degree in chemistry and physics. As an undergraduate, his interests were wide-ranging and included a concern for social problems. By his final year he had realized that his life would be devoted to psychology and so, against the advice of his physical science classmates, he pursued an advanced degree and a career in psychology. In 1929 he received a Ph.D. from the University of London and in 1937 was awarded an honorary D.Sc. from the same school. As a graduate student, he worked in the laboratory of Charles Spearman, the noted British quantitative psychologist, who was then at work on his monumental studies of human abilities. After finishing his degree, Cattell found that his friends from undergraduate days were right—there were no jobs available in academic psychology.

Consequently, he took a position as an "educationist" at Exeter University, where he remained until 1932, when he moved to Leicester, a city that was beginning a child guidance clinic. His five years as Director of the Psychological Clinic at Leicester were spent mostly in administration and clinical work, but he was able to conduct research on intelligence testing and to publish several articles and a book during this time. By 1937 Cattell realized that his research plans could only be realized in a university setting. However, there were only six psychology professorships in all of England and the same "hale and hearty" professors occupied those positions as had 10 years earlier (Cattell, 1974a).

As a consequence, he decided to accept E. L. Thorndike's offer to journey to the United States and become a research assistant at Columbia University. Thus Cattell followed in the steps of Abraham H. Maslow (Chapter 16), who had been Thorndike's assistant two years earlier. Cattell was reluctant to leave his beloved England and intended to remain in the United States for only one year. After leaving Columbia, however, he accepted the G. Stanley Hall professorship at Clark University in Worcester, Massachusetts. That position, unfortunately, did not allow him a relaxed atmosphere for psychological research and he soon moved to neighboring Harvard as a lecturer.

During World War II he worked with the Adjutant General's office developing personality tests for use in the selection of officers. His work there taught him the advantages of the team approach, which was generally lacking in most universities. After the war he finally found the academic position that allowed him the opportunity to conduct research in the manner he had long desired. This was at the University of Illinois, where he was to spend 30 years as Director of the Laboratory of Personality and Group Analysis. Most of Cattell's productive years were spent at Illinois where he eventually was honored as Distinguished Research Professor. At Illinois he helped found the Institute for Personality and Ability Testing (IPAT) in 1949, which has served as an outlet for the many tests developed by Cattell and his colleagues.

In 1973 Cattell retired from the University of Illinois and moved to Boulder, Colorado, where he established the Institute for

Research on Morality and Adjustment. This institute, coupled with his book *A New Morality from Science: Beyondism* (1972a), points toward his interest in a morality that finds ethical values based not on faith in an unseen Being but on the principles of science, especially the social science of psychology. Since 1977 Cattell has been Resident in the Department of Psychology at the University of Hawaii, as well as Professor Emeritus at Illinois.

Early in his career, while still in England and even before completion of his Ph.D., Cattell set a plan for his life's work, much as Skinner (Chapter 10) had outlined his goals for the years 1930–1960. Cattell's strategy, which took only a year to design but a lifetime to execute, was to measure and describe personality structure objectively from three media of observation—ratings of life behavior, questionnaires, and objective test data (Cattell, 1974b). These concepts are more fully discussed below.

Cattell's early professional life was not always easy. His long hours of work, poor pay, and residence in a damp basement flat had adverse effects on both his health and his marriage (Cattell, 1974a). He developed, as a result of his work schedule and eating habits, a functional stomach disorder, from which he never completely recovered. Also, his wife of two years, Monica Rogers, not being accustomed to such a Spartan life, left him. Cattell had one son by his first marriage and three daughters and another son by his second marriage to Karen Schuettler, a mathematician whom he married in 1946.

Cattell has been a prolific writer, having published some three dozen books and 400 articles. He has also won many awards including the Darwin Fellowship, the Wenner Gren Prize of the New York Academy of Sciences, presidency of the Society of Multivariate Experimental Psychology, a distinguished foreign honorary membership in the British Psychological Society, and the American Psychological Association Award for Distinguished Service to Measurement. Now nearing the tenth decade of life, Cattell continues an active and productive work schedule. He has recently applied his structured learning theory to the process of psychotherapy (Cattell, 1987).

CATTELL'S TRAIT THEORY

Cattell has opposed the clinical methods of earlier personality theorists as being unscientific and based more on unsupported speculation than on hard data. In his scientific analysis of personality he uses an **inductive method** as opposed to a **hypothetico-deductive method.** In the latter approach the investigator has some hypothesis or theory in mind *before* gathering data. In other words, the nature of the scores that enter the correlation matrix is determined by some previous ideas as to what traits are to be measured. With Cattell's inductive approach a large body of data is collected with no preexisting hypotheses dictating the kind of data that will be used. With the inductive method, hypotheses are drawn *after* factor analyses have been run, since they are suggested by the results of the analysis.

BASICS OF FACTOR ANALYSIS

How does factor analysis identify traits? A comprehensive knowledge of the mathematical operations involved in factor analysis is not essential to our understanding of trait and factor theories of personality. Nevertheless, a general description of factor analysis should be helpful. To use factor analysis we first begin by making specific observations on many individuals. These observations are then quantified in some manner; for example, height is measured in inches; weight in pounds; aptitude in test scores; job performance by rating scales; and so on. Let us assume that we have 1000 such measures on 5000 people. Our next step is to determine which of these variables (scores) are related to which other variables and to what extent. To do this, we would calculate the **correlation coefficient** between each variable and each of the other 999 scores.

As a result, we would have a table of intercorrelations or a matrix with 1000 rows and 1000 columns. Some of these correlations would be high and positive, some near zero, and some would be negative. For example, we might observe a high positive correlation between leg length and height, since one is partially a measure of the other. We may also find a positive correlation between a measure of leadership ability and ratings on social poise. This relationship might be due to the fact that they are each part of a more basic underlying trait—self-confidence.

With 1000 separate variables, our table of intercorrelations would be too cumbersome. At this point we would turn a factor analysis. The general purpose of factor analysis is to account for a large number of variables with a smaller number of more basic dimensions. For our purposes, these more basic dimensions can be called *traits,* which represent a cluster of variables that are closely related to each other. For example, we may find high positive intercorrelations among test scores in algebra, geometry, trigonometry, and calculus. We have now identified a cluster of scores, or a factor that we might call M for mathematics. In similar fashion we can identify a number of other **factors,** but that number, of course, will be smaller than the original number of observations.

Our next step is to determine the extent to which each individual score contributes to the various factors. Correlations of scores with factors are called **factor loadings.** For example, if scores for algebra, geometry, trigonometry, and calculus contribute highly to Factor M, but not to other factors, they will have high factor loadings on M. Factor loadings give us an indication of the purity of the various factors and enable us to interpret their meanings.

Traits generated through factor analysis may be either **unipolar** or **bipo-**

lar. Unipolar traits are scaled from zero to some large amount. Height, weight, and general intelligence are examples of unipolar traits. Bipolar traits, on the other hand, extend from one pole to an opposite pole, with zero representing a midpoint. Introversion vs. extraversion, liberalism vs. conservatism, and social ascendancy vs. timidity are examples of bipolar traits.

CATTELL'S METHODS OF INVESTIGATION

An understanding of Cattell's scientific analysis of personality is enhanced by an acquaintance with his methods of investigation and with the rationale underlying them. Therefore, the reader is given an introduction to oblique rotation, P technique, and the three media of observation.

Oblique Rotation

Earlier we said that the general purpose of factor analysis is to reduce a multiplicity of data to fewer and, therefore, more manageable factors. We also defined factor loading as the correlation of one score with one factor. Now, in order for mathematically derived factors to have psychological meaning, the axes on which the scores are plotted are usually turned or *rotated* into a specific mathematical relationship with each other. There are two basic different ways of performing this rotation—orthogonal and oblique. Most factor analysts favor the **orthogonal rotation,** while Cattell has pioneered the method of **oblique rotation.** Mathematically, orthogonally rotated axes are at right angles to each other, which means that the intercorrelation between

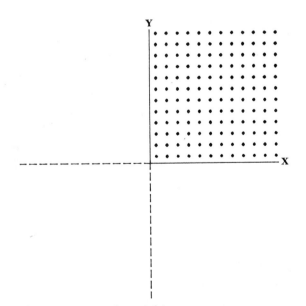

Figure 13.1   Orthogonal Axes

the factors is zero; that is, they are independent of one another. The oblique method assumes some positive or negative correlation and refers to an angle of less than or more than 90°. Figure 13.1 shows a scattergram of scores for two variables (x and y) that are totally uncorrelated ($r = .00$). As scores on the x variable increase, scores on the y axes may have any value; that is, they are completely independent of scores on the y axis.

Figure 13.2 depicts a scattergram of scores when x and y are positively correlated with one another; that is, as scores on the x variable increase, scores on the y axis have a tendency also to increase. (Note that the correlation is not perfect; that is, some people may score high on the x variable, but relatively low on y and vice versa.) A perfect correlation ($r = 1.00$) would result in x and y occupying the same line. In the factor analytical technique of Eysenck and others, the orthogonal axes are maintained throughout rotation, while Cattell keeps the axes in the oblique position.

Psychologically, orthogonal rotation usually results in only a few meaningful traits, whereas oblique methods ordinarily produce a larger number. This partially explains why Cattell has extracted more traits than has Eysenck, but the psychological meanings of his traits are not directly comparable to those produced through orthogonal methods. Since traits identified by Cattell are themselves intercorrelated (oblique), it is possible to factor analyze the results of the original factor analysis. In this way *high-order factors* are produced. Cattell has utilized this possibility to extract second-, third-, and even fourth-stratum factors, which are increasingly smaller in number but broader in scope.

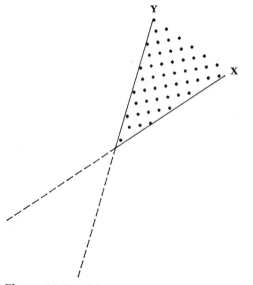

Figure 13.2   Oblique Axes

P Technique

When Cattell was a lecturer at Harvard during the early 1940s he often lunched with Gordon Allport (Chapter 14) and the relationship between the two proved to be productive. Allport, a strong advocate of individual or *unique traits,* chided factor analysts in general and Cattell in particular for limiting investigations to *common traits,* that is, traits extracted from the study of many people. At that time the correlational method typically used was the so-called R technique, which involves many persons taking two or more tests on essentially one occasion. Results of factor analytical studies using the R technique can only identify traits that are common to a large number of people. Allport's criticisms stimulated Cattell to begin thinking of ways by which the single case could be extensively and objectively studied. The result was the **P technique,** a correlational method that involves one person taking two or more tests on many occasions. Actually, as used by Cattell, the technique employs 30 or more variables obtained from one person on more than 100 occasions. In the beginning, that one person was Cattell's wife, Karen, who understandably grew tired after nine weeks of daily testing with "electric shocks and other indignities of the experiment" (Cattell, 1974b, p. 106). Cattell, of course, has since found other volunteers and has continued to use the P technique.

As a companion to the P technique, Cattell devised the dR (differential R) technique, which correlates the scores of a large number of people on many variables obtained at two different occasions. The P and dR techniques should complement one another in the determination of common state or mood patterns. The P technique alone is susceptible to sampling errors with regard to subjects while the dR technique is open to error in the sampling of occasions. In other words, although the P technique satisfies Allport's call for methods of studying the single case, factors derived from it cannot be generalized to other people. On the other hand, although the dR technique allows for generalization to other people, it samples only two points in time, either one of which might be affected by some unusual event. Only when P is combined with the dR technique does it yield information about moods or states that are shared by many people.

Cattell distinguishes between mood states and traits. The concept of **state** refers to temporary changes in behavior as the result of immediate environmental changes. Examples of psychological mood states include anxiety, stress, anger, fear, and arousal. Physiological states include heart rate, body temperature, and blood pressure. Fluctuations in these behavioral and physiological states are most reliably calculated by the P and dR techniques. A **trait,** on the other hand, is a relatively permanent property or disposition, defined by Cattell (1979–1980, Vol. 1, p. 14) as "that which defines what a person will do when faced with a defined situation." Traits are revealed by the traditional R technique, a correlational procedure Cattell has continued to employ.

Media of Observation

From the beginning of his professional career Cattell has concentrated his psychometric procedures on three different media of observation, that is, three sources of data that enter the correlation matrix (Cattell, 1983). The first is one's life record, or **L data,** which comes from observation made by other people. It includes both objective information, called L(T) data and more subjective information based on ratings, termed L(R) data. An example of L(T) data might be a number of residences in a 20-year period, while an example of L(R) data would be an evaluation of a worker by a supervisor.

The second source of information is the person's self-reports, or **Q data,** which are based on questionnaires that call for a person to respond to questions or statements on the basis of self-observation and introspection. Most personality inventories, for example, yield Q data. Since Q data rely on self-observations they are subject to deliberate faking and self-delusion. Therefore, they should be corroborated by correlations with behavioral data. Unverified self-reports are regarded as Q' data, while only those which have been corroborated by objective behavioral scales can truly be called Q data (Cattell & Kline, 1977).

The third medium of observation is **T data,** or information obtained from objective tests, that is, tests where the true purpose is hidden from the subject or where answers cannot be faked. Cattell and Warburton (1967) have identified over 200 objective tests, including both behavioral and physiological measures. Ability tests that require subjects to do as well as they can obviously yield T data, but so too do personality inventories such as the Rorschach and other "projective" instruments where the subject is unaware of the purpose of the test. These latter tests, however, are not favored by Cattell since a measure of subjectivity enters into their scoring (Cattell & Kline, 1977). Cattell's use of L, Q, and T data gives his investigations a false appearance of being unrelated, but viewed from the perspective of his entire career, one can see that all these studies have been attempts to measure the global concept of personality.

SOURCE TRAITS

Cattell (1950, p. 2) defines personality as "that which permits a prediction of what a person will do in a given situation." How can these predictions most accurately be made? Cattell's answer, of course, is to measure and describe the source traits underlying behavior. *Source traits* must be distinguished from *surface traits.* In Cattell's system, surface traits are not very important except as starting points and as indicators of source traits. Allport and Odbert (1936) identified nearly 18,000 trait-names in an unabridged dictionary, then reduced the list to more than 4500, most of which could be considered as *surface traits.* Correlational techniques, however, would reveal that many of these traits cluster together. For example, the surface traits of *gregariousness, humor,* and *unselfishness* may be found to be intercorrelated. If so, then there must be some underlying source of these three traits.

The underlying factor that is responsible for the intercorrelation among surface traits is called a *source trait*. Source traits are smaller in number than surface traits, but they are better predictors of behavior. Figure 13.3 shows the three surface traits of humor, gregariousness, and unselfishness clustering together with considerable overlap or intercorrelation among them. What holds these surface traits together; that is, what do these three traits have in common? If surface traits consistently cluster together, then there must be some common trait underlying them. In this example, the source trait, represented by the shaded area in Figure 13.3, might be called *friendliness*.

Source traits can be identified through each of the three media of observation. Ideally, if measurement techniques in L, Q, and T data were perfectly

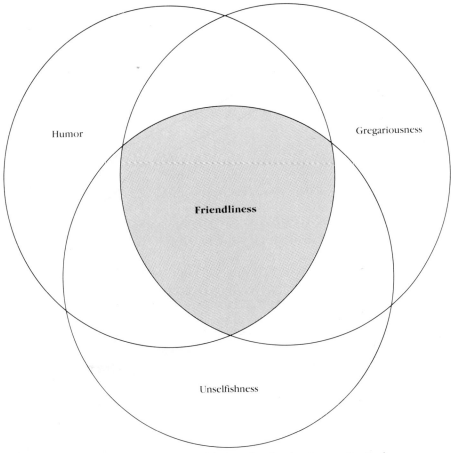

Figure 13.3   Three Surface Traits Held Together by the Source Trait of Friendliness

reliable and valid, then information from any one of the three would yield exactly the same factors or source traits as data from the other two. Practically, of course, this state of infallibility has not yet been reached, but Cattell (1957, 1979–1980) has discovered some significant overlap among the various media of observation, with especially good matches in factors obtained from L and Q data.

Temperament Traits

We have seen that traits can be divided into *common* (shared by many) and *unique* (peculiar to one individual). Also, *source* traits can be distinguished from trait indicators called *surface* traits. A third dimension for dividing traits is by classifying them into *temperament, motivation* (dynamic), and *ability*. Traits of temperament are concerned with *how* a person behaves, motivation deals with *why* one behaves, and ability refers to *how far* or *how fast* one can perform. (A discussion of abilities need not detain us here, but the interested reader is referred to Cattell [1971] for a lengthy discussion on the structure of abilities.)

Over the years Cattell and his associates have identified some 35 primary or first-order traits measuring personality. Twenty-three of these factors characterize the normal population and 12 measure the pathological dimension. Temperament traits have been isolated using L and Q data obtained from both adult and child samples (Cattell, 1983).

Normal Traits

The largest and most frequently studied of the normal traits are the 16 personality factors found on Cattell's 16 PF scale (Cattell, Eber, & Tatsuoka, 1970). Because the 16 PF is a personality inventory of a questionnaire format, each of the 16 traits, of course, is obtained through Q media. The seven additional factors that make up the total of 23 normal traits were originally identified only through L data, though some of them, particularly J (Zeppia) and K (Social unconcern), are beginning to show up in the more sophisticated measures of Q data (Cattell, 1979–1980). Table 13.1 depicts the 23 primary source traits found in normal personality of both adults and children.

As seen in Table 13.1, normal primary source traits in L and Q data are lettered from A through Q_7. (Traits identified through T media are numbered according to the Universal Index system, for example, U.I.1, U.I.2, U.I.3, etc.). Traits are lettered in descending order of magnitude. In other words, Factor A (Sizia/Affectia) is the largest factor, meaning that it emerges the most clearly from factor analyses and accounts for the largest amount of variance. The size of this factor agrees with clinical practice and with everyday observation, which suggests that an obvious dimension of personality is flatness of affect (sizia) vs. proneness to affect (affectia). Likewise, Factor B (Intelligence) is a substantial factor easily noted in the measurement of personality. Incidentally, Factor B represents the ability dimension of personality, while the other primary source traits are basically temperament traits.

TABLE 13.1   Cattell's 23 Normal Primary Source Traits

Factor	Low Score Description	High Score Description
A	SIZIA Reserved, detached, critical, aloof	AFFECTIA Warmhearted, outgoing, easygoing, participating
B	LOW INTELLIGENCE[1] Low mental capacity, dull, quitting	HIGH INTELLIGENCE High mental capacity, bright, persevering
C	LOW EGO STRENGTH Affected by feelings, easily upset, changeable	HIGH EGO STRENGTH Emotionally stable, faces reality, calm
D	PHLEGMATIC TEMPERAMENT[2] Undemonstrative, deliberate, inactive, stodgy	EXCITABILITY Excitable, impatient, demanding, overactive, unrestrained
E	SUBMISSIVE Obedient, mild, easily led, docile, accommodating	DOMINANCE Assertive, aggressive, competitive, stubborn
F	DESURGENCY Sober, taciturn, serious	SURGENCY Enthusiastic, heedless, happy-go-lucky
G	LOW SUPEREGO STRENGTH Disregards rules and group moral standards, expedient	HIGH SUPEREGO STRENGTH Conscientious, persistent, moralistic, staid
H	THRECTIA Shy, timid, restrained, threat-sensitive	PARMIA Adventurous, "thick-skinned," socially bold
I	HARRIA Tough-minded, rejects illusions	PERMSIA Tender-minded, sensitive, dependent, overprotected
J	ZEPPIA[2] Zestful, liking group action	COASTHENIA Circumspect individualism, reflective, internally restrained
K	SOCIAL UNCONCERN[2] Socially untutored, unconcerned, boorish	SOCIAL-ROLE CONCERN Socially mature, alert, self-disciplined
L	ALAXIA Trusting, accepting conditions	PROTENSION Suspecting, jealous, dogmatic
M	PRAXERNIA Practical, has "down to earth" concerns	AUTIA Imaginative, bohemian, absent-minded
N	NAIVETE Forthright, unpretentious	SHREWDNESS Astute, worldly, polished, socially aware
O	UNTROUBLED ADEQUACY Self-assured, placid, secure, complacent	GUILT PRONENESS Apprehensive, self-reproaching, insecure, troubled
P	CAUTIOUS INACTIVITY[2] Melancholy, cautious, takes no risks	SANGUINE CASUALNESS Sanguine, speculative, independent
Q_1	CONSERVATISM Disinclined to change, respects traditional values	RADICALISM Experimenting, analytic, free thinking
Q_2	GROUP DEPENDENCY A "joiner," sound follower	SELF-SUFFICIENCY Self-sufficient, resourceful, prefers own decisions

TABLE 13.1   Continued

Factor	Low Score Description	High Score Description
Q_3	LOW SELF-SENTIMENT Uncontrolled, lax, follows own urges	HIGH SELF-SENTIMENT Controlled, exacting will power, socially precise, compulsive, follows self-image
Q_4	LOW ERGIC TENSION Relaxed, tranquil, unfrustrated, composed	HIGH ERGIC TENSION Tense, frustrated, driven, overwrought, fretful
Q_5	LACK OF SOCIAL CONCERN[2] Does not volunteer for social service, experiences no obligation, self-sufficient	GROUP DEDICATION WITH SENSED INADEQUACY Concerned with social good works, not doing enough, joins in social endeavors
Q_6	SELF EFFACEMENT[2] Quiet, self-effacing	SOCIAL PANACHE Feels unfairly treated by society, self-expressive, makes abrupt antisocial remarks
Q_7	LACKS EXPLICIT SELF-EXPRESSION[2] Is not garrulous in conversation	EXPLICIT SELF-EXPRESSION Enjoys verbal-social expression, likes dramatic entertainment, follows fashionable ideas

[1] Factor B (INTELLIGENCE) is an ability trait rather than a temperament trait.
[2] One of the "seven missing factors," so termed because they were not identified by the original 16 PF.
SOURCE: R. B. Cattell, *Personality and learning theory*, Vol. 1. New York: Springer Publishing Company, 1979–1980, pp. 61–73. Copyright 1979 by Springer Publishing Company, Inc., New York 10012. Adapted by permission.

Because each succeeding factor becomes "fuzzier" or more difficult to extract, Factors N through Q_7 are termed traits of lesser variance (Cattell, 1979–1980). These latter factors are successively weaker and more difficult for the factor analyst to identify with certainty.

The 23 traits reveal a complete picture of normal personality, at least in terms of temperament traits. All measures of normal temperament, whether from Cattell's laboratory or from some other source, whether obtained from adult samples or from children, should match with one or more of these 23 primary traits. In other words, probably all the important personality traits have now been identified by Cattell and his associates. Cattell, in fact, stated some time ago that "the pioneer years of hewing out the major human personality structures are essentially over" (Cattell, 1974a, p. 86). Additional work is now aimed at identifying traits across the three media sources within each of the various age groups and across cultures, and at refining the precise psychological meaning of these 23 traits.

Abnormal Traits

Cattell believes that pathological individuals possess the same traits as normal people, but, in addition, exhibit certain abnormal traits. However, there is some overlap of normal and abnormal traits. For example, some factors such as low ego strength and guilt proneness are strongly characteristic of

TABLE 13.2   Cattell's 12 Abnormal Primary Source Traits

Factor	Low Score Description	High Score Description
D_1	LOW HYPOCHONDRIASIS Is happy, mind works well, does not find ill health frightening	HIGH HYPOCHONDRIASIS Shows overconcern with bodily functions, health, or disabilities
D_2	ZESTFULNESS Is contented about life and surroundings, has no death wishes	SUICIDAL DISGUST Is disgusted with life, harbors thoughts or acts of self-destruction
D_3	LOW BROODING DISCONTENT Avoids dangerous and adventurous undertakings, has little need for excitement	HIGH BROODING DISCONTENT Seeks excitement, is restless, takes risks, tries new things
D_4	LOW ANXIOUS DEPRESSION Is calm in emergency, confident about surroundings, poised	HIGH ANXIOUS DEPRESSION Has disturbing dreams, is clumsy in handling things, tense, easily upset
D_5	HIGH ENERGY EUPHORIA Shows enthusiasm for work, is energetic, sleeps soundly	LOW ENERGY DEPRESSION Has feelings of weariness, worries, lacks energy to cope
D_6	LOW GUILT AND RESENTMENT Is not troubled by guilt feelings, can sleep no matter what is left undone	HIGH GUILT AND RESENTMENT Has feelings of guilt, blames self for everything that goes wrong, is critical of self
D_7	LOW BORED DEPRESSION Is relaxed, considerate, cheerful with people	HIGH BORED DEPRESSION Avoids contact and involvement with people, seeks isolation, shows discomfort with people
Pa	LOW PARANOIA Is trusting, not bothered by jealousy or envy	HIGH PARANOIA Believes is being persecuted, poisoned, controlled, spied on, mistreated
Pp	LOW PSYCHOPATHIC DEVIATION Avoids engagement in illegal acts or breaking rules, sensitive	HIGH PSYCHOPATHIC DEVIATION Has complacent attitude toward own and others' antisocial behavior, is not hurt by criticism, likes crowds
Sc	LOW SCHIZOPHRENIA Makes realistic appraisals of self and others, shows emotional harmony and absence of regressive behavior	HIGH SCHIZOPHRENIA Hears voices or sounds without apparent source outside self, retreats from reality; has uncontrolled and sudden impulses
As	LOW PSYCHASTHENIA Is not bothered by unwelcome thoughts and ideas or compulsive habits	HIGH PSYCHASTHENIA Suffers insistent, repetitive ideas and impulses to perform certain acts
Ps	LOW GENERAL PSYCHOSIS Considers self as good, dependable, and smart as most others	HIGH GENERAL PSYCHOSIS Has feelings of inferiority and unworthiness, timid, loses head easily

Cattell believes that pathological individuals possess the same traits as normal people, but, in addition, exhibit certain abnormal traits such as depression.

neurotic and psychotic individuals, though they appear among the 23 normal factors (Cattell, 1979–1980).

Cattell (1973) hypothesizes two forms of pathology. The first is an imbalance of normal function. For example, affectia (Factor A) carried to extreme would result in a manic-depressive disorder. The second is a separate and distinct disease process, characterized by traits not found among the 23 normal factors. The abnormal traits listed in Table 13.2 represent the second category, that is, pathological traits as separate factors. The first seven, symbolized by the letter D, represent depressive traits. The last five (Pa, Pp, Sc, As, Ps) are not only more serious clinically, but, as factors, they are also more readily identified than the depressive traits.

Cattell isolated these 12 factors using primarily Q data obtained from items on the Minnesota Multiphasic Personality Inventory (MMPI) (Hathaway & McKinley, 1951). In addition, he has used textbook descriptions of abnormal behavior and he and his associates have written new items as their work continued. Subjects from whom measures were obtained included samples from both normal and abnormal populations. Interestingly, factor analysis of these "abnormal" items revealed the same normal traits found with nonpathological items when used with normal subjects. Alongside these 23 traits, though, were the 12 pathological factors. This lends some support to the hypothesis

TABLE 13.3   Cattell's Second-Stratum Source Traits

Factor	Name	Primary Factors		Descriptive Label
QI	EXVIA (Extraversion)	A	Affectia	Sociable
		F	Surgency	Enthusiastic
		H	Parmia	Adventurous
		Q_2-	Group Dependency	Dependent
QII	ANXIETY	$C-$	Low Ego Strength	Easily upset
		$H-$	Threctia	Shy, Timid
		L	Protension	Suspicious
		O	Guilt Proneness	Apprehensive
		Q_3-	Low Self-Sentiment	Uncontrolled
		Q_4	High Ergic Tension	Tense
QIII	CORTERIA (Cortical Alertness)	$A-$	Sizia	Unsociable
		$I-$	Harria	Insensitive
		M·	Praxernia	Practical
QIV	INDEPENDENCE	E	Dominance	Dominant
		F	Surgency	Enthusiastic
		H	Parmia	Adventurous
		L	Protension	Suspicious
QV	DISCREETNESS	A	Affectia	Sociable
		N	Shrewdness	Astute, Socially aware
QVI	SUBJECTIVITY	M	Autia	Unconcerned
		Q_1	Radicalism	Radical
QVII	INTELLIGENCE	B	Intelligence	Intelligent
QVIII	GOOD UPBRINGING	$E-$	Submissive	Obedient, Docile
		$F-$	Desurgency	Taciturn
		G	High Superego Strength	Emotionally stable
		Q_3	High-Self-Sentiment	Controlled

SOURCE: This table is based on the mean pattern loadings from 14 studies summarized in R. B. Cattell, *Personality and learning theory,* Vol. 1. New York: Springer Publishing Company, 1979–1980, p. 80. Copyright 1979 by Springer Publishing Company, Inc., New York 10012. Adapted by permission.

that abnormal people are, first of all, people like everyone else, but with some additional traits that happen to be pathological (Cattell, 1979–1980).

Second-Stratum Traits

Because Cattell's oblique rotation assumes an intercorrelation among the primary source traits, it is possible to factor analyze the results of the original factor analysis and determine which of the first-order traits tend to cluster together. The result has been the consistent identification of eight second-stratum traits and the tentative isolation of at least seven more. Since these last seven still need more cross-validation, we will be concerned here only with the more firmly established original eight second-stratum factors and the primary factors that contribute most heavily to their makeup. Second-stratum factors are assigned roman numerals and the Q preface signifies Q data (questionnaire).

In interpreting Table 13.3 the reader should note that four primary factors contribute to second-stratum Factor QI (Exvia). Primary Factors A, F, and H are positively correlated with QI and Primary Factor Q_2 (group dependency) is negatively correlated with it. Also, realize that exvia (extraversion) has an opposite pole called invia (introversion). Again, second-stratum source traits are numbered in descending order of magnitude, so that QI (Exvia/Invia) and QII (Anxiety) are the strongest and most readily identified of these factors. This is consistent with other personality theorists such as Jung who, using clinical methods, identified extraversion and introversion as basic types, and with Freud, Sullivan, and others who noted the importance of anxiety in shaping different personalities. Likewise, Eysenck, employing a different factor analytic technique, has recognized the importance of extraversion/introversion plus an anxiety factor he terms "neuroticism."

Measurement of Traits

To measure normal traits Cattell (1949) developed the Sixteen Personality Factor Questionnaire, usually called the 16 PF. Different forms of the 16 PF are available for the various age groups: PSPQ (Pre-School Personality Questionnaire, ages 4–6); the ESPQ (Early School Personality Questionnaire, ages 6–8); the CPQ (Child Personality Questionnaire, ages 8–12); and the HSPQ (High School Personality Questionnaire, ages 12–18). These questionnaires asks subjects to select from one of two alternatives such as, "Can you spell as well as other children or do most children spell better," and "Would you rather play with your toys or with friends."

In addition, Delhees and Cattell (1971) have constructed the Clinical Analysis Questionnaire (CAQ), an instrument designed to assess the 12 abnormal traits along with the 16 normal personality traits and nine second-order factors. Scores are reported in terms of *stens,* that is, a 10-unit scale ranging from low scores of 1 to high scores of 10. The profile for Holly, our 24-year-old case study, is seen in Figure 13.4. Second-order factors were not scored. One can see how Holly's high scores on radicalism and self-sufficiency coupled with low scores on conformity, shrewdness, and self-discipline might lead to trouble with any superior who demands conformity and submissiveness.

Dynamic Traits

Besides temperament, Cattell recognizes motivation traits that underlie the *dynamics of personality.* The general personality traits discussed above include ability (Factor B, Intelligence), and some generalized dynamic traits (Cattell, 1979–1980). However, they are largely temperament traits. We turn

NORMAL PERSONALITY TRAITS

Factor	Low Score Description	High Score Description	raw	sten
A: WARMTH	reserved, detached, aloof	warm, personable, easygoing	9	5
B: INTELLIGENCE	concrete-thinking	abstract-thinking	7	6
C: EMOTIONAL STABILITY	easily upset, emotional	emotionally stable, calm	13	7
E: DOMINANCE	submissive, accommodating	dominant, assertive, competitive	12	8
F: IMPULSIVITY	prudent, sober, serious	impulsive, happy-go-lucky	11	7
G: CONFORMITY	expedient, disregards rules	conforming, conscientious, persistent	7	3
H: BOLDNESS	shy, timid, threat-sensitive	bold, venturesome	10	7
I: SENSITIVITY	tough-minded, insensitive	sensitive, tender-minded, unrealistic	10	6
L: SUSPICIOUSNESS	trusting, adaptable	suspicious, hard-to-fool, jealous	12	8
M: IMAGINATION	practical, "down-to-earth"	imaginative, absent-minded	13	8
N: SHREWDNESS	forthright, unpretentious	shrewd, polished, calculating	5	3
O: INSECURITY	confident, self-satisfied	insecure, apprehensive	9	6
Q_1: RADICALISM	conservative, traditional	experimenting, innovative	12	9
Q_2: SELF-SUFFICIENCY	group-adherent, sociable	self-sufficient, resourceful	13	8
Q_3: SELF-DISCIPLINE	undisciplined, uncontrolled	self-disciplined, controlled, precise	6	3
Q_4: TENSION	relaxed	tense, frustrated, driven	8	6

THE CLINICAL FACTORS

Factor	Low Score Description	High Score Description	raw	sten
D_1: HYPOCHONDRIASIS	few somatic complaints	obsessed by ill health	0	2
D_2: SUICIDAL DEPRESSION	contented	despondent, thinks of self-destruction	0	2
D_3: AGITATION	restrained	craves excitement, hypomanic	15	8
D_4: ANXIOUS DEPRESSION	composed	shaky, frightened, clumsy	6	5
D_5: LOW ENERGY DEPRESSION	energetic	gloomy, wornout, sad	5	5
D_6: GUILT & RESENTMENT	untroubled	guilty, self-critical, resentful	4	4
D_7: BOREDOM & WITHDRAWAL	seeks relationships with others	seclusive, feels useless	10	8
Pa: PARANOIA	reasonable	unreasonable, feels persecuted	9	8
Pp: PSYCHOPATHIC DEVIATION	inhibited	uninhibited, unsocialized	22	12
Sc: SCHIZOPHRENIA	reality-oriented	retreats from reality, withdrawn	5	6
As: PSYCHASTHENIA	noncompulsive	obsessive, compulsive	7	6
Ps: PSYCHOLOGICAL INADEQUACY	feels competent, has sense of self-worth	feels inferior and unworthy	6	6

Figure 13.4 Profile for a 24-Year-Old Female on the Clinical Analysis Questionnaire (CAQ) (Adapted from the CAQ™ Individual Record Folder, © 1980 by the Institute for Personality and Ability Testing, Inc. All rights reserved. Reproduced by permission.)

now to a more specific discussion of motivation, that is, the dynamics of personality.

Attitudes

The cornerstone of Cattell's dynamic traits is the concept of **attitude.** An attitude is not an opinion for or against something, but a concept with a much more basic definition. It is a specific course of action, or desire to act, in response to a given situation (Cattell & Child, 1975). For example, let us consider a college student, Monica, whose desire to study French with a particular classmate would be an attitude. It includes a particular stimulus or situation, an interest (intensity level of the desire), the response, and an object. In this example it makes no difference whether or not Monica actually studies with the classmate. The attitude is present in either case and serves as a motive for behavior.

Cattell assumes that motivation is complex and that a network of motives, or **dynamic lattice,** is involved with nearly any attitude. A variety of motives, not all of which are conscious, would doubtless enter into the above example. Monica may desire to do well in French in order to maintain her reputation as a good student, she may wish to spend time with a potential sexual partner, or she may be lonely and simply desire the company of another person. In addition to this network of motives, a **subsidiation chain** underlies nearly all motivation. This simply means that some motives are subsidiary to others; that is, they are directed toward subgoals that must be reached in order to attain the next goal. Assuming motivation to be conscious (which is not always so), a subsidiation chain could be revealed by asking the person a series of "Why" questions. In our example with Monica, the first question would be "Why do you want to study French with Glenn?" Answer: To pass French. "Why?" To graduate from college. "Why?" To get a job. "Why?" To be able to eat. At this point, an innate drive (hunger) is reached and no further questions are needed. Each motive in the chain is subsidiary to the next and all eventually lead to the innate drive for food.

Ergs

Innate drives or motives are called **ergs** (Cattell, 1983). The term erg refers to the energy inherent in primary or unlearned drives such as sex, hunger, curiosity, anger, and other motives, most of which are not limited to humans, but are also found in the primates and higher mammals. In identifying dynamic traits, Cattell began with no preconceived biases as to their nature or their number. Unlike other personality theorists such as Freud (Chapter 2) and Dollard and Miller (Chapter 9), he did not presuppose the existence of primary and secondary (learned) drives. Rather, he started with a heterogeneous array of objective test items (T data), administered them to children and adults in different cultures, factor analyzed the results, and thereby mapped out human motivation mathematically rather than logically (Cattell, 1983).

As a consequence of this approach, Cattell has extracted with a high level of confidence some 10 ergs, most of which are also found in the other mammals. There is reason to believe, therefore, that these dynamic traits are not acquired through enculturation. In fact, Cattell (1979–1980) suggests that ergic factors are the human equivalents of animal instinctual patterns. The presently mapped human ergic goals and their corresponding emotions are shown in Table 13.4. The first 10 have been consistently identified as independent factors; the next four are of uncertain independence; and the final two are even more questionable as factors.

TABLE 13.4   List of Experimentally Presently Indicated Human Ergs

Goal Title	Emotion	Status of Evidence
Food-seeking	Hunger	
Mating	Sex	
Gregariousness	Loneliness	
Parental protectiveness	Pity	
Exploration	Curiosity	
Escape to security	Fear	Consistently identified
Self-assertion	Pride	
Narcistic sex	Sensuousness	
Pugnacity	Anger	
Acquisitiveness	Greed	
Appeal	Despair	
Rest-seeking	Sleepiness	
Constructiveness	Creativity	Uncertain independence
Self-abasement	Humility	
Disgust	Disgust	
Laughter	Amusement	Questionable factors

SOURCE. R. B. Cattell and P. Kline, (1977). *The scientific analysis of personality and motivation.* Orlando, FL: Academic Press, p. 181. Copyright 1977 by Academic Press. Used by permission of Academic Press and R. B. Cattell.

Sems

The third component in Cattell's theory of motivation are **sems,** which are *learned* or acquired dynamic traits. Sems receive their energy from the ergs and give some organization and stability to the attitudes. The acquired traits have traditionally been called **sentiments,** but more recently (Cattell, 1983, 1985) he has termed them sems, an acronym for socially shaped ergic manifolds. Sems are socially acquired and, ordinarily, satisfy several ergs at the same time. We have seen that an attitude is an action, or desire to act, in response to a particular situation, and that attitudes ordinarily can be traced to primary, innate drives called ergs. The intermediate goals between attitudes and ergs are the sems. In the preceding example of our student, Monica, and her desire to study French with a classmate, we saw that her strong wish to study represented her attitude and that her ultimate goal of food was an erg. The network of subgoals bridging the span between attitude and erg is comprised of various sems (see Figure 13.5). For example, Monica's wish to maintain her reputation as a diligent student is part of her self-sentiment and her motivation to study French with a friend connects directly with the loneliness erg. This example shows that several sems can be subsidiated in one erg. For example, self and superego are both connected to pride. With the complexity of human motivation, it is also quite likely that several ergs will be involved with one sem. For example, the family and home sem may relate to the ergs of sex and loneliness.

Attitude Level　　　　　　　**Sem Level**　　　　　　　**Ergic Level**

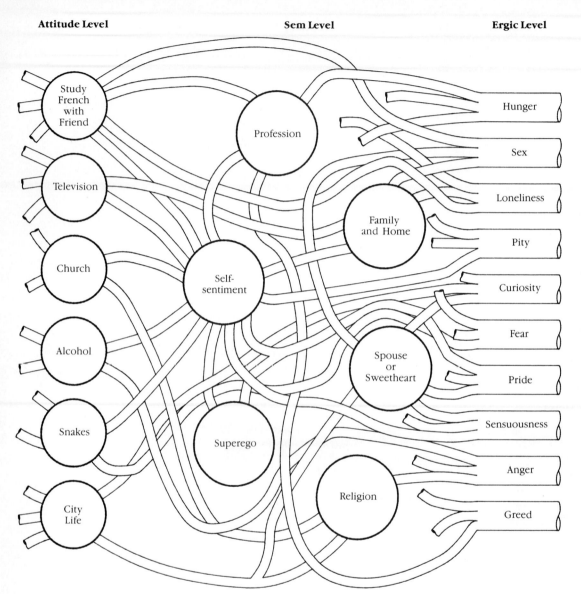

Figure 13.5　Fragments of a Person's Dynamic Lattice, Illustrating Subsidiation Chains and Their Component Attitudes, Sems and Ergs

　　Because sems are learned, they may be either unique or common traits. Unique factors, remember, are peculiar to the individual and are determined through the P correlational technique. Common traits are those found in many people and emerge through factor analyses of correlations obtained through the R technique. Though unique motivational traits are important in psychotherapy or vocational guidance where the psychologist is working with one person, they do not have a separate factor analytical existence. In other words, the dynamic factors that are extracted through the use of the P technique should be the same as those obtained through the R technique (Cattell & Cross, 1952).

It is more difficult to identify a fixed number of sems than it is to extract a specific list of ergs. Since sems are culturally acquired, their number differs with different cultures and among various age groups. Cattell has thus far identified some 27 sems. The strongest mathematically and most important clinically are those shown in Figure 13.5, namely profession, family and home, spouse or sweetheart, self-sentiment, superego, and religion. The *self-sentiment* has some special importance because of its crucial position in integrating other sems. The self-sentiment is the psychometric equivalent of the clinically derived term of self-concept. However, it is no different from the other sems in quality and origin. Like the others, it is peculiarly human and learned through one's culture.

Each of the semic subgoals has a pattern of attitudes that correlate (positively or negatively) to it. For example, three attitudes that load heavily on the Religious Factor are a desire to feel in touch with God, a wish to maintain or increase standards of organized religion, and an interest in seeking and heeding advice from one's parents. Attitudes that contribute to the self-sentiment include the desire to attain control of impulses and mental processes, to maintain self-respect, to excel in one's career, and to maintain a good reputation (Cattell & Child, 1975).

The Dynamic Lattice

The interrelationships among the attitudes, ergs, and sems of an individual can be expressed pictorially by the **dynamic lattice** (see Figure 13.5), which consists of a complex network of attitudes, ergs, and sems underlying a person's motivational structure. To understand the dynamic lattice shown in Figure 13.5, begin with the ergs—the innate human drives—on the right side of the diagram. Each erg affects one or more of the sems (depicted in large circles in the center). Recall that sems are learned dynamic traits that can satisfy one or more ergs. Notice that the profession sem is subsidiary to, that is, receives its basic energy from, both hunger and greed. The small circles at the left of the diagram represent attitudes, that is, a person's tendency to action in a particular situation. Monica's attitude toward studying French with Glenn is energized directly by the sex erg, indirectly by hunger, through the profession sem, and also indirectly by pride, through the self-sentiment.

THE DYNAMIC CALCULUS

In the broad sense of the word, Cattell is a behaviorist, that is, his ultimate aim is to understand and predict behavior. Traits of temperament, ability, and motivation are measured not in terms of properties owned by an individual but rather in terms of behavior. How can behavior be predicted most accurately? Cattell's response is to employ the **dynamic calculus,** a complex procedure for determining the strength and direction of attitudes.

In the dynamic calculus, ergs and sems are considered to be the roots of all motivation and they enter into the **behavioral equation,** which allows one to predict the behavior of a given individual (Cattell & Child, 1975). Cattell's early work of identifying various source traits, as well as the different ergs and sems (sentiments), simply provided the structure of personality. As Cattell (1982, p. 14) put it, "This unitary trait structure research yields a description of the pieces on the chess board, but not of the rules of the game." The dynamic calculus provides those rules. It allows for the prediction of strength of attitudes and is sufficiently practical to enable the clinician, for example, to recommend equally satisfying but less destructive and fatiguing ways of behaving. It also permits the specific calculation of such previously amorphous concepts as conflict, repression, and decision making. Through precise mathematical means, the exact weights attached to the various ergs and sems can be known and, when fit into the behavioral formulas, an accurate prediction of attitude can be made, that is, one's specific course of action or desire to act (Cattell, 1982, 1985).

THE HERITABILITY OF TRAITS

Cattell has long been interested in behavior genetics and the heritability of the various source traits, but in recent years he has accelerated his research output in this area. Using factor analytic methods and a sample of over 3000 related and unrelated subjects, Cattell and his associates have provided tentative answers to such questions as: Is intelligence acquired or inherited? How much of ego strength and superego strength are due to heredity and how much to environmental factors?

Estimates of heritability (H) of the various source traits have been provided by Cattell and his colleagues. Heritability (H) of a trait is the ratio of the genetically determined variance to the total variance so that an H of .60 for intelligence, for example, would mean that 60 percent of the total variance of intelligence is accounted for by genetic factors. Variance refers to the extent to which scores spread out over the entire scale. If everyone in a sample obtained the same score, that variance would be zero. If they do not all score the same, the difference must be due to something—heredity, environment, or an interaction of the two. Cattell's H is simply an estimate of the extent to which the variance of a given trait is due to heredity. The statistical technique used to obtain an H is Multiple Abstract Variance Analysis or MAVA (Cattell, 1979–1980, 1983).

Cattell feels that MAVA is superior to the older twin methods, which simply compared differences among identical twins, fraternal twins, and siblings. Multiple Abstract Variance Analysis has the advantage, among other things, of being sensitive to differences in the environment for identical twins as compared to fraternal twins. It also allows analysis within families as well as between families. The technique has the capacity to measure genetic, environmental, and total variances for pairs of children (or other people) in the following family constellations: (1) identical twins reared together; (2) fraternal twins reared together; (3) siblings reared together; (4) half siblings reared together; (5) unrelated children reared together; (6) siblings reared apart; (7) unrelated children (adopted) reared apart; and so on. In addition, identical twins reared apart could also be included, but due to their relative scarcity (MAVA only utilizes large sample sizes), this constellation has not been included by Cattell.

Cattell and his associates have published several studies that have used some or all of a total sample of more than 3000 boys aged 12 to 18. All must be of the same sex since identical twins are necessarily same-sexed. Most of the 2973 unrelated boys living apart were from the original norm group for the American edition of the High School Personality Questionnaire (HSPQ), a form of the 16 PF.

In one study, Cattell, Schuerger, and Kline (1982) investigated the heritability of three primary source traits: Ego Strength (Factor C), Superego Strength (Factor G), and Self-sentiment (Factor Q_3). These three factors, sometimes called the "controlling triumvirate," were chosen because of their substantial interest to clinicians. A 10-hour battery of tests was administered to 94 identical twins reared together, 124 fraternal twins reared together, 470 brothers reared together, and 2973 unrelated children reared apart. This latter category was considered as a general population group. Using the MAVA method, the authors found, as one might expect, that very little of the variance for superego strength (Factor G) was accounted for by heredity. For the general population the H was .05, which indicates the superego is mostly a function of education or environment. For ego strength (Factor C) and self-sentiment (Factor Q_3), however, the H values were considerably higher. For the general population, heritability of ego strength was about .40, while the within-family H was a little lower, between .30 and .40. For self-sentiment, the heritability for the general population was even higher, .63. This is an interesting finding in view of Cattell's assumption that sentiments are culturally acquired. However, in looking at the H values for within- and between-families, the authors found that self-sentiment has a higher heritability for between-families (.65) than for within-families (.46). This suggests that brothers have a similar exposure to cultural influences within the family, at least as far as self-sentiment (self-concept) is concerned.

Cattell (1979–1980) has averaged results from earlier studies and has compiled estimates of H for 18 primary- and 13 second-stratum source traits. Interestingly, the H for both sizia/affectia and exvia/invia is estimated at 50 percent. Sizia/affectia is a basic primary source trait that describes people in terms of reserved and detached vs. outgoing and warmhearted. Exvia/invia is a second-stratum source trait roughly equivalent to Jung's concept of extraversion/introversion. For both these strong traits, Cattell estimates that approximately half the variance is accounted for by heritability factors and about half by the environment.

Before looking at the controversial issue of the heritability of intelligence, we should understand that Cattell differentiates between fluid and crystallized intelligence. *Fluid intelligence* is that which enables one to adapt to new kinds of material regardless of previous experiences with it, whereas *crystallized intelligence* is that which depends on previous learnings to solve present problems. Primary Factor B is considered as crystallized intelligence and Cattell estimates its heritability value of 60 percent. For fluid intelligence, a second-stratum trait, the estimate of .65 (Cattell, 1979–1980). These relatively high heritability values suggest that intelligence is probably due more to heredity than to environment.

EYSENCK'S FACTOR THEORY

Eysenck's approach to theory building differs from Cattell's in several respects. First, he is more likely to use the *hypothetico-deductive* method of theorizing *before* factor analyzing data. Second, because he tends to favor *orthogonal* rotation, he has identified far fewer factors. Third, Eysenck uses factor analysis as only one means of answering important questions on personality theory. In an interview with Richard Evans he said,

> I think probably of all the factor analysts you may know, I'm the one who thinks least of it. I regard it as a useful adjunct, a technique that was invaluable under certain circumstances, but one which we must leave behind as soon as possible in order to get a proper causal type of understanding of the factors and to know just what they mean (Evans, 1976, p. 259).

Eysenck, then, is a generalist, not merely a factor analyst. His range of interests is broad; his willingness to step into a controversy is legendary. He has been a gadfly to the conscience of psychology since he first entered its ranks. He upset many psychoanalysts and other therapists in the early 1950s with his contention that there is no evidence to suggest that psychotherapy is more effective than spontaneous remission. In other words, those people who receive no therapy are just as likely to get better as are those who undergo expensive, painful, prolonged psychotherapy with expertly trained psychoanalysts and psychologists (Eysenck, 1952a). Eysenck is not afraid to take an unpopular stand, as witnessed by his defense of Arthur Jensen and his contention that IQ cannot be significantly increased by well-intentioned social programs, but is largely genetically determined. Eysenck's book *The IQ Argument* (1971) was so controversial that elements in the United States "threatened booksellers with arson if they dared to stock the book; well-known 'liberal' newspapers refused to review it; and the outcome was that it was largely impossible in the land of free speech to discover the existence of the book or to buy it" (Eysenck, 1980a, p. 175).

In England he was "attacked and beaten up by some left-wing hooligans" while preparing to deliver a speech on a separate topic (Eysenck, 1980a, p. 175). Eysenck's enemies and critics, however, do not only come from the political left; his battles with the fascist right go back even further.

BIOGRAPHY OF HANS J. EYSENCK

Hans Jurgen Eysenck was born in Berlin, Germany, on March 4, 1916, the child of a theatrical family. His father was a comedian, singer, and actor. His mother was a starlet at the time of his birth and later became a German silent film star under the stage name of Helga Molander. When Hans was two his mother and father divorced and he went to live with his maternal grandmother, who had also been in the theater, but whose promising career in opera was cut short by a crippling fall (Eysenck, 1982). Neither his father nor his mother was religious, though his grandmother was a devout Catholic. Religion, however, has never played an important role in Eysenck's life (Gibson, 1981).

Eysenck suffered the deprivation of many post-World War I Germans who were faced with astronomical inflation, mass unemployment, and near starvation. Eysenck's future appeared no brighter after Hitler came to power. As a condition of studying at a university, he was told that he would have to join the Nazi secret police, an idea he found so repugnant that he decided to leave Germany.

This encounter with the fascist right and his later battles with the radical left suggested to him that the trait of tough-mindedness was equally prevalent in both extremes of the political spectrum. This hypothesis was supported in a later study that demonstrated that, though Communists were radical and Fascists conservative on one dimension of personality, on the tough-minded vs. tender-minded dimension both groups were more authoritarian, rigid, and intolerant of ambiguity (tough-minded) than a control group (Eysenck & Coulter, 1972).

As a consequence of Nazi tyranny, Eysenck, at age 18, left Germany and eventually settled in England where he tried to enroll in the University of London. He was an avid reader, interested in both the arts and the sciences, but his first choice of curriculum was physics. Bandura (see Chapter 12) speaks of fortuitous events that have a profound and permanent effect on people's lives. With Eysenck, a chance event altered the flow of his life and, consequently, the course of the history of psychology. In order to be accepted at the university he was required to pass an entrance examination, which he took after a year's study at a commercial college. After passing the exam, he confidently enrolled in the University of London intending to major in physics. However, he was told that he had taken the wrong subjects in his exam and therefore was not eligible to pursue a course in physics. Rather than wait another year to take the right subjects, he inquired if there were not some scientific subject that he was qualified to pursue. When told he could take psychology, he asked, "What on earth is psychology?" (Eysenck, 1982, p. 290).

The University of London's psychology department was basically pro-Freudian, but it was also psychometrically oriented, with Charles Spearman having just left and with Cyril Burt still president. Eysenck received his bachelor's degree in 1938, about the same time he married Margaret Davies, a Canadian woman with a degree in mathematics. In 1940 he was awarded the Ph.D. from the University of London, but by this time England and most of Europe were at war.

As a German national, he was

considered an enemy alien and not allowed to enter the Royal Air Force (his first choice) or any other branch of the military. Instead, with no training as a psychiatrist or as a clinical psychologist, he went to work at the Mill Hill Emergency Hospital, treating patients who were suffering from a variety of psychological symptoms, including anxiety, depression, and hysteria. Eysenck, however, was not comfortable with most of the traditional clinical diagnostic categories. Using factor analysis, he found that two major personality factors—neuroticism and extraversion/introversion—could account for all the traditional diagnostic groups. These early theoretical ideas led to the publication of his first book, *Dimensions of Personality* (Eysenck, 1947). After the war he became director of the Psychology Department at Maudsley Hospital and later became a Reader in Psychology at the University of London.

In 1949 Eysenck traveled to North America to examine the clinical psychology programs in the United States and Canada with the idea of setting up a clinical psychology profession in Great Britain. He obtained a visiting professorship at the University of Pennsylvania for the year 1949–1950, but spent much of that year traveling throughout the United States and Canada appraising clinical psychology programs, which he found to be totally unscientific (Eysenck, 1980a).

Returning to England, Eysenck established a clinical psychology department at the University of London and in 1955 became professor of psychology. While in the United States he had begun *The Structure of Human Personality* (1952b), in which he argues for the efficacy of factor analysis as the best method of representing the known facts of human personality.

Prior to his trip to North America his first marriage came to an end and he married Sybil Rostal, also a quantitative psychologist and the daughter of a famous violinist. Hans and Sybil Eysenck have coauthored several publications, and their marriage has produced three sons and a daughter. In addition, Eysenck has one son, Michael, from his previous marriage.

Eysenck equals if not surpasses Cattell for volume of published works. Along with hundreds of technical writings, he has published some 40 books, several of which have titles with popular appeal such as *Uses and Abuses of Psychology* (1953), *Sense and Nonsense in Psychology* (1956), *Fact and Fiction in Psychology* (1965a), *Psychology Is about People* (1972b), *You and Neurosis* (1977c), and *Sex, Violence and the Media* (with D. K. B. Nias, 1978). In 1983 Eysenck retired as professor of psychology at the Institute of Psychiatry, University of London, and as senior psychiatrist at the Maudsley and Bethlehem Royal hospitals. His current work centers on developing behavioral interventions in cancer and heart disease (see Box—"Does Personality Cause Disease?"). He continues to enjoy his favorite hobby, tennis, and is currently writing his autobiography.

Does Personality Cause Disease?

During the 1950s Eysenck upset the psychological world with his conclusions that evidence showed a total lack of effectiveness for most major systems of psychotherapy. Then in the 1970s he angered many people, especially American psychologists, with his contention that low intelligence is largely inherited and not due to poor socioeconomic background. Now in the 1990s, Eysenck may shake the world of medicine and psychology with his report that personality type is a much better predictor of death from cancer than is cigarette smoking. In addition, Eysenck believes that cognitive behavioral therapy can mold personality types in ways that prevent both cancer and coronary heart disease.

Eysenck's (1987, 1988) stunning claims are based on research findings of Yugoslav physician and psychologist, Ronald Grossarth-Maticek. During the 1960s, Grossarth-Maticek began to find a marked relationship between such personality traits as hopelessness and helplessness and death from cancer. He also noted that angry, aggressive, hostile people are more likely to die from coronary heart disease than are people who do not have these characteristics.

Grossarth-Maticek's early findings were so astounding that he was accused of falsifying data. His research fell on hard times financially, and when funds were exhausted he applied for and received a grant from R. J. Reynolds, an American tobacco company. In 1980 Eysenck agreed to become chairman of the project, and with his knowledge of behavior therapy and personality types, the research took on a new dimension.

Using a short questionnaire and a long personal interview, about 90 percent of the subjects could be placed into one of four personality groups. Type I included those people who want to get close to others and who have a helpless/hopeless reaction to stress. These people also have a rational, nonemotional reaction to life events and do not readily express strong feelings such as fear or anger. Eysenck (personal communication, November 17, 1987) believes that Type I people would score high on his neuroticism (N) scale.

Type II persons are easily frustrated by other people and by events, and they blame others for their distress and unhappiness. They typically react to frustration with anger, aggression, and emotional arousal.

Type III people are ambivalent, shifting from the typical reaction of Type I individuals to the typical reaction of Type IIs, and back again.

People in Type IV are characterized by personal autonomy. They regard their own autonomy and the autonomy of others as important conditions for their personal well-being and happiness.

In the original study in Yugoslavia, 1353 subjects were recruited by selecting the oldest person in every second household in a town of 14,000 people. Most of the subjects were between 59 and 65 years old. Ten years later the incidences of death from cancer and heart disease were measured and compared with the four personality types. Astonishingly, more than 45 percent of the deaths among Type I personalities were due to cancer, but only 5 percent of deaths among Type II people were the result of cancer. For heart disease, the proportions were reversed. About 30 percent of deaths among Type II persons were attributed to cardiovascular disease, while less than 10 percent of Type II deaths were due to cancer.

For Type III individuals only 5 percent had died from cancer and 10 percent from heart disease. The incidence of death from cancer and cardiovascular disease among Type IV people was less than 5 percent for both diseases combined.

Grossarth-Maticek replicated this study in Heidelberg, Germany, using somewhat younger subjects. Because the people were younger, death rates (especially from cancer) were lower. However, the results were quite consistent with those found in Yugoslavia. In Heidelberg, the researchers studied both a group of normal subjects as well as a group of subjects nominated by friends and relatives as being "highly stressed." Once again, cancer was overwhelmingly the leading cause of death among Type I people, while heart disease was much more likely to be the cause of death for people with Type II personalities. The results were even more pronounced in the stressed group.

Eysenck and Grossarth-Maticek have used behavior therapy techniques to teach Type I people to express their emotions more readily. In this study (Eysenck, 1987, 1988), 100 subjects from the Heidelberg stressed group were randomly divided into a control and a therapy group. The 50 people in the therapy group received individual cognitive behavior therapy designed to *change* their behavior from that typical of Type I people to that characteristic of Type IV. Socially acceptable expressions of emotions were encouraged and subjects were taught coping behaviors appropriate to their particular experience of stress. People in the control group received no therapy.

A 13-year follow-up traced all 100 subjects, living or dead. Of people in the control group, only 19 were still living; 17 had died of cancer and 14 from other causes. Of the people who had received therapy, 45 were still living; none had died of cancer and five had died from other causes. These results are genuinely amazing and strongly suggest that cognitive behavior therapy can reshape personality and thereby prolong life.

If these findings can be replicated, it would revolutionize our way of looking at the link between personality and disease. Type I personalities can be identified and taught more appropriate ways of expressing emotion. These changes then may lead to a nearly complete protection against cancer.

MEASUREMENT OF PERSONALITY

Eysenck's theory of personality is spotlighted by three men who have had the greatest influence on his thinking—Cyril Burt, Charles Spearman, and Ivan Pavlov. Burt, his professor, and Spearman, whose lectures he attended, showed him that personality could best be investigated psychometrically. Pavlov, whom he never knew personally, taught him that there is a biological basis for personality structure (Cohen, 1977).

Criteria for Identifying Factors

Psychometric sophistication alone is not sufficient to measure the structure of human personality. Traits and types arrived at through factor analytic methods are sterile and meaningless unless they have been shown to possess a biological existence. Eysenck, in fact, lists four criteria for the identification of a factor. First, there must be *psychometric evidence* for the factor's existence. A corollary to this criterion is that the factor must be reliable and replicable. Other investigators, from separate laboratories, must also be able to find the factor. A second criterion is that the factor must also possess *heritability;* it must fit an established genetic model. This criterion eliminates learned characteristics, such as the ability to mimic the voices of well-known people or a religious or political belief. Third, the factor *must make sense from a theoretical view.* Eysenck employs the deductive method of investigation, beginning with a theory and proceeding to gather data which are logically meaningful to that theory. The resultant factors should be consistent with some reasonable theory of personality. The final criterion for the existence of a factor is that it must *possess social relevance;* that is, it must be demonstrated that mathematically derived factors have a relationship (not necessarily causal) with such socially relevant variables as drug addiction, accident proneness, outstanding performance in sports, psychotic behavior, criminality, and so on (Eysenck, 1977b).

Hierarchy of Measures

Eysenck recognizes at least four levels of behavior organization. At the lowest level are *specific responses,* individual behaviors that may or may not be characteristic of the person. A student finishing a reading assignment would be an example of a specific response. At the second level are the *habitual responses,* or a combination of specific responses that recur under similar conditions. For example, if a student frequently keeps at an assignment until it is finished, then this behavior becomes a habitual response. As opposed to specific responses, habitual responses must be reasonably reliable or consistent.

Several related habitual responses form a *trait*—the third level of behavior. Eysenck (1981, p. 3) defines traits as "important semi-permanent personality disposition." For example, students who habitually finish class assignments and persist in their endeavors on the job, with hobbies, and in social relations can be said to possess the trait of persistence. Though traits can be identified intuitively, trait and factor theorists, of course, rely on a more systematic approach, namely factor analysis. Trait-level behaviors are extracted through factor analysis of habitual-level responses just as habitual-level responses are mathematically extracted through factor analysis of specific responses. Cattell ordinarily works with factors at this third level of organization.

Eysenck, in contrast, concentrates on the fourth level, that of *types* or superfactors. Types represent interrelated traits. For example, persistence may be related to inferiority, poor emotional adjustment, social shyness, and several other traits, with the entire cluster forming the introverted type. These four levels of behavior organization are shown in Figure 13.6. It is important to keep in mind that Eysenck's structure of personality rests on the

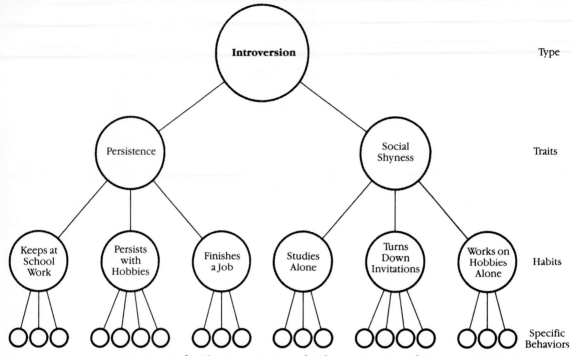

Figure 13.6   The Organization of Behavior into Specific Actions, Habitual Responses, Traits, and Types. Besides Persistence and Social Shyness, other traits such as Inferiority, Low Activity, and Serious-Mindedness contribute to Introversion.

more generalized type level factors, while Cattell's theory is based largely on trait-level factors (Eysenck & Eysenck, 1979).

TYPES

Eysenck has extracted three general types or superfactors—**extraversion** (E), **neuroticism** (N), and **psychoticism** (P). Neuroticism and psychoticism are not limited to pathological individuals, though disturbed people score high on scales measuring these two factors. Eysenck regards all three types as part of normal personality structure. All three types are bipolar, with extraversion being on one end of Factor E and introversion occupying the opposite pole. Similarly, neuroticism is opposed to stability, while psychoticism is opposed to the superego function.

The bipolarity of Eysenck's factors does not imply that most people are on one end or the other of the three main poles. Each type is unimodally, rather than bimodally, distributed. Extraversion, for example, is fairly normally distributed in much the same fashion as intelligence or height. Most people are near the center of a bell-shaped (unimodal) distribution, which means that Eysenck (1976a) does not hold to the outmoded notion that people can be neatly divided into mutually exclusive types. Despite important differences between Cattell and Eysenck at the trait level, there is considerable agreement among them at the type level (Royce, 1973). Eysenck's E (Extraversion), for example, appears to be comparable to Cattell's QI (Exvia/Envia); and his N (Neuroticism) may be the same factor as Cattell's QII (Anxiety).

Extraversion

In Chapter 5 we saw that Jung conceptualized two broad personality types called "extraversion" and "introversion." We also noted some differences between his definitions and the prevailing notion of these two terms. Jung saw extraverted people as having an objective or nonpersonalized view of the world, while introverts have essentially a subjective or individualized way of looking at things. Eysenck's concepts of extraversion and introversion are closer to the popular usage. Extraverted types are characterized primarily by sociability and impulsiveness, but also by jocularity, liveliness, quickwittedness, optimism, and other traits indicative of people who are rewarded for their association with others (Eysenck & Eysenck, 1969). Our case study, Holly, is somewhat more extraverted than introverted. She enjoys high-risk activities such as mountain climbing and sky diving. In addition, she is willing to gamble her health against the pleasures of smoking, drinking, and using marijuana.

Introverts are characterized by traits opposite to those of extraverts. They can be described as quiet, passive, unsociable, careful, reserved, thoughtful, pessimistic, peaceful, sober, and controlled (Eysenck, Nias, & Cox, 1982). According to Eysenck (1982), however, the principal differences between extraversion and introversion are not behavioral, but rather biological and genetic in nature.

Eysenck believes that the primary cause of differences between extraverts and introverts is one of cortical arousal level, a physiological condition that is largely inherited rather than learned. He has found evidence that extraverts are characterized by a lower level of cortical arousal than introverts. Consequently, they have higher sensory thresholds and, thus, lesser reactions to sensory stimulation. Introverts, conversely, are characterized by a higher level of arousal and, as a result of a lower sensory threshold, they experience greater reactions to sensory stimulation (Eysenck, 1967, 1968, 1981; Eysenck & Eysenck, 1969). In order to maintain an optimal level of stimulation, therefore, introverts with their congenitally low sensory threshold must seek to avoid situations that will cause too much excitement. Hence, introverts should be expected to shun such activities as wild social events, downhill skiing, sky diving, competitive sports, leading a fraternity or sorority, or playing practical jokes.

On the other hand, since extraverts have a habitually low level of cortical arousal, it takes a high level of sensory stimulation to cross the threshold and consequently to maintain an optimal level of stimulation. Therefore, it could be hypothesized that extraverts would more likely be found participating in

Extraverts enjoy exciting and stimulating activities.

exciting and stimulating activities. Taking only one example, Eysenck (1976b) hypothesizes that extraverts, as opposed to introverts, will engage in sexual intercourse earlier, more frequently, with more different partners, in more different positions, with a greater variety of sexual behaviors, and will indulge in longer precoital love play. Because extraverts have a lower level of cortical arousal, however, they become more quickly accustomed to strong stimuli (sexual or other) and respond less and less to the same stimuli, while introverts are less likely to become bored and uninterested in routine activities carried on with the same people.

Neuroticism

The second type extracted by Eysenck is neuroticism/stability (N). Like extraversion/introversion, Factor N has a strong hereditary component. Eysenck (1967) reports several studies that have found evidence of a genetic basis for such neurotic traits as anxiety, hysteria, and obsessive-compulsive disorders. In addition, he has found a much greater agreement among identical twins than among fraternals on a number of antisocial and asocial behaviors such as adult crime, childhood behavior disorders, homosexuality, and alcoholism (Eysenck, 1974).

How can neurotics be described? No single syndrome can define neurotic behavior, since neuroticism can be combined with different points on the extraversion scale to produce at least three classes of neurotic behavior. Eysenck's orthogonal rotation assumes the independence of types, which means that the neuroticism scale is at right angles (signifying zero correlation) to the extraversion scale. This means that different people, all scoring high on N, might display quite different symptoms, depending on their degree of introversion or extraversion. Figure 13.7 shows the extraversion/introversion pole with zero correlation with the neuroticism/stability pole. Consider subjects A, B, and C, all equal on the neuroticism scale, but representing three distinct points on the extraversion scale. Subject A, an introverted neurotic, is characterized by anxiety, depression, phobias, and obsessive-compulsive symptoms; subject B is neither introverted nor extraverted and is likely to be characterized by hysteria (a neurotic disorder associated with emotional instability), suggestibility, and somatic symptoms; subject C, an extraverted neurotic, has been found to manifest psychopathic qualities, namely, criminality and delinquent tendencies (Eysenck, 1967). Consider, also, subjects A, D, and E, all equally introverted, but with three different levels of emotional stability. Subject A is the introverted neurotic described above; D is equally introverted, but is neither severely neurotic nor emotionally stable; and E is both psychologically healthy and extremely introverted.

Figure 13.7 shows only five subjects, all of whom have at least one extreme score. Most subjects, of course, score near the mean on both scales and are, therefore, near the center of the figure. As one moves toward the outer limits of the diagram, scores would become increasingly less and less frequent.

Eysenck has developed two widely used personality inventories that measure E and N. The first, the Maudsley Personality Inventory or MPI (Eysenck, 1959), appeared to yield some correlation between E and N. For this reason,

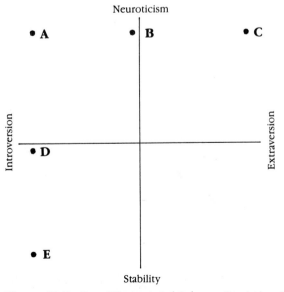

Figure 13.7   Two-Dimensional Scheme Depicting Several Extreme Points on Eysenck's E and N Scales

Eysenck began work on another test, the Eysenck Personality Inventory or EPI (Eysenck & Eysenck, 1964), which is an improved version of the MPI. This later inventory measures extraversion (E) and neuroticism (N) independently and also contains a lie (L) scale to detect faking.

Psychoticism

Eysenck's original theory of personality was based on only two types— extraversion and neuroticism. After several years of alluding to psychoticism (P) as an independent personality type, he finally elevated it to a position equal to E and N (Eysenck & Eysenck, 1976). This is reminiscent of Freud elevating aggression to an equal place with sex. In both cases a long-held theory received a substantial addition, and in both cases colleagues and followers were slow to accept the change (Broadbent, 1981).

The psychoticism/superego dimension is independent of both E and N. Figure 13.8 shows the three factors at right angles with one another. (Since three-dimensional space cannot be faithfully produced on a two-dimensional plane, the reader is asked to look at Figure 13.8 as if the solid lines represent the corner of a room where two walls meet the floor. Each line can then be seen as perpendicular to the other two.) Eysenck's view of personality, therefore, allows each person to be measured on three independent factors and resultant scores to be plotted in space having three coordinates. Figure 13.8 subject F, for example, is very high on superego, somewhat high on extraversion, and near the midpoint on the neuroticism/stability scale.

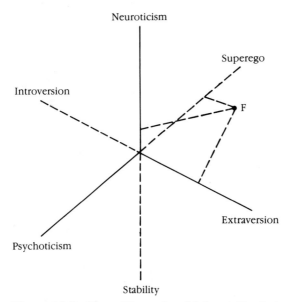

Figure 13.8   Three-Dimensional Scheme Depicting One Individual's Scores on Each of Eysenck's Major Dimensions of Personality

Psychoticism, like extraversion and neuroticism, has a strong genetic component with about three-fourths of the variance of all three factors accounted for by heredity and about one-fourth by environmental factors. Eysenck describes high P scorers as egocentric, cold, nonconforming, aggressive, impulsive, hostile, suspicious, and antisocial. Low P scorers (in the direction of superego function) tend to be empathetic, caring, cooperative, and highly socialized (Eysenck, Nias, & Cox, 1982, p. 3). In addition, high P scorers tend to be male and low scorers female. To date, not as much research has been conducted on the psychoticism scales as on the two older ones, but Fulker (1981) has reported some evidence for a high heritability of psychoticism as well as extraversion and neuroticism.

CONCEPT OF HUMANITY

How do trait and factor theorists view humanity? Cattell and Eysenck are not concerned with traditional themes such as *determinism vs. free choice, optimism vs. pessimism,* and *teleological vs. causal influences.* In fact, their theories do not even lend themselves to speculation on these topics. What, then, can we say concerning their view of humanity?

First, we know that Cattell and Eysenck see humans as being different from other animals. From a psychometric view, people can be differentiated from other beings on the basis of their ability to report data about themselves. Animal data can be collected by life records (L data) and by objective measurement of performance (T data). However, only humans are capable of answering questions about themselves (Q data). From this fact, it can be inferred that Cattell and Eysenck believe that humans possess not only *consciousness* but self-consciousness as well. People are also able to evaluate their performance and to render reasonably reliable reports concerning their attitudes, temperament, needs, interests, and behaviors.

Second, both Cattell and Eysenck, place heavy emphasis on *genetic factors* of personality. Eysenck insists that the traits of extraversion, neuroticism, and psychoticism all have strong hereditary components. Cattell, likewise, has found significant heritability for the various traits he has identified. On the dimension of biological vs. social influences, therefore, trait and factor theories tend to favor biology.

A third dimension, which is applicable to trait theories, is that of *individual differences vs. similarities.* Factor analysis rests on the premise of differences among individuals and variability in their scores. If scores on individuals did not differ, correlations would be impossible and factor analysis unthinkable. Even though common factors are ordinarily derived from factor analysis, this does not subtract from the emphasis that trait theorists place on individual differences. Eysenck (1981, p. xi), for instance, says that "people are above all else *individuals*." Common traits do not require that similarities be emphasized. Individual differences can be accentuated by plotting one person's scores on each of several traits. In addition, Cattell has pioneered the use of the P technique, which begins with a large pool of scores obtained from a single individual and results in the identification of individual traits. For these reasons it can be said that trait theorists are more concerned with individual differences than with similarities among people.

CRITIQUE OF TRAIT AND FACTOR THEORIES

The trait and factor theories of Cattell and Eysenck are examples of a strictly empirical approach to personality investigation. Both theories were built by collecting as much data as possible on a large number of people, intercorrelating the scores, factor analyzing correlation matrices, and applying appropriate psychological significance to the resultant factors. Psychometrics, rather than clinical judgment, is the cornerstone of trait and factor theories. The approach is scientifically sound; the results, though promising, are nevertheless disappointing. Hypothetically, if two factor analysts set out to measure the same entity (human personality), they should report the same findings just as two chemists should each find the same chemical elements when conducting an analysis of a single compound. However, Cattell has set out trying to measure the entire sphere of human personality, while Eysenck has limited himself to only a small area of personality. Therefore, Cattell and Eysenck do not arrive at the same destination after setting out on their journeys to discover the structure of personality.

It would be an error, however, to discard trait and factor theories simply because they have not yet produced a single description of human personality. To reject the theories on the grounds of their collective disagreement would be comparable to throwing out the works of Freud, Adler, and Jung merely because their clinically produced theories have not yielded identical results.

Just as Freud, Adler, and Jung sometimes squabbled among themselves, so too have Cattell and Eysenck. But while the former three were often vicious and personal, the latter two are more likely to raise technical issues and to disagree in the spirit of scientific kinship (Cattell, 1972b; Eysenck, 1972a, 1977b). Despite disagreements and discrepancies among trait and factor theorists, their works can be combined for purposes of critical evaluation.

Allport (Chapter 14) has criticized the concept of "factor" on at least four counts. First, he said, factors represent a composite picture of people in general and in no way resemble any single individual. Second, Allport claimed that individual identity is lost in the "statistical grinder" that mixes one person's scores with everyone else's. The third difficulty arises in the naming of factors. Factor theorists themselves recognize this difficulty and sometimes resort to the use of letters such as A, B, C, N, or P to represent factors. Finally, Allport contended that factor analysis cannot produce anything that is not first put into it. What often goes into a correlation matrix are scores obtained by instruments subject to errors of measurement and to sampling error (Allport, 1961).

While Allport's criticisms sound reasonable, they do not represent the standards by which trait and factor theories must be judged. Rather, the five criteria of a useful theory provide the bases for a critique of the theories of Cattell and Eysenck.

First, do trait and factor theories *organize knowledge?* On this criterion they receive a very high rating. Anything that is truly *known* about personality should be reducible to some quantity. Anything that can be quantified can be factor analyzed. The extracted factors then provide a convenient and accurate description of personality in terms of traits. These traits, in turn, can present a framework for organizing many disparate observations about human personality. Traits possess a high level of versatility. They can be viewed as highly specific factors, not much broader than a habit, or they can be clustered to form generalized dispositions or types; they can be seen as individual traits (peculiar to one person) or as common traits (shared by many); and they can be viewed as unitary (unrelated to other traits). In addition, people can be seen in terms of normal or pathological traits and also in terms of learned or inherited traits. Trait and factor theories, then, have the power to give meaning to much of what is known about personality.

Do these theories *generate research?* On this second criterion of a useful theory, trait and factor theories must be rated high. Cattell, especially, has built his theory inductively, without reliance on a preconceived notion of what personality ought to be. This highly empirical procedure may appear to some to be atheoretical, but it is actually a sound method of building a theory. In this manner, theory and observation never become estranged. Factor analytic methods not only *create* hypotheses, they are capable of *testing* them as well. Cattell and Eysenck have each constructed several personality inventories that have generated a prodigious amount of research. Though many of these investigations are not direct tests of the theory on which the inventories are based, an impressive measure of research has been generated by trait and factor theories.

A third criterion of a useful theory is the power to *guide the actions of practitioners.* On this criterion, trait and factor theories receive mixed reviews. In general, they provide a comprehensive and structured taxonomy or classification. A taxonomy, though impotent in generating testable hypotheses, is a necessary condition for theory and for science. The classification system provided by trait theorists, particularly Cattell, serves as a useful guide to the researcher and the theory builder, but it is less useful to psychotherapists, teachers, and parents who look toward a sound theoretical system to answer many of their everyday questions.

Are trait and factor theories *internally consistent?* Again, the rating must be equivocal. Each theory alone is a model of consistency, but the two theories taken together are somewhat inconsistent. This presents a problem, especially since factor analysis is a precise mathematical procedure and factor theories are heavily empirical. Inconsistencies arise for several reasons. First, different data are collected. This is due partly to differences in opinion as to the importance of the various data and partly to the inevitable errors of measurement and to sampling errors. Second, orthogonal and oblique rotations almost always result in some differences in number and nature of factors extracted. Third, and perhaps most important, subjective judgments enter the process in at least three places. First is the decision on the number of rotations and thus the number of factors extracted. The second involves the criteria for establishing the magnitude of factor loadings and thus the purity of each factor. Finally, personal values influence the naming of each factor and thus the psychological significance of each trait.

The final criterion of a useful theory is *parsimony*. Ideally, trait and factor theories should receive an excellent rating on this standard since factor analysis is predicated on the idea of the fewest number of explanatory factors possible. In other words, the very purpose of factor analysis is to reduce a large number of variables to as few as possible. This is the essence of parsimony. Eysenck, with only three factors, certainly has epitomized parsimony. Cattell, on the other hand, has not only extracted many more factors but has also applied neologistic labels to most of them, thus rendering his language troublesome for the uninitiated.

CHAPTER SUMMARY

A summary of the assumptions underlying trait and factor theories has been provided by Eysenck (1981, p. 3), who believes that eight statements have now been firmly established and are acceptable not only to him but also to Cattell.

1. Individuals differ with respect to their location on important semipermanent personality dispositions, known as "traits."
2. Personality traits can be identified by means of correlational (factor analytical) studies.
3. Personality traits are importantly determined by hereditary factors.
4. Personality traits are measurable by means of questionnaire data.
5. The interactive influence of traits and situations produces transient internal conditions, known as "states."
6. Personality states are measurable by means of questionnaire data.
7. Traits and states are intervening variables or mediating variables that are useful in explaining individual differences in

behavior to the extent that they are incorporated into an appropriate theoretical framework.

8. The relationship between traits or states and behavior is typically indirect, being affected or "moderated" by the interactions that exist among traits, states, and other salient factors.

Cattell's theory of personality is psychometrically, rather than clinically, based. He began with no preconceived ideas on the structure of human personality; proceeded *inductively* to gather quantified information from life reports (L data), self reports (Q data), and objective test performance (T data); obtained intercorrelations of scores; and then extracted *primary factors* from the correlation matrices. These factors emerged as psychologically meaningful traits within three modalities of personality— *temperament, ability,* and *motivation.*

In all, 35 *first-order personality traits* have been identified—23 within the realm of normal personality, plus 12 pathological traits. These factors themselves are intercorrelated, thus allowing for further factoring and the extraction of at least 15 *second-stratum factors.* These primary and secondary factors are called "general personality traits," but they are largely traits of *temperament.*

Cattell has also been able to classify ability and motivation traits. Motivation or *dynamic traits* are divided into innate drives or *ergs* and culturally acquired motives called sentiments or *sems.* Both are part of the *dynamic lattice,* which also includes the more fundamental concept of *attitudes.* After 50 years of work, Cattell, who set out to explore the entire sphere of human personality, has succeeded in mapping a comprehensive taxonomy of personality structure and suggesting possible means of predicting behavior.

In contrast, Eysenck has had more modest goals. Relying more on a *hypothetico-deductive* approach and an *orthogonal* method of factoring, he has extracted only three bipolar factors—extraversion/introversion, neuroticism/stability, and psychoticism/superego.

Extraversion is characterized by sociability and impulsiveness—*introversion* by passivity and thoughtfulness; *neuroticism* by anxiety and compulsivity—*stability* by their absence; *psychoticism* by antisocial behavior—*superego* by empathy and cooperation.

Both Cattell and Eysenck place heavy emphasis on biological components of personality.

Suggested Readings

CATTELL, R. B. (1974a). An autobiography. In G. Lindzey (Ed.), *A history of psychology in autobiography* (Vol. 6) (pp. 59–100). Englewood Cliffs, N.J.: Prentice-Hall.
   Although this autobiography is several years old, it provides an interesting account of Cattell's early life in England, his settling in the United States, and his lengthy search for various components of personality.
CATTELL, R. B. (1983). *Structured personality–learning theory: A wholistic multivariate research approach.* New York: Praeger.
   Although sections of this book, with their complicated mathematical formulas, are difficult to comprehend, Cattell offers much to the interested reader.
EYSENCK, H. J. (1982). Personality. In H. J. Eysenck, *Personality, genetics, and behavior: Selected papers* (pp. 49–109). New York: Praeger.
   A selection of six papers on personality including a brief discussion of the three superfactors—extraversion, neuroticism, and psychoticism.
GIBSON, H. B. (1981). *Hans Eysenck: The man and his work.* London: Peter Owen.
   Until Eysenck's full-length autobiography becomes available, this interesting account of a fascinating man will remain recommended reading.

ALLPORT

The Psychology of the Individual

As she lay in her bed in a home for aged women, Jenny was unable to sleep. The lights from a saloon across the street, the pain from a recent broken foot, and the constant worry about money and the honesty of her caretakers all made her restless. Suddenly, she felt a hand on her neck and back. Terrified with fright, she struck out at her intruder, hitting her on the breast and head and calling her an assortment of foul names. Jenny was sure that the nurse was trying to steal her money. People at the "home" couldn't be trusted. They were a bunch of hypocrites, liars, and double dealers.

The next morning when Jenny apologized for her attack, the nurse explained that she was only trying to see if Jenny was warm enough. Jenny didn't believe her. In fact she trusted almost no one. She detested the other residents and turned her face to the wall when meeting them in the corridor. She was suspicious of the staff, accusing them of opening her mail, inadequately feeding her, and trying to steal her money. Jenny's animosity was especially virulent against women, but men too were not spared her wrath.

Jenny was nearly 70 years old and had less than a year to live. Except for the pleasure she received from reading great literature, visiting art museums, and viewing beautiful sunsets, her life now had few pleasant moments.

Jenny was the oldest in a family of seven children that included five sisters and a brother. When she was 18 her father died, so Jenny was forced to quit school and go to work to help support her family. After her brothers and sisters became self-supporting, Jenny, who had always been considered rebellious, married a divorced man. This further alienated her from her conservatively religious family.

After only two years of marriage her husband died, and her son, Ross, was born a month later. The next 17 years were somewhat contented ones for Jenny. Her world revolved around her son, and she worked hard to ensure that he had everything he wanted. She told Ross that, aside from art, the world was a miserable place, and that it was her duty to sacrifice for him because she was responsible for his existence.

When Ross moved away to attend college, Jenny continued to scrimp in order to pay all his bills. As Ross began to become interested in women, his idyllic relationship with his mother came to an end. The two quarreled often and bitterly over his women friends. Jenny referred to all of them as prostitutes or whores, including the woman Ross married. With that marriage, Jenny and Ross became temporarily estranged.

At about that same time, Jenny began to correspond with Ross's former college roommate, Glenn, and his wife, Isabel. During the next 11 1/2 years Jenny wrote a series of 301 letters to the young couple in which she revealed much about both her life and her personality. The early letters showed that she was deeply concerned with money, death, and Ross. She felt that Ross was ungrateful and that he had abandoned her for another woman, and a prostitute at that. She continued her bitterness toward him until he and his wife were divorced. She then moved to the apartment next to Ross and, for a short time, Jenny was happy. But soon Ross was seeing other women and Jenny inevitably found something wrong with each. Her letters to Glenn and Isabel were filled with animosity for Ross, a suspicious and cynical attitude toward others, and a morbid yet dramatic approach to life.

Three years into the correspondence, Ross suddenly died. Now Jenny's letters expressed a somewhat more favorable attitude toward him. Now she did not have to share him with anyone; now he was safe—no more prostitutes.

For the next eight years, Jenny continued writing to Glenn and Isabel, and they usually answered her. However, they served mostly as neutral listeners and not as advisors or confidantes. Jenny continued to be overly concerned with death and money. She increasingly blamed others for her misery and intensified her suspicions and hostility toward her caregivers. After Jenny died Isabel commented that, in the end, Jenny was "the same only more so."

OVERVIEW

Later in this chapter we will learn more about Jenny. Her letters represent the kind of personal documents used by Gordon W. Allport to support his ideas that personality should be studied from the individual's point of view. Allport insisted that the study of the person must take into consideration the uniqueness of every individual. This concern for individuality makes Allport himself rather unique among personality theorists, most of whom look for general laws based on common elements among people. In contrast, Allport advocated the study of the individual.

Allport was concerned with uniqueness and individuality because he firmly believed that the psychology of personality must occupy an intermediate position between universal laws and generalities on the one hand and the anarchy of complete individuality on the other. He leaned far in the direction of individuality in order to balance existing theories that he believed were overly inclined toward a generalized concept of humanity.

In 1937, when Allport completed his first major work, *Personality: A Psychological Interpretation,* most existing schools of psychology (with the notable exception of Adler's Individual Psychology) favored an analysis of personality based on traits or characteristics people have in common. Foremost among these theories were psychoanalysis, Analytical Psychology, factor theories, and the various learning theories. By 1961 when he published

Pattern and Growth in Personality, Allport was able to note several new movements, namely existentialism, phenomenology, and client-centered therapy, which had adopted the humanistic or individualistic viewpoint. However, Allport believed the basic question still existed: What is the proper balance between universal laws and individual uniqueness?

The major thrust of Allport's work was to examine individual uniqueness and to elevate it to a legitimate position in the psychology of personality. If at times he seems to have gone to extremes in his emphasis on the individual life style and the uniqueness of each action, it was for the purpose of achieving a balance between the general and specific. There already existed enough theories concerned chiefly with universal factors.

As a reaction to psychoanalysis and learning theory, Allport's psychology of the individual attempted to swing the pendulum back to a middle position—a position that even he might find more satisfying than the completely individualistic one he sometimes advocated. His intention was to supplement rather than supplant the findings of psychoanalysis, stimulus-response theories, operant conditioning, and social psychology.

Allport was eclectic in his acceptance of certain observations produced by these older schools, but he feared that they might hide the individual essence of personality. He believed that only by using the findings of psychoanalysis, learning theory, and social psychology, in conjunction with the findings and procedures of his individual psychology, could the psychology of personality strike a happy middle ground. Many of his writings, therefore, are controversial and overstated, but this was his intention. He once wrote, "I know in my bones that my opponents are partly right" (Allport, 1968, p. 405).

BIOGRAPHY OF GORDON ALLPORT

Gordon W. Allport was born on November 11, 1897, in Montezuma, Indiana, the youngest of four sons. His father, a country doctor, and his mother, a former schoolteacher, moved their family to the Cleveland, Ohio area where Gordon received his first 12 years of schooling.

The youngest child by five years, Gordon developed an early interest in philosophical and religious questions and more facility for words than for games. Though he graduated second in his high school class of 100, he did not consider himself an inspired scholar (Allport, 1967).

In the fall of 1915 Allport entered Harvard, following in the footsteps of his older brother, Floyd, who had graduated two years earlier and was at that time a graduate assistant in psychology. His enrollment at Harvard marked the beginning of a 50-year association with that university, which was interrupted only briefly on several occasions. He received his bachelor's degree in 1919 with a major in philosophy and economics. However, he was still uncertain about a future career. He had taken undergraduate courses in psychology and social ethics, and both disciplines had made a lasting impression on him. When he received an opportunity to teach in Turkey, he saw it as a chance to find out whether or not he would enjoy teaching. He spent the academic year of 1919–1920 in Europe teaching English and sociology at Robert College in Istanbul.

Allport returned to Harvard in 1920 with a fellowship for graduate study, but not before an interesting meeting with Sigmund Freud. With a certain audacity, the 22-year-old Allport wrote to Freud announcing his intention to visit Vienna and offered the father of psychoanalysis an opportunity to meet with him. The encounter was significant to Allport who, not knowing what to talk about, told Freud about seeing a small boy on the train that same day who had displayed a dirt phobia, constantly complaining to his mother about the filthy conditions on the train. After Allport completed the story, Freud looked at him and said, "And was that little boy you?"

This single response was to have great meaning for Allport. Though not an anti-Freudian, he was later to evolve a personality theory that had an almost diametrically opposite view from psychoanalysis concerning the importance of unconscious and conscious motivation. While Freud assumed an underlying unconscious meaning to such stories, Allport was inclined to accept self-reports at face value. This simple anecdote reveals a basic dichotomy between Allport and Freud in their approach to the scientific study of behavior.

Back at Harvard, Allport quickly finished his work, receiving his Ph.D. in psychology in 1922 at age 24. The following two years he spent in Europe studying under the great German psychologists, Max Wertheimer, Wolfgang Kohler, William Stern, Heinz Werner, and others in Berlin and Hamburg. The latter half of his European experiences were spent in Cambridge, England, where he had a chance to absorb what he had learned in Germany.

In 1924 he returned again to Harvard to teach among other classes a new course in the psychology of personality. After two years he took a position at Dartmouth College, but four years later he returned to Harvard where he remained until his death. He died on October 9, 1967, of lung cancer.

In 1925 Allport married Ada Lufkin Gould, whom he had met when both were graduate students in psychology. Their son, Robert, became a pediatrician, thus sandwiching Allport between two generations of physicians, a fact that seems to have pleased him in no small measure (Allport, 1967). In 1939, at the age of 41, Allport was elected president of the American Psychological Association and in 1966 he was honored as the first Richard Clarke Cabot Professor of Social Ethics at Harvard.

ALLPORT'S APPROACH

Allport criticized older theories of personality for losing sight of the normal, psychologically healthy individual. Most people, he believed, are motivated by present drives rather than past events. They are aware of what they are doing and have some understanding of why they are doing it. They not only seek to reduce tensions but to establish new ones as well. They have the potential to learn new patterns of behavior and to grow during any period of their lives.

In his approach to personality, Allport adopted an *open system* and was *eclectic* in his construction of a personality theory. Both terms are explained below.

Open System

We have said that Allport advocated an **open system** in the study of personality, by which he meant that any adequate theory of personality must take into consideration the fact that persons not only react to their environment but also that they shape the environment and cause it to react to them. Personality is a growing system, allowing new elements constantly to enter into and change the person.

Allport (1960) believed that many theories of personality are not based on an open system, but rather on a partially closed one, which does not adequately allow for possibilities of growth. Theories such as psychoanalysis and learning theory are basically homeostatic and view humanity as a quasiclosed system. These theories can also be called *reactive theories* because they treat human personality as basically reactive; that is, people are seen as being motivated primarily by needs to reduce tension and to return to a state of equilibrium.

A truly open system of personality must allow for **proactive** behavior, that is, the notion that people are capable of consciously acting upon their environment in new and innovative ways that permit them to grow toward psychological health. Also an open system must meet four criteria, the first two of which also apply to partially closed systems.

1. "There is intake and output of both matter and energy" (Allport, 1960, p. 303). Any system, whether machine, animal, or human, meets this criterion. In fact, this is the basic definition of a system.
2. "There is achievement and maintenance of steady (homeostatic) states, so that intrusion of outer energy will not seriously disrupt internal form and order" (Allport, 1960, p. 303). Theories based on reduction of tensions, satisfaction of needs, and other homeostatic concepts meet this criterion, but usually do not go beyond this point. (An exception is Maslow's theory [see Chapter 15], which is based on satisfaction of needs, but which allows for psychological growth.) Theories that meet only the first two criteria regard the person as an essentially static animal, constantly driven by internal or external forces to seek a state of equilibrium.

No theory of personality is based on a completely closed system. Openness is a matter of degree. Allport believed that most theories of personality meet these first two criteria. However, those which satisfy only these two are quasiclosed or merely partially open. Allport, of course, advocated an open system in personality theory, one which meets the third and fourth criteria as well as the first two.

3. "There is generally an increase of order over time, owing to an increase in complexity and differentiation of parts" (Allport, 1960, p. 303). An open system of personality must meet this third criterion; that is, it must allow for fundamental change and growth within the organism. Allport's theory repeatedly emphasizes the point that people not only attempt to reduce tension but they also, at times, actually *seek* tension and enjoy its maintenance. Other theories that postulate growth, notably those of Jung (Chapter 5), Maslow (Chapter 16), and Rogers (Chapter 17), also meet this key criterion.

4. "There is more than mere intake and output of matter and energy; there is extensive transactional commerce with the environment" (Allport, 1960, p. 303). This criterion points toward the importance of culture or society. The person and the environment are seen as one mutually inter-active system. Field theories, which insist that people cannot be viewed apart from their surroundings, meet this fourth criterion.

Allport suggested that present controversies in personality theory arise from two basic opposing views: first, the *homeostatic position* espoused by Freud, Dollard and Miller, Skinner, and others, and second, the *growth theories* advocated by Maslow, Rogers, and others. The homeostatic theorists emphasize the first two criteria of an open system, the growth theorists stress the latter two, especially the third criterion. Although he advocated an open system, Allport emphasized that any adequate theory of personality must be able to incorporate the explanation of *reactive theories,* while at the same time it must make allowances for *proactive theories* that stress change and growth. In other words, a complete personality theory must meet all four criteria of an open system. Allport, therefore, argued for a psychology which, on the one hand, studies behavioral patterns and general laws (the subject matter of traditional psychology) and, on the other, growth and individuality. Pattern (consistency) and growth (uniqueness) cannot be separated. Hence, the title of one of Allport's most important works, *Pattern and Growth in Personality* (1961).

Eclecticism

Because an adequate theory of personality must explain proactive as well as reactive behavior, it must be sufficiently broad in scope and procedure to encompass the growing, evolving person on the one hand, and the static, adjustive person on the other. It is for this reason that Allport advocated an **eclectic** approach to theory building. He argued against particularism, that is, those theories which emphasize a single approach, and went on to warn theorists not to "forget what you have decided to neglect" (Allport, 1968, p. 23). In other words, no theory at this time can be completely comprehensive and one should always realize that much of human nature is not included in any single theory.

The closed theories usually exclude everything that does not fit neatly into their static concepts of humanity. Growth theories, such as Jungian psychology, existentialism, or self-actualization, may be somewhat more open-minded, but they too can become closed and exclusive. For example, when a theory insists that all motivation is directed toward self-actualization it runs the risk of overlooking much of human behavior that is adjustive and homeostatic.

Allport accepted the contributions of Freud, Cattell, Skinner, and others, but he believed that they stopped short in their theory of the total personality. The growth theories of Maslow, Rogers, and Allport himself add to the earlier foundation formed by psychoanalysis and learning theory, but none is complete by itself. Allport (1968), therefore, favored eclecticism over particularism because it is less restrictive and offers more hope in understanding the complete and unique person. Broader theories, even when they do not generate specific testable hypotheses, are preferable to narrow ones because they organize known facts from all kinds of research as well as from intuition.

PERSONALITY DEFINED

Few psychologists are as painstaking and exhaustive as Allport in defining terms. His pursuit of a definition of personality is a classic. He traced the etymology of the word *persona* back to early Greek roots including the Old Latin and Etruscan meanings. As was seen in Chapter 1, the word personality probably comes from **persona**, which refers to the theatrical mask used in ancient Greek drama by Roman actors during the first and second centuries before Christ. After tracing the history of the term, Allport spelled out 49 definitions of personality as used in theology, philosophy, law, sociology, and psychology. He then offered a 50th definition. In 1937 he defined personality as

> the dynamic organization within the individual of those psychophysical systems that determine his unique adjustments to his environment (Allport, 1937, p. 48).

By 1961 he had changed the last phrase to read "that determine his characteristic behavior and thought" (Allport, 1961, p. 28). The change was significant and reflected Allport's penchant for accuracy. By 1961 he realized that the phrase "adjustments to his environment" could imply that people merely adapt to their environment. In his later definition Allport conveys the idea that behavior is *expressive* as well as adaptive. People not only adjust to their environment but also reflect on it and interact with it in such a way as to cause their environment to adjust to them.

Each phrase of his definition was carefully chosen. Each word conveys precisely what Allport was saying. The term *dynamic organization* implies an integration or interrelatedness of the various aspects of personality. There is an organized pattern to personality. However, the organization is always subject to change, hence the qualifier "dynamic." Personality is not a static organization; it is constantly growing or changing. Organization also implies disorganization, a term used to describe so-called abnormal personalities.

The term *psychophysical* is used to emphasize the importance of both the psychological and the physical aspects of personality.

Allport (1960, p. 302) defined the word *system* as a "complex of elements in mutual interaction." Traits, for example, are systems. So too are habits and sentiments. System implies activity, either as potentiality or as action itself.

Another word in the definition which implies action is *determine*. This term, however, must not be confused with determinism or predeterminism. Allport (1961, p. 29) chose the word "determine" to indicate that "personality *is* something and *does* something." In other words, personality is not merely the mask we wear; nor is it simply behavior. It refers to the person behind the façade, the organism behind the action.

By *characteristic* Allport meant individual or unique. It comes from the word "character," which originally meant marking or engraving. All persons stamp their unique mark on their personality. Their characteristic behavior and thought set them apart from all other people. Characteristics are marked with a unique engraving, a stamp or marking that no one else can duplicate.

The words *behavior and thought* simply refer to anything the person does. They are omnibus terms meant to include internal behaviors (thoughts) as well as external behaviors such as words and actions. In other words, everything a person does (actions, thoughts, feelings, language) is a part of personality.

Allport's definition of personality is nothing if not comprehensive. In it he proposes that human personality is both product and process; people have some organized structure while, at the same time, they possess the capability of change. Pattern coexists with growth; order with diversification.

Personality is everything, both physical and psychological; it includes both overt behaviors and covert thoughts; it not only *is* something, but it *does* something. Personality is both substance and change; both product and process; both structure and growth.

STRUCTURE OF PERSONALITY

The structure of personality refers to its basic units or building blocks. To Freud the basic units are instincts; to Dollard and Miller they are habits; to Cattell and Eysenck they are traits. To Allport, the most important structures are those which permit the description of the person in terms of individual characteristics. The two basic units of personality are personal disposition and the proprium.

Personal Dispositions

The term traits and the name Gordon Allport are often closely associated. This association, however, represents a misconception of Allport's general theory of personality and his specific concept of traits. In a conversation with Richard Evans, Allport rejected the label of trait psychologist and with good reason (Evans, 1976). Allport, of course, placed supreme importance on the uniqueness of the individual. The term trait, on the other hand, too often implies a general characteristic held in common by several people (Zuroff, 1986).

Allport was careful to distinguish between common traits and individual traits or *personal dispositions.* **Common traits** are those aspects of human personality which lend themselves to interindividual comparisons. They provide the means by which characteristics of people within a given culture can be compared. While common traits are important in interperson comparative studies, **personal dispositions** (p.d.'s) are of even greater importance because they permit intrapersonal study.

Allport used the term personal dispositions rather than individual traits because it is more descriptive and less likely to be confused with common traits. He defined a personal disposition as "a generalized neuropsychic structure (peculiar to the individual), with the capacity to render many stimuli functionally equivalent, and to initiate and guide consistent (equivalent) forms of adaptive and stylistic behavior" (Allport, 1961, p. 373).

The most important distinction between a personal disposition and a common trait is indicated by the parenthetical phrase "peculiar to the individual." Personal dispositions are individual; common traits are shared by several people.

How many personal dispositions are there? By definition there would be more p.d.'s than there are people, since personal dispositions are not shared, and everyone has some. Practically, there are as many p.d.'s as there are words in the language to describe personal behavior. Allport and Odbert (1936) counted approximately 18,000 such words in the English language. However, personal dispositions seldom are accurately described in a single word, but may require a phrase such as, "She's generous with her money but not her time," or simply, "Joe is just Joe. There's no one else like him."

A more important question is: How many p.d.'s does a single person have? This question cannot be answered without reference to the degree of dominance the p.d. has in the individual's life. If one counts those personal dispositions which are central to a person, then each person probably has ten or fewer. However, if all tendencies or dispositions are included, then each person may have hundreds of p.d.'s.

Levels of Personal Dispositions

Allport placed personal dispositions on a continuum from those which are most central to those which are of only peripheral importance to the person.

Cardinal Traits.   Some people possess an eminent trait or ruling passion so outstanding that it dominates their lives. Allport (1961) called these personal dispositions **cardinal traits.** They are so outstanding that they cannot be hidden; nearly every action in a person's life revolves around this one cardinal disposition. Most people do not have a cardinal trait, but those few people who do are often known by that single trait.

Allport identified several historical or fictional characters who have possessed a disposition so outstanding that they have become associated with that trait name. Some examples of these traits include quixotic, narcissistic, sadistic, a Don Juan, and so forth. The reader should remember that personal dispositions are individual and are not shared with any other person. Therefore, only Don Quixote was truly quixotic; only Narcissus was completely narcissistic; only the Marquis de Sade possessed the cardinal disposition of sadism. When these names are used to describe characteristics in others they become changed into common traits.

Central Traits.   Few people have cardinal dispositions, but everyone has several **central traits.** Central dispositions are the five to ten most outstanding characteristics around which a person's life focuses. Allport (1961) described central dispositions as those which would be listed in a carefully written letter of recommendation. Almost any trait name could be a central disposition. We began this chapter with the story of Jenny, the woman with strong love/hate feelings for her son, Ross. Through Jenny's letters to Ross's friends we find that she possessed seven or eight central traits that characterized the last 12 years of her life, if not her entire life. She was aggressive, suspicious, possessive, aesthetic, sentimental, morbid, dramatic, and self-centered. These central dispositions were sufficiently powerful so that she was described in terms similar to these both by Isabel, who knew her well, and by independent researchers, who studied her letters (Allport, 1965).

Similarly, most people who knew Gordon Allport described him as reserved, prim, and orderly (see interview with Abraham Maslow by Mary H. Hall, 1968). Allport's reputation as "Mr. Clean Personality" (Elms, 1972) has raised interesting questions about his single encounter with Sigmund Freud (see Box—"Mr. Clean Meets Dr. Freud").

Secondary Traits.   Less conspicuous than central traits are the **secondary traits** or dispositions. The same trait names that can be used with central traits can also be employed to describe secondary traits. Everyone has many secondary dispositions. They are p.d.'s that are not central to the personality, yet they occur with some regularity and are responsible for much of one's specific behaviors.

These three traits are, of course, arbitrary points on a continuous scale from most appropriate to least appropriate. Cardinal dispositions are exceedingly prominent in a person and they shade into central dispositions which, though not dominating the person, nevertheless distinguish him or her as a unique person and guide much adaptive and stylistic behavior. Central p.d.'s blend into secondary dispositions, which are of lesser importance to the individual. One cannot say, however, that one person's secondary dispositions are less intense than another's central p.d.'s. Interpersonal comparisons are inappropriate to personal dispositions and any attempt to make such com-

Mr. Clean Meets Dr. Freud

Though he was not an anti-Freudian, Allport advocated views on the importance of unconscious motivation that were directly opposite to those of Freud. According to Allport, mentally disturbed people may frequently be driven by unconscious strivings, but most adults are aware of their reasons for acting and there is seldom need to go beyond the surface to detect the meaning of other people's behavior.

In his autobiography, Allport (1967) reported that the incident that taught him that psychoanalysis was mistaken in its penchant for looking beneath the surface was his own single meeting with Freud in Vienna. When Allport could not think of anything to say to Freud, he told him of seeing a young boy on the train earlier that same day who had displayed an obvious dirt phobia. Allport's apparent purpose in choosing this particular incident was to get Freud's reaction to a dirt phobia in a child so young. He was quite flabbergasted, however, when Freud "fixed his kindly therapeutic eyes upon [him] and said, 'And was that little boy you?'" (Allport, 1967, p. 8). Allport told this story many times as an illustration of the silliness of psychoanalytic procedures. How could Freud have been so blind as to overlook the obvious? Why read hidden meaning into a story that was selected more or less at random? Freud obviously was accustomed to looking for underlying significance in even the most innocent and innocuous statements. Allport thought that the misunderstanding of his motivation was amusing and that his manifest motivation had escaped Freud. But did it?

Some psychoanalytically oriented writers have taken Allport to task for his naivete. M. D. Faber (1970, p. 61), writing in *The Psychoanalytic Review,* contends that "Allport missed and misinterpreted the significance of the entire incident." Faber believes that Freud, indeed, made exactly the correct interpretation in suggesting that the little boy was, in fact, Gordon Allport. He suggests that Allport chose that particular story because of his preconception that Freud liked to hear "dirty" stories. Allport was "naughty" in presuming to call on Freud and he manifested his naughtiness by "pulling a dirty trick" on Freud. Freud immediately saw that it was Allport who was dirty and his question was an attempt to put the conversation on an honest level. What is more, Faber says, Allport unconsciously knew before he arrived at Freud's house that Freud would be psychoanalyzing him and, after the incident, he unconsciously knew that Freud had seen through him.

Alan Elms (1972), in a later article in the same publication, adds to Faber's interpretation of the incident. He looks to Allport's childhood for clues concerning his motivation in telling Freud about the clean little boy. In his autobiography, Allport (1967, p. 4) writes that his early life "was marked by plain Protestant piety." His father was a physician who, lacking adequate outside facilities, turned the Allport household into a miniature hospital. Both patients and nurses were found in the home and a clean, sterile atmosphere prevailed. With this background, Elms asserts, Allport was preoccupied with cleanliness and, in fact, was later known as "Mr. Clean Personality." Elms believes that Freud immediately saw through Allport's "pathological" concern with dirt. Allport admitted that he felt guilty when Freud asked if the little boy was him and he therefore contrived to change the subject. This is seen by Elms as evidence that Allport knew unconsciously that Freud was right.

How convincing is such evidence? Are people ordinarily aware of the reasons for their actions, as Allport contended, or are they motivated by hidden forces beneath their consciousness? Can such incidents as Allport's meeting with Freud be taken at face value or must one look for sinister intentions behind these stories? Was Freud really so perceptive that he could immediately see Allport's true intentions, as Faber and Elms claim?

It is not necessary to adopt either the psychoanalytic or the Allport view of this incident. It is quite possible that Allport's choice of the clean little boy story was not entirely random, but a reflection of his personality and his early training in cleanliness. But at the same time, it is not necessary to imbue Freud with superhuman powers of perception. After all, Freud *asked* if the little boy was Allport; he did not state it as a fact. In other words, he was guessing that his young visitor was intentionally disguising himself, a strategy not uncommon in psychotherapeutic patients. Allport was *not* the little boy, but the selection of that particular incident may not have been an entirely chance event.

parison transforms the personal dispositions into common traits (Allport, 1961).

Motivational and Stylistic Traits

All personal dispositions are dynamic in the sense that they have motivational power. Nevertheless, some are much more strongly felt than others, and those most intensely experienced are said to be *motivational*. Basic needs and drives supply the motivation for those personal dispositions which are strongly felt. Those p.d.'s which are less intensely experienced, though possessing some motivational power, are said to be more *stylistic*. They guide action, whereas those p.d.'s which are more intensely felt initiate action. An example of a stylistic p.d. might be impeccable personal appearance. One is motivated to dress because of a *need* to stay warm, but the *manner* in which one attires one's self is determined by a stylistic personal disposition (Allport, 1961).

There is no sharp line between motivational and stylistic personal dispositions. All p.d.'s have some motivational power. Though some are clearly stylistic, others are obviously based on a strongly felt need. Politeness, for example, is a stylistic trait, whereas eating is more motivational. How one eats (the style) depends at least partially on how hungry one is, but it also depends on the strength of the stylistic disposition. A usually polite but hungry person may forego manners while eating alone, but if the politeness trait is strong enough and if others are present, that person may eat with etiquette and courtesy, despite being famished.

Whether motivational or stylistic, some personal dispositions are close to the core of personality while others are more on the periphery. Those which are at the center of personality are experienced by the person as being an important part of self. They are the ones an individual refers to in such terms as, "That is me," or "this is mine." All characteristics that are "peculiarly mine" are said to belong to proprium (Allport, 1955).

Proprium

Allport used the term **proprium** to refer to those behaviors and characteristics which we regard as warm, central, and important in our lives. The proprium, however, is not the whole of personality. Many characteristics and behaviors of a person are not warm and central; they exist on the periphery of personality. These peripheral aspects include basic drives and needs that are ordinarily met and satisfied without much trouble; tribal customs such as saying "hello" to people, wearing clothes, and driving on the right side of the road; and habitual behaviors that are performed automatically and are not crucial to the person's sense of self. These behaviors might include smoking, biting one's fingernails, referring to older people as "madam" or "sir," and brushing one's teeth after every meal.

Allport (1955) preferred the term proprium to self or ego for three reasons. First, the concept of self or ego sometimes evokes the image of a homunculus or small man inside the person pulling strings that determine behavior. For example, Freud's concept of ego could imply that there is some *thing* inside the person that is responsible for realistic behavior and rational thinking. A second reason Allport preferred proprium is that the terms self and ego are used in different ways by different authors, but usually in some restricted fashion. For example, self might refer to my physical body, my image or concept of me, my self-esteem, and so on. The proprium includes these and other aspects of self and is not limited to a specific component of personhood. Finally, Allport pointed to the ambiguity of using self as both object and subject. When I think of my self, I can think of my physical being, my reputation, or my self-concept. But who is the "I" doing the thinking? This must also be my self. However, I cannot be aware of this subjective self; any aspect of self of which I am aware is, by definition, an objective self. This problem of the self as subject is not thoroughly discussed by most personality theorists, but Allport recognized it and, in his discussion, limited the term proprium to the objective self while he used the term "self as knower" to refer to the subjective self (Allport, 1955, 1961).

As the warm center of personality, the proprium includes those aspects of a person which are regarded as important to a sense of self-identity and self-enhancement (Allport, 1955). My proprium includes my values, at least those which are important to me. It also includes part of my conscience, that part which is personal and consistent with my adult beliefs. A generalized conscience (one shared by most people within a given culture) may be only peripheral to my sense of personhood. I may rigidly follow a generalized conscience, but it still remains outside my proprium. For example, I may believe that it is wrong to steal, a belief which prevents me from taking another's property. Yet, because this precept is common to most people in my culture, I do not acquire uniqueness, self-identity, or self-enhancement by my belief. I take this aspect of my personality for granted and it remains on the outskirts of my concept of me; that is, it is not part of my proprium.

GROWTH OF PERSONALITY

Allport's theory of personality rests on a dual system of motivation. People are driven by both the need to *adjust* to their environment *and* by the tendency to *grow* or to become more and more self-actualized. Adjustment needs and growth needs exist side by side within the same person and any adequate theory of personality, Allport said, must take into consideration the fact that people are both reactive and proactive.

The Developing Person

Allport (1961) believed that people are not born with personalities, but rather develop them. At birth, infants have only potential personality, one based on genetic endowment. Since infants possess no characteristic modes of behavior and thought, they cannot be said to have a personality. Unlike most psychologists, Allport believed that the first year of life is the *least* important one.

The sense of self evolves from birth to adulthood in seven overlapping stages. These stages are cumulative so that in adulthood all seven are experienced. The beginning three or four years of life are called the early self and comprise the first three aspects of selfhood. The first to evolve is the *bodily sense* (Allport, 1961). The infant learns the physical "me" from the "not me." "This thumb is part of me; this nipple is not." The bodily sense continues to develop and becomes an important, though by no means the sole, component of the proprium. Throughout our lives our bodies provide us with a reference for self-awareness. If I scrape my arm, I know that the blood and the pain are "peculiarly mine." They belong to no other person and give me a bodily sense of self. However, what is physically mine may not remain so permanently. I maintain a warm and propriate attachment to my fingernails as long as they are part of me. But when they are cut, the clippings can be discarded with no anxiety or concern.

A second early aspect of the developing proprium is the sense of continuing *self-identity* (Allport, 1961). This feeling of who I am includes my thoughts and actions, as well as my memory of them and the acceptance of them as mine. At first, the sense of self-identity is weak and children may accept imaginary characteristics as their own. Their self-identity is closely bound to their social surroundings, especially the family. "This is *my* house" or "That tricyle is *mine*." The words "I," "me," and "mine" dominate the vocabulary of young children.

The third aspect of early self is *ego-enhancement* or *self-esteem* (Allport, 1961). Self-esteem can be both positive and negative. It is that property of

During the early years, an infant develops a sense of me and not me.

the proprium which involves pride, selfishness, narcissism, and other behaviors and sentiments related to exaltation of the ego.

From ages four to six children are extremely egocentric. The world exists for them alone. The bodily sense, self-identity, and self-esteem continue to grow, but a fourth and fifth stage of the proprium emerge during this period. The fourth is the *extension of self* and the fifth is the *self-image.* Children broaden their sense of self to include possessions (clothes, toys, and pets), as well as mother, father, sisters, and brothers. Self-image refers to one's view of present abilities, status, and roles and also to one's aspirations or future goals. It consists largely of the child's image of self as a "good" or "bad" person—in Freudian terms, one's ego-ideal and conscience (Allport, 1961).

The years from six to twelve gain importance from children's entrance into school, which extends their experiences beyond the family. This is a period of reality-testing in which society challenges and modifies the child's self-identity, self-esteem, and self-image. The sixth stage, the *rational-self,* which develops during these early school years, is capable of rationalization and denials, but it is also capable of reasoning correctly and finding solutions to the problems of living. It is responsible for formal and reflective thought and reconciling inner needs with demands of the external world (Allport, 1961).

Adolescence brings about a seventh and final aspect of the *self as object,* namely **propriate strivings.** It is at this level that the person emerges as a truly unique individual with a clearly defined sense of personhood. In other words, the individual now has a well-developed proprium, which unifies the other six aspects of self, gives some consistency to actions and thoughts, and allows the person to set goals that maintain tension rather than merely reduce it (Allport, 1961).

Propriate strivings are those which are close to the person; that is, they are experienced as "peculiarly mine." They rely on memory of past experiences, but they also include thoughts of the future which take the form of realistic planning and intention. The problems of selecting a mate and choosing a career can be successfully pursued only through propriate strivings, though some people stumble into choosing a spouse or a job without any sense of purpose. When people drift into decisions their striving is called "opportunistic," since it is not part of the proprium and exists only on the periphery of personality (Allport, 1961). In a real sense, the goals of propriate strivings are not attainable since people constantly seek to maintain tension and to strive for goals they may never reach (Allport, 1955).

There is an eighth aspect of self called the *self as knower* or the subjective self. However, only the first seven aspects of self belong to the proprium (Allport, 1961). As noted earlier, the self as knower is that "I" which is aware of the objective "me."

The proprium is not only limited to self as object but it also excludes other components of personality that are merely peripheral to the person. Personality and proprium, then, are not synonymous. Personality includes many habits, emotions, traits, tribal customs, opportunistic strivings, adjustment patterns, and chance factors, such as heredity and environment, which are not warm and central to the person. Some skills such as typing and driving a car may be propriate in the beginning, but later they lose their central importance and become opportunistic. Others, such as language, are not ordinarily propriate, but when denied to a person or when accomplished only through great difficulty, they can become part of the proprium.

Motivation

Allport contended that a single theory of motivation is inadequate. Peripheral motives and propriate strivings are not of the same order. The first requires a theory based on need *reduction* while propriate strivings demand a theory that accommodates the *maintenance* of tension and disequilibrium. Adult behavior is both reactive and proactive and an adequate theory of personality must be able to explain both. Theories of unchanging motives, Allport (1961) maintained, are incomplete because they are limited to an explanation of reactive behavior. The mature person, however, is not motivated merely to seek pleasure and reduce pain. Much of adult behavior is functionally autonomous; that is, it seeks goals that are functionally independent from the original motivation.

Functional Autonomy

The concept of **functional autonomy** represents Allport's most distinctive and, at the same time, most controversial postulate. It is the capstone of his theory of motivation. Functional autonomy is Allport's (1961) explanation for the myriad human motives that seemingly are not accounted for by hedonistic or drive-reduction principles. It represents a theory of changing, rather than unchanging, motives.

In general, the concept of functional autonomy holds that some, but not all, human motives are functionally independent from the original motive responsible for the behavior. If a motive is functionally autonomous it is *the* explanation for behavior. We cannot look beyond it for hidden or primary causes. In other words, if hoarding money is a functionally autonomous motive, we cannot say that the miser's behavior is traceable to anal needs or to childhood experiences with reward and punishment. We should look no further than the explanation that the miser simply *likes* money. This idea that much of our behavior is based on interests and on conscious preference is in harmony with the commonsense belief of many people who hold that we do things simply because we like to do them.

Functional autonomy is a reaction to what Allport called theories of unchanging motives, namely Freud's pleasure principle and the drive-reduction hypothesis of stimulus-response psychology. Allport held that both theories are concerned with *historical* facts rather than *functional* facts. He believed that adult motives are built primarily on conscious, self-sustaining, contemporary systems. Functional autonomy represents his attempt to explain these conscious, self-sustaining contemporary motivations.

Though some motivations are unconscious and others are the result of drive reduction, Allport contended that it is only necessary to show that some behavior is functionally autonomous in order to postulate a theory of changing motives and to demonstrate the inadequacy of Freudian and drive-reduction explanations.

Allport listed four requirements of any adequate theory of motivation. Functional autonomy, of course, meets each criterion.

1. An adequate theory of motivation *"will acknowledge the contemporaneity of motives."* In other words, "Whatever moves us must move now" (Allport, 1961, p. 220). The past per se is unimportant. The history of an individual is significant only when it has a present effect on motivation.
2. It must *"be a pluralistic theory—allowing for motives of many types"* (Allport, 1961, p. 221). On this point, Allport was critical of Freud and his two-instinct theory, Adler and the single striving for success, and of all theories that emphasize self-actualization as the ultimate motive. Allport was emphatically opposed to the reduction of all human motivation to one master drive. He contended that adult motives are basically different from those of children and that the motivation of neurotic individuals is not the same as that of normal people. In addition, some motivation is conscious, some unconscious; some transient, some recurring; some peripheral, some propriate; and some is tension-maintaining. Apparently different motives really are different, not only in form but also in substance.
3. *It must attribute dynamic power to the cognitive processes of planning and intention* (Allport, 1961).

   We conclude that while human beings are busy living their lives into the future, much psychological theory is busy tracing these lives backward into the past. And while it seems to each of us that we are spontaneously *active,* many psychologists are telling us that we are only *reactive* (Allport, 1961, p. 206).

Though intention is involved in all motivation, this third requirement refers more generally to long-range intention. A young woman declines an offer to see a movie because she *prefers* to study anatomy. This preference is consistent with her *purpose* of making good grades at college. This relates to her *plans* of being admitted to medical school, which is necessary in order for her to fulfill her *intention* of being a doctor. The lives of healthy adults are future-oriented, involving preferences, purposes, plans, and intentions. These, of course, are not always completely rational processes, but represent a fusion of reason and emotion.

4. An adequate theory of motivation is one that *"will allow for the concrete uniqueness of motives"* (Allport, 1961, p. 225). A concrete unique motive is opposed to an abstract, generalized one. The latter has more to do with fitting into a preexistent theory than with describing the actual motivation of one person. There is an endless number of concrete unique motives, one for every motivation of each individual. Duane is interested in improving his bowling game. This is a concrete motive and his manner of seeking improvement is unique to him. It may involve reading, observing, practicing, and taking lessons. Some theories of motivation may ascribe Duane's behavior to an aggressive need, others to an inhibited sexual drive, and still others to a secondary drive learned on the basis of a primary drive. Allport would simply say that Duane wants to improve his bowling game. This is Duane's unique, concrete, and functionally autonomous motive.

By this time the reader has some idea that a functionally autonomous motive is one that is contemporary, self-sustaining, growing out of an earlier motive, but now functionally independent of it. Allport (1961, p. 229) defined functional autonomy as *"any acquired system of motivation in which the tensions involved are not of the same kind as the antecedent tensions from which the acquired system developed."* In other words, what begins as one motive may grow into a new one that is historically continuous with the original, but functionally autonomous from it. For example, a person may plant a garden originally to satisfy a hunger drive, but eventually, the person becomes interested in gardening for its own sake and now plants flowers (which cannot be eaten) and asparagus (which is given to the neighbors).

Allport (1961) recognized two levels of functional autonomy—*perseverative* and *propriate.*

Perseverative Functional Autonomy.   The more elementary of the two is **perseverative functional autonomy.** Allport borrowed this term from the word "perseveration," which is the tendency of an impression to leave an influence on subsequent experience. Perseverative functional autonomy is found in animals as well as humans and is based on simple neurological principles. As an example of perseverative functional autonomy Allport spoke of

A person might begin an exercise program as a means of weight control, but may continue simply because running is enjoyable. This is an example of a functionally autonomous motive.

a rat that has learned to run a maze in order to be fed, but then continues to run the maze even after it has become satiated. Why does it continue to run? Allport would say that the rat runs the maze just for the fun of it!

Allport (1961) listed other examples of perseverative functional autonomy that involve human rather than animal motivation. The first is an addiction to alcohol, tobacco, or other drugs when there is no physiological hunger for them. Alcoholics continue to drink though their current motivation is functionally independent from original motives.

Another example concerns incompleted tasks. A problem once started, but then interrupted, will perseverate, creating a new tension to finish the task. This new tension is different from the initial motivation. For example, college students are offered 10 cents for every piece of a 500-piece jigsaw puzzle they successfully put together. Assume that these students do not have a preexisting interest in solving jigsaw puzzles and that their original motivation is solely for the money. Also assume that their monetary reward is limited to $45.00, so that after they have completed 450 pieces they will no longer be paid. Will these students finish the remaining 50 pieces in the absence of monetary reward? If a new tension is created, which motivates them to complete the task, then this could serve as an example of perseverative functional autonomy.

Propriate Functional Autonomy.   The master system of motivation that confers unity on personality is **propriate functional autonomy.** It is the highest level of functional autonomy and refers to those self-sustaining motives which are related to the proprium. Jigsaw puzzles and alcohol are seldom regarded as "peculiarly mine." They are not part of the proprium, but exist only on the periphery of personality. On the other hand, occupation, hobbies, and interests are closer to the core of personality and many of our motivations concerning them become functionally autonomous. For example, a woman may originally take a job because she needs money. At first, the work is uninteresting, perhaps even distasteful. As the years pass, however, she develops a consuming passion for the job itself, spending some vacation time at work and, perhaps, even developing a hobby that is closely related to her occupation.

Criterion for Functional Autonomy.   In general, a *present motive is functionally autonomous to the extent that it seeks new goals.* This means that the behavior will continue even as the motivation for it changes. For example, children first learning to walk are perhaps motivated by some maturational drive, but later they may walk to increase mobility or to build self-confidence. Similarly, scientists may be dedicated to searching for answers to difficult problems. Their satisfaction comes more from the search than from the solution, and their method of searching may vary as the problem changes. As one problem is solved, scientists search for another area of inquiry even though the new field may be somewhat different from the previous one. New tensions are now established which are separate and autonomous from the antecedent ones. Each new finding leads to higher levels of aspiration and to the establishment of new goals.

Limitations of Functional Autonomy.   Functional autonomy is not an explanation for all human motivation. Allport (1961) listed several processes that are not functionally autonomous. Biological drives, such as eating, breathing, and sleeping, are not functionally autonomous, nor are motives directly linked to the reduction of basic drives. Other processes outside the scope of functional autonomy include reflex actions such as an eye blink; constitutional equipment, namely physique, intelligence, and temperament; habits in the process of being formed; patterns of behavior that require primary reinforcement; nonproductive behaviors such as compulsions, fixations, and regressions; and finally, sublimations that can be tied to childhood sexual desires.

   Not all pathological symptoms, however, lie beyond the range of functional autonomy. Some serve a contemporary life style and are presently independent of an earlier trauma. Many, however, are traceable to childhood experiences and, therefore, are not functionally autonomous. At first glance, compulsions may seem similar to perseverative functional autonomy. Compulsions, however, are not self-sustaining, but can be eliminated through behavior modification or some other method of therapy. Any symptom that cannot be extinguished through psychotherapy or does not change as the self-concept is altered is said to be functionally autonomous.

Conscious and Unconscious Motivation

Probably more than any other personality theorist, Allport emphasized the importance of conscious motivation; healthy adults are generally aware of what they are doing and their reasons for doing it.

This does not mean, however, that Allport ignored the existence or even the importance of unconscious processes. He agreed that there is some truth to Freud's picture of the unconscious mind. He recognized the fact that much motivation that appears to be a function of consciousness is, in reality, unconscious and driven by hidden impulses and sublimated drives. However, he objected to Freud's idea that the unconscious controls and dominates personality. For the healthy individual, Allport (1961) said, consciousness is in control. Freud's concept of the power of unconscious motivation may be an accurate description of the abnormal personality, but, Allport insisted, it misses the mark as an explanation for normal healthy behavior.

Allport (1961) believed that symptomatic behaviors are automatic repetitions, usually self-defeating, which are motivated by unconscious tendencies. They often have their origins in childhood and retain a childish flavor into adult years. Normal behavior is functionally autonomous and is motivated by conscious processes. Allport insisted that conscious motivation is not only separate from unconscious motivation but also that it has its own ignition and spark and is not dependent upon power generated by the id or the unconscious mind. The mature personality is motivated principally by conscious thoughts; unconscious processes play only a minor role in the behavior of the healthy adult.

The Mature Personality

Allport saw a dichotomy between the psychologically mature personality and the one who is immature or neurotic. Because mature individuals are motivated by conscious processes, they are more flexible and autonomous than the immature who remain dominated by unconscious motives springing from childhood experiences. Mature people are also characterized by activity, security, and freedom of choice. Ordinarily they have experienced a relatively trauma-free childhood, even though their later years may be tempered by conflict and suffering. Mature individuals are not without foibles and idiosyncrasies. In fact, individuality and uniqueness would be expected. Age is not a requisite for maturity, though healthy persons seem to become more mature as they get older.

What are the requirements for psychological health? Allport (1961) identified six criteria for the mature personality. The number is somewhat arbitrary, yet the list is descriptive of the healthy personality as seen by Allport.

The first criterion of maturity is an *extension of the sense of self.* Mature people continually seek to identify with and participate in events outside themselves. They are not self-centered, but rather are able to become involved in problems and activities that are not centered on themselves. They develop a nonegotistical interest in work, play, and recreation. Social inter-

*People are sometimes
motivated to seek tension, not
merely reduce it.*

est, family, and spiritual life are important to them. Eventually, these outside activities become part of the proprium. Allport (1961 p. 285) summed up this first criterion by saying: "Everyone has self-love, but only self-extension is the earmark of maturity."

Second, mature personalities are characterized by a *"warm relating of self to others"* (Allport, 1961, p. 285). They have the capacity to love others in an intimate and compassionate manner. Warm relating, of course, is dependent on the ability to extend the sense of self. Only by looking beyond themselves can mature people love others nonpossessively and unselfishly. Psychologically healthy individuals treat other people with respect and realize that the needs, desires, and hopes of others are not completely foreign to their own. In addition, they have a healthy sexual attitude and do not exploit others for personal gratification.

A third criterion is *emotional security* or *self-acceptance*. Mature individuals accept themselves for what they are and they possess what Allport (1961) called emotional poise. These psychologically healthy people are not overly upset when things do not go as planned or when they are simply "having a bad day." They do not allow themselves to be overly concerned over minor irritations; they recognize that frustrations and inconveniences are a part of living and do not overreact to imagined insults or injuries.

Realistic perception is another measure of maturity. Healthy people do not live in a fantasy world nor do they bend reality to fit their own perceptions. They are problem-oriented rather than self-centered, in touch with the world as most others see it, and are capable of supporting themselves economically (Allport, 1961).

A fifth criterion is *insight and humor.* Mature people know themselves and, therefore, have no need to attribute their own sins and weaknesses to others. They possess insight into their own personalities. Maturity is also character-ized by a nonhostile sense of humor. Mature persons have the capacity to laugh at self and seldom rely on sexual or aggressive themes to elicit laughter from others. Allport believed that insight and humor are closely related and may be aspects of the same thing, namely self-objectification. Mature individ-uals see themselves objectively. They are able to perceive the incongruities and absurdities in life and have no need to pretend or to put on airs (Allport, 1961).

The final criterion of maturity is a *unifying philosophy of life.* Healthy peo-ple have a clear view of the purpose of life. Without this, their insight would be empty and barren and their humor would be trivial and cynical. The uni-fying philosophy of life may or may not be religious, but Allport (1954, 1963), on a personal level, seemed to have felt that a mature religious orientation is a crucial ingredient in lives of most mature individuals. Although many, or even most, churchgoing people have an immature religious philosophy and quite often they have narrow racial and ethnic prejudices, a mark of maturity is often a strong religious motivation. Allport was never far from a consider-ation of religion and published six lectures on the subject under the title *The Individual and His Religion* (1950). The person with a mature religious atti-tude and a unifying philosophy of life has a well-developed conscience and, quite likely, a strong desire to serve others (see Box—"Allport and the Sci-entific Study of Religion").

Cultural Influences

The growth of personality always takes place within a cultural setting. The emphasis Allport placed on cultural or social factors must be described as moderate. He recognized the importance of environmental influences in helping to shape personality, but he cannot be called a social psychologist. The heavy concern with culture in the Allport family rests mainly with his brother Floyd. Gordon's writings seek a balance between those theorists who emphasize individual development separate from culture and those who stress the point that the individual is but a mirror of society. Allport (1955) believed that culture is important, but he insisted that personality has some life of its own. On the one hand, the individual can change while society remains relatively stable, while, on the other hand, personality often main-tains its consistency even in the face of great social upheaval.

Allport, of course, did recognize cultural influences in the lives of people. Though each person is a unique individual, culture leads to certain similar-ities among personalities. Culture can influence our language, our morals,

Allport and the Scientific Study of Religion

More than any other personality theorist, Gordon Allport maintained a lifelong active interest in the scientific study of religion (Allport, 1950). On a personal level, Allport was a deeply religious person and from 1938 to 1966 he offered a series of 33 meditations in Appleton Chapel, Harvard University (Allport, 1978).

We have seen that Allport believed that a deep religious commitment was a mark of a mature individual. However, not all churchgoers have a mature religious orientation. Some, in fact, are highly prejudiced. Allport and Ross (1967) looked at earlier studies that had found a **curvilinear** relationship between church attendance and various forms of prejudice. That is, many previous investigations had reported that some churchgoers were highly prejudiced while others had very little prejudice.

In order to understand this curvilinear relationship, Allport and Ross (1967) developed a Religious Orientation Scale (ROS) to measure types of religious commitment. The scale assumes both an *extrinsic* and an *intrinsic* orientation toward religion. People with an extrinsic orientation have a utilitarian view of religion, that is, they see it as a means to an end. Theirs is a self-serving religion of comfort and social convention. Their beliefs are lightly held and easily reshaped when convenient. On the other hand, people with an intrinsic orientation *live* their religion and find their master motive in their religious faith. Rather than using religion for some end, they bring other needs into harmony with their religious values. They have an internalized creed and follow it fully.

With this distinction in mind, Allport and Ross (1967) developed two subscales for ROS—one consisting of Extrinsic (E) items and the other of Intrinsic (I) items. An example of an Extrinsic item is, "What religion offers me most is comfort when sorrow and misfortune strike" (Allport & Ross, 1967, p. 436). People who definitely disagree or tend to disagree with this statement are scored in the direction of Intrinsic orientation. People who definitely agree or tend to agree with the item are scored in an Extrinsic direction. An example of an Intrinsic item is, "My religious beliefs are what really lie behind my whole approach to life" (Allport & Ross, 1967, p. 436). Agreement with this statement yields an Intrinsic score, while disagreement gives one an Extrinsic score.

Although Allport originally thought that religious orientation would be a bipolar trait, he soon realized that not everyone could easily be fit into either the Extrinsic or the Intrinsic pole. Some people endorsed *both* the Extrinsic *and* the Intrinsic statements. These people formed a third group called *indiscriminately proreligious.* Others tended to disagree with both the Extrinsic and the Intrinsic items, and these people made up a fourth group called *indiscriminately antireligious* or nonreligious. All subjects in Allport and Ross's (1967) study, however, were churchgoers, so this fourth category does *not* include people who never attend church.

Allport and Ross (1967) found that high E scorers were more prejudiced than high I scorers, but that churchgoers who were indiscriminately proreligious were more prejudiced than either of these two groups. This last finding may account for the fact that previous studies had found a curvilinear relationship between church attendance and prejudice. It seems that some churchgoers harbor a great deal of prejudice, but that those who live their religion (Intrinsics) are far less prejudiced.

Since its development, the Religious Orientation Scale has been refined (Hood, 1970) and employed in dozens of studies on religious commitment. Donahue (1985) reviewed many of these studies and analyzed their combined findings. He reported that the ROS is a generally useful measure of religious orientation. In conclusion, he stated, "Intrinsic religiousness serves as an excellent measure of religious commitment as distinct from religious belief, church membership, liberal-conservative theological orientation, and related measures" (Donahue, 1985, p. 415).

Allport, undoubtedly, would be pleased that in recent years psychology and religion have become less estranged. In its infancy psychology had an intimate relationship with both religion and philosophy, but then during the behaviorist influence, religion ceased to be regarded as an important psychological variable. Gorsuch (1988) has recently traced psychologists' interest in religion and found that, while the psychology of religion is still not well integrated within psychology in general, there has been a resurgence of research activity. Much of the activity is due to Allport's passionate interest in both psychology and religion.

our values, and our fashions, to name but a few. But how each of us reacts to cultural forces depends on our unique personality. Culture and individuality are antagonistic to one another; in truth, however, one does not exist without the other.

RESEARCH METHODS

We have seen that Allport steadfastly held to the belief that personality theory must be concerned with the study of the individual. Common factors must be complemented with that which is unique to the single person. Because psychology has historically dealt with general laws and characteristics that people have in common, Allport repeatedly advocated the development and use of research methods that study the individual. To balance the predominant normative or group approach, he suggested that psychologists employ methods that study the motivational and stylistic behaviors of the single case.

Morphogenic Science

Early in his writings Allport distinguished between two scientific approaches: the **nomothetic,** which seeks general laws, and the **idiographic,** referring to that which is peculiar to the single case. Because the term idiographic was so often misused, misunderstood, and misspelled (being confused with "ideographic," or the representation of ideas by graphic symbols), Allport (1968) abandoned the term in his later writings and spoke of **morphogenic** procedures. Both idiographic and morphogenic pertain to the individual, but the former term does not suggest structure or pattern, while morphogenic refers to patterned properties of the whole organism and allows for intraperson comparisons. The pattern or structure of one's traits are important. For example, Jim may be intelligent, introverted, and strongly motivated by achievement needs, but the unique manner in which his intelligence is related to his introversion and his needs for achievement form a structured pattern. These individual patterns are the subject matter of morphogenic science.

What are the methods of morphogenic psychology? Allport (1962) listed many; some completely morphogenic, some partly so. Examples of wholly morphogenic, first-person methods include autobiographies; verbatim recordings, including interviews, dreams, and confessions; diaries, letters, personalized questionnaires, self-anchoring scales; and expressive and projective documents, including literary works, art forms, automatic writings, doodles, handshakes, voice patterns, body gestures, handwriting, and gait. Semimorphogenic approaches include self-rating scales, such as the adjective checklist; standardized tests using ipsative scores whereby people are compared to themselves rather than a norm group; the Allport-Vernon-Lindzey *Study of Values* (1960); and the Q sort technique of Stephenson (1953).

Consistent with common sense, but contrary to many psychologists, Allport was willing to accept at face value the self-disclosure statements of most subjects. If one wishes to learn the personal dynamics of people, one simply needs to ask them what they think of themselves. Answers to direct questions should be accepted as valid unless subjects are young children, psychotic, or extremely defensive. Allport (1962, p. 413) said that, "Too often we fail to consult the richest of all sources of data, namely, the subject's own self-knowledge."

Allport's belief that the scientific study of humans must rely in large part on morphogenic techniques is unacceptable to some hard-nosed psychologists (see Box—"Critique of Morphogenic Methods"). However, Allport insisted that if we are to understand human personality it cannot be otherwise. "Whatever contributes to a knowledge of human nature is an admissible method to science" (Allport, 1942, p. 140).

Letters from Jenny

We introduced this chapter with an unusually illuminating example of the morphogenic method, namely letters written by Jenny to her son's former roommate, Glenn, and his wife, Isabel. These letters came into Allport's possession during the early 1940s and were later published as *Letters from Jenny* (Allport, 1965). For years these personal documents were subjected to close analysis and study by Allport and his students who sought to build the structure of a single personality by identifying central traits or dispositions.

The letters from Jenny Gove Masterson (a fictitious name) reveal the story of an older woman and her intense love/hate feelings toward her son, Ross.

Critique of Morphogenic Methods

It has been more than a half-century since Allport picked up the gauntlet to do battle against the prevailing trends in psychology. His fight on the side of the uniqueness of the individual and the use of methods that study the single case has been constant and determined. But how successful has his struggle been? For the most part, his voice has been heard, but his advice unheeded. Morphogenic studies are no more prevalent in psychology today than they were during the mid-1920s when Allport began teaching at Harvard. Some years ago, Sanford (1963, p. 547) reported that "By and large, psychologists seem to have been rather unimpressed by Allport's argument and plea." He went on to say that even those psychologists involved in the study of the individual, that is, those doing assessment, diagnosis, and psychotherapy, "have acted as if they had never heard of Allport."

In response to Sanford, Allport (1966, p. 9) himself somewhat reluctantly concluded, "Well, if this is so in spite of 4 decades of labor on my part, and in spite of my efforts in the present paper—I suppose I should in all decency cry 'uncle' and retire to my corner." Sadly, the following year Allport was dead and the cause of morphogenic psychology lost its most passionate advocate.

An important question, however, remains. Do morphogenic methods make a meaningful contribution to psychological science?

The answer to the questions is a qualified "Yes." The case study method has a long history in psychology. Its legitimacy is widely accepted and its future in psychology is assured. One must remember, however, that the study of the single case is scientific only to the extent that the individual is *not* unique. Holt (1962) contended that if behavior is truly unique it would be impossible to learn anything from its study. He believed that the division between nomothetic and morphogenic approaches is a false dichotomy and that the two terms should be dropped from the psychological lexicon.

The letters from Jenny are interesting and informative only because we recognize in others some similarity of traits we find in Jenny. Unless we can generalize from Jenny to people in general, or at least to some group of people, or to some one other person, it does us little good to study Jenny. It may conceivably help Jenny, but no non-Jenny can possibly profit from it.

On the other hand, the same limitations apply to the study of groups. Nomothetic studies are useful only when their results can be generalized to other subjects, in other places, and at other times. The study of groups helps illuminate the individual just as an investigation of the single case aids our understanding of people in general.

Between March, 1926 (when she was 58) and October, 1937 (when she died), Jenny wrote a series of 301 letters to Glenn and Isabel. These letters represent an unusually rich source of morphogenic material for several reasons. First, all 301 letters were preserved by the recipients, which is itself an unusual occurrence. Second, Jenny was a gifted and interesting writer, avoiding everyday mundane matters while revealing her innermost thoughts in an open unself-conscious manner. Third, the content of the letters is not a reflection of a growing relationship between the writer and the recipients. Indeed, the relationship did not seem to change over the years. The young couple simply provided Jenny with a forum to pour forth her feelings toward life in general and her son, Ross, in particular. A fourth serendipitous circumstance was the discovery of the letters by an erudite psychologist with a pre-existing, passionate interest in personal documents.

One of Allport's students, Alfred Baldwin (1942) developed a technique called *personal structure analysis* by which he originally analyzed approximately one-third of the letters. The purpose of this technique was to analyze the structure of Jenny's personality from her letters. Baldwin used two strictly morphogenic procedures, *frequency* and *contiguity,* for gathering evidence. The first simply involves a notation of the frequency with which an item appears in the case material. For example, how often did Jenny mention Ross, or money, or herself? Contiguity refers to the proximity of two items in the letters. How often did the category "Ross—unfavorable" occur in close correspondence with "herself—self-sacrificing"? This technique of contiguity was used intuitively by Freud and other psychoanalysts to discover an association between two items in a subject's unconscious mind. Baldwin, however, refined it to some extent by determining statistically those correspondences which occur more frequently than could be expected by chance alone.

Using the personal structure analysis, Baldwin identified three clusters of categories in Jenny's letters. The first related to *Ross, women, the past,* and *herself—self-sacrificing.* The second dealt with Jenny's *search for a job* and the third cluster revolved around her attitude toward *money* and *death.* The three clusters are independent of each other even though a single topic, such as money, may appear in all three clusters.

The reader will note that Baldwin's original clusters resembled those which might be found in factor analysis (see Chapter 13). Indeed, Jeffrey Paige, another student of Allport, later published a factor analytic study of Jenny's letters. A total of eight factors were extracted and identified: aggression, possessiveness, affiliation, autonomy, familial acceptance, sexuality, sentience, and martyrdom (Paige, 1966).

Paige's study is interesting for a couple of reasons. First, the number of factors identified—eight—corresponds very well with the number of central dispositions or traits—five to ten—that Allport had earlier hypothesized would be found in most people. Second, the results are quite similar to those Allport (1965) found when he used a somewhat common-sense approach.

In this latter study, Allport asked 36 judges to list what they thought were Jenny's essential characteristics. As a result, 198 descriptive adjectives were obtained, many of which were synonymous and overlapping. Allport then grouped the terms into eight clusters. Listed in order of frequency of occurrence they were: quarrelsome—suspicious; self-centered; independent—autonomous; dramatic—intense; aesthetic—artistic; aggressive; cynical—morbid; and sentimental.

Comparing this commonsense, clinical approach with Paige's factorial study, Allport (1966) presented the following parallel:

Commonsense Traits (Allport)	Factorial Traits (Paige)
Quarrelsome—suspicious Aggressive	Aggression
Self-centered (possessive)	Possessiveness
Sentimental	Need for affiliation Need for family acceptance
Independent—autonomous	Need for autonomy
Aesthetic—artistic	Sentience
Self-centered (self-pitying)	Martyrdom
(No parallel)	Sexuality
Cynical—morbid	(No parallel)
Dramatic—intense	("Overstate," that is, the tendency to be dramatic and to overstate her concerns)

The close agreement between the clinical, commonsense approach and the factor analytic method does not prove the validity of either. It does, however, indicate the feasibility of morphogenic studies. The individual can be analyzed and central dispositions identified with consistency even when two different procedures are employed.

CONCEPT OF HUMANITY

The reader with an *optimistic* and hopeful view of life will find much in Allport to admire. The psychoanalytic and behavioral views of humanity were rejected by Allport as being too deterministic and too mechanistic. Our fate and our characteristics are not determined by unconscious motives originating in early childhood, but by conscious choices made in the present. We are not simply automatons blindly reacting to the forces of reward and punishment. Instead, we are able to interact with our environment and make it reactive to us. This view is similar to that of Bandura (see Chapter 12), the social cognitive theorist, who believes that cognition is at least partially responsible for shaping behavior.

Allport believed that people not only seek to reduce tensions, but to establish new ones. Healthy individuals desire both change and challenge. They are active, purposive, flexible, and enjoy the new and the unexpected.

Because people have the potential to learn a variety of responses and traits in many situations, growth can take place at any age. Personality is not established in early childhood, even though for some people strong infantile influences remain. Early childhood experiences are important only to the extent that they exist in the present. Though early security and love leave lasting marks, children need more than love; they need an opportunity to shape their own existence creatively, to resist conformity, and to be free, self-directed individuals.

Though *society* has some power to mold personality, Allport believed that social psychology does not hold the answer to the nature of humanity. The factors shaping personality, Allport held, are not as important as personality itself. Heredity, environment, and the nature of the organism are important, but one must not overlook the basic fact that people are essentially proactive. Each of us is a unique individual, free to follow the prevailing dictates of society or to chart our own course.

People, however, are not completely free. Allport (1961) adopted a *limited-freedom* approach. He was often critical of the existential view that allows for absolute freedom, but he also opposed the psychoanalytic and behavioral views he regarded as denying free will. Allport's position was somewhere in the middle. Though free will exists, some people are more capable of making choices than are others. A mature personality (discussed earlier) has more freedom than a child or a severely disturbed person. The intelligent, reflective person has more capacity for free choice than the non-reflective, mentally deficient one. Again, this stance is similar to the one adopted by Bandura (1986), who holds that people are partially free and that different individuals have different degrees of freedom.

Even though freedom is limited, Allport maintained that it can be expanded. The more self-insight a person develops, the greater the freedom of choice. The more objective a person becomes, that is, the more the blindfolds of self-concern and egotism are removed, the greater one's degree of freedom. As serious compulsions and restrictive habits are overcome (as in successful therapy or some other growth process) the person becomes more and more free to engage in spontaneous and flexible behavior.

Education and knowledge also expand the amount of freedom we have. The greater our knowledge of a particular area, the broader becomes our freedom in that area. To have a broad general education means that, to some extent, one has a wider choice of jobs, recreational activities, reading materials, and friends. Finally our freedom can be expanded by our mode of choosing. If we stubbornly adhere to a familiar course of action simply because it is more comfortable, our freedom remains largely restricted. On the other hand, if we adopt an open-minded mode of solving problems, then we broaden our perspective and increase our alternatives, that is, we expand our freedom to choose (Allport, 1955).

Allport's view of humanity is more *teleological* than causal. Personality, to some extent, is influenced by past experiences, but the behaviors that make us human are those which are motivated by our expectations of the future. In other words, we are healthy individuals to the extent that we set up and seek future purposes and aspirations. Those factors which make one person different from another are not so much the basic drives, but rather self-erected goals and intentions.

In summary, Allport holds an optimistic view of humanity, maintaining that people have at least limited freedom. Human beings are goal-oriented, proactive, and motivated by a variety of forces, most of which are within their realm of awareness. Early childhood experiences are of relatively minor importance and significant only to the extent that they exist in the present. Both differences and similarities among people are important, but *individual differences and uniqueness* receive far greater emphasis in Allport's psychology.

CRITIQUE OF ALLPORT

Allport's theory is based more on philosophical speculation and common sense than on original scientific investigations. Unlike Bandura and Cattell, Allport did not conduct a vast number of investigations testing hypotheses drawn from his own theory. Nevertheless, he was quite familiar with much of the literature and his theorizing never ventured too far beyond what was then known about human personality. Remember, it was not Allport's intention to construct a completely new theory of personality. He was an eclectic, carefully borrowing from older theories those elements which were consistent with his conviction that most people, are best thought of as conscious, forward-looking, tension-seeking individuals. To those who are offended by the deterministic theories of Freud and Skinner, Gordon Allport's view of humanity is philosophically quite refreshing. As with any other theory, however, it must be evaluated on a scientific basis.

The first consideration is whether or not Allport's approach is truly a theory of personality. It certainly deals with personality. In fact, Allport had probably done more than any other psychologist to define personality and to categorize other definitions of the term. But does he have a *theory?* Is his a set of related assumptions that generate testable hypotheses? On this criterion Allport's exhortations rate a qualified "Yes." It is a limited theory, offering explanations for a fairly narrow scope of personality, namely, certain kinds of motivation. The functionally autonomous motives of psychologically healthy adults are covered quite adequately by Allport's theory. But what of the motives of children and of psychotic and neurotic adults? What moves them and why? What about ordinarily healthy adults who uncharacteristically behave in a strange manner? What accounts for these inconsistencies? What explanation is there for the bizarre dreams, fantasies, and hallucinations of mature individuals? Unfortunately, Allport's account is not broad enough to adequately answer these questions.

A useful theory provides an *organization for observations.* Does Allport's theory meet this criterion? Again, only for a narrow range of adult motives does the theory offer a meaningful organization for observations. Much of what is known about human personality cannot be easily integrated into Allport's theory. Specifically, behaviors motivated by unconscious forces, as well as those that are stimulated by primary drives, do not belong to the proprium and are not adequately explained by Allport. He recognizes the existence of these kinds of motivations, but seems content to allow the psychoanalytical and behavioral explanations to stand without further elaboration. This limitation, however, does not devastate Allport's theory. To accept the validity of other theoretical concepts is a legitimate approach to theory building. Nevertheless, Allport might have been more specific in identifying those elements of earlier theories which he accepted and those which he rejected.

Has the theory *generated* much *research?* On this criterion Allport's theory receives a moderate rating. His development of the Religious Orientation Scale has led to more than 100 research studies on the scientific study of religion. Aside from this area of inquiry, however, research into the theory has been limited largely to that conducted by Allport himself and some of his students. Moreover, much of their research has been undertaken to demonstrate the feasibility of morphogenic methods rather than to test hypotheses drawn from the theory.

As a *guide for the practitioner,* the theory has moderate usefulness. It certainly serves as a beacon to the teacher and the therapist, illuminating the view of personality which suggests that people should be treated as individuals. The details, unfortunately, are left unspecified. On the fourth and fifth criteria of a useful theory, Allport's psychology of the individual is highly rated on each. His precise language renders the theory both *internally consistent* and *parsimonious.*

Despite its limitations as a useful theory, Allport's approach to personality is both stimulating and illuminating. For anyone interested in building a theory of personality, the reading of Allport would be a recommended first step. Few others have made such an effort to place personality theory in perspective; few have been as careful in defining terms, in categorizing previous definitions, or in questioning what units should be employed in personality theory. The work of Allport has set a standard for clear thinking and precision that future theorists would do well to emulate.

CHAPTER SUMMARY

Allport's psychology of the individual is an attempt to restore balance to the study of personality. Allport objected to the psychoanalytic theories of Freud and Jung and the learning theories of Skinner and others for being too mechanistic and for losing sight of the uniqueness of each individual. He wished to swing the pendulum away from these *reactive* theories and toward a more *proactive* stance.

Allport did not discount the insights from psychoanalysis and learning theory; he was *eclectic* in his acceptance of ideas from a variety of sources. None of these earlier theories, however, could meet the criteria he established for an *open system* approach to personality. They did not allow for fundamental *growth* and *change* within the individual. Allport believed that people are motivated both to *reduce tension* and to *seek new tensions.*

Allport's emphasis on uniqueness led him to deemphasize common traits and to espouse individual traits or *personal dispositions.* Three levels of personal dispositions are (1) *cardinal traits,* (2) *central traits,* and (3) *secondary traits.* Few people have a cardinal personal disposition, that is, a trait so outstanding that it cannot be hidden. Most of us have six to ten central traits, characteristics that would be used in an honest description of us by people who know us very well. Central traits blend into secondary traits, which are less reliable but far more numerous.

All individual traits are dynamic, but those that initiate actions are called *motivational,* while those that guide actions are called *stylistic.*

The *proprium* refers to those behaviors and personal dispositions which we regard as peculiarly our own. Not all personality belongs to the proprium, only those aspects that are warm, central, and important to our lives.

Childhood is relatively unimportant in Allport's theory. Ordinarily, it is not until adolescence that people develop a clearly defined sense of personhood, a well-developed proprium, and become motivated by *propriate strivings.*

Probably Allport's most controversial concept is that of *functional autonomy.* This postulate holds that some motives are functionally independent from the original motivation responsible for the development of those acquired behaviors. *Perseverative functional autonomy* refers to those habits and behaviors that are not part of one's proprium, while *propriate functional autonomy* includes all those self-sustaining motivations that are related to the proprium.

Allport believed that *mature persons* are motivated largely by conscious processes, have an extended sense of self, relate warmly to others, accept themselves, have a realistic perception of the world, and possess insight, humor, and a unifying philosophy of life.

Research methods that emphasize general laws, Allport insisted, must be balanced by *morphogenic procedures* that stress the study of the individual. Personal documents, such as the famous *Letters from Jenny* (Allport, 1965), provide insights into the whole of humanity by revealing outstanding characteristics of the single individual.

Allport's concept of humanity is optimistic, and is welcomed by those who believe that common sense has been abandoned by some of the earlier personality theorists. Throughout our lifetime, Allport insisted, we have some freedom to grow and to seek new challenges.

Allport's psychology of the individual receives high ratings for its internal consistency and parsimony, but on the more critical criteria of a useful theory its marks are not as high. It is rated low on both its capacity to organize knowledge and its ability to generate research. As a guide to action, it is moderately practical.

Suggested Readings

ALLPORT, G. W. (1955). *Becoming: Basic considerations for a psychology of personality.* New Haven, CT: Yale University Press.

    Allport's perceptive thinking and cogent writing are evidenced in this brief book that discusses a wide range of topics pertinent to personality.

ALLPORT, G. W. (1961). *Pattern and growth in personality.* New York: Holt, Rinehart and Winston.

A completely revised edition of Allport's classic 1937 book on personality, this volume once again focuses on the study of the individual. The book is essential to an understanding of Allport's conception of personality.

ALLPORT, G. W. (1965). *Letters from Jenny.* New York: Harcourt, Brace & World.

A fascinating account of Jenny, our case study, as seen though her eyes and from the view of others who knew her.

ALLPORT, G. W. (1967). An autobiography. In E. G. Boring & G. Lindzey (Eds.), *A history of psychology in autobiography* (Vol 5). New York: Appleton-Century-Crofts.

Allport's interesting account of his life, including his encounter with Sigmund Freud.

Part Five
HUMANISTIC/ EXISTENTIAL THEORIES

15

The Psychology of Personal Constructs

Like many other college students, Arlene works hard—not necessarily on school work, but on her job. Arlene works 30 to 40 hours a week at a convenience store and carries a full load of classwork as a political science major. Despite a hectic schedule that calls for driving to morning classes, then across town to her job, and then back to her apartment, Arlene had been able to keep up with her studies, her job, and an active social life—that is, until her 10-year-old car broke down.

Now she has been told by the garage mechanic that her repair bill will be almost as much as the car is worth. Arlene had planned to buy a new car after she graduated and has saved some money for the purchase. Should she buy a new car now? How about another used car? Should she have her old car fixed? What if it breaks down again? If she buys a new car, what kind should she get? What color? What brand? How much can she afford?

Are there other alternatives? Could she use public transportation? Depend on friends for a ride? Quit her job and find one closer to her apartment and school? Walk to work? Quit school and move back home with her parents? The number of possibilities goes on and on.

How did Arlene solve this problem? According to the personal construct theory of George Kelly, Arlene made her decision in much the same manner that a scientist makes decisions. She observed her environment, asked questions, anticipated answers, perceived relationships between events, hypothesized about possible solutions to her dilemma, asked more questions, and predicted potential outcomes. In addition, she attempted to control her environment and the behavior of others just as a psychologist tries to control behavior.

Many of the steps in Arlene's "scientific" process were not put into words. For example, she did not consciously think about walking the four miles to work, or about relying on friends for transportation. Yet each of these possibilities, on some level, was considered. Each was rejected just as a scientist might reject some hypotheses as being unworthy of experimental testing. On a more overt level, Arlene considered most of the other options. She looked at new-car advertisements, visited several dealers, bargained over price, compared her bank account and current income against possible monthly payments, and then rejected that course of action. She repeated (replicated) that same procedure with reference to used cars. The resulting evidence supported the hypothesis that she would be able to afford a late model Honda. When she found the car she liked, she tested it by driving it, then took it to a mechanic to cross-validate the word of the dealer and her own opinion. After reviewing all the evidence, Arlene purchased the car.

With the purchase, Arlene's scientific quest did not stop. She continued to evaluate her decision. Was her evidence complete? Was it valid? Was a Honda the right choice? Before she bought the car she had no particular preference for a Honda, but having committed herself (in the form of a down payment and a promise to pay monthly notes) she became convinced that Hondas are superior to other cars of comparable price. In other words, like all other people (including "professional" scientists), her perceptions of reality were colored by her *personal constructs,* that is, her way of looking at, explaining, and interpreting events in her world.

OVERVIEW

Kelly's theory of personal constructs is like no other personality theory. It has been variously called a cognitive theory, a behavioral theory, an existential theory, and a phenomenological theory. Yet it is none of these. Perhaps the most appropriate term would be metatheory, or a theory about theories. According to Kelly, all people (including those who build personality theories) anticipate events by the meanings or interpretations they place on events. These meanings or interpretations are called *constructs.* People exist in a real world, but their behavior is shaped by their gradually expanding interpretation or *construction* of that world. They construe the world in their own way and every construction is open to revision or replacement. People are not victims of circumstances. They need not paint themselves into a corner. There are always alternative constructions available, a philosophical position Kelly calls *constructive alternativism.*

Constructive alternativism is implied by Kelly's theory of personal constructs. The theory itself is expressed in a basic postulate and 11 supporting corollaries. The basic postulate assumes that people are constantly active and that their activity is guided by the way they anticipate events.

BIOGRAPHY OF GEORGE KELLY

George Alexander Kelly was born April 28, 1905, on a farm near Perth, Kansas, a small town 35 miles south of Wichita. George was the only child of Theodore V. Kelly, an ordained Presbyterian minister and Elfleda M. Kelly, a former schoolteacher. By the time George was born, his father had given up the ministry in favor of becoming a Kansas farmer. Both parents were well-educated and both helped in the formal education of their son. This was fortunate for George because his schooling was rather erratic.

When George was four the family moved to eastern Colorado, where his father staked a claim on some of the last free land in that part of the country. While in Colorado George attended school only irregularly, seldom for more than a few weeks at a time (Thompson, 1968).

Lack of water drove the family back to Kansas, where George attended four different high schools in four years. At first he commuted to high school, but, at age 13, he was sent to school in Wichita and, from that time on, he mostly lived away from home. After graduation he spent three years at Friends University in Wichita and one year at Park College in Parkville, Missouri. Both schools had religious affiliations, which may account for the fact that many of Kelly's later writings are sprinkled with biblical references.

Kelly was a man of many and varied interests. His undergraduate degree was in physics and math, but he was also a member of the college debate team and, as such, became intensely concerned with social problems. This interest led him to the University of Kansas, where he received a master's degree with a major in educational sociology and a minor in labor relations and sociology.

During the next few years Kelly moved several times and held a variety of positions. First, he moved to Minneapolis, where he taught soap-box oratory at a special college for labor organizers, conducted classes in speech for the American Bankers Association, and taught government to an Americanization class for prospective citizens (Kelly, 1969a). In 1928 he moved to Sheldon, Iowa, were he taught at a junior college and coached drama. While there he met his future wife, Gladys Thompson, an English teacher at the same school. After a year and a half he moved back to Minnesota, where he taught a summer session at the University of Minnesota. Next, he returned to Wichita to work for a few months as an aeronautical engineer. From there he went to the University of Edinburgh in Scotland as an exchange student, receiving an advanced professional degree in education.

At this point in his life Kelly "had dabbled academically in education, sociology, economics, labor relations, biometrics, speech pathology, and anthropology, and had majored in psychology for a grand total of nine months" (Kelly, 1969a, p. 48). After returning from Edinburgh, however, he began in earnest to pursue a career in psychology. He enrolled at the State University of Iowa in 1930 and the following year completed a Ph.D. with a dissertation on common factors in speech and reading disabilities.

Once again Kelly returned to Kansas, beginning his academic career in 1931 at Fort Hays Kansas State College teaching physiological psychology. With the dust bowl and the Great Depression, however, he soon became convinced that he should "pursue something more humanitarian than physiological psychology" (Kelly, 1969a, p. 48). Consequently, he decided to become a psychotherapist, counseling college and high school students in the community. True to his psychology of personal constructs, Kelly (1969a) quickly points out that it wasn't the circumstances that dictated his decision, but rather his interpretation of events. It was neither duty nor a calling that determined his change in focus, but his own construction of reality.

Everything around us "calls," if we choose to heed. Moreover, I have never been completely satisfied that becoming a psychologist was even a very good idea in the first place. . . . The only thing that seems clear about my career in psychology is that it was I who got myself into it and I who have pursued it (Kelly, 1969a, p. 49).

Now a psychotherapist, Kelly obtained legislative support for a program of traveling psychological clinics in Kansas. He and his students traveled widely throughout the state, providing psychological services during those hard times. During this period he evolved his own approach to therapy, abandoning the Freudian techniques which he had been using.

During World War II Kelly joined the Navy as an aviation psychologist. After the war he taught at the University of Maryland for a year and then, in 1946, joined the faculty at Ohio State University as a professor and director of the Psychological Clinic, where he worked with Julian Rotter (see Chapter 11), who succeeded him as director of the clinic. Kelly had been gradually formulating his theory of personality, and in 1955 his most important work, *The Psychology of Personal Constructs,* was published in two volumes.

Many of his summers were spent as a visiting professor at such schools as the University of Chicago, the University of Nebraska, Southern California, Northwestern, Brigham Young University, Stanford, and City College of New York. During these postwar years Kelly became a major force in clinical psychology in the United States. He was president of both the Clinical and the Consulting Divisions of the American Psychological Association and was also head of the American Board of Examiners in Professional Psychology.

In 1965 he accepted a position at Brandeis University, where, for a brief time, he was a colleague of A. H. Maslow (see Chapter 16). Kelly died on March 6, 1967, before he could complete revisions of his theory of personal constructs.

Although Kelly's popularity with American psychologists has waned somewhat since the time of his death, his ideas are widely known among psychologists in England. The late Donald Bannister was instrumental in spreading Kelly's theories throughout Britain (Bannister, 1970, 1975, 1977; Bannister & Fransella, 1966, 1971; Bannister & Mair, 1968). The Center of Personal Construct Psychology, with a mission to train clinicians in the theory and practice of personal construct psychology, was opened in London during the past decade under the direction of Fay Fransella. In addition, British psychologists have applied Kelly's ideas to industrial and organizational settings. In the United States, Alvin Landfield of the University of Nebraska has championed personal construct theory (Landfield, 1971; Landfield & Epting, 1987; Landfield & Leitner, 1980).

Kelly's diverse life experiences, from the wheat fields of Kansas to some of the major universities of the world, from education to labor relations to drama and debate to psychology, are consistent with his theory of personality, which emphasizes the possibility of interpreting events from many possible angles.

KELLY'S PHILOSOPHICAL POSITION

Is human behavior (such as Arlene's decision to buy a late model used car) based on reality or on our perception of reality? George Kelly would say *both*. He did not accept Skinner's (see Chapter 10) position that behavior is shaped by the environment, that is, reality. On the other hand, he also rejected a strictly **phenomenological** approach (see Combs & Snygg, 1959) that holds that the only reality is our perceptions. Kelly (1955) believed that the universe is real, but that different people construe it in different ways. Thus, our **personal constructs,** or ways of interpreting and explaining events, hold the key to predicting our behavior.

Personal construct theory does not try to explain *nature*. Rather it is a theory of our *construction* of events, that is, our personal inquiry into our world. It is "a psychology of the human quest. It does not say what has or will be found, but proposes rather how we might go about looking for it" (Kelly, 1970, p. 1).

Person as Scientist

From our case study we saw that when her car broke down, Arlene acted in much the same manner as a scientist does. She asked questions, formulated hypotheses, tested them, and drew conclusions. She attempted to predict future events ("If I buy a reliable car I will be able to continue my job.") and to control them ("By purchasing this car I will be free to drive to work and earn enough money to stay in school."). In a similar manner, all of us, in our quest for meaning, make observations, construe relationships among events, formulate theories, generate hypotheses, test those that are plausible, and reach conclusions from our experiments. As with any scientist our conclusions are not fixed or final. They are open to question and reconsideration. Kelly was hopeful that people individually as well as humanity in general would find better ways of restructuring their lives through imagination and foresight.

Scientist as Person

If people can be seen as scientists, then scientists must be seen as people. Therefore, the pronouncements of scientists must be regarded with the same skepticism with which we view any behavior. Every scientific observation can be looked at from a different perspective. Every theory can be slightly tilted and viewed from a new angle. This means, of course, that Kelly's theory is not exempt from restructuring. Kelly (1969b) presented his theory as a set of half-truths and recognized the inaccuracy of its constructions. Like Carl Rogers (see Chapter 17), Kelly hoped that his theory would be overthrown and replaced by a better one. Indeed, Kelly, more than any other personality theorist, formulated a theory that encourages its own demise. Just as all of us can use our imagination to see everyday events differently, personality theorists can use their ingenuity to construe better theories.

Constructive Alternativism

As already mentioned, Kelly began with the assumption that the universe really exists and that it functions as an integral unit, with all its parts interacting precisely with each other. Moreover, the universe is constantly changing so that something is happening all the time. Added to these basic assumptions is the notion that people's thoughts also really exist and that people strive to make sense out of their continuously changing world. Different people construe reality in different ways and the same person is capable of changing his or her view of the world.

In other words, there are alternative ways of looking at things. Kelly (1965, p. 15) assumed *"that all of our present interpretations of the universe are subject to revision or replacement."* He referred to this assumption as **constructive alternativism** and summed up the notion with these words: "The events we face today are subject to as great a variety of constructions as our wits will enable us to contrive" (Kelly, 1970, p. 1). The piece by piece accumulation of facts does not add up to truth. The philosophy of constructive alternativism assumes that facts can be looked at from different perspectives. Kelly agreed with Adler (see Chapter 4) that our interpretation of events is more important than the events themselves. In contrast to Adler, however, Kelly stressed the notion that interpretations have meaning in the dimension of time, and what is valid at one time becomes false when construed differently. For example, when Freud (see Chapter 2) originally heard his patients' accounts of childhood seduction, he believed that early sexual experiences were responsible for later hysterical reactions. If Freud had continued to construe his patients' reports in this fashion, the entire history of psychoanalysis would have been quite different. But then, for a variety of reasons, Freud restructured his data and gave up his seduction hypothesis. Shortly thereafter, he tilted the picture a little and saw a very different view. Now he concluded that these reports merely represented childhood fantasies. His alternative hypothesis was the Oedipus complex, a concept that permeates all of current psychoanalytic theory, and one that is 180 degrees removed from his original seduction theory. If Freud's observations are viewed from yet another angle, such as Erikson's perspective (see Chapter 3), then a still different conclusion might be reached.

Kelly believed that it is the *person,* not the facts, that holds the key to an individual's future. Facts and events do not dictate conclusions, but rather they carry meanings for us to discover. We all have responsibility for how we construe our worlds. We are constantly faced with alternatives which we can explore if we choose. We are victims neither of our history nor our present circumstances. That is not to say that we can make of our world whatever we wish. We are "limited by our feeble wits and our timid reliance upon what is familiar" (Kelly, 1970, p. 3). We do not always welcome new ideas. Like scientists in general and personality theorists in particular, we often find restructuring disturbing and thus hold on to ideas that are comfortable and theories that are well-established.

PERSONAL CONSTRUCTS

We have seen that Kelly's philosophy assumes the existence of a unified, ever-changing real world and also the reality of our interpretation of that world. "Man looks at his world through transparent patterns or templates which he creates and then attempts to fit over the realities of which the world is composed"(Kelly, 1955, pp. 8–9). Although these patterns or templates do not always fit accurately, they are the means by which we make sense out of the world. Kelly referred to these patterns as *personal constructs.*

> They are ways of construing the world. They are what enables man, and lower animals too, to chart a course of behavior, explicitly formulated or implicitly acted out, verbally expressed or utterly inarticulate, consistent with other courses of behavior or inconsistent with them, intellectually reasoned or vegetatively sensed (Kelly, 1955, p. 9).

A personal construct is our way of seeing how things (or people) are alike and yet different from other things (or people). For example, we may see how Betty and Jane are alike and how they are different from Carol. The comparison and the contrast must occur within the same context. For example, we cannot say that Betty and Jane are attractive and Carol is religious. That would not be a personal construct because attractiveness is one dimension and religiosity is another. A construct would be formed if we see that Betty and Jane are attractive and Carol is unattractive, or if we view Betty and Jane as irreligious and Carol as religious. Both the comparison and the contrast are essential.

Whether they are clearly perceived or dimly felt, personal constructs shape an individual's behavior. As an example, consider Arlene, our case study. After her old car broke down, her personal constructs molded her subsequent course of action, but not all constructs were clearly defined. For instance, she may have decided to buy a late model Honda because she interpreted the dealer's friendliness and persuasiveness as reliability for the car. Arlene's personal constructs may be accurate or inaccurate, but, in either case, they are her means of predicting and controlling her environment.

Arlene tried to increase the accuracy of her predictions (that the car would provide reliable, economical, and comfortable transportation) by increasing her store of information. She researched her purchase, asked others' opinions, tested the car, and had it checked by a mechanic. In much the same manner, all of us attempt to improve our constructs. We look for better fitting templates, not worse fitting ones. We strive for progression rather than regression. However, individual progress is not inevitable. Personal investment in an established construct blocks the path of forward development. The world, remember, is constantly changing so that what is accurate at one time may not be accurate at another. The reliable blue bicycle once rode during childhood should not be construed to mean that all blue vehicles are reliable.

Kelly's basic theory is expressed in one fundamental postulate or assumption and elaborated by means of 11 supporting corollaries.

Basic Postulate

The fundamental postulate of personal construct theory is: *"A person's processes are psychologically channelized by the ways in which he [or she] anticipates events"* (Kelly, 1955, p. 46).

This statement assumes that our behavior (thoughts and actions) are directed by the way we see the future. The postulate is not intended as an absolute statement of truth, but is a tentative assumption open to question and scientific testing.

Kelly (1955, 1970) clarified this fundamental assumption by defining its key terms. First, the phrase *person's processes* refers to a living, changing, moving human being. Kelly was not concerned here with animals, with society, or with any part or function of the person. He did not recognize motives, needs, drives, or instincts as forces underlying motivation. Life itself accounts for our movement. "The person is not an object which is temporarily in a moving state but is himself a form of motion" (Kelly, 1955, p. 48).

The term *channelized* was chosen to suggest that people move with a direction through a network of pathways or channels. The network, however, is flexible. It both facilitates and restricts one's range of action. In addition, the term avoids the implication that some sort of energy is being transformed into action. People are already in movement; they merely channelize or direct their processes toward some end or purpose.

The next key phrase is *ways of anticipating events*. This suggests that people guide their actions according to the ways they predict the future. Neither the past nor the future per se determine behavior. Rather it is our present view of the future that is important. Arlene did not buy a blue Honda because she had a blue bicycle when she was a child, although that fact may have helped her construe the present so that she anticipated that her Honda would be a reliable car in the future. "It is the future which tantalizes man, not the past. Always he reaches out to the future through the window of the present" (Kelly, 1955 p. 49).

Supporting Corollaries

Kelly's personal construct theory is elaborated by 11 supporting corollaries, all of which can be inferred from his basic postulate.

Similarities among Events

No two events are exactly alike, yet we construe similar events so that they are perceived as being the same. One sunrise is never identical to another, but our construct *dawn* conveys our recognition of some similarity or some replication of events. Two dawns are never exactly alike, although they may be similar enough for us to construe them as the same event. Kelly (1955, 1970) referred to this similarity among events as the **construction corollary.**

The construction corollary states that "*a person anticipates events by construing their replications* (Kelly, 1955, p.50). This corollary again points out that people are forward-looking; their behavior is molded by their anticipation of future events. It also emphasizes the notion that people construe or interpret future events according to recurrent themes or replications.

The construction corollary may seem little more than common sense. We see similarities among events and use a single concept to describe the common properties. Kelly, however, felt that it was necessary to include the obvious when building a theory.

Differences among People

Kelly's second corollary is equally obvious. *"Persons differ from each other in their construction of events"* (Kelly, 1955, p. 55). Kelly called this emphasis on individual differences the **individuality corollary.**

People have different experiences and construe things in different ways. Even when two constructions appear the same, they are not identical. In addition, they are not put together in the same way. In other words, both the substance and the form of the construct are different. For example, a philosopher may subsume the construct *truth* under the rubric of eternal values; a lawyer may view *truth* as a relative concept, useful for a particular purpose; and a scientist may construe *truth* as an ever-elusive goal, something to be sought, but never attained. For the philosopher, the lawyer, and the scientist *truth* has a different substance, a different meaning. Moreover, each person arrived at his or her particular construction in a different manner.

Even identical twins living in nearly identical environments do not construe events exactly the same. Part of the environment for Twin A includes Twin B, an experience not shared by Twin B. In addition, each twin experiences a unique self as the central figure of life.

Although Kelly (1955) emphasized individual differences, he pointed out that experiences can be shared and that people can find a common ground for construing experiences. This allows people to communicate both verbally and nonverbally. However, due to individual differences, the communication is never perfect.

Relationships among Constructs

Kelly's third corollary emphasizes relationships among constructs. It is called the **organization corollary** and states that *people "characteristically evolve, for [their] convenience in anticipating events, a construction system embracing ordinal relationships between constructs"* (Kelly, 1955, p. 56).

The first two corollaries assume similarities among events and differences among people. The third emphasizes that different people organize similar events in a manner than minimizes incompatibilities and inconsistencies. We arrange our constructions so that we may move from one to another in an orderly fashion. This allows us to anticipate events in ways that transcend contradictions and avoid needless conflicts.

The organization corollary also assumes an ordinal relationship of constructs so that one construct may be subsumed under another. Figure 15.1 illustrates a hierarchy of constructs as they might apply to Arlene, our case study. In deciding a course of action after her car broke down, Arlene may have seen her situation in terms of dichotomous superordinate constructs such as good vs. bad. These constructs (as interpreted by Arlene) include much more than *independence vs. dependence.* For example, intelligence and health are good, while stupidity and illness are bad. Likewise, independence and dependence have a multitude of subordinate constructs. But for Arlene in this situation, continuation in school was construed as independence while returning home meant dependence. In order to remain in school and continue her job, Arlene needed transportation. There are many means of transportation, but Arlene considered only four: riding a public bus, walking, relying on friends, or driving her own car. Subsumed under the construct of car were three subordinate constructs: repairing her old car, buying

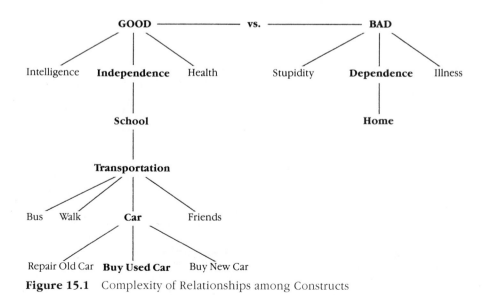

Figure 15.1   Complexity of Relationships among Constructs

People can find a common ground for construing experiences.

a new one, or purchasing a late model used car. This example not only suggests that constructs have a complex ordinal relationship with each other but a dichotomous one as well.

Dichotomy of Constructs

Now we come to a corollary that is not so obvious. In fact, at first thought most people might find it completely unbelievable. The **dichotomy corollary** states that *"a person's construction system is composed of a finite number of dichotomous constructs"* (Kelly, 1955, p. 59).

Kelly insisted that a construct is an either/or proposition—black or white, with no shades of grays. In nature things may not be either/or, but natural events have no meanings other than those attributed to them by an individual's personal construct system. In nature the color blue may have no opposite pole (except on a color chart), but people attribute contrasting qualities to blue, such as *light* blue vs. *dark* blue or *pretty* vs. *ugly*.

In order to form a construct we must be able to see similarities between events, but we also contrast those events with their opposite pole. Kelly (1955, p. 61) stated it this way: "In its minimum context a construct is a way in which at least two elements are similar and contrast with a third." As an example, let us return to Figure 15.1. How are *intelligence* and *independence* alike? Their common element has no meaning without contrasting it to an opposite. Intelligence and independence have no overlapping element when compared to *purple* or *modern*. By contrasting intelligence with stupidity and independence with dependence, we see how they are alike and how they can be organized under the construct "good" as opposed to "bad."

Choice between Dichotomies

If people construe events in dichotomized fashion, then it follows that they have some choice in following alternative courses of action. This is Kelly's **choice corollary,** paraphrased as follows: *People choose for themselves that alternative in a dichotomized construct through which they anticipate the greater possibility for extension and definition of future constructs.*

This corollary assumes much of what is stated in Kelly's basic postulate and in the preceding corollaries. People make choices on the basis of how they anticipate events and those choices are between dichotomous alternatives. In addition, the choice corollary assumes that people choose those actions that are most likely to extend their future range of choices.

Arlene's decision to buy a used car was based on a series of previous choices, each of which was between dichotomized alternatives and each of which broadened her range of future choices. First she chose the independence of school over the dependence of going home to live with her parents. Next, buying a car offered more freedom than relying on friends or on bus schedules or walking (which she perceived as time consuming). Repairing her old car was financially *risky* compared to the greater *safety* of buying a used one. Purchasing a new car was too *expensive* compared to the relatively *inexpensive* used car. Each choice was between alternatives in a dichotomized construct and with each Arlene anticipated the greater possibility for extending and defining future constructs.

Range of Convenience

Kelly's **range corollary** assumes that personal constructs are finite. They are not relevant to everything. *"A construct is convenient for the anticipation of a finite range of events only"* (Kelly, 1955, p. 68). In other words, a construct is limited to a particular *range of convenience.*

The construct "independence" was within Arlene's range of convenience when she was deciding to buy a car, but on other occasions it would be outside those boundaries. Independence carries with it the notion of dependence. Within the independence/dependence range of convenience would be Arlene's freedom to remain in school, to continue her job, and to move quickly from place to place without relying on others. However, Arlene's construct of independence excludes all irrelevancies such as up/down, light/dark, or wet/dry, that is, it is convenient only for a finite range of events.

The range corollary allowed Kelly to distinguish between the notion of a *concept* and his view of a *construct.* A concept includes all elements having a common property and excludes all others. The concept *tall* includes all those people and objects having extended height and excludes all other concepts, even those that are outside its range of convenience. Therefore, *fast* or *independence* or *dark* are all excluded from the concept *tall* because they do not have extended height. But such exclusions are both endless and needless. The idea of construct contrasts tall with short, thus limiting its range of convenience. "That which is outside the range of convenience of the construct is not considered part of the contrasting field but simply an area of irrelevancy" (Kelly, 1955, p. 69). Thus we see that dichotomies limit a construct's range of convenience.

Experience and Learning

Basic to personal construct theory is the anticipation of events. We look to the future and make guesses as to what will happen. Then, as events become revealed to us, we either validate our existing constructs or restructure them to match our experience. The restructuring of events allows us to learn from our experiences.

The **experience corollary** states: *"A person's construction system varies as he [or she] successively construes the replications of events"* (Kelly, 1955, p. 72). Kelly used the word "successively" to point out that we pay attention to only one thing at a time. "The events of one's construing march single file along the path of time" (Kelly, 1955, p. 73).

Experience consists of the successive construing of events. The events themselves do not constitute experience—it is the meaning we attach to them that changes our lives. To illustrate this point let us return to Arlene and her personal construct, *independence.* When her old car (a high school graduation gift from her parents) broke down, Arlene decided to remain in school rather than to return to the security and dependent status of living at home. As subsequent events were successively encountered and Arlene had to make decisions without benefit of parental consultation, she restructured her notions of independence. Earlier she had construed independence as freedom from outside interference. After deciding to go into debt for a used car, she began to alter her meaning of independence to include responsibility and anxiety. The events themselves did not force a restructuring. Arlene could have become a spectator in the events surrounding her. Instead, her existing constructs were flexible enough to allow her to adapt to experience.

Adaptation to Experience

Arlene's flexibility illustrates Kelly's **modulation corollary.** *"The variation in a person's construction system is limited by the permeability of the constructs within whose range of convenience the variants lie"* (Kelly, 1955, p. 77). This corollary follows from and expands the experience corollary. It assumes that the extent to which we revise our constructs is related to the degree of **permeability** of our existing constructs. A construct is permeable if new elements can be added to it. Impermeable or concrete constructs do not admit new elements. If a man believes that women are inferior to men, then contradictory evidence will not find its way into his range of convenience. The achievements of women will be attributed to luck or unfair social advantage. A change in events means a change in constructs only if those constructs are permeable.

Arlene's personal construct of *independence vs. dependence* was sufficiently permeable to take in new elements. When, without parental consultation, she made the decision to buy a used car, the construct of *maturity vs. childishness* penetrated *independence vs. dependence* and added a new flavor to it. Previously the two constructs had been separated and Arlene's notion of independence was limited to the idea of doing as she chose, while dependence was associated with parental domination. Now she construed independence as meaning mature responsibility and dependence as signifying a childish leaning on parents. In such a manner constructs are modulated or adjusted.

Incompatible Constructs

Although Kelly assumed an overall stability or consistency of one's construction system, his **fragmentation corollary** allows for the incompatibility of specific elements. *"A person may successively employ a variety of constructive subsystems which are inferentially incompatible with each other"* (Kelly, 1955, p. 83).

At first it may seem as if personal constructs must be compatible, but if we look to our own behavior and thinking we can easily see some inconsistencies. We may be brave while confronting a vicious dog, but cowardly when confronting a boss or teacher. A man might be protective of his wife, yet encourage her to be more independent. Protection and independence may be incompatible with each other on one level, but on a larger level both are subsumed under the superordinate construct of *love.*

Superordinate systems may also change, but those changes take place within a still larger system. In the above example, for instance, the man's love for his wife may gradually shift to hatred, but that change remains within a larger construct of *self-interest.* The previous love for his wife and the present hatred are both consistent with his view of self-interest. If incompatible constructs could not coexist, people would be locked into a fixed construct and change would be nearly impossible.

Similarities among People

Recall that Kelly's second supporting corollary assumed that people are different from each other. Now we see that he also assumed similarities among people. His slightly revised **commonality corollary** reads: *"To the extent that one person employs a construction of experience which is similar to that employed by another, his [or her] processes are psychologically similar to those of the other person"* (Kelly, 1970, p. 20).

It is not necessary for two people to experience the same event or even *similar* events in order for their processes to be psychologically similar. It is only necessary that they *construe* their experiences in a similar fashion. People may have similar constructions even though their experiences have been quite different. This is possible because people actively construe events; they ask questions, form hypotheses, draw conclusions, and then ask more questions. Thus two people with widely different experiences may construe events in very similar ways. For example, two people might arrive at similar political views although they come from disparate backgrounds. One may have come from a wealthy family, having lived a life of leisure and contemplation, while another may have survived a destitute childhood, struggling constantly for survival. Yet both adopt a liberal political view.

Although people of different backgrounds can have similar constructs, people with similar experiences are more likely to construe events along similar lines. Americans tend to construe *democracy* in a somewhat similar manner, and one that differs from the construction of democracy held by people from the Soviet Union.

Within a given social group people may employ similar constructions, but it is always the individual, never society, that construes events. Moreover, no two people ever interpret experiences exactly the same. Americans may have a similar construction of *democracy*, but no two individuals see it in identical terms.

Social Processes

"People belong to the same cultural group, not merely because they behave alike, nor because they expect the same things of others, but especially because they construe their experience in the same way" (Kelly, 1955, p. 94).

The final supporting corollary, the **sociality corollary** states: *"To the extent that one person construes the construction processes of another, he [or she] may play a role in a social process involving the other person"* (Kelly, 1955, p. 95).

We do not communicate with one another simply on the basis of common experiences or even similar construction; we communicate because we construe the constructions of each other. In our interpersonal relations, we not only observe the behavior of the other person, we also interpret what that behavior means to that person. When Arlene was negotiating with the used car dealer, she was not only aware of his words and actions, but also their meanings. She realized that, to him, she was a potential buyer, someone who might provide him with a nice commission. She construed his words as exaggerations and, at the same time, realized that he construed her indifference as an indication that she construed his motivations differently from her own.

All this seems rather complicated, but Kelly is simply suggesting that we are actively involved in interpersonal relations and realize that we are part of the other person's construction system.

Kelly also introduced the notion of **role** with his sociality corollary. A role refers to a pattern of behavior that results from a person's understanding of the constructs of others with whom that person is engaged in a task. For example, when Arlene was negotiating with the used car dealer, she construed her role as that of a potential buyer because she understood that that was his expectation of her. At other times and with other people, she construes her role as student, employee, daughter, girlfriend, and so on.

Kelly construed roles from a psychological rather than a sociological per-

In our interpersonal relationships, we not only observe the behavior of the other person, we also interpret what that behavior means to that person.

spective. One's role does not depend on one's place or position in a social setting, but rather on how one interprets that role. For example, Arlene, in her interaction with Chris, construes her role as girlfriend although neither Chris nor others interpret her role as such. Kelly also stressed the point that one's construction of a role need not be accurate in order for the person to play that role. This is apparent from Arlene's role as girlfriend to Chris. Her perceptions differ from his, yet she continues to play the role because she construes his construction of her as that of a girlfriend.

Arlene's roles as student, employee, and girlfriend would be considered *peripheral roles.* More central to her existence would be her *core role.* With our core role we define ourselves in terms of who we really are. It gives us a sense of identity and provides us with guidelines for everyday living.

APPLICATIONS OF PERSONAL CONSTRUCT THEORY

Like most personality theorists, Kelly's theoretical formulations evolved from his practice as a therapist. He spent more than 20 years conducting psychotherapy before he published *The Psychology of Personal Constructs* in 1955. In this section we look at his views of abnormal development, his approach to psychotherapy, and, finally, his Role Construct Repertory (Rep) Test.

Abnormal Development

In Kelly's view, psychologically healthy people validate their personal constructs against their experience with the real world. They are like competent scientists who test reasonable hypotheses, accept the results without denial or distortion, and then willingly alter their theories to match available data. Healthy individuals not only anticipate events but are also able to make satisfactory adjustments when things don't turn out as they expected.

Unhealthy people, on the other hand, stubbornly cling to outdated personal constructs, fearing invalidation because it might upset their present comfortable view of the world. They are similar to incompetent scientists who test unreasonable hypotheses, reject or distort legitimate results, and refuse to amend old theories that are no longer useful. Kelly (1955, p. 831) defined a disorder as *"any personal construction which is used repeatedly in spite of consistent invalidation."*

A person's construction system exists in the present—not the past or future. Psychological disorders, therefore, exist in the present. They are caused neither by childhood experiences nor by future events. Because construction systems are *personal,* Kelly objects to traditional classifications of abnormalities. Labeling a person as a manic-depressive or a paranoid schizophrenic is likely to result in misconstruing the person's unique constructions.

Disordered persons, like everyone else, possess a complex construction system. Their personal constructs, however, often fail the test of permeability in one of two ways: They may be either too impermeable or too flexible. In the first instance, new experiences do not penetrate the construction system so that the person fails to adjust to the real world. For example, an abused child may construe intimacy with parents as bad and solitude as good. Psychological disorders result when the child's construction system rigidly denies the value of any intimate relationship and clings to the notion that either withdrawal or attack is a preferred mode of solving interpersonal problems. On the other hand, a construction system that is too loose or flexible leads to disorganization, an inconsistent pattern of behavior, and a transient set of values. Such an individual is too easily "shaken by the impact of unexpected minor daily events" (Kelly, 1955, p. 80).

Although Kelly did not use traditional labels in describing psychopathology, he identified four common elements in most human disturbance: threat, fear, anxiety, and guilt.

Threat

Threat is experienced when people perceive that the stability of their basic constructs is likely to be shaken. Kelly (1955, p. 489) defined threat as *"the awareness of imminent comprehensive change in one's core structures."* We can be threatened by either people or events and sometimes the two cannot be separated. For example, during psychotherapy clients often feel threat from the prospect of change, even change for the better. A therapist who is seen as the instigator of change is therefore viewed as threatening. Clients frequently resist change and construe their therapist's behavior in a negative fashion. Such resistance and "negative transference" are means of reducing threat and maintaining existing personal constructs.

Fear

By Kelly's definition, threat involves a *comprehensive* change in a person's core structures. **Fear,** on the other hand, is more specific and incidental. Kelly (1955) illustrated the difference between threat and fear with the following example. A man may drive his car dangerously as the result of anger or exuberance. These impulses become *threatening* when the man realizes that he may run over a child, be arrested for reckless driving, and end up as a criminal. In this case, a comprehensive portion of his personal constructs is threatened. However, if he is suddenly confronted with the probability of crashing his car, *fear* is the result. Threat demands a comprehensive restructuring—fear an incidental one. Psychological disturbance results when either threat or fear persistently prevent a person from feeling secure.

Anxiety

Kelly (1955, p. 495) defined **anxiety** as *"the recognition that the events with which one is confronted lie outside the range of convenience of one's construct system."* We are likely to feel anxious when we are experiencing a new event. For example, when Arlene, our case study, was bargaining with the used car dealer she was not sure what to do or say. She had never before negotiated over such a large amount of money and therefore this experience was outside the range of her convenience. As a consequence, she felt anxiety, but it was a normal level of anxiety and did not result in incapacitation.

Pathological anxiety exists when incompatible constructs can no longer be tolerated and one's construction system breaks down. Recall that Kelly's fragmentation corollary assumes that people can evolve construction subsystems that are incompatible with one another. For example, when a person who has erected the rigid construction that all people are trustworthy is blatantly cheated by a colleague, that person may for a time tolerate the ambiguity of the two incompatible subsystems. However, when evidence of the untrustworthiness of others becomes overwhelming, the person's construct system may break down. The result is a relatively permanent and debilitating experience of anxiety.

Guilt

Kelly's sociality corollary assumes that people construe a core role that gives them a sense of identity within a social environment. When that core role is weakened or dissolved we develop a feeling of guilt. Kelly (1970, p. 27) defined **guilt** as *"the sense of having lost one's core role structure."* In other words, we feel guilty when we behave in ways inconsistent with our sense of who we are.

People who have never developed a core role do not feel guilty. They may be anxious or confused, but without a sense of personal identity they do not experience guilt. For example, people without a conscience have no integral sense of self, no core role structure. Such people have no stable guidelines to violate and hence will not feel guilty regardless of their behavior.

Psychotherapy

Psychological distress exists whenever an individual has difficulty validating personal constructs, anticipating future events, and controlling present environment. When distress becomes unmanageable, the person may seek outside help in the form of psychotherapy.

In Kelly's view, people should be free to choose those courses of action most consistent with their prediction of events. In therapy this means that clients, not the therapist, select the goal. Clients are active participants in the therapeutic process, and the therapist's role is to assist them to alter their construct systems in order to improve efficiency in making predictions.

As a technique for altering the clients' constructs, Kelly used a procedure called *fixed-role therapy*. The purpose of fixed-role therapy is to help clients change their outlook on life (personal constructs) by acting out a predetermined role, first within the relative security of the therapeutic setting and then in the environment beyond therapy where they enact the role continuously over a period of several weeks. Together with the therapist, clients work out a role, one that includes attitudes and behaviors not currently part of their core role. In writing the fixed-role sketch the client and therapist are careful to include the construction systems of other people. How is one's spouse or parents or boss or friends likely to react? How will they construe this new role? Will their reactions help the client reconstrue events more productively?

This new role is then tried out in everyday life in much the same manner that a scientist tests a hypothesis—cautiously and objectively. In fact, the fixed-role sketch is typically written in the third person, with the actor assuming a new identity. The client is not trying to *be* another person, but is merely playing the part of someone worth knowing. The role should not be taken too seriously. It is only an act, something that can be altered as evidence warrants.

Fixed-role therapy is not aimed at solving specific problems or "repairing" obsolete constructs. It is a creative process that allows clients to discover previously hidden aspects of themselves. The discovery does not come quickly, and, in the early stages, only peripheral roles are introduced. Change in the core roles comes only after clients have had time to become comfortable with minor changes in personality structure (Kelly, 1955).

Prior to developing the fixed-role approach, Kelly (1969) stumbled on an unusual procedure which strongly resembles fixed-role therapy. After becoming uncomfortable with Freudian techniques, he decided to offer his clients "preposterous interpretations" for their complaints. Some were farfetched Freudian interpretations, but nevertheless, most clients accepted these "explanations" and used them as guides to future action. For example, Kelly might tell a client that strict toilet training has caused him to construe his life in a dogmatically rigid fashion, but that he need not continue to see things in this way. To Kelly's surprise, many of his clients began to function better! The key to change was the same as with fixed-role therapy: clients must begin to interpret their lives from a different perspective and see themselves in a different role.

The Rep Test

Another procedure used by Kelly, both inside and outside therapy, was the *Role Construct Repertory (Rep) Test.* The purpose of the Rep Test is to discover ways in which people construe significant people in their lives.

A subject is given a Role Title List and asked to designate people who fit the role titles by writing their names on a card. For example, for "a teacher you liked" the subject must supply a particular name. The number of role titles can vary but Kelly (1955) listed 24 on one version (see Table 15.1).

TABLE 15.1 Example of a List of Role Titles Used for the Rep Test

1. A teacher you liked. (Or the teacher of a subject you liked.)
2. A teacher you disliked. (Or the teacher of a subject you disliked.)
3. Your wife or present girl friend.
3a. (for women) Your husband or present boy friend.
4. An employer, supervisor, or officer under whom you worked or served and whom you found hard to get along with. (Or someone under whom you worked in a situation you did not like.)
5. An employer, supervisor, or officer under whom you worked or served and whom you liked. (Or someone under whom you worked in a situation you liked.)
6. Your mother. (Or the person who has played the part of a mother in your life.)
7. Your father. (Or the person who has played the part of a father in your life.)
8. Your brother nearest your age. (Or the person who has been most like a brother.)
9. Your sister nearest your age. (Or the person who has been most like a sister.)
10. A person with whom you have worked who was easy to get along with.
11. A person with whom you have worked who was hard to understand.
12. A neighbor with whom you get along well.
13. A neighbor whom you find hard to understand.
14. A boy you got along well with when you were in high school. (Or when you were 16.)
15. A girl you got along well with when you were in high school. (Or when you were 16.)
16. A boy you did not like when you were in high school. (Or when you were 16.)
17. A girl you did not like when you were in high school. (Or when you were 16.)
18. A person of your own sex whom you would enjoy having as a companion on a trip.
19. A person of your own sex whom you would dislike having as a companion on a trip.
20. A person with whom you have been closely associated recently who appears to dislike you.
21. The person whom you would most like to be of help to. (Or whom you feel most sorry for.)
22. The most intelligent person whom you know personally.
23. The most successful person whom you know personally.
24. The most interesting person whom you know personally.

SOURCE: *The psychology of personal constructs* by G. A. Kelly, 1955 (pp. 221–222), New York: Norton. Copyright 1955 by W. W. Norton & Company. Used by permission.

Next, the subject is given three names from the list and asked to judge which two people are alike and yet different from the third. Recall that for a construct there must be both a similarity and a contrast. Therefore, three is the minimum number for any construct. Say, for example, that the subject construes Number 1 ("A teacher you liked") and Number 6 ("Your mother") as similar and Number 9 ("Your sister nearest your age") as different. Then the subject is asked how mother and favorite teacher are alike and yet different from sister. The *reason* a person gives for the similarity and contrast constitutes the construct. If the subject gives a superficial response such as "They're both old and my sister is young," the examiner will say, "That's one way they are alike. Can you think of another?" The subject might then say, "My mother and favorite teacher are both unselfish and my sister is very self-centered." The examiner records the construct and then asks the subject to sort three more cards. Not all combinations of sorts are elicited and the examiner has some latitude in determining which combinations will be used.

After a number of sorts are completed, the information is transferred to a repertory grid (see Figure 15.2 for an example). In this particular grid, 19 role titles are listed along the horizontal axis and 22 personal constructs along the vertical axis. On Sort Number 1 this subject construed Persons 17 and 18 alike because they don't believe in God and Person 19 as being dif-

CONSTRUCTS

Role titles (columns 1–19): 1. Self, 2. Mother, 3. Father, 4. Brother, 5. Sister, 6. Spouse, 7. Ex-flame, 8. Pal, 9. Ex-pal, 10. Rejecting Person, 11. Pitied Person, 12. Threatening Person, 13. Attractive Person, 14. Accepted Teacher, 15. Rejected Teacher, 16. Boss, 17. Successful Person, 18. Happy Person, 19. Ethical Person

SORT NO.	EMERGENT POLE	IMPLICIT POLE
1	Don't believe in God	Very religious
2	Same sort of education	Complete different education
3	Not athletic	Athletic
4	Both girls	A boy
5	Parents	Ideas different
6	Understand me better	Don't understand at all
7	Teach the right thing	Teach the wrong thing
8	Achieved a lot	Hasn't achieved a lot
9	Higher education	No education
10	Don't like other people	Like other people
11	More religious	Not religious
12	Believe in higher education	Not believing in too much education
13	More sociable	Not sociable
14	Both girls	Not girls
15	Both girls	Not girls
16	Both have high morals	Low morals
17	Think alike	Think differently
18	Same age	Different ages
19	Believe the same about me	Believe differently about me
20	Both friends	Not friends
21	More understanding	Less understanding
22	Both appreciate music	Don't understand music

Figure 15.2 Example of a Repertory Grid (From *The Psychology of personal constructs,* by G. A. Kelly, 1955, p. 270, New York: Norton. Copyright 1955 by W. W. Norton & Company. Used by permission.)

ferent because he or she is very religious. The subject also checked Persons 7, 10, and 12 because they are construed as similar to the two people in the emergent pole, that is, they too do not believe in God. Similarly, each row is checked until the entire grid is completed.

There are several versions of the Rep Test and the repertory grid, but all are designed to assess personal constructs. A subject, for example, can see how her father and boss are alike or different; whether or not she identifies with her mother; how her boyfriend and father are alike; or how she construes members of the opposite sex. Also the test can be given early in therapy and then again at the end. Changes in personal constructs reveal the nature and degree of movement made during therapy.

Kelly and his colleagues have used the Rep Test in a variety of forms and no set scoring rules apply. Reliability and validity of the instrument are not very high and its usefulness depends largely on the skill and experience of the examiner (Adams-Webber, 1970; Fransella & Bannister, 1977).

CONCEPT OF HUMANITY

Kelly had an essentially *optimistic* view of human nature. He saw people as anticipating the future and living their lives in accordance with those anticipations. People are capable of changing their personal constructs at any time of life, but those changes are seldom easy. Kelly's modulation corollary suggests that constructs are permeable or resilient, meaning that new elements can be admitted. Not all people, however, have equally permeable constructs. Some accept new experiences and restructure their interpretations accordingly; others possess concrete constructs that are very difficult to alter. Nevertheless, Kelly was quite optimistic in his belief that therapeutic experiences can help people live more productive lives.

On the dimension of *determinism vs. free choice,* Kelly's theory leans toward free choice. The environment, although it has a real existence, can never make us free. No one can grant us freedom. No event can unloose our chains. Only within our own personal construct system are we ever free to make a choice (Kelly, 1980). We choose between alternatives within a construct system that we ourselves have built. We make those choices on the basis of our anticipation of events. But more than that, we choose those alternatives that appear to offer us the greater opportunity for further elaboration of our anticipatory system. Kelly (1980) referred to this as the **elaborative choice,** that is, in making present choices, we look ahead and pick the alternative that will increase our range of future choices.

Kelly adopted a *teleological* as opposed to a causal view of human personality. He repeatedly insisted that childhood events per se do not shape current personality. Our present construction of past experiences may have some influence on present behavior, but that influence is quite limited. Personality is much more likely to be guided by our present anticipation of future events. Kelly's fundamental postulate, the one on which all corollaries and assumptions stand, is that *all human activity is directed by the ways in which we anticipate events* (Kelly, 1955, p. 46). There can be no question, then, that Kelly's theory is essentially teleological.

Kelly emphasized *conscious processes* more than unconscious ones. However, we cannot say that he stresses conscious *motivation* because motivation itself plays no part in personal construct theory. Kelly speaks of *levels of cognitive awareness.* High levels of awareness refer to those psychological processes that are easily symbolized in words and can be accurately expressed to other people. Low-level processes are incompletely symbolized and are difficult or impossible to communicate.

There are several reasons why some processes are at low levels of awareness. First, some constructs are preverbal, formed before a person acquires meaningful language and hence not capable of being symbolized even to one's self. Second, some processes are at a low level of awareness because a person sees only similarities and fails to make meaningful contrasts. For example, a person may construe all people as trustworthy. However, the implicit pole of untrustworthiness is denied. Because the person's superordinate construction system is rigid, the person fails to adopt a realistic construct of trustworthy/untrustworthy and tends to see the actions of others as completely trustworthy. Third, some subordinate constructs may remain at a low level of awareness as superordinate constructs are changing. In the above example, for instance, even after changing one's view to the notion that people are not trustworthy, the person may be reluctant to construe one particular individual as untrustworthy. This means that a subordinate construct has not yet caught up to a superordinate one. Finally, some events may lie outside our range of convenience so that certain experiences do not become part of our construct system. For example, such automatic processes as heart beat, circulation, eye blink, and digestion are ordinarily outside our range of convenience and we are usually not aware of them.

On the issue of *biological vs. social influences,* Kelly was inclined more toward the social but it would be a mistake to say that he placed heavy emphasis on social forces. His sociality corollary assumes that, to some extent, we are influenced by others and in turn have some impact on them. When we accurately construe the constructions of another person, we may play a role in a social process involving that other person. Kelly assumed that our interpretation of the construction systems of important other people (such as parents, spouse, and friends) may have some influence on our future constructions. Recall that in fixed-role therapy the client adopts the identity of a fictitious person and, by trying out that role in various social settings, may come to experience some change in personal constructs. However, it is not the actions of others that shape behavior—it is one's view or interpretation of events.

On the final dimension for a conception of humanity—*uniqueness vs. similarities*—Kelly's emphasis was on the uniqueness of personality. This emphasis, however, is tempered by his commonality corollary, which assumes that people from the same sociocultural background tend to have had the same kinds of experience and therefore construe events similarly. Nevertheless, Kelly holds that it is our individual interpretation of events that counts and that no two persons ever have precisely the same personal constructs.

CRITIQUE OF KELLY

Kelly's personal construct theory is like no other personality theory discussed in this book. We have included it with the humanistic theories only because it is less antagonistic to the humanistic perspective than to any of the other major views. On the surface, Kelly's theory seems to be remarkably open-minded. He repeatedly states that all theories, including his own, should be open to reconstruction. Basic to his theory is his insistence that events can always be construed differently. There are alternative ways of looking at things. Contrary to this broadminded stance, however, is Kelly's lack of toleration for existing theories. As Holland (1970) pointed out, Kelly frequently attacked Freudian theory, behavior theories, cognitive theories, existentialism, and phenomenology. He seems to have been rather nonacceptant of these constructive alternatives.

Most of Kelly's professional career was spent working with relatively normal, intelligent college students. Understandably, his theory seems most applicable to such people. He makes no attempt to elucidate early childhood experiences (as did Freud) or maturity and old age (as did Erikson). To him, people live solely in the present, with one eye always on the future. This view, while somewhat optimistic, fails to account for developmental and cultural influences on personality.

How does his theory rate on the five criteria of a useful theory? First, does it *organize knowledge* about human behavior? On this criterion, personal construct theory must be rated very low. Kelly's avoidance of the problems of motivation, developmental influences, and cultural forces limits his theory's ability to give meaning to much of what is currently known about the complexity of personality.

Second, has personal construct theory *generated research* in significant amounts? On this criterion, Kelly would be rated a little higher. The Rep Test and the repertory grid have generated some research, especially in Great Britain, but these instruments are not used much by psychologists in the United States.

Despite the relative parsimony of Kelly's basic postulate and 11 supporting corollaries, the theory does not easily lend itself to the formation of testable hypotheses. Therefore, little research is currently being conducted on specific hypotheses drawn from personal construct theory.

The theory also falls short as a *guide to action*. Kelly's ideas on psychotherapy are rather innovative and suggest to the practitioner some interesting techniques. Playing the role of a fictitious person, someone the client would like to know, is indeed an unusual and practical approach to therapy. Kelly relied heavily on "common sense" in this therapeutic practice and what worked for him might not work for someone else. That would be quite acceptable to Kelly, however, because he viewed therapy as a scientific experiment. The therapist is like a scientist, using imagination to test a variety of hypotheses, that is, to try out new techniques and to explore alternate ways of looking at things. Nevertheless, Kelly's personality theory offers few specific suggestions to parents, therapists, researchers, and others who are trying to understand human behavior.

Fourth, is the theory *internally consistent,* with a set of operationally defined terms? On the first part of this question, personal construct theory rates very high. Kelly was exceptionally careful in choosing terms and concepts to explain his fundamental postulate and the 11 corollaries. His language, though frequently difficult, is both elegant and precise. Although *The Psychology of Personal Constructs* (Kelly, 1955) contains over 1200 pages, the entire theory is pieced together like a finely woven fabric. Kelly always seems to have been aware of what he had already said and what he was going to say.

On the second half of this criterion, Kelly's theory falls short. Like most theorists discussed in this book, Kelly did not define his terms operationally. However, he was exemplary in writing comprehensive and exacting definitions of nearly all terms used in the basic postulate and supporting corollaries.

Finally, is the theory *parsimonious?* Despite the length of Kelly's two-volume book, the theory of personal constructs is exceptionally straightforward and economical. The basic theory is stated in one fundamental postulate and then elaborated by means of 11 corollaries. All other concepts and assumptions can be easily related to this relatively simple structure.

CHAPTER SUMMARY

According to Kelly, our personality is shaped by our idiosyncratic interpretation of events. Although the outside world is real, it does not directly influence our behavior. Instead, our actions are guided by the way we anticipate events, and we anticipate events by our *personal constructs,* that is, the meanings or interpretations we place on our experience.

Kelly sees people as scientists, asking questions, testing hypotheses, formulating theories, asking additional questions, and making interpretations.

Basic to Kelly's theory is the idea of *constructive alternativism,* that is, the notion that our present interpretations are subject to change.

Kelly's theory can be summarized in his one fundamental postulate and 11 supporting corollaries. His *basic postulate* assumes that all our psychological processes are directed by the ways in which we anticipate events.

The 11 corollaries derive from and elaborate the one fundamental postulate.

1. *Construction Corollary.* We anticipate future events according to our interpretations of recurrent themes.
2. *Individuality Corollary.* People have different experiences and therefore construe events in different ways.
3. *Organization Corollary.* We organize our personal constructs in a hierarchical system, with some constructs in superordinate positions and others subordinate to them. This organization allows us to minimize incompatible constructs.
4. *Dichotomy Corollary.* All personal constructs are dichotomous, that is, we construe events in an either/or manner.
5. *Choice Corollary.* We choose the alternative in a dichotomized construct that we see as extending our range of future choices.
6. *Range Corollary.* Constructs are limited to a particular range of convenience, that is, they are not relevant to all situations.
7. *Experience Corollary.* We continually revise our personal constructs as the result of experience.
8. *Modulation Corollary.* Not all new experiences lead to a revision of personal constructs. To the extent that constructs are permeable they are subject to change through experience. Concrete or impermeable constructs resist modification regardless of our experience.
9. *Fragmentation Corollary.* Our behavior is sometimes inconsistent because our construct system can readily admit incompatible elements.
10. *Commonality Corollary.* To the extent that we have had experiences similar to others, our personal constructs tend to be similar to the construction systems of those people.
11. *Sociality Corollary.* We communicate with others because we are able to construe their constructions. We not only observe the behavior of others but we interpret what that behavior means to them as well.

The application of Kelly's theory can be divided into (1) *abnormal development,* (2) *psychotherapy,* and (3) *the Role Construct Repertory (Rep) Test.*

In Kelly's view, unhealthy people are like incompetent scientists who test unreasonable hypotheses and refuse to modify their constructs in the light of contradictory evidence. They persist in using personal constructs that have repeatedly failed the test of validation.

Kelly's psychotherapeutic approach relies heavily on the clients' ability to actively participate with the therapist in restructuring their construct systems and making them more efficient predictors of future events. *Fixed-role therapy* calls for clients to act out predetermined roles continuously for a couple of weeks. The clients' peripheral and core roles may gradually change as significant others begin reacting differently to them.

The purpose of the *Rep Test* is to discover ways in which people construe important people in their lives.

Kelly has an optimistic view of humanity and sees people as forward-looking and ultimately in charge of their lives.

Unfortunately, personal construct theory falls short on the most crucial standards for a useful theory. Aside from the Rep Test, it has generated very little research, and its ability to organize knowledge is limited by Kelly's avoidance of developmental issues and his rejection of such concepts as learning and motivation.

Suggested Readings

KELLY, G. A. (1963). *A theory of personal constructs: The psychology of personal constructs.* New York: Norton.

This brief paperback contains the first three chapters of Kelly's *The psychology of personal constructs* (1955). These three chapters present the essence of Kelly's theory—constructive alternativism, the basic theory, and the nature of personal constructs.

KELLY, G. A. (1969). The autobiography of a theory. In B. Maher (Ed.), *Clinical psychology and personality: The selected papers of George Kelly* (pp. 46–65). New York: Wiley.

Perhaps the most interesting of all of Kelly's writings, this chapter combines personal glimpses with theoretical insights to produce the story of how personal construct theory came into being.

KELLY, G. A. (1970). A brief introduction to personal construct theory. In D. Bannister (Ed.), *Perspectives in personal construct theory* (pp. 1–29). London: Academic Press.

Written the year preceding Kelly's death, this chapter was originally intended as an introduction to a book Kelly never finished. It presents an updated but briefer version of his 1955 book.

LANDFIELD, A. W., & EPTING, F. R. (1987). *Personal construct psychology: clinical and personality assessment.* New York: Human Sciences Press.

Although intended mainly for the clinician, this book can be easily understood by students interested in the practical applications of personal construct theory.

MASLOW

16

Holistic-Dynamic Theory

When Julius was 39 years old his wife died, leaving him with two small children and a large farm. During the next dozen years Julius devoted much time to his daughters, while struggling to hold on to his farm during years of drought, grasshoppers, and low prices. Finally, after four consecutive years of losing money, he sold his farm and moved to town.

After a series of odd jobs, Julius, at age 58, found regular work with one of the local farmers. For another 20 years he drove a tractor, worked with cattle, fixed fences, repaired farm machinery, and performed dozens of other jobs required of a farm laborer.

At age 55, six years after his younger daughter had left home, Julius married again. Unlike many older widowers, he was not driven into marriage by loneliness or the need to have someone look after him. He had always been very independent and quite capable of caring for himself. He and Anna were married simply because they both wanted it.

Julius found pleasure in little things. He enjoyed his work on the farm and looked forward each morning to the day's activities. He worked long hours, six days a week during the spring and summer, but fewer hours the rest of the year. On Sunday, he often drove his pick-up truck to the farm to look after his employer's land, cattle, and fences. He never considered charging for his time, he simply enjoyed farming and ranching. Julius also enjoyed growing his own vegetables and flowers. He spent many hours of his free time in his garden, sometimes with Anna, sometimes alone. His appreciation for growth and change extended to his grandchildren whom he saw only a few times a year. He was greatly fond of them and took a keen interest in their academic, social, and emotional development. Julius was not well known by the people of his town. Except for church, he seldom attended social functions. His close friends were limited to his boss and his coworkers. The people who knew him well regarded him as no one special, simply a pleasant old man with a refreshing sense of humor and an optimistic attitude toward life. Abraham H. Maslow might have regarded him as self-actualizing.

OVERVIEW

The concept of self-actualization and the name Abe Maslow have been closely associated for nearly 40 years. While Maslow did not coin the term and is not the only personality theorist to use it, he has done more than any other psychologist to popularize the notion of self-actualization.

Maslow's theory of personality, however, goes far beyond a consideration of self-actualization. His **holistic-dynamic** theory holds that people are constantly being motivated by one need or another. Few of us ever reach self-actualization. Instead, we are motivated by lower level needs such as hunger, safety, love, and self-esteem. In addition, other dimensions of needs, namely, cognitive and aesthetic, help shape our behavior. Moreover, some of us are driven by neurotic needs to perpetuate the status quo rather than to move in the direction of psychological health or self-actualization.

Holistic-dynamic theory was, in part, built on concepts of earlier theories, but Maslow added new ideas of his own. He carefully selected those principles from Freud, Adler, Allport, the behaviorists, and others which were logically consistent with his own fresh, innovative theory and blended them together in one self-consistent package. The result has been a theory that is comprehensive, appealing, and quite useful to anyone trying to comprehend the complexities of human motivation.

Though often thought of as being the father of the *Third Force* in psychology (the first force is psychoanalysis and its modifications; the second is behaviorism), Maslow (1971) did not regard himself as either anti-Freudian or antibehavioristic. In fact, he perceived himself to be both a psychoanalyst and a behaviorist. He repudiated neither, seeing much of value in both of these earlier theories. However, he held that both had a limited view of humanity. Neither psychoanalysis nor behaviorism spent enough time studying the normal healthy person, such as Julius. Neither of the older theories gave humans enough credit for reaching toward higher values and goals. Only relatively recently, Maslow believed, has psychology in particular and science in general paid much attention to people's higher nature. Maslow (1970a) called this the "unnoticed revolution" and he found evidence for its existence in various scientific disciplines as well as in philosophy. Maslow believed that humans have a higher nature than was formerly thought and he spent the last years of his life trying to discover what it is like to achieve the ultimate in psychological health.

BIOGRAPHY OF ABRAHAM MASLOW

Abraham Harold Maslow was born on April 1, 1908, in Brooklyn, New York. The oldest of seven children, he was not especially close to either parent, but felt more affection toward his father, a Russian Jewish immigrant from Kiev. Toward his mother he felt hatred and deep-seated animosity, not only during his childhood, but until the day she died just a couple of years before Maslow's own death. His mother was a very religious woman who often threatened young Abe with punishment from God, and from her Maslow learned to hate and mistrust religion. Though never a practicing Jew, his felt the sting of anti-Semitism from a young age onward.

His feelings of persecution were not as intense as those of Freud, but, nevertheless, were probably somewhat exaggerated (Hoffman, 1988). Throughout early childhood Maslow was extremely lonely, shy, and depressed. He felt ugly and inferior and later described himself as being neurotic during this time (Wilson, 1972).

Possibly as a defense against the anti-Semitic attitudes of his classmates, he turned to books and scholarly pursuits. He spent little time at home, preferring either the company of a maternal uncle who lived nearby or the confines of the public library, where he spent many hours reading on a variety of subjects.

Being intellectually gifted, Maslow found some happiness during his four years at Boys High School in Brooklyn. At the same time he developed a close friendship with his cousin Will Maslow, an outgoing, socially oriented person. Through this relationship, Abe himself became more sociable. He now had the courage to get involved with school activities, and became editor of both the Latin and the physics magazines as well as a member of the chess team.

During Abe's childhood the Maslow family gradually rose from the slums to lower-middle-class respectability. In later years his three younger brothers became financially independent as owners of the Maslow Cooperage Corporation.

Maslow's father wanted him to be a lawyer and, while attending City College of New York, Maslow also enrolled in law school. However, he walked out of law classes one night leaving his books behind. Significantly, he felt that law dealt too much with evil people and was not sufficiently concerned with the good. His father, though initially disappointed, eventually accepted Abe's decision to quit law school (Hall, 1968).

Maslow was only a mediocre student at CCNY, and after three semesters, he transferred to Cornell University. There, too, his scholastic work was poor. His introductory psychology professor was Edward B. Titchener, a renowned pioneer in psychology who taught all his classes in full academic robes. Titchener's "bloodless" approach to psychology left Maslow cold and indifferent (Hoffman, 1988).

After one semester Maslow returned to City College, partly to be nearer his first cousin, Bertha Goodman. He loved Bertha in a distant, bashful sort of way, having never touched her nor expressed his feelings. Then, suddenly a fortuitous event changed his life. While visiting his Aunt Pearl (Bertha's mother), his cousin, Anna (Bertha's older sister), shoved Abe toward Bertha, saying, "For the love of Pete, kiss her, will ya!" (Hoffman, 1988, p. 29). He did, and to his surprise Bertha did not fight back. She kissed him, and from that time on his life became meaningful.

Abe and Bertha were married during Christmas recess, 1928, when he was 20 and she was 19. Maslow's parents stubbornly resisted the marriage fearing hereditary defects in any possible offspring. This resistance was ironic in light of the fact that Abe's parents themselves were first cousins and had had seven healthy children.

Maslow had earlier enrolled at the University of Wisconsin and, after their marriage, Bertha went west to join him. At Wisconsin, Maslow became interested in psychology and his grades showed a marked improvement. His life, by his own reckoning, began at this time (Hall, 1968). His marriage and his academic experiences at Wisconsin profoundly altered the course of his life.

As a student, Maslow was greatly influenced by two forces which, at first glance, seem far removed from the holistic and humanistic leanings that so strongly characterize his later works. The first of these was behaviorism. The influence of John B. Watson was strong on American campuses during the 1930s and Maslow became excited about the potential of behaviorism to remake the world. The second influence was Harry Harlow and his experiments with monkeys. Maslow not only worked in Harlow's laboratories, but made some important discoveries on dominance and sexual behavior among monkeys.

Though Maslow's later researches on self-actualizing people seem far removed from either behaviorism or experiments with monkeys, these two early experiences played an important role in the evolution of his thinking. For example, after studying the sexual behavior of monkeys, Maslow moved easily to the field of human sexuality and

made important contributions to that area several years before Kinsey's (Kinsey, Pomeroy, & Martin, 1948) landmark research appeared. The destruction wrought by World War II moved him to devote his life to the study of the best in human beings and his experiences gained from interviewing people on sexual behavior proved useful in interviewing healthy individuals.

Maslow's work with Harlow on the intelligence of monkeys led to his first publication while he was still an undergraduate. Seeing his name in print captivated him and served as motivation to do more. It was at this time that he became enthusiastically interested in psychology as a profession as well as a science. This early training as an experimental psychologist proved to be valuable throughout the remainder of his life. Though sometimes seen by others as somewhat of a philosopher, Maslow always regarded himself as a scientist, albeit a scientist who scouts out ahead, freely speculates, then leaves to others the task of systematically testing his hypotheses.

After receiving his Ph.D. from Wisconsin in 1934, he could not find an academic position due in part to the Great Depression and to anti-Semitic prejudice still strong on American campuses in those years. Consequently, he continued to teach at Wisconsin for a short time and even enrolled in medical school there. Medical school bored him and he felt that, like law school, it reflected a dispassionate and negative view of people. Whenever Maslow became bored with something he usually quit it and medical school was no exception.

In 1935 he returned to New York to become E. L. Thorndike's research assistant at Teacher's College, Columbia University. Because Maslow scored 195 on an intelligence test, Thorndike, demonstrating confidence in both Maslow and his own test, gave Maslow free reign to do as he wished. This was precisely the situation in which Maslow's fertile mind thrived. After a year and a half of doing research on human sexuality, however, he left Columbia to join the faculty of Brooklyn College.

Living in New York during the 1930s and 1940s afforded Maslow an opportunity to come into contact with many of the European psychologists who had escaped Nazi rule. Among others he met Erich Fromm, Karen Horney, Max Wertheimer, Kurt Goldstein, and Ruth Benedict, an anthropologist. Maslow was influenced by each of these as well as by Alfred Adler, who was living in New York at that time. Adler held seminars in his home on Friday nights and Maslow was a frequent visitor to these sessions, as was Julian Rotter (see Chapter 11). In a personal letter to Frank Goble, Maslow wrote:

> I think it's fair to say that I have had the best teachers, both formal and informal, of any person who ever lived, just because of being in New York City when the cream of

European intellect was migrating away from Hitler. . . . I learned from all of them. . . . So I could not be said to be a Goldsteinian nor a Frommian nor an Adlerian or whatever. I never accepted any of the invitations to join any of these parochial and sectarian organizations. I learned from all them and refused to close any doors (Goble, 1970, pp. 11–12).

While at Brooklyn College, Maslow taught a full load, conducted research, and did personal counseling with the young, precocious students whom he greatly admired. At the same time he underwent a partial psychoanalysis with Emil Oberholzer, a New York psychiatrist. Despite this and later psychoanalytic treatments, Maslow never lost his hatred for his mother and even refused to attend her funeral.

During the mid-1940s Maslow's health began to deteriorate. In 1946, at age 38, he suffered a strange illness that left him weak, faint, and "barely able to stand for more than a few minutes at a time" (Hoffman, 1988, p. 176). In 1947 he took a medical leave and, with Bertha and their two daughters, moved to Pleasanton, California, where, in name, he was plant manager of a branch of the Maslow Cooperage Corporation. His light work schedule enabled him to read biographies and histories in a search for information on self-actualizing people. By 1949 his health had improved and he went back to teaching at Brooklyn College.

In 1951 Maslow took a position as chairman of the psychology department at the recently established Brandeis University in Waltham, Massachusetts. It was during his Brandeis years that his name emerged as the leading figure of the Third Force in psychology. It was also during this time that he began writing extensively in his journals. Beginning in 1959 and continuing until a month before his death, Maslow wrote down at irregular intervals his thoughts, opinions, and feelings. Also included in these semiautobiographical diaries are his social activities, important conversations, and concerns over his health (Maslow, 1979).

Despite his achievement of fame, the decade of the 1960s was not always easy for him. He became increasingly disenchanted with students and faculty at Brandeis. Some students rebelled against his teaching methods, demanding more experiential involvement and less of an intellectual and scientific approach. In addition Maslow suffered a severe but nonfatal heart attack in December of 1967. He then learned that his strange malady more than 20 years earlier had been an undiagnosed heart attack.

In poor health and disappointed with the academic atmosphere at Brandeis, Maslow accepted W. P. Laughlin's offer to join the Saga Administrative Corporation in Menlo Park, California. Maslow had no particular job there and was free to think and write as he wished. He enjoyed the freedom, but on June 8, 1970, while slowly jogging, he suddenly collapsed and died of a massive heart attack. He was 62.

Maslow's professional career can be roughly divided into four periods. The early phase, including the period from 1933 until December 7, 1941, was marked by his experiments with monkeys, his studies on dominance, and his research on sexual behavior in females. The attack on Pearl Harbor and the subsequent entry of the United States into World War II profoundly altered Maslow's life. From that moment, he realized that the problems of war and peace could only be understood by the study of human motivation. In an interview with Mary Hall he said, "I wanted to prove that human beings are capable of something grander than war and prejudice and hatred" (Hall, 1968, p. 54). This second phase of his career, however, was not formally recognized until July of 1943, when he published his theory of human motivation (Maslow, 1943). This article, which has been reprinted dozens of times, is important because it contains Maslow's original formulation of the famous hierarchy of needs concept.

The third period of his life began in 1950 with his publication "Self-actualizing people: A study of psychological health" (Maslow, 1950). This work was a milestone in Maslow's career, elevating him to a position of prominence among the humanistic psychologists. Finally, toward the end of his life, Maslow spent increasing time on the study of peak experiences. This topic, of course, grew out of the studies on self-actualization, just as those latter studies evolved from the concept of a hierarchy of needs. The four phases in Maslow's life represent a movement from objective psychology toward a more and more subjective approach; from experimental details toward more and more philosophical speculation. They also demonstrate his life-long tendency as a scientist to jump from one problem to another. Reaching out to the edges of psychology was a favorite pleasure of his.

Maslow received many honors during his lifetime, including his election to the presidency of the American Psychological Association for the year 1967–68. At the time of his death he was well known, not only within the profession of psychology, but among educated people generally, particularly in business management, marketing, theology, counseling, education, nursing, and other health-related fields.

Maslow's personal life was filled with pain, both physical and psychological. As an adolescent he was terribly shy, unhappy, isolated, and self-rejecting. His love for Bertha made him miserable because he didn't know how to act or what Bertha felt toward him. Those problems were solved by his marriage, but he continued to be painfully shy. He was terrified of public speaking and was past 50 before he was able to overcome some of his stage fright. He never overcame the intense hatred of his mother. In 1969 he wrote in his journal these thoughts concerning his mother.

What I had reacted against and totally hated and rejected was not only her physical appearance, but also her values and world view, her stinginess, her total selfishness, her lack of love for anyone else in the world, even her own husband and children . . . her assumption that anyone was wrong who disagreed with her, her lack of concern for her grandchildren, her lack of friends, her sloppiness and dirtiness, her lack of family feeling for her own parents and siblings. . . . I've always wondered where my Utopianism, ethical stress, humanism, stress on kindness, love, friendship, and all the rest came from. I knew certainly of the direct consequences of having no mother-love. But the whole thrust of my life-philosophy and all my research and theorizing also has its roots in a hatred for and revulsion against everything she stood for (Maslow, 1979, p. 958).

Maslow's physical health was never robust, and he suffered from a series of ailments, including chronic fatigue, hypoglycemia, an arthritic hip, and chronic heart problems. His journals (Maslow, 1979) are sprinkled with references to ill health. In his last journal entry (May 7, 1970, one month before his death) he complained about people expecting him to be a courageous leader and spokesperson. He wrote: "I am not temperamentally 'courageous.' My courage is really an *overcoming* of all sorts of inhibitions, politeness, gentleness, timidities—and it always cost me a lot in fatigue, tension, apprehension, bad sleep" (Maslow, 1979, p. 1307).

MOTIVATION

The basis of Maslow's theory of personality rests on his view of motivation. An appreciation of his most famous concept—self-actualization—depends on some understanding of several basic assumptions regarding motivation.

First, Maslow (1970a) adopted a holistic approach to motivation, repeatedly pointing out that the whole person, not any single part or function, is motivated. For example, it is not just the genitals that are motivated during sexual intercourse, but also the brain, the intestines, the self-concept, the entire organism. Similarly, every motivation involves the whole person and must be considered in the context of the complete personality. Any attempt to isolate a drive or to study a motive apart from the whole person is inaccurate and incomplete.

Second, motivation is usually complex. Surface behavior is often an expression of a hidden basic need. For example, the desire to use a telephone may actually be an expression of the need for love or belongingness. Complexity of motivation is often due to the unconscious components of drives. One important way in which Maslow differed from Allport was in his emphasis on unconscious motivation. While Allport might say that one plays golf "just for the fun of it," Maslow would look beneath the surface for hidden and often complex reasons for playing.

A third assumption is that people are continually motivated by one need or another. When one need is satisfied it ordinarily loses its motivational power and is replaced by another one. For example, so long as one's hunger needs are frustrated the person will strive for food, but whenever enough food is received the person will then become motivated to secure shelter, to cultivate companionship, or to satisfy some other need.

Another assumption is that all people everywhere are motivated by the same basic needs or desires. The *manner* in which people in different cultures obtain food, build shelter, express friendship, and so forth may vary widely, but the fundamental needs for food, safety, and friendship are common to the entire species.

A final assumption concerning motivation is that needs can be arranged on a hierarchy (Maslow, 1943, 1970a).

Hierarchy of Needs

The basic idea behind Maslow's hierarchy of needs concept is that basic lower level needs must be satisfied or relatively satisfied before higher level needs become motivators. Needs can be arranged on a hierarchy or staircase, with each ascending step representing a higher need, but one less basic to survival (see Figure 16.1). The hierarchy of needs is also referred to as the theory of prepotent needs. Lower level needs have prepotency over higher level needs; that is, when they are frustrated the person will stop striving (at least temporarily) for the higher need and will return to the unsatisfied lower

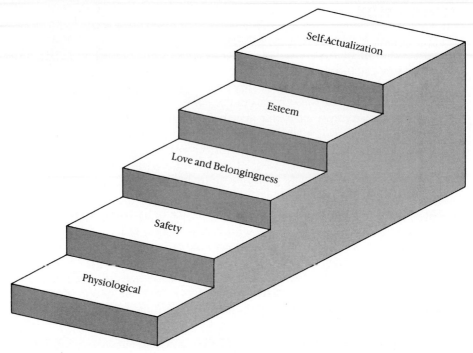

Figure 16.1   Maslow's Hierarchy of Needs. One must reach self-actualization one step at a time.

need. For example, an artist at work in his studio may be satisfying an esteem or self-actualization need (higher level needs), but eventually he will become hungry and leave his work to find food (a lower level need). Hunger, then, has prepotency over esteem or self-actualization.

Maslow (1970a) listed the following needs in order of their prepotency: physiological, safety, love and belongingness, esteem, and self-actualization.

Physiological Needs

The most basic needs of any person are physiological, including food, water, oxygen, maintenance of body temperature, and so on. Physiological needs are the most prepotent of all. Hungry people are motivated to eat, not to make friends or gain self-esteem. They do not see beyond food, and so long as this need remains unsatisfied, their primary motivation is to obtain something to eat. Perpetually hungry people come to believe that food is the ultimate goal. They delude themselves with the belief that if only they can get enough to eat, they will be forever happy.

In advanced societies most people satisfy their hunger needs as a matter of course. They usually have enough to eat so that when they say they are hungry they are really speaking of appetites, not hunger. A truly hungry person will not be overly particular about taste, smell, temperature, or the texture of the food.

Maslow (1970a, p. 38) said; "It is quite true that man lives by bread alone—when there is no bread." When people do not have their physiological needs satisfied they live primarily for those needs and their constant motivation is to satisfy them. Starving prisoners in concentration camps have been known to be preoccupied with food, plotting to obtain it, creating new recipes in their minds, and even dreaming of it nightly.

Physiological needs differ from other needs in at least two important respects. First, they are the only needs that can be completely satisfied or even overly satisfied. One can get enough to eat so that food completely loses its motivational power. For someone who has just finished a large meal, the thought of more food can have a nauseating effect. A second characteristic peculiar to physiological needs is their recurring nature. After we have eaten we will eventually become hungry again; we constantly need to replenish our water supply; and one breath of air must be followed by another. Other level needs do not constantly recur. Once love and esteem needs are relatively met they remain satisfied, but physiological needs continually reappear.

Safety Needs

When one's physiological needs are satisfied or relatively well satisfied, then the person becomes motivated by needs for safety. These include physical security, stability, dependency, protection, and freedom from such threatening forces as illness, fear, anxiety, danger, and chaos. The need for law, order, and structure are also safety needs (Maslow, 1970a).

Safety needs differ from physiological needs in that they cannot be overly satiated; one can never have too much safety. Therefore, safety needs can never be completely satisfied as can physiological needs. If people fear atomic warfare, for example, they can live in a bomb shelter, but the ceiling may collapse or an earthquake may swallow them. One can never be completely protected from meteorites, fires, floods, or the dangerous acts of others.

In societies not at war most healthy adults have their safety needs relatively well satisfied most of the time. Therefore, safety needs are relatively unimportant. Children, however, are more often motivated by these needs, living with such threats as darkness, animals, strangers, and punishments from parents. Neurotic adults also feel relatively unsafe. Fears from childhood may irrationally persist so that neurotic adults act as if they were afraid of parental punishment. They imagine their physical well-being to be threatened and therefore constrict themselves to the safe and the familiar. They spend far more energy than do healthy people trying to satisfy safety needs, and when they are not successful in their attempts they suffer from what Maslow (1970a) called **basic anxiety.**

For anyone, the healthy as well as the unhealthy, safety needs become activated during emergency situations. Natural disasters, injury, accidents, and war cause safety needs to become active. At least during short periods of immediate danger higher level needs such as love, esteem, and self-actualization lose their potency and a person becomes motivated primarily by safety needs.

Love and Belongingness Needs

For most of us physiological and safety needs are fairly well satisfied and do not dominate our lives. Love and belongingness needs, however, are a different matter. Most of us get caught at this level and strive more or less constantly to be accepted and loved by other people (Maslow, 1970a).

Belongingness and love needs become motivators after physiological and safety needs are relatively well satisfied. These needs include the desire for friendship, the wish for a mate and children, the need to belong to a family, a club, a neighborhood, or a nation. It also includes some aspects of sex, human contact, and the need to both give and receive love.

Motivation for love is ordinarily strongest when the need is partially denied. People who have never received love, who have never been kissed or cuddled, can go for long periods without these things and not panic. The absence of love is taken for granted and eventually the need can become devalued. Conversely, people who have had love and belongingness needs adequately satisfied from early years also will not panic when denied love. Such persons have confidence that they are accepted by those who are important to them. Hence, when they are rejected by others they are not devastated by this rejection.

On the other hand, people who have tasted love only in small doses will be strongly motivated to seek satisfaction of love and belongingness needs. It seems, therefore, that the motivation for someone who has received only a small amount of love to gain affection and acceptance is stronger than for someone who has received either a healthy amount of love or none at all (Maslow, 1970a).

Without love, a child would not grow to psychological health. Adults, however, sometimes become proficient at disguising their need for love just as they may also be adept at hiding the fact that their safety is threatened. Adults who do not give and receive love often engage in self-defeating behavior. Some become cynical, cold, and calloused in interpersonal relationships, often pretending to be aloof from other people. They may give the appearance of self-sufficiency and independence, but in reality they have a strong need to be accepted and loved by other people. Other adults whose love needs remain largely unsatisfied adopt a more obvious method of trying to gain love. They undermine their own needs by striving too hard to obtain affection. Their constant supplications for acceptance and affection leave others suspicious, unfriendly, and impenetrable.

If people have had love needs gratified from childhood, they gain a feeling of esteem and may become self-actualizing adults. Once that level is reached, they are no longer dependent upon the continual love and acceptance of

Love and belongingness should be encouraged early in a child's relationship with the mother.

other people. They then become independent and can maintain feelings of esteem and continue to be self-actualizing even though scorned, rejected, and dismissed by other people. In other words, esteem and self-actualization are no longer dependent upon the satisfaction of love and belonging needs; that is, they are now functionally autonomous from the lower level needs that gave them birth.

Esteem Needs

To the extent that love and belongingness needs are satisfied people are free to pursue esteem needs. These needs include self-respect, confidence, competence, and the esteem of others (Maslow, 1970a).

There are two levels of esteem needs. The first is *reputation,* which is the perception of the prestige, recognition, or fame one has achieved in the eyes of other people; the second is *self-esteem,* defined as the person's own feelings of worth and confidence (Maslow, 1970a). In most cases, reputation must be satisfied before self-esteem, so that one's feelings of self-worth are somewhat dependent on the recognition that one is highly regarded by other people. However, once self-esteem is reached, it seems to exist independently of the need for recognition. In other words, people who have attained self-confidence and strong feelings of self-worth will retain positive feelings toward themselves even when being criticized, defamed, or deprecated by others. On the other hand, it appears to be nearly impossible to secure self-esteem unless people first perceive that they have gained approval in the eyes of others.

Once esteem needs are met, a person stands on the threshold of self-actualization, the highest need recognized by Maslow.

Self-Actualization Needs

When lower level needs are satisfied one proceeds more or less automatically to the next level. However, once esteem needs are met one does not always move to the level of self-actualization. Originally, Maslow assumed that self-actualization needs become potent whenever esteem needs have been met. However, during the 1960s he came to realize that many of the young students at Brandeis and other campuses around the country had all their basic needs gratified, including reputation and self-esteem, and yet they did not become self-actualizing (Frick, 1971, 1982; Maslow, 1967, 1971). Why some people step over the threshold from esteem to self-actualization and others do not is a matter of whether or not they embrace the **B-values** (B-values will be discussed later). Those who hold in high respect such values as truth, beauty, justice, and the other B-values become self-actualizing after their esteem needs are met, while those who do not embrace these values are frustrated in their self-actualization needs even though they have satisfied each of their other basic needs.

Self-actualization is the desire for self-fulfillment, to realize all of one's potentials, to become everything that one can, and to become creative in the full sense of the word (Maslow, 1970a). People who have reached the level of self-actualization become fully human, satisfying needs that others merely glimpse or never view at all. They are natural in the same sense that animals and infants are natural; that is, their basic human needs are allowed expression and are not hidden or suppressed by culture. (A more complete sketch of self-actualizing people will follow the present discussion of needs.)

The five needs comprising the foregoing hierarchy are **conative needs,** which Maslow often refers to as basic needs. There are, however, other needs, which are sometimes preconditions for the satisfaction of basic needs, but nevertheless they operate on a separate dimension. The first of these are **aesthetic needs** and the second are **cognitive needs.** In addition, there are **neurotic needs,** which tend to oppose basic needs and block psychological health.

Aesthetic Needs

Unlike conative needs, aesthetic needs are not universal, but at least some people in every culture seem to be motivated by the need for beauty and aesthetically pleasing experiences (Maslow, 1967). Historically, humanity has produced art for art's sake from the days of the cave dweller down to the present time.

People with strong aesthetic needs desire beautiful and orderly surroundings and when these needs are not met they become sick in the same way that frustration of basic needs leads to pathology. Healthy people prefer beauty to ugliness, and there is some evidence to suggest that people living in squalid, disorderly environments become physically and spiritually ill more often than those surrounded by beauty and harmony. However, cause and effect are difficult to determine.

There is some overlapping of needs and it is not always a simple matter to properly place a particular need. For example, the need for order and symmetry may be an aesthetic need, but it might also satisfy the conative need for safety. Then again, it could also satisfy cognitive needs, especially those involving mathematics and numbers (Maslow, 1970a).

Cognitive Needs

In addition to conative and aesthetic needs, people also possess a desire to know, to solve mysteries, to understand, and to be curious (Maslow, 1970a). These are the cognitive needs and, though they have an interdependence with conative ones, they belong to a different dimension. When cognitive needs are blocked, all other needs are threatened. Knowledge is necessary to satisfy each of the five conative needs. Physiological needs can be gratified by knowing the answer to the question, "Where is the food?" Safety needs require knowledge of how to build a shelter. Belongingness needs can be satisfied by impressing other people with one's knowledge. Self-esteem and reputation can only be attained if one has some knowledge and some level of self-confidence with that knowledge. Self-actualization depends on utilizing fully one's cognitive potentials, though self-actualizing people need not have outstanding inherent intellectual powers.

Thwarting cognitive needs results in pathology just as does the frustration of conative and aesthetic needs (Maslow, 1970a). Ignorance, dishonesty, and secrecy all frustrate our need to know and undermine our psychological health. We become sick, paranoid and depressed when we are consistently lied to, denied knowledge, or deprived of curiosity. Our physical health may suffer when our work does not challenge our intellectual capacities and we may become skeptical, disillusioned, and cynical when we do not hear the whole truth.

Besides having a synergic relationship with conative needs, cognitive needs have a separate existence. The need to know is important in itself and is not always specifically related to the satisfaction of another need. Knowledge brings with it the desire to know more, to theorize, to test hypotheses, or to find out how something works just for the satisfaction of knowing (Maslow, 1968b).

Neurotic Needs

The satisfaction of conative, aesthetic, and cognitive needs is basic to one's physical and psychological health; their frustration leads to some level of illness. On the other hand, there is a fourth category of needs that results only in stagnation and pathology, whether the needs are satisfied or not. These are called neurotic needs (Maslow, 1970a).

By definition, neurotic needs are nonproductive. They perpetuate an unhealthy style of life and have no value in the striving for self-actualization. Neurotic needs are usually reactive; that is, they serve as compensation for unsatisfied basic needs. When safety needs are not met, for example, a person may have a strong desire to hoard money or property. The hoarding drive is a neurotic need; it is worthless as a motivator toward health. When love and belongingness needs are not fulfilled, one may become overly aggressive and hostile toward others. Aggression and hostility are also neurotic needs.

Neurotic needs are distinguishable from basic needs in that their satisfaction does not foster health. As Maslow (1970a, p. 274) said:

> Giving a neurotic power seeker all the power he wants does not make him less neurotic, nor is it possible to satiate his neurotic need for power. However much he is fed he still remains hungry (because he's really looking for something else). It makes little difference for ultimate health whether a neurotic need be gratified or frustrated.

General Discussion of Needs

Maslow (1970a) estimated that the hypothetical average person has his or her needs satisfied to approximately these levels: physiological, 85 percent; safety, 70 percent; love and belongingness, 50 percent; esteem, 40 percent; and self-actualization, 10 percent. The more a lower level need is satisfied, the greater the emergence of the next level need. For example, if love needs are only 10 percent satisfied, esteem needs may not be active at all. But if love needs are 25 percent satisfied, esteem may emerge 5 percent as a need. If love is 75 percent satisfied, then esteem may emerge 50 percent, and so on. Needs, therefore, emerge gradually and a person may be simultaneously motivated by needs from two or more levels. For example, a self-actualizing person may be the honorary guest at a dinner given by close friends in a peaceful restaurant. The act of eating gratifies a physiological need, but at the same time safety, love, esteem, and self-actualization needs are also being satisfied.

Reversed Order of Needs

Even though the order of needs is generally the same, there are certain exceptions. For some people, the drive for creativity (a self-actualization need) may take precedence over safety and physiological needs. An enthusiastic artist may risk safety and health in order to complete an important work. The late sculptor Korczak Ziolkowski for years risked his life, endangered his health, and abandoned companionship to work on carving a mountain in the Black Hills into a monument to Crazy Horse, the Indian chief.

For other people esteem may come before love; or safety may be prepotent to food. Then, again, some seem to stop at one level and not proceed to the next. For example, people overwhelmed with despair may not aspire beyond the safety level. They may take no interest in possible friends, in prestige, or in creativity. Their safety needs may be adequately satisfied, but they lack the hope and courage to relate to other people. This situation, of course, is pathological and may be caused by lack of previous positive interpersonal relationships. They do not try the usual, neurotic techniques of satisfying love and belongingness needs; they are not overly aggressive to other people, but neither do they adopt the opposite, though equally self-defeating, approach of timidly withdrawing from others. Instead, they display no interest in people and seem to be truly unmotivated by love and belongingness needs (Maslow, 1970a).

Other examples of reversals might include martyrs who sacrifice physiological needs for a belief and heroes who risk their lives to save others. Maslow (1970a) believed that, ordinarily, people capable of martyrdom are those who have received gratification of basic needs from early life onward. On the other hand, some who have been greatly deprived as children build a frustration tolerance to starvation and danger and are also capable of sacrificing their lives for their beliefs.

Reversals, however, are sometimes more apparent than real. Some seemingly obvious deviations in the order of needs are not variations at all, as would be revealed by an understanding of the underlying unconscious motivation.

Unconscious Motivation

Unlike Allport, Maslow believed that motivation is more often unconscious than conscious. Most behavior has several causes and therefore serves to gratify needs on several levels. For example, the desire for a new car might represent the desire for respect, which, in turn, could be equivalent to the need for love. At the same time, safety and prestige needs are usually considered in the purchase of a new automobile.

Much surface behavior is, in reality, an expression of a more basic though often unconscious need. This can be observed frequently at the level of love and belongingness needs. When these needs are not met some persons engage in self-defeating behavior, but their actions may appear to be motivated by esteem or self-actualization needs. On the surface, they may disdain social contact and pretend not to care whether or not others accept them. They may boast about their accomplishments and possessions in an apparent move to satisfy competence and prestige needs. In reality, however, they are attempting an indirect approach to get people to like them, albeit an unsuccessful and self-defeating one.

Unmotivated Behavior

Maslow believed that all behavior has a cause, but that some behaviors are not motivated. In other words, not all determinants are motives. Some behavior is not caused by needs, but by other factors such as conditioned reflexes, maturation, or drugs. Motivation is limited to the striving for the satisfaction of some need. Much of what Maslow (1970a) called "expressive behavior" is unmotivated.

Expressive and Coping Behavior

Maslow (1970a) made a distinction between expressive behavior, which is often unmotivated, and coping behavior, which is always motivated and which serves the purpose of satisfying a need.

Expressive behavior is often an end in itself. It serves no other purpose than to be. It is often unconscious and usually takes place naturally and with little effort. Also, it is usually unlearned, spontaneous, and determined by forces within the person rather than the environment. Expressive behavior has no goals or aim, but is merely the person's mode of expression. It includes such behaviors as slouching, looking stupid, being relaxed, showing anger, and expressing joy. Expressive behavior need not be reinforced or rewarded in order for it to continue. For example, a frown, a blush, or a twinkle of the eye are not ordinarily specifically reinforced.

Expressive behaviors also include one's gait, gestures, voice, and smile (even while alone). A person, for example, may express a methodical, compulsive personality simply because he is what he is and not because of any need to do so. Other examples of expression include art, play, enjoyment, appreciation, wonder, awe, and excitement.

On the other hand, coping behavior is usually conscious, effortful, learned, and determined by the external environment. It involves the individual's attempts to cope with the environment, to secure food and shelter, to make friends, and to receive acceptance, appreciation, and prestige from others. Coping behavior serves some aim or goal (though not always conscious or known to the person) and is always motivated by some deficit need (Maslow, 1970a).

Deprivation of Needs

Lack of satisfaction of any of the basic needs leads to some kind of pathology. Deprivation of the physiological need results in fatigue, loss of energy, malnutrition, obsession with sex, and so on. Threat to safety leads to fear, insecurity, and dread. When love needs go unfulfilled the person becomes defensive, overly aggressive, or socially shy. Lack of esteem also results in illness. The person becomes doubtful of self-worth and ability, and suffers from self-depreciation and lack of confidence. Deprivation of self-actualization needs likewise leads to pathology, or more accurately, **metapathology.** Maslow (1967) defined metapathology as the absence of values, lack of fulfillment, and the loss of meaning in life. If the deprivation of basic needs leads to sickness, then their gratification leads to psychological health. In fact, the satisfaction of needs may be considered as the definition of health. Traditionally, many philosophers and even psychologists have held the opposite view; that is, health and happiness come from the renunciation of basic needs. For example, fasting and other forms of self-sacrifice are advocated by some as a means of self-control and spiritual growth. To Maslow (1967), however, self-actualization (the essence of psychological health) is characterized by full enjoyment of food, sex, and other sensuous pleasures.

Instinctoid Nature of Needs

Maslow (1970a) rejected the classical instinct theories of Freud and William McDougall, but he also refused to accept the newer, anti-instinct concepts of the behaviorist school of psychology. Instead, he proposed a middle position, which hypothesizes that some human needs are innately determined even though they can be modified by learning. These are called **instinctoid needs.** The criterion of separating instinctoid from noninstinctoid needs is the level of pathology upon frustration. The thwarting of instinctoid needs produces pathology; the frustration of other needs does not. For example, when people are denied sufficient love, they become sick and are blocked from achieving psychological health. Likewise, the frustration of physiological, safety, esteem, and self-actualization needs results in pathology. These needs therefore are instinctoid. On the other hand, the need to comb one's hair or to speak one's native tongue are learned and their frustration does not ordinarily produce illness. If persons become psychologically ill as the result of not being able to comb their hair or to speak their native language, then we know that the frustrated need is in reality a basic instinctoid need, perhaps love and belongingness or possibly esteem.

In addition to the fact that instinctoid needs produce pathology when frustrated, there is a second but related criterion for distinguishing them from noninstinctoid needs. Instinctoid needs are persistent and their satisfaction leads to psychological health; noninstinctoid needs are ususaly temporary and their satisfaction is not a prerequisite for health.

Instinctoid needs are basic and not learned on the basis of secondary reinforcement. Moreover, instinctoid behavior is species-specific and, therefore, animal instincts cannot be used as a model for their study. On the other hand, not all instinctoid needs are unchangeable. Some can be molded, inhibited, or altered by environmental influences. Because many instinctoid needs (for example, love) are weaker than cultural forces (for example, aggression in the form of crime or war), Maslow (1970a, p. 82) insisted that society should "protect the weak, subtle, and tender instinctoid needs if they are not to be overwhelmed by the tougher more powerful culture." Stated another way, even though instinctoid needs are basic unlearned drives, they can be changed and even destroyed by the more powerful forces of civilization. Hence, society would be well advised to seek ways in which its members can receive satisfaction not only for physiological and safety needs but for love, esteem, and self-actualization needs as well.

Comparison of Higher and Lower Needs

There are important similarities and differences between higher level needs (love, esteem, and self-actualization) and lower level needs (physiological and safety).

Higher needs are similar to lower ones in that they are all instinctoid. Love, esteem, and self-actualization are just as biological as thirst, sex, and hunger (Maslow, 1970a).

The differences between higher needs and lower ones are those of degree and not of kind. First, higher level needs are later on the phylogenetic or evolutionary scale. For instance, only humans (a relatively recent species) have the need for self-actualization. Also, higher needs appear later during the course of individual development; lower level needs must be cared for in infants and children before higher level needs become operative.

Another distinction between the levels is that higher level needs produce more happiness, more peak experiences, though satisfaction of lower level needs may produce a degree of pleasure. This hedonistic pleasure, however, is usually temporary and not comparable to the quality of happiness produced by the satisfaction of higher needs. Also, satisfaction of higher level needs is more subjectively desirable to those who have experienced both higher and lower level needs. In other words, for one who has reached the level of self-actualization, there is no motivation to return to a lower stage of development (Maslow, 1970a).

SELF-ACTUALIZATION

Maslow's devotion to the study of health rather than illness is most clearly visible in his research on self-actualizing people. His ideas on self-actualization began soon after he received his Ph.D., when he became puzzled as to why two of his teachers in New York City, Ruth Benedict and Max Wertheimer, were so different from average people. His love and admiration for each of these two unusual people led him to take notes describing fundamental characteristics of each. Soon it became clear to him that, though the two were different, a single pattern seemed to characterize their lives. He began to look for others who fit this pattern and found many. To him, these people represented the highest level of human development and he called that level "self-actualization."

Values of Self-Actualizers

Maslow held that self-actualizing people are motivated by the "external verities" or what he called **B-values.** These "Being" values are indicators of psychological health and are opposed to deficiency needs, which motivate nonself-actualizers. B-values are not needs in the same sense as food, shelter, or companionship. They are called "metaneeds"; that is, they are ultimate or the highest level needs. Maslow distinguished between ordinary need motivation and the motives of self-actualizing people, which he called **metamotivation.**

Metamotivation is characterized by expressive rather than coping behavior and is associated with the B-values. It differentiates self-actualizing people from those who are not. The concept of metamotivation was Maslow's tentative answer to the problem of why some people, who have their lower needs satisfied, are capable of giving and receiving love, and hence possess a great amount of confidence and self-esteem, and yet fail to pass over the threshold to self-actualization. Their lives are meaningless and lacking in B-values. Only those who live among the B-values are self-actualizing and they alone are capable of metamotivation.

Maslow identified 14 B-values, though the number is not important because ultimately all become one, or at least there is a high correlation among them. The values of self-actualizing people include *truth, goodness, beauty, wholeness or the transcendence of dichotomies, aliveness, unique-*

ness, perfection, completion, justice and order, simplicity, richness or total-ity, effortlessness, playfulness and humor, and self-sufficiency or autonomy (see Figure 16.2). These values distinguish self-actualizing people from those whose psychological growth is stunted after they reach esteem needs. Maslow (1971) hypothesized that when metaneeds are not met, we experi-ence illness, an existential sickness. We all have a holistic tendency to move toward completeness or totality and when this movement is thwarted we suf-fer feelings of inadequacy, disintegration, and unfulfillment. Absence of the B-values leads to pathology just as surely as lack of food results in malnutri-tion. When denied the truth we suffer from paranoia; when we live in ugly surroundings we become physically ill; without justice and order we expe-rience fear and anxiety; without playfulness and humor we become stale, rigid, and somber. Deprivation of any of the B-values results in metapathol-ogy, or the lack of a meaningful philosophy of life.

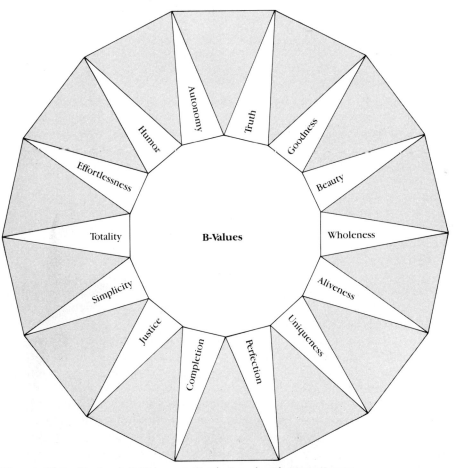

Figure 16.2 Maslow's B-Values: A Single Jewel with Many Facets

Definition and Description

Using research methods described later, Maslow (1970a) identified a self-actualizing syndrome while studying healthy people. These individuals, to a greater or lesser extent, possessed characteristics consistent with that syndrome. Finally, a pattern of self-actualization emerged. Maslow (1970a, p. 150) define self-actualization as the "full use and exploitation of talents, capacities, potentialities, etc."

In identifying self-actualizing people Maslow used both negative and positive criteria. First, these people must not be neurotic; they must not have psychopathic personalities, psychoses, or a tendency toward them. This is an important negative criterion because some neurotic and psychotic individuals have some things in common with self-actualizing people, namely such characteristics as a heightened sense of reality, mystical experiences, creativity, and detachment from other people. When any of Maslow's subjects showed definite signs of psychopathology (excepting some psychosomatic illnesses) they were eliminated from the list of possible self-actualizing people.

Second, self-actualizing people have progressed through the hierarchy of needs. Therefore, they live above the subsistence level of existence and have no ever-present threat to their safety. More importantly, they must have experienced love and have a well-rooted sense of self-worth and esteem. Because they have had lower level needs satisfied, self-actualizing people are better able to tolerate the frustration of these needs. Even when hungry, self-actualizing persons do not panic when food is not immediately available. They do not have the desperate need for money or security often found in people operating at the level of physiological and safety needs. Because they feel loved, they have no neurotic need to have everyone love them. They can tolerate rejection and their esteem remains intact even in the face of criticism and scorn. They are capable of loving a wider variety of people than are non-self-actualizing persons, but they do not feel an obligation to love everyone they meet.

The third criterion for self-actualization is the full realization of one's needs to grow, to develop, and to become more and more what one is capable of becoming. This, in essence, is Maslow's definition of self-actualization. However, in order to fully utilize their capacities, self-actualizing people must also embrace the B-values.

Julius, the farm laborer we introduced in our case study, seems to have met these criteria. He was free from psychopathology, had his lower level needs relatively well satisfied, and was motivated to use his talents and potentialities. In many ways he was childlike (but not childish). He was unpretentious, spontaneous, creative, and naive. He enjoyed work for its own sake, taking a keen interest in the various farm activities and performing many jobs with no expectation of pay. He approached work as if it were a game, something enjoyable for its own sake. As we will soon see, Julius had other characteristics of self-actualizing people.

Characteristics of Self-Actualizing People

Most people identified by Maslow as being self-actualizing were private individuals, not widely known to the general public. However, he did study some historical and several then-living public persons whom he regarded as being self-actualizing. These included Thomas Jefferson, Abraham Lincoln (in his later years), Albert Einstein, Jane Addams, William James, Albert Schweitzer, Aldous Huxley, Benedictus de Spinoza, and Eleanor Roosevelt, our case study in Chapter 3. What characteristics do these and other self-actualizing people tend to have in common? In his 1970 publication *Motivation and Personality,* Maslow listed 15 tentative qualities that characterize these people to at least some degree.

More Efficient Perception of Reality

Self-actualizing people can more easily detect phoniness in others. They can discriminate between the genuine and the fake not only in people but also in literature, art, and music. They are not fooled by façades and can see both positive and negative underlying traits in others, which are not readily apparent to most people. They perceive ultimate values more clearly than nonself-actualizing people and are less prejudiced and less likely to see the world as they wish it to be.

Related to this clear perception is the finding that self-actualizing people are less afraid and more comfortable with the unknown. They not only have a greater tolerance of ambiguity, they actively seek it. They feel comfortable with problems and puzzles that have no definite right or wrong solution. They welcome doubt, uncertainty, indefiniteness, and uncharted paths. These qualities make self-actualizing people particularly well suited to be philosophers, explorers, or scientists.

Julius was not a philosopher, an explorer, or a scientist; he had worked on a farm his entire life. Yet, in many ways, he possessed an efficient perception of reality. He had a knack for seeing solutions to the problems of construction and repairs frequently faced by farmers. Although not gifted as a mechanic or a carpenter, he could see better than others how parts could be successfully fit together. Also, he would usually be the first to realize that some problems had no solutions, while other people would have their perceptions clouded by wishful thinking.

Acceptance of Self, Others, and Nature

Self-actualizing people can accept themselves the way they are. They lack defensiveness, phoniness, and self-defeating guilt. They have good hearty animal appetites for food, sleep and sex. They are not overly critical of their own shortcomings and are not burdened by undue anxiety or shame. In similar fashion, they are accepting of others. They have no compelling need to instruct, inform, or convert. They can tolerate weaknesses in others and are not threatened by their strengths. They accept nature as it is. Also, they are accepting of human nature in general, not expecting perfection in either themselves or in others. They realize that people suffer, grow old and die.

While other farm people complained about the weather being too hot, too cold, too dry, and occasionally too wet, Julius always accepted weather conditions, knowing that he could not change them. He also accepted his own mortality. As an old man in his late seventies, he was heard to say, "Well, this will probably be my last winter." This was said without intent to draw out sympathy or protest; it was simply a matter-of-fact, realistic statement. (Incidentally, he first made that statement three years before he died, so he wasn't quite able to predict his own death.)

Spontaneity, Simplicity, and Naturalness

Self-actualizing people are natural, not artificial. They are unconventional, but not compulsively so. They are highly ethical, though at times they may appear to be unethical or nonconforming. They usually behave conventionally, either because the issue is not of great importance or out of deference to others. But when the situation warrants it, they can be unconventional and uncompromising even at the price of ostracism and censure. The similarity between self-actualizing people and children and animals is in their spontaneous and natural behavior. They ordinarily live simple lives in the sense that they have no need to erect a fancy but complex veneer designed to deceive the world. Julius was completely unpretentious. He was not afraid or ashamed to express his joy and awe toward a beautiful sunrise or sunset.

Problem-Centered

A fourth characteristic of self-actualizing people is their interest in problems outside themselves. Neurotics and, to a lesser extent, average people are self-centered, tending to see all the world's problems in relation to themselves. All conversation quickly leads back to self; any problem worthy of concern must be personal and emotional. Self-actualizing people, however, are task-oriented, ordinarily concerned with problems outside themselves. This interest allows them to develop a mission in life, a purpose for living that spreads beyond self-aggrandizement. Their occupation is not merely a job, a means to earning a living, but a vocation, a calling, an end in itself. As noted earlier, Julius frequently used his own time and transportation to look after cattle and crops that he did not own.

Self-actualizing people extend their frame of reference far beyond self. They are concerned with eternal problems and adopt a solid philosophical and ethical basis for handling these problems. They are not petty, but rather unconcerned with the trivial. Their realistic perception enables them to clearly distinguish between the important and the unimportant issues in life.

The Need for Privacy

Self-actualizing persons have a quality of detachment. They can be alone without being lonely. Unlike neurotics, who often have difficulty with interpersonal relations but yet must be surrounded by others, healthy individuals feel relaxed and comfortable either with people or when they are alone. They enjoy solitude and privacy and have no desperate need for others since their love and belongingness needs are already satisfied.

Unfortunately, this quality of detachment is not always understood or accepted by others. Self-actualizing people may be seen as aloof or uninterested, but, in fact, their uninterest is limited to minor matters. They have a global concern for the welfare of others without becoming entangled in minute and insignificant problems. Because they spend little energy attempting to impress others or trying to gain love and acceptance, they have more ability to make responsible choices. They are self-movers, resisting society's attempts to make them adhere to convention. Being alone was never a problem for Julius. He often spent up to 14 hours a day driving a tractor, isolated from the rest of the world and listening to nothing but the roar of the engine. But when the occasion called for him to work cooperatively with others, he always enjoyed that also.

Autonomy

A related characteristic is autonomy or the ability to be independent of culture and environment. Self-actualizing people depend on themselves for growth even though some time in the past they had to have received love and security from others. No one is born autonomous and therefore no one is completely independent of people. Autonomy can be achieved only through satisfactory relations with others. However the confidence that one is loved and accepted for what one is, without conditions or qualifications, can be a powerful force in contributing to feelings of self-worth. Once that confidence is attained the person no longer has a dependency on other people for self-esteem. Self-actualizing people have that confidence and therefore a large measure of autonomy. This independence allows them to be not only unperturbed by negative criticism but also unmoved by flattery. It gives them an inner peace and serenity not enjoyed by those who live for the approval of others.

When his first wife died, Julius had no desperate need to immediately remarry. He had loved his wife and enjoyed her companionship, but he was also quite capable of living without her. After his daughters married and left his home, he lived alone for six years without being lonely. Then, he married Anna because he wanted to, not because he was incapable of caring for himself.

Continued Freshness of Appreciation

Maslow (1970a, p. 163) said that "self-actualizing people have the wonderful capacity to appreciate again and again, freshly and naively, the basic goods of life, with awe, pleasure, wonder, and even ecstasy." The most intense of these feelings comes only occasionally, but they are experienced more often by healthy people than by others. Self-actualizers are constantly aware of their good fortune, health, friends, and political freedom. Unlike others who take their blessings for granted, healthy individuals see with a fresh vision such everyday phenomena as flowers, food, and friends. They have an appreciation of their possessions and do not waste time complaining about a boring, uninteresting existence.

The Peak Experience

As Maslow's study of self-actualizers continued, he made the unexpected discovery that many of his subjects had had experiences that were mystical in nature and which somehow gave them a feeling of transcendence. These so-called "peak experiences" are not experienced by all self-actualizing people, but they are far more common among them than among nonself-actualizers (see Box—"Peak Experiences: Those Mystical Moments of Transcendence"). These are not theological or supernatural experiences, though they are religious at their core (Maslow, 1970b). They are not all of equal intensity; some are only mildly felt, others moderately, and some are quite intensely experienced. In their mild form these peak experiences probably occur in everyone, though they are seldom noticed. For example, long-distance runners often report a sort of transcendence, a loss of self, or a feeling of being separated from their body. Sometimes during periods of intense pleasure or satisfaction, for example, the sexual orgasm, mystical or peak experiences are felt. Viewing a sunset or some other grandeur of nature may precipitate a peak experience, but these experiences cannot be brought on by an act of the will and sometimes they occur at unexpected, quite ordinary moments (Maslow, 1970a). Julius apparently was a "nonpeaker." He seemed to have had no comprehension of what was meant by the term "peak experience."

Gemeinschaftsgefühl

Self-actualizing people possess ***Gemeinschaftsgefühl,*** Adler's term for social interest or a feeling with humanity. Maslow found that his healthy subjects had a kind of brotherly attitude toward other people. Though they often feel like aliens in a foreign land, self-actualizers nevertheless identify with all others and have a geniune interest in helping people, strangers as well as friends.

Profound Interpersonal Relations

Related to *Gemeinschaftsgefühl* is a special quality of interpersonal relations that involves deep profound feelings for individuals. Self-actualizers have a big-brotherly feeling toward people in general, but their close friendships are limited to only a few. They have no neurotic need to be friends with everyone, but the few important interpersonal relationships they do have are quite deep and intense. For the most part, this level of depth and intensity limits the actualizer's partners to other very healthy people. Self-actualizing people do not have close interpersonal relations with dependent or neurotic people, though their social interest allows them to have a special feeling of empathy for less healthy persons.

We have seen that self-actualizers are often misunderstood and sometimes

Peak Experiences: Those Mystical Moments of Transcendence

What is it like to have a peak experience? Would you know whether or not you have ever had one? Maslow (1970b) described several guidelines that may help you answer this question. First, though peak experiences have a religious core, they are not supernatural events. They are quite natural and are part of our human makeup. Second, during the experience, the whole universe is seen as unified or all in one piece and people clearly see their place in that universe. Also, during this mystical time, peakers feel both more humble and more powerful at the same time. They feel passive, receptive, more desirous of listening, and more capable of hearing. Simultaneously, they feel more responsible for their activities and perceptions, more active, and more self-determined. Peakers experience a loss of fear, anxiety, and conflict. They become more loving, more accepting, more spontaneous, less an object, and less likely to want to get something practical from the experience. Peakers often report such emotions as awe, wonder, rapture, ecstasy, reverence, humility, and surrender. There is often a disorientation in time and space, with persons less conscious of self or ego, more unselfish, and more able to transcend everyday polarities. Also, the peak experience is unmotivated, nonstriving and nonwishing. At that time, the person experiences no needs, wants, or deficiencies and feels gratified in all things. In addition, Maslow says "the peak experience is seen only as beautiful, good, desirable, worthwhile, etc. and is never experienced as evil or undesirable" (Maslow, 1970b, p. 63). Maslow also believes that the peak experience often has a lasting effect on a person's life.

Since Maslow's original description, an increasing amount of literature has been devoted to the peak experience. Some of it has been supportive, some critical. Consistent with Maslow's hypothesis, Panzarella (1980) found that musically and artistically oriented people claim that a peak experience has had a lasting effect on their lives and has deepened their appreciation of music and art. At the same time, they describe these mystical moments as providing a sense of renewal and as producing an urge to be more creative.

Ravizza (1977) found that during peak experiences that accompanied participation in sports, athletes felt no fear, were totally immersed in the activity, experienced a temporary loss of ego, felt a unity with the experience and with the universe, and experienced a disorientation of time and space. Because the moment is experienced as perfect, they felt passive and saw their activity as effortless and described it in terms of awe, wonder, and ecstasy. However, contrary to Maslow, they did not see the experience as pivotal in their lives and generally gave it a narrower focus of attention than that described by Maslow.

Many writers have been critical of Maslow's notion of peak experience. For example, Blanchard (1969) claimed that the peak experience is not always pleasant and good, and that Maslow contaminated his results by asking his subjects for their "most wonderful experiences." Blanchard suggested that the peak experience is neither good nor bad, but rather the presence of creative possibility.

Rowan (1983) suggested that Maslow had a too narrow view of the peak experience. He identified seven separate and distinct mystical experiences, with Maslow's concept being only the first. Other mystical moments include the experience of a surge or flow of pure energy or power; the realization that one is in touch with the real self; being in contact with a higher spirit or higher self, such as a guardian angel or spirit guide; experiencing the Deity as subject or substance, for example, talking with God, Allah, or Jehovah; and experiencing the Deity as process. This latter experience may also be negative or evil, as when the Devil is experienced as process. For this to be a mystical moment, the person must realize that God or Devil is not a projection of the parents, but a separate entity. Finally, Rowan listed a seventh mystical experience that he admitted may be a level that does not even exist. He described this experience as a sense of falling into the Void or Ultimate, a sense "of being everything and nothing at the same time" (Rowan, 1983, p. 19). If you have been unable to identify with Maslow's description of the peak experience, perhaps you will have experienced one of these six mystical moments.

despised by others. On the other hand, many are greatly loved and attract a large group of admirers and even worshipers. This seems to be especially true for those who have made a special contribution to their business or professional fields. Those healthy people studied by Maslow (1970a) felt uneasy and embarrassed by this veneration, preferring instead relationships that were mutual rather than one-sided.

The Democratic Character Structure

Maslow found that all his subjects possessed democratic values; that is, they could be friendly and considerate with anyone regardless of class, color, age, or sex. Moreover, they had the ability to learn from anybody without adopting a superior or authoritarian attitude. In fact, they seemed to be less aware of superficial differences among people than were other people.

Each of the three previous characteristics was descriptive of Julius, at least to some extent. He seemed to have genuine feelings of empathy for people he saw on television who were starving or who had lost their homes to wars or natural disasters. He had few close friends among the townfolk, but he enjoyed the love of his wife, daughters, and grandchildren. He made no distinction among people based on social class, gender, or skin color. His employer was a friend, not a superior; his grandchildren were individuals, not inferiors.

Discrimination between Means and Ends

Self-actualizing people have a clear sense of right and wrong conduct. They have little conflict about basic values and do not confuse means and ends. They set their sights on ends rather than means and have an unusual ability to distinguish between the two. What is conventionally considered a means, for example, eating or exercise, may be, for self-actualizing people, an end in itself. They enjoy doing something for its own sake and not just because it is a means to some other end.

Philosophical Sense of Humor

Another distinguishing characteristic of self-actualizing people is their philosophical, nonhostile sense of humor. Most of what passes for humor or comedy is basically hostile or scatological. The laugh is usually at someone else's expense. Healthy persons see little humor in putdown jokes. They may poke fun at themselves, but not masochistically. They make fewer tries at humor than others, but their attempts serve a purpose beyond making people laugh. They amuse, inform, point out ambiguities, provoke a smile rather than a guffaw.

The humor of a self-actualizing person is intrinsic to the situation rather than contrived; it is spontaneous rather than planned. Because it is situation-dependent, it usually cannot be repeated. For those who demand examples of the philosophical sense of humor, disappointment is inevitable. A retelling of the incident almost invariably loses its original quality of amusement. One must "be there" to appreciate it.

Julius had a marvelous sense of humor. One example shows the nonsexual, nonaggressive nature of his humor. After he and his fellow workers looked long and hard for a particular wrench, Julius, upon finding it, quietly remarked, "Let's use this one until we can find the other one." The statement elicited no roaring laughter, but it was genuinely funny.

Creativeness

All self-actualizing subjects studied by Maslow were creative in some sense of the word. In fact, he suggested that creativity and self-actualization may be one and the same. This does not mean that all self-actualizers are talented or creative in the arts, but each one is creative in his or her own way. Each is unique in the conduct of interpersonal relationships; each brings a fresh approach to her or his job whether it be carpenter, teacher, homemaker, or lawyer. Each has a keen perception of truth, beauty, and reality—ingredients that form the foundation of true creativity (Maslow, 1970a).

The self-actualizing person need not be a poet or an artist to be creative. In speaking of his mother-in-law, whom he regarded as self-actualizing, Maslow vividly pointed out this fact. He said that while his mother-in-law had no special talents as a writer or artist, she was truly creative in preparing home-made soup. Maslow (1968a) remarked that first-rate soup was more creative than second-rate poetry any day!

In a similar, unspectacular manner, Julius was creative. His solution to problems were often innovative and refreshingly simple.

Resistance to Enculturation

A final characteristic identified by Maslow is resistance to enculturation. Self-actualizing people have a detachment from their surroundings and are able to transcend any particular culture. They are neither antisocial nor consciously nonconforming. Rather, they are autonomous, following their own standards of conduct and not blindly obeying the rules of others.

They do not waste energy fighting against insignificant customs and regulations of society. Such folkways as dress, hair style, and traffic laws are relatively arbitrary and unimportant and self-actualizing people do not make a conspicuous show of defying these conventions. Because they accept the conventional style and dress, they are not too different in appearance from anyone else. However, on important matters they can become strongly aroused to seek social change and to resist society's attempts to enculturate them. Self-actualizing people do not merely have different social mores, but, Maslow (1970a, p. 174) hypothesized, they are "less enculturated, less flattened out, less molded."

For this reason, these healthy people are more individualized and less homogenized than others. They are not alike. In fact, the term "self-actualization" means to become everything that one can become, to actualize or fulfill all one's potentials. When this is accomplished, people become more unique, more heterogeneous, and less shaped by a given culture (Maslow, 1970a).

This last characteristic does not seem to apply to Julius. His personal standards of conduct were congruent with those of his society and he had no history of fighting for social change.

Love, Sex, and Self-Actualization

Before people can become self-actualizing, love needs must be satisfied. It follows then that self-actualizing people are capable of both giving and receiving love and are no longer motivated by the kind of deficiency love (**D-love**) that characterizes people motivated by lower level needs. They are capable of **B-love,** which is love for the essence or "Being" of the other. B-love is mutually felt and shared. It is not motivated by a deficiency or incompleteness within the lover. In fact, it is unmotivated, expressive behavior. Self-actualizing people do not love because they expect something in return. They do not love because of weaknesses or shortcomings within the other person. For example, a self-actualizing mother would not say, "I must love my baby because he is so small and helpless." Then again, self-actualizing people do not love because of the strength, attractiveness, or power of the other person. They simply love and are loved. Their love is never harmful. It never creates anxiety, but rather reduces it. It is the kind of love that allows one to be oneself, to be relaxed, to be open and nonsecretive (Maslow, 1970a).

Self-actualizers are capable of a deeper level of love, and hence sex between two B-lovers often becomes a kind of mystical experience. Sex, or the thought of sexual intercourse, with one who is not loved seems to be unimportant and undesirable according to Maslow (1970a). Though they are lusty people, fully enjoying sex, food, and other sensuous pleasures, self-actualizers are not dominated by sex. They can more easily tolerate the absence of sex (as well as other basic needs) because they have no deficiency need for it. Sexual activity between B-lovers is not always a heightened emotional experience. Sometimes it is taken quite lightly, in the spirit of playfulness and humor. But this is to be expected since playfulness and humor are B-values and, like the other B-values, they characterize all aspects of a self-actualizer's life, including sexual relationships.

ABNORMAL DEVELOPMENT

According to Maslow (1970a), everyone is born with a will toward health, a tendency to grow toward self-actualization. Failure of personal growth results in neurosis and abnormal development. Strictly considered, anything less than self-actualization is abnormal. That which is usually considered "normal" in psychology is merely descriptive of the majority. The average person falls short of full human potential and is therefore "abnormal." The normal human condition is health; the usual condition is somewhat less than that.

Maslow (1970a) rejected the medical model of illness and saw psychopathology as people's weak, clumsy way of groping toward psychological health. Neurotics are fearful and lacking in courage and are thus prevented from reaching toward self-actualization. But what causes some people to be blocked in their movement toward growth while others become more and more healthy? Conflict and frustration are not the answer. They do not inevitably produce pathology, though sometimes they do. Healthy people experience conflict and frustration, but they are not chronically thwarted in their strivings for basic needs. Conversely, severely neurotic individuals often give up hope and therefore feel no great conflict or frustration.

Growth toward normal healthy personality is blocked by an absence of basic need gratification. If one cannot provide for food and shelter, full potential growth cannot be reached. Most Americans, however, have physiological and safety needs relatively satisfied. The major obstacle is typically at the level of love and belongingness needs. Many people have difficulty giving and receiving love and developing a feeling of belongingness because, as children, they did not experience healthy parental love. Even when love needs are satisfied and the person gains self-esteem and confidence, self-actualization does not automatically follow (Maslow, 1970a).

One abnormal syndrome that blocks growth toward self-actualization is the **Jonah complex** or the fear of being one's best. It is characterized by attempts to run away from our destiny just as the biblical Jonah tried to escape from his fate. The Jonah complex, which is found in nearly everyone, represents a fear of success, a fear of being one's best, and a feeling of awesomeness in the presence of beauty and perfection (Maslow, 1971).

Why do people run away from greatness and self-fulfillment? Maslow offered the following rationale. First, the human body is simply not strong enough to endure the ecstasy of fulfillment for any length of time, just as peak experiences and sexual orgasms would be overly taxing if they lasted too

Can You Fake Self-Actualization?

Now that you have some information about Maslow and his list of characteristics found in the self-actualizing person, would it be possible for you to fake self-actualization? Since authenticity or naturalness is one of the characteristics of self-actualizing people, and since authenticity cannot be faked, the answer would appear to be "no."

There would, of course, be other difficulties as well. First one would need to have love and belongingness needs satisfied. If people do not like you and if you do not like people, it would be extremely difficult to maintain any pretense of love or affection. Another problem in simulating self-actualization involves the question, "What should I do; that is, how should I behave?" Though Maslow reported 15 generalized characteristics of self-actualizing people, he did not tell us much about how they specifically *behave*. Since, by definition, the concept means to actualize that self which one truly is, it follows that different self-actualizers would behave in different ways. In fact, it can be argued that there would be greater individual behavioral differences among self-actualizers than there would be among normal or neurotic people. For these reasons, then, it is safe to say that self-actualization per se cannot be faked.

A somewhat different, but related question, is: Can one fake the right answers on standardized intruments designed to measure self-actualization? The most widely used of these instruments is the **Personal Orientation Inventory** (Shostrom, 1974) and research indicates that the POI is extremely resistant to faking—unless one is familiar with Maslow's description of a self-actualizing person. Before looking at some of the literature, it might be interesting to point out that Maslow encouraged and approved the construction of the POI and when he filled out the inventory his scores were in the direction of self-actualization, but not nearly as high as self-actualized subjects (Shostrom, 1974).

In the POI Manual, Shostrom (1974) cites several studies in which subjects were asked to "fake good" or "make a favorable impression" in filling out the inventory. When subjects followed these instructions they generally scored lower (in the direction away from self-actualization) than they did when responding honestly to the statements. This, indeed, is an interesting finding. Why should subjects lower their scores when trying to look good? The answer lies in Maslow's concept of self-actualization. Statements that might be true for self-actualizers are not necessarily socially desirable and do not always conform to cultural standards. For example, the item "I must strive for perfection in everything I undertake" might seem like a desirable goal to someone trying to simulate self-actualization, but an actualizer probably would not feel the necessity to constantly strive for perfection. Since one of the characteristics of self-actualizing people is resistance to enculturation, it should not be surprising that attempts by naive subjects to make a good impression usually results in failure.

long. Therefore, the intense emotion which accompanies perfection and fulfillment carries with it a shattering sensation such as "this is too much," or "I can't stand it anymore" (Maslow, 1971).

A second explanation for the evasion of growth is the necessity of humility. Maslow (1971) reasoned that most of us have a private ambition to be great, to write a great novel, to be a movie star, to become a world famous scientist, and so on. However, when we compare ourselves with those who have accomplished greatness we are appalled by our own arrogance. "Who am I to think I could do as well as this great person?" As a defense against this grandiosity or "sinful pride" we lower our aspirations, feel stupid and humble, and adopt the self-defeating approach of running away from the realization of our full potentials (Maslow, 1971).

Maslow also suggested that the Jonah complex may be caused by the fact that the metaneeds—truth, beauty, justice, and the like—carry with them both an impulse toward, and a defense against, that need. For example, though we seek the truth we are simultaneously apprehensive about attaining it. The built-in responsibility that would accompany our knowing the truth creates anxiety and often makes it more comfortable to accept less than the complete truth. A parallel course applies to each of the other metaneeds. We seek excellence while belittling those who have achieved it; we love beauty but feel anxious around it; we secretly aspire to greatness, but we delight in seeing the mighty fall.

Though the Jonah complex stands out most sharply in neurotic people, nearly all of us have some timidity toward seeking perfection and greatness. We allow false humility to stifle creativity and thus prevent ourselves from becoming self-actualizing.

PSYCHOTHERAPY

Maslow's (1970a) approach to psychotherapy followed from his hierarchy of needs theory. Since physiological and safety needs are prepotent, they must be met before the needs for love, self-confidence, and self-actualization can become activated. It follows, then, that a starving person will not ordinarily be motivated to seek psychotherapy, but rather to obtain nourishment. Most who come for therapy have difficulty satisfying love and belongingness needs. Therefore, psychotherapy is largely an interpersonal process. Through a warm, loving interpersonal relationship with the therapist, the client gains satisfaction of love and belongingness needs and thereby acquires feelings of confidence and self-worth. A healthy interpersonal relationship between client and therapist is therefore the best psychological medicine. It gives the client the feeling of being worthy of love and acceptance and makes it easier for her or him to establish other healthy relationships outside therapy.

Even though some therapeutic growth takes place in any healthy human relationship, not all healthy people are automatically effective therapists. In addition to psychological health, a therapist needs intelligence, self-insight, and understanding as well as specific training in the modern techniques and tools of psychotherapy.

The aim of Maslovian therapy is to free the person from dependency on others so that the natural impulse toward growth and self-actualization can become active. Psychotherapy cannot be value-free, but must take into consideration the fact that everyone has an inherent tendency to move toward a better, more enriching condition, namely self-actualization. Therapists must be willing to admit that it is better for clients to gratify their needs than to have them thwarted; it is better to love and be loved than never to have experienced it; it is better to have self-respect than self-abhorrence; and self-actualization is to be valued over pathology and stagnation (Maslow, 1970a).

PHILOSOPHY OF SCIENCE

Traditional science, Maslow (1966) contended, has been too limited to properly study human personality. It does not help us understand people because its philosophy has been value-free and its methodology has been sterile and nonemotional. Maslow argued for a different philosophy of science, a humanistic, holistic approach that is not value-free and where the scientist *cares* about the subject studied. He agreed with Allport (see Chapter 14) that psychological science should stress the importance of idiographic procedures as opposed to nomothetic ones. Subjective reports should be favored over rigidly objective ones. People should be allowed to tell about themselves in a holistic fashion instead of the more orthodox approach that studies people in bits and pieces. Traditional psychology has dealt with sensations, intelligence, attitudes, stimuli, reflexes, test scores, and hypothetical constructs from an external point of view. It has not concerned itself much with the whole person as seen from that person's subjective view.

Maslow was critical of scientists who have **"desacralized"** science; that is, they have removed the emotion, joy, wonder, awe, and rapture from their study in order to purify and objectify it. There is no ritual or ceremony in orthodox science. Scientists should put values, emotion, and ritual back into their work. They must be creative in their pursuit of knowledge and not narrowly bound to traditional methodology. They must be willing to **"resacralize"** science or to instill it with human values, emotion, and ritual. Astronomers must not only study the stars, they must be awestruck by them; psychologists must not only study human personality, they must do so with enjoyment, excitement, wonder, and affection.

Maslow (1966) argued for a **Taoistic attitude** for psychology, one which is noninterfering, passive, and receptive. This new psychology would abolish prediction and control as the major goals of science and replace them with sheer fascination and the desire to release people from controls so that they can grow and become less predictable. The proper response to mystery, Maslow (1966) said, is not analysis but awe.

The new scientific psychologists must themselves be healthy people, free from blinding anxiety and excessive defensive behaviors. They must be able to tolerate ambiguity and uncertainty, be intuitive and nonrational, and be insightful and courageous enough to ask the right questions. They must also be willing to flounder, to be imprecise, to question their own procedures, and to take on the important problems of psychology. Maslow (1966) contended that there is no need to do well that which is not worth doing. Rather it is better to do poorly that which is important.

RESEARCH METHODS

In his study of self-actualizing people and peak experiences, Maslow employed research methods consistent with his philosophy of science. He began intuitively, often "skating on thin ice," then attempted to verify his hunches using idiographic and subjective methods. He often left to others the technical work of gathering evidence. His personal preference was to "scout out ahead," leaving one area when he grew tired of it and going on to explore new ones (Hall, 1968). This accounts for many shifts of interest through his career—from monkeys to dominance to human sexuality to hierarchy of needs to self-actualization, and finally to peak experiences.

Maslow's (1970a) approach to studying self-actualizing people was to begin by selecting from among friends, acquaintances, and public and historical persons those people who appeared to him to be healthy, strong, creative, saintly, and wise. In addition, he attempted to study 3000 college students, but found only one who was definitely self-actualizing. He later searched for relatively self-actualizing people, arbitrarily defined as the healthiest one percent of Brandeis University students. After selecting his original subjects on the basis of somewhat arbitrary and unscientific definitions, Maslow carefully studied these people so that a syndrome for psychological health could be established. Next, he refined the original definition and then reselected the subjects, retaining some, eliminating others, and adding new ones. Then the entire procedure was repeated with the second group. Further changes were made in the definition and criteria of self-actualization, and a third group of subjects was selected. This cyclical process was continued until Maslow was satisfied that he had refined a vague unscientific concept into a precise operational definition and that his study of self-actualization was indeed scientific.

Maslow's methods of investigation, however, are subject to severe criticism. In his study of self-actualizing people he selected subjects from among personal acquaintances, friends, and public and historical persons. Therefore, most of his subjects were from the middle and upper classes, highly intelligent, and well educated. No specific set of criteria is reported for classifying a person into the "highly probable," "fairly sure," or merely "possible" categories of self-actualization. In addition, several important questions concerning self-actualization are left unanswered by Maslow.

First, is self-actualization limited to the bright and highly intelligent? Are feeble minded people capable of full use of their capacities and talents? Maslow, in an interview with Willard Frick (1971), said that he did not know what self-actualization means in feeble-minded people.

A second question not fully answered involves the possibility of intentionally striving toward self-actualization. Can people consciously and willfully move themselves in the direction of high-level motivation? In the same interview, Maslow alluded to certain people who consciously set metamotivation as a goal. He said, however, that "they're doing it stupidly and inefficiently and incapably and they want it *now*" (Frick, 1971, p. 36).

Another question concerns replication, a critical ingredient in scientific methodology. Because no operational definition of self-actualization was presented and because sampling procedures were not adequately described other than the comment that "contacts were fortuitous" (Maslow, 1970a, p. 152), it would be difficult to repeat Maslow's original study and be certain that the same syndrome of self-actualization had been identified.

In addition, Daniels (1982) had criticized Maslow for not comparing his group of self-actualizers with a control group and for his failure to renounce earlier formulations of self-actualization as he continued to expand and reshape the concept. Consequently, Daniels claims, there exists an inconsistency between the earlier notion that self-actualization is rooted in biology and the later concept of self-actualization in terms of self-transcendence, metamotivation, and a spiritual phenomenon.

CONCEPT OF HUMANITY

In Maslow's view, people are not inherently evil, hostile, or destructive, but rather neutral or good. The basic needs that motivate us are not negative or pathological, but precisely those which ultimately result in positive growth and health. Human nature is structured in such a happy way that the basic needs are exactly what people desire most. For example, children first want food, then protection, love, praise, and finally self-fulfillment.

Though Maslow was generally optimistic and hopeful, he recognized that people are capable of great evil and destruction. Evil, however, stems from the frustration or thwarting of basic needs, not from the basic nature of people. When basic needs are not met, people may steal, cheat, lie, or kill. Maslow held that human perfection is not possible, but certain individuals are capable of far greater growth and improvement than is presently supposed. Society, too, can be improved though not perfected. Growth, both individually and culturally, is slow and painful, but it seems to be part of our evolutionary history.

Maslow (1970a, p. 70) insisted on the ultimate improvability of humans, but he also realized that "most men are doomed to wish for what they do not have." In other words, though all people have the potential for self-actualization, most will live out their lives struggling for food, safety, or love. Most societies, Maslow believed, stress these lower level needs and are therefore based on an invalid concept of humanity. Education and politics have failed to take into account the scientific fact that people are capable of self-actualization. Truth, love, beauty, and the like are instinctoid and are just as basic to our nature as hunger, sex, and aggression. All people have the potential to strive toward self-actualization just as they have the motivation to seek food and protection. Because Maslow held that basic needs are structured the same for everyone, but that people satisfy these needs at their own rate, his holistic-dynamic theory of personality can be seen as placing moderate emphasis on the dimension of *uniqueness vs. similarities.*

From both a historical and an individual point of view, we are an evolutionary animal. We are in the process of becoming more and more fully human, that is, more motivated by metaneeds. High-level needs exist, at least as potentiality, in everyone. Since people aim toward self-actualization, Maslow's view can be considered *teleological and purposive.*

Because Maslow's view of humanity is comprehensive, it is difficult to classify it on such dimensions as *determinism vs. free choice,* optimism vs. pessimism, conscious vs. unconscious, or biological vs. social determinants of personality. In general, the more a person is motivated by physiological and safety needs, the more one's behavior is determined by outside forces; the more self-actualizing one becomes, the more one is motivated by internal forces.

As noted earlier, Maslow was basically *optimistic,* but he was also realistic enough to recognize that most people never achieve self-actualization and their lives are not as fulfilling as they might have been under different circumstances.

On the dimension of *consciousness vs. unconscious,* Maslow held that self-actualizing people are ordinarily more aware than others of what they are doing and why. However, motivation is so complex that a person may be driven by several needs at the same time and even healthy people are not always fully aware of all the reasons underlying their behavior.

As for *biological vs. social influences,* Maslow would insist that this is a false dichotomy. Individuals are shaped by both biology and society and the two cannot be separated. Inadequate genetic endowment does not condemn a person to an unfulfilled life just as a poor environment does not preclude growth. When self-actualization is reached there is a wonderful synergy among the biological, social, and spiritual lives of the person. Self-actualizers receive more physical enjoyment from the sensuous pleasures; they experience deeper and richer interpersonal relationships; and they receive pleasure from spiritual qualities such as beauty, truth, goodness, justice, and perfection.

CRITIQUE OF MASLOW

A useful theory of personality must give organization to known observations, generate research, serve as a guide to action, have internal consistency, and be parsimonious. How does Maslow's theory rate on these five criteria?

First, much of what is known about human behavior can be conveniently organized within the hierarchy of needs framework. For this reason, Malsow's theory of personality is quite consistent with common sense. It seems reasonable that a person must have enough to eat before being motivated by other matters. Starving people care little about political philosophy. Their primary motivation is for food, not philosophical differences between one form of government or another. Because Maslow's theory provides a broad framework that may offer some explanations for almost all human motivation, it receives a very high rating on its ability to *give organization to known facts.*

A second criterion of a useful theory is that it must *generate research.* Maslow's personality theory is quite fruitful on this basis. Tenets of the theory suggest an almost unlimited number of testable hypotheses. A large body of research exists on Maslow's hierarchy of needs concept, and self-actualization remains one of the most frequently studied topics in psychology.

Does Maslow's theory serve as a *guide to the practitioner?* On this criterion, the theory must be rated as highly useful. A psychotherapist adhering to Maslow's theory knows that if a client's safety needs are perceived as threatened, as, for example, in paranoia, then attempts to enhance self-esteem are premature and the patient must first be provided with a safe and secure environment. Once physiological and safety needs are satisfied, the therapist must work to provide the patient with feelings of love and belongingness. This suggests a relationship in therapy similar to that proposed by Carl Rogers (see Chapter 17) and others.

Likewise, industrial managers can use Maslow's theory to motivate workers. They know that increases in pay can, at best, satisfy only physiological and safety needs and that, since these needs are already largely gratified by the average American worker, wage increases per se will not permanently increase worker morale and productivity. Only when pay raises are seen by the worker as recognition for a job well done do they satisfy a higher level need. In *The Human Side of Enterprise,* Douglas McGregor (1960) suggested that workers will produce more when their esteem and self-actualization needs are activated. This means that workers should be allowed to have more responsibility and freedom, their ingenuity and creativity in solving problems must be utilized, and they must be allowed to use their intelligence and imagination on the job. Maslow's theory should suggest to the industrial manager many techniques for motivating workers on the level of esteem and self-actualization.

Is the theory *internally consistent?* Unfortunately, Maslow's arcane and often unclear language makes important parts of his theory ambiguous and inconsistent. Apart from the problem of idiosyncratic language, however, Maslow's theory ranks high on the criterion of internal consistency. The hierarchy of needs follow a logical progression and are hypothesized to be the same for everyone, though the possibility of certain reversals is not overlooked. Maslow built his theory step by step largely on empirical and clinical observations. Though he often did not report his methodology in enough detail for accurate replication, he insisted that his data were based on scientifically obtained facts and that anyone else investigating the same phenomena would confirm his observations. Aside from these methodological weaknesses, his theory has a consistency and precision that give it popular appeal.

Is Maslow's theory *parsimonious* or does it contain superfluous fabricated concepts and models? At first glance the theory seems quite simplistic. A hierarchy of needs model with only five steps gives the theory a deceptive appearance of simplicity. A full understanding of Maslow's total theory, however, suggests a far more complex model. Overall, the theory receives a moderate rating on parsimony.

CHAPTER SUMMARY

Maslow's holistic-dynamic theory of personality is largely a theory of human motivation. It assumes that (1) the *whole person* is motivated, (2) motivation is *complex* and often *unconscious,* (3) people are *continually motivated* by one need or another, and (4) the *same basic needs* apply to all people.

Maslow recognized four major dimensions of needs: (1) the *conative needs;* (2) *cognitive needs,* including knowledge; (3) *aesthetic needs,* including love of beauty and order; and (4) *neurotic needs,* which produce neuroses whether or not they are satisfied.

The *conative needs* can be arranged on a hierarchy, meaning that one need must be relatively satisfied before the next one can become active. The most basic needs are *physiological,* including food, water, oxygen, and so forth. After physiological needs are satisfied, people are motivated to seek *safety.* Once safety needs are relatively satisfied, *love and belongingness needs* become motivators. The more people satisfy their needs for love, the greater their level of *self-esteem.* When esteem needs are adequately met, people will either remain on that level or cross the threshold to *self-actualization.*

Occasionally, needs on the hierarchy can be *reversed,* but ordinarily people from all cultures proceed in the same order through the hierarchy. *Unconscious motivation* frequently blurs one's view of the true need underlying a particular behavior.

All behavior has a cause, but not all behavior is motivated. *Coping behavior,* which stems from basic needs, is motivated; much of *expressive behavior* is not. Expressive behavior has no goal; it's simply our way of expressing ourselves.

Conative needs, including self-actualization, are *instinctoid,* that is, their deprivation leads to pathology. The frustration of self-actualization needs results in *metapathology.*

Self-actualizing people are motivated by the B-values. In fact, acceptance of B-values (truth, beauty, humor, etc.) is the criterion that separates self-actualizing people from those who are merely healthy, but mired at the level of self-esteem.

In addition, self-actualizers are characterized by (1) a more efficient perception of reality; (2) acceptance of self, others, and nature; (3) spontaneity, simplicity, and naturalness; (4) a problem-centered approach to life; (5) the need for privacy; (6) autonomy; (7) freshness of appreciation; (8) peak experiences, although not all actualizers are peakers; (9) social interest; (10) profound interpersonal relations; (11) a democratic attitude; (12) the ability to discriminate means from ends; (13)

a philosophical sense of humor; (14) creativeness; and (15) resistance to enculturation.

In addition, self-actualizers are capable of *B-love,* or love for the essence of another. Maslow also hypothesized that sex between two actualizers is both more mystical and more pleasurable.

Abnormal development is brought about by the frustration of basic needs, usually love and belongingness, but it could stem from the deprivation of any need. The *Jonah complex* is the fear of being or doing one's best. *Therapy* to rectify abnormal development should be directed at the need level currently being thwarted.

In his philosophy of science Maslow argued for a *Taoistic attitude,* one which is noninterfering, passive, receptive, and subjective. The subject matter of psychology must be viewed with joy, wonder, awe, and affection.

Maslow's own *research methods* followed a Taoistic approach, but he was less than careful in reporting his procedures. Replication of his studies on self-actualization would be extremely difficult.

Nevertheless, Maslow's holistic-dynamic theory is quite useful in organizing knowledge, generating research, and serving as a guide to the practitioner. Maslow's language is not always clear, but his theory is rated adequate on both internal consistency and parsimony.

Suggested Readings

FRICK, W. B. (1971). Interview with Dr. Abraham Maslow. In W. B. Frick, *Humanistic psychology: Interviews with Maslow, Murphy and Rogers* (pp. 18–49). Columbus, OH: Merrill.
  During the last years of his life Maslow granted many interviews. This one with Willard Frick is stimulating, comprehensive, and well organized.

HOFFMAN, E. (1988). *The right to be human: A biography of Abraham Maslow.* Los Angeles: Tarcher.
  Hoffman interviewed dozens of Maslow's family members, friends, and associates to write this fascinating biography of the father of the Third Force in psychology. The result is a very readable, informative, and comprehensive book.

MASLOW, A. H. (1970a). *Motivation and personality.* (2nd. ed.). New York: Harper & Row.
  Maslow's basic theory of motivation and self-actualization are presented. Required reading for anyone interested in Maslow's holistic-dynamic theory.

MASLOW, A. H. (1971). *The farther reaches of human nature.* New York: Viking Press.
  Published after his death, this work is an extension of Maslow's (1968b) *Toward a Psychology of Being.* Among other topics, Maslow discusses B-values, metamotivation, creativeness, and peak experiences.

Rogers

17

Person-Centered Theory

Mrs. Oak is miserable. Quarrels with her husband seem both endless and pointless. She is filled with self-doubts, despair, and hostility. She romanticizes the sexual aspects of her marital relationship, but does not enjoy the sex act and has some confusion over her sexual identity.

Mrs. Oak has not worked outside the home since her marriage and feels extremely dependent upon her husband. She is also deeply disturbed over her relationship with her teenage daughter, blaming herself for her daughter's recent serious illness. In fact, Mrs. Oak has a strong sense of duty toward others, but does little to make her own life more fulfilling.

She is a dependent, passive person who feels rejected both at home and in social groups. Lonely, unhappy, and without friends, she harbors deep resentment toward others, especially women. Although lacking in feelings of self-worth and self-confidence, she has high aspirations for some great achievement. Her daydreams of accomplishment occupy her time and prevent her from dealing realistically with daily problems. Actually, she has almost no self-generated goals, but allows others or "society" to determine her responsibilities. She resents these outside forces, not realizing that they are mostly of her own creation.

In her late thirties, feeling unattractive, guilty, frustrated, and generally miserable, Mrs. Oak decided to seek psychotherapy. Consequently, she entered the Counseling Center at the University of Chicago, received help, and, in turn, helped Carl Rogers better understand the process of personality change that seems to take place during client-centered therapy.

OVERVIEW

The process of growth experienced by Mrs. Oak and dozens of other people as a result of client-centered psychotherapy was studied in depth by a research team at the University of Chicago, and these studies helped lay the foundation for Rogers's person-centered theory of personality. Later in this chapter, we will look again at Mrs. Oak and chart her progress toward becoming what Rogers has called "a fully functioning person."

Though he is best known as the founder of client-centered therapy, Rogers also developed a theory of personality that grew out of his experiences as a practicing psychotherapist. Unlike Freud, who was primarily a theorist and secondarily a therapist, Rogers was a consummate therapist but only a reluctant theorist (Rogers, 1959). He was more concerned with helping people than in discovering why they behaved as they did. He was more likely to ask, "How can I help this other person grow and develop?" than he was to ponder the question "What caused this person to develop in this manner?"

Even though he formulated a rigorous internally consistent theory of personality, Rogers did not feel comfortable with theory. His personal preference was to be a helper of people and not a constructor of theories. To him, theories seemed to make things too cold and external and he worried that his theory might imply a measure of finality.

During the 1950s, at a midpoint in his career, Rogers was invited to write what was then called the "client-centered" theory of personality and his original statement is found in Volume 3 of Sigmund Koch's *Psychology: A Study of a Science* (see Rogers, 1959). Even at that time he realized that 10 or 20 years hence his theories would be different, but unfortunately, throughout the intervening years he never systematically reformulated his theory of personality. Even though subsequent experiences have altered those earlier ideas, his current theory of personality continues to stand on that original foundation.

BIOGRAPHY OF CARL ROGERS

Rogers was born on January 8, 1902, in Oak Park, Illinois, the fourth of six children born to Walter and Julia Cushing Rogers. Carl was closer to his mother than to his father who, during the early years, was often away from home working as a civil engineer. His father eventually became a successful businessman so that Rogers was truly a product of middle-class, midwestern America. Walter and Julia Rogers were both devoutly religious and Carl became interested in the Bible, reading from it and other books even as a preschool child.

As a child in Oak Park, Rogers attended school with Ernest Hemingway, who was two years older, and with the children of Frank Lloyd Wright, the great American architect. Carl was an excellent student, but also a dreamer who loved adventure books. Although from a large family, he was a loner and quite unsocial at school. Being a sensitive boy, he was easily hurt by teasing from classmates and siblings.

At the beginning of his high school years Carl moved with his family to a farm 25 miles west of Chicago. His father was not a farmer, but by this time was running a successful construction company. The move to the farm was intended by the parents to provide a more wholesome and religious atmosphere for the Rogers children. The house was more of a mansion than a farmhouse, with eight bedrooms, five baths, a tile roof, and a tennis court. In this environment young Carl developed a passionate interest in nature and adopted a scientific attitude toward farming, taking detailed notes of his observations of both plants and animals. This scientific attitude was to remain with him for a lifetime and his early interest in plants became a satisfying hobby in his later years.

Upon graduation from high school Rogers intended to become a farmer, and when he entered the University of Wisconsin in 1919 he selected agriculture as his major. During his freshman year at the university he made the first close friendships outside his family. That year also marked the beginning of a more intense interest in religion and a lessening of his desire to become a farmer.

By his third year at Wisconsin he was deeply involved with religious activities on campus and spent six months during his junior year traveling to the Orient to attend a student religious conference in China. The trip made a lasting impression on Rogers. The interaction with other young religious leaders changed him into a more liberal thinker and moved him toward independence from his parents' religious views. The experiences in the Orient with his fellow leaders gave him more self-confidence in social relationships; but he also returned from the journey with an ulcer. He spent a year recuperating by working on the farm and at a local lumberyard. After returning to Wisconsin, he joined a fraternity, displayed more self-confidence, and, in general, was a changed student from his pre-China days.

Rogers's early shyness had restricted his experiences with girls so that when he originally went to Wisconsin he had only enough courage to ask out a young lady whom he had known earlier in Oak Park. This woman turned out to be Helen Elliott, whom he married in 1924 at the age of 22. Carl and Helen had two children—David, born in 1926 and Natalie, born in 1928.

After their marriage Carl and Helen traveled to New York where Carl entered the Union Theological Seminary. While at the seminary, he enrolled in several psychology and education courses at neighboring Columbia University. He was influenced by the progressive education movement of John Dewey, which was then strong at Teachers College, Columbia. Gradually, he became disenchanted with the doctrinaire attitude of religious work. Even though Union Theological Seminary was quite liberal, Rogers decided that he did not wish to express a fixed set of beliefs, but desired more freedom to explore new ideas. Finally, in the fall of 1926 he crossed the street to attend Teachers College on a full-time basis with a major in clinical and educational psychology. From that point on he never returned to formal religion. His life would now take a new direction—toward psychology and education.

In 1927 he served as a Fellow at the new Institute for Child Guidance in New York City and continued to work there while completing his doctoral degree. At the institute he gained an elementary knowledge of Freudian psychoanalysis, but was not much influenced by it, even though he tried it out in his practice. At the institute he also attended a lecture by Alfred Adler who shocked Rogers and the other staff members with his contention that an elaborate case history was unnecessary for psychotherapy.

Rogers received his Ph.D. from Columbia in 1931, after having already moved to Rochester, New York, to work with the Rochester Society for the Prevention of Cruelty to Children. During this early phase of his professional career he was strongly influenced by the practice, but not the theory, of Otto Rank and his students. Rogers was mostly unconcerned then with theoretical formulations and gradually developed his own techniques for treating problem children. Not surprisingly, he had little awareness that his practice of psychotherapy was either unique or novel.

Rogers spent 12 years at Rochester working at a job that might easily have isolated him from a successful academic career. He had harbored a desire to teach in a university after a rewarding teaching experience during the summer of 1935 at Teachers College. Later he taught courses in sociology at the University of Rochester. It was during this period also that he wrote his first book, *The Clinical Treatment of the Problem Child* (1939), the publication of which led to a teaching offer from Ohio State University. Despite his fondness for teaching he might have turned down the offer if his wife had not urged him to accept and if the university had not agreed to start him at the top, with the academic

rank of full professor. In January 1940, at the age of 38, Rogers moved to Columbus to begin a new career.

Pressed by his graduate students at Ohio State, Rogers gradually conceptualized his own ideas on psychotherapy, not intending them to be unique and certainly not controversial. These ideas were put forth in his book *Counseling and Psychotherapy,* published in 1942. This work was a reaction to the older psychoanalytic and diagnostic approaches to therapy. He minimized causes of disturbances and the identification and labeling of disorders and, instead, emphasized the importance of growth within the patient (called by Rogers the "client").

In 1944, as part of the war effort, he took a leave from Ohio State to move back to New York as Director of Counseling Services for the United Services Organization. After one year he took a position at the University of Chicago, where he established a counseling center and was allowed more freedom to do research on the process and outcome of psychotherapy. The years 1945 to 1957 at Chicago were the most productive and creative of his career. His therapy evolved from one that emphasized methodology, or what in the early 1940s was called the "nondirective" technique, to one in which the sole emphasis was on the client/therapist relationship. Always the scientist, Rogers, along with his students and colleagues, produced the most original and sophisticated research on the process and effectiveness of psychotherapy published to that date. Mrs. Oak, our case study, was one of the subjects of that research.

Wanting to expand his research and his ideas to psychiatry, Rogers accepted a position at the University of Wisconsin in 1957. He was disappointed with his stay at Wisconsin because he was unable to unite the professions of psychiatry and psychology and because he felt there was dishonest and unethical behavior in his own research staff (Kirschenbaum, 1979). However, he did have an opportunity to influence both psychiatry and psychology and also to work with both normal and psychotic clients as opposed to the largely neurotic subjects he encountered at Chicago and Ohio State.

Rogers's next move was to California, where, in 1964, he joined the Western Behavioral Sciences Institute (WBSI). There he became increasingly interested in encounter groups and dealt less with individual therapy. He also became interested in expanding the "person-centered" approach to education and to larger social issues including politics and international affairs (Heppner, Rogers, & Lee, 1984; Rogers, 1982b). He resigned from WBSI when he felt it was becoming less democratic and, along with about 75 others from the institute, formed the Center for Studies of the Person. He continued to work with encounter groups, but extended his person-centered methods to education (including the training of physicians) and to international politics. During the last years of his life he led workshops in such countries as

Hungary, Brazil, South Africa, and the Soviet Union (Gendlin, 1988). He died on February 4, 1987, following surgery for a broken hip. At the time of his death he was still active at the Center for the Study of the Person.

The personal life of Carl Rogers was characterized by change and openness to experience. As a youth he was a shy loner with an active fantasy life which, he later believed, probably would have been diagnosed as "schizoid" (Rogers, 1980, p. 30). This socially inept youngster grew to become a leading proponent of the notion that the interpersonal relationship between two individuals is a powerful ingredient that cultivates psychological growth within both persons. The transition, however, was not easy. He abandoned the formalized religion of his parents, gradually shaping a humanistic, and then an existential, philosophy that he hoped would bridge the gap between Eastern and Western thought.

Rogers received many honors during his long professional life. He was the first president of the American Association for Applied Psychology and helped bring that organization and the American Psychological Association back together. He served as president of APA for the year 1946–1947 and served as first president of the American Academy of Psychotherapists. In 1956 he was cowinner, along with Kenneth Spence and Wolfgang Kohler, of the first Distinguished Scientific Contribution Award presented by the American Psychological

Association. This award was especially satisfying to Rogers because it highlighted his skill as a researcher.

Rogers originally saw little need for a theory of personality, but under pressure from others and also to satisfy an inner need to be able to explain the phenomena he was observing, he evolved his own theory. It was first tentatively expressed in his APA presidential address (Rogers, 1947), then more fully espoused in *Client-Centered Therapy* (1951). His theory received a fuller expression in the Koch series (Rogers, 1959). However, Rogers always insisted that the theory would remain tentative. It is with this thought that one must approach any discussion of Rogerian personality theory.

PERSON-CENTERED THEORY

The therapy and theory of Rogers have undergone several changes in name, but no substantive changes in philosophy have occurred from his early years as a "nondirective" therapist. He used the terms client-centered, student-centered, and group-centered in referring to the various aspects of his work. He had also expressed a fondness for the term person to person, which is perhaps more descriptive than the label **client-centered** (Frick, 1971; Rogers & Stevens, 1967), since the latter term implies that the client is the more important person in Rogers' therapy. This is misleading because Rogers advocates a type of relationship therapy where *both* client *and* therapist must be deeply and personally involved. Nevertheless, in the present work, the label "client-centered" will be used in reference to therapy, while the more inclusive term **person-centered** will be employed where Rogerian personality theory is discussed.

Person-centered theory is a holistic theory and, like other holistic theories, it can be outlined and divided only arbitrarily. Each assumption is interrelated with every other concept and cannot be considered apart from the whole of the theory. Rogers, however, was able to state many of the assumptions of his theory in an if-then framework. An example might be: *If* certain conditions exist, *then* a process will occur; *if* this process occurs, *then* certain outcomes can be expected. A specific example might be found in therapy: *If* the therapist possesses unconditional positive regard (a concept to be discussed in the section on therapy), *then* therapeutic change will occur; *if* therapeutic change occurs, *then* the client will experience more self-acceptance, greater trust of self, and so on. Person-centered theory is one of very few personality theories stated in such a precise fashion (see Rogers, 1959).

Basic Assumptions

What are the basic assumptions of person-centered theory? Rogers postulated two broad assumptions—the formative tendency and the actualizing tendency.

Formative Tendency

Rogers (1978, 1980) believed that there is a tendency for all matter, both organic and inorganic, to evolve from simpler to more complex forms. For the entire universe, a creative process, rather than a disintegrative one, is in operation. Rogers called this the **formative tendency** and pointed to many examples from nature. For instance, complex galaxies of stars form from a less well-organized mass; crystals such as snowflakes emerge from formless vapor; complex organisms develop from single cells; and human consciousness evolves from primitive unconsciousness to a highly organized awareness.

Actualizing Tendency

An interrelated, and here more pertinent, assumption is the **actualizing tendency,** the tendency within all human beings to move toward completion or fulfillment of potentials (Rogers, 1980). Individuals have within themselves the creative power to solve problems, to alter their self-concepts, and to become increasingly self-directed. The source of psychological growth and maturity resides within the individual and is not found in outside forces. Individuals perceive their experiences as reality and they know their reality better than anyone else. They do not need to be directed, controlled, exhorted, or manipulated in order to spur them toward actualization.

Though individuals have a variety of needs and behave in many different ways, all behavior is relative to this single actualizing tendency. The organism moves as a whole toward actualization. Since the person operates as one complete organism in striving for fulfillment, it follows then that actualization involves the whole person, not merely the emotional or intellectual spheres. The need to satisfy one's hunger drive, as well as the need to accept one's self, are but two examples of the single motive of actualization.

If everyone possesses the same actualization tendency, why then is not everyone completely actualized? The answer is that there are certain *conditions* which must exist in order for individuals to be able to activate their capacities for growth. Specifically, a person must be involved in a relationship in which the partner possesses the characteristics of *genuineness, unconditional acceptance,* and *empathy.* These three characteristics will be more fully discussed below in the section on therapy, but it is important to emphasize here that the possession of these three qualities by a partner does not *cause* people to move toward constructive personal change, but they permit people to actualize their own tendency toward self-fulfillment. In fact, Rogers (1961) contended that when these three conditions are present in a relationship, psychological growth *invariably* occurs. For this reason, genuineness, acceptance, and empathy are regarded as *necessary* and *sufficient* conditions for growth.

The Self

The self begins to develop early in infancy when a portion of one's experiences becomes personalized and differentiated as "I" or "me" experiences.

Infants gradually become aware of their own identity (Rogers, 1959). They begin to learn what tastes good and what tastes bad, what feels pleasant and what does not, and they begin to evaluate experiences as positive or negative using as a criterion the actualizing tendency. Since nourishment is a require-ment for actualization, infants value food and devalue hunger. They also value sleep, air, physical contact, and health since all of these are needs through which the actualization tendency is expressed.

Once the self structure becomes established, there also evolves a tendency to actualize the self. **Self-actualization** is a subsystem of the actualization tendency and is therefore not synonymous with it. The actualization ten-dency refers to organismic experiences of the individual, whereas self-actu-alization is the tendency to actualize the self as perceived. When an organism and the self are in harmony, the two tendencies are identical; but when there is incongruence beween what one truly is and one's self-perception, then there is a discrepancy between the two actualization tendencies, resulting in conflict and inner tension (Rogers, 1959).

To Rogers (1959), a person does not possess a self, but rather the term self refers to the entire organism—what one really is on an organismic level. Also, there are two subsystems of the self, both of which are pertinent to the self as perceived. These are the self-concept and the ideal self.

Self-Concept

The **self-concept** includes all those aspects of one's being and one's expe-riences which are perceived in awareness (though not always accurately) by the individual. The self-concept can ordinarily be expressed in statements beginning with, "I am a person who. . . ." The blanks can be filled in by pos-itive, negative, or ambivalent self-descriptions.

Self-concept is not identical with the real self, that is, the organismic self. Portions of the organismic self may be beyond our awareness or simply not owned by us. My stomach is part of my organismic self, but unless it mal-functions and causes concern, it is not likely to be part of my self-concept. Similarly, it is possible to disown certain aspects of self, for example, experiences of dishonesty when they are not consistent with our self-concept.

Once the self-concept is formed, change and significant learnings become difficult. Experiences that are inconsistent with the self-concept usually are either denied or accepted only in distorted forms (Rogers, 1959). Take for example a man who sees himself as a faithful husband who could not possi-bly be attracted to any woman other than his wife. If, on an organismic level, he experiences sexual feelings for another woman, he will either deny the feelings to his awareness or reshape them, possibly by projecting them onto the woman. "I'd better be wary of this woman. She's trying to seduce me."

An established self-concept does not make change impossible, merely dif-ficult. Change most readily occurs in an atmosphere of acceptance by others, which allows the person to reduce anxiety and threat and to take ownership of previously rejected experiences.

Ideal Self

The second subsystem of the self is the **ideal self,** defined as one's view of oneself as one would like to be. It contains all those attributes, usually positive, which one aspires to possess. Operationally, both self-concept and ideal self can be measured by such psychometric devices as the **Q sort** (an instrument that will be more fully discussed later). A wide gap between the ideal self and the perceived self indicates an incongruent and unhealthy personality. **Incongruence,** in fact, can be defined as a discrepancy between the self-concept and the ideal self. Psychologically healthy individuals perceive little discrepancy between what they truly perceive themselves to be and what they ideally would like to be.

Awareness

The self-concept and the ideal self have existence only to the extent that a person is aware of those aspects of experience which are regarded as "I" or "me" experiences. Without awareness, therefore, there would be no self-concept or self-ideal. *Awareness* is defined as "the symbolic representation (not necessarily in verbal symbols) of some portion of our experience" (Rogers, 1959, p. 198). The term is used synonymously with consciousness and with symbolization.

Levels of Awareness

There are three levels of symbolization. First, some events are experienced below the threshold of awareness and are said to be either *ignored or denied.* There are many examples of ignored experiences. For instance, in walking down a busy street, there are many potential stimuli, particularly of sight and sound. Because one cannot attend to all of them, many remain ignored. An example of denied experience might be seen in a mother who never wanted children, but from guilt and fear becomes oversolicitous to them. Her anger and resentment toward her children may be hidden to her for years, never reaching consciousness, but yet remain a part of her experience and color her conscious behavior toward them. Those experiences which are discriminated but not yet accepted into awareness are said to be subceived. The term **subception** refers to the process of perceiving stimuli without an awareness of the perception (Rogers, 1959).

Second, Rogers (1959) hypothesized that some experiences are *accurately symbolized* and freely admitted to the self-structure. Such experiences are both nonthreatening and consistent with the existing self-concept. For example, if pianists who have full confidence in their ability are told by friends that their playing is excellent, they can easily hear these words, accurately symbolize them, and freely admit them to their self-concept.

A third possibility is that experiences are perceived in *distorted* form. When our experience is not consistent with our view of self, we reshape the experience so that it can be assimilated into our existing self-concept (Rogers, 1959). If gifted pianists from the above example were to be told by a

An incongruence between the perceived self and the ideal self can result in dissatisfaction and unhappiness.

distrusted competitor that their playing was excellent, there might transpire a very contrasting set of circumstances from that which followed after hearing the same words from trusted friends. First, their experience in hearing the words would be quite different. They may hear the remarks but distort the meaning because they feel threatened. "Why is this person trying to flatter me?" This doesn't make sense." Their experiences are inaccurately symbolized in awareness and, therefore, can be made to conform to an existing self-concept which, in part, says, "I am a person who does not trust my piano-playing competitors, especially ones who are trying to trick me."

Denial of Positive Experiences

It is not only the negative or derogatory experiences that are distorted or denied to awareness; many people have difficulty accepting genuine compliments and positive feedback even when they are deserved. Students who feel inadequate, but yet make a superior grade, might say to themselves, "I know this grade should be evidence of my scholastic ability, but somehow I just don't feel that way. This class was the easiest on campus. The other students were idiots who didn't try. My teacher did not know what she was doing," etc., etc. Compliments, even those genuinely dispensed, seldom have a positive influence on the self-concept of the recipient (Rogers, 1961). They may be distorted because the person distrusts the giver; or they may be denied because the recipient does not feel deserving of them; and in all cases, a compliment from another also implies the right of that person to criticize or condemn, and thus the compliment carries an implied threat.

Needs

We have seen that people possess an inherent tendency to move toward actualization. Experiences that are seen as either maintaining or enhancing that movement are positively valued; those that are not are negatively valued. The basic needs of all of us, therefore, are **maintenance** and **enhancement** (Rogers, 1959).

Maintenance

The need to maintain our organismic self includes the satisfaction of basic needs such as food, air, and safety, but it is also seen in the tendency to resist change and to seek the status quo. The conservative nature of maintenance needs finds expression in our desire to protect our current, comfortable self-concept. We fight against new ideas; we distort experiences that do not quite fit; we find change painful and growth frightening.

Enhancement

Even though we have a strong desire to maintain the status quo, we are still willing to learn and to change. This need to become more, to develop, and to achieve growth is called enhancement. The need for enhancing the self is manifested in our willingness to learn things that are not immediately rewarding. Other than enhancement, what motivation does a child have in learning to walk? Crawling can satisfy the need for mobility, while walking is associated with falling and pain. Rogers's position is that we are willing to face threat and pain because of a biologically based tendency for the organism to fulfill its basic nature.

Enhancement needs are expressed in a variety of forms. Curiosity, playfulness, self-exploration, maturation, and friendship are ordinarily enhancement needs. Even food and sex are usually expressions of the organism's need to enhance itself. Both might also be maintenance needs, particularly when they are largely unsatisfied. However, for most people, the pursuit of food and sex is conducted in ways that enhance the self-concept.

Positive Regard

As the awareness of self emerges, the infant begins to develop a need to be loved, liked, or accepted by another person, a need Rogers (1959) referred to as **positive regard.** The need for positive regard is found in all human beings and remains a strong and persistent motivator throughout our lives. We value those experiences that satisfy our needs for positive regard. Unfortunately, the expression of positive regard by a significant other may be more powerful than the reward we receive from meeting our organismic needs. For example, a child who, on an organismic level is afraid of a large dog, may hear the father say, "Show me how brave you are. Go ahead and touch the dog." The child may then deny or distort fear in order to receive the praise (positive regard) from the father.

Self-Regard

After the self emerges, we begin to develop the need for **self-regard** as the result of our experiences with the satisfaction or frustration of our need for positive regard. In the above example, praise from the father may teach the child positive self-regard for being brave and negative self-regard for acting cowardly. Positive self-regard is similar to Maslow's concept of self-esteem and includes feelings of self-confidence and self-worth.

How does one acquire positive self-regard? Originally, the need is dependent upon the perception that others, especially significant others, care for, prize, or value you. If you perceive that you are liked or loved by others, then your need to receive positive regard is at least partially satisfied. Positive regard is a prerequisite for self-regard, but once positive self-regard is established it becomes independent of the continual need to be loved (Rogers, 1959). This conception is quite similar to Maslow's notion that love and belongingness needs must be satisfied prior to the activation of self-esteem, but once one begins to feel confident and worthy, it is no longer necessary that one receive a replenishing supply of love and approval from others.

The source of positive self-regard, then, lies in the positive regard received from others, but once established, it is autonomous and self-perpetuating. As Rogers (1959, p. 224) stated it, the person then "becomes in a sense his own significant social other."

Conditions of Worth

Instead of unconditional acceptance, most of us receive **conditions of worth;** that is, we feel that we are loved and accepted only if we meet the other person's expectations and approval. "A condition of worth arises when the positive regard of a significant other is conditional, when the individual feels that in some respects he is prized and in others not" (Rogers, 1959, p. 209).

Even though maintenance and enhancement are basic needs, conditions of worth can also become a criterion by which experiences are accepted or rejected by the self-structure. We gradually assimilate into our self-structure the attitudes we perceive others as expressing toward us. In time, we come to evaluate our experiences on this basis.

As the self begins to evolve during early childhood, we learn to attach worth and value to our experience. An experience is valued if it is perceived to meet the approval of parents and significant others. If we perceive that our behavior is disapproved, we feel rejection not merely of that specific behavior; rather, the entire person feels unworthy since rejection is seen as a gestalt or whole. Eventually, we come to believe those reflections of others which are consistent with our view of self. We ignore our own primary sensory and visceral perceptions and gradually become less acquainted with our real or organismic self.

Acceptance by others is so important that when it is not forthcoming, we desperately seek it, even at the expense of our own enhancement. From early childhood forward, most of us, to some extent, learn to disregard our own organismic valuations and, instead, look beyond ourselves for direction and guidance. To the degree that we introject the values of others, that is, accept conditions of worth, we tend to be incongruent or out of balance. Others' values can be assimilated only in distorted fashion or at the risk of creating disequilibrium and conflict within the self (Rogers, 1959).

Inner conflict and incongruence, then, are due to the disparity between one's own values, which are formed from direct organismic experience, and the more or less distorted values that one has introjected from others. External evaluations, either positive or negative ("You're a good girl when you eat your carrots" or "That's bad of you to hit your baby brother"), do not foster psychological health, but rather prevent one from being completely open to one's own experiences. "That felt good to me, but others may not approve; therefore, it is not good." When one's own experiences are distrusted, further symbolization becomes distorted and the person solidifies the discrepancy between organismic evaluation and introjected values. The result is a psychologically maladjusted person (Rogers, 1959).

Psychological Maladjustment

To understand Rogers's view of abnormal development, one must recall that the organism and the self are two separate entities that may or may not be congruent with one another. Also remember that actualization refers to the organism's tendency to move toward fulfillment, while self-actualization is the desire of the perceived self to reach fulfillment. These two tendencies are sometimes at variance with one another.

Incongruence

Psychological disequilibrium begins when experiences on an organismic level are not recognized as self-experiences; that is, they are not accurately symbolized into awareness because they are seen as inconsistent with the emerging self-concept. This **incongruence** between self and experience is the source of psychological maladjustment. Conditions of worth received during early childhood result in a somewhat false self-concept, that is, one based on distortions and denials. The self-concept that emerges includes subceived perceptions that are not in harmony with organismic experiences. This incongruence between self and experience leads to discrepant and seemingly inconsistent behavior. Sometimes a person behaves in ways that maintain or enhance the actualizing tendency of the organism, and at other times the person behaves in a manner designed to maintain or enhance a self-concept founded on other people's expectations and evaluations.

The greater the incongruence between self and organismic experience, the more **vulnerable** the person. People are said to be vulnerable when they are unaware of the discrepancy between self and experience (Rogers, 1959). Vulnerable people, because of the lack of awareness of their incongruence, often behave in ways that are incomprehensible not only to others but also to themselves. For example, a person may say, "I don't know why I say such childish things to my boss. I know she must think I'm an idiot. I don't want to do it, but every time I open my mouth I say something stupid." The person fails to understand her own behavior because she is unaware of the incongruence between her organismic self and her perceived self (Rogers, 1959).

Anxiety and Threat

When a person becomes dimly aware, that is, subceives that the discrepancy between experience and self may become conscious, then a feeling of anxiety exists. Rogers (1959, p. 204) defined **anxiety** as "a state of uneasiness or tension whose cause is unknown." Anxiety is seen from a phenomenological point of view, that is, from the individual's own frame of reference. I feel anxious when I subceive that my experience is incongruent with my concept of self. On the other hand, **threat** is the same phenomenon from an external viewpoint (Rogers, 1959). Anxiety refers to my perceived feeling; threat to my perception of the unsettling nature of the experience itself. If threatening experiences are accurately symbolized, a state of anxiety will exist because the self-concept would be seen as inconsistent.

Defensiveness

In order to prevent this inconsistency from occurring a person reacts in a defensive manner. **Defensiveness** is the protection of the self-concept against anxiety and threat by the denial or distortion of experiences inconsistent with it (Rogers, 1959). Since the self-concept consists of many self-descriptive statements, it is a many-faceted phenomenon. When an experience is inconsistent with one part of the self-concept, a person behaves in a defensive manner to protect the current structure of self.

The two chief defenses are **distortion** and **denial.** Distortion involves the misinterpretation of an experience so that it is seen to fit some aspect of the self-concept. The experience is perceived in awareness, but its true meaning is not understood. With denial, an experience is not perceived in awareness or at least some aspect of it fails to reach symbolization. Denial is not as common as distortion since most experiences can be twisted or reshaped to fit the current self-concept. According to Rogers (1959), both distortion and denial serve the same purpose—keeping the person's perception of organismic experiences consistent with self-concept.

Distortion and denial lead to absolutistic and rigid behaviors, such as rationalization (giving reasonable-sounding but invalid explanations for one's behavior), compensation (making up for feelings of inadequacy by pretending to be somebody other than what one truly is), paranoia, delusions, hallucinations, and a multitude of other "neurotic" or "psychotic" behaviors.

When one's defenses fail to operate properly, disorganized or psychotic behavior results.

Disorganization

Defensiveness is characteristic of so-called normal and neurotic individuals. When one's defenses fail to operate properly, disorganized or psychotic behavior results. But why would one's defenses fail to function?

In answering this question, it is helpful to trace the course of disorganized behavior. Disorganization has the same origins as normal defensive and neurotic behaviors, namely discrepancy between one's organismic experience and one's view of self. In normal and neurotic cases denial and distortion prevent a person from recognizing this discrepancy. With disorganization there is a large degree of incongruence between perceived self and experience, and this discrepancy is either too obvious to be denied or distorted or it occurs so suddenly that it becomes overwhelming. Thus the incongruence is threatening to the self-structure and is experienced as anxiety. Since the defenses could not adequately handle the discrepancy, this otherwise inconsistent experience is accurately symbolized in awareness and the previously unified self-structure becomes broken. The resulting disorganization can occur either suddenly or gradually over a long period of time. Ironically, a person may be particularly vulnerable to disorganization during therapy, especially if a therapist not only makes accurate interpretations but also insists that the client face the experience prematurely (Rogers, 1959).

In a state of disorganization, a person may at times behave consistently with organismic experience and at other times in accordance with the shattered self-concept. The first case is seen in the example of a previously prudish and proper person who now uses language explicitly sexual and scato-logical. The second case can be illustrated by a person who, because the self-concept is no longer a gestalt or unified whole, behaves in a confused, incon-sistent, and totally unpredictable manner. Behavior is still consistent with the self-concept, but the self-concept has been broken and thus the behavior appears bizarre and confusing.

Though Rogers was even more tentative than usual when he first put forth his views of disorganized behavior in 1959, he made no important revisions in this portion of his theory. He never wavered in his disdain for using diag-nostic labels for people. Traditional classifications such as hypochondriasis, paranoid schizophrenia, homosexuality, or manic-depression have never been part of the vocabulary of person-centered theory. In fact, Rogers always remained uncomfortable with the terms neurotic and psychotic, preferring instead to speak of defensive and disorganized behaviors, terms which more accurately convey the idea that psychological maladjustment is on a contin-uum from the slightest discrepancy between self and experience to the most incongruent.

THERAPY

Client-centered therapy is deceptively simple in statement, but decidedly difficult in practice. Briefly, the client-centered approach holds that in order to effect psychological growth, it is only necessary that a client who is vul-nerable or anxious come into contact with a therapist who is congruent and whom the client perceives as providing an atmosphere of unconditional acceptance and accurate empathy. But therein lies the difficulty. To be con-gruent and to have unconditional positive regard and empathic understand-ing for another are not easily obtainable goals.

Schematically, client-centered counseling can be stated in an if-then fash-ion. If the *conditions* of therapist congruence, empathic listening, and unconditional positive regard are present in a client/counselor relationship, then the *process* of therapy will transpire. If the process of therapy takes place, then certain predictable *outcomes* can be noted. Rogerian therapy, therefore, can be viewed in terms of conditions, process, and outcomes.

Conditions

Rogers (1959) postulated that in order for therapeutic growth to take place, the following conditions are necessary and sufficient. First, an anxious or vul-nerable client must come into contact with a congruent therapist who also possesses empathy and unconditional positive regard for the client. Second, the client must perceive these characteristics in the therapist. Third, contact between client and therapist must be of some duration.

The significance of the Rogerian hypothesis is revolutionary. It is a safe assumption that in any psychotherapy the first and third conditions are pres-ent; that is, the client or patient is motivated by some sort of tension to seek help and the relationship between client and therapist will last for some period of time. Client-centered therapy is unique in its insistence that the conditions of *counselor congruence, unconditional positive regard,* and *empathic listening* are necessary and sufficient (Rogers, 1957).

Even though all three conditions are necessary for psychological growth, Rogers (1980) believed that congruence is more basic than either unconditional positive regard or empathic listening. Congruence is a general quality possessed by the therapist, while the other two conditions are specific and represent feelings or attitudes the therapist has for an individual client.

Counselor Congruence

The first necessary and sufficient condition for therapeutic change is a congruent therapist. **Congruence** exists when a person's organismic experiences are matched by an awareness of them and by an ability and willingness to openly express these feelings (Rogers, 1980). To be congruent means to be real or genuine, to be whole or integrated, to be what one truly is. A congruent counselor is not a warm milquetoast, but rather a complete human being with feelings of joy, anger, frustration, confusion, and so on. When these feelings are experienced, they are neither denied nor distorted, but flow easily into awareness and are freely expressed. A congruent therapist, therefore, is not passive, not aloof, and not "nondirective" (Rogers, 1980).

Congruence is opposed to stagnation. A congruent person would not be static since there are always new experiences going on within the organism and a congruent individual allows these into awareness and, as a result, experiences growth and change.

A congruent therapist wears no mask, does not attempt to fake a pleasant façade, and avoids any pretense of friendliness and affection where these are not truly felt. Also, there is no simulation of anger, toughness, or ignorance; no covering up of feelings of joy, elation, or happiness. A congruent therapist matches feelings with awareness and both with honest expression.

Since congruence involves feelings, awareness, and expression, incongruence can arise from either of two points. First, there can be a breakdown between feelings and awareness. A person may be feeling angry and the anger may be obvious to others but not to the person experiencing it ("I'm not angry. How dare you say I'm angry!"). The second source of incongruence is a discrepancy between awareness of an experience and the ability or willingness to express it to another ("I know I'm feeling bored by what is being said, but I don't dare verbalize my disinterest or my client will think I am not a good therapist"). Rogers stated that therapists will be more effective if they communicate genuine feelings even when those feelings are negative or threatening. To do otherwise would be dishonest and clients will detect (though not necessarily consciously) any significant indicators of incongruence (Rogers, 1961).

Though congruence is a necessary ingredient in successful therapy, Rogers (1980) did not believe that it is essential that a therapist be congruent in relationships outside the therapeutic process. One can be less than perfect and yet become an effective psychotherapist. Also, a therapist need not be absolutely congruent in order to facilitate some growth within a client. As with empathic listening and unconditional positive regard, there are different degrees of congruence and the more it is perceived to be a quality of the therapist, the more successful will be the therapeutic process.

Unconditional Positive Regard

Positive regard has been defined as the need to be liked, prized, or accepted by another. When this need exists without any conditions or qualifications, **unconditional positive regard** occurs (Rogers, 1980). Therapists have unconditional positive regard when they are "experiencing a warm, positive and acceptant attitude toward what *is* the client" (Rogers, 1961, p. 62). The attitude is without possessiveness, without evaluations, and without reservations.

The therapist shows a nonpossessive warmth and acceptance, not an effusive, effervescent persona. To have nonpossessive warmth means to care about another without smothering or owning that person. It includes the attitude "Because I love you or care about you, I can permit you to be autonomous and independent of my evaluations and restrictions. You are a separate person with your own feelings and opinions regarding what is right or wrong. The fact that I care for you does not mean that I must guide you in making choices, but that I can allow you to be yourself and to decide what is best for you." This kind of permissive attitude earned for Rogers the undeserved reputation of being passive or nondirective in therapy, but, as seen above, a client-centered therapist must be actively involved in a relationship with the client.

Unconditional positive regard means that a therapist does not attach any external evaluations or conditions of worth onto a client. No differentiation of client behaviors is made in terms of worth or morality. One action is not accepted and another rejected. External evaluation, whether positive or negative, is always restricting and leads to client defensiveness rather than growth. "My therapist thinks I'm so brilliant. However, I don't feel very smart so I'm having a hard time fitting together her evaluation of me and my own feelings about myself." When a client-centered therapist experiences unconditional positive regard for a client, no conditions of worth exist and no evaluations are made.

Unconditional positive regard involves a warm acceptance of the client without any restrictions or reservations. Regardless of the client's behavior, the therapist continues to prize that person. This does not imply that every behavior is valued equally. It does mean, however, that whether a client is frightened, obnoxious, angry, or loving, a therapist's positive regard remains constant and unwavering (Rogers, 1959).

Although unconditional positive regard is a somewhat awkward term, all three words carry important meaning. "Regard" means that there is a close relationship and that the therapist sees the client as an important person; "positive" indicates that the direction of the relationship is toward warm and loving feelings; and "unconditional" suggests that the positive regard is no longer dependent on specific client behaviors and does not have to be continually earned.

Empathic Listening

The third necessary and sufficient condition of psychological growth is **empathic listening.** Empathy exists when therapists accurately sense the feelings of clients and are able to communicate these perceptions so that the clients know that another has entered their world of feelings without prejudice, projection, or evaluation. To Rogers (1980, p. 142) empathy "means temporarily living in the other's life, moving about in it delicately without making judgments." Empathy is not interpretation or the uncovering of another's unconscious feelings. This would entail an external frame of reference and threat to the client; empathy suggests an internal frame of reference and safety.

Client-centered therapists do not take empathy for granted, but check the accuracy of their sensings by trying them out on the client. "You seem to be telling me that you feel a great deal of resentment toward your father." Valid empathic understanding is often followed by an exclamation from the client along these lines: "Yes, that's it exactly! I really do feel resentful."

Empathic listening is a powerful tool which, along with genuineness and caring, facilitates personal growth within the client. What, precisely, is the role of empathy in psychological change? How does an empathic therapist help a client move toward wholeness and self-actualization? Rogers's (1980, p. 156) own words provide the best answer to these questions.

> When persons are perceptively understood, they find themselves coming in closer touch with a wider range of their experiencing. This gives them an expanded referent to which they can turn for guidance in understanding themselves and directing their behavior. If the empathy has been accurate and deep, they may also be able to unblock a flow of experiencing and permit it to run its uninhibited course.

Empathy is effective because it enables clients to listen to themselves and, in effect, become their own therapists (Rogers, 1980).

Empathy is not to be confused with sympathy. The latter suggests a feeling *for* the client, while empathy connotes a feeling *with* another. Sympathy is never therapeutic since it stems from external evaluation and usually leads to clients feeling sorry for themselves. Self-pity is a deleterious attitude that weakens the self-concept and creates disequilibrium within the self-structure. Also empathy does not mean that a therapist has the same feelings as the client. A therapist does not feel anger, frustration, confusion, resentment, or sexual attraction at the same time a client experiences them. Rather, a therapist is experiencing the depth of the client's feeling, while permitting the client to be a separate person. A therapist has an emotional, not merely cognitive, reaction to a client's feelings, but the feelings *belong* to the client, not the therapist. A therapist does not take ownership of the client's experiences, but yet is able to convey to the client an understanding of what it means to *be* the client at that particular moment (Rogers, 1961).

Effective client-centered therapy is characterized by a congruent therapist who feels empathy and unconditional positive regard for the client.

Process

If the conditions of therapist congruence or genuineness, unconditional positive regard or caring, and accurate empathy are present, then the process of therapeutic change is set in motion. Though each person seeking psychotherapy is unique, there is a certain lawfulness that characterizes the process of therapy.

The process of constructive personality change can be placed on a continuum from most defensive to most integrated. Rogers has arbitrarily divided this continuum into seven stages.

Stage One is characterized by an unwillingness to communicate anything about oneself. People at this stage ordinarily do not seek help, but if for some reason they come to therapy, they are extremely rigid and resistant to change. They do not recognize any problems and refuse to own any personal feelings or emotions.

In *Stage Two* there is a slight loosening of rigidity. External events are discussed; other people are talked about and personal feelings are still unrecognized or disowned, though they may be talked about as if they were objective phenomena.

As clients enter into *Stage Three* they can more freely talk about self, though still as an object. "I'm doing the best I can at work, but my boss still doesn't like me." Feelings and emotions are talked about in the past or future tense. Present feelings are avoided and all emotions seem to be unacceptable and distant from the here and now situation. Personal choice and individual responsibility are only vaguely perceived.

With *Stage Four* clients begin to talk of deep feelings, but not ones presently felt. "I was really burned up when my teacher accused me of cheating." When feelings are expressed in present form they usually take the client by surprise. Experiences are mostly denied or distorted, although there is some dim recognition that emotions can be felt in the present. Clients begin to question some values that have been introjected from others and there is an emerging realization of incongruence between self and experience. Clients accept more freedom and responsibility than in Stage Three and begin to tentatively allow themselves to become involved in a relationship with the therapist.

By the time clients reach *Stage Five* significant change and growth have begun. Feelings are now expressed in the present, though not yet accurately symbolized. Clients are beginning to rely on an internal locus of evaluation for feelings and to make fresh and new discoveries about themselves. There is also greater differentiation of feelings and more appreciation for nuances among them. Freedom of choice and self-responsibility become increasingly important.

Stage Six is characterized by dramatic growth. At this stage people are moving irreversibly closer to becoming fully functioning or self-actualizing individuals. Previously denied or distorted experiences are now freely allowed into awareness and experienced deeply and richly in the immediate present. Clients become more congruent, real, or genuine. Experiences are matched with awareness and with open expression. External evaluation disappears and the organismic self becomes the criterion for evaluating experiences. Clients are now developing unconditional self-regard, which means a feeling of genuine caring and affection for the person they are becoming.

An interesting concomitant to this stage is a physiological loosening. The organism is experienced as one: muscles relax, tears flow, circulation improves, and many physical symptoms disappear.

In many ways Stage Six signals an end to therapy. Indeed, if therapy were to be terminated at this point, clients would still progress to the next level.

Stage Seven can occur outside the therapeutic encounter, since growth at Stage Six seems to be irreversible. Clients are now fully functioning "persons of tomorrow" (a concept more fully explained later). Stage Seven entails a generalization of in-therapy experiences to the world beyond therapy. People now possess the confidence to be themselves at all times, to own and to feel deeply the totality of their experiences. Experiences are lived in the present and the organismic self, now unified with the self-concept, remains the locus for evaluation. Accompanying this is a pleasure in knowing that these evaluations are fluid and that change and growth continue. Clients become congruent, possess unconditional self-regard, and are able to be loving and empathic toward others.

Now that the dynamics of therapeutic change have been described, what theoretical formulations are evoked to explain this process? Rogers's (1980) explanation follows this line of reasoning. When persons come to experience themselves as prized and unconditionally accepted, they realize, perhaps for the first time, that they are lovable. The example of the therapist enables them to prize and accept themselves, to have *unconditional positive self-regard*. As clients perceive that they are empathically understood, they are freed to listen to themselves more accurately, to have *empathy* for their own feelings. As a consequence, when persons come to prize themselves and to accurately understand themselves, the perceived self becomes more *congruent* with organismic experiences. They now possess the same three therapeutic characteristics as any effective helper and, in effect, they become their own therapists.

Outcomes

If the process of therapeutic change is set in motion, then certain observable outcomes can be expected. Rogers (1959) elaborated these predictable outcomes with enough precision to allow for research on the effectiveness of psychotherapy.

The most basic outcome of successful client-centered therapy is a congruent client who is less defensive and more open to experience. Each of the remaining outcomes is a logical extension of this basic one.

As a result of being more congruent and less defensive, clients have a clearer picture of themselves and a more realistic view of the world. They are better able to assimilate experiences into the self on the symbolic level; they are more effective in solving problems; and they have a higher level of positive self-regard.

Being more realistic, they have a more accurate view of their potentials. This permits them to narrow the gap between ideal self and real self which, at the beginning of therapy, is typically quite wide. This discrepancy is lessened through movement by both the ideal self and the true self. Clients, because they are more realistic, lower their expectations of what they should be or would like to be and, because of increased positive self-regard, they raise their view of what they really are.

Because ideal self and real self are more congruent, clients experience less physiological and psychological tension, are less vulnerable to threat, and have less anxiety. They are less likely to look to others for direction and less likely to use others' opinions and values as the criteria for evaluating self-experiences. Instead, they become more self-directed and more likely to perceive the locus of evaluation within themselves. They no longer feel compelled to please other people and to meet external expectations. They feel sufficiently safe to take ownership of an increasing number of their experiences and comfortable enough with themselves to lessen the need for denial and distortion.

Their relationships with others are also changed. They become more accepting of others, make fewer demands, and simply allow others to be themselves. Because they have less need to distort reality, they have less desire to force others to meet their expectations. They are also perceived by others as being more mature, more likable, and more socialized. Their genuineness, positive self-regard, and empathic understanding are extended beyond therapy and they become better able to participate in other growth-facilitating relations (Rogers, 1959, 1961).

THE PERSON OF TOMORROW

The interest shown by Rogers in the psychologically healthy individual is rivaled only by that of Maslow (see Chapter 16). While Maslow, the researcher, was more intensely dedicated to the study of the self-actualizing person, Rogers, the psychotherapist, was more concerned with formulating a theory of the fully functioning person, which was a logical extension of his general theory. In 1951 Rogers first briefly put forward his "characteristics of the altered personality," then enlarged on the concept of the "fully function-ing person" in an unpublished paper (Rogers, 1953). A few years hence his theory of the healthy personality was expounded in the Koch series (Rogers, 1959). He returned to the topic frequently during the early 1960s (Rogers, 1961, 1962, 1963). Somewhat later he described both the world of tomorrow and "the person of tomorrow" (Rogers, 1980).

Characteristics

If the three necessary and sufficient therapeutic conditions of congruence, unconditional positive regard, and empathy are optimal, what kind of theo-retically possible person would emerge? Rogers (1961, 1980) listed five characteristics.

Constant State of Change

First, persons of tomorrow would be in a constant state of change. They would not be end products, but emerging, evolving individuals. They would have self-structures that are fluid and flexible. They would be comfortable with change and confident that the present, for all its richness of feeling, is not the final goal. They would realize that they have not "arrived" and that life will continue to open before them, bringing new and unexpected expe-riences and an accompanying change in the self-structure.

Older theories, which speak of drive reduction, psychological adjustment, or homeostasis, do not apply to Rogers's persons of tomorrow. Here Rogers is in complete agreement with Allport (see Chapter 14), who steadfastly maintained that healthy people seek an ongoing state of tension rather than its reduction.

An Increasing Openness to Experience

Persons of tomorrow would be open to their experiences (Rogers, 1961). They would not be defensive, that is, experiences would be accurately sym-bolized in awareness rather than denied or distorted.

This simple statement is pregnant with meaning. For the person open to experience, all stimuli, whether stemming from within the organism or from the external environment, are freely received by the self. The preexisting self-concept no longer dictates which experiences will be received and which will be blocked. Instead, experiences are openly accepted, thus allowing the self-structure to be in a continual state of change and growth. For the average person this might be a rather frightening situation, for it signifies that outside events cannot be completely controlled.

Persons of tomorrow have no defensive mechanism with which to sift out undesirable experiences and to color other ones. Rather than relying on the mechanism of subception these people prefer to travel uncharted waters, courageously participating in experiences that assuredly reshape their self-concept and render impossible the prediction of specific future behaviors.

Freshness of Attitude and Approach

A related characteristic of persons of tomorrow is a freshness of attitude and approach. Because these people are open to their experiences, they are in a constant state of fluidity and change. What they experience in each moment is new and unique, something never before experienced by that evolving self (Rogers, 1961).

Each experience is seen with a new freshness and appreciated fully in the present moment. The experience may not be pleasant or even welcome, but it is openly lived in the here and now. Rogers (1961) refers to this tendency to live in the moment as **existential living.** This freshness of attitude and approach to each new situation becomes possible as the need for defensiveness declines. Defensiveness forces us to fit uncomfortable experiences into awareness only in a rigid, self-deceptive manner. Persons of tomorrow would permit even undesirable and repugnant experiences to be symbolized in consciousness, having no need to deceive themselves and no need to impress others. They are young in mind and spirit, with no preconceptions about how the world should be. They discover what an experience means to them by living that experience without the prejudice of prior expectations. They do not live by "shoulds" and "oughts" but by what is. They are unique and creative in their search for new means of adopting new solutions to problems and new ways of being.

Trust in Self

A fourth characteristic of persons of tomorrow is a trust in their organismic selves (Rogers, 1961, 1980). They do not depend on others for guidance. They realize that their own experiences can only be evaluated in terms of their organismic selves and not in accordance with the values of others. They have discovered that when they do what feels right for themselves, they are following the proper course of action. Their own inner feelings are a more trustworthy guide than the pontifications of parents or the rigid rules of society. Not that persons of tomorrow would be oblivious to the rights and feelings of other people. These rights and feelings would be perceived clearly and, along with other internal data, become the material from which choices are made.

If people relied singly on their organismic selves for guidance, would there not be much self-seeking behavior, social chaos, and constant confusion and conflict? At the present evolutionary period in history, the answer, unfortunately, is "yes." This is simply a reflection of the existing defensiveness and self-deception of most people. When most of us look within ourselves, we see a cloudy picture, colored by memories and expectations of events that should not be there and by an absence of things that should be in view. Persons of tomorrow, however, would assimilate experiences without denial and distortion so that their own perceptions would prove to be the most reliable guide to action. The meanings they have discovered in present experiences, though not infallible, are more trustworthy than the values or opinions of any other person and would lead to harmonious relationships with others.

Harmonious Relations with Others

Persons of tomorrow may find themselves at times removed from the mainstream of social opinion, but they would remain confident of their own ability to experience harmonious relations with at least some others. It would not be necessary for them to be liked or loved by everyone since they already know that they are unconditionally prized and accepted by someone. They would seek intimacy with another person who is probably equally healthy. The relationship itself would be productive since it would contribute to the continual growth of each partner. Both persons would receive positive self-regard from the assurance that the other has unconditional positive regard for them. The relationship is thus mutually rewarding and productive (Rogers, 1959).

Persons of tomorrow would be authentic in their relations with others. They would be what they appear to be, without deceit or fraud, without defenses and façades, without hypocrisy and sham. They would care about others, but in a nonjudgmental manner. They would value individuals above institutions and healthy relationships above material goods. They would not be selfish or individualistic, however, but would seek meaning in life beyond themselves. They would yearn for the spiritual life and would seek for inner peace in a variety of ways (Rogers, 1980).

Implications

If individuals experience the necessary conditions for growth they will become more and more fully functioning and perhaps will emerge as persons of tomorrow. What implications does this hypothesis have for the individual and for society? Rogers (1961, 1972, 1980) listed at least four.

Greater Integration of the Individual

Persons of tomorrow become more integrated, more whole, more "all one piece" (Rogers, 1962). The artificial boundaries between consciousness and unconsciousness vanish; all experiences are symbolized accurately in awareness. There is no longer a dichotomy between what is and what should be; the organismic self becomes the criterion for evaluation of experiences. The distance between real self and ideal self disappears; persons of tomorrow have no need for inflated self-ideals and they receive pleasure in being their real selves. Integrated individuals manifest no façades; they confidently are what they appear to be and they can openly express whatever feelings they are experiencing (Rogers, 1962).

More Adaptable

From an evolutionary view, the persons of tomorrow are more adaptable, more likely to survive. Hence the title, "persons of tomorrow." Fully functioning persons are not conformists and they do not adjust to a static environment; conformity and adjustment to a fixed condition, in the long run, have little survival value. Persons of tomorrow live creatively and are able to form new relationships with their environment. They can afford to be adaptable because they feel comfortable with change; their self-structures are fluid and their behaviors are flexible. They live in harmony with other people and balance their contributions to society with the satisfaction of their own needs (Rogers, 1980).

Basic Trustworthiness of Human Nature

Implicit in the description of persons of tomorrow is the assumption that human nature is basically trustworthy. There is no need to worry about persons of tomorrow destroying other people, since one of the strongest needs of humanity is that of affiliation with others. Fully functioning persons care about others and are ready to help when needed, but "they are suspicious of the professional 'helpers'" (Rogers, 1980, p. 351). They experience anger, but they can be trusted not to strike out unreasonably against others when they are angry. They feel aggression, but they channel it in appropriate directions. Their behavior would be rational, socialized, and self-controlled. They can be relied on to live in harmony both with themselves and with others (Rogers, 1961).

Greater Richness of Life

Since persons of tomorrow are open to all experiences, they enjoy a greater richness in life than do others. They do not distort internal stimuli nor do they buffer their emotions. Consequently, they feel more deeply than others. Both negative and positive emotions are experienced to the fullest extent. Anger, pain, and sorrow are vividly felt, but so too are joy, elation, pleasure, and love. These persons live in the present and thus participate more richly in the ongoing moment. The greater confidence they have in themselves allows them to enjoy lives that are "enriching, exciting, rewarding, challenging, meaningful" (Rogers, 1961, p. 32).

The Rogers/Skinner Debate

One of the most famous debates in the history of American psychology took place during the mid-1950s and early 1960s between Rogers and B. F. Skinner. Philosophical differences between Rogers and Skinner led to three face-to-face confrontations between them concerning the problem of freedom and control.

The initial confrontation was the most famous. It took place during the 1956 convention of the American Psychological Association, where Rogers had just received the Distinguished Scientific Contribution Award. Skinner was already one of the best known psychologists in the country and so the debate created much interest and excitement among those attending the convention and those reading the account of it later that year in *Science* (Rogers & Skinner, 1956). The two men were worthy adversaries. Each held firm opinions, possessed an easy command of the language, and had a good sense of humor. The symposium, entitled "Some Issues Concerning the Control of Human Behavior," followed the style of a formal debate, with Skinner first presenting the behaviorist's side of the controversy, then Rogers reading his paper and reacting to Skinner's presentation, and finally Skinner giving his rebuttal to Rogers's remarks. Two less publicized meetings followed. The first took place in December 1960, and was sponsored by the American Academy of Arts and Sciences; the second took place in June 1962 on the Duluth campus of the University of Minnesota.

In general, Skinner, during these meetings and in *Beyond Freedom and Dignity* (1971), argued that people are always controlled, whether they realize it or not, by the contingencies of reinforcement. Since current control is usually haphazard and without an external design, people often have the illusion that they are free. Though they struggle for freedom, the struggle is not the result of an inherent free will, but rather a desire to avoid or escape from punitive conditions within the environment.

Rogers recognized the validity of much of Skinner's argument. He conceded that much of human behavior is controlled by hereditary and environmental forces. He contended, however, that people retain some measure of freedom, some degree of subjective choice, and some capacity to be self-directed. The portion of human behavior that is controlled, predictable, and lawful comes under the province of science, while the major values and choices that people make are outside science's realm. Since science can be a powerful tool in shaping human behavior, Rogers argued, the issue of control is of grave concern to everyone. He worried about such questions as: "Who will control?" "Who will be controlled?" "What type of control will be used?" and, perhaps, most importantly, "For what purpose will control be exercised?" (Rogers, 1968; Rogers & Skinner, 1956).

Rogers summed up the implications of fully functioning living with these words:

This process of healthy living is not, I am convinced, a life for the fainthearted. It involves the stretching and growing of becoming more and more one's potentials. It involves the courage to be. It means launching oneself fully into the stream of life. Yet the deeply exciting thing about human beings is that when the individual is inwardly free, he chooses this process of becoming (Rogers, 1962, p. 32).

RESEARCH

At the beginning of his professional career at the Institute for Child Guidance in New York City, and later at the Rochester Society for the Prevention of Cruelty to Children, Rogers practiced a fairly standard and traditional method of psychotherapy. Then gradually, he began to develop a unique form of therapy based on the assumption that individuals have the resources within themselves for effecting change.

As his ideas continued to take shape, he felt a need to test them scientifically. First at Ohio State, then especially at Chicago, and later at Wisconsin, he conducted elaborate, well-designed research, the results of which tended to confirm his earlier hunches and encouraged him to set forth his first tentative theory of personality. Once his theoretical position was elucidated, he instigated more research designed specifically to test the principal assumptions of the theory.

We have seen that Freud, Adler, Jung, and Sullivan each combined the clinical practice of psychotherapy with the need to build an attendant theory of personality. Rogers has gone a step beyond this, becoming a researcher as well as a therapist and theorist. The vast magnitude of sophisticated research conducted by Rogers, and his colleagues made him unique among psychotherapists and the amount of time he spent in individual and group therapy give him a unique position among scientific researchers.

Philosophy of Science

According to Rogers (1968) science begins and ends with the subjective experience. Scientists must be inclined to look within, to be in tune with internal feelings and values, be intuitive and creative, be open to experiences, able to change, have a fresh outlook, and possess a solid trust in self. In other words, scientists themselves must be fully functioning people.

In addition, scientists should be completely involved in the phenomena being studied. They must not view that phenomena too objectively, as detached outsiders. A research psychologist cannot be merely a disinterested observer, but must also be fully immersed in the phenomena being observed. Rogers (1968) wrote that if one does research on psychotherapy, for example, it is first necessary that the researcher have had a long career as a therapist. A scientist must care about and care for newly born ideas and nurture them lovingly through their fragile infancy.

Science begins when an intuitive scientist starts to perceive patterns among phenomena. At first, these dimly seen relationships may be too vague to be communicated to others, but they are nourished by a caring scientist until eventually they can be formulated into testable hypotheses. These hypotheses, then, are the consequence of the open-minded personal experiences of the scientist and not the result of preexisting stereotypical thought. The scientist formulates hypotheses not to fit existing tools of measurement, but in accordance with the phenomena being investigated.

At this point methodology enters the picture. Though the creativity of a scientist may yield innovative methods of research, these procedures themselves must be rigorously controlled, empirical, and objective. The precise nature of the methodology should prevent a scientist from self-deception and from intentionally or unintentionally manipulating the observations. But this precision should not be confused with science. It is only the *methodology* of science that is precise and objective.

The findings of scientific methodology are then communicated to others, but the communication itself is subjective. The people receiving the communication bring their own degrees of open-mindedness or defensiveness into this process. They have varying levels of readiness to receive the findings depending on the prevailing climate of scientific thought and the personal subjective experiences of each individual. The findings are seen subjectively and differently by each person receiving them.

Consistent with his philosophy of science, Rogers did not permit methodology to dictate the nature of his research. In his investigations of the outcomes of client-centered psychotherapy, he allowed the problem to take precedence over methodology and measurement. He did not formulate hypotheses simply because the tools for testing them were readily available. Instead, he began by sensing vague impressions from clinical experience and gradually forming these into testable hypotheses. It was only then that he dealt with the task of finding or inventing instruments by which these hypotheses could be tested (Rogers & Dymond, 1954).

Research Design

Scientifically, the years Rogers spent at the University of Chicago were his most productive, though throughout his entire career he was fervently devoted to science and its findings. During his Wisconsin period he was deeply involved with a major study of psychotherapy with schizophrenics (Rogers, et al., 1967) and in California he continued to conduct research on the person-centered approach to teaching and learning (Rogers, 1974, 1983). However, his research (Rogers & Dymond, 1954) at the Counseling Center at Chicago best exemplifies his scientific work. The research design of this project is presented here as an illustration of Rogers' approach to the problem of identifying change during psychotherapy. Each of the three sides of Rogers, the warm-hearted therapist, the hard-headed scientist, and the systematic theorist, came into play during this research.

The purpose of the studies was to investigate both the process and the outcomes of client-centered therapy. The therapists were of a "journeyman" level. They included Rogers and other faculty members, but graduate students also served as therapists. Though they ranged widely in experience and ability, all were basically client-centered in approach (Rogers, 1955; 1961; Rogers & Dymond, 1954).

Hypotheses

Research at the Counseling Center was built around the basic client-centered hypothesis, which states that all persons have within themselves the capacity, either active or latent, for self-understanding and the capacity and tendency to move in the direction of self-actualization and maturity. This tendency will become realized provided the therapist creates the proper psychological atmosphere (Rogers, 1954).

More specifically, it was hypothesized that during therapy clients would assimilate into their self-concepts feelings and experiences previously denied to awareness; the discrepancy between real self and ideal self would lessen as a concomitant of therapy; the observed behavior of clients would become more socialized and mature as a result of therapy; during and after therapy clients would become both more self-accepting and more accepting of others. These hypotheses, in turn, became the foundation for several more specific hypotheses, which were operationally stated and then tested.

Selection of Instruments

Since the hypotheses of the study dictated that subtle subjective personality changes be measured in an objective fashion, the selection of measurement instruments was a difficult one. To assess change from an external viewpoint the Thematic Apperception Test (TAT), the Self-Other Attitude Scale (S-O Scale), and the Willoughby Emotional Maturity Scale (E-M Scale) were employed. The TAT, a projective personality test developed by Henry Murray during the 1930s (Murray, 1938), was used to test hypotheses that called for a standard clinical diagnosis; the S-O Scale, an instrument compiled at the Counseling Center from several earlier sources, measures antidemocratic trends and ethnocentrism; the E-M Scale was used to compare descriptions of clients' behavior and emotional maturity as seen by two close friends and by the clients themselves.

To measure change from the client's point of view (a procedure quite consistent with client-centered theory) the Research Group relied on the then new Q technique developed by William Stephenson of the University of Chicago (Stephenson, 1953). The Q technique begins with a universe of 100 self-referent statements printed on 3 × 5 cards, which subjects are requested to sort into nine piles from "most like me" to "least like me." Some of the items were judged by an independent group of clinicians to describe the well-adjusted person, some the poorly adjusted person, and for others the clinicians could not agree. Examples of these self-referent items include: "I express my emotions freely"; "My personality is attractive to the opposite sex"; "I put on a false front"; "I really am disturbed"; and "I am a submissive person" (Dymond, 1954a). The subjects were required to sort the cards into piles of 1, 4, 11, 21, 26, 21, 11, 4, and 1. The resulting distribution approximates a normal curve and allows the data to be analyzed by correlation and factor analysis. At various points throughout the study, subjects were requested to sort the cards to describe the self, the ideal self, and the ordinary person.

Subjects and Procedure

Subjects for the study were 29 clients, 18 men and 11 women, who had sought therapy at the Counseling Center of the University of Chicago. They ranged in age from 21 to 40 with a mean of 27. More than half were university students, while others were from the surrounding community. These subjects, called the experimental or therapy group, were randomly selected from the population of adult clientele at the Counseling Center. They were, however, stratified for sex and student–nonstudent status. All subjects in the experimental group received at least six therapeutic interviews and each session was electronically recorded and transcribed, a procedure Rogers had pioneered as early as 1938 and one which typically required approximately 700 hours of data gathering per subject (Grummon, 1954).

Two different methods of control were used in the study. First, half the people in the *therapy group* were asked to wait 60 days before they would receive therapy. These subjects were known as the own-control or *wait group*. The rationale for the wait group was obvious. Do people seeking therapy undergo change simply because they are motivated to get better? If the wait group were to change significantly during the wait period, then motivation to change rather than therapy itself might be the therapeutic ingredient. The other half of the therapy group, called the *no-wait group*, received therapy immediately.

The second control consisted of a separate group of "normals," who had volunteered to serve as subjects for "research on personality." This group was matched with the therapy group on sex, student–nonstudent status, and approximate socioeconomic level. The separate control group was used to determine the effects of such variables as passage of time, knowledge that one is part of an experiment (the placebo effect), and the impact of repeated testing. The 23 subjects in the *control group* were divided into *wait* and *nonwait* subgroups corresponding to the wait and nonwait therapy groups. For both the therapy and the control group, the wait group was tested four times, at the beginning of the 60-day wait period, prior to therapy, immediately after therapy, and after a 6- to 12-month follow-up period. The nonwait groups were administered the tests on the same occasions, except, of course, prior to the wait period. The follow-up period was used as a check for the permanence of any change that might take place during therapy. The overall design of the study is shown in Figure 17.1.

Findings

Some of the more pertinent findings are summarized here. As hypothesized, the therapy group showed less discrepancy between self and self-ideal after therapy than before. Prior to counseling the correlation between self and self-ideal was $-.01$, indicating an almost total lack of relationship. After therapy the correlation was .34, demonstrating a significant degree of congruence between self and self-ideal. At the end of the follow-up period most of the gains had been retained, as indicated by a positive correlation of .31.

How about the control group? They showed almost no change from the

Testing Points

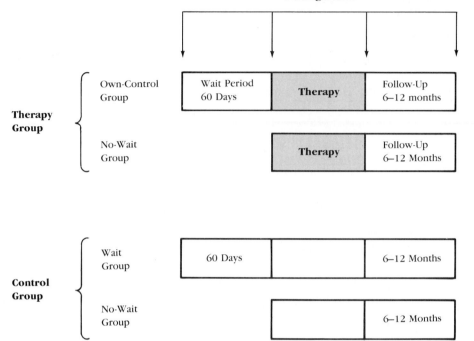

FIGURE 17.1 Design of the Chicago Study. (From C. R. Rogers and R. F. Dymond (Eds.), *Psychotherapy and personality change,* p. 38, © 1954 by The Univeristy of Chicago.

initial testing until the final follow-up. The corresponding correlations between self and self-ideal for the control group were .58 and .59. This indicates a higher level of congruence at the beginning and also greater agreement at the conclusion of the study. The higher correlations were expected since these were normal subjects, not seeking therapy, but merely volunteering for a research study. It was also hypothesized that the real self of the therapy group would change more than the ideal self. Though the gap between the two narrowed because the ideal self became more "realistic" and the real self became healthier, the greater change took place in the real self, thereby supporting the hypothesis (Butler & Haigh, 1954).

The real self also changed more than the clients' perception of the ordinary person. This means that, although clients showed little change in their notion of what the average person was like, they manifested marked change in their perceptions of self. In other words, intellectual insight does not equate with growth (Rudikoff, 1954).

Using the TAT as a criterion for change, the researchers found that the therapy group, which prior to therapy was more disturbed than the control group, showed marked improvement at the post-therapy point and also at the end of the follow-up period. No corresponding gains were made by the control group. This is an important finding, since the TAT is based on theoretical grounds nearly 180 degrees removed from Rogerian theory (Dymond, 1954b).

As the result of therapy, it was hypothesized, clients would change their attitudes toward others. The S-O Scale, designed to measure prejudicial and authoritarian attitudes toward others, was the principal instrument used to test this hypothesis. No significant changes in the experimental group from pretherapy to posttherapy to follow-up were found. Also, there were no significant differences between the therapy group and the control group in authoritarian attitudes. In other words, there was no support for the hypothesis that clients receiving client-centered therapy would demonstrate a greater acceptance of and respect for others (Gordon & Cartwright, 1954).

Does therapy bring about noticeable changes in clients' behavior as perceived by close friends? All subjects in both the therapy and control groups were asked to supply the experimenters with names of two intimate friends who would be in a position to judge overt behavioral changes. Contact was made by mail and the friends did not know the true nature of the study. Subjects and friends alike filled out the Willoughby E-M Scale, rating the subject for emotional maturity in several everyday situations. Overall, it was found that there were no significant behavioral changes in clients, as seen by their friends, from the pretherapy period to posttherapy. However, this global rating of no change was due to counterbalancing effect. Clients judged by their therapists as being most improved received higher posttherapy maturity scores by their friends, while those rated as least improved were scored lower by their friends following therapy than they were prior to therapy. Interestingly, before therapy, clients typically rated themselves as more immature than their friends rated them. As therapy progressed, clients rated themselves higher and, therefore, more in agreement with their friends' ratings. Subjects in the control group showed no changes throughout the study in emotional maturity as judged by friends (Rogers & Dymond, 1954).

Effectiveness of Client-Centered Therapy

The Chicago studies continue as some of the best-designed investigations of the outcomes of psychotherapy. The studies demonstrated that people receiving client-centered therapy, in general, show some growth or improvement. However, improvement fell short of the optimum. The therapy group began treatment as less healthy than the control group, then showed growth during therapy and retained most of it throughout the follow-up period. However, they never attained the level of psychological health demonstrated by those in the control group.

Looking at these outcomes another way, the typical person receiving client-centered therapy probably never approaches Stage Seven hypothesized by Rogers and discussed above. A more realistic expectation might be for the client to advance to Stage Three or Four. Client-centered therapy is effective, but it does not result in the fully functioning person.

The Case of Mrs. Oak

In our introduction we saw that when Mrs. Oak sought help at the University of Chicago Counseling Center, she was frustrated, miserable, and generally unhappy.

At the time of therapy, Mrs. Oak (a fictitious name) was a housewife in her late thirties who had an antagonistic relationship with her husband and who also felt guilty over her adolescent daughter's psychosomatic illness. During the early stages of therapy she talked mostly about other people and spoke of herself objectively as someone who was burdened with problems and who wanted to find the causes of her unhappiness. She had unrealistically high aspirations and a strong need to be perfect. At this time she felt unattractive, rebellious, useless, and deeply conflicted over her sexual identity. Her therapist saw her as shy, almost nondescript, and nearly incoherent. She expressed herself in "jumbled analogies, half-sentences, and incomplete thoughts" (Rogers, 1954a, p. 164). As therapy progressed Mrs. Oak became less problem-oriented, better able to express herself, and more self-confident.

Once she realized that the therapist *cared* for her, she began to experience herself in a more positive way. "She gradually became aware of the fact that, though she had searched in every corner of herself, there was nothing fundamentally bad but, rather, at heart she was positive and sound" (Rogers, 1954a, p. 263).

At the end of 40 counseling interviews Mrs. Oak had experienced considerable change in her self-concept. She saw herself as being more self-sufficient, more integrated or whole, and less threatened by people. She was still in conflict over her sexuality and continued to be somewhat pessimistic and depressed. Nevertheless, she was confident that she would continue to make progress even in the absence of further psychotherapy.

However, Mrs. Oak did receive more counseling. Seven months after therapy she returned for follow-up testing and at that time decided to resume therapy in order to clear up a few things. Subsequently, she received eight additional counseling sessions.

When therapy was over Mrs. Oak had divorced her husband, taken a job, and improved her relationship with her daughter. She was no longer striving to be perfect, but was content to relax and enjoy life.

Many months before this case study was completed, Rogers (1951, p. 195) had written a theoretical statement that predicted the changes that took place within Mrs. Oak during the process of therapy.

Thus therapy produces a change in personality organization and structure, and a change in behavior, both of which are relatively permanent. It is not necessarily a reorganization which will serve for a lifetime. It may still deny to awareness certain aspects of experience, may still exhibit certain patterns of defensive behavior. There is little likelihood that any therapy is in this sense complete. Under new stresses of a certain sort, the client may find it necessary to seek further therapy, to achieve further reorganization of self. But whether there be one or more series of therapeutic interviews, the essential outcome is a more broadly based structure of self, an inclusion of a greater proportion of experience as part of self, and a more comfortable and realistic adjustment to life.

CONCEPT OF HUMANITY

Rogers evolved a basically positive and *optimistic* view of human- ity. He believed that people are essentially forward moving and, under proper conditions, will grow toward self-actualization. Peo- ple are basically trustworthy, socialized, and constructive. They ordinarily know what is best for themselves and will strive for completion provided they are prized and understood by another healthy individual.

This tendency toward growth and self-actualization has a biological basis. Just as plants and animals have in their basic nature some tendency toward growth and fulfillment, so too do human beings. All organisms actualize themselves, but only humans can become self-actualizing. Humans are dif- ferent from plants and animals primarily because they have self-awareness. To the extent that we have awareness, we are able to make free choices and to play an active role in forming our personalities. Other organisms do not possess this power. Rogers, then, is rated high on the dimension of *free choice.*

Rogers's person-centered theory is also rated high on *teleology* since peo- ple are seen as striving with purpose toward goals they freely set for them- selves. Again, under therapeutic conditions, people consciously desire to become more fully functioning, more open to their experiences, and more accepting of self and others.

Rogers placed more emphasis on individual differences and *uniqueness* than on similarities. If plants have individual potential for growth, people have even greater uniqueness and individuality. Within a nurturant environ- ment, people can grow in their own fashion toward the process of being more fully functioning. Though common elements can be extracted from an ana- lytical study of this process, people themselves are becoming more unique and more completely themselves as this process continues.

Though Rogers did not deny the importance of unconscious processes, his primary emphasis was on the ability of people to *consciously* choose their course of action. Fully functioning people are ordinarily aware of what they are doing and have some understanding of their reasons for doing it.

On the dimension of *biological vs. social influences,* Rogers favored the latter. Psychological growth is not automatic. In order to move toward actu- alization, one must experience empathic understanding and unconditional positive regard from another person who is genuine or congruent. Rogers firmly held that, while much of our behavior is determined by heredity and environment, we have within us the capacity to choose and to become self- directed. Not only do we possess the ability to choose, but under nurturant conditions "choice always seems to be in the direction of greater socialization, improved relationships with others" (Rogers, 1982a, p. 8).

People are not by nature ego-centered, socially dangerous, or evil (Rogers, 1982a, p. 8), but neither do they possess an innate morality. Rogers did not claim that, if left alone, people would be righteous, virtuous, or honorable. However, in an atmosphere without threat, people are free to become what they potentially can be. This is neither good nor bad, for these terms imply some standard of evaluation. No evaluation in terms of morality applies to the nature of humanity. People simply have the potential for growth, the need for growth, and the desire for growth. By nature they will strive for completion even under unfavorable conditions, but under poor conditions they do not realize their full potential for psychological health. However, under the most nurturant and favorable conditions, people will become more aware of self, trustworthy, congruent, and self-directed. They will become psychologically adjusted, rational, realistic, and will move toward becoming the persons of tomorrow.

CRITIQUE OF ROGERS

If one were to be assigned the task of constructing a personality theory that meets the five criteria of a useful theory enumerated in Chapter 1, the consequence might be an endeavor similar to Rogers' person-centered theory. But, in a real sense, that was precisely Rogers's motivation. He wished to clearly and efficiently express a theory built on empirical observation. The result was a theory of personality, therapy, and interpersonal relationships reported within the confines of about 80 pages in the Koch (1959) series (Rogers, 1959).

How well does Rogerian theory satisfy the five criteria of a useful theory? Does it *organize knowledge* into a meaningful framework? While the theory is unusually systematic and well constructed, much of the research generated by it has been limited to those aspects of personality that are the direct result of interpersonal relations. Not everything that is known about human personality can be fit into a meaningful framework by Rogerian theory, but this is true of all other theories as well. Refreshingly, Rogers's theoretical speculations are not far removed from the observations upon which they are based.

Because its data base was limited to psychotherapeutic experiences and to teacher–student relationships, it is fair to say that person-centered theory is valuable in its ability to organize knowledge of the process and outcomes of psychotherapy and education, but less successful in explaining the development of personality outside these two endeavors.

The second criterion of a useful theory is the ability to *generate research* and testable hypotheses. Though Rogerian theory has generated much research in the realm of psychotherapy and classroom learning (see Rogers, 1983), there has been less interest in testing the theory in settings outside these two areas. This does not reflect an inherent weakness of the theory itself, but it is an indication of the theory's ability to spark an abundance of research activity within the general field of personality.

How does person-centered theory serve as a *guide for the solution of practical problems?* For the psychotherapist, the answer is unequivocal. To effect personality change it is only necessary that the therapist possess congruence and be able to demonstrate empathic understanding and unconditional positive regard for the client. Rogers suggested that these three conditions are necessary and sufficient to effect growth in any interpersonal relationship, including those outside therapy. But what is the evidence for this assumption?

In the Chicago studies described above it was found that therapy was associated with positive personality change. However, after an average of 33 weeks of receiving client-centered therapy, people in the experimental group were still not as healthy as those in the control group. What factors explain this? Was the length of therapy insufficient? Did some of the counselors lack the three therapeutic conditions? Did people in the control group have many years of experience with the therapeutic conditions in their relationships with others? If this is so, why is a nontherapeutic setting more conducive to growth than a therapeutic one? Where is the evidence that changes experienced by the therapy group were due specifically to these three conditions? Perhaps growth was the result of counseling itself and therefore nearly any system of therapy would be equally effective. Since the study did not control for the specific kind of therapy, it is not possible to conclude that change is related to any particular ingredient of client-centered counseling. These problems limit the usefulness of person-centered theory even in its strongest setting—the therapeutic situation.

The fourth criterion of a useful theory is *internal consistency* and a set of operational definitions. Person-centered theory must receive a very high rating for its consistency and its carefully worked-out operational definitions. Future theory builders can learn a valuable lesson from Rogers's pioneering work in constructing a theory of personality.

Finally, is Rogerian theory *parsimonious* and free from cumbersome concepts and language? The theory itself is unusually clear and economical, but some of the language seems needlessly awkward and vague. For example, the term unconditional positive regard, while precise, possibly could have been expressed in more everyday language. Other concepts such as "organismic experiencing," "becoming," "symbolization," and "fully functioning" are too broad and imprecise to have any scientific meaning. This is a small criticism, however, in comparision with the overall tightness and parsimony of person-centered theory.

CHAPTER SUMMARY

Rogers's person-centered theory of personality grew out of his experience as a client-centered therapist and is an expression of his fundamental belief that, under proper conditions, people will move inevitably toward psychological growth and fulfillment.

This assumption follows from a more general notion that all matter, both organic and inorganic, tends to evolve from simple to more complex forms. Rogers called this the *formative tendency.*

Somewhat more specific is the *actualizing tendency,* or the tendency found within all people to move toward completion of fulfillment of potentials. During early infancy, a person begins to evolve a self-system, eventually including a *self-concept* (perceived self) and an *ideal self.* At that point the person also seeks *self-actualization,* or fulfillment of the self as perceived. *Incongruence* develops when the organismic (real) self, perceived self, and ideal self do not match.

In order to bring the organismic self and the perceived self together, the person distorts or denies certain aspects of experience. Experiences not accepted into awareness are said to be *subceived.*

Rogers postulated that we are guided by two basic needs—*maintenance* and *enhancement* of our perceived selves. In addition, we need positive regard, first from others, then from ourselves. Conditions of worth and external evaluation prevent us from experiencing *unconditional positive regard* and may lead to psychological maladjustment.

Maladjusted people are characterized by incongruence between self and experience; *vulnerability,* or an unawareness of their incongruence; and *anxiety, threat,* and *defensiveness.* When the defenses of *denial* and *distortion* are insufficient to block out incongruence, *disorganization* or psychosis results.

Rogerian therapy can be stated quite simply. If certain conditions are present, then the process of therapy will transpire and predictable outcomes will be noted. The *three necessary and sufficient therapeutic conditions* are (1) *counselor congruence,* (2) *empathic listening,* and (3) *unconditional positive regard.*

The *process* of therapeutic personality change ranges from extreme defensiveness, or unwillingness to talk about self, to the final stage where clients are their own therapists and are able to continue psychological growth outside the therapeutic setting.

The basic *outcomes* of client-centered counseling are a congruent client who is open to experiences and with no need to be defensive. Ideal self and real self come closer together and the client moves closer to becoming the *person of tomorrow.*

Rogers's fully functioning person, or person of tomorrow, would be characterized by (1) a constant state of change, (2) an increasing openness to experience, (3) a fresh attitude and approach toward life, (4) trust in self, and (5) harmonious relations with others.

Despite Rogers's optimistic view that people can become self-actualizing, his own evidence from research on client-centered therapy suggests that therapeutic experience was insufficient to move disturbed people to even the level of a control group of people who had average psychological health. Nevertheless, this same research yielded generally positive results for client-centered counseling.

Rogers's view of humanity was basically positive and optimistic. Through proper conditions people will move toward becoming more open to their experiences and more self-actualizing.

Person-centered theory receives only a moderate rating on its ability to organize knowledge and to serve as a useful guide to the practitioner. However, it rates high as a generator of research and very high on internal consistency and parsimony.

Suggested Readings

Evans, R. I. (1981). *Dialogue with Carl Rogers.* New York: Praeger.

Evans's book contains not only his lively discussion with Rogers but also the Rogers/Skinner debate, a tribute to Rogers by Richard Farson, Rogers's 1973 address to the APA, and his more recent paper on "the emerging person."

Kirschenbaum, H. (1979). *On becoming Carl Rogers.* New York: Delacorte Press.

The best and most complete source for biographical information on Rogers, Kirschenbaum's book adopts a highly favorable attitude toward the father of client-centered therapy and person-centered theory.

Rogers, C. R. (1959). A theory of therapy, personality, and interpersonal relationships, as developed in the client-centered framework. In S. Koch (Ed.), *Psychology: A study of a science* (Vol. 3) (pp. 184–246). New York: McGraw-Hill.

The essence of Rogers's personality theory is contained within these relatively few pages. Rogers remained disappointed that this frequently referenced chapter was not more widely read.

Rogers, C. R. (1961). *On becoming a person: A therapist's view of psychotherapy.* Boston: Houghton Mifflin.

Rogers's most popular book, this volume is actually a collection of papers written during the previous decade.

Rogers, C. R. (1980). *A way of being.* Boston: Houghton Mifflin.

Reflecting changes that occurred in his life and work during the decade of the 1970s, this book presents Rogers's most recent thoughts.

18

Existential Psychology

Twice married, twice divorced, Philip was struggling through yet another relationship. A successful architect in his midfifties, Philip could offer Nicole both love and financial security.

Six months after Philip met Nicole, a writer in her midforties, the two spent an idyllic summer together at his retreat. Nicole's two small sons were with their father and Philip's three children were by then young adults who could care for themselves. At the beginning of the summer Nicole talked about the possibility of marriage, but Philip replied that he was against it, citing his two previous unsuccessful marriages as his reason. Aside from this brief disagreement, the time they spent together that summer was completely pleasurable. Their intellectual discussions were gratifying to Philip and their lovemaking was the most satisfying he had ever experienced, often bordering on ecstasy. In addition to the intellectual and sexual stimulation, both Philip and Nicole were able to work productively, he on his architectural designs, she on her writing.

At the end of this romantic summer, Nicole returned home alone to put her children in school. The day after she arrived home Philip telephoned her, but somehow her voice seemed strange. The next morning he called again and got the feeling that someone else was with Nicole. That afternoon he called several more times but kept getting a busy signal. When he finally got through, he asked her if someone had, indeed, been with her that morning. Without hesitation, Nicole reported that Craig, an old friend from her college days, had been staying with her and that she had fallen in love with him. Moreover, she planned to marry Craig at the end of the month and move to another part of the country.

Philip was devastated. He felt betrayed and abandoned. He lost weight, resumed smoking, and suffered from insomnia. When he saw Nicole again he expressed his anger at her "crazy" plan. This outburst of rage was rare for Philip. He seldom showed anger, perhaps for fear of losing the one he loved. To complicate matters, Nicole said she still loved Philip and continued to see him whenever Craig was not available. Eventually, Nicole lost her infatuation for Craig and told Philip that, as he well knew, she could never leave him. This surprised Philip because he knew no such thing. Nevertheless, he accepted her statement because he needed to be desired by Nicole.

About a year later, Philip learned that Nicole had had another affair, but before he could confront her and break off their relationship, he had to leave for a five-day business trip. By the time he returned he was able to reason that, perhaps, he could accept Nicole's right to sleep with other men. Also, Nicole convinced him that the other man didn't mean anything to her and she loved only Philip.

A little later, there was a third affair, one which Nicole made sure Philip would discover. Once again, Philip was filled with anger and jealousy. But once again, Nicole reassured him that the man meant nothing to her.

Though on one level Philip wished to accept Nicole's behavior, on another he felt betrayed by her affairs. Yet, he did not seem to be able to leave her and to search for some other woman to love. He was paralyzed—unable to change his relationship with Nicole, but also unable to break it off. At this point in Philip's life, he sought therapy from Dr. Rollo May.

OVERVIEW

Shortly after World War II a new psychology—existential psychology—began to spread from Europe to the United States. Existential psychology is rooted in the philosophy of Søren Kierkegaard, Friedrick Nietzsche, Martin Heidegger, Jean-Paul Sartre, and other European writers. The first existential psychologists were also Europeans and these included Ludwig Binswanger, Medard Boss, Victor Frankl, and others.

For the past 40 years the foremost spokesperson for existential psychology in the United States has been Rollo May. During his years as a psychotherapist, May evolved a new way of looking at human beings. His approach is not based on any controlled scientific research, but rather on clinical experience. He sees people as living in the world of present experiences and ultimately being responsible for what they become. May's penetrating insights and profound analyses of the human condition have made him a popular writer among lay people and professional psychologists.

Many people, May believes, lack the courage to face their destiny and in the process of fleeing from it they give up much of their freedom. Having negated their freedom, they likewise abrogate their responsibility. Not being willing to make choices, they lose sight of who they are and develop a sense of insignificance and alienation. Healthy people, on the other hand, challenge their destiny, cherish their freedom, and live authentically with other people and with themselves. They recognize the inevitability of death and have the courage to live life in the present.

BIOGRAPHY OF ROLLO MAY

Rollo Reese May was born April 21, 1909, in Ada, Ohio, the first son of the six children born to Earl Tittle and Matie Boughton. Neither parent was very well educated and May's early intellectual climate was virtually nonexistent. In fact, when his older sister had a psychotic breakdown some years later, May's father attributed it to too much education! (Bilmer, 1978).

At an early age, May moved with his family to Marine City, Michigan, where he spent most of his childhood. May's parents had frequent arguments and eventually they separated. As a child Rollo was not particularly close to either parent. His father was a YMCA secretary who moved frequently during Rollo's youth. His mother, according to May's description, was a "bitch-kitty on wheels" and he attributed his own two failed marriages to her unpredictable behavior and to his older sister's psychotic episode (Rabinowitz, Good, & Cozad, 1989, p. 437). During his childhood Rollo found solitude and relief from family strife by playing on the shores of the St. Clair River. The river became his friend, a serene place to swim during the summer and ice skate during the winter. He claimed to have learned more from the river than from the school he attended in Marine City (Rabinowitz, Good, & Cozad, 1989). As a youth he acquired an interest in art and literature, interests which never left him. He attended college at Michigan State where he majored in English. However, he was asked to leave school soon after he became editor of a radical student magazine. May then transferred to Oberlin College in Ohio and received his bachelor's degree from there in 1930.

For the next three years, May followed a course very similar to the one traveled by Erik Erikson (see Chapter 3) some 10 years earlier. He roamed throughout eastern and southern Europe as an artist painting pictures and studying native art (Harris, 1969). Actually, the nominal purpose for May's trip was to tutor English at Anatolia College, in Saloniki, Greece. This job provided him time to work as an itinerant artist in Turkey, Poland, Austria, and other countries. However, by his second year, May was beginning to become lonely. As a consequence, he poured himself into his work as a teacher, but the harder he worked the less effective he became.

> Finally in the spring of that second year I had what is called, euphemistically, a nervous breakdown. Which meant simply that the rules, principles, values, by which I used to work and live simply did not suffice anymore. I got so completely fatigued that I had to go to bed for two weeks to get enough energy to continue my teaching. I had learned enough psychology at college to know that these symptoms meant that something was wrong with my whole way of life. I had to find some new goals and purposes for my living and to relinquish my moralistic, somewhat rigid way of existence (May, 1985, p. 8).

From that point May began to listen to his inner voice, the one that spoke to him of beauty. "It seems it had taken a collapse of my whole former way of life for this voice to make itself heard" (May, 1985, p. 13).

A second experience in Europe also left a lasting impression on him, namely, his attendance at

Alfred Adler's summer seminars at a resort in the mountains above Vienna. May greatly admired Adler and learned a lot about human beings and about himself during that time (Rabinowitz, Good, & Cozad, 1989).

After May returned to the United States he enrolled at Union Theological Seminary in New York, the same seminary Carl Rogers had attended 10 years earlier. Unlike Rogers, however, May did not enter the seminary to order to become a minister, but rather to ask the ultimate questions concerning the nature of human beings (Harris, 1969). While at the Union Theological Seminary he met the renowned existential theologian and philosopher Paul Tillich, then a recent refugee from Germany and a faculty member at the seminary. May learned much of his philosophy from Tillich and the two remained friends for over 30 years.

Though May had not gone to seminary to be a preacher, after he received his Bachelor of Divinity degree in 1938 he served as a minister for two years in Montclair, New Jersey. However, he found parish work meaningless so he quit in order to pursue his interest in psychology. He studied psychoanalysis at the William Alanson White Institute of Psychiatry, Psychoanalysis, and Psychology while working as a counselor to male students at the City College of New York. At about this time he met Harry Stack Sullivan (see Chapter 6), president and cofounder of the William Alanson White Institute. May was impressed with Sullivan's notion that the therapist is a participant observer and that therapy is a human adventure capable of enhancing the life of both patient and therapist. He also met and was influenced by Erich Fromm (see Chapter 8), who at that time was a faculty member at the William Alanson White Institute.

In 1946 May opened his own private practice and later joined the faculty of the William Alanson White Institute. In 1949, at the relatively advanced age of 40, he earned the first Ph.D. in clinical psychology awarded by Columbia University.

Prior to receiving his doctorate, May underwent the most profound experience of his life. While still in his early thirties, he contracted tuberculosis and spent three years at the Saranac Sanitarium in upstate New York. At that time there was no medication for the disease, and for a year and a half May did not know whether he would live or die. He felt helpless and had little to do except wait for the monthly X-ray that would tell whether the cavity in his lung was getting larger or smaller (May, 1972).

At that point, he began to develop some insight into the nature of his illness. He realized that the disease was taking advantage of his helpless and passive attitude. He saw that the patients around him who accepted their illness were the very ones who tended to die, while those who fought against their condition tended to survive. "Not until I developed some 'fight,' some sense of personal responsibility for the fact that it was *I* who had the tuberculosis, an assertion of my own will to live, did I make lasting progress" (May, 1972, p. 14).

As May learned to listen to his body he discovered that healing is an active, not a passive, process. The person who is sick, be it physiologically or psychologically, must be an active participant in the therapeutic process. May realized this truth for himself as he recovered from tuberculosis, but it was only later that he was able to see that his psychotherapy patients also had to fight against their disturbance in order to get better (May, 1972).

During his illness and recovery May was writing a book on anxiety. To better understand the subject he read both Freud and Søren Kierkegaard, the great Danish existential philosopher and theologian. He admired Freud, but was more deeply moved by Kierkegaard's view of anxiety as a struggle against *nonbeing,* that is, loss of consciousness (May, 1969a).

After he recovered from his illness he wrote his dissertation on the subject of anxiety and the next year published it under the title *The Meaning of Anxiety* (May, 1950). Three years later he wrote *Man's Search for Himself* (May, 1953), the book that gained for him some recognition, not only in professional circles, but among other educated people as well. In 1958 he collaborated with Ernest Angel and Henri Ellenberger to publish *Existence: A New Dimension in Psychiatry and Psychology.* This book introduced American psychotherapists to the concepts of existential therapy and continued the popularity of the existential movement. May's best-known work, *Love and Will* (1969c), became a national best seller and won the 1970 Ralph Waldo Emerson Award for humane scholarship.

May has been a visiting professor at both Harvard and Princeton and has lectured at such institutions as Yale, Dartmouth, Columbia, Vassar, Oberlin, and the New School for Social Research. In addition, he has been an adjunct professor at New York University, chairman for the Council for the Association of Existential Psychology and Psychiatry, president of the New York Psychological Association, and a member of the Board of Trustees of the American Foundation for Mental Health. He has two daughters and a son from his first marriage and currently lives in Tiburon, California.

Through his books, articles, and lectures May has become the best-known American spokesperson for the existential movement. Nevertheless, he has spoken out against the tendency of some existentialists to slip into an antiscientific or even antiintellectual posture (May, 1962). He has been critical of any attempt to dilute existential psychology into a painless method of reaching self-fulfillment. People can aspire to psychological health only through coming to grips with the unconscious core of their existence. Though philosophically aligned with Carl Rogers (see Chapter 17), May takes issue with what he sees as Rogers's naive view that evil is a cultural phenomenon. To May (1982), human beings are both good and evil, prompting them to create cultures that are both good and evil.

BACKGROUND OF EXISTENTIALISM

Modern existential psychology has it roots in the writings of Søren Kierkegaard (1813–1855), Danish philosopher and theologian. Kierkegaard was concerned with the increasing trend in modern societies toward the dehumanization of people. He opposed any attempt to see people merely as objects, but at the same time he opposed the view that subjective perceptions are one's only reality. Instead, Kierkegaard was concerned with *both* the experiencing person and the person's experience. He wished to understand people as they exist in the world as thinking, active, and willing beings. As May (1967, p. 67) put it, "Kierkegaard sought to overcome the dichotomy of reason and emotion by turning men's attentions to the reality of the immediate experience which underlies both subjectivity and objectivity."

Kierkegaard, like later existentialists, emphasized an equilibrium between *freedom* and *responsibility*. People acquire freedom of action through expanding their self-awareness and then by assuming responsibility for their actions. The acquisition of freedom and responsibility, however, is achieved only at the expense of anxiety. As people realize that, ultimately, they are in charge of their own destiny, they experience the burden of freedom and the pain of responsibility.

Kierkegaard's views had little effect on philosophical thought during his comparatively short lifetime (he died at age 44), but the work of two German philosophers, Friedrick Nietzsche (1844–1900) and Martin Heidegger (1899–1976), helped carry existential philosophy into the twentieth century. Heidegger, especially, exerted considerable influence on two Swiss psychiatrists, Ludwig Binswanger and Medard Boss. Binswanger and Boss, along with Karl Jaspers, Victor Frankl, and others, adapted the philosophy of existentialism to the practice of psychotherapy.

Existentialism has also permeated modern literature through the work of the French writer, Jean-Paul Sartre and the French-Algerian novelist, Albert Camus; religion through the writings of Martin Buber, Paul Tillich, and others; and the world of art through the work of Cezanne, Matisse, and Picasso, whose paintings break through the boundaries of realism and demonstrate a freedom of being rather than the freedom of doing (May, 1981).

After World War II European existentialism in its various forms spread to the United States and became even more diversified as it was taken up by an assorted collection of writers, artists, dissidents, college professors and students, playwrights, clergy, and others. The variety of interpretations threatened the existence of existentialism as a meaningful entity. In more recent years, however, existentialism has lost some of its popularity and, paradoxically, has strengthened its position as an alternate means of understanding humanity.

What Is Existentialism?

Though there are still a variety of interpretations of existentialism, some common elements are found among most existential thinkers. First, *exis-*

tence takes precedence over *essence*. Existence means to emerge or to become; essence implies a static immutable substance. Existence suggests process; essence refers to a product. Existence is associated with growth and change; essence signifies stagnation and finality. Western civilization, and particularly Western science, has traditionally valued essence over existence. It has sought to understand the essential composition of things, including humans. Existentialists, on the other hand, affirm that people's essence is their existence, their power to continually define themselves through the choices they make.

Second, existentialism opposes the split between subject and object. May (1958b, p. 11) defines existentialism as *"the endeavor to understand man by cutting below the cleavage between subject and object."* As we have seen, Kierkegaard opposed those who saw the person only as a subjective thinking being. May (1969a, p. 6) quotes Kierkegaard as saying "Truth exists for the individual only as he himself produces it in action." In other words, people find the truth by living honest and authentic lives and not by armchair contemplation. On the other hand, Kierkegaard also criticized those who wished to make people into machines or objects. Each individual is a unique being and must not be viewed as a mere cog in the machinery of an industrialized society.

Third, people search for some meaning to their lives. They ask (though not always consciously) the important questions concerning their being. Who am I? Is life worth living? Does it have a meaning? How can I realize my humanity?

Fourth, existentialists hold that ultimately each of us is responsible for who we are and what we become. We cannot blame parents, teachers, employers, God, or circumstances. As Sartre (1957, p. 15) said, "Man is nothing else but what he makes of himself. Such is the first principle of existentialism." Though we may associate with others in productive and healthy relationships, in the end, we are each alone. We can choose to become what we can be, or we can choose to avoid commitment and choice. But ultimately it is our choice.

Fifth, existentialists are basically antitheoretical. To them, theories further dehumanize people and render them as objects. As we saw in Chapter 1, theories are constructed, in part, to explain phenomena. Existentialists are generally opposed to this. Authentic experience takes precedence over artificial explanations. When experiences are molded into some preexisting theoretical model, they lose their authenticity and become divorced from the individual who experienced them.

Basic Concepts

Before proceeding to Rollo May's view of humanity, we will pause to look at two basic concepts of existentialism, namely, being-in-the-world and nonbeing.

Being-in-the-World

Existentialists adopt a phenomenological approach to understanding humanity. We exist in a world that can be best understood from our own perspective. Studying people from an external frame of reference violates both the subjects and their world. The essential unity of person and environment is expressed in the German word *Dasein*, meaning to exist there. Hence, *Dasein* literally means to exist in the world and is generally written as **being-in-the-world.** The hyphens in this term imply a oneness of subject and object, of person and world.

Many people suffer from anxiety and despair brought on by their alienation from themselves and/or from their world. They either have no clear image of self or they feel isolated from a world that seems distant and foreign. They have no sense of *Dasein*, no unity of self and world. As people strive to gain power over nature they lose touch with their relationship to the natural world. As they come to rely on the products of the industrial revolution, they become more alienated from the stars, the soil, and the sea. Alienation from the world includes one's own body as well. Recall that Rollo May began his recovery from tuberculosis only after realizing that it was *he* who had the illness.

This feeling of isolation and alienation of self from the world is suffered not only by pathologically disturbed individuals but also by most individuals in modern societies. It is the illness of our time and it manifests itself in three areas: (1) separation from nature, (2) lack of meaningful interpersonal relations, and (3) alienation from one's authentic self. Thus, there are three simultaneous aspects or modes of world that characterize people in their being-in-the-world. The first of these is **Umwelt,** or the environment around us. The second is **Mitwelt** (literally, the with world) that refers to our relations with other people. Third is **Eigenwelt,** or our relationship with our self.

Umwelt is the world of objects and things and would exist even if people had no awareness. It is the world of nature and natural law. It includes our biological drives, such as hunger and sleep, and such natural phenomena as birth and death. We cannot escape *Umwelt;* we must learn to live in the world around us and to adjust to changes within this world. Freud's theory with its emphasis on biology and instincts deals mostly with *Umwelt.*

But we do not live only in *Umwelt.* We also live in the world with people, that is, *Mitwelt.* We must relate to people as people, not as things. If we treat people as objects, then we are living solely in *Umwelt.* The difference between *Umwelt* and *Mitwelt* can be seen by contrasting sex with love. If I use another as an instrument for sexual gratification, then *Umwelt* dominates my life in relation to that person. However, love demands that I make a commitment to the other person. If I love someone, then I respect that person's being-in-the-world; I don't try to mold or change that person. If I relate to a person with love, then I am living in *Mitwelt.* Not every *Mitwelt* relationship necessitates love. The essential criterion is that the *Dasein* of the other person is respected. The theories of Sullivan and Rogers, with their emphasis on interpersonal relations, deal mostly with *Mitwelt.*

Eigenwelt refers to our relationship with our self. It is a world not usually explored by other personality theorists. To live in *Eigenwelt* means to be aware of our self as a human being and to grasp who we are as we relate to the world of things and to the world of people. What does this sunset mean to *me?* How is this other person a part of *my* life? What characteristics of *mine* allow me to love this person? How do *I* perceive this experience?

Healthy people live in *Umwelt, Mitwelt,* and *Eigenwelt* simultaneously. They adapt to the natural world, relate to others as humans, and have a keen awareness of what all these experiences mean to them (May, 1958a).

Nonbeing

Being-in-the-world necessitates an awareness of self as a living, emerging being. This, in turn, leads to the dread of not being, that is, **nonbeing** or **nothingness.** May (1958a, pp. 47–48) writes that

> to grasp what it means to exist, one needs to grasp the fact that he might not exist, that he treads at every moment on the sharp edge of possible annihilation and can never escape the fact that death will arrive at some unknown moment in the future.

Death is not the only avenue of nonbeing, but it is the most obvious one. Life becomes more vital, more meaningful when we confront the possibility of our death. May (1958, p. 49) views death as "the one fact of my life which is not relative but absolute, and my awareness of this gives my existence and what I do each hour an absolute quality."

When nonbeing is not courageously confronted through contemplation of death, it manifests itself in a variety of other forms, including addiction to alcohol or other drugs, promiscuous sexual activity, and other compulsive behaviors. Nonbeing is also expressed by a blind conformity to society's expectations and by a generalized hostility that pervades our relationships.

Self-awareness is dimmed and nonbeing approached when we flee from making active choices, that is, choices based on a consideration of who we are and what we want. Nonbeing prevents us from realizing our potentials and from seeing ourself as a unique individual.

ANXIETY

The failure to confront death serves as a temporary escape from the anxiety or dread of nonbeing. But the escape cannot be permanent. Death is the one absolute of life that sooner or later everyone must face. We experience **anxiety** when we become aware that our existence or some value identified with it might be destroyed (May, 1977a). May (1958a, p. 50) defined anxiety as "the subjective state of the individual's becoming aware that his existence can be destroyed, that he can lose himself and his world, that he can become 'nothing'." At another time he defined anxiety as a threat to some important *value.* Anxiety, May (1967, p. 72) said, is *"the apprehension cued off by a threat to some value which the individual holds essential to his existence as a self."*

The dread of nonbeing can take the form of isolation and alienation.

Anxiety, then, can spring either from an awareness of our nonbeing or from a threat to some value essential to our existence. But anxiety also arises from growth and change. The acquisition of freedom inevitably leads to anxiety. Freedom cannot exist without anxiety, nor can anxiety exist without an awareness of the possibility of freedom. May (1981, p. 185) quotes Kierkegaard as saying that "anxiety is the dizziness of freedom." Anxiety, like dizziness, can be either pleasurable or painful, constructive or destructive. It can give us energy and zest, but it can also paralyze and panic us. Moreover, anxiety can be either normal or neurotic.

Normal Anxiety

We live in an age of anxiety. No one can escape its effects. To grow and to change one's values means to experience constructive or normal anxiety. May (1967, p. 80) defined **normal anxiety** as that "which is proportionate to the threat, does not involve repression, and can be confronted constructively on the conscious level."

As we grow from infancy to old age our values change and with each step normal anxiety is experienced. "All growth consists of the anxiety-creating surrender of past values" (May, 1967, p. 80). Normal anxiety is also experienced during those creative moments when an artist, a scientist, or a philosopher suddenly achieves insight. Insight leads to a recognition that one's life, and perhaps the lives of countless others, will be permanently changed. For example, scientists who witnessed the first atomic bomb tests in Alamogordo, New Mexico, experienced normal anxiety with the realization that from that moment, everything had been changed (May, 1981).

Neurotic Anxiety

Normal anxiety, the type experienced during periods of growth or of threat to one's values, is experienced by everyone. It can be constructive provided it remains proportionate to the threat. But anxiety can become neurotic or sick. May (1967, p. 80) defined **neurotic anxiety** as "a reaction which is disportionate to the threat, involves repression and other forms of intrapsychic conflict, and is managed by various kinds of blocking-off of activity and awareness."

While normal anxiety is felt whenever values are threatened, neurotic anxiety is experienced whenever values become transformed into dogma. To be absolutely right in our beliefs provides us with temporary security, but it is security "bought at the price of surrendering [our] opportunity for fresh learning and new growth" (May, 1967, p. 80).

Philip, the case study introduced at the beginning of this chapter, suffered from neurotic anxiety. Like others who experience neurotic anxiety, Philip behaved in a nonproductive, self-defeating manner. Though he was deeply hurt by Nicole's unpredictable and "crazy" behavior, he became paralyzed with inaction and could not break off their relationship. Nicole's actions seemed to engender in Philip a sense of duty toward her. Because she obviously needed him, he felt obligated to take care of her.

Philip's attachment to unpredictable and "crazy" women began in early childhood. During the first two years of his life, his world was inhabited primarily by just two other people—his mother and a sister two years older than him. His mother was a borderline schizophrenic whose behavior toward Philip alternated between tenderness and cruelty. His sister was definitely schizophrenic, and later spent some time in a mental hospital.

> Thus, Philip endured his first years in the world learning to deal with two exceedingly unpredictable women. Indeed, he must have had inescapably imprinted on him that he needed not only to rescue women, but that one of his functions in life was to stick by them, especially when they acted their craziest. Life, then, for Philip would understandably not be free, but rather would require that he be continuously on guard or on duty (May, 1981, p. 30).

We will return to Philip later in this chapter, but at this point his story can be used to illustrate how neurotic anxiety blocks growth and productive action. Philip could find no new way of behaving toward Nicole. His approach seemed to be a recapitulation of childhood behaviors toward his mother and sister.

GUILT

Just as May uses the term anxiety to refer to large issues dealing with our being-in-the-world, so too does he employ the concept of **guilt.** In this sense, both anxiety and guilt are **ontological,** that is, they refer to the nature of being and not to feelings arising from specific situations or transgressions.

May (1958a) recognized three forms of ontological guilt, each corresponding to the three modes of being-in-the-world—*Umwelt, Mitwelt,* and *Eigenwelt.*

The first form of guilt arises out of our separation from the natural world *(Umwelt).* As civilization advances technologically and scientifically we become further and further removed from nature. This form of ontological guilt is especially prevalent in "advanced" societies where people live in heated or cooled dwellings, use motorized means of transportation, and consume food gathered and prepared by others.

The second form of guilt stems from our inability to perceive accurately the world of others *(Mitwelt).* We can only see other people through our own eyes and thus can never perfectly judge their needs. Because we cannot unerringly anticipate the needs of others, we feel inadequate in our relations with them. This leads to a pervasive condition of guilt, one experienced by all of us to some extent.

The third form of ontological guilt is associated with our denial of our own potentialities or with our failure to fulfill them. In other words, it is grounded in our relationship with self *(Eigenwelt).* Again, this form of guilt is universal since none of us can completely fulfill all our potentials.

Ontological guilt can have either a positive or a negative effect on personality. We can use it to develop a healthy sense of humility, to improve our relations with others, and to creatively use our potentialities. However, when we refuse to accept ontological guilt it becomes neurotic or morbid. Neurotic guilt, like neurotic anxiety, then leads to nonproductive or neurotic symptoms such as sexual impotency, depression, cruelty to others, or inability to make a choice.

INTENTIONALITY

The ability to make a choice implies some underlying structure upon which that choice is made. The structure that gives meaning to our experience and allows us to make decisions about the future is called **intentionality** (May, 1969c). Without intentionality we could neither choose nor act upon our choice. Action implies intentionality, just as intentionality implies action. The two are inseparable: "The act is in the intention, and the intention in the act" (May, 1969c, p. 242).

May uses the term intentionality to bridge the gap between subject and object. Intentionality is "the structure of meaning which makes it possible for us, subjects that we are, to see and understand the outside world, objective as it is. In intentionality, the dichotomy between subject and object is partially overcome" (May, 1969c, p. 225).

To illustrate how intentionality partially bridges the gap between subject and object, May (1969c) used a simple example of a man (the subject) seated at his desk observing a piece of paper (the object). The man can write on the paper, fold it into a paper airplane for his grandson, or sketch a picture on it. In all three instances the subject and object are identical, but the man's actions depend on his intentions and on the meaning he gives to his experience. That meaning is a function of both himself (subject) and his environment (object).

Intentionality is not always conscious. It "goes below levels of immediate awareness, and includes spontaneous, bodily elements and other dimensions which are usually called 'unconscious'" (May, 1969c, p. 234). Unconscious intentionality can be illustrated with our case study, Philip, who felt a duty to take care of Nicole despite her unpredictable and "crazy" behavior. Philip did not see that his actions were in some way connected to his early experiences with his unpredictable mother and his "crazy" sister. He was trapped in his unconscious belief that unpredictable and "crazy" women must be cared for, and this intentionality made it impossible for him to discover new ways of relating to Nicole.

CARE, LOVE, AND WILL

Philip had a history of taking care of others, especially women. He had given Nicole a "job" with his company that permitted her to work at home and earn enough money to live on. In addition, after she ended her affair with Craig and gave up her "crazy" plan to move across country, Philip gave her several thousand dollars. He previously had felt a duty to take care of his two wives and, before that, his mother and sister.

In spite of Philip's pattern of taking *care of* women, he never really learned to *care for* them. To care for someone means to recognize that person as a fellow human being, to identify with that person's pain or joy, guilt or pity. Care is an active process, the opposite of apathy. "Care is a state in which something does *matter*" (May, 1969c, p. 289).

Care is not the same as love, but it is the source of love. To love means to *care,* to recognize the essential humanity of the other person, to have an active regard for that person's development. May (1953, p. 206) defined love as a "delight in the presence of the other person and an affirming of his value and development as much as one's own." Without care there can be no love—only empty sentimentality or transient sexual arousal.

Care is also the source of **will.** May (1969, p. 218) defined will as *"the capacity to organize one's self* so that movement in a certain direction or toward a certain goal may take place." May distinguished between will and *wish,* the latter simply meaning *"the imaginative playing with the possibility* of some act or state occurring" (May, 1969c, p. 218). More forcefully he stated:

"Will" requires self-consciousness; "wish" does not. "Will" implies some possibility of either/or choice; "wish" does not. "Wish" gives the warmth, the content, the imagination, the child's play, the freshness, and the richness to "will." "Will" gives the self-direction, the maturity to "wish." "Will" protects "wish," permits it to continue without running risks which are too great (May, 1969c, p. 218).

Union of Love and Will

Modern society, May (1969c) claims, is suffering from an unhealthy division of love and will. Love has become associated with sensual love or sex, while will has come to mean a dogged determination or will power. Neither concept captures the true meaning of these two terms. When love is seen as sex, it becomes temporary and lacking in commitment; there is no will, but only wish. When will is seen as will power, it becomes self-serving and lacking in passion; there is no care, but only manipulation.

Love and will "are not united by automatic biological growth but must be part of our conscious development" (May, 1969c, p. 283). In fact, there are biological reasons why love and will are separated. When we first come into the world we are at one with the universe *(Umwelt),* our mother *(Mitwelt),* and ourself *(Eigenwelt).* "Our needs are met without self-conscious effort on our part, as, biologically, in the early condition of nursing at the mother's breast. This is the 'first freedom,' the first 'yes' " (May, 1969c, p. 284).

Then, when will begins to develop, it manifests itself as opposition, the first "no." The blissful existence of early infancy is now opposed by the emerging willfulness of late infancy. The "no" should not be seen as a statement against the parents, but rather a positive assertion of self. Unfortunately, parents often interpret the "no" negatively and therefore stifle the child's self-assertion. As a result, children learn to disassociate will from the blissful love they had previously enjoyed.

Our task, says May, is to unite love and will. This is not an easy task, but it is a possible one. Neither blissful love nor self-serving will have a role in the uniting of love and will. For the mature person, both love and will mean a reaching out toward another person. Both involve care, both necessitate choice, both imply action, and both require responsibility.

Forms of Love

Love is obviously more than sex, but sex is one form of love. May (1969c) identifies four kinds of love in Western tradition—sex, eros, philia, and agape.

Sex

Sex is a biological function that can be satisfied through sexual intercourse or some other release of sexual tension. Although it has become cheapened in modern Western societies, "it still remains the power of procreation, the drive which perpetuates the race, the source at once of the human being's most intense pleasure and his most pervasive anxiety" (May, 1969c, p. 38).

May believes that in ancient times sex was taken for granted, just as eating and sleeping were taken for granted. In modern times sex has become a problem. First, there was a denial of sexual feelings that took place during the Victorian period, when sex was not a topic of conversation in polite company. Then came a reaction against sexual suppression. Beginning with the 1920s, sex suddenly came into the open, and since then our preoccupation with sex has caused it to become trivialized. As May (1969c) points out, we went from a period when *having* sex was frought with guilt and anxiety to a time when *not having* it brought about guilt and anxiety.

Eros

In our society sex is frequently confused with **eros.** Sex is a physiological need that seeks gratification through the release of tension. Eros is a psychological desire that seeks procreation or creation through an enduring union with a loved one.

In comparing eros to sex, May (1969c, p. 74) writes:

Eros, on the other hand, takes wings from human imagination and is forever transcending all techniques, giving the laugh to all the "how to" books by gaily swinging into orbit above our mechanical rules, making love rather than manipulating organs.

Eros is built on care and tenderness. It longs to establish an enduring union with the other person, such that both partners experience delight and passion and both are broadened and deepened by the experience. Eros is the kind of love that draws two people together to form a lasting relationship, for example, in marriage. Because the human species could not survive without desire for a lasting union, eros can be regarded as the salvation of sex.

Philia

While eros is the salvation of sex, it in turn is built on the foundation of **philia.** Philia refers to an intimate but nonsexual friendship between two people, for example, brother and sister. Philia cannot be rushed; it takes time to grow, to develop, to sink its roots. "Philia does not require that we do anything for the beloved except accept him, be with him, and enjoy him. It is friendship in the simplest, most direct terms" (May, 1969a, p. 31).

In Chapter 6 we saw that Harry Stack Sullivan placed great importance on preadolescence, that developmental epoch characterized by the need for a chum, someone who is more or less like oneself. According to Sullivan, chumship or philia is a necessary requisite for healthy erotic relationships during early and late adolescence. May, who was influenced by Sullivan, agrees that philia makes eros possible. The gradual, relaxed development of true friendship is a prerequisite for the enduring union of two people.

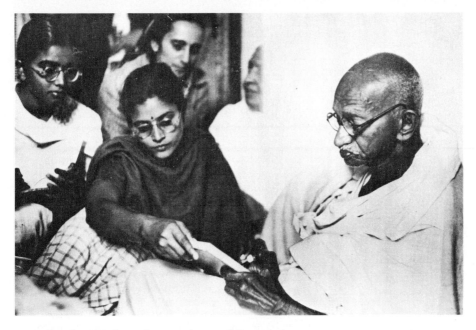

Agape is altruistic love that requires nothing in return.

Agape

Just as eros depends on philia, so philia needs **agape.** May (1969c, p. 319) defines agape as "esteem for the other, the concern for the other's welfare beyond any gain that one can get out of it; disinterested love, typically, the love of God for man."

Agape is altruistic love. It is a kind of spiritual love that carries with it the risk of playing God. It does not depend on any behaviors or characteristics of the other person. In this sense, it is undeserved and unconditional.

Healthy adult relationships, May believes, blend all four forms of love. They are based on sexual satisfaction, a desire for an enduring union, genuine friendship, and an unselfish concern for the welfare of the other person. Such authentic love, unfortunately, is quite difficult. It requires self-affirmation and the assertion of oneself. "At the same time it requires tenderness, affirmation of the other, relaxing of competition as much as possible, self-abnegation at times in the interests of the loved one, and the age-old virtues of mercy and forgiveness" (May, 1981, p. 147).

FREEDOM AND DESTINY

We have seen that a blend of the four forms of love requires both self-assertion and an affirmation of the other person. It also requires an assertion of one's *freedom* and a confrontation with one's *destiny*. Healthy individuals are able both to assume their freedom and to face their destiny.

Freedom Defined

In an early definition May (1967, p. 175) said that "freedom is the individual's capacity to *know that he is the determined one.*" The word "determined" in this definition is synonymous with what May (1981) would later call *destiny.* Freedom, then, comes from an understanding of our destiny; an understanding that death is a possibility at any moment, that we are male or female, that we have inherent weaknesses, that early childhood experiences dispose us toward certain patterns of behavior.

Freedom is the possibility of changing, though we may not know what those changes might be. Freedom "entails being able *to harbor different possibilities in one's mind even though it is not clear at the moment which way one must act*" (May, 1981, pp. 10–11). This condition often leads to increases in anxiety, but it is normal anxiety, the kind that healthy people welcome and are able to manage.

Forms of Freedom

May (1981) recognized two forms of freedom—freedom of doing and freedom of being. The first he calls **existential freedom;** the latter, **essential freedom.**

Existential Freedom

Existential freedom, May insists, should not be identified with existential philosophy. It is the freedom of action—the freedom of doing. Most middle-class adult Americans enjoy large measures of existential freedom. They are free to travel across state lines, to choose their associates, to vote for their representatives in government, and so on. On a more trivial scale, they are free to push their shopping carts through a supermarket and select from among thousands of items. Existential freedom, then, is the freedom to act on the choices that one makes.

Essential Freedom

Freedom of action, however, does not insure freedom of being. At times, in fact, it seems that existential freedom makes essential freedom more difficult. May (1981) cites several examples of prisoners and inmates in concentration camps who speak enthusiastically of their "inner freedom." Perhaps solitary confinement or the denial of liberty allows people to face their destiny and to gain their freedom of being. May (1981, p. 60) framed this question in these words: "Do we get to essential freedom only when our everyday existence is interrupted?"

May's answer is: "No." One need not be imprisoned to attain essential freedom, that is, freedom of being. Destiny itself is our prison—our concentration camp that allows us to be less concerned with freedom of doing and more concerned with essential freedom.

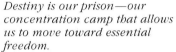

Destiny is our prison—our concentration camp that allows us to move toward essential freedom.

Does not the engaging of our destiny—which is the design of our life—hedge us about with the confinement, the sobriety, indeed, often the cruelty, which forces us to look beyond the limits of day-to-day action? Is not the inescapable fact of death . . . the concentration camp of us all? Is not the fact that life is a joy and a bondage at the same time enough to drive us to consider the deeper aspect of being (May, 1981, p. 61)?

Destiny Defined

May (1981, p. 89) defines destiny "as the pattern of limits and talents that constitutes the 'givens' in life." Destiny is *"the design of the universe speaking through the design of each one of us"* (May, 1981, p. 90). Our ultimate destiny is death, but on a lesser scale our destiny includes other biological properties such as intelligence, gender, size and strength, and genetic predisposition toward certain illnesses. In addition, psychological and cultural factors contribute to our destiny.

Destiny does not mean preordained or foredoomed. It is our destination, our terminus, our goal. Within the boundaries of our destiny we have the power to choose, and this freedom allows us to confront and challenge our destiny. It does not, however, permit any change we wish. We cannot be successful at any job, conquer any illness, enjoy a fulfilling relationship with any person. "Our destiny cannot be cancelled out; we cannot erase it or substitute anything else for it. But we can choose how we shall respond, how we shall live out our talents which confront us" (May, 1981, p. 89).

May suggests that freedom and destiny, like love–hate, life–death, are not antithetical but rather a normal paradox of life. "The paradox is that freedom owes its vitality to destiny, and destiny owes its significance to freedom" (May, 1981, p. 17). Freedom and destiny are thus inexorably intertwined; one cannot exist without the other. Freedom without destiny is license. Ironically, license leads to anarchy and the ultimate destruction of freedom. Without destiny, then, there is no freedom, but without freedom destiny is meaningless.

Freedom and destiny give birth to each other. As we challenge our destiny we gain freedom and as we achieve freedom we push at the boundaries of destiny.

Philip's Destiny

When Philip, our case study, first walked into Rollo May's office he was paralyzed with inaction because he refused to accept his destiny. He saw no connection between his adult pattern of relating to women and the strategy that, as an infant, he had adopted in order to survive in an unpredictable and "crazy" world. His destiny was not fixed by those early experiences. Philip, like other people, had the freedom to change his destiny. First he had to recognize his biological, social, and psychological limitations and then he had to possess the courage to make choices within those limitations. Philip lacked both the understanding and the courage to confront his destiny. Up to the point of seeking therapy, he had tried to compensate for his destiny, to consciously deny it. "He had been searching for someone who would make up for his having been born into an unwelcoming world consisting of a disturbed mother and a schizophrenic sister, a destiny that he did not in the slightest choose" (May, 1981, p. 88). Philip's denial of his destiny "only contributed to resentment, a longing and yearning that he could not understand" (May, 1981, p. 89).

Philip's inability or unwillingness to face his destiny robbed him of personal freedom and kept him tied to his mother. He treated his wives and Nicole in the same way that earlier had proven successful with his mother and sister. He could not dare express his anger to women, but instead, he adopted a charming though somewhat possessive and protective attitude toward them. May (1981, p. 89) insists that "the freedom of each of us is in proportion to the degree with which we confront and live in relation to our destiny." After several weeks of psychotherapy Philip was able to stop blaming his mother for not doing what he thought she should have done. When he began to see the positive things she *did* do, he began to change his attitude toward her. The objective facts of his childhood had not changed, but his subjective perceptions had. As Philip came to terms with his destiny, he began to be able to express his anger, to feel less trapped in his relationship with Nicole, and to become more aware of his possibilities. In other words, he gained his freedom of being.

PSYCHOPATHOLOGY

May's ideas on psychopathology have grown out of 50 years' experience as a psychotherapist. During that time he evolved a way of looking at psychological disturbance which differs widely from the traditional perspective that relies on diagnostic labels and specific disorders. According to May, apathy and emptiness are the malaise of our time—not anxiety and guilt. When people deny their destiny, they lose their purpose for being, they become directionless. Without some goal or destination people become sick and engage in a variety of self-defeating and self-destructive behaviors. "The human being cannot live in a condition of emptiness for very long: if he is not growing *toward* something, he does not merely stagnate; the pent-up potentialities turn into morbidity and despair, and eventually into destructive activities" (May, 1953, p. 24).

Many people in modern Western societies feel alienated from the world *(Umwelt);* from others *(Mitwelt);* and especially from themselves *(Eigenwelt).* They experience a sense of helplessness to avoid nuclear war, to reverse industrialization, or to make contact with another human being. They feel insignificant in a world that increasingly dehumanizes the individual. This sense of insignificance leads to *apathy* and to a state of diminished consciousness (May, 1967).

May sees psychopathology as lack of communicativeness. It is the "inability to participate in the feelings and thoughts of others or to share oneself with others" (May, 1981, p. 21). Psychologically disturbed individuals deny their destiny and, in the process, lose their freedom. They erect a variety of neurotic symptoms, not to regain their freedom, but as methods of renouncing it. Symptoms narrow the person's phenomenological world to the size that makes coping easier. The compulsive person adopts a rigid routine, thereby making new choices unnecessary.

Symptoms may be temporary, as when stress produces a headache, or they may be relatively permanent and stem from early childhood experiences. Philip's psychopathology was tied to his early environment with a disturbed mother and a schizophrenic sister. These experiences did not *cause* his pathology in the sense that they alone produced it. However, they did set up Philip to learn to adjust to his world by containing his anger, by developing a sense of apathy, and by trying to be a "good little boy." Neurotic symptoms, therefore, do not represent a failure of adjustment, but rather a proper and necessary adjustment by which one's *Dasein* can be preserved. Philip's behavior toward his two wives and Nicole represents an abrogation of his freedom and a self-defeating attempt to escape from his destiny.

PSYCHOTHERAPY

Unlike Freud, Adler, Rogers, and other clinically oriented personality theorists, May has not established a school of psychotherapy that has yielded avid followers and identifiable techniques. He has, however, written extensively on the subject.

As noted above, May does not regard anxiety and guilt as the primary ingredients in psychopathology and, consistent with this view, he does not believe that the goal of therapy should be their alleviation. In fact, he does not think that psychotherapy should be aimed at curing patients of a particular disorder, or eliminating a specific problem. Instead, he suggests that the purpose of therapy is to make people more human, to help them expand and develop their consciousness so that they will be in a better position to make choices (Hall, 1967). These choices, then, lead to the simultaneous growth of freedom and responsibility.

May (1981, pp. 19–20) states that *"the purpose of psychotherapy is to set people free. . . .* I believe that the therapist's function should be to help people become free to be aware of and to experience their possibilities." Therapists who concentrate on a patient's symptoms, May believes, are missing the more important picture. Neurotic symptoms, as we have seen, are simply ways of running away from freedom. They indicate that a patient has inner possibilities that are not being used. When a patient becomes more free, that is, more human, frequently neurotic symptoms disappear, neurotic anxiety gives way to normal anxiety, and neurotic guilt is replaced by normal guilt. But these are secondary gains and not the central purpose of therapy. May insists that psychotherapy must be concerned with helping people experience their existence and that "any cure of symptoms which will last must be a by-product of that" (May, 1967, p. 86).

How does a therapist help patients become free, responsible human beings? May does not offer many specific directions for therapists to follow. Existential therapists have no special set of techniques or methods that can be applied to all patients. Instead, they have only themselves, their own humanity to offer. They must establish a one-to-one relationship *(Mitwelt)* that enables patients to become more aware of self and to live more fully in their own world *(Eigenwelt)*. This may mean challenging patients to confront their destiny, to experience despair, anxiety, and guilt. But it also means establishing an I-thou encounter where both therapist and patient are viewed as subjects rather than objects. "In this encounter," May (1967, p. 108) writes, "I have to be able, to some extent, to experience what the patient is experiencing. My job as a therapist is to be open to his world."

Therapists must be able and willing to risk participating fully in a human encounter, an encounter that may produce despair, anxiety, and guilt for them as well as for the patient. The encounter may also produce joy and ultimately growth for both partners.

> Genuine encounter with another person always shakes our self-world relationship: our comfortable temporary security of the moment before is thrown into question . . . shall we risk ourselves, take the chance to be enriched by this new relationship? . . . Or shall we brace ourselves, throw up a stockade, hold out the other person and miss the nuances of his perceptions, feelings, intentions? Encounter is always a potentially creative experience; it normally should ensue in the expanding of con-

sciousness, the enrichment of the self. . . . In genuine encounter both persons are changed, however minutely (May, 1967, pp. 121–122).

Philosophically, May holds many of the same beliefs as Carl Rogers (see Chapter 17). Basic to both approaches is the notion of therapy as a human encounter, that is, an I-thou relationship with the potential to facilitate growth within both therapist and patient. In practice, however, May is much more likely to ask questions, to delve into a patient's early childhood, and to suggest possible meanings of present behavior. For example, he explained to Philip that his relationship with Nicole was an attempt to hold on to his mother. Rogers would reject such a technique because it emanates from an external (that is, the therapist's) frame of reference. May, however, believes in making interpretations, insisting that they can be an effective means of confronting patients with information that they have been hiding from themselves.

Another technique May used with Philip was the suggestion that he hold a fantasy conversation with his dead mother. In this conversation Philip spoke for both himself and his mother. When talking for his mother he was able for the first time to empathize with her, to see himself from her point of view. Speaking for his mother, he said that she was very proud of him and that he had always been her favorite child. Then talking for himself, he told his mother that he appreciated her courage and recalled an incident when her courage saved his eyesight. When Philip finished the fantasy conversation he said, "'I never in a thousand years would have imagined *that* would come out'"(May, 1981, p. 39).

May also asked Philip to bring a photo of himself when he was a little boy. Philip then had a fantasy conversation with "Little Philip." As the conversation ensued, "Little Philip" explained that he had triumphed over the problem that had most troubled grown Philip, namely, the fear of abandonment. "Little Philip" become Philip's friendly companion and helped him overcome his loneliness and allay his jealousy of Nicole.

At the end of therapy Philip did not become a new person, but he did become more conscious of a part of himself that had been there all the time. Awareness of new possibilities allowed him to move in the direction of personal freedom. For Philip, the end of therapy was the beginning of "the uniting of himself with that early self that he had had to lock up in a dungeon in order to survive when life was not happy but threatening" (May, 1981, p. 41).

CONCEPT OF HUMANITY

Like Erik Erikson (see Chapter 3), May has offered a new way of looking at things. His view of humanity is both broader and deeper than those of most other personality theorists. He sees people as complex beings, capable of both tremendous good and immense evil.

According to May, people have become estranged from the natural world, from other people, and, most of all, from themselves. The threat of nuclear war has turned impotence into anxiety, *"anxiety into regression and apathy, these in turn into hostility, and the hostility into an alienation of man from man"* (May, 1967, p. 32).

As people become more alienated from other people and from themselves, they surrender portions of their consciousness. They become less aware of themselves as a subject, that is, the person who is aware of the experiencing self. As the subjective self becomes obscured, people lose some of their capacity to make choices. This progression, however, is not inevitable. May believes that people, within the confines of their destiny, have the ability to make free choices. Each choice pushes back the boundaries of determinism and permits new choices. People generally have much more potential for freedom than they realize. However, free choice does not come without anxiety. Choice demands the courage to confront one's destiny, to look within and to recognize the evil as well as the good.

Choice also implies action. Without action, choice is merely a wish, an idle desire. With action comes responsibility. Freedom and responsibility are always commensurable. A person cannot have more freedom than responsibility, nor can one be shackled with more responsibility than freedom. Healthy individuals welcome both freedom and responsibility, but they realize that choice is often painful, anxiety-provoking, and difficult. Although May believes that many people have surrendered some of their ability to choose, he holds that that capitulation itself constituted a choice. Ultimately, each of us is responsible for the choices we make and those choices define us as unique human beings. May, therefore, must be rated high on the dimension of *free choice.*

Is May *optimistic* or *pessimistic?* Although he sometimes paints a rather gloomy picture of humanity, May is not pessimistic. He sees the present age as merely a plateau in humanity's quest for new symbols and new myths that will engender the species with renewed spirit.

Although May recognizes the potential impact of childhood experiences on adult personality, he clearly favors *teleology* over causality. In a comment on Clement Reeves's (1977) book, May stated: "I believe in a teleological approach—that each person, by virtue of his being a person, has certain potentialities that he is required, by life itself, to live out" (May, 1977b, pp. 303–304). Each of us has a particular destiny that we must discover and challenge or else risk alienation and neurosis.

May assumes a moderate stance on the issue of *conscious vs. unconscious* forces in personality development. By their nature, people have enormous capacity for self-awareness, but often that capacity remains fallow. People sometimes lack the courage to face their destiny or to recognize the evil that exists within their culture as well as within themselves.

Consciousness and choices are interrelated. As people make more free choices, they gain more insight into who they are, that is, they develop a greater sense of being. This sharpened sense of being, in turn, facilitates the ability to make further choices. Awareness of self and capacity for free choice are hallmarks of psychological health.

May also takes an intermediate position on *social vs. biological* influences. Society contributes to personality principally through interpersonal relationships. One's relations with other people can have either a freeing or an enslaving effect. Sick relationships, such as Philip experienced with his mother and sister, can stifle personal growth and leave one with an inability to participate in a healthy encounter with another person. Without the capacity to relate to people as people, life becomes meaningless and a person develops a sense of alienation, not only from others, but from one's self as well.

Biology also contributes to personality. Biological factors such as gender, physical size, predisposition to illnesses, and ultimately death itself, shape a person's destiny. Everyone must live within the confines of destiny, even though those confines can be expanded.

On the dimension of *uniqueness vs. similarities,* May's view of humanity leans toward uniqueness. Each of us is responsible for shaping our own personality within the limits imposed by destiny. No two of us make the same sequence of choices and no two develop identical ways of looking at things. May's emphasis on phenomenology implies individual perceptions and therefore unique personalities.

CRITIQUE OF MAY

Existentialism in general and May's psychology in particular have been criticized as being antiintellectual and antitheoretical. May acknowledges the claim that his views do not conform to the traditional concept of theory, but he staunchly defends his psychology against the charge of being antiintellectual or antiscientific. He points to the sterility of conventional scientific methods and their inability to unlock the ontological character of willing, caring, and acting human beings. May agrees with Allport, Maslow, and Rogers that a new science is needed in order to grasp the total, living person. People must be seen as subjects, not merely objects. The *Dasein* or being-in-the-world of the observer has an influence on the reactions of the people being observed, an influence that is often overlooked by traditional psychology. Both the observer and the observed are changed by their encounter with each other.

A new scientific psychology must recognize such human characteristics as uniqueness, personal freedom, destiny, phenomenological experiences, and especially our capacity to relate to ourselves as both object and subject. A new science of humans must also include *ethics.* "The actions of living, self-aware human beings are never automatic, but involve some weighing of consequences, some potentiality for good or ill" (May, 1967, p. 199).

May concludes his position on a new psychology with these words:

The outlines of a science of man we suggest will deal with man as the symbol-maker, the reasoner, the historical mammal who can participate in his community and who possesses the potentiality of freedom and ethical action. The pursuit of this science will take no less rigorous thought and wholehearted discipline than the pursuit of experimental and natural science at their best, but it will place the scientific enterprise in a broader context. Perhaps it will again be possible to study man scientifically and still see him whole (May, 1967, p. 199).

Until that new science acquires greater maturity, we must evaluate May's views by the same criteria used for each of the other personality theorists.

First, does May's philosophically oriented psychology help *organize what is currently known about human nature?* On this criterion May would receive a high rating. Compared to most theorists discussed in this book, May has more closely followed Allport's dictum, "Do not forget what you have decided to neglect" (Allport, 1968, p. 23). May has not forgotten that he has excluded discourses on developmental stages, basic motivational forces, and other factors that tend to segment the human experience. Yet May's philosophical writings have reached deep into the far recesses of the human experience and have explored aspects of humanity not examined by other personality theorists. His popularity is due in part to his ability to touch individual readers, to connect with their humanity. May's use of certain concepts are at times inconsistent and confusing, yet his ideas affect people in ways that other theorists do not.

Second, have May's ideas *generated scientific research?* May has not formulated his views in a theoretical structure and a paucity of hypotheses are suggested by his writings. On this criterion, therefore, May's existential psychology receives a very low score.

Similarly, May's psychology is quite weak as a *practical guide to action.* Though May possesses a keen understanding of human personality, his writings are more philosophical than scientific. May, in fact, has no objection to being called a philosopher and frequently refers to himself as a philosopher-therapist.

On the criterion of *internal consistency,* May's existential psychology, again, falls short. He offers a variety of definitions for such concepts as anxiety, guilt, intentionality, will, and destiny. Unfortunately, none of these terms are ever operationally defined. This imprecise terminology has also contributed to the lack of research on May's ideas.

The final criterion of a useful theory is *parsimony* and on this standard May's psychology receives a moderate rating. His writings, at times, are cumbersome and awkward, but, to his credit, he deals with complex issues and does not attempt to oversimplify human personality.

CHAPTER SUMMARY

During the past 40 years existential psychology, which began in Europe, has secured a hold in the United States. Rooted in the philosophy of Kierkegaard, Nietzsche, Sartre, and others, existential psychology holds that people are largely responsible for their own personalities. Existence is given priority over essence; growth and change are seen as being more important than stable and fixed characteristics; and process receives preference over product.

At the vanguard of existential psychology in the United States is Rollo May, a philosophically oriented psychologist who came to existentialism from a background of art and psychotherapy. May, like other existentialists, believes that (1) existence precedes essence, meaning that what people *do* is more important than what they *are;* (2) people are both subjective and objective, that is, they are thinking as well as acting beings; (3) people are motivated to search for answers to important questions regarding the meaning of life; (4) *freedom* and *responsibility* are always balanced, that is, a person cannot have one without the other; and (5) fixed personality theories tend to dehumanize people and turn them into objects, things to be observed.

Existentialists generally take a *phenomenological* approach, insisting that people can best be understood from their own point of view. The unity of people and their phenomenological world is expressed by the term *Dasein,* or *being-in-the-world.*

There are three modes of being-in-the-world: *Umwelt,* our relationship with the world of objects or things; *Mitwelt,* our world with people; and *Eigenwelt,* our relationship with ourself. Healthy people live in all three worlds simultaneously.

If people are aware of their being-in-the-world, then they are also aware of the possibility of *nonbeing* or nothingness. Life becomes more meaningful when we confront the inevitability of death or nonbeing.

The awareness of nonbeing contributes to the experience of *anxiety,* but anxiety is also increased when people realize that they are free to choose and have responsibility for their actions. *Normal anxiety* is experienced by everyone. It is proportionate to the threat and can be managed constructively on a conscious level. *Neurotic anxiety* is

disportionate to the threat, involves repression, and is handled in a self-defeating manner.

Just as anxiety is a normal aspect of the human condition, so too is *guilt.* People experience guilt as a result of their (1) separation from the natural world, (2) inability to judge the needs of others, and (3) denial of their own potentials.

Intentionality is the underlying structure that gives meaning to experience and allows people to make decisions about the future. Intentionality implies action, not merely idle wishing.

Both *love* and *will* involve *care,* both necessitate choice, and both require responsibility. Love means taking delight in the presence of the other person and affirming that person's value as much as one's own; will calls for a conscious commitment to action. May identifies four aspects of love: (1) *sex,* which is a physiological function; (2) *eros,* which seeks an enduring union with a loved one; (3) *philia,* or nonsexual friendship between two people; and (4) *agape,* or an altruistic love that demands nothing in return.

May holds that freedom comes from one's confrontation with *destiny* and with an understanding that death or nonbeing is a possibility at any moment. Many people have *freedom of action,* but a deeper, more rare kind of freedom is *freedom of being.* People can be free within themselves even though they may be physically imprisoned.

Although May has been a psychotherapist for many years, he has not written extensively on techniques or methods of existential therapy. Because psychopathology results from alienation from nature, others, and self, May asserts that the purpose of therapy is to help people expand their consciousness so that they can make free choices and be at one with nature, other people, and self.

In his concept of humanity, May places high emphasis on uniqueness, free choice, and teleology. Existential psychology receives high marks for its ability to organize that which is known about human personality, but it falls short as a scientific theory, having little heuristic value either in generating research or in guiding the practitioner.

Suggested Readings

HALL, M. H. (1967, September). An interview with "Mr. Humanist": Rollo May. *Psychology Today,* pp. 25–29, 72–73.

  Although this article is more than 20 years old, it reflects many ideas that are appropriate today.

MAY, R. (1958b). The origins and significance of the existential movement in psychology. In R. May, E. Angel, & H. F. Ellenberger (Eds.), *Existence: A new dimension in psychiatry and psychology* (pp. 3–36). New York: Basic Books.

  With this chapter, May introduced existential psychology to many American readers. The philosophical background, rationale, and terminology of existential psychology are presented.

MAY, R. (1969a). The emergence of existential psychology. In R. May (Ed.), *Existential psychology* (2nd ed.) (pp. 1–48). New York: Random House.

  Another introductory chapter in which May discusses the meaning of existentialism and the implications of existential psychology for science and psychotherapy.

MAY, R. (1969c). *Love and will.* New York: Norton.

  May's most popular book, this volume discusses the failure of modern culture to understand the meaning of love and will. Included are chapters on intentionality and care.

Part Six
CONCLUDING REMARKS

19

A Final Word

In the years since Freud began seriously formulating the first modern theory of personality, the world has seen unprecedented change. When Breuer and Freud published *Studies in Hysteria* in 1895, Henry Ford had not yet mass-produced the automobile, the Wright brothers had not flown at Kitty Hawk, Marconi had not yet built the wireless radio, and bleeding was a treatment sometimes still used in medicine.

What progress has personality theory made in the intervening decades? Obviously the advances have not been as dramatic as those in technology. To some, it may appear that no advances have been made since Freud's elaborate and fascinating description of human personality. From a scientific view, however, considerable progress has been made. Consider, for example, the work of Bandura, currently the most active theory-builder discussed in these pages. Bandura's cautious mixture of research and theoretical speculation serve as a model for correct theory building. While his theory may lack the breadth and the colorful appeal of Freud's psychoanalysis, it is, nevertheless, several steps in front as a rigorous scientific theory. If personality theory is to serve as a tool for explaining, predicting, and controlling human behavior, it must be modeled more on the pattern of current theorists than on the highly speculative formulations of the original triumvirate, namely, Freud, Adler, and Jung.

CONCEPTS OF HUMANITY SUMMARIZED

In the opening chapter we listed six broad dimensions on which the various personality theorists can be rated. These basic beliefs can be stated in the form of the following questions. First, does each personality theorist believe that behavior is determined by forces outside the individual or that humans can freely decide for themselves how they are to live their lives? This is the issue of *determinism vs. free choice.* Second, does each theorist have a basically *optimistic* view of humanity or a *pessimistic* one? Third, does the theorist have a *causal* or a *teleological* view of development; that is, does he or she emphasize past experiences or present expectations of future goals? A fourth question concerns the role of *conscious vs. unconscious* forces in shaping personality. Fifth, are *biological* or *social* factors more important to the formation of the individual? And finally, can personality best be conceptualized in terms of *unique* patterns of behavior or in terms of *similar* elements among people?

Table 19.1 presents a summary of these six dimensions as seen from the view of the 17 major theories discussed in preceding chapters. When examining the combined ratings for these theories, one is impressed by how closely the group approximates a "Moderate" score on most of the basic issues. Only on the Pessimistic vs. Optimistic and the Uniqueness vs. Similarities dimension do the combined scores move away from the center position. As a whole, our personality theories tend to be somewhat optimistic and to emphasize the uniqueness of human personalities.

EVALUATION OF PERSONALITY THEORIES

In Chapter 1 we defined scientific theory as a set of related assumptions from which, by logical deductive reasoning, testable hypotheses can be drawn. In Chapters 2–18 we examined in some detail the leading theories of personality and evaluated each on the basis of five criteria of a useful theory. Now it is time to judge the usefulness of contemporary personality theory in general.

First, do current personality theories adequately organize knowledge? Are most findings from psychological research explainable by one or more of these theories? The answer to each question is a resolute "yes." Human behavior, from the most mundane to the most fanciful, from the simplest to the most complex, from the most altruistic to the most sadistic, from the most healthy to the most psychotic, can be explained by at least one, but usually most, of these theories. Not all explanations, of course, would be the same and some may be quite unsatisfactory to an individual reader. That is under-

TABLE 19.1   Summary of Major Personality Theorists' Concept of Humanity

	Freud	*Erikson*	*Adler*	*Jung*	*Sullivan*	*Horney*	*Fromm*	*Dollard and Miller*	*Skinner*	*Rotter*	*Bandura*	*Trait and Factor Theories*	*Allport*	*Kelly*	*Maslow*	*Rogers*	*May*
Free Choice	VL	M	H	M	M	H	M	L	VL	M	M	NA	H	H	H	H	H
Optimistic	L	H	VH	M	M	H	M	M	M	M	H	NA	H	H	H	VH	M
Causality	VH	H	VL	H	M	M	L	H	VH	L	M	NA	L	VL	L	L	L
Unconscious	VH	M	H	VH	H	H	M	H	VH	L	L	M	VL	L	H	L	M
Social Influences	VL	H	H	L	VH	H	VH	H	H	VH	VH	VL	M	M	M	H	M
Uniqueness	M	H	H	L	VL	L	M	H	H	M	H	H	VH	H	H	H	H

VH = Very High   H = High   M = Moderate   L = Low   VL = Very Low   NA = Not Applicable

standable since each reader has a personal preference, which allows for the rejection of explanations not compatible with one's philosophical orientation.

Explanation is precisely what personality theories do best. They are considerably more useful and accurate in explaining behavior than they are in predicting or controlling behavior. Encouragingly, the more recently developed theories are becoming more sophisticated at predicting human behavior and they are also more effective at suggesting the means to control it. The earlier theories, especially those of Freud, Adler, and Jung, are extremely useful in explaining what is already known about human behavior, but they are less proficient at predicting it.

Second, what is the heuristic value of contemporary personality theory? That is, how well does the field of personality generate research and investigation? Though much of current psychological research is without theoretical focus, a significant portion has been stimulated by attempts to test hypotheses drawn from established theories, including those within the scope of personality. Freud's theory alone has generated thousands of research studies and continues to stimulate dozens of important studies each year. The theories of Adler, Skinner, Bandura, Cattell, and Maslow have also been exceptionally productive of research and Rotter's notion of locus of control continues to be a popular topic in the psychological literature. Taken as a totality, personality theory has sparked a substantial amount of research and is largely responsible for much of what is now known about human behavior.

The third criterion for evaluating personality theory is the extent to which it serves as a guide for the practitioner. Here the theories as a whole would receive a moderate to high rating. This criterion presupposes that the practitioner, be it a psychotherapist, plant manager, parent, politician, or teacher, has extensive knowledge of at least one theory, since without that knowledge theory would have no value as a practical tool. Even with that knowledge, however, the practitioner will sometimes face problems for which contemporary personality theory offers no ready-made solutions. Despite these shortcomings, knowledge of personality theory continues to serve as a practical guide for those who must understand, explain, control, or predict human behavior. This third criterion of a useful theory is sometimes overlooked by those who believe that theory and practice are necessarily antithetical and that theory exists only in some abstract realm far removed from practical concerns. For the person making daily decisions about human behavior, knowledge of one or more personality theories can eliminate endless floundering and serve as a practical guide to action.

The fourth criterion of a useful theory is internal consistency. Taken as a whole, the personality theories discussed in these pages would not, of course, have much internal consistency, but are more accurately characterized by diversity. As a group, personality theorists would also receive low ratings for consistency of terminology, with some employing the same word in different ways and others using different terms to express the same concept. At the present stage of personality theorizing, these discrepancies are preferable to unanimity and orthodoxy. A variety of theories, representing different philosophical orientations, will more likely stimulate a diversity of research than would a single unified theory. At the present time, divergent theories also offer more flexibility for synthesizing knowledge and for guiding action. In summary, though present personality theories lack consistency, their diversification makes them more useful than a single circumscribed theory.

Finally, is personality theory parsimonious? Actually, the law of parsimony cannot be applied when considering personality theory as a whole, since it states that when two or more theories are equal, the simpler one is preferred. By combining all theories into one, no comparisons on parsimony are possible. If one were to evaluate personality theory on the basis of simplicity, one must judge it as extremely complex and diversified, just as personality itself is quite complex and diversified.

A summary of the current ratings for these 17 theories is provided in Table 19.2. A word or two is in order. First, it should be pointed out that the ratings are both arbitrary and approximate. They merely represent the author's judgment of where each theory falls on the five criteria of a useful theory. Second, the table is but a synopsis of the ratings. A more detailed discussion is found in the "Critique" section of the 17 preceding chapters. Notice also that individually these personality theories receive the highest marks on their ability to organize knowledge and to explain what is known about human behavior. Only Horney, Allport, and Kelly fail to receive at least a "Moderate" rating on this first criterion. Freud's psychoanalysis, which can accommodate nearly anything human, receives a "Very High" score on its ability to organize and explain. So too does Adler's theory, since nearly all behavior can be seen as either useless or useful attempts to gain superiority or success. Maslow's the-

TABLE 19.2 Ratings of 17 Theories on the Criteria of a Useful Theory

	Freud	Erikson	Adler	Jung	Sullivan	Horney	Fromm	Dollard and Miller	Skinner	Rotter	Bandura	Trait and Factor Theories	Allport	Kelly	Maslow	Rogers	May	Average Rating
Organize Knowledge	VH	M	VH	H	M	L	H	H	M	H	VH	VH	L	VL	VH	M	H	H
Generate Research	VH	H	H	M	L	VL	VL	H	H	M	VH	H	M	L	VH	H	VL	M+
Guide Action	H	M	H	L	M	M	L	H	VH	M	H	M	M	L	H	M	VL	M−
Internally Consistent	L	H	L	L	M	M	L	H	VH	H	VH	M	H	VH	M	VH	L	M
Parsimonious	M	M	M	L	L	M	L	M	H	H	VH	H	H	VH	M	VH	M	M+

VH = Very High   H = High   M = Moderate   L = Low   VL = Very Low

ory is also rated "Very High," since it is able to organize most of behavior in terms of the hierarchy of needs concept. Viewing behavior as an attempt to satisfy the various need levels provides an explanation for almost all human activity.

Useful theories are practical. Not only do they explain data and offer guidance to the researcher, but they also help the clinician, teacher, parent, and administrator make decisions that involve human behavior.

THEORISTS OF PERSONALITY

In the present volume we have devoted a little more space to the lives of the theorists than is typically found in personality textbooks. One reason for this is the author's hypothesis that personality differences among the theorists account, at least in part, for differences among their theories. Differences in birth order, family size, religious and socioeconomic backgrounds, closeness to mother or father, training, and education, in part, account for differences in the manner in which these theorists view the world and also their concepts of humanity.

On the other hand, these theorists have also been similar in some respects. For one, each of these persons has been motivated to construct and publish a personal view of human personality. Not every observer of human behavior is so disposed. What other characteristics do these theorists have in common? Without indulging in too much groundless speculation, it can be said that all of them have possessed superior intelligence, nearly all have been highly creative, and most have had outstanding literary skills. Several of the theorists have been unusually romantic, almost to the point of sentimentality. Many were lonely, at least at one time or another during their lives. Freud remained somewhat distrustful of outsiders throughout his life; Jung retreated into extreme isolation during the early part of his midlife; Maslow was painfully shy during his youth; Rogers, who like Maslow came from a large family, spent most of his childhood and adolescence as a loner; and Sullivan, an only child, had difficulties with interpersonal relationships during most of his life. Another characteristic shared by most of these theorists is the fervent belief that they were scientists and were making observations and constructing theories within the framework of science.

FUTURE DIRECTIONS

Perhaps the only accurate statement one can make about the future is this: "No accurate statements can be made about the future." Nevertheless, I will venture a few guesses about the future direction of personality theory.

First, I foresee that there will be few clinicians formulating grand, all-encompassing theories based largely on their therapeutic experiences. This was the procedure followed by many early theorists—Freud, Erikson, Adler, Jung, Sullivan, Horney, Fromm, and Kelly. In the future personality theories will be built piece by piece on the foundation of *empirical research*. These theories will be less inclusive, less speculative, and less philosophical than those emanating from the consulting rooms and libraries of the above-mentioned theorists.

These narrow, low-level theories will be developed by academic, research-oriented psychologists studying one variable at a time and developing a limited model to explain that variable. Being less philosophical, these theories will be little concerned with such topics as free will vs. determinism and causality vs. teleology. They will avoid postulating a single master motive such as self-actulization or striving for success. Conscious vs. unconscious motivation will be a matter of empirical research, not personal opinion. Hard data will replace philosophical speculation as the cornerstone of future personality theories.

A second and related direction is theories will become more of a *team* effort rather than the work of a single person. The vast research on which future theories will be constructed can only be conducted by a well-coordinated group effort. Carl Rogers initiated this procedure more than 40 years ago by relying on graduate students and colleagues for assistance in conducting research on client-centered psychotherapy. Albert Bandura has refined this approach, but has been much more empirical. Bandura is building a cognitive learning theory in small increments as he gathers data from studies carried out by him and his colleagues.

No single individual will be able to conduct enough research to support an adequate theory of personality. At the very least, it would take a lifetime of solid empirical research by one person before a theory can begin to have firm underpinnings. For one person to come up with insightful, comprehensive, consistent, and researchable ideas concerning the nature of human personality is one thing; but it may be impossible for that same person to sin glehandedly conduct research, compile data, and publish results covering the full range of personality. Only a cooperative team approach can provide sufficient data for even a moderate comprehensive theory of personality.

For the immediate future at least, I see a continuing trend toward cognitive theories of personality. This is the direction in which Bandura is proceeding, and it is also a favorite topic of research and theory building for many younger students of personality. At the front of this group is the not-so-young Walter Mischel, born in 1930. Mischel's (1977, 1981, 1986) cognitive-social learning theory, like Bandura's social cognitive learning theory, emphasizes the interaction of cognition with personal factors and environmental stimuli. Other relatively young proponents of the cognitive approach include Nancy Cantor, Hazel Markus, David Buss, Robert Nisbett, Oliver John, and others.

Another promising field of personality theory is that of a revitalized self-concept. Again, Bandura's self-efficacy leads the way; but others, including Markus's possible selves, Seymour Epstein's experiential-cognitive self-theory, and William Swann's self as architect, have the potential to help elucidate our understanding of self. Research in this area has the benefit of being comprehensive and relevant to issues of motivation, emotion, cognition, and behavior. Self-theory, therefore, has the potential of serving as a unifying force and preventing personality theory from becoming fragmented and trivialized.

Glossary

accusation Adlerian safeguarding tendency whereby one protects magnified feelings of self-esteem by blaming others for one's own failures.

acrophobia An intense fear of high places.

active imagination Technique used by Jung to uncover collective unconscious material. Subjects are asked to concentrate on an image until a series of fantasies are produced.

activity (Adler) Degree of activity is the level of energy or interest with which one moves toward finding solutions to life's problems.

actualizing tendency (Rogers) Tendency within all people to move toward completion or fulfillment of potentials.

adolescence (Erikson) An important psychosocial stage when ego identity should be formed. Adolescence is characterized by puberty and the crisis of identity vs. identity confusion.

adulthood (Erikson) The ages from about 31 to 60 which are characterized by the psychosexual mode of procreativity and the crisis of generativity vs. stagnation.

aesthetic needs (Maslow) Needs for art, music, beauty, and the like. Though they may be related to the basic conative needs, aesthetic needs are a separate dimension.

agape Altruistic love.

aggression (Adler) Safeguarding tendencies that may include depreciation or accusation of others, as well as self-accusation, all designed to protect exaggerated feelings of personal superiority by striking out against other people.

aggression (Freud) One of two primary instincts or drives that motivate people. Aggression is the outward manifestation of the death instinct and is at least a partial explanation for wars, personal hostility, sadism, masochism, and murder.

amnesia The inability to recall past experiences. May be due to physical or psychological trauma.

Analytical Psychology Theory of personality and approach to psychotherapy founded by Carl Jung.

anal phase (Freud) (see **sadistic-anal phase**)

anal-urethral-muscular Erikson's term for the young child's psychosexual mode of adapting.

anima Jungian archetype that represents the feminine side in the personality of males and originates from men's inherited experiences with women.

animus Jungian archetype that represents the masculine component in the personality of females and originates from women's inherited experiences with men.

anticipatory response (Dollard & Miller) Responses that have a tendency to occur earlier than they did in the original learning situation.

anxiety A felt, affective, unpleasant state accompanied by physical sensation.

anxiety (Kelly) The recognition that the events with which one is confronted lie outside the range of convenience of one's construct system.

anxiety (May) Experience of the threat of imminent nonbeing.

apathy (Sullivan) Dynamism that reduces tensions of needs through the adoption of an indifferent attitude.

approach-avoidance conflict (Dollard & Miller) Conflict arising whenever the same stimulus carries both a positive and a negative value.

approach gradient (see **gradient of approach**).

archetypes Jung's concept that refers to the contents of the collective unconscious. Archetypes, also called primordial images or collective symbols, represent psychic patterns of inherited behavior and are thus distinguished from instincts, which are physical impulses toward action. Typical archetypes are the anima, animus, and shadow.

attention (Bandura) First of four processes that govern modeling, attention refers to the active perception of others' behavior.

attitude (Cattell) A motivational trait that refers to a specific course of action in response to a given situation. In Cattell's definition, an attitude includes a particular situation, interest, response, and object.

attitude (Jung) A predisposition to act or react in a characteristic manner, that is, in either an introverted or an extraverted direction.

authoritarianism (Fromm) The tendency to give up one's independence and to unite with another person or persons in order to gain strength. Takes the form of masochism or sadism.

autism Pathological condition characterized by the tendency to perceive the world in terms of one's own personality rather than in terms of reality. Withdrawal from real life through daydreams, bizarre fantasies, and private language.

autistic language (Sullivan) Private or parataxic language that makes little or no sense to other people.

autoeroticism Self-gratification. In Freudian theory, infants are seen as exclusively autoerotic since their interest in pleasure is limited to themselves.

aversive stimulus A painful or undesired stimulus which, when associated with a response, decreases the tendency of that response to be repeated in similar situations.

avoidance-avoidance conflict (Dollard & Miller) Conflict arising whenever a person is trapped midway between two negative stimuli of equal value.

avoidance gradient (see **gradient of avoidance**).

axiology That realm of philosophy dealing with the nature of values.

B-love (Maslow) Love between self-actualizing people characterized by the love for the *being* of the other.

B-values (Maslow) The values of self-actualizing people, including beauty, truth, goodness, justice, wholeness, and the like.

basic anxiety (Fromm) The feeling of being alone and isolated, separated from the natural world.

basic anxiety (Horney) Feelings of isolation and helplessness in a potentially hostile world.

basic anxiety (Maslow) Anxiety arising from inability to satisfy physiological and safety needs.

basic conflict (Horney) The incompatible tendency to move toward, against, and away from people.

basic strength The ego quality that emerges from the conflict between antithetical elements in Erikson's stages of development.

behavior potential (Rotter) Refers to the possibility of a particular response occurring at a given time and place as calculated in relation to the reinforcement of that response.

behavioral equation Cattell's basic formula for representing and predicting behavior.

behaviorism A "school" of psychology that limits its subject matter to observable behavior. John B. Watson is usually credited with being the founder of behaviorism, with B. F. Skinner its most notable proponent.

being-in-the-world (see *Dasein*)

bimodal distribution A set of scores with two distinct modes.

biophilia Love of life.

bipolar factors Factors with two poles, that is, those scaled from a minus point to a positive point, with zero representing the midpoint.

cardinal traits (Allport) (see **disposition, cardinal**).

castration anxiety (Freud) (see **castration complex**).

castration complex (Freud) Condition that accompanies the Oedipus complex, but takes different forms in the two sexes. In boys it takes the form of *castration anxiety,* or fear of having one's penis removed, and is responsible for shattering the Oedipus complex. In girls it takes the form of *penis envy,* or the desire to have a penis, and precedes and instigates the Oedipus complex.

causality An explanation of behavior in terms of past experiences.

central traits (Allport) (see **disposition, central**).

chance encounters (Bandura) An unintended meeting of persons unfamiliar to each other.

character (Fromm) Relatively permanent acquired qualities through which people relate themselves to others and to the world.

choice corollary Kelly's assumption that people choose the alternative in a dichotomized construct that they perceive as extending their range of future choices.

client-centered therapy Approach to psychotherapy originated by Rogers, which is based on respect for the person's capacity to grow within a nurturant climate.

cognitive needs (Maslow) Needs for knowledge and understanding; related to basic or conative needs, yet operate on a different dimension.

collective unconscious Jung's idea of an inherited unconscious. He believed that many of our acts are motivated by unconscious ideas that are beyond our personal experiences and originate with repeated experiences of our ancestors.

common traits (Allport) (see **trait, common**).

commonality corollary (Kelly) The personal

constructs of people with similar experiences tend to be similar.

complex (Jung) An emotionally toned conglomeration of ideas that comprise the contents of the personal unconscious. Jung originally used the Word Association Test to uncover complexes.

compulsion The irresistible repetition of an act.

compulsion neurosis Neurotic reaction characterized by phobias, obsessions, and compulsions.

conative Pertaining to willful, purposive striving.

conditioned reinforcer (Skinner) Environmental event that is not by nature satisfying, but becomes so because it is associated with unlearned or unconditioned reinforcers such as food, sex, and the like.

conditions of worth (Rogers) Restrictions or qualifications attached to one person's regard for another.

conformity (Fromm) Means of escaping from isolation and aloneness by giving up one's self and becoming whatever others desire.

congruence (Rogers) The matching of organismic experiences with awareness, and with the ability to express those experiences. One of three "necessary and sufficient" therapeutic conditions.

conscience (Freud) The part of the superego which results from experience with punishment and which, therefore, tells a person what is wrong or improper conduct.

conscious (Freud) Refers to those mental elements in awareness at any given time.

consensual validation The agreement of two or more people on the meaning of experiences, especially language. In Sullivan's theory, consensually validated experiences are said to operate on the syntaxic level of cognition.

constructing obstacles (Adler) Safeguarding tendency characterized by a person creating a barrier to success so that self-esteem can be protected by either using the barrier as an excuse or by overcoming it.

construction corollary Kelly's assumption that people anticipate events according to their interpretations of recurrent themes.

constructive alternativism Kelly's view that events can be looked at or construed from a different (alternative) perspective.

continuous schedule (Skinner) The reinforcement of an organism for every correct trial; opposed to the intermittent schedule in which only certain selected responses are reinforced.

conversion hysteria Neurotic reaction characterized by the transformation of repressed psychological conflicts into overt physical symptoms.

copying (Dollard & Miller) A form of imitative behavior in which one person attempts to minimize perceived differences between her or his behavior and that of another.

correlation coefficient A mathematical index used to measure the direction and magnitude of the relationship between two variables.

cosmology That realm of philosophy dealing with the nature of causation.

countertransference Strong undeserved feelings the therapist develops toward the patient during the course of treatment. These feelings can be either positive or negative and are considered by most writers to be a hindrance to successful psychotherapy.

cue (Dollard & Miller) Any stimulus distinctive enough to guide responses, but not strong enough to serve as a drive.

cue-producing responses (Dollard & Miller) A series of responses, each of which produces cues which, in turn, lead to additional responses.

curvilinear A relationship between two variables in which scores on the first variable increase with increases of scores on the second, but only to a certain point where they then begin to decrease.

D-love (Maslow) Deficiency love or affection (attachment) based on the lover's specific *deficiency* and the loved one's ability to satisfy that deficit.

Dasein An existential term meaning a sense of self as a free and responsible person whose existence is embedded in the world of things, of people, and of self-awareness.

death instinct (Freud) One of two primary drives or impulses, the death instinct is also known as Thanatos or aggression.

deductive method Approach to factor analytical theories of personality that gathers data on the basis of previously determined hypotheses or theory. Reasoning from the general to the particular.

defense mechanisms (Freud) Techniques such as repression, reaction formation, sublimation, and the like, whereby the ego defends itself against the pain of anxiety.

defensiveness (Rogers) Protection of the self-concept against anxiety and threat by denial and distortion of experiences inconsistent with it.

degree of activity (Adler) (see **activity**).

denial (Rogers) The blocking of an experience or some aspect of an experience from awareness because it is inconsistent with the self-concept.

dependent variable A variable within an experimental design whose value is hypothesized to change as a result of changes in the independent variable.

depreciation Adlerian safeguarding tendency whereby another's achievements are undervalued and one's own are overvalued.

desacralization (Maslow) The process of removing respect, joy, awe, and rapture from an experience resulting in the purification or objectifying of that experience.

destructiveness (Fromm) Method of escaping from freedom by eliminating people or objects, thus restoring feelings of power.

dichotomy corollary Kelly's assumption that people construe events in an either/or (dichotomous) manner.

differential R (dR technique) Correlational procedure pioneered by Cattell, which correlates scores of a large number of people on many tests obtained at two different occasions. The dR technique measures consistency of the scores.

disengagement of behavior (Bandura) Justification of otherwise reprehensible behavior through one of four techniques: (1) redefinition of behavior, (2) distortion of the effects of behavior, (3) denial of responsibility, or (4) dehumanization or blaming the victim.

disengagement of internal control (Bandura) The displacement or diffusion of responsibility for the injurious effects of one's actions.

disposition, cardinal (Allport) Personal traits so dominating in an individual's life that they cannot be hidden. Most people do not have a cardinal disposition.

disposition, central (Allport) The five to ten traits around which an individual's life focuses.

disposition, secondary (Allport) The least characteristic and reliable of the personal traits that still appear with some regularity in an individual's life.

dissociation (Sullivan) The process of separating unwanted impulses, desires, and needs from the self-system.

distortion (Rogers) Misinterpretation of an experience so that it is seen as fitting some aspect of the self-concept.

double approach-avoidance conflict (Dollard & Miller) Conflict arising whenever a person is trapped midway between two stimuli, each of which has both a negative and a positive value.

drive (Dollard & Miller) Any stimulus strong enough to impel action.

dynamic calculus Cattell's complex procedure for determining the strength and direction of attitudes. The dynamic calculus includes the more specific behavioral equation, which permits the specific prediction of behavior.

dynamic lattice Cattell's term for a network of motives that includes attitudes, sentiments (sems), and ergs.

dynamics of personality Refers to motivation or those units which drive people to respond.

dynamisms (Sullivan) Relatively consistent patterns of action which characterize the person throughout a lifetime. Similar to traits or habit patterns.

dystonic Erikson's term for the negative element in each pair of opposites that characterize the eight stages of development.

earliest recollections Technique proposed by Adler to understand the pattern or theme that runs throughout a person's style of life.

early childhood (Erikson) The second stage of psychosocial development—one characterized by the anal-urethral-muscular psychosexual mode and by the crisis of autonomy vs. shame and doubt.

eclecticism Approach that allows selection of usable elements from different theories or approaches and combines them in a consistent and unified manner.

ego (Freud) The province of the mind that refers to the "I" or those experiences which are owned (not necessarily consciously) by the person. As the only region of the mind in contact with the real world, the ego is said to serve the reality principle.

ego (Jung) The center of consciousness. In Jungian psychology the ego is of lesser importance than the more inclusive self and is limited to consciousness.

ego-ideal (Freud) That part of the superego which results from experiences with reward and which, therefore, teach a person what is right or proper conduct.

eidetic personifications (Sullivan) Imaginary traits attributed to real or imaginary people in order to protect one's self-esteem.

Eigenwelt Term used by existentialists to refer to the world of one's relationship to self. One of three simultaneous modes of being-in-the-world.

elaborative choice (Kelly) Making choices that will increase a person's range of future choices.

empathic listening (Rogers) The accurate sensing of the feelings of another and the communication of these perceptions. One of three "necessary and sufficient" therapeutic conditions.

empathy (Sullivan) An indefinite process through which anxiety is transferred from one person to another, for example, from mother to infant.

empirical Based on experience, systematic observation, and experiment rather than on logical reasoning or philosophical speculation.

empirical law of effect (Rotter) Principle that states that behaviors which move people in the direction of their goals are more likely to be reinforced.

energy transformations (Sullivan) Overt or covert actions designed to satisfy needs or reduce anxiety.

enhancement needs (Rogers) The need to develop, to grow, and to achieve.

entropy The principle of entropy states that when objects of differing temperatures meet, heat flows from the hotter to the colder, bringing about an equalization of temperature. Jung emphasized that tension is generated by the meeting of opposites.

epigenetic principle Erikson's term meaning that one component grows out of another in its proper time and sequence.

epistemology That branch of philosophy which deals with the nature of knowledge.

equivalence The principle of equivalence states that when a given quantity of energy is expended in the performance of an activity, an equal amount of energy will appear elsewhere. Jung emphasized that psychic energy cannot be destroyed, but is merely displaced.

ergs Energy inherent in primary or innate drives or motives. In Cattell's theory, ergs are contrasted to sentiments or sems, which are learned motives.

erogenous zones Organs of the body that are especially sensitive to the reception of pleasure. In Freudian theory, the three principal erogenous zones are the mouth, anus, and genitals.

eros The desire for an enduring union with a loved one.

essential freedom (May) The freedom of being or the freedom of the conscious mind. Essential freedom cannot be limited by chains or bars.

excuses Adlerian safeguarding tendencies whereby the person, through the use of reasonable sounding justifications, becomes convinced of the reality of self-erected obstacles.

existential freedom (May) The freedom of doing one's will. Existential freedom can be limited by chains or bars.

existential living Rogers's term indicating a tendency to live in the moment.

existential needs (Fromm) Peculiarly human needs aimed at moving people toward a reunification with the natural world. Fromm listed relatedness, transcendence, rootedness, a sense of identity, and a frame of orientation as existential or human needs.

expectancy (Rotter) The subjective probability held by a person that any specific reinforcement or set of reinforcements will occur in a given situation.

experience corollary Kelly's view that people continually revise their personal constructs as the result of experience.

exploitative orientation (Fromm) Refers to people who take from others, either by force or cunning.

external evaluation (Rogers) Conditions of worth placed on a person, which may then serve as a criterion for evaluating one's own conduct. Conditions of worth block growth and interfere with one's becoming fully functioning.

external reinforcement (Rotter) The positive or negative value of any reinforcing event, as seen from the view of societal or cultural values.

extinction The tendency of a previously acquired response to become progressively weakened upon nonreinforcement.

extraversion (E) (Eysenck) One of three types of superfactors, identified by Eysenck, and consisting of two opposite poles—extraversion and introversion. Extraverts are characterized behaviorally by sociability and impulsiveness and physiologically by a low level of cortical arousal. Introverts, by contrast, are characterized by unsociability and caution and by a high level of cortical arousal.

extraversion (Jung) An attitude or type characterized by the turning outward of psychic energy so that the person is oriented toward the objective.

factor A unit of personality derived through factor analysis, though the term is sometimes used more generally to include any underlying aspect of personality.

factor analysis A mathematical procedure for reducing a large number of variables to a few. Used by Cattell and Eysenck to identify personality traits.

factor loadings The amount of correlation that a score contributes to a given factor.

fear (Kelly) A specific threat to one's personal constructs.

feeling (Jung) A rational function that tells us the value of something. The feeling function can be either extraverted (directed toward the objective world) or introverted (directed toward the subjective world).

fiction (Adler) A belief or expectation of the future, which serves to motivate present behavior. The truthfulness of a fictional idea is immaterial since the person acts as if the idea were true.

fixation (Freud) A defense mechanism that arises when psychic energy is blocked at one stage of development, thus making change or psychological growth difficult.

fixation (Fromm) The nonproductive form of rootedness characterized by a reluctance to grow beyond the security provided by one's mother.

fixed-interval (Skinner) Intermittent reinforcement schedule whereby the organism is reinforced for its first response following a designated period of time (for example, FI 10 means that the animal is reinforced for its initial response after 10 minutes have elapsed since its previous reinforcement).

fixed-ratio (Skinner) Reinforcement schedule in which the organism is reinforced intermittently according to a specified number of responses it makes (for example, FR 7 means that the organism is reinforced for every seventh response).

formative tendency (Rogers) Tendency in all matter to evolve from simpler to more complex forms.

fortuitous events (Bandura) Environmental events that are unexpected and unintended.

fragmentation corollary Kelly's assumption that behavior is sometimes inconsistent because one's construct systems can admit incompatible elements.

frame of orientation (Fromm) The need for humans to develop a unifying philosophy or consistent way of looking at things.

freedom of movement (Rotter) The mean expectancy of being reinforced for performing all those behaviors which are directed toward the satisfaction of some general need.

frustration-aggression hypothesis Dollard and Miller's original contention that frustration inevitably leads to aggression and that aggression is always produced by frustration. Later amended to read that frustration may lead to a variety of responses, aggression being one of them.

fully functioning person (Rogers) (see **person of tomorrow**).

functional autonomy (Allport) The tendency for some motives to become independent from the original motive responsible for the behavior.

Gemeinshaftsgefühl (see **social interest**).

generalization The transfer of the effects of one learning situation to another.

generalized expectancy (Rotter) Expectation based on similar past experiences that a given behavior will be reinforced.

generalized reinforcer (Skinner) A conditioned reinforcer that has been associated with several primary reinforcers. Money, for example, is a generalized reinforcer because it is associated with food, shelter and other primary reinforcers.

genital-locomotor Erikson's term for the preschool child's psychosexual mode of adopting.

genital stage (Freud) Period of life beginning with puberty and continuing through adulthood. This second sexual stage of the person's life should not be confused with the phallic phase, which takes place during the first sexual stage, that is, during infancy.

genitality (Erikson) The psychosexual mode of

young adulthood characterized by mutual trust and a sharing of sexual satisfactions.

gradient of approach (Dollard & Miller) Refers to the observation that the tendency to approach a goal becomes stronger as a person nears the goal.

gradient of avoidance (Dollard & Miller) Refers to the observation that the tendency to avoid a feared stimulus becomes stronger as a person nears it. The gradient of avoidance is steeper (progressively stronger) than the gradient of approach.

gradient of reinforcement (Dollard & Miller) Refers to the sequence of responses leading to the final reinforced one. Each response in the sequence is progressively strengthened by reinforcement.

great mother Jungian archetype of the opposing forces of fertility and destruction.

guilt (Kelly) The sense of having lost one's core role structure.

guilt (May) An ontological characteristic of human existence arising from our separation from the natural world *(Umwelt),* from other people *(Mitwelt),* or from ourself *(Eigenwelt).*

hero A Jungian archetype representing the myth of the godlike man who conquers or vanquishes evil, usually in the form of a monster, dragon, or serpent.

hesitating (Adler) Safeguarding tendency characterized by vacillation or procrastination designed to provide a person with the excuse "It's too late now."

heuristic Pertaining to a method or theory that leads to the discovery of new information.

hierarchy of needs (Maslow) Idea that needs are ordered in such a manner that those on a lower level must be satisfied before higher level needs become activated.

hierarchy of response (Dollard & Miller) The order of response probabilities. In any learning situation ordinarily several potential responses may occur. These can be placed on a hierarchy of response according to their probability of occurrence.

holistic-dynamic Maslow's theory of personality, which stresses both the unity of the organism and the motivational aspects of personality.

hoarding characters (Fromm) People who seek to save and not let go of material possessions, feelings, or ideas.

humanistic psychology Ill-defined term referring to those theories and systems of psychology which, in general, emphasize the power of the individual to make conscious rational decisions and which stress the primacy of humans to other beings.

hypochondriasis Exaggerated attention to and anxiety about one's health.

hypothesis An assumption or educated guess that can be scientifically tested.

hysteria (Freud) A mental disorder characterized by conversion of repressed psychical elements into somatic symptoms such as impotency, paralysis, or blindness, where no physiological bases for these symptoms exist.

id (Freud) That region of personality which is alien to the ego in that it includes experiences that have never been owned by the person. The id is the home base for all the instincts and its sole function is to seek pleasure, regardless of consequences.

ideal self (Rogers) One's view of self as one would like to be.

idealistic principle (Freud) Refers to the demands of the superego that the ego oppose the pleasure-seeking id and instigate, instead, behaviors consistent with the child's perception of parental standards.

idealization Adlerian safeguarding tendency whereby the individual, in order to maintain exaggerated feelings of inferiority, sets up an ideal model so that any real person, by comparison, will inevitably fall short and thus be depreciated.

idealized image (Horney) An attempt to solve basic conflicts by adopting a belief in one's godlike qualities.

identity crisis Erickson's term for a crucial period or turning point in the life cycle which may result in either more or less ego strength. Identity crises can be found in Erikson's later stages of development.

idiographic Approach to the study of personality, which is based on the single case.

incestuous symbiosis (Fromm) Extreme dependence on a mother or mother substitute.

incongruence (Rogers) The perception of discrepancies between organismic self, self-concept, and ideal self.

independent variable A variable that is manipulated by the experimenter in order to assess its possible effects on behavior, that is, on the dependent variable.

Individual Psychology Theory of personality and approach to psychotherapy founded by Alfred Adler.

individuality corollary Kelly's assumption that people have different experiences and therefore construe events in different ways.

individuation Jung's term for the process of becoming a whole person, that is, an individual with a high level of psychic development. Similar to Maslow's concept of self-actualization.

inductive method Approach to factor analytic theories of personality that gathers data with no preconceived hypotheses or theory in mind. Reasoning from the particular to the general.

infancy (Erikson) The first stage of psychosocial development—one characterized by the oral-sensory mode and by the crisis of basic trust vs. basic mistrust.

infantile stage (Freud) First four or five years of life characterized by autoerotic or pleasure-seeking behavior and consisting of the oral, anal, and phallic substages.

inferiority complex (Adler) Exaggerated or abnormally strong feelings of inferiority, which usually interfere with socially useful solutions to life's problems.

instinct (Freud) From the German *Trieb* meaning drive or impulse, this term refers to an internal stimulus that impels action or thought. The two primary instincts are sex and aggression.

instinct (Jung) An unconscious physical impulse toward action. Instincts are the physical counterpart of archetypes.

instinctoid needs (Maslow) Needs that are innately determined, but can be modified through learning. The frustration of instinctoid needs leads to pathology.

intentionality (May) The underlying structure that gives meaning to our experience.

intermittent schedule (Skinner) The reinforcement of an organism on only certain selected occurrences of a response. Opposed to a continuous schedule, where the organism is reinforced for every correct trial. The four most common intermittent schedules are: fixed-ratio, variable-ratio, fixed-interval, and variable-interval.

internal reinforcement (Rotter) The individual's perception of the positive or negative value of any reinforcing event.

interpersonal trust (Rotter) A generalized expectancy held by a person that other people can be relied on to keep their word. The Interpersonal Trust Scale attempts to measure degree of interpersonal trust.

intimacy (Erikson) The ability to fuse one's identity with that of another person without fear of losing it. The syntonic element of young adulthood.

intimacy (Sullivan) Conjunctive dynamism characterized by a close personal relationship with another person who is more or less of equal status.

introversion (Eysenck) (see **extraversion, Eysenck**).

introversion (Jung) An attitude or type characterized by the turning inward of psychic energy with an orientation toward the subjective.

intuition (Jung) An irrational function that involves perception of elementary data that are beyond our awareness. Intuitive people "know" something without understanding how they know.

ipsative A method of measurement that uses the person's own behavior or scores as a standard of reference; opposed to the normative method, which compares a person's scores to those obtained by a norm group.

irrational functions (Jung) Methods of dealing with the world without evaluation or thinking. Sensing and intuiting are the two irrational functions.

isolation (Erikson) The inability to share true intimacy or to take chances with one's identity. The dystonic element of young adulthood.

isolation (Freud) A defense mechanism; also a type of repression, whereby the ego attempts to isolate an experience by establishing a period of blacked-out affect immediately following that experience.

Jonah complex The fear of being one's best.

L data Cattell's term for life record or information collected on a person by objective observation.

latency (Erikson) The psychosexual mode of the school-age child. A period of little sexual development.

latency stage (Freud) The time between infancy and puberty when psychosexual growth is at a standstill.

latent dream content (Freud) The underlying, unconscious meaning of a dream. Freud held that the latent content, which can only be revealed through dream interpretation, was more important than the surface, or manifest dream content.

libido (Freud) Psychic energy of the life instinct; sexual drive or energy.

life instinct (Freud) One of two primary drives or impulses, the life instinct is also called Eros or sex.

locus of control (Rotter) Refers to the belief people have that their attempts to reach a goal are within their control (internal locus of control) or primarily due to powerful events such as fate, chance, or other people (external locus of control). Locus of control is measured by the Internal-External Control Scale.

love (Fromm) A union with another person in which a person retains separateness and integrity of self.

love (May) To delight in the presence of the other person and to affirm that person's value and development as much as one's own.

lust (Sullivan) Isolation dynamism characterized by impersonal sexual interest in another.

maintenance needs (Rogers) Those basic needs which protect the status quo. They may be either physiological (for example, food), or interpersonal (for example, the need to maintain the current self-concept).

malevolence Sullivan's term for those destructive behavior patterns characterized by the attitude that people are evil and harmful and that the world is a bad place to live.

malignant aggression (Fromm) The destruction of life for reasons other than survival. Peculiar to the human species.

mandala (Jung) Symbol representing the striving for unity and completion. It is often seen as a circle within a square or a square within a circle.

manifest dream content (Freud) The surface or conscious meaning of a dream. The manifest content of a dream is the story the dreamer can describe to others. Freud believed that the manifest level of a dream has no deep psychological significance and that the unconscious or latent level holds the key to the dream's true meaning.

marketing characters (Fromm) People who see themselves as commodities, with their personal value dependent on their ability to sell themselves.

masculine protest Adler's term for the neurotic and erroneous belief held by some men and women that males are superior to females.

masochism A condition characterized by the reception of sexual pleasure from suffering pain and humiliation inflicted either by self or others.

matched-dependent behavior (Dollard & Miller) A form of imitative behavior in which one person uses another's responses as cues for her own behavior.

maturity (Freud) The final psychosexual stage following infancy, latency, and the genital period. Maturity would be characterized by a strong ego in control of the id and superego and by an ever-expanding realm of consciousness.

mean The arithmetic average score in a distribution.

mechanisms of defense (Freud) (see **defense mechanisms**)

mediation The cognitive or mental process ensuing between the physical stimulus and the subsequent response.

metamotivation (Maslow) The motives of self-actualizing people including especially the B-values.

metapathology (Maslow) Illness characterized by absence of values, lack of fulfillment, and loss of meaning of life and resulting from deprivation of self-actualization needs.

metaphysics That branch of philosophy dealing with the nature of reality.

metavalues (Maslow) (see **B-values**).

minimal goal level (Rotter) Lowest possible reinforcement accepted as positive.

Mitwelt Term used by existentialists to refer to the world of one's relationship to other people. One of three simultaneous modes of being-in-the-world.

mode The most frequent score in a distribution.

modeling (Bandura) One of two basic sources of learning, modeling involves the observation of others and thus learning from their actions. More than simple imitation, modeling entails the addition and subtraction of specific acts and the observation of consequences of others' behavior.

modulation corollary (Kelly) To the degree that personal constructs are permeable (resilient) they are subject to change through experience.

moral hypochondriasis (Fromm) Preoccupation with guilt about things one has done wrong.

morphogenic Allport's concept of science,

which deals with idiographic or individual methods of data gathering.

motor production (Bandura) Third of four processes that affect modeling, motor production entails the conversion of cognitive representations into appropriate actions.

moving against people One of Horney's neurotic trends. It is characteristic of neurotics who protect themselves against the hostility of others by adopting an aggressive stragegy.

moving away from others One of Horney's neurotic trends. It is characteristic of neurotics who protect themselves against feelings of isolation by adopting a detached attitude.

moving backward (Adler) Safeguarding inflated feelings of superiority by reverting to a more secure period of life.

moving toward people One of Horney's neurotic trends. It is characteristic of neurotics who need others as a protection against feelings of helplessness.

narcism (Cattell) An erg or innate drive to be interested in one's own body and appearance (see also **narcissism**).

narcissism Love of self or the attainment of erotic pleasure from viewing one's own body.

necrophilia Love of death.

need potential (Rotter) Refers to the possible occurrence of a set of functionally related behaviors directed toward the satisfaction of the same goal or a similar set of goals.

need value (Rotter) The degree to which a person prefers one set of reinforcements to another.

negative reinforcement The removal of any aversive stimulus which, when removed from a situation, increases the probability that a given behavior will occur.

neurasthenia Neurotic condition characterized by excessive fatigue, chronic aches and pains, and low motivational level.

neurosis Somewhat dated term signifying mild personality disorders, as opposed to the more severe psychotic reactions. Neuroses are generally characterized by one or more of the following: anxiety, hysteria, phobias, obsessive-compulsive reactions, depression, chronic fatigue, and hypochondriacal reactions.

neurotic anxiety (May) A reaction that is disproportionate to the threat and that leads to repression and defensive behaviors.

neurotic claims (Horney) Unrealistic demands and expectations of neurotics to be entitled to special privilege.

neurotic needs (Horney) Original 10 defenses against basic anxiety.

neurotic needs (Maslow) Nonproductive needs that are opposed to the basic needs and that block psychological health whether or not they are satisfied.

neurotic pride (Horney) A false pride based on one's idealized image of self.

neurotic search for glory Horney's concept for the comprehensive drive toward actualizing the ideal self.

neurotic trends Horney's term for the three basic attitudes toward self and others—moving toward people, moving against people, and moving away from people; a revision of her original list of 10 neurotic needs.

neuroticism (N) (Eysenck) One of three types or superfactors identified by Eysenck. Neuroticism is a bipolar factor consisting of neuroticism at one pole and stability at the other. High scores on N may indicate anxiety, hysteria, obsessive-compulsive disorders, or criminality.

nomothetic Approach to the study of personality which is based on general laws or principles.

nonbeing The awareness of the possibility of one's not being through death or loss of awareness.

normal anxiety (May) The experience of threat that accompanies growth or change in one's values.

nothingness (see **nonbeing**).

oblique rotation A method of rotating the axes in factor analysis which assumes some intercorrelation among primary factors.

obsession A persistent or recurrent idea, usually involving an urge toward some action.

Oedipus complex (Freud) Term used by Freud to indicate the situation in which the child of either sex develops feelings of love and/or hostility for the parent. In the simple male Oedipus complex, the boy has incestuous feelings of love for the mother and hostility toward the father. The simple female Oedipus complex exists when the girl feels hostility for the mother and sexual love for the father.

old age (Erikson) The eighth and final stage of the life cycle, characterized by the psychosocial crisis of integrity vs. despair and the basic strength of wisdom.

old wise man Jungian archetype of wisdom and meaning.

ontology That branch of philosophy dealing with the nature of being.

open system (Allport) Any approach to personality that takes into consideration the observation that people are not only reactive to their environment but also act upon the environment and are capable of causing the environment to react to them. An open system permits growth and change within the individual that is independent of environmental determinants.

operant conditioning (Skinner) A type of learning in which reinforcement is contingent upon the occurrence of a particular response. Reinforcement increases the probability that the same response will occur again.

operant discrimination (Skinner) As a consequence of an organism's reinforcement history, it learns to respond to some elements in the environment, but not to others. Operant discrimination does not exist within the organism, but is a function of environmental variables and the organism's previous history of reinforcement.

operant extinction (Skinner) The loss of an operantly conditioned response due to systematic withholding of reinforcement.

operational definition A definition of a concept in terms of specific operations to be carried out by the observer.

oral phase (Freud) The earliest phase of the infantile period. This stage is characterized by attempts to gain pleasure through the activity of the mouth, especially sucking, eating, and biting; corresponds roughly to the first 12–18 months of life.

oral-sensory Erikson's term for the infant's first psychosexual mode of adapting.

organ dialect (Adler) The expression of a person's underlying intentions or style of life through a diseased or dysfunctioning bodily organ.

organismic That approach to psychological theories which emphasized that the entire organism develops in a unified manner.

organismic self (Rogers) A more general term than self-concept, the organismic self includes the entire person, including those aspects of existence beyond awareness.

organizational corollary Kelly's notion that people arrange their personal constructs in a hierarchical system.

orthogonal rotation A method of rotating the axes in factor analysis that assumes the independence of primary factors.

overt inhibition (Dollard & Miller) The blocking of a response or action not under verbal control (for example, when unacceptable responses are inhibited by guilt or anxiety. Differs from repression, which refers to *thoughts* rather than actions).

overt restraint (Dollard & Miller) The blocking of a response or action not under verbal control (for example, when unacceptable responses are inhibited by guilt or anxiety). Differs from repression, which refers to *thoughts* rather than actions.

P technique Correlational procedure pioneered by Cattell, which utilizes variables from one person taken at many different occasions.

paranoia Mental disorder characterized by unrealistic feelings of persecution, grandiosity, and suspicious attitude toward others.

parataxic (Sullivan) Mode of cognition characterized by attribution of cause and effect when none is present; private language not consensually validated (that is, not able to be accurately communicated to others).

parataxic distortion (Sullivan) The process of seeing a cause and effect relationship between two events in close proximity when there is no such relationship.

parsimony Criterion of a useful theory, which states that when two theories are equal on other criteria, the simpler one is preferred.

peak experience (Maslow) An intense, mystical experience often characteristic of self-actualizing people, but not limited to them.

penis envy (Freud) (see **castration complex**).

perceptual-conscious (Freud) The system that perceives external stimuli through sight, sound, taste, and the like, and communicates them to the conscious system.

perseverative functional autonomy (Allport) Functionally independent motives that are not part of the proprium (for example, addictions and incompleted tasks).

person of tomorrow (Rogers) The psychologically healthy individual in the process of evolving into all that he or she can become.

person-centered The theory of personality founded by Carl Rogers as an outgrowth of his client-centered psychotherapy.

persona Jungian archetype that represents that side of personality one shows to the rest of the world. Also, the mask worn by ancient Roman actors in the Greek theater, and thus the root of the word "personality."

personal constructs (Kelly) A person's way of interpreting, explaining, and predicting events.

personal disposition (Allport) Relatively permanent neuropsychic structure peculiar to the individual, which has the capacity to render different stimuli functionally equivalent and to initiate and guide personalized forms of behavior.

Personal Orientation Inventory (POI) Test designed by E. L. Shostrom to measure Maslow's concept of self-actualizing tendencies in people.

personal unconscious Jung's term for those repressed experiences which pertain exclusively to one particular individual; opposed to the collective unconscious which pertains to unconscious experiences that originate with repeated experiences of our ancestors.

personality A global concept referring to all those relatively permanent traits, dispositions, or characteristics within the individual, which give some degree of consistency to that person's behavior. At present, no one definition of personality is acceptable.

personifications (Sullivan) Images a person has of self or others, such as "good-mother," "bad-mother," "good-me," and "bad-me."

phallic phase (Freud) The third and latest stage of the infantile period, this period is characterized by the Oedipus complex. Though anatomical differences between the sexes are responsible for important differences in the male and female Oedipal periods, Freud used the term phallic phase to signify both the male and the female developmental stage.

phenomenology A philosophical position that holds that all behavior is caused by one's perceptions rather than by external reality.

philia Brotherly or sisterly love. Friendship.

placebo effect Changes brought about by people's beliefs or expectations.

play age (Erikson) The third stage of psychosocial development, encompassing the time from about three to five and characterized by the genital-locomotor psychosexual mode and the crisis of initiative vs. guilt.

play construction Erikson's projective technique for assessing personality dynamics in children through the use of toys.

pleasure principle (Freud) Refers to the motivation of the id to seek immediate reduction of tension through the gratification of instinctual drives.

positive freedom (Fromm) Spontaneous activity of the whole, integrated personality. Positive freedom signals a reunification with others and with the world.

positive regard (Rogers) The need to be loved, liked, or accepted by another.

positive reinforcer Any stimulus which, when added to a situation, increases the probability that a given behavior will occur.

preconscious (Freud) Those mental elements that are currently not in awareness, but which can become conscious with varying degree of difficulty.

primary narcissism (Freud) The infant's investment of libido upon its own ego; self-love or autoerotic behavior of the infant (see **narcissism**).

primary process (Freud) Refers to the id, which houses the primary motivators of behavior called instincts.

primary traits First-order traits extracted through factor analysis of more specific behaviors.

principle of entropy (Jung) (see **entropy**).

principle of equivalence (Jung) (see **equivalence**).

proactive (Allport) Concept that presupposes that people are capable of consciously acting upon their environment in new and innovative ways which, in turn, feed new elements into the system, thus permitting psychological growth.

procreativity (Erikson) The drive to have children and to care for them.

progression (Jung) The forward flow of psychic energy. Involves the extraverted attitude and movement toward adaptation to the external world.

projection A defense mechanism whereby the ego reduces anxiety by attributing an unwanted impulse to another person or object.

projective techniques Various methods used to discover conscious or unconscious motivations and attitudes through the analysis of responses to unstructured or ambiguous stimuli. The Rorschach (inkblot) test is, perhaps, the best known projective instrument, but Freud's technique of free association, Adler's early recollections, and Jung's active imagination are other examples.

propriate functional autonomy (Allport) Allport's concept of a master system of motivation which confers unity on personality by relating self-sustaining motives to the proprium.

propriate strivings (Allport) Motivation toward goals which are consistent with an established proprium and which are uniquely one's own.

proprium (Allport) All those characteristics which a person sees as peculiarly his or hers and which are regarded as warm, central, and important.

prototaxic Primitive, presymbolic, undifferentiated mode of experience which cannot be communicated to others.

psychoanalysis Theory of personality, approach to psychotherapy, and method of investigation founded by Sigmund Freud.

psychoanalytical social theory Horney's theory of personality that emphasizes cultural influence in shaping both normal and neurotic development.

psychodynamic Loosely defined term usually referring to those psychological theories which heavily emphasize unconscious motivation. The theories of Freud, Adler, Jung, Sullivan, Horney, and Fromm are usually considered to be psychodynamic.

psychoid unconscious Jung's term for those elements in the unconscious which are not capable of becoming conscious.

psychological situation (Rotter) That part of the external and internal world to which an individual is responding.

psychoneurosis (See **neurosis**).

psychopathology General term referring to various levels and types of mental disturbances or behavior disorders, including neuroses, psychoses, and psychosomatic ailments.

psychosis Severe personality disorders, as opposed to the more mild neurotic reactions. Psychoses interfere seriously with the usual functions of life and include both organic brain dysfunctions and functional or learned conditions.

psychoticism (P) (Eysenck) One of three superfactors or types identified by Eysenck. Psychoticism is a bipolar factor consisting of psychoticism at one pole and superego function at the other. High P scores indicate hostility, self-centeredness, suspicion, and nonconformity.

punishment The presentation of an aversive stimulus or the removal of a positive one. Punishment sometimes, but not always, weakens a response.

Q data Cattell's term for questionnaire information or self-report data.

Q sort Inventory technique originated by William Stephenson in which the subject is asked to sort a series of self-referent statements into several piles, the size of which approximates a normal curve.

quaternity (Jung) An archetype symbolized by figures with four equal sides or four elements.

range corollary Kelly's assumption that personal constructs are limited to a finite range of convenience.

rational functions (Jung) Methods of dealing with the world which involve thinking and feeling, that is, valuing.

reaction formation A defense mechanism characterized by the repression of one impulse and the adoption of the exact opposite form of behavior. Reactive behavior is ordinarily exaggerated and ostentatious.

reactive (Allport) Term for those theories which view people as being motivated by tension reduction and by the desire to return to a state of equilibrium.

reality principle (Freud) Refers to the ego, which must realistically arbitrate the conflicting demands of the id, the superego, and the external world.

receptive orientation (Fromm) Refers to people who relate to the world through receiving love, knowledge, and material possessions.

reciprocal determinism (Bandura) Scheme that includes environment, behavior, and person as mutually interacting to determine personal conduct.

regression (Freud) A defense mechanism whereby the person returns to an earlier stage in order to protect the ego against anxiety.

regression (Jung) The backward flow of psychic energy. Regression involves the introverted attitude and movement toward adaptation to the internal world.

reinforcement (Dollard & Miller) Any event that strengthens the connection between a cue and a response, thereby increasing the tendency for a response to be repeated.

reinforcement (Skinner) Any condition within the environment that strengthens a behavior (see also **negative reinforcer** and **positive reinforcer**).

reinforcement-reinforcement sequences Rotter's term which indicates that the value of a reinforcement is a function of one's expectation that this reinforcement will lead to future reinforcements.

reinforcement value (Rotter) The preference a person attaches to any reinforcement when the probabilities are equal for the occurrence of a number of different reinforcements.

relatedness (Fromm) The need for union with another person or persons. Expressed through submission, power, or love.

reliable The extent to which a test or other measuring instrument yields consistent results.

repetition compulsion (Freud) The tendency of an instinct, especially the death instinct, to repeat or recreate an earlier condition, particularly one that was frightening or anxiety-arousing.

repression (Freud) The forcing of unwanted, anxiety-laden experiences into the unconscious in order to defend the person against the pain of that anxiety.

resacralization (Maslow) The process of returning respect, joy, awe, rapture, and the like to an experience in order that the experience is more subjective and personal.

respondent conditioning Often called classical conditioning and sometimes Pavlovian conditioning. In respondent conditioning a neutral (conditioned) stimulus is paired with, that is, immediately precedes, an unconditioned stimulus a number of times until it is capable of bringing about a previously unconditioned response, now called the conditioned response.

respondent extinction The loss of any behavior acquired through respondent conditioning. Respondent extinction takes place when the conditioned stimulus is presented several times in the absence of the unconditioned stimulus.

response (Dollard & Miller) Behavior that occurs as a reaction to drives and cues.

response consequences (Bandura) One of two basic sources of learning. Response consequences involve the observation of the effects of a response.

retention (Bandura) Second of four steps that affect modeling. Retention refers to the symbolic representation in memory of a response pattern observed in another person.

role (Kelly) A person's pattern of behavior that results from his or her understanding of the constructs of others with whom he or she is engaged in some tasks.

role repudiation (Erikson) The inability to synthesize different self-images and values into a workable identity.

rootedness (Fromm) The human need to establish roots, that is, to find a home again in the world.

sadism A condition characterized by the reception of sexual pleasure through inflicting pain or humiliation on another person.

sadistic-anal phase (Freud) Sometimes called the anal phase, this is the second stage of the infantile period and is characterized by attempts to gain pleasure from the excretory function and such related behaviors as destroying or losing objects, stubbornness, neatness, and miserliness. Corresponds roughly to the second year of life.

safeguarding tendencies (Adler) Protective mechanisms such as aggression, withdrawal, and the like, which maintain exaggerated feelings of superiority.

same behavior (Dollard & Miller) A form of behavior in which each person learns to respond in the same way to a given pattern of cues. May or may not involve imitation.

schizophrenia Psychotic disorder characterized by fundamental disturbances in perception of reality, severe apathy, and loss of affect.

school age (Erikson) The fourth stage of psychosocial development. School age covers the period from about six to 12 or 13 and is characterized by psychosexual latency and the psychosocial crisis of industry vs. inferiority.

secondary traits (Allport) (see **disposition, secondary**).

secondary narcissism (Freud) Self-love or

autoerotic behavior in an adolescent (see **narcissism**).

secondary process (Freud) Refers to the ego which, chronologically, is the second region of the mind (after the id or primary process). Secondary process thinking is in contact with reality.

secondary reinforcement Learned reinforcement. If a previously ineffective event—for example, money—increases the likelihood that learning will take place, then that event is a secondary reinforcer.

security operations (Sullivan) Behaviors aimed at reducing interpersonal tension.

selective activation Refers to Bandura's belief that self-regulatory influences are not automatic, but rather operate only if they are activated.

selective inattention (Sullivan) The control of focal awareness, which involves a refusal to see those things one does not wish to see.

self (Jung) The most comprehensive of all archetypes, the self includes the whole of personality, though it is mostly unconscious. The self is often symbolized by the mandala motif.

self-accusation Adlerian safeguarding tendency whereby the person aggresses indirectly against others through self-torture and guilt.

self-actualization (Maslow) The highest level of human motivation characterized by full development of all of one's capacities.

self-actualization (Rogers) A subsystem of the actualizing tendency. The tendency to actualize the self as perceived.

self-concept Those aspects of one's experiences which are perceived by the individual.

self-efficacy (Bandura) One's expectation that he or she is capable of performing the behaviors that will produce desired outcomes in any particular situation.

self-hatred (Horney) The powerful tendency for neurotics to despise their real self.

self-realization (Jung) The highest possible level of psychic maturation. It necessitates a balance between conscious and unconscious, ego and self, masculine and feminine, and introversion and extraversion. All four functions would be fully developed.

self-regard (Rogers) The need to accept, like, or love oneself.

self system (Bandura) Cognitive structure of personality that provides reference for perceiving, evaluating, and regulating behavior.

self-system (Sullivan) Complex of dynamisms that protect the person from anxiety and maintain interpersonal security.

sems (Cattell) Learned dynamic traits or sentiments.

sense of identity (Fromm) The distinctively human need to develop a feeling of "I."

sensation (Jung) An irrational function that receives physical stimuli and transmits them to perceptual consciousness. People may rely on either extraverted sensing (outside perceptions) or on introverted sensing (internal perceptions).

sentiments Learned dynamic traits. In Cattell's theory, sentiments are contrasted to ergs, which refer to energy inherent in innate drives. Also called *sems.*

shadow Jungian archetype representing the inferior or dark side of personality.

shaping Conditioning a response by first rewarding gross approximations of the behavior, then closer approximations, and finally the desired behavior itself.

social interest (Adler) Translation of the German *Gemeinschaftsgefühl,* meaning a community feeling or a sense of feeling at one with all human beings.

sociality corollary Kelly's notion that people can communicate with others because they are able to construe their constructions.

solicitude Adlerian safeguarding tendency whereby the individual depreciates others and receives an inflated feeling of superiority by acting as if other people are incapable of caring for themselves.

somnolent detachment (Sullivan) Dynamism that protects the person from increasingly strong and painful effects of severe anxiety.

standing still (Adler) Safeguarding tendency characterized by lack of action as a means of avoiding failure.

states Temporary conditions within an individual such as anger, stress, sexual arousal, or fear; opposed to traits which are more permanent.

stereotypes (Sullivan) Imaginary traits attributed to a group of people.

stimulus generalization (see **generalization**).

structure of personality The basic units or building blocks of personality.

style of life (Adler) A person's individuality expressing itself in any circumstance or environment; the "flavor" of a person's life.

subception (Rogers) The process of perceiving stimuli without an awareness of the perception.

sublimation A defense mechanism that involves the repression of the genital aim of eros and its substitution by a cultural or social aim.

subsidiation chain Cattell's term for the complex of subgoals underlying motivation. A subsidiation chain generally traces motivation to some innate drive.

successive approximations Procedure used to shape an organism's behavior; entails the rewarding of behaviors as they become closer and closer to the target behavior.

superego (Freud) The province of the mind which refers to the moral or ethical processes of personality. The superego has two subsystems—the conscience, which tells us what is wrong, and the ego-ideal, which tells us what is right.

superiority complex (Adler) Exaggerated and unrealistic feelings of personal superiority as an overcompensation for unusually strong feelings of inferiority.

suppression The blocking or inhibiting of an activity by either a conscious act of the will or by an outside agent such as parents or other authority figures. Not to be confused with *repression*, which is the unconscious blocking of anxiety-producing experiences.

syndrome A group of concurrent symptoms or characteristics.

synergy The combined effectiveness of two or more actions.

systematic desensitization A behavior therapy technique used to inhibit or extinguish phobias and fears through the use of relaxation.

syntaxic (Sullivan) Consensually validated experiences. As the highest level of cognition, syntaxic experiences can be accurately communicated to others, usually through language.

syntonic Erikson's term for the positive element in each pair of opposites that characterize his eight stages of development.

T data Cattell's term for test scores or objective information obtained from observation of performance.

Taoistic attitude (Maslow) Noninterfering, passive, receptive attitude that includes awe and wonder toward that which is observed.

taxonomy A system of classification of data according to their natural relationships.

teleology An explanation of behavior in terms of future goals or purposes.

temperament An inherited quality that refers to the manner in which one typically performs an activity.

tenderness (Sullivan) Tension within the mothering one, which is aroused by the manifest needs of the infant. Within the child tenderness is felt as the need to receive care.

tension (Sullivan) The potentiality for action, which may or may not be experienced in awareness.

theory A scientific theory is a set of related assumptions from which, by logical deductive reasoning, testable hypotheses can be drawn.

thinking (Jung) A rational function that tells us the meaning of a sensation that originates either from the external world (extraverted) or from the internal or subjective world (introverted).

third force Somewhat vague term referring to those approaches to psychology that have reacted against the psychodynamic and behavioristic theories. The third force is usually thought to include humanistic, existential, and phenomenological theories.

threat (Kelly) The anticipation of danger to the stability of one's personal constructs.

threat (Rogers) Results from the perception of an experience that is inconsistent with one's organismic self.

trait A relatively permanent disposition of an individual, which is inferred from behavior. Cattell, Eysenck, and Allport each have slightly different definitions.

trait, common (Allport) Relatively permanent neuropsychic structure with the capacity to render disparate stimuli functionally equivalent and to initiate and guide action.

transcendence (Fromm) The need for humans to rise above their passive animal existence through either creating or destroying life.

transference (Freud) Strong, undeserved feelings the patient develops toward the analyst during the course of treatment. This feeling may be either sexual or hostile and stems from the patient's earlier experiences with parents.

transformation Psychotherapeutic approach used by Jung wherein the therapist is transformed into a healthy individual who can aid the patient in establishing a philosophy of life.

types (Factor theorists) A cluster of primary

traits. Eysenck recognized three general types—extraversion (E), neuroticism (N), and psychoticism (P).

types (Jung) Classification of people based on the two-dimensional scheme of attitudes and functions. The two attitudes of extraversion and introversion and the four functions of thinking, feeling, sensing, and intuiting combine to produce eight possible types.

tyranny of the should (Horney) A key element in the neurotic search for glory. It includes an unconscious and unrelenting drive for perfection.

Umwelt Term used by existentialists to refer to the world of things or objects. One of three simultaneous modes of being-in-the-world.

unconditional positive regard (Rogers) The need to be accepted and prized by another without any restrictions or qualifications. One of three "necessary and sufficient" therapeutic conditions.

unconscious (Freud) All those mental elements of which a person is unaware. Two levels of the unconscious are the unconscious proper and the preconscious. Unconscious ideas can become conscious only through great resistance and difficulty.

undoing (Freud) A defense mechanism, closely related to repression, involving the ego's attempt to do away with unpleasant experiences and their consequences by an expenditure of energy on compulsive ceremonial activities.

unimodal distribution A set of scores with only one mode.

unipolar factors Factors with only one pole, that is, those scaled from zero to some large amount, rather than from a minus point, through zero, to a positive point.

valid The extent to which a test or other measuring instrument measures what it is supposed to measure; accurate.

variable-interval (Skinner) Intermittent reinforcement schedule in which the organism is reinforced after a lapse of random and varied periods of time (for example, VI 10 means that the animal is reinforced for its first response following random-length intervals that average 10 minutes).

variable-ratio (Skinner) Intermittent reinforcement schedule whereby the organism is reinforced for every nth response on the average (for example, VR 50 means that the animal is reinforced on the average of one time for every 50 responses).

variance A measure of the extent to which individual scores differ from one another.

vicarious experience Learning through the observation of consequences of others' behavior.

voyeurism The reception of sexual pleasure from viewing certain objects, persons, or activities.

vulnerable (Rogers) A condition that exists when people are unaware of the discrepancy between their organismic selves and their experiences. Vulnerable people often behave in ways incomprehensible to themselves and to others.

will (May) A conscious commitment to action.

withdrawal (Adler) Safeguarding one's exaggerated sense of superiority by establishing a distance between oneself and one's problems.

young adulthood (Erikson) The age from about 19 to 30 which is characterized by mature genitality and the crisis of intimacy vs. isolation.

References

Adams-Webber, J. R. (1970). An analysis of the discriminant validity of several repertory grid indices. *British Journal of Psychology, 60,* 83–90.

Adler, A. (1907/1917). *Study of organ inferiority and its psychical compensation.* New York: Nervous and Mental Disease Publishing Co.

Adler, A. (1925/1968). *The practice and theory of Individual Psychology.* Totowa, NJ: Littlefield, Adams.

Adler, A. (1927). *Understanding human nature.* New York: Greenberg.

Adler, A. (1929/1964). *Problems of neurosis.* New York: Harper Torchbooks.

Adler, A. (1929/1969). *The science of living.* New York: Anchor Books.

Adler, A. (1930). Individual Psychology. In C. Murchinson (Ed.), *Psychologies of 1930.* Worcester, MA: Clark University Press.

Adler, A. (1956). *The Individual Psychology of Alfred Adler: A systematic presentation in selections from his writings.* H. L. Ansbacher & R. R. Ansbacher (Eds.). New York: Basic Books.

Adler, A. (1964). *Superiority and social interest: A collection of later writings.* H. L. Ansbacher & R. R. Ansbacher (Eds.). New York: Norton.

Allport, G. W. (1937). *Personality: A psychological interpretation.* New York: Henry Holt.

Allport. G. W. (1942). *The use of personal documents in psychological science.* New York: Social Science Research Council, Bulletin 49.

Allport, G. W. (1950). *The individual and his religion.* New York: Macmillan.

Allport, G. W. (1954). *The nature of prejudice.* Reading, MA: Addison-Wesley.

Allport, G. W. (1955). *Becoming: Basic considerations for a psychology of personality.* New Haven, CT: Yale University Press.

Allport, G. W. (1960). The open system in personality theory. *Journal of Abnormal and Social Psychology, 61,* 301–310.

Allport, G. W. (1961). *Pattern and growth in personality.* New York: Holt, Rinehart and Winston.

Allport, G. W. (1962). The general and the unique in psychological science. *Journal of Personality, 30,* 405–422.

Allport, G. W. (1963). Behavioral science, religion and mental health. *Journal of Religion and Health, 2,* 187–197.

Allport, G. W. (1965). *Letters from Jenny.* New York: Harcourt, Brace & World.

Allport, G. W. (1966). Traits revisited. *American Psychologist, 21,* 1–10.

Allport, G. W. (1967). An autobiography. In E. G. Boring & G. Lindzey (Eds.), *A history of psychology in autobiography* (Vol. 5). New York: Appleton-Century-Crofts.

Allport, G. W. (1968). *The person in psychology.* Boston: Beacon Press.

Allport, G. W. (1978). *Waiting for the Lord: 33 meditations on God and man.* New York: Macmillan.

Allport, G. W., & Odbert, H. S. (1936). Trait-names: A psycho-lexical study. *Psychological Monographs, 47,* 1–171.

Allport, G. W., & Ross, J. M. (1967). Personal religious orientation and prejudice. *Journal of Personality and Social Psychology, 5,* 432–443.

Allport, G. W., Vernon, P. E., & Lindzey, G. (1960). *A study of values.* Boston: Houghton Mifflin.

Altman, K. E. (1973). The relationship between social interest dimensions of early recollections and selected counselor variables (Doctoral dissertation, University of South Carolina). *Dissertation Abstracts International, 34,* 5613A. (University Microfilm No. 74–05, 364).

Ansbacher H. L. (1985). The significance of Alfred Adler for the concept of narcissism. *American Journal of Psychiatry, 142,* 203–207.

Bachofen, J. J. (1861/1967). *Myth, religion, and mother right: Selected writings of Johann Jacob Bachofen* (R. Manheim, Trans.). Princeton, NJ: Princeton University Press.

Baldwin, A. F. (1942). Personal structure analysis: A statistical method for investigating the single personality. *Journal of Abnormal and Social Psychology, 37,* 163–183.

Balmary, M. (1979/1982). *Psychoanalyzing psychoanalysis.* Baltimore: Johns Hopkins University Press.

Bandura, A. (1977a). Self-efficacy: Toward a unifying theory of behavior change. *Psychological Review, 84,* 191–215.

Bandura, A. (1977b). *Social learning theory.* Englewood Cliffs, NJ: Prentice-Hall.

Bandura, A. (1978a). On paradigms and recycled ideologies. *Cognitive Therapy and Research, 2,* 79–103.

Bandura, A. (1978b). The self system in reciprocal determinism. *American Psychologist, 33,* 344–358.

Bandura, A. (1979). Self-referent mechanisms in social learning theory. *American Psychologist, 34,* 439–441.

Bandura, A. (1981). Self-referent thought: A developmental analysis of self-efficacy. In J. H. Flavell & L. D. Ross (Eds.), *Cognitive social development: Frontiers and possible futures.* New York: Cambridge University Press.

Bandura, A. (1982a, July). Model of causality in social learning theory. Paper presented at the meeting of the Japanese Psychological Association, Kyoto.

Bandura, A. (1982b). The psychology of chance encounters and life paths. *American Psychologist, 37,* 747–755.

Bandura, A. (1982c). Self-efficacy mechanisms in human agency. *American Psychologist, 37,* 122–147.

Bandura, A. (1983). Self-efficacy determinants of anticipated fears and calamities. *Journal of Personality and Social Psychology, 45,* 464–469.

Bandura, A. (1984). Recycling misconceptions of perceived self-efficacy. *Cognitive Therapy and Research, 8,* 231–255.

Bandura, A. (1986). *Social foundations of thought and action: A social cognitive theory.* Englewood Cliffs, NJ: Prentice-Hall.

Bandura, A. (1988a, August). *Human agency in social cognitive theory.* Paper presented at the XXIV International Congress of Psychology, Sydney, Australia.

Bandura, A. (1988b). Self-regulation of motivation and action through goal systems. In V. Hamilton, G. H. Bower, & N. H. Fryda (Eds.), *Cognitive perspectives on emotion and motivation.* Dordrecht: Kluwer Academic Publishers.

Bandura, A. (1988c). Social cognitive theory. In R. Vasta (Ed.), *Annals of child development* (Vol. 6). Greenwich, CT: JAI Press.

Bandura, A. (1988d). Social cognitive theory of moral thought and action. In W. M. Kurtiness & J. L. Gewirty (Eds.), *Moral behavior and development: Advances in theory, research, and applications* (Vol. 1). Hillsdale, NJ: Erlbaum.

Bandura, A., & Adams, N. E. (1977). Analysis of self-efficacy theory of behavioral change. *Cognitive Therapy and Research, 1,* 287–310.

Bandura, A., Adams, N. E., Hardy, A. B., & Howells, G. N. (1980). Tests of the generality of self-efficacy theory. *Cognitive Therapy and Research, 4,* 39–66.

Bandura, A., Blanchard, E. B., & Ritter, B. (1969). The relative efficacy of desensitization and modeling approaches for inducing behavioral, affective, and attitudinal changes. *Journal of Personality and Social Psychology, 13,* 173–199.

Bandura, A., & Cervone, D. (1983). Self-evaluative and self-efficacy mechanisms governing the motivational effects of goal systems. *Journal of Personality and Social Psychology, 45,* 1017–1028.

Bandura, A., Ross, D., & Ross, S. A. (1963). Imitation of film-mediated aggressive models. *Journal of Abnormal and Social Psychology, 66,* 3–11.

Bandura, A., & Walters, R. H. (1959). *Adolescent aggression.* New York: Ronald Press.

Bannister, D. (1970). *Perspectives in personal construct theory.* London: Academic Press.

Bannister, D. (Ed.). (1975). *Issues and approaches in the psychological therapies.* London: Wiley.

Bannister, D. (1977). *New perspectives in personal construct theory.* London: Academic Press.

Bannister, D., & Fransella, F. (1966). A grid test of schizophrenic thought disorder. *British Journal of Social and Clinical Psychology, 5,* 95–102.

Bannister, D., & Fransella, F. (1971). *Inquiring man: The theory of personal constructs.* Harmondsworth, England: Penguin Books.

Bannister, D., & Mair, J. M. M. (1968). *The evaluation of personal constructs.* London: Academic Press.

Benson, H. (1975). *The relaxation response.* New York: Morrow.

Berkowitz, L. (1958). Expression and reduction of hostility. *Psychological Bulletin, 55,* 257–283.

Berkowitz, L. (1962). *Aggression: A social psychological analysis.* New York: McGraw-Hill.

Berkowitz, L. (1969). The frustration-aggression hypothesis revisited. In L. Berkowitz (Ed.), *Roots of aggression: A re-examination of the frustration-aggression hypothesis.* New York: Atherton.

Berkowitz, L. (1978). Whatever happened to the frustration-aggression hypothesis? *American Behavioral Scientist, 21,* 691–708.

Bettelheim, B. (1982, March 1). Freud and the soul. *The New Yorker,* pp. 52–93.

Bilmes, M. (1978). Rollo May. In R. S. Valle & M. King (Eds.), *Existential-phenomenological alternatives for psychology* (pp. 290–294). New York: Oxford University Press.

Black, R. (1940). *Eleanor Roosevelt: A biography.* New York: Duell, Sloan and Pearce.

Blanchard, W. H. (1969). Psychodynamic aspects of the peak experience. *Psychoanalytic Review, 46,* 87–112.

Bottome, P. (1939). *Alfred Adler: Apostle of freedom.* London: Faber & Faber.

Borkovec, T. D. (1978). Self-efficacy: Cause or reflection of behavioral change. In S. Rachman (Ed.), *Advances in behavior research and therapy* (Vol. 1). Oxford: Pergamon Press.

Breuer, J., & Freud, S. (1895/1955). *Studies on hysteria.* In J. Strachey (Ed. and Trans.), *The standard edition of the complete psychological works of Sigmund Freud* (Vol. 2). London: Hogarth Press.

Brown, I., Jr., & Inouye, D. K. (1978). Learned helplessness through modeling: The role of perceived similarity in competence. *Journal of Personality and Social Psychology, 36,* 900–908.

Buss, A. H. (1961). *The psychology of aggression.* New York: Wiley.

Butler, J. M., & Haigh, G. V. (1954). Changes in the relation between self-concepts and ideal concepts consequent upon client-centered counseling. In C. R. Rogers & R. F. Dymond (Eds.), *Psychotherapy and personality change. Co-ordinated research studies in the client-centered approach.* Chicago: University of Chicago Press.

Byck, R. (Ed.). (1974). *Cocaine papers by Sigmund Freud.* New York: Meridian.

Carlson, R. (1980). Studies of Jungian typology: II, Representation of the personal world. *Journal of Personality and Social Psychology, 38,* 801–810.

Carroll, W. R., & Bandura, A. (1982). The role of visual monitoring in observational learning of action patterns: Making the observable observable. *Journal of Motor Behavior, 14,* 153–167.

Carroll, W. R., & Bandura, A. (1985). Role of timing of visual monitoring and motor rehearsal in observational learning of action patterns. *Journal of Motor Behavior, 17,* 269–281.

Cattell, R. B. (1949). *Manual for Forms A and B: Sixteen Personality Factors Questionnaire.* Champaign, IL: IPAT.

Cattell, R. B. (1950). *Personality: A systematic, theoretical and factual study.* New York: McGraw-Hill.

Cattell, R. B. (1957). *Personality and motivation structure and measurement.* Yonkers-on-Hudson, NY: World Book.

Cattell, R. B. (1971). *Abilities: Their structure, growth, and action.* Boston: Houghton Mifflin.

Cattell, R. B. (1972a). *A new morality from science: Beyondism.* New York: Pergamon Press.

Cattell, R. B. (1972b). The 16 P.F. and basic personality structure: A reply to Eysenck. *Journal of Behavioral Science, 1,* 169–187.

Cattell, R. B. (1974a). An autobiography. In G. Lindzey (Ed.), *A history of psychology in autobiography* (Vol. 6). Englewood Cliffs, NJ: Prentice-Hall.

Cattell, R. B. (1974b). Travels in psychological hyperspace. In T. S. Krawiec (Ed.), *The Psychologists* (Vol. 2). New York: Oxford University Press.

Cattell, R. B. (1979–1980). *Personality and learning theory: Vol. 1. The structure of personality in its environment: Vol. 2. A systems theory of maturation and structure learning.* New York: Springer.

Cattell, R. B. (1983). *Structured personality—learning theory: A wholistic multivariate research approach.* New York: Praeger.

Cattell, R. B. (1985). *Human motivation and the dynamic calculus.* New York: Praeger.

Cattell, R. B. (1987). *Psychotherapy by structured learning theory.* New York: Springer.

Cattell, R. B., & Child, D. (1975). *Motivation and dynamic structure.* New York: Halsted Press.

Cattell, R. B., & Cross, P. (1952). Comparison of the ergic and self-sentiment structures found in dynamic traits by R and P techniques. *Journal of Personality, 21,* 250–270.

Cattell, R. B., Ebert, H. W., & Tatsuoka, M. M. (1970). *Handbook for the sixteen personality factor questionnaire.* Champaign, IL: IPAT.

Cattell, R. B., & Kline, P. (1977). *The scientific analysis of personality and motivation.* New York: Academic Press.

Cattell, R. B., Schuerger, J. M., & Klein, T. W. (1982). Heritabilities of ego strength (Factor C), superego strength (Factor G), and self-sentiment (Factor Q_3) by multiple abstract variance analysis. *Journal of Clinical Psychology, 38,* 769–779.

Cattell, R. B., & Warburton, E. W. (1967). *Objective personality and motivation tests.* Urbana, IL: University of Illinois Press.

Chambliss, C. A., & Murray, E. J. (1979). Cognitive procedures for smoking reduction: Symptom attribution versus efficacy attribution. *Cognitive Therapy and Research, 3,* 91–95.

Chapman, A. H. (1976). *Harry Stack Sullivan: His life and his work.* New York: Putnam.

Clark, R. W. (1980). *Freud: The man and the cause.* New York: Random House.

Cohen, D. (1977). *Psychologists on psychology.* New York: Taplinger.

Coles, R. (1970). *Erik H. Erikson: The growth of his work.* Boston: Little, Brown.

Combs, A. W., & Snygg, D. (1959). *Individual behavior: A perceptual approach to behavior.* New York: Harper & Row.

Crandall, J. E. (1975). A scale for social interest. *Journal of Individual Psychology, 31,* 187–195.

Crandall, J. E. (1981). *Theory and measurement of social interest: Empirical tests of Alfred Adler's concept.* New York: Columbia University Press.

Crandall, J. E. (1984). Social interest as a moderator of life stress. *Journal of Personality and Social Psychology, 47,* 164–174.

Crandall, J. E., & Putnam, E. L. (1980). Relations between measures of social interest and psychological well-being. *Journal of Individual Psychology, 36,* 156–168.

Croake, J. W. (1975). An Adlerian view of life style. *Journal of Clinical Psychology, 31,* 513–518.

Daniels, M. (1982). The development of the concept of self-actualization in the writings of Abraham Maslow. *Current Psychological Review, 2,* 61–76.

Davis, A., & Dollard, J. (1940). *Children of bondage: The personality development of Negro youth in the urban South.* Washington, DC: American Council on Education.

Delhees, K. H., & Cattell, R. B. (1971). *Manual for the Clinical Analysis Questionnaire* (CAQ). Champaign, IL: IPAT.

Dement, W. (1960). The effects of dream deprivation. *Science, 131,* 1705–1707.

Dollard, J. (1935). *Criteria for the life history.* New Haven: CT: Yale University Press.

Dollard, J. (1937). *Caste and class in a southern town.* New Haven, CT: Yale University Press.

Dollard, J. (1942). *Victory over fear.* New York: Reynal & Hitchcock.

Dollard, J. (1943). *Fear in battle.* New Haven, CT: Yale University Press.

Dollard, J., & Auld, F. (1959). *Scoring human motives.* New Haven, CT: Yale University Press.

Dollard, J., Doob, L. W., Miller, N. E., Mowrer, O. H., & Sears, R. R. (1939). *Frustration and aggression.* New Haven, CT: Yale University Press.

Dollard, J., & Miller, N. E. (1950). *Personality and psychotherapy: An analysis in terms of learning, thinking, and culture.* New York: Knopf.

Donahue, M. J. (1985). Intrinsic and extrinsic religiousness: Review and meta-analysis. *Journal of Personality and Social Psychology, 48,* 400–419.

Dymond, R. F. (1954a). Adjustment changes over therapy from self-sorts. In C. R. Rogers & R. F. Dymond

(Eds.), *Psychotherapy and personality change: Co-ordinated research studies in the client-centered approach*. Chicago: University of Chicago Press.

Dymond, R. F. (1954b). Adjustment changes over therapy from Thematic Apperception Test ratings. In C. R. Rogers & R. F. Dymond (Eds.), *Psychotherapy and personality change: Co-ordinated research studies in the client-centered approach*. Chicago: University of Chicago Press.

Eastman, D., & Marzillier, J. S. (1984). Theoretical and methodological difficulties in Bandura's self-efficacy theory. *Cognitive Therapy and Research, 8,* 231–229.

Ellenberger, H. F. (1970). *The discovery of the unconscious*. New York: Basic Books.

Elms, A. C. (1972). Allport, Freud, and the clean little boy. *The Psychoanalytic Review, 59,* 627–632.

Elms, A. C. (1981). Skinner's dark year and *Walden Two*. *American Psychologist, 36,* 470–479.

Erikson, E. H. (1950). *Childhood and society*. New York: Norton.

Erikson, E. H. (1958). *Young man Luther: A study in psychoanalysis and history*. New York: Norton.

Erikson, E. H. (1963). *Childhood and society*. (2nd ed.). New York: Norton.

Erikson, E. H. (1968). *Identity: Youth and crisis*. New York: Norton.

Erikson, E. H. (1969). *Gandhi's truth: On the origins of militant nonviolence*. New York: Norton.

Erikson, E. H. (1974). *Dimensions of a new identity: The 1973 Jefferson Lectures in the Humanities*. New York: Norton.

Erikson, E. H. (1975). *Life history and the historical moment*. New York: Norton.

Erikson, E. H. (1977). *Toys and reasons: Stages in the ritualization of experience*. New York: Norton.

Erikson, E. H. (1979). Reflections on Dr. Borg's life cycle. In D. D. Van Tassel (Ed.). *Aging, death, and the completion of being* (pp. 29–67). Philadelphia: University of Pennsylvania Press.

Erikson, E. H. (1980). *Identity and the life cycles*. New York: Norton.

Erikson, E. H. (1982). *The life cycle completed: A review*. New York: Norton.

Erikson, E. H. (1987). Problems of infancy and early childhood. In S. Schlien (Ed.), *A way of looking at things: Selected papers from 1930 to 1980: Erik H. Erikson* (pp. 547–568). New York: Norton.

Erikson, E. H., Erikson, J. M., & Kivnick, H. Q. (1986). *Vital involvement in old age*. New York: Norton.

Evans, R. I. (1966). *Dialogue with Erich Fromm*. New York: Harper & Row.

Evans, R. I. (1967). *Dialogue with Erik Erikson*. New York: Harper & Row.

Evans, R. I. (1976). *The making of psychology: Discussion with creative contributors*. New York: Knopf.

Evans, R. I. (1981). *Dialogue with Carl Rogers*. New York: Praeger.

Eysenck, H. J. (1947). *Dimensions of personality*. London: Routledge & Kegan Paul.

Eysenck, H. J. (1952a). The effects of psychotherapy: An evaluation. *Journal of Consulting Psychology, 16,* 319–324.

Eysenck, H. J. (1952b). *The structure of human personality*. London: Methuen.

Eysenck, H. J. (1953). *Uses and abuses of psychology*. Baltimore: Penguin.

Eysenck, H. J. (1956). *Sense and nonsense in psychology*. London: Penguin.

Eysenck, H. J. (1959). *Manual for the Maudsley Personality Inventory*. London: University of London Press.

Eysenck, H. J. (1964). *Crime and personality*. Boston: Houghton Mifflin.

Eysenck, H. J. (1965). *Fact and fiction in psychology*. London: Penguin.

Eysenck, H. J. (1967). *The biological basis of personality*. Springfield, IL: Charles C Thomas.

Eysenck, H. J. (1971). *The IQ argument*. New York: The Library Press. (British edition: *Race, intelligence and education*. London: Maurice Temple Smith, 1971).

Eysenck, H. J. (1972a). Primaries or second-order factors: A critical consideration of Cattell's 16 PF battery. *British Journal of Social and Clinical Psychology, 11,* 265–269.

Eysenck, H. J. (1972b). *Psychology is about people*. London: Allen Lane.

Eysenck, H. J. (1976a). Genetic factors in personality development. In A. R. Kaplan (Ed.), *Human behavior genetics*. Springfield, IL: Charles C Thomas.

Eysenck, H. J. (1976b). *Sex and personality*. Austin: University of Texas Press.

Eysenck, H. J. (1977). Personality and factor analysis: A reply to Guilford. *Psychological Bulletin, 84,* 405–411.

Eysenck, H. J. (1977b). *You and neurosis*. London: Temple Smith.

Eysenck, H. J. (1978). Expectations as causal elements in behavioral change. In S. Rachman (Ed.), *Advances in behavior research and therapy* (Vol. 1). Oxford: Pergamon Press.

Eysenck, H. J. (1980). An autobiography in G. Lindzey (Ed.), *A history of psychology in autobiography* (Vol. 7). San Francisco: Freeman.

Eysenck, H. J. (Ed.). (1981). *A model for personality.* New York: Springer.

Eysenck, H. J. (1982). *Personality, genetics and behavior: Selected papers.* New York: Praeger.

Eysenck, H. J. (1987, November). *Personality, stress and cancer: Prediction and prophylaxis.* Paper presented at the meeting of the Louisiana Psychological Association, New Orleans.

Eysenck, H. J. (1988, December). Health's character. *Psychology Today,* pp. 28–35.

Eysenck, H. J., & Coulter, T. (1972). The personality and attitudes of working class British Communists and Fascists. *Journal of Social Psychology, 87,* 59–73.

Eysenck, H. J., & Eysenck, S. B. G. (1964). *Manual of the Eysenck Personality Inventory.* London: University of London Press.

Eysenck, H. J., & Eysenck, S. B. G. (1969). *Personality structure and measurement.* San Diego: R. R. Knapp.

Eysenck, H. J., & Eysenck, S. B. G. (1976). *Psychoticism as a dimension of personality.* London: Hodder & Stoughton.

Eysenck, H. J., & Nias, D. K. B. (1978). *Sex, violence and the media.* New York: Harper & Row.

Eysenck, H. J., Nias, D. K. B., & Cox, D. N. (1982). Sport and personality. *Advances in behavior research and therapy, 4,* 1–56.

Faber, M. D. (1970). Allport's visit with Freud. *The Psychoanalytic Review, 57,* 60–64.

Ferster, C. B., & Skinner, B. F. (1957). *Schedules of reinforcement.* New York: Appleton-Century-Crofts.

Fransella, F., & Bannister, D. (1977). *A manual for repertory grid technique.* London: Academic Press.

Freud, A. (1946). *The ego and the mechanisms of defense.* New York: International Universities Press.

Freud, E. (Ed.). (1960). *Letters of Sigmund Freud.* New York: Basic Books.

Freud, S. (1896/1962). *The aetiology of hysteria.* In J. Strachey (Ed. and Trans.), *The standard edition of the complete psychological works of Sigmund Freud* (Vol. 3). London: Hogarth Press.

Freud, S. (1900/1953). *The interpretation of dreams.* In *Standard edition* (Vols. 4 & 5).

Freud, S. (1901/1953). On dreams. In *Standard edition* (Vol. 5).

Freud, S. (1901/1960). *Psychopathology of everyday life.* In *Standard edition* (Vol. 6).

Freud, S. (1905/1953a). On psychotherapy. In *Standard edition* (Vol. 7).

Freud, S. (1905/1953b). Three essays on the theory of sexuality. In *Standard edition* (Vol. 7).

Freud, S. (1905/1960). *Jokes and their relation to the unconscious.* In *Standard edition* (Vol. 8).

Freud, S. (1910/1957). Leonardo da Vinci and a memory of his childhood. In *Standard edition* (Vol. 11).

Freud, S. (1913/1953). *Totem and taboo.* In *Standard edition* (Vol. 13).

Freud, S. (1914/1953). The Moses of Michelangelo. In *Standard edition* (Vol. 13).

Freud, S. (1914/1957). On narcissism: An introduction. In *Standard edition* (Vol. 14).

Freud, S. (1915/1957a). Instincts and their vicissitudes. In *Standard edition* (Vol. 14).

Freud, S. (1915/1957b). The unconscious. In *Standard edition* (Vol. 14).

Freud, S. (1917/1955). A difficulty in the path of psycho-analysis. In *Standard edition* (Vol. 17).

Freud, S. (1917/1963). *Introductory lectures on psychoanalysis.* In *Standard edition* (Vol. 15 & 16).

Freud, S. (1920/1955). *Beyond the pleasure principle.* In *Standard edition* (Vol. 18).

Freud, S. (1922/1955). Some neurotic mechanisms in jealousy, paranoia and homosexuality. In *Standard edition* (Vol. 18).

Freud, S. (1923/1961a). *The ego and the id.* In *Standard edition* (Vol. 19).

Freud, S. (1923/1961b). The infantile genital organization: An interpolation into the theory of sexuality. In *Standard edition* (Vol. 19).

Freud, S. (1924/1961). The dissolution of the Oedipus complex. In *Standard edition* (Vol. 19).

Freud, S. (1925/1959). *An autobiographical study.* In *Standard edition* (Vol. 20).

Freud, S. (1925/1961). Some psychical consequences of the anatomical distinction between the sexes. In *Standard edition* (Vol. 19).

Freud, S. (1926/1959). Inhibitions, symptoms and anxiety. In *Standard edition* (Vol. 20).

Freud, S. (1931/1961). Female sexuality. In *Standard edition* (Vol. 21).

Freud, S. (1933/1964). *New introductory lectures on psychoanalysis.* In *Standard edition* (Vol. 22).

Freud, S. (1940/1964). *An outline of psychoanalysis.* In *Standard edition* (Vol. 23).

Freud, S. (1950/1966). *Project for a scientific psychology.* In *Standard edition* (Vol. 1).

Freud, S. (1985). The complete letters of Sigmund Freud to Wilhelm Fleiss, 1887–1904 (J. M. Masson, Ed. and Trans.). Cambridge, MA: Harvard University Press.

Freud, S., & Bullitt, W. C. (1967). Thomas Woodrow Wilson: *A psychological study.* Boston: Houghton Mifflin.

Frick, W. D. (1971). *Humanistic psychology: Interviews with Maslow, Murphy, and Rogers.* Columbus, OH: Merrill.

Frick, W. B. (1982). Conceptual foundations of self-actualization: A contribution to motivation theory. *Journal of Humanistic Psychology, 22,* 33–52.

Fromm, E. (1941). *Escape from freedom.* New York: Holt, Rinehart and Winston.

Fromm, E. (1947). *Man for himself: An inquiry into the psychology of ethics.* New York: Holt, Rinehart and Winston.

Fromm E. (1950). *Psychoanalysis and religion.* New Haven, CT: Yale University Press.

Fromm, E. (1951). *The forgotten language: An introduction to the understanding of dreams, fairy tales and myths.* New York: Rinehart.

Fromm, E. (1955). *The sane society.* New York: Holt, Rinehart and Winston.

Fromm, E. (1956). *The art of loving.* New York: Harper & Brothers.

Fromm, E. (1959). *Sigmund Freud's mission.* New York: Harper & Brothers.

Fromm, E. (1962). *Beyond the chains of illusion.* New York: Simon and Schuster.

Fromm, E. (1964). *The heart of man.* New York: Harper & Row.

Fromm, E. (1973). *The anatomy of human destructiveness.* New York: Holt, Rinehart and Winston.

Fromm, E. (1976). *To have or be.* New York: Harper & Row.

Fromm, E. (1986). *For the love of life* (H. J. Schiltz, Ed.: R. Kimber & R. Kimber Trans.). New York: Free Press. (Original works published 1972, 1974, 1975, 1983).

Fromm, E., & Maccoby, M. (1970). *Social character in a Mexican village.* Englewood Cliffs, NJ: Prentice-Hall.

Fromm, E. (1981). *On disobedience and other essays.* New York: Seabury Press.

Fulker, D. W. (1981). The genetic and environmental architecture of psychoticism, extraversion and neuroticism. In H. J. Eysenck (Ed.), *A model for personality.* New York: Springer.

Funk, R. (1982). *Erich Fromm: The courage to be human.* New York: Continuum.

Furtmuller, C. (1964). Alfred Adler: A biographical essay. In H. L. Ansbacher & R. R. Ansbacher (Eds.), *Superiority and social interest: A collection of later writings.* Evanston, IL: Northwestern University Press.

Gay, P. (1988). *Freud: A life for our time.* New York: Norton.

Gendlin, E. T. (1988). Carl Rogers (1902–1987). *American Psychologist, 43,* 127–128.

Gibson, H. B. (1981). *Hans Eysenck: The man and his work.* London: Peter Owen.

Gilgen, A. R. (1982). *American psychology since World War II: A profile of the discipline.* Westport, CT: Greenwood.

Goble, F. G. (1970). *The third force: The psychology of Abraham Maslow.* New York: Grossman.

Gordon, T., & Cartwright, D. (1954). The effects of psychotherapy upon certain attitudes toward others. In C. R. Rogers & R. F. Dymond (Eds.), *Psychotherapy and personality change: Co-ordinated research studies in the client-centered approach.* Chicago: University of Chicago Press.

Gorsuch, R. L. (1988). Psychology of religion. In M. R. Rosenzweig & L. W. Porter (Eds.), *Annual Review of Psychology* (Vol. 39, pp. 201–221). Palo Alto, CA: Annual Review.

Greever, K. B., Tseng, M. S., & Friedland, B. U. (1973). Development of the social interest index. *Journal of Consulting and Clinical Psychology, 41,* 454–458.

Greever, K. B., Tseng, M. S., & Friedland, B. U. (1974). Measuring change in social interest in community college freshmen. *Individual Psychologist, 11,* 4–6.

Grummon, D. L. (1954). Design, procedures, and subjects for the first block. In C. R. Rogers & R. F. Dymond (Eds.), *Psychotherapy and personality change: Co-ordinated research studies in the client-centered approach.* Chicago: University of Chicago Press.

Hall, E. (1983, June). A conversation with Erik Erikson. *Psychology Today,* pp. 22–30.

Hall, M. H. (1967, September). An interview with "Mr. Humanist": Rollo May. *Psychology Today,* pp. 25–29, 72–73.

Hall, M. H. (1968, July). A conversation with Abraham Maslow. *Psychology Today,* pp. 35–37, 54–57.

Hamachek, D. E. (1988). Evaluating self-concept and ego development within Erikson's psychosocial framework: A formulation. *Journal of Counseling and Development, 66,* 354–360.

Harris, T. G. (1969, August). The devil and Rollo May. *Psychology Today,* pp.13–16.

Hartmann, H. (1939/1958). *Ego psychology and the problem of adaptation.* (D. Rapaport, Trans.). New York: International Universities Press.

Hathaway, S. R., & McKinley, J. C. (1951). *The Minnesota Multiphasic Personality Inventory Manual (Revised).* New York: The Psychological Corp.

Hausdorff, D. (1972). *Erich Fromm.* New York: Twayne.

Heppner, P. L., Rogers, M. E., & Lee, L. A. (1984). Carl Rogers: Reflections on his life. *Journal of Counseling and Development, 63,* 14–20.

Hoffman, E. (1988). *The right to be human. A biography of Abraham Maslow.* Los Angeles: Tarcher.

Holland, R. (1970). George Kelly: Constructive innocent and reluctant existentialist. In D. Bannister (Ed.), *Perspectives in personal construct theory.* London: Academic Press.

Holt, R. R. (1962). Individuality and generalization in the psychology of personality. *Journal of Personality, 30,* 377–402.

Hood, R. W., Jr. (1970). Religious orientations and the report of religious experiences. *Journal for the Scientific Study of Religion, 9,* 285–291.

Horney, K. (1917/1968). The technique of psychoanalytic therapy. *American Journal of Psychoanalysis, 28,* 3–12.

Horney, K. (1937). *The neurotic personality of our time.* New York: Norton.

Horney, K. (1939). *New ways in psychoanalysis.* New York: Norton.

Horney, K. (1942). *Self-analysis.* New York: Norton.

Horney, K. (1945). *Our inner conflicts: A constructive theory of neurosis.* New York: Norton.

Horney, K. (1950). *Neurosis and human growth: The struggle toward self-realization.* New York: Norton.

Horney, K. (1967). The neurotic need for love. In H. Kelman (Ed.). *Feminine Psychology.* New York: Norton.

Horney, K. (1987). *Final lectures.* D. H. Ingram (Ed.). New York: Norton.

Isbister, J. N. (1985). *Freud: An introduction to his life and work.* Cambridge, England: Polity Press.

Jacobson, E. (1938). *Progressive relaxation: A physiological and clinical investigation of muscle states and the significance in psychology and medical practice* (2nd ed.). Chicago: University of Chicago Press.

Janeway, E. (1971). *Man's world, woman's place.* New York: Morrow.

Jankowicz, A. D. (1987). Whatever became of George Kelly? Applications and implications. *American Psychologist, 42,* 481–487.

Jones, E. (1953, 1955, 1957). *The life and work of Sigmund Freud* (Vols. 1–3). New York: Basic Books.

Jung, C. G. (1916/1953). *The structure of the unconscious.* In H. Read, M. Fordham, & G. Adler (Eds.), R. F. C. Hull (Trans.), *The collected works of C. G. Jung* (Vol. 7). New York: Pantheon Books.

Jung, C. G. (1916/1960). General aspects of dream psychology. In *Collected works* (Vol. 8).

Jung, C. G. (1921/1971). *Psychological types.* In *Collected works* (Vol. 6).

Jung, C. G. (1928/1960). On psychic energy. In *Collected works* (Vol. 8).

Jung, C. G. (1931/1954a). The aims of psychotherapy. In *Collected works* (Vol. 16).

Jung, C. G. (1931/1954b). Problems of modern psychotherapy. In *Collected works* (Vol. 16).

Jung, C. G. (1931/1960a). The stages of life. In *Collected works* (Vol. 8).

Jung, C. G. (1931/1960b). The structure of the psyche. In *Collected works* (Vol. 8).

Jung, C. G. (1934/1954). The development of personality. In *Collected works* (Vol. 17).

Jung, C. G. (1934/1960). The soul and death. In *Collected works* (Vol. 8).

Jung, C. G. (1935/1968). The Tavistock lectures. In *Collected works* (Vol. 18).

Jung, C. G. (1937/1959). The concept of the collective unconscious. In *Collected works* (Vol. 9, pt. 1).

Jung, C. G. (1939/1959). Conscious, unconscious, and individuation. In *Collected works* (Vol. 9, pt. 1).

Jung, C. G. (1943/1953). *The psychology of the unconscious.* In *Collected works* (Vol. 7).

Jung, C. G. (1945/1953). *The relations between ego and the unconscious.* In *Collected works* (Vol. 7).

Jung, C. G. (1946/1964). The fight with the shadow. In *Collected works* (Vol. 10).

Jung, C. G. (1948/1960a). Instinct and the unconscious. In *Collected works* (Vol. 8).

Jung, C. G. (1948/1960b). On the nature of dreams. In *Collected works* (Vol. 8).

Jung, C. G. (1950/1959). Concerning rebirth. In *Collected works* (Vol. 9, pt. 1).

Jung, C. G. (1951/1959a). *Aion: Researches into the phenomenology of the self.* In *Collected works* (Vol. 9, pt. 2).

Jung, C. G. (1951/1959b). The psychology of the child archetype. In *Collected works* (Vol. 9, pt.1).

Jung, C. G. (1952/1956). *Symbols of transformation.* In *Collected works* (Vol. 5).

Jung, C. G. (1952/1968). *Psychology and alchemy* (2nd ed.). In *Collected works* (Vol. 12).

Jung, C. G. (1954/1959a). Archetypes and the collective unconscious. In *Collected works* (Vol. 9, pt. 1).

Jung, C. G. (1954/1959b). Concerning the archetypes, with special reference to the anima concept. In *Collected works* (Vol. 9, pt. 1).

Jung, C. G. (1954/1959c). Psychological aspects of the mother archetype. In *Collected works* (Vol. 9, pt. 1).

Jung, C. G. (1961). *Memories, dreams, reflections.* A. Jaffé (Ed.). New York: Random House.

Jung, C. G. (1964). *Man and his symbols.* Garden City, NY: Doubleday.

Jung, C. G. (1979). *Word and image.* A. Jaffé (Ed.). Princeton, NJ: Princeton University Press.

Jung, C. G., & Riklin, F. (1904/1973). The associations of normal subjects. In *Collected works* (Vol. 2).

Kazdin, A. E. (1978). Conceptual and assessment issues raised by self-efficacy theory. In S. Rachman (Ed.), *Advances in behavior research and therapy* (Vol. 1). Oxford: Pergamon Press.

Kelly, G. A. (1955). *The psychology of personal constructs* (Vols. 1 and 2). New York: Norton.

Kelly, G. A. (1963). *A theory of personality: The psychology of personal constructs.* New York: Norton.

Kelly, G. A. (1969a). The autobiography of a theory. In B. Maher (Ed.), *Clinical psychology and personality: The selected papers of George Kelly.* New York: Wiley.

Kelly, G. A. (1969b). Man's construction of his alternatives. In B. Maher (Ed.), *Clinical psychology and personality: The selected papers of George Kelly.* New York: Wiley.

Kelly, G. A. (1970). A brief introduction to personal construct theory. In D. Bannister (Ed.), *Perspectives in personal construct theory.* London: Academic Press. Also in J. C. Mancuso (Ed.), *Readings for a cognitive theory of personality.* New York: Holt, Rinehart and Winston.

Kelly, G. A. (1980). A psychology of the optimal man. In A. W. Landfield & L. M. Leitner (Eds.), *Personal construct psychology: Psychotherapy and personality.* New York: Wiley.

Kinsey, A. C., Pomeroy, W., & Martin, C. (1948). *Sexual behavior in the human male.* Philadelphia: Saunders.

Levy, N., & Ridley, S. E. (1987). Stability of Jungian personality types within a college population over a decade. *Psychological Reports, 60,* 419–422.

Kirsch, I. (1980). "Microanalytic" analyses of efficacy expectations as predictors of performance. *Cognitive Therapy and Research, 4,* 259–262.

Kirsch, I. (1982). Efficacy expectations or response predictions: The meaning of efficacy ratings as a function of task characteristics. *Journal of Personality and Social Psychology, 42,* 132–136.

Kirsch, I. (1990). *Changing expectations: A key to effective psychotherapy.* Monterey, CA: Brooks/Cole.

Kirsch, I., & Wickless, C. V. (1983). Concordance rates between self-efficacy and approach behavior are redundant. *Cognitive Therapy and Research, 7,* 179–188.

Kirschenbaum, H. (1979). *On becoming Carl Rogers.* New York: Delacorte Press.

Kline, P. (1984). *Psychology and Freudian theory: An introduction.* London: Methuen.

Krumboltz, J. D., & Thoresen, C. E. (1976). *Counseling methods.* New York: Holt, Rinehart and Winston.

Landis, B., & Tauber, E. S. (1971). Erich Fromm: Some biographical notes. In B. Landis & E. S. Tauber, *In the name of life: Essays in honor of Erich Fromm.* New York: Holt, Rinehart and Winston.

Landfield, A. W. (1971). *Personal construct systems in psychotherapy.* Chicago: Rand-McNally.

Landfield, A. W., & Epting, F. R. (1987). *Personal construct psychology: Clinical and personality assessment.* New York: Human Sciences Press.

Landfield, A. W., & Leitner, L. M. (Eds.), (1980). *Personal construct psychology: Psychotherapy and personality.* New York: Wiley.

Lang, P. J. (1978). Self-efficacy theory: Thoughts on cognitive and unification. In S. Rachman (Ed.), *Advances in behavior research and therapy,* (Vol. 1). Oxford: Pergamon Press.

Lefcourt, H. M. (1982). *Locus of control: Current trends in theory and research.* Hillsdale, NJ: Erlbaum.

Lerman, H. (1986). *A mote in Freud's eye: From psychoanalysis to the psychology of women.* New York: Springer.

Marcia, J. E. (1966). Development and validation of ego-identity status. *Journal of Personality and Social Psychology, 3,* 551–558.

Marcia, J. E. (1976). Identity six years after: A follow-up study. *Journal of Youth and Adolescence, 5,* 145–160.

Marcia, J. E. (1980). Identity in adolescence. In J. Adelson (Ed.), *Handbook of adolescent psychology* (pp. 159–187). New York: Wiley.

Marzillier, J., & Eastman, C. (1984). Continuing problems with self-efficacy theory: A reply to Bandura. *Cognitive Therapy and Research, 8,* 257–262.

Maslow, A. H. (1941). Deprivation, thirst, and frustration. *Psychological Review, 48,* 364–366.

Maslow, A. H. (1943). A theory of human motivation. *Psychological Review, 50,* 370–396.

Maslow, A. H. (1950). Self-actualizing people: A study of psychological health. *Personality Symposia: Symposium #1 on Values* (pp. 11–34). New York: Grune & Stratton.

Maslow, A. H. (1966). *The psychology of science.* New York: Harper & Row.

Maslow, A. H. (1967). A theory of metamotivation: The biological rooting of the value-life. *Journal of Humanistic Psychology, 7*(2), 93–127.

Maslow, A. H. (1968a). Self-actualization (Film). Santa Ana, CA: Psychological Films.

Maslow, A. H. (1968b). *Toward a psychology of being* (2nd ed.). New York: Van Nostrand.

Maslow, A. H. (1970a). *Motivation and personality* (2nd ed.). New York: Harper & Row.

Maslow, A. H. (1970b). *Religions, values, and peak-experiences.* New York: Viking.

Maslow, A. H. (1971). *The farther reaches of human nature.* New York: Viking Press.

Maslow, A. H. (1979). *The Journals of A. H. Maslow* (2 vols.). R. J. Lowry (Ed.). Monterey, CA: Brooks/Cole.

Masson, J. M. (1984). *The assault on truth: Freud's suppression of the seduction theory.* New York: Farrar, Straus, and Giroux.

May, R. (1950). *The meaning of anxiety.* New York: Ronald Press.

May, R. (1953). *Man's search for himself.* New York: Norton.

May, R. (1958a). Contributions of existential psychotherapy. In R. May, E. Angel, & H. F. Ellenberger (Eds.), *Existence: A new dimension in psychiatry and psychology.* New York: Basic Books.

May, R. (1958b). The origins and significance of existential movement in psychology. In R. May, E. Angel, & H. F. Ellenberger (Eds.), *Existence: A new dimension in psychiatry and psychology.* New York: Basic Books.

May, R. (1962). Dangers in the relation of existentialism to psychotherapy. In H. M. Rultenbeek (Ed.), *Psychoanalysis and existential philosophy.* New York: Dutton.

May, R. (1967). *Psychology and the human dilemma.* Princeton, NJ: Van Nostrand.

May, R. (1969a). The emergence of existential psychology. In R. May (Ed.), *Existential psychology* (2nd ed.). New York: Random House.

May, R. (1969b). Existential bases of psychotherapy. In R. May (Ed.), *Existential psychology* (2nd ed.). New York: Random House.

May, R. (1969c). *Love and will.* New York: Norton.

May, R. (1972). *Power and innocence: A search for the sources of violence.* New York: Norton.

May, R. (1977a). *The meaning of anxiety* (Rev. Ed.). New York: Norton.

May, R. (1977b). Reflections and commentary by Rollo May. In C. Reeves, *The psychology of Rollo May* (pp. 295–309). San Francisco: Jossey-Bass.

May, R. (1981). *Freedom and destiny.* New York: Norton.

May, R. (1982). The problem of evil: An open letter to Carl Rogers. *Journal of Humanistic Psychology, 22*(3), 10–21.

May, R. (1985). *My quest for beauty.* San Francisco: Saybrook.

May, R., Angel, E., & Ellenberger, H. F. (Eds.). (1958). *Existence: A new dimension in psychiatry and psychology.* New York: Basic Books.

McGregor, D. (1960). *The human side of enterprise.* New York: McGraw-Hill.

McGuire, W. (Ed.). (1974). *The Freud/Jung letters: The correspondence between Sigmund Freud and C. G. Jung.* Princeton, NJ: Princeton University Press.

Menninger, K. (1942). *Love against hate.* New York: Harcourt, Brace & World.

Miller, N. E. (1941). The frustration-aggression hypothesis. *Psychological Review, 48,* 337–342.

Miller, N. E. (1944). Experimental studies of conflict behavior. In J. McV. Hunt (Ed.), *Personality and behavior disorders* (Vol. 1). New York: Ronald Press.

Miller, N. E. (1951). Learnable drives and rewards. In S. S. Stevens (Ed.), *Handbook of experimental psychology.* New York: Wiley.

Miller, N. E. (1959). Liberalization of basic S-R concepts: Extensions to conflict behavior, motivation and social learning. In S. Koch (Ed.), *Psychology: A study of science* (Vol. 2). New York: McGraw-Hill.

Miller, N. E. (1982). John Dollard (1900–1980): Obituary. *American Psychologist, 37,* 587–588.

Miller, N. E. (1983). Behavioral medicine: Symbiosis between laboratory and clinic. In M. R. Rosenzweig & L. W. Porter (Eds.), *Annual Review of Psychology, 34,* 1–31.

Miller, N. E. (1984a). *Bridges between laboratory and clinic.* New York: Praeger.

Miller, N. E. (1984b). Learning: Some facts and needed research relevant to maintaining health. In J. D. Matarazzo, S. M. Weiss, J. A. Herd, N. E. Miller, & S. M. Weiss (Eds.), *Behavioral health: A handbook of health enhancement and disease prevention* (pp. 199–208). New York: Wiley.

Miller, N. E., & Dollard, J. (1941). *Social learning and imitation.* New Haven, CT: Yale University Press.

Mischel, W. (1977). The interaction of person and situation. In D. Magnusson & N. S. Endler (Eds.), *Personality at the crossroads: Current issues in interactional psychology.* Hillsdale, NJ: Erlbaum.

Mischel, W. (1981). Personality and cognition: Something borrowed, something new? In N. Cantor & J. F. Kihlstrom (Eds.), *Personality, cognition, and social interaction.* Hillsdale, NJ: Erlbaum.

Mischel, W. (1986). *Introduction to personality: A new look* (4th ed.). New York: Holt, Rinehart and Winston.

Mozdzierz, G. J., & Semyck, R. W. (1980). The social interest index: A study of construct validity. *Journal of Clinical Psychology, 36,* 417–422.

Murray, H. A. (1938). *Explorations in personality.* New York: Oxford University Press.

Myers, I. B. (1972). *Myers-Briggs Type Indicator Manual.* Palo Alto, CA: Consulting Psychologists Press.

Myers, I. B., & McCaulley, M. H. (1985). *Manual: A guide to the development and use of the Myers-Briggs Type Indicator.* Palo Alto, CA: Consulting Psychologists Press.

Newman, B. M., & Newman, P. R. (1987). *Development through life: A psychosocial approach* (4th ed.). Chicago: Dorsey Press.

Olds, J., & Milner, P. (1954). Positive reinforcement produced by electrical stimulation of septal area and other regions of rat brain. *Journal of Comparative and Physiological Psychology, 47,* 419–427.

Olsen, L. A. (1979). Bandura's self system sans Sullivan. *American Psychologist, 34,* 439.

Paige, J. M. (1966). Letters from Jenny: An approach to the clinical analysis of personality structure by computer. In P. J. Stone (Ed.), *The general enquirer: A computer approach to content analysis.* Cambridge, MA: M.I.T. Press.

Panzarella, R. (1980). The phenomenology of aesthetic peak experiences. *Journal of Humanistic Psychology, 20* (1), 69–85.

Pereboom, A. C. (1979). Bandura's self system: Some reservations. *American Psychologist, 34,* 438–439.

Perry, H. S. (1982). *Psychiatrist of America: The life of Harry Stack Sullivan.* Cambridge, MA: The Belknap Press.

Pines, M. (1978, September). Invisible playmates. *Psychology Today,* pp. 38–42, 106.

Prager, K. (1986). Identity development, age, and college experience in women. *Journal of Genetic Psychology, 147,* 31–36.

Quinn, S. (1987). *A mind of her own: The life of Karen Horney.* New York: Summit Books.

Rabinowitz, F. E., Good, G., & Cozad, L. (1989). Rollo May: A man of meaning and myth. *Journal of Counseling and Development, 67,* 436–441.

Rattner, J. (1983). *Alfred Adler* (H. Zohn, Trans.). New York: Frederick Ungar. (Original work published 1983).

Ravizza, K. (1977). Peak experiences in sport. *Journal of Humanistic Psychology, 17* (4), 35–40.

Reeves, C. (1977). *The psychology of Rollo May.* San Francisco: Jossey-Bass.

Rimm, D. C., & Masters, J. C. (1979). *Behavior therapy: Techniques and empirical findings.* New York: Academic Press.

Roazen, P. (1976). *Erik H. Erikson: The power and limits of a vision.* New York: Free Press.

Rogers, C. R. (1939). *The clinical treatment of the problem child.* Boston: Houghton Mifflin.

Rogers, C. R. (1942). *Counseling and psychotherapy: Newer concepts in practice.* Boston: Houghton Mifflin.

Rogers, C. R. (1947). Some observations on the organization of personality. *American Psychologist, 2,* 358–368.

Rogers, C. R. (1951). *Client-centered therapy: Its current practice, implications, and theory.* Boston: Houghton Mifflin.

Rogers, C. R. (1953). *A concept of the fully functioning person.* Unpublished manuscript, University of Chicago Counseling Center, Chicago.

Rogers, C. R. (1954a). The case of Mrs. Oak: A research analysis. In C. R. Rogers & R. F. Dymond (Eds.), *Psychotherapy and personality change: Co-ordinated research studies in the client-centered approach.* Chicago: University of Chicago Press.

Rogers, C. R. (1954b). Introduction. In C. R. Rogers & R. F. Dymond (Eds.), *Psychotherapy and personality change: Co-ordinated research studies in the client-centered approach.* Chicago: University of Chicago Press.

Rogers, C. R. (1955). Personality change in psychotherapy. *The International Journal of Social Psychiatry, 1,* 31–41.

Rogers, C. R. (1957). The necessary and sufficient conditions of therapeutic personality change. *Journal of Consulting Psychology, 21,* 95–103.

Rogers, C. R. (1959). A theory of therapy, personality, and interpersonal relationships, as developed in the client-centered framework. In S. Koch (Ed.), *Psychology: A study of a science* (Vol. 3). New York: McGraw-Hill.

Rogers, C. R. (1961). *On becoming a person: A therapist's view of psychotherapy.* Boston: Houghton Mifflin.

Rogers, C. R. (1962). Toward becoming a fully functioning person. In A. W. Combs (Ed.), *Perceiving, behaving, becoming: Yearbook* (pp. 21–33). Washington, DC: Association for Supervision and Curriculum Development.

Rogers, C. R. (1963). The concept of the fully functioning person. *Psychotherapy: Theory, Research, and Practice, 1*(1), 17–26.

Rogers, C. R. (1968). Some thoughts regarding the current presuppositions of the behavioral sciences. In W. R. Coulson & C. R. Rogers (Eds.), *Man and the science of man.* Columbus, OH: Merrill.

Rogers, C. R. (1978). The formative tendency. *Journal of Humanistic Psychology, 18* (1), 23–26.

Rogers, C. R. (1980). *A way of being.* Boston: Houghton Mifflin.

Rogers, C. R. (1982a). Notes on Rollo May. *Journal of Humanistic Psychology, 22* (3), 8–9.

Rogers, C. R. (1982b). A psychologist looks at nuclear war: Its threat; its possible prevention. *Journal of Humanistic Psychology, 22* (4), 9–20.

Rogers, C. R. (1983). *Freedom to learn for the 80's.* Columbus, OH: Merrill.

Rogers, C. R., & Dymond, R. F. (Eds.). (1954). *Psychotherapy and personality change: Co-ordinated research studies in the client-centered approach.* Chicago: University of Chicago Press.

Rogers, C. R., & Skinner, B. F. (1956). Some issues concerning the control of human behavior. *Science, 124,* 1057–1066.

Rogers, C., Gendlin, E., Kiesler, D., & Truax, C. (1967). *The therapeutic relationship and its impact: A study of psychotherapy with schizophrenics.* Madison, WI: University of Wisconsin Press.

Rogers, C. R., & Stevens, B. (1967). *Person to person: The problem of being human: A new trend in psychology.* Lafayette, CA: Real People Press.

Rosenthal, T. L., & Bandura, A. (1978). Psychological modeling: Theory and practice. In S. L. Garfield & A. E. Bergin (Eds.), *Handbook of psychotherapy and behavior change: An empirical analysis.* New York: Wiley.

Rotter, J. B. (1954). *Social learning and clinical psychology.* Englewood Cliffs, NJ: Prentice-Hall.

Rotter, J. B. (1964). *Clinical psychology.* Englewood Cliffs, NJ: Prentice-Hall.

Rotter, J. B. (1966). Generalized expectancies for internal versus external control of reinforcement. *Psychological Monographs, 80* (Whole No. 609).

Rotter, J. B. (1967). A new scale for the measurement of interpersonal trust. *Journal of Personality, 35,* 651–665.

Rotter, J. B. (1970). Some implications of a social learning theory for the practice of psychotherapy. In D. J. Levis (Ed.), *Learning approaches to therapeutic behavior change.* Chicago: Aldine.

Rotter, J. B. (1971). Generalized expectancies for interpersonal trust. *American Psychologist, 26,* 443–452.

Rotter, J. B. (1975). Some problems and misconceptions related to the construct of internal vs. external control of reinforcement. *Journal of Consulting and Clinical Psychology, 43,* 56–67.

Rotter, J. B. (1978). Generalized expectancies for problem solving and psychotherapy. *Cognitive Therapy and Research, 2,* 1–10.

Rotter, J. B. (1980). Interpersonal trust, trustworthiness, and gullibility. *American Psychologist, 35,* 1–7.

Rotter, J. B. (1982). *The development and applications of social learning theory: Selected papers.* New York: Praeger.

Rotter, J. B., Chance, J. E., & Phares, E. J. (1972). *Applications of a social learning theory of personality.* New York: Holt, Rinehart and Winston.

Rotter, J. B., & Hochreich, D. J. (1975). *Personality.* Glenview, IL: Scott, Foresman.

Rowan, J. (1983). The real self and mystical experiences. *Journal of Humanistic Psychology, 23*(2), 9–27.

Royce, J. R. (1973). The conceptual framework for a multi-factor theory of individuality. In J. R. Royce (Ed.), *Multivariate analysis and psychological theory.* London: Academic Press.

Rubins, J. L. (1978). *Karen Horney: Gentle rebel of psychoanalysis.* New York: Dial Press.

Rudikoff, E. C. (1954). A comparative study of the changes in the concepts of the self, the ordinary person, and the ideal in eight cases. In C. R. Rogers & R. F. Dymond (Eds.), *Psychotherapy and personality change: Co-ordinated research studies in the client-centered approach.* Chicago: University of Chicago Press.

Rule, W. R. (1972). The relationship between early recollections and selected counselor and life style characteristics (Doctoral dissertation, University of South Carolina). *Dissertation Abstracts International, 33,* 1448A–1449A (University Microfilms No. 72–25, 921).

Rule, W. R., & Traver, M. D. (1982). Early recollections and expected leisure activities. *Psychological Reports, 51,* 295–301.

Rychlak, J. F. (1979). A nontelic teleology? *American Psychologist, 34,* 435–438.

Sanford, N. (1963). Personality: Its place in psychology. In S. Koch (Ed.), *Psychology: A study of a science* (Vol. 5). New York: McGraw-Hill.

Sartre, J. P. (1957). *Existentialism and human emotions.* New York: Wisdom Library.

Schur, M. (1972). *Freud: Living and dying.* New York: International Universities Press.

Sheffield, F. D. (1966a). A drive theory of reinforcement. In R. N. Haber (Ed.), *Current research in motivation.* New York: Holt, Rinehart and Winston.

Sheffield, F. D. (1966b). New evidence on drive-induction theory of reinforcement. In R. N. Haber (Ed.), *Current research in motivation.* New York: Holt, Rinehart and Winston.

Shostrom, E. (1974). *Manual for the Personal Orientation Inventory.* San Diego: Educational and Industrial Testing Service.

Skinner, B. F. (1938). *The behavior of organisms: An experimental analysis.* Englewood Cliffs, NJ: Prentice-Hall.

Skinner, B. F. (1945). The operational analysis of psychological terms. *Psychological Review, 52,* 270–277, 291–294.

Skinner, B. F. (1948). *Walden two.* New York: Macmillan.

Skinner, B. F. (1953). *Science and human behavior.* New York: Macmillan.

Skinner, B. F. (1967). An autobiography. In E. G. Boring & G. Lindzey (Eds.), *A history of psychology in autobiography* (Vol. 5). New York: Appleton-Century-Crofts.

Skinner, B. F. (1969). *Contingencies of reinforcement: A theoretical analysis.* New York: Appleton-Century-Crofts.

Skinner, B. F. (1971). *Beyond freedom and dignity.* New York: Knopf.

Skinner, B. F. (1974). *About behaviorism.* New York: Knopf.

Skinner, B. F. (1976). *Particulars of my life.* New York: Knopf.

Skinner, B. F. (1978). *Reflections on behaviorism and society.* Englewood Cliffs, NJ: Prentice-Hall.

Skinner, B. F. (1979). *The shaping of a behaviorist.* New York: Knopf.

Skinner, B. F. (1983). *A matter of consequences.* New York: Knopf.

Skinner, B. F. (1987a). *Upon further reflection.* Englewood Cliffs, NJ: Prentice-Hall.

Skinner, B. F. (1987b). Whatever happened to psychology as the science of behavior? *American Psychologist, 42,* 780–786.

Skinner, B. F. (1989). The origins of cognitive thought. *American Psychologist, 44,* 13–18.

Skinner, B. F., & Vaughan, M. E. (1983). *Enjoy old age: A program for self-management.* New York: Norton.

Sobel, D. (1980, March 19). Erich Fromm. *The New York Times.* p. B11.

Solso, R. L. (1987). Recommended readings in psychology over the past 33 years. *American Psychologist, 42,* 1130–1132.

Steele, R. S., & Kelley, T. J. (1976). Eysenck Personality Questionnaire and Jungian Myers-Briggs Type Indicator correlations of extraversion-introversion. *Journal of Consulting and Clinical Psychology, 44,* 690–691.

Steinberg, A. (1958). *Mrs. R: The life of Eleanor Roosevelt.* New York: Putnam.

Stephenson, W. (1953). *The study of behavior: Q-technique and its methodology.* Chicago: University of Chicago Press.

Stephenson, W. (1953). *The study of behavior.* Chicago: University of Chicago Press.

Strickland, B. R. (1989). Internal-external control expectancies: From contingency to creativity. *American Psychologist, 44,* 1–12.

Sullivan, H. S. (1953a). *Conceptions of modern psychiatry.* New York: Norton.

Sullivan, H. S. (1953b). *The interpersonal theory of psychiatry.* New York: Norton.

Sullivan, H. S. (1954). *The psychiatric interview.* New York: Norton.

Sullivan, H. S. (1956). *Clinical studies in psychiatry.* New York: Norton.

Sullivan, H. S. (1962). *Schizophrenia as a human process.* New York: Norton.

Sullivan, H. S. (1964). *The fusion of psychiatry and social science.* New York: Norton.

Sullivan, H. S. (1972). *Personal psychopathology.* New York: Norton.

Sulloway, F. J. (1979). *Freud, biologist of the mind: Beyond the psychoanalytical legend.* New York: Basic Books.

Suzukl, D. T., Fromm, E., & DeMartino, R. (1960). *Zen Buddhism and psychoanalysis.* New York: Grove Press.

Thompson, G. G. (1968). George A. Kelly (1905–1967). *Journal of General Psychology, 79,* 19–24.

Thorn, F. C. (1975). The life style analysis. *Journal of Clinical Psychology, 31,* 236–240.

Vaihinger, H. (1911/1925). *The philosophy of "as if."* New York: Harcourt, Brace & Co.

Vitz, P. C. (1988). *Sigmund Freud's Christian unconscious.* New York: Guilford Press.

Walston, K. A., Wallston, B. S., & DeVellis, R. F. (1978). Development of the Multidimensional Health Locus of Control (MHLC) Scales. *Health Education Monographs, 6,* 161–170.

Warren, C. (1982). The relationship between early recollections and behavior pattern. *Journal of Individual Psychology, 38,* 223–237.

Weisz, J. R., & Stipek, D. J. (1982). Competence, contingency, and the development of perceived control. *Human Development, 25,* 250–281.

Wheelright, J. B., Wheelwright, J. A., & Buehler, J. A. (1974). *Jungian Type Survey Manual.* San Francisco: Society of Jungian Analysts of Northern California.

Wilson, C. (1972). *New pathways in psychology: Maslow and the post-Freudian revolution.* New York: Taplinger.

Winson, J. (1985). *Brain and psyche: The biology of the unconscious.* Garden City, NY: Anchor Press/Doubleday.

Woehlke, P. A., & Piper, R. B. (1980). Factorial validity of the Jungian Type Survey. *Educational and Psychological Measurement, 40,* 1051–1058.

Wolpe, J. (1973). *The practice of behavior therapy.* New York: Pergamon Press.

Wolpe, J. (1978). Self-efficacy theory and psychotherapeutic change: A square peg for a round hole. In S. Rachman (Ed.), *Advances in behavior research and therapy* (Vol. 1). Oxford: Pergamon Press.

Woolfolk, R. L., & Lazarus, A. A. (1979). Between laboratory and clinic: Paving the two-way street. *Cognitive Therapy and Research, 3,* 239–244.

Youniss, J. (1980). *Parents and peers in social development: A Sullivan-Piaget perspective.* Chicago: University of Chicago Press.

Zarski, J. J., Sweeney, T. J., & Barcikowski, R. S. (1977). Counseling effectiveness as a function of counselor social interest. *Journal of Counseling Psychology, 24,* 1–5.

Zarski, J. J., West, J. D., & Bubenzer, D. L. (1982). Social interest, running, and life adjustment. *Personnel and Guidance Journal, 61,* 146–149.

Zuroff, D. (1986). Was Gordon Allport a trait theorist? *Journal of Personality and Social Psychology, 51,* 993–1000.

Name Index

Subject Index